TERENCE
RATTIGAN

TERENCE RATTIGAN

GEOFFREY WANSELL

Fourth Estate · London

For my daughter, Molly

First published in Great Britain in 1995 by
Fourth Estate Limited
6 Salem Road
London W2 4BU

A catalogue record for this book is available
from the British Library

ISBN 1–85702–207–1

Typeset by Rowland Phototypesetting Ltd
Bury St Edmunds, Suffolk
Printed in Great Britain by
Clays Ltd, St Ives plc

Contents

Preface

Why does anyone write a biography? Does the biographer see himself in his subject? Is there some hidden chord struck that leads the one to the other? I am not sure, but I do know that my father looked astonishingly like Terence Rattigan. They shared the same sleek short haircut, just as they both invariably wore a collar and tie. They were also born within a few years of each other, on either side of the Great War. Indeed both Rattigan and my father were Londoners, though my father was unmistakably a cockney from Islington, while Rattigan was just as unmistakably a toff from Kensington.

Terence Rattigan and my father shared a common heritage, and culture, even though they were forever separated, both by the divides of the English class system and by success. By the time my father had become a serious young theatregoer of eighteen, Rattigan, at twenty-five, was already established as the West End's brightest new playwright, the author of London's latest comedy sensation, *French Without Tears*. But the divide between them did nothing to lessen my father's admiration for his slightly older contemporary. Throughout his life, my father loved the plays of Terence Rattigan almost as much as he loved the theatre itself.

It was a love that he passed on to me. Almost my first memory as a child was of being taken to the pantomime *Mother Goose* at the Finsbury Park Empire, much as Rattigan's was of being taken to see *Cinderella*. By the time I was ten, I had been inside almost every London theatre, though more often in the upper circle than the stalls. But by then, the summer of 1955, the London theatre was on the brink of a cataclysmic change.

Look Back in Anger opened in London in May 1956, two months before my eleventh birthday, and inevitably I became a child of the Osborne generation, weaned at the Royal Court, on the *Observer* reviews of Kenneth Tynan, and on a diet of Arnold Wesker, Joan Littlewood and Harold Pinter. For his part, my father loathed the

new 'angry young men'. He remained unrepentantly a member of the
Rattigan generation, fervent in his admiration for *The Deep Blue Sea*,
The Browning Version and *Separate Tables*. And we argued incessantly
as a result. I was convinced that the world of drawing-rooms and
french windows, of elegant dresses and gentlemen in dinner jackets,
was doomed. My father was equally convinced that the kitchen sink
would eventually disappear down its own plughole; and that, in any
case, it did not hold a candle to Rattigan.

For a long time it seemed that I was right. Terence Rattigan was
consigned to the footnotes of British drama, while Osborne, Pinter,
and Tynan held the stage. Tragically, by the time I began to realise
that perhaps I had been too hasty, too anxious to follow the theatrical
fashion, it was too late. My father was dead. He died so suddenly in
the summer of 1985 that I never had the opportunity to put it to him
that perhaps we had both been right. Osborne and Pinter were good,
but so too was Rattigan, and a great deal better than I had ever been
prepared to accept.

More than any other, then, my father is the reason I chose to write
a book about Terence Rattigan. But it was not simply the memories
of our violent arguments that spurred me on. There was another reason.
Because my father was a child of Rattigan's generation, so he too shared
the publicly stiff upper lip, the steadfastly cautious public persona. Like
Rattigan, my father chose to hide himself away in a pinstripe suit. For
their generation of Englishmen, emotion was always kept strictly under
control. To talk about emotions, even worse to reveal them, was not
my father's way. That too he shared with Rattigan.

In particular, my father was sensitive about any discussion of sexuality. And when it came to homosexuality, my father, my mother, and
indeed most other people I knew in postwar Britian, were adamantly
of the same mind. To them homosexuality was a repellent, disgusting
deviation, not to be tolerated at any price; a threat to society and to
the young, which no right-thinking person could possibly tolerate or
condone. It was truly the love that dared not speak its name. If that now
seems hardly credible, indeed itself almost repellent, let me illustrate my
point with another personal experience.

When I was a small boy still discovering Enid Blyton and Richmal
Crompton in the local library, one of the librarians was particularly
kind to me. He gradually became a friend of the family, dropping in
on Saturdays after the library closed, or when it was half-day closing.
My mother liked him, though my father did not meet him all that
often. One Saturday, the librarian did not appear. He was missing on
Wednesday as well, and the following Saturday. Finally, my mother

struggled to tell me, through agonies of embarrassment, that he had
been arrested in a public lavatory at Arnos Grove underground station
for 'indecency'. Though I had no idea at all what that meant, my
parents decided that they, and I, should never see him again. The
librarian in question had never made the slightest step towards
seduction, but even the possibility that he might have done so was too
much for my parents. An exposed homosexual, particularly one who
had been arrested for cottaging, was not a person to be invited into
the house.

If my father had had the slightest inkling of Terence Rattigan's own
sexual preferences, it would have coloured his views about him, but
fortunately he never had. Rattigan was careful to disguise the truth
about his own sexuality for the simple and compelling reason that to
have revealed it would have endangered his appeal to my father, and
to millions of other ordinary British theatregoers like him. It was a
precise reflection of the time.

But it was not the potential prejudice of the ordinary members of
the theatre audience, like my father, that ultimately destroyed Terence
Rattigan's reputation as a dramatist in Britain and around the world –
far from it. Rattigan was denied his place at the pinnacle of contemporary English drama by the bigotry, jealousy and shortsightedness of an
influential group of individuals in what came to be the English theatrical
establishment. As a result of their prejudice, and for no sound reason,
he was suddenly, unforgivably and unreasonably dismissed as a playwright of no consequence. It was to break his spirit, I believe, and
shorten his life.

Like many Scots, and I was born on the Clyde even though I was
brought up in North London, I have a passion for underdogs. And
for me, Terence Rattigan became the ultimate theatrical underdog, a
playwright whose work was blithely dismissed by the members of
what we would nowadays call the 'chattering classes' for no reason
other than its lack of 'fashionability'. As Rattigan himself pointed out
plaintively towards the end of his life, he did not mind people not
liking his plays, but he thought that it ought to be for a rather more
serious reason than that he had become 'unfashionable'. Though his
work never lost its appeal to the ordinary theatregoer, it did so to those
who commanded the heights of the British theatre in the years after
1956. This biography is an attempt, not only to put his life and career
into perspective, but also to redress that balance, and in doing so to
atone for my own initial misjudgement of him.

When I began this book, I had no idea how many people shared my
view that Terence Rattigan was a unique playwright, whose talents

had been unfairly scorned. But as my research progressed I realised that there were literally hundreds of men and women in the theatre today who thought exactly as I did. The playwright Harold Pinter is probably the most distinguished among his present-day admirers, but there are many others. Two, in particular, stand out: one the American critic and academic Holly Hill, who, almost single-handedly, has kept the Rattigan flag flying in the academic world for two decades, the other Peter Carter-Ruck, the English lawyer who runs the Rattigan Trust and has shrewdly managed the playwright's estate and painstakingly collated his papers over the past eighteen years. Both have given me enormous support and encouragement.

This is the first biography of Rattigan to make use of the Rattigan papers, which are now lodged at the British Library under the care of the curator of modern manuscripts, Sally Brown, without whom this book could not have been written. Two substantial bookcases of boxes and files house a mountain of Rattigan records and memorabilia, which took me almost a year to work my way through. While working there I was also given access to the Kenneth Tynan papers, and to the remarkable records of the Lord Chamberlain, whose office was responsible for censorship in the British theatre until 1968.

But there were many other unlikely sources of valuable material. Rattigan's publisher, Hamish Hamilton, for example, donated his firm's archive to the special library collections at the University of Bristol, where the librarian, Nick Lee, took considerable trouble to unearth material for me. The Theatre Museum in Covent Garden proved another treasure trove, as did its sister archive, the H.M. Tennent collection, housed in the vast Victoria and Albert Museum warehouse just off Brook Green in West London, and I am particularly indebted to both Barry Norman and Sarah Woodcock for their assistance there. In the United States, the Billy Rose collection at the New York Public Library at Lincoln Center houses an equally valuable cache of Rattigan material.

Terence Rattigan's twenty-three West End plays, fifteen of which also played on Broadway (*Grey Farm*, written with Hector Bolitho, was only ever played in New York, making the Broadway total properly sixteen), were not his only work, however. He also wrote twenty-two produced screenplays, and five original television plays. Here the libraries of the American Academy of Motion Picture Arts and Sciences in Los Angeles and the British Film Institute library in London were invaluable.

Rattigan's school and university records were every bit as fascinating. I am enormously grateful to the archivist at Sandroyd, as well as to

Alasdair Hawkyard and Clare Hopkins, the archivists at Harrow and Trinity College, Oxford respectively, for their help. The details they enabled me to discover added dimensions to the portrait that could not have come from anywhere else. The advice of Miss Elizabeth Oliver, the secretary to the Trustees of Albany, proved similarly illuminating.

Equally I could not have survived the research without the support and help of the Garrick Club's library and its dedicated librarian Mrs Enid Foster, who helped me find all manner of material which I was convinced I could never unearth. The same patience was not quite in evidence at the Public Record Office in London, but the assistance I received there was almost as valuable.

Helpful though the institutions that housed Rattigan material were, however, they could not help me to bring the man himself back to life. For that I had to rely on his friends and former colleagues, who were without exception most generous with their time and reminiscences. I am enormously grateful to each and every one of them for their kindness and time, and if there are any of this numerous company whom I have neglected to mention by name, I trust they will accept my heartfelt apologies.

This biography could not have been written without the help of B.A. 'Freddie' Young, who not only knew Rattigan but also wrote an account of his life; nor could it have been written without the advice and encouragement of his former colleague Anthony Curtis, who was at one stage considering writing a biography of Rattigan himself. It also could not have been written without the work of the film-maker Michael Darlow, who produced a television obituary and then a book with Gillian Hodson about Rattigan shortly after his death in 1977.

Sadly Michael Franklin, Rattigan's lover throughout the second half of his life, was dead by the time I started out on this book, as too were Cuthbert Worsley and Billy Chappell, two of Rattigan's longest-standing friends. Equally, many of the actors and directors who worked with him had died before I had the chance to speak to them. Anthony Asquith was dead, so were Kenneth More and Peggy Ashcroft, Eric Portman and Emlyn Williams, Vivien Leigh and Margaret Leighton, Roland Culver and Laurence Olivier.

Fortunately, however, a large group who knew Terence Rattigan particularly well are still alive, and to each and every one of them I owe a special debt. Harold Pinter, Holly Hill and Peter Carter-Ruck I have already mentioned, but this group also includes Sir John 'Jimmy' Stow, who together with John Ivimy knew Rattigan at Harrow; Peter Osborn, who knew Rattigan intimately in the thirties and forties; Jack Watling, who shared a psychiatrist with Rattigan as a young man;

Frith Banbury, who directed *The Deep Blue Sea*; Harold French, who directed *French Without Tears* and whose wife Pegs did so much to look after Rattigan in the last years of his life; Bunny Roger, who knew Rattigan from his first day at Oxford until the end of Rattigan's life forty-five years later; Stephen Mitchell, who presented *The Browning Version* and *Separate Tables* and played golf with Rattigan for so many years; Jean Dawnay, later Princess Galitzine, for so long a friend of Rattigan's; Mary Herring, Rattigan's secretary for no less than seventeen years; and the critic and columnist Bernard Levin.

I also received help and advice from an extraordinary and diverse group of Terence Rattigan's friends and colleagues in the theatre, including Sir John Gielgud and Sir John Mills, Kenneth Griffith, George Cole, Frederick Treves, Terence Longden, Robert Flemyng, Donald Sinden, William Fox and Paul Scofield. I am extremely grateful to them all, just as I am to the directors James Cellan Jones, for his reminiscences of Rattigan's experiences in feature films, and Alvin Rakoff, for his memories of three television plays with Rattigan. I should also thank the agent Michael Sissons, whose predecessor A.D.Peters for so long represented Rattigan.

There was another group of Terence Rattigan's friends, however, who asked particularly to remain anonymous, and to them I also offer my grateful, and heartfelt, thanks. Many of them echoed the words of Sir John Gielgud to me: 'He was a generous and affectionate friend as well as a brilliant playwright, and I miss him very much.'

I am also grateful to the few surviving relatives of Terence Rattigan, and particularly to Mrs Roxanne Senior, who took the trouble to consult one another about their memories of a man whom they had hardly seen for more than half a century.

The work of a handful of British critics and academics has also been enormously helpful. Professor Christopher Innes's *Modern British Drama* and Richard Foulkes's contributions on Rattigan in a recent collection on British dramatists were vastly encouraging, while the critics Michael Billington, John Lahr and Irving Wardle have also written sensitively and seriously about Rattigan in the past few years.

Finally, I must thank my agent and first editor, Rivers Scott, for seeing me through this initially daunting project, and his associate Gloria Ferris, whose belief in it almost rivalled my own. I also owe a debt to my editor at Fourth Estate, Christopher Potter, for his patience and encouragement, and to the television director Donald Sturrock, whose enthusiasm for Rattigan, and our television biography of him, all but equalled my own. Each in their own way contributed distinctively to this biography. Most of all, it could not have been written without the help and support of my wife, Jan, and the forbearance of my son Dan and my daughter Molly, who came to live with Terence Rattigan every day of their lives and bore the experience with hardly a moment's complaint.

Not one of the above should be held responsible for my conclusions, however; those are mine alone. And that, perhaps, is the answer to the question that I posed at the beginning of this preface. Terence Rattigan's life struck some chord in my own, which made the journey to bring it to life all the more exciting, and all the more challenging. His need for affection from a father who could never quite offer it has its parallel in my own life, along, I must confess, with a determination to conceal that need behind a mask of British restraint. Perhaps it also takes one underdog to recognise another, I am not sure. But I am certain that the work of Terence Rattigan has been unfairly, and unreasonably, overlooked for far too long. It is time he was acknowledged, and accepted, as one of Britain's greatest playwrights, and not just of this twentieth century.

Geoffrey Wansell
Wiltshire, England
May 1995

Nature's Shift

◆

No mask like open truth to cover lies,

As to go naked is the best disguise.

WILLIAM CONGREVE

◆

In the watery winter sunshine, the sound of Puccini's *Madame Butterfly* floods the drawing-room of a sumptuous flat in Eaton Square. It is a little after eleven o'clock on a cool November morning in 1951 and a tall, elegant, forty-year-old man is lying on the sofa. With a Dunhill Crystal cigarette holder clenched in his left hand and a ballpoint pen in his right, he is writing rapidly on sheet after sheet of lined foolscap paper on a velvet-covered 'writing table' on his knee.

The telephone rings, but the man continues to write, pausing only to flick fallen ash from the sleeve of his jacket on to the Aubusson carpet. The ringing stops: the phone has clearly been answered elsewhere. The man seems oblivious to the music, to the trees in the square outside, indeed to the world.

The voice of Cio-Cio-San rises in anguish, but the man's clear blue eyes never leave the lined pages in front of him as the words flood quickly across the sheets in his spidery upright scrawl. He has no use for a typewriter. The brutal tapping of a keyboard, the ring of the bell at the end of each line would break the spell.

There is a Vuillard and a Lautrec on the walls, and a pair of Venetian giltwood mirrors above the mantel; the sofa, like the writing-table, is covered in velvet, the curtains are heavy brocade, the decanters crystal. There is a Rolls-Royce parked in front of the house, and the tall man's tailored jacket is of the finest Savile Row cut.

He has already made a fortune, and a reputation, as one of the glittering figures in the theatre of the twentieth century. Successor to Maugham and Pinero, a threat to his older contemporary Noël Coward, winner of two Ellen Terry awards, he has been a success since 1936, when the London production of his light comedy *French Without Tears* rocketed him to fame at the age of just twenty-five. Later, during the war, he was to become the only playwright ever to have three plays running simultaneously in adjoining West End theatres.

Recently he has had two flops, but his position still seems secure, and now he is working on a play that he believes will confirm his reputation and put him back on Shaftesbury Avenue, in the place that is rightfully his.

The sofa, the clothes, the paintings, the cigarette holder, all could be props in a Terence Rattigan play, and in a sense they are. For the model of the charming, diplomatic, upper-class Englishman that he has taken such trouble to present to the world is every bit as much his creation as anything he has ever written for the theatre.

The scene changes. This time the room is smaller: panelled in wood, with a bed folded away in one corner. The initials of hundreds of schoolboys are carved into the dark walls, and the occupant is sitting – this time in a chair – but he is still writing furiously.

There is a copy of the day's *Times* at his feet, and a canvas cricket bag standing guard in one corner. On the back of the door hangs a white flannel jacket, the mark of a Harrow boy who plays for the school's cricket eleven. No one would dare to call it the first eleven, it is simply the Eleven.

It is a May evening in 1930, and in a few days' time Harrow's annual match against its oldest rival, Eton, takes place at Lord's, the headquarters of English cricket. Terence Rattigan is to open the batting for Harrow. But still he is writing, by candlelight, the embers of the day filtering through his window, which looks far out across the lights of London towards the Thames, Windsor and the opposing school.

There is a brief knock at the door. For a moment, the writing ceases. But he does not speak.

The scene changes again. The Eaton Square flat is dark, and the only sound comes from the chime of a magnificent ormolu clock on the mantel. The doorbell rings, but there is no response. It rings again, and again. Finally, Terence Rattigan appears in a silk dressing-gown, cigarette holder clasped in his hand.

He opens the door slowly, and looks levelly at the young man standing in front of him. The visitor is small, young enough to be Rattigan's nephew, with a round cherub's face, and a slightly mischievous grin. Without uttering a word, they embrace and move into the darkened shadows of the flat. The door closes behind them.

This time the scene is a large house in Sunningdale, on the very edge of the golf course. It is Sunday morning, and the house is full of laughter. There are weekend guests, some of them preparing to play golf, some still in bed. The housekeeper has laid the sideboard with an enormous breakfast. There is champagne as well as fruit juice.

It is the summer of 1960, and Terence Rattigan is standing by the french windows reading a copy of the *Observer*. He is shaking visibly: so much so that when a strikingly beautiful woman comes quietly into the room, she is convinced he is about to suffer some form of heart attack. When she speaks, he turns round abruptly and laughs.

'These critics,' he tells her, smiling with every part of his face except his eyes. 'I don't know why I read them.' Margaret Leighton returns his smile, but she does not believe him. As she watches him put his golf-clubs into the boot of his Rolls, she looks down. The review by Kenneth Tynan has been crumpled into a small ball. It lies at her feet.

The scene changes to a hospital room, and the man writing is having difficulty sitting. His face is pallid, the skin taut against his cheekbones, and now pain is clear in his eyes. It is the summer of 1977, and Terence Rattigan is dying of cancer. He has come to London for the opening of his new play, *Cause Célèbre*. He knows it will be his last first night.

As he looks out of the hospital window across the rooftops of central London, towards Piccadilly Circus and Shaftesbury Avenue, he knows that the theatre he knew and loved is dead. Binkie has gone, and with him the glittering days of H.M. Tennent. Puffin Asquith is dead, and so are Kay and Vivien. Even his mother, who seemed almost indestructible, died six years ago.

His eyes fill with tears. There is no way back, no way to recover those heady days when everything he touched turned to gold. And he cannot quite understand why. To find out, we must return to the beginning.

CHAPTER 1

Land of Heart's Desire

◆

I remember my youth and the feeling that will
never come back any more — the feeling that I could
last forever, outlast the sea, the earth, and all men;
the deceitful feeling that lures us on to perils, to
love, to vain effort — to death.

JOSEPH CONRAD

◆

The Rattigan family were Irish bred, Protestant by religion, and imbued with a distinctive spirit of adventure and determination. Their rise began in the 1840s, when Bartholomew Rattigan of County Kildare decided to exchange the mist and peat fires of his native Ireland for more exciting prospects. He emigrated to India with his new young wife and their first child, a son, after accepting a post in the ordnance department of the East India Company. Two years later a second son was born.

Both sons prospered in their adopted land. The elder, Henry Adolphus Rattigan, became an advocate and author of standard works on Indian law, notably as it applied to divorce among Christians and Indians, and ended his career as Chief Justice of the Punjab. But his fame was eclipsed by that of his younger brother William, the real founder of the Rattigan family's reputation.

'A self-made man, without advantage of family influence' was how the *Dictionary of National Biography* was to describe this archetypally resolute and gifted Victorian after his death in 1904, at the age of sixty-one. Educated at the High School in Agra, William Henry

Rattigan went straight into Government service as an assistant commissioner in the Punjab. Before the age of twenty he was acting as a judge in the 'small causes' court in Delhi.

A year after his marriage to an English colonel's daughter, Teresa Matilda Higgins, whose father was examiner of accounts in the public works department, he resigned his post with the Government and started to study the law in India, recognising how important a sound legal system would become to the country so rapidly developing around him. When the Punjab Chief Court was established in 1866, William Rattigan rapidly built himself a successful advocacy practice. He was twenty-four.

In 1871, at the age of twenty-nine he was well enough established to return to London to complete his legal education. He was admitted as a student at King's College in the University of London and at Lincoln's Inn, where he was called to the Bar in June 1873, having passed his law examinations with first class honours. England did not attract him, however, and with his growing family of four sons and two daughters, he lost no time in returning to India. Within four years he was Government Advocate, and therefore chief prosecutor, in Lahore, a position that put him, in the words of a later Indian Government report, 'at the height of his profession'. During the 1880s he also acted (in between his periods of advocacy) as Judge of the Chief Court of Lahore.

Both in association with a colleague, Charles Boulnois, and on his own, William also helped to construct the first reference books on Punjab law. His book *The Civil and Customary Law for the Punjab*, first published in 1880, is still the standard text on the subject, with editions published well into the 1960s. He also found time to write books on Hindu law, including *The Hindu Law of Adoption*, as well as to complete a treatise on the history of India from the invasion of Alexander 'to the latest times' – 'with introductory remarks on the mythology, philosophy and science of the Hindus'.

An exceptional linguist, Rattigan had mastered the five major European languages within a few years of the end of his schooldays in Agra, and went on to learn not only several Indian dialects – and their vernacular – but also Persian. Shortly after his fortieth birthday, and while still acting as Chief Advocate in Lahore, he found time to take a doctorate in German at the University of Göttingen.

His enthusiasm for the Indian Bar was beginning to wane, however. In November 1886 he resigned his judgeship to concentrate on advocacy, but within three months had accepted the vice-chancellorship of the then all but bankrupt (and only recently founded) Punjab University. In the next five years he saved it from financial ruin, for which its grateful Court awarded him a Doctorate of Law and reappointed him biennially until he resigned in 1895. He also became President of the Khalsa College Committee, and thereby helped to establish education among the Sikh community. A hospital named in his memory in the college was established after his death by the Sikhs of Amritsar in recognition of his work.

Knighted by Queen Victoria in 1895 and elected a QC in 1897, he eventually decided to return to England to practise before the Privy Council as one of the few barristers with substantial experience in the Indian courts. He was by now long remarried. His first wife had died in 1876 and two years later he had married her younger sister Evelyn, with whom he proceeded to have a further three sons, bringing the total number of his children to nine. Encouraged by Evelyn, he entered politics, but his career in the House of Commons was short-lived.

In the 'khaki election' of October 1900, Sir William Rattigan stood 'in the liberal unionist interest' as a candidate for the Scottish seat of North East Lanarkshire, and went so far as to name his new London residence (a large house recently constructed in Cornwall Gardens, South Kensington) Lanarkslea, in the constituency's honour. He failed to get elected at the first attempt, but shortly afterwards, in September 1901, he won the seat at a by-election, with a majority of 904.

But his health was weakening. The intense demands he had put upon himself in India had taken their toll, and by the beginning of 1904 he was too ill even to speak in the House. In the spring of that year he told the Government whips that he was going to take the summer off and retire to his Scottish constituency in an effort to recuperate. On the morning of 4 July 1904 he and Lady Rattigan set off for Scotland in the back of their chauffeur-driven Darracq. Sir William had not returned from India loaded with wealth, but he adored new inventions, and particularly the motor car, even though these contraptions, in the words of the historian Sir Robert Ensor, aroused intense feelings about the 'selfishness of arrogant wealth' as they dashed along the old narrow untarred carriageways, 'frightening the passer-by on their approach and drenching him in dust as they receded'. Sir William's Darracq would certainly have done that. On this occasion, while passing Langford, a village near Biggleswade in Bedfordshire, on the way north, however, the spokes of the rear wheel shattered as the car rounded a corner, and the vehicle overturned.

Sir William was thrown out of the open car. His neck was broken instantly. Lady Rattigan and the chauffeur, John Young, survived because they remained inside, crumpled together in a heap. The

Coroner suggested two days later that the car may have been in need of some mechanical attention, which Sir William had refused to allow it to have, and that the luggage piled on the roof at the rear had made it unstable. He nevertheless recorded a verdict of accidental death. Three days later, Sir William Rattigan KC, MP, the founder of the Rattigan dynasty, was buried in Kensal Green Cemetery in London.

The headship of the family now passed to his eldest son, William Frank, always called Frank, a young man who displayed the familiar Rattigan loquacity and charm but totally lacked his father's gravitas. Frank had already embarked on a promising diplomatic career, and at the moment of his father's death was about to take up his second posting, as an attaché at The Hague. Handsome and distinctly dashing, and with an eye for pretty girls, he realised, however, that a young diplomat with ambitions needs a wife, and on 2 December 1905, at Christ Church in Paddington, Frank Rattigan married Vera Houston, daughter of Arthur Houston KC, barrister, bankruptcy expert, authority on English drama and former don, the child of another itinerant Irish Protestant family. Vera Houston, who lived with her father at 22 Lancaster Gate on the northern edge of Hyde Park, was then just twenty, with flaming red hair that streamed down to her shoulders in waves, and a slight lilt to her voice. Slim, effervescent, and undeniably pretty, she was to be Frank Rattigan's long-suffering wife throughout the rest of his life.

The union of these two Irish families provides the first clues to the character of their second son. Irish though they were, neither Frank nor Vera thought much about religion. An Irish Protestant does not perhaps suffer the haunting guilt that his Scottish equivalent might. The Rattigans lived life to the full, and that is how their second son, Terence, was to be brought up.

Frank Rattigan had spent the first ten years of his life with his father in Lahore, looked after by a full complement of servants but not overly supplied with much in the way of hard cash. Sir William Rattigan was more likely to present his eldest son with a rifle and six cartridges – to shoot whatever food he could – than to give him money. Around Christmas Sir William would take two or three week holidays to go shooting in the Himalayas, and years later Frank was to recall, 'I sometimes sat up with him all night, waiting for the tigers and leopards, and learnt to control my nerves.' It gave the boy an appetite for shooting which he was never to lose. It also gave him a taste for a life surrounded by servants.

Frank came to England in 1888, at the age of ten, to study at a preparatory school, Elstree near Newbury in Berkshire, in preparation for Harrow. Presents of books from his father and mother would arrive from time to time to alleviate the austere school lifestyle. Like other boys in his position, he travelled home to India only rarely, though there was no sign that he suffered – as so many of his contemporaries did – from the fear that he would never recognise his parents when he saw them again. He was a confident boy, who turned into a fine cricketer. The masters at Elstree were 'nearly all famous cricketers', he recalled later, and their coaching stood him in good stead.

Frank arrived at Harrow in 1893, sweeping into the school with effortless assurance and charm. He was no Tom Brown, frightened of the shadow of Flashman, but a boy happy in the knowledge that he was one of England's chosen few. So great was his enjoyment of his time at the school that a decade later he donated a plaque to the chapel when his father was killed in the summer of 1904.

His two brothers also went to Harrow. Gerald, the next senior, who stayed for just two years, from 1896 to 1898, was the only one of the three not to go on to university. He became a clerk in the Principal Probate Registry. Like his father, he was killed in a motor accident, in 1934.

Cyril, the youngest, stayed at the school for the full five years, from 1898 until the summer of 1904. He became a Monitor (Harrow's equivalent of a prefect), was picked to play against Eton in the annual cricket match at Lords (though he missed the game through illness), and played for the school cricket eleven in 1903 and 1904 before going on to Trinity College, Cambridge. He was killed in Flanders in 1916, serving as a captain in the Royal Fusiliers.

Neither brother could rival Frank's success, and particularly his success on the cricket field. In his first year, at the age of barely fourteen, there was a strong possibility that Frank might be asked to play for the Eleven against Eton in June. In the end, he was adjudged too young, but the following summer he made the Eleven and was awarded his 'flannels', a significant honour. Like Cyril, he was to miss the first match through illness, but was to play against Eton in the next three matches, in 1896, 1897 and 1898, with considerable distinction. The swashbuckling Frank Rattigan became something of a Harrow cricketing legend.

In 1898 he went up to Magdalen College, Oxford, where he played cricket in the Freshmen's match, scoring a century, but did not get a trial for the University side in his first year. By then he had decided to leave Oxford and join the Diplomatic Service, which his father had urged upon him. This necessitated going abroad to learn French and German. He went first to Hanover and then to Compiègne.

In Hanover he lodged with a stern German lady used to 'young English gentlemen preparing for the Diplomatic', and made friends with another student, Lionel de Rothschild. Both young men experienced the wave of Anglophobia that was sweeping Germany in the first years of the century, but neither was unduly disconcerted by it. At Compiègne the hostile atmosphere he had experienced in Germany did nothing to prevent Frank from indulging his favourite pastimes – gambling, shooting and flirting with pretty girls. On his return to London he finished his course of cramming under the tutelage of the formidable and renowned W.B.Scoones, and in the autumn of 1902 he filled the third of the three places available to entrants for the Diplomatic Service in the autumn examinations. He joined the service, spent a year as Foreign Office clerk in London, and in March 1904 was posted to Vienna as a junior attaché.

This was the life. 'The Vienna season,' he was to reminisce later, 'was an endless whirl of gaiety, what with the numerous Court Balls, those given by the leading Austrian families, and the picnic dances subscribed for by the bachelors in society.' The new attaché was also to gain a moment of fame dancing the polka with the future Queen Mary, wife of George V. ('I was far from being an expert at this particular dance; my royal partner and I created some devastation in the ballroom, by bumping into other couples and sending them flying.')

A mere three months later he was posted to The Hague. 'It was in Holland,' he was to write later, 'that I first developed an interest in collecting antiques of all kinds, and I travelled all over the country in the search for Delft, old books, furniture and prints.' He augmented his modest income by discreet dealing in furniture and pictures. It was here too that he brought his new young wife Vera in 1906.

Frank Rattigan was an embroiderer of the truth. In his memoirs, *Diversions of a Diplomat*, published in 1924, he writes that his new young wife was 'seventeen when they married', yet the marriage certificate he signed shows clearly that she was twenty. This trait was one of many that Vera Rattigan was to discover about her new husband. For the moment she was more than enchanted to be whisked off to The Hague, there to be fêted by other diplomatic wives, smiled at by ambassadors and introduced to the many pleasures of this glittering world. The idyll was interrupted only by her pregnancy. On 24 October 1906, nine months after her arrival in The Hague, Vera gave birth in London to a boy, Brian William Arthur.

The child was born with a physical deformity. His left leg was severely shorter than the right, and there were indications that there might be some brain damage. Vera was desolate. She felt she had failed, but Frank seemed unperturbed. His smile was still as warm, his words as consoling. There was no question, however, of taking the baby back with them to The Hague. Brian would stay in Kensington with Lady Rattigan, to be looked after by a nanny and given all necessary medical care.

By the time Frank Rattigan got round to officially registering his son's birth – something he did not manage until 1 December – he knew that he and his wife were already destined for a new posting, the Tangier Legation. After the New Year celebrations in England, and a brief trip to Holland, they set off for Morocco.

Just getting to Tangier proved to be an adventure. The city had no formal harbour, which forced visiting steamships to anchor on the tide and wait for flat-bottomed rafts to be rowed out to transport the passengers and their luggage ashore. The wife of a French chargé d'affaires and his children had been drowned in the process, and when the Rattigans arrived in a storm they were in fear for their lives. 'We had a terrible time during the row to the shore,' Frank wrote,

and were several times nearly swamped by the tremendous following waves. However, we did eventually reach the quay, soaked to the skin but alive. Under the escort of Legation soldiers, who had been sent to meet us, we fought our way through the hordes of yelling donkey boys, mounted the horses provided for us, and clattered up the slippery cobble-paved streets to our hotel. It was too rough to land our baggage for two days, and we were obliged to remove our soaking clothes and retire to bed, until our chief and his wife kindly came to our assistance with spare clothes.

Frank and Vera Rattigan were to become popular members of the distinctive expatriate community of Tangier over the next four years. They won the mixed doubles in the Moroccan tennis championship – incidentally beating their chief, Sir Gerald Lowther, and his pretty American wife in the process – and travelled throughout the country. When Lowther left, to be replaced by the bachelor Sir Richard Lister, Vera effectively became hostess of the Legation. There were servants, parties, and an exciting diplomatic life, with the rebel Rasouli still in command of vast sections of the country, his actions and escapades chronicled by the veteran correspondent of *The Times*, Walter Harris, who himself had been kidnapped by the chieftain and ransomed for £10,000.

There was so much to do that there were few trips home. Brian had to remain in his grandmother's house in Cornwall Gardens. Vera loved her son, but she had made her mind up. Supporting Frank was more important. Other diplomats' wives had made the same decision, but Vera had another reason. She did not want to leave her handsome husband unsupervised.

Had she been a little older, Vera would have realised that there was little she could do to reduce her husband's appetite for girls. She was still in her twenties, beautiful in her own right, and with a slightly imperious air, as well as something of an Irish temper. She was not going to be outdone without a fight. However, her absence abroad was not to provide an auspicious start to Brian Rattigan's life. He was to become a morbid, unhappy boy, an outsider with a self-destructive urge, depressed at his inability to live up to the Rattigan tradition. In the stiff surroundings of Cornwall Gardens, where he was ushered at teatime into his grandmother's presence to be inspected – properly dressed in velvet and lace – he was denied the affection that he so obviously craved. Brian was left to sink into his own painful loneliness: the boy who was never talked about.

On the afternoon of 6 May 1910, King Edward VII died at Biarritz and the golden age of Edwardian England came to an end. Frank and Vera Rattigan were already discussing a return to England. There was talk of a second child, and Vera was determined to see the new baby born safely at home. By the end of the year Vera knew that she was pregnant. A second child was due in June 1911, only days before the date fixed for the Coronation of the new King. In May Frank and Vera returned to Cornwall Gardens, and to Brian, who was now almost five.

By then Frank had found that his posting to Tangier had produced an unexpected benefit. He was appointed Gold Staff Officer at the Coronation of King George V, with the special task of looking after the ex-Grand Vizier of Morocco, Sid el Menebhi, one of his old tennis friends from his days at the Legation, who would be one of the official guests. The prospect thrilled him much more than his wife's pregnancy. He thoroughly enjoyed showing London to the Moroccan. His guest was 'much interested and excited by the shops, and I had great difficulty in preventing him from buying vast quantities of useless objects'. Frank also took the former Grand Vizier to a number of smart parties, introducing him to the strikingly beautiful young Lady Diana Cooper, whom they met at Belvoir Castle on a visit to the Duke of Rutland.

It was against this backdrop that Terence Rattigan, the second and last son of Frank and Vera Rattigan, was born.

CHAPTER 2

Father of the Man

◆

What you see is the Never Land. You have

often half-seen it before, or even three quarters,

after the nightlights were lit, and you might then

have beached your coracle on it if you had

not always at the great moment fallen asleep.

J.M.BARRIE, *Peter Pan*, Act II

◆

The first thing to note about Terence Rattigan's birth is that no reference book seems to give the date correctly. Rattigan was not born on 10 June 1911, though he, himself, never corrected the error. In fact Vera Rattigan gave birth to her second son in an upstairs room at Lanarkslea, her mother-in-law's house in Cornwall Gardens, shortly before midnight on 9 June, as his birth certificate at the Kensington Register Office and the announcement in *The Times* two days later duly stated. The birth certificate bore just the single Christian name Terence, though he was to adopt the extra Christian name of Mervyn as a young man.

Frank Rattigan did not register his second son's birth for three weeks. Like almost every other man in England, he was caught up in the excitement of King George V's coronation. The whole country was preparing to celebrate. In London the streets had been specially cleaned and new flowers had been planted in the gardens. Two official Coronation bank holidays had been announced, and visitors to the capital could purchase tickets to watch the Coronation procession from a covered grandstand for prices between four guineas and fifteen guineas.

While they were waiting, both visitors and Londoners could divert themselves by going to see George Robey at the Empire in Leicester Square or Gerald du Maurier and Irene Vanbrugh in a new play by C. Haddon Chambers at Wyndham's.

Vera was not sufficiently recovered from giving birth to attend the celebrations taking place almost beneath her window, but Frank was in the thick of them, conducting his charge, the former Grand Vizier of Morocco, to parties and tennis tournaments, balls and shooting weekends, with an eye to the advancement of his own career. He was no doubt proud of his new and perfectly healthy son, whom his wife had presented to him the day after his birth. Frank had not been present at the birth itself, but in the book he wrote thirteen years later, about his time in the diplomatic service, the child's arrival, like that of his firstborn almost five years earlier, merits not even a line. In its place there are lists of tennis scores and dinner guests, alongside lengthy references to his own many and varied talents.

In the days to come, while Vera exulted in the new baby and Lady Rattigan looked magisterially over her shoulder, Frank was occupied by his life as Gold Staff Officer at the Coronation. There were costume fittings, and seating plans, dinners to be attended and Sid el Menehbi to be ushered to all the right places. He took the Moroccan to 'one of the great balls of the season', at Derby House, where the former Grand Vizier, on being introduced to the Duchess, uttered, much to her amusement, one of his few English phrases, 'It looks like rain.'

Throughout the two days of official celebrations Frank Rattigan marched around the capital, a gilded figure dressed in his Gold Staff Officer's uniform. Then it was time to return to Tangier. Hardly had he arrived there – joined by Vera as soon as she felt well enough – than he received his reward for his efforts in The Hague. He was to be promoted to Second Secretary and posted to the British Embassy in Cairo, to work for the Ambassador, the famously irascible Lord Kitchener. Frank and Vera left Tangier in a P & O steamship and reached the Egytian capital in December, having stopped at Gibraltar, Marseilles and Malta on the way. But they did not take their new son Terence with them.

Cairo proved a magical posting. An extraordinary Ambassador reigned over an opulent and extravagant court. There were 'balls every night' and a 'delightful country club'. 'One could play any game one liked, including polo, cricket, golf, tennis, squash racquets and croquet.' Frank was in his element, and was also captivated by Kitchener himself. 'Certainly under the magic wand of his tremendous energy and force of character, and his faculty of bringing out all that was best in his subordinates, difficulties and obstacles would melt away like snow. I know that I myself was inspired by him with a spirit of zeal and devotion which filled me with a desire to do my best.' His best came out at the outset, when Kitchener demanded that he write the annual report on the Sudan, a massive work of detail, almost immediately after his arrival. 'Have you any comment to make?' Frank was asked. 'No sir, except that for the moment I know nothing about the Sudan.' 'Then you are in luck,' retorted the Ambassador, 'for when you have finished you should know everything that can be known about it.' He was given a fortnight to complete the task, and he took just ten days.

The two years that Frank Rattigan and his wife spent in Cairo were among the happiest of their life in the Diplomatic Service. Frank's ability as a tennis player earned him an enormous reputation at the country club, where he consistently defeated the reigning German champion to the obvious delight of the British community. Indeed, his prowess as a tennis player is almost the only aspect of his posting that Frank later recorded of his life there: apart, that is, from his formidable expertise as a shot – '184 Quail before 4 pm' a record for the previous ten years.

His gambling continued, as did his collecting. He even induced Kitchener to take trips into the souk with him in pursuit of Egyptian antiquities. He embarked on a 'dig' for Greco-Roman remains at the delta outside the city and unearthed 'three large mosaics in practically unspoilt condition', as well as 'a few small statuettes and a large number of Roman coins of base silver'. Statuettes, vases, screens, bronze tables, rugs, daggers, earthenware pots, fragments of marble frescos all lined the Rattigans' apartment, and Frank was not above offering particular treasures to his Ambassador – at the right price. Nor was Kitchener above buying them.

His summer leaves were spent partly in England, on visits to see Terence and Brian and his mother in Cornwall Gardens, but these fleeting visits never delayed him long, for his amiable conversation as well as his sporting skills ensured invitations to shooting parties all over Europe. In the summer of 1913, for example, though he spent a little time in England, he spent much longer shooting on the banks of the Danube, in a villa he and his younger brother Cyril had rented on the Hungarian side of the Austro-Hungarian border.

That autumn Frank learnt he was to be transferred from Cairo to a new posting in Berlin. He and Vera returned to London for a brief leave before travelling to the German capital, where they arrived on 31 December 1913. Totally unaware of the impending Armageddon,

they had had their antiques and furniture shipped over from England,
where they had been stored on their return from Cairo. 'I had little
idea,' Frank wrote, 'that all this furniture would have to be abandoned
in Berlin and that it would be nearly six years before I got it back in
a damaged and battered condition.' For Frank Rattigan the lights were
certainly not going out all over Europe. They were shining more
brightly than ever. 'It was the height of the Berlin season and we were
at once plunged into a whirl of social engagements . . . The Berlin
Court Balls were even more magnificent than those of Vienna.' They
were followed by more embassy receptions, more liaisons with glamorous women, and more tennis competitions.

His two sons, meanwhile, lived the life customary for children of
the rich, a life circumscribed by servants and nannies, and, in this case,
a severe grandmother. There is no record that either Brian or Terence
ever joined Frank and Vera at any of their earlier postings, and it is
most unlikely that they did so. Vera was still determined to devote
herself to her husband, and she relished the diplomatic life. But now,
in 1914, for just a few months, Frank Rattigan had his young son
Terence with him in Berlin. Perhaps Vera insisted on it, in the hope
that her son would keep her company and prove to her husband that
he had responsibilities to his family; perhaps it was simply a whim.
For whatever reason, the youngest Rattigan spent the period between
March and early July 1914 in the German capital, at the end of which
time he was just over three years old.

Years later Terence Rattigan could 'still conjure up vague memories
of being given an immense bottle of brightly coloured sweets by Crown
Prince William, embraced by him, and consoled for not in the least
resembling either of my beautiful parents'. The story formed part of
the folklore of his childhood – one of the few happier memories amid
the harsher recollections of the nursery at Cornwall Gardens. 'My
mother tells me this story is apocryphal, but the Crown Prince had by
then become a great friend of theirs, I don't, unhappily, look much
like either of them, and someone did give me those sweets. I still think
it was the Crown Prince.'

In the middle of July, only three weeks before war was declared,
Frank took his customary month's leave – to go back to England with
his wife and son. 'The crisis had then not become acute,' he wrote,
'and the usual summer leave was not stopped.' Scarcely a week after
his arrival he was back on the train to Berlin. War was declared on 4
August and shortly before dawn the next morning he was waiting in
the Embassy for the official train which the German Government had
reluctantly agreed to lay on for the departing diplomats. He crossed

the English Channel safely and returned to Cornwall Gardens, only to find the house almost deserted – as his wife and family, as well as his mother, had departed for a seaside holiday.

Frank immediately sought out his old Cairo boss, Lord Kitchener, to ask for a post on his general staff, and within two days he had been offered a captaincy, 'provided he could be ready to leave for France tomorrow'. On 9 August 1914 the thirty-five-year-old diplomat purchased a 'ready-to-wear' khaki captain's uniform in London, and summoned Vera and the children from the seaside.

His military adventures in France were brief and bizarre. He got lost on several occasions, was almost blown up after getting lost on his way to the front, and seemed forever to be attaching himself to whatever command happened to be nearest. Within four months, after having been slightly wounded in an explosion, he was back at the Foreign Office in London, working from midnight to eight in the morning monitoring incoming cables and telegrams.

He was rescued from this position by a new diplomatic posting, this time to the Legation in Bucharest, where he was again to be a Second Secretary. Though officially neutral, Romania was nevertheless hemmed in on every side by Germany and her allies, the Austrians, Bulgarians and Turks. Frank set off for Bucharest alone, but Vera joined him only 'a little later'. It was their first experience of a neutral country in wartime, and he recorded later that they found 'the conditions of life curious and disconcerting'. The majority of the Romanian population were pro-British, but there was a strongly Germanophile minority, including the leading families, the army officers and a substantial section of the Jewish community. From time to time the British found themselves abused in the streets.

Even here there were still receptions, tennis matches – and gambling. There were big poker and baccarat schools in the Bucharest clubs, as well as a strong tradition of horse-racing, relying on imported British and American jockeys. Game included the remarkable three-foot-high cock Great Bustard, and there were regular trips to the marshes for woodcock.

In the middle of September 1916 Romania entered the war on the Allied side, and two months later Frank heard the news that his brother Cyril had been killed on the Somme. As usual, he later romanticised the details, describing Cyril's death in imaginary and Homeric terms and bringing the date forward to 1 July, the first day of the battle, when in fact it had occurred on 13 November. Nevertheless Cyril was almost certainly one of the very few people whom Frank genuinely loved. He had joined the Royal Fusiliers shortly after the outbreak of war, and in August 1916 was offered a staff appointment, which would have taken him away from the front. Cyril declined, saying that he 'could not leave his regiment and the men he loved, all of whom are such fine fellows'.

By comparison, Frank Rattigan did not even consider the lives of his two sons. In spite of the one brief trip to Berlin, neither Brian nor Terry had spent more than a few months with their father throughout their lives, and very little more with their mother. Theirs was an isolated world of starched aprons and prim mouths, of strict teatimes and prayers before bed. Their parents were almost strangers. Affection was not dispensed in large warm handfuls at Lanarkslea in Cornwall Gardens. Lady Rattigan did not believe in spoiling the child by sparing the rod, indeed she may even have wished she had displayed a firmer hand towards her eldest son, Frank, so different was he in temperament from his public-spirited father. This lack of affection, when it was added to their isolation, taught Brian and his younger brother Terence never to give too much away for fear of a ferocious reprisal. It bred an obsessive, wilful secrecy.

Terence Rattigan was to fill the vacuum with romance, and his own imaginings, and the New Year of 1918 gave his longings an impetus which, young though he was, sowed the seeds of a lifelong passion. He was taken to his first pantomime. Thirty-one years later, in a talk for the BBC's Home Service, he described, with a little philosophical hindsight, what it had meant to him.

> So what would I say had been my greatest thrill in the theatre to date? Well I suppose my answer to that would be much the same as anyone else's – namely the first time in my life that I ever went to the theatre. I was seven, and the piece I saw was *Cinderella* . . .
>
> What was it that so thrilled me about *Cinderella*? Well, first it told a story . . . and a good one too – heaven knows it's been stolen often enough. Then it told it clearly and simply, in terms that the most nit-witted member of the audience – which was probably me – could easily understand.

It was not only the story that captured his imagination, however. There was something else.

> It was about people – not about things – and, what is more, about people I cared for. It was important to me, as a member of that audience, that Cinderella should go to the ball and marry the prince. Just as, at a later age, it was important to me that Hamlet should succeed in avenging his father. Why was it important, do

you suppose? Well, I think, in both cases because the character had completely captured the audience's imagination, and mine with it, as no inanimate object like a theme or an idea or a moral could ever do . . . I do remember that I believed implicitly everything I saw on that stage. Belief in the play – belief in what is happening on the stage – that's the life blood of the theatre. I believed that Cinderella did go to that ball. Why? Because I was made to believe . . . And what, after all, is the theatre but the art of make-believe?

In short, he was transported as far from his real life in the nursery in Cornwall Gardens as the Darling children were from their imaginary nursery not a mile away in *Peter Pan*. As his friend the critic B. A. Young was to say of him many years later, Terence Rattigan, like Peter Pan, was 'the boy who never grew up'.

Not that Frank and Vera Rattigan noticed. They returned from Bucharest later in 1918, for Frank to have treatment for a severe attack of arthritis, but Terence was well aware by now that they would not stay for long. He was right. They left again for the Romanian capital soon after Christmas, with thirty-seven pieces of luggage and no idea that the world had changed for ever. To them it was as it had always been. Indeed, Frank's career was about to receive its first public recognition. At the age of forty-one Frank Rattigan was made a Companion of the Order of St Michael and St George, a CMG, for his services to the cause of Britain's diplomacy. It was the first step on the ladder which normally led up to a KCMG, a GCMG and the crowning honour of an ambassadorship. Simultaneously with the award he was appointed Counsellor at the Romanian Embassy, and within a few months was offered the sensitive and demanding post of Assistant High Commissioner at the British Embassy in Constantinople.

To mark his departure the Bucharest Jockey Club organised a banquet in his honour – 'the only occasion, so I was informed, that anything of the kind has been done for a departing diplomat'. The idea that his enthusiasm not merely for its race meetings but for the betting which accompanied them might have something to do with this does not seem to have crossed his mind. This endlessly charming, self-deceiving symbol of the Edwardian era swept out of Bucharest on a cloud of self-congratulation, to proceed to Turkey with, as ever, barely a thought for anyone other than himself.

By the time of their final return from Bucharest in 1920, however, their eight-year-old son, Terence, was ready to announce to his parents that he had decided to become a playwright. They responded by telling him that he would be joining his brother at Sandroyd, a preparatory school near Cobham in Surrey, run by an old-style but respected pedagogue called W.M.Hornby.

Terence and his brother overlapped for just one term. They were a study in contrasts. Brian, at thirteen, was now a huge boy, almost six feet tall, coarse and vigorous. Club foot or no, he kept wicket for the school's first eleven and led the batting averages. His brother, slight and rather shy, would take a term or two to establish his sporting prowess. Nonetheless, he already knew his own mind. He insisted on being called Terry rather than Terence by his fellow pupils, and loathed being called 'Rattigan Minor' by the staff. And he continued to explore his private world of make-believe.

By the time he had been at the school two years, he had written a short story called 'Self-Sacrifice', described by its author as an 'enthralling novelette by the famous playwrite and author T.M.Rattigan' (the additional Christian name Mervyn having been added in Cornwall Gardens, probably to annoy Lady Rattigan rather than his parents). He commented forty years later that the work 'seems to show signs of another literary ambition; but it appears to have been abandoned on page three, both novelette and ambition, for thereafter there are no indications among my fairly extensive juvenilia of anything but the dialogue form'.

At Sandroyd, Terry was as oblivious to his father's adventures as his father was to his. Brian had moved on to Harrow, and he was relishing school life, particularly anything to do with plays and acting. When his parents came home on leave from Bucharest he persuaded one or other of them to take him to the theatre whenever he could, provoking his mother Vera to remark, 'If he had his way he would have got there long before the dust sheets were removed from the seats.' Some thirty years later he wrote, 'By the age of eleven I was already a confirmed and resolute playgoer.' He was also a confirmed and resolute 'playwrite' in the making, determined to rediscover the magic he had witnessed in the theatre itself. He had already written two short plays, *Lady Hermione's Secret* and *Shoot to Kill*, and was planning several more.

Writing plays, and going to plays, were an obsession, and became his whole life. 'The only reason that, from the age of eleven to the age of twenty-three, I continually persisted in raising the imagined curtain to disclose a non-existent stage, was that there was really no way I could have kept the darn thing down.' Plays were his secret, an experience that he need share with no one. They were a passion that he need not share or explain, but that, in turn, induced a sense of guilt.

He explained the dilemma to an American magazine many years afterwards.

As I invariably suffered acute guilt about such jaunts, feeling that any pleasure so intensely felt must be somehow immoral, I would lie to my parents with, apparently, some early signs of creative invention, anyway with invariable success, to explain why my pocket money had so quickly disappeared and why I needed another shilling to indulge myself in the more conventional pleasures of childhood. My parents must have thought me a very greedy, careless and over-generous little boy (my three main excuses) but they never caught me in Shaftesbury Avenue.

The theatre, and the Shaftesbury Avenue theatre in particular, gave him a home, a place where he felt, for the first time in his life, a sense of belonging.

All of which, no doubt, sounds very foolish – seemingly no more than an expression, in a rather absurd form, of the ordinary child's urge to ape the grown-ups . . . Yet I don't think it was only that. Up in my galleries (or, as my pocket money increased proportionately with my snobbishness, down in my pits), I was experiencing emotions which, though no doubt insincere of origin in that they were induced and coloured by the adult emotions around me, were none the less most deeply felt.

It was those sensations that he was to try to recapture in his own work.

When I came, therefore, to try to reproduce, as a precocious playwright, the emotions that had been aroused in myself as a precocious member of any audience, the results, though no doubt ludicrous, were at least instinctively theatrical. It was by no cold and conscious exercise that I was able to act as an audience to my own plays, I could not have written them otherwise.

Almost the only other thing which engaged his imagination in a similar way was cricket. It too was a world where heroes reigned. There had been stories at Cornwall Gardens of his father's exploits at Harrow, and tales of his uncle's misfortune at never being able to play against Eton. Cricket was in the Rattigan blood. He had seen his brother keep wicket and bat for Sandroyd's first eleven in his first term at the school, and Terry was determined to match the achievement. In August 1921, in his first summer vacation away from Sandroyd, he had been taken to see the legendary C.G.Macartney play at the

Somerset county ground at Taunton, where his hero was, alas, bowled for 19 by J.G.White.

More than forty years later Rattigan wrote that:

> The analogy between theatre and cricket is truthful, if inexact. At the Oval we had queued to see great drama certainly – but we wouldn't have queued so long or so happily if Dexter (and O'Neill, Trueman and Simpson) hadn't been in the cast. At Chichester we queued to see Shakespeare's *Othello* certainly – but with Olivier standing down with a pulled tendon (and in that performance he is apt to pull almost anything) might the audience have wondered whether to sit in a dark theatre for three hours to watch a familiar drama unfold . . . was really the best way to spend a sunny Saturday afternoon.

Frank and Vera Rattigan were quite oblivious to these dreams of their sensitive son. By now they were firmly established in Constantinople, Frank promoted from Assistant to Acting High Commissioner on the departure of Sir Horace Rumbold. In August 1922 Vera returned to England for her customary summer holiday, taking both boys to stay in a rented cottage belonging to the drama critic Hubert Griffiths, where the only books seemed to be plays. For the three weeks they were there Terence read nothing else. He was hypnotised.

Though neither knew it at the time, that summer of 1922 was to be the last that Terence Rattigan or his brother would spend alone with their mother. A non-theatrical nemesis was about to overtake Frank Rattigan, wrecking his career as a rising diplomat and deeply affecting the lives of his wife and sons. Two causes underlay it. First came the Chanak crisis of 1922, when Turkish forces, poised to invade the European side of the Turkish frontier, near Constantinople, threatened to spark off a major international conflagration less than four years after the last had come to an end. In London, Lloyd George and Churchill were in favour of resisting them by force. Lord Curzon, the Foreign Secretary, took the opposite view. Reflecting the feelings of the majority of the nation, who showed no enthusiasm for embarking on another war, he issued a statement explaining that he looked 'with favour' on Turkish claims. The danger was averted when the British commander in the field made a pact with the Turks, who agreed to respect a neutral zone around Chanak. Then, shortly afterwards, Lloyd George was forced to resign as prime minister for more domestic reasons. Frank Rattigan, who had already supported the Lloyd George/ Churchill policy, found himself suspended as Acting High Commissioner in Constantinople at the end of September 1922.

Frank Rattigan's behaviour had certainly been unwise for an ambitious diplomat, but it was not the sole cause of his downfall in the diplomatic service. Although in the years to come he would steadfastly maintain that his views had cost him his career, the real reason was spicier. His womanising had increased steadily, and in Bucharest he had embarked on an affair with Princess Elisabeth of Romania which, even by his standards, was ambitious. When Elisabeth became Queen of Greece, the British Foreign Office decided that enough was enough. Frank Rattigan was politely, but firmly, asked to resign: not for his principles but for his philandering. If he agreed he would be given a small pension. Reluctantly, he agreed.

Suddenly deprived of all the trappings that had made their life so glamorous, Frank and Vera found themselves renting a top-floor flat at 19 Stanhope Gardens, South Kensington, only a short walk from the far grander Lanarkslea. The dreary climb up four flights of stairs was a painful reminder of all that they had lost. With his pension, a few investments, and his antique dealing, Frank could scrape together an income of about £1,000 a year. It was hardly abject poverty, and for the moment the schooling of his two sons would remain undisturbed – not least with the financial support of his mother – but it was a tight squeeze. It was the disgrace that was difficult to face.

For a time Frank tried to pretend he was just 'on leave' when he went to his club, the Bath, to have dinner. To bolster his confidence he took to calling himself 'Major Rattigan', his rank at the end of his brief period of military service. But, as ever, his salvation lay in his capacity for self-deception. In his own estimation he was still a great diplomat ('who had had the misfortune to fall out with Curzon'), a magnificent sportsman, a key figure in the events of his times. He even attempted to confirm his importance by writing a memoir of his career, *Diversions of a Diplomat*, published in 1924. This rich fantasy of his past importance sustained him throughout the rest of his life. It also served to hypnotise the striking young blondes whose presence his younger son Terence increasingly came to resent as an insult to his mother.

Brian Rattigan's reaction, on the other hand, was more akin to envy. This strong, strapping, almost overweight sixteen-year-old liked pretty girls too. Indeed, his sexual appetite was to cost him almost as much as it did his father. His career at Harrow, which had begun in the autumn of 1920, was threatened when as a monitor he was rumoured to have made one of the maids in his House pregnant. Certainly he did not complete his fifth and final year at the school, leaving instead in the summer of 1924, when he was still only seventeen. His brother Terence called him 'naughty Brian' from that day forward.

Sandroyd, like Harrow, was a privileged world. The school received Winston Churchill's son Randolph at the same time as Terry Rattigan. Both were taught history and cricket by a remarkable Scot called Donald MacLachlan, known as 'Cluckie', who gave his young pupils a taste for dramatic readings – particularly from the diaries of famous men. English was the responsibility of the equally eccentric Priscilla Matthews, famous for her orange clothes and an undisguisable black moustache.

Sport at Sandroyd was at least as important as study. The younger Rattigan's appetite for cricket recalled that of his father before him. He played for the school's second eleven in his first summer, and became its dominant member the following year, before graduating to the first eleven. He also shone at football, keeping goal for the school first team for two full seasons.

Like his brother, he was also a member of one of the Sandroyd scout troops, becoming troop leader in his final year. The hearty all-male atmosphere of the school was punctuated by one or two fumbling sexual scandals among the boys. One master left abruptly, because, rumour had it, he had made a sexual approach to Randolph Churchill, news of which reached his father's ears in London. Terry himself admitted to experimenting with one or two other boys, 'but he didn't think it was particularly significant'.

His theatrical activities continued unabated. At one point his headmaster complained that he was neglecting his studies because of his obsession, offering him the choice between abandoning a part he particularly wanted to play and taking a beating from his notorious cane, nicknamed Fustis. Terry chose the cane. In spite of the demands of Common Entrance and the forthcoming Scholarship examinations to Harrow, he took inordinate pleasure in playing the lead in a pair of one-act plays presented at the school's Supper Night in the autumn of his final year. The first was a school favourite, *The Bathroom Door*, the second another comedy, *Ici on Parle Français*, based on experiences in a crammer's in France, and a distant forebear of *French Without Tears*.

Though he was still only a little over five feet two inches tall, Terry Rattigan was one of the oldest boys in the school when, in the spring of 1925, he won the Seventh Entrance Scholarship to Harrow, with distinctions in Latin and French. He had made every effort to win the scholarship, as his parents' financial plight was becoming increasingly clear. It was one of only ten awarded by Harrow to preparatory school boys that summer. He was to go on to Harrow at the beginning of the summer term. Terence Rattigan was on the brink of having to grow up. But he knew he did not intend to do it conventionally.

Sandroyd's headmaster, W.M.Hornby, recorded in the school magazine after he left that Rattigan 'has quick perceptions and a natural sense of style, and is gaining rapidly the power to use them wisely and effectively. He has taken a leading part here in things grave and gay.'

CHAPTER 3

Harrow

◆

Oh, as I trace again the winding hill

Mine eyes admire, my heart adores thee still,

Thou drooping Elm! beneath whose boughs I lay,

And frequent mused the twilight hours away.

LORD BYRON, *Hours of Idleness*, 1807

◆

When Terence Rattigan arrived at Harrow in the first week of May 1925, at the age of not quite fourteen, he was, in the words of one contemporary, 'spectacularly handsome'. But he was more than just a good-looking and immaculately turned-out new boy in yellow boater, dark blue jacket and grey trousers. Beneath the firm straw hat and behind the soft cherubic face was a boy who knew exactly what he wanted.

His father's dismissal from the diplomatic service, which might well have shattered his confidence completely, had, in fact, the opposite effect. 'He seemed,' according to another contemporary, 'very much the man of the world. He knew everything that was going on in high society.' Whether for this reason, or as a result of administrative chance, instead of being put into one of the 'Small Houses', which customarily looked after the newest boys, he was placed straight away in one of the school's main houses, the Park, which stood not far from the Head-master's residence on the High Street.

Founded in the sixteenth century for the education of the poor, Harrow had become, as it has remained, one of England's renowned public schools. The country's then prime minister, Stanley Baldwin, had been a pupil, as had his predecessors Robert Peel and Lord

Palmerston. Galsworthy and Trollope had been taught there, as had Sheridan, while the sixth Lord Byron had been inspired by his experiences as a pupil to write his first collection of verse.

The very act of attending this great school, perched on a hill in Middlesex ten miles north of London, gave its 650 pupils a sense of self-importance. Legend had it that if a boy climbed the tower of Harrow's church, which stood at the top of its hill, and looked east, there was no higher point in Europe. According to the school atlas the line of sight would stretch across Holland, the north German and Polish plains, the Pripet marshes, and just south of Minsk and Moscow before it encountered its first obstacle, the Urals. Whatever the truth, there was no denying that on almost any clear day a boy could certainly see across London, or westwards towards Windsor Castle and Britain's other pre-eminent public school, Eton. Harrow inspired confidence.

The uneven concrete steps, worn thin by generations of boys; the top hats, *de rigueur* on Sundays; the red fezes with tassels that distinguished the Park football players; the white blazers of the cricket 'flannels' who played for the Eleven – all these marks and traditions of a great public school fascinated Rattigan. So did the arcane and inviolable custom whereby boys in their first year must fasten all three buttons on their blue jackets, in their second year only one, and thereafter none at all. Terence Rattigan had always felt special, and Harrow convinced him that he had every right to that feeling.

He was in good company. Cecil Beaton, who had only just left, had cut no mean figure at the school, 'walking proudly down the the middle of the High Street with an umbrella', 'wearing a high-winged stiff collar and fur-lined gloves', in the words of one of Rattigan's contemporaries, Aidan Crawley, later to become chairman of Independent Television News and London Weekend Television. Rattigan was Crawley's fag in his first year at the Park, though Crawley remembered him later only as a 'small round-faced boy'.

The horrors of fagging and bullying had not troubled Beaton, and neither were they to trouble Rattigan. He quickly realised that the school favoured boys confident enough to be eccentric, and this gave him his cue. He did not quite affect Beaton's silk pyjamas or mauve-painted walls, but he was good-looking and he was popular. And like his brother Brian, he was not averse to a little 'naughtiness', as the school always styled it.

'Naughtiness' at Harrow, as at every other major English public school, was not restricted to adventures with the school's maids. The onset of adolescence among the all-male population found more predictable outlets and, as one of his contemporaries later recalled, 'I think

we were all homosexual for a while at Harrow.' This caused no great
sensation. It was not even all that noteworthy. In his biography of
Cecil Beaton, Hugo Vickers records, 'One boy found himself in
another's bed on his first night at the school, while another crossed the
hill . . . for the same purpose. The situation varied from house to
house, in some there was "open naughtiness", in others very little.'

Neither the watchful eye of Rattigan's housemaster, B. Middleditch
– known as B. Mid – nor the equally careful gaze of the then headmaster,
the Reverend Lionel Ford MA, PhD, seemed to have much effect.
Cecil Beaton powdered his face, put on lipstick, and affected surprise
that people took him for 'a little tart'. Terence Rattigan went less far.
He knew that he was attractive to other boys, just as he knew that
he was attracted to them. The first stirrings of that recognition had
taken place at Sandroyd, but the atmosphere of his preparatory school,
among boys of eight to thirteen, was more asexual than flirtatious.
It was Harrow that saw the flowering of Terence Rattigan's nascent
sexuality.

Rattigan was a scholar, and – as he proved in his first term – a
cricketer of some ability, opening the batting for the Park against the
Knoll. His father and uncles were still remembered by some of the
staff and Terence, as one of the second generation of Rattigans to go
to the school, was keen to do at least as well at both study and sport.
His determination impressed several young men who were to become
his close friends, including George Nathaniel Rous, son of the third
Earl of Stradbroke; N.M.V. (Victor, later Lord) Rothschild, and
J.M.Stow, who was known as James, even though his first Christian
name was John.

Terence Rattigan could now, for the first time in his life, start to
explore his emotions and individuality. The strain of having to control
his emotions, to conceal his feelings from his grandmother, to pretend
to be a conformist – and in command of every situation – abated, at
least within the walls of the school. He felt comfortable – more
comfortable than he had ever done with his contemporaries, confident
in the knowledge that they respected him and liked him. They shared
his jokes. They admired his worldliness. What more could a fourteen-
year-old schoolboy want?

Within a year he had his own room in the Park, as most of the other
boys did, with its small coal fire and a bed that folded up in one corner
to allow the room to be used as a study during the day. As he progressed
through the school he moved on to the White Passage, and then to the
prized Bottom Passage, the usual domain of the seniors. The boys
would carve their names on the wooden walls, and 'would wolf-whistle

at the girls in the tailor's shop opposite' from the window at the end of each passage, which looked out on to the High Street.

Mr Middleditch, 'a rather lacklustre but charming man', reigned over his house in a bumbling, disorganised way. Having never been to a boarding school himself, he had no clear idea of the pressures on or the temptations faced by the young men in his care. The school provided him with a butler and a staff of servants, including a cook and a series of maids, to look after him in his own quarters. Mrs Middleditch was responsible for the catering, which was not regarded as the finest in the school – rumour had it that she saved on her catering allowance. She encouraged her charges to take a vitamin supplement, hence their nickname, 'the Bemax Boys', among the rest of the school. They had a daughter, Margaret, a handful of years older than Terence, who came to inspire, though she would not discover it for many years, a string of predatory young women in Rattigan plays in the years to come.

In his first month at Harrow, he completed a ten-minute playlet that had started to form in his mind during the Easter holidays after leaving Sandroyd. 'Even in my first term I seem to have risked punishment by deciding to write a play about the Borgias in hours in which I should have been writing about Homer.' *The Parchment,* inspired by the current success of the historical novelist Rafael Sabatini, was set in a contemporary English sitting-room, from which the action flashed back to the Borgias' Palace in Rome in 1549. 'Particularly turgid and ill-written,' he later decided.

At the time, however, he was sufficiently proud of the play to provide cardboard covers and an inscription stating that 'the Author' apologised for any historical inaccuracies. In 'portentous green ink' he added: 'the author wishes it known that the following cast would be eminently suitable for a presentation of this work'. The cast he had in mind included Godfrey Tearle, Gladys Cooper, Marie Tempest, Matheson Lang, Isobel Elsom, Henry Ainley and 'a promising young actor over whom I hesitated long before finally giving him the five-line role of a comic poet – Noël Coward'. The excuse for this impertinent exercise 'was simply that, as I had composed my feeble lines, I had quite genuinely visualised them as being spoken by the actors and actresses of my choice; and I claim that the green-inked note was really more wistful than arrogant, more touching than offensive'. In fact, he was simply starting as he meant to go on. Throughout his writing life, he thought of actors as he created their parts, just as he thought of the actual theatres that they might play in. His was an imagination nurtured in the pits and galleries of many a Shaftesbury Avenue theatre.

He lay on his 'hard school bed, his soul split between the rival dreams of making witty first night speeches to wildly cheering houses (after being kissed by Marie Tempest and Gladys Cooper simultaneously) and of bowling out the entire Australian eleven for thirteen (eight of which I usually conceded to my hero, Macartney, the rest being byes)'.

'In the first term too, I discovered that in the school library they had the collected plays of Galsworthy, Barrie and Shaw and that, if one made a friend of the librarian (not too difficult), one could get a copy of *Plays Unpleasant*, which was not supposed to be shown to boys under seventeen, and was kept under lock and key.' Reading the play fuelled his imagination, and his ambition, still further. 'The pleasures of seeing plays may have been great, but the pleasures of reading them, I found, even greater . . . Quite a lot of other things too I absorbed or disregarded as they suited or didn't suit my ambitions.'

In his first term he wrote another play beside *The Parchment*, this time at the command of the French master, who set form Lower Remove B2, of which Terence was a member, the prep of writing a one-page playlet. While his twelve colleagues created straightforward dramas, allowing them full use of what preparatory school French they could recall, Rattigan instead 'seized the theatrical opportunity with both hands – for it is rare that an ambitious dramatist of fourteen is given such a chance to display his talents'. He plunged straight into the final scene of a tragedy in which the Comte de Boulogne, driven mad by his wife's passion for a handsome young gendarme, rushes into her boudoir – where her hair was being done by no fewer than three maids – and announces that her lover 'is none other than her long lost brother Armand' (the gendarme being hidden in the cupboard at the time). His curtain line was simplicity itself.

COMTESSE: (*souffrant terriblement*) Non! non! non! Ah non! Mon Dieu, non!

The Comtesse was then to faint, because 'in my plays of the period my heroine always fainted at such moments. How else could one bring down the second act curtain?'

The French master scrawled across the top of the first page, in red ink, 'French execrable.' But he added, 'Theatre sense first class.' His marks: two out of ten. Terence was not in the least taken aback. 'I remember clearly being no more surprised at the time by the master's appraisal of my theatrical talents than by his condemnation of my French. Both judgements, I felt, were correct, and I accepted my marks, or lack of them, with equanimity.'

At the end of his first term Rattigan came third out of the thirteen

boys in Lower Remove B2, Classical Divisions, and he was acknowledged as 'a boy with a future at the school'. Speech day at the end of
the term, itself a great event, was addressed by the playwright Sir
Arthur Wing Pinero, whose 'hawk-like eyes under heavy black eye-
brows' had made a considerable impression on the actress Irene Vanbrugh. Pinero had much that Rattigan was to admire in a playwright.
For a start, he was a storyteller, and as the critic J.C.Trewin put it: 'In
marshalling a plot, he insisted upon suspense, never letting a play strike
twelve in the middle of its first act and thereafter run down.' He was
concerned with the sins of society, the 'woman with a past' and the
'odd, odd triangle', but he was also a craftsman, ordered and careful
with every detail. *The Second Mrs Tanqueray*, one of his greatest successes, provided part of the inspiration for one of Rattigan's own future
plays. Rattigan had listened entranced to Pinero's speech.

The following academic year he wrote plays bearing titles such as
The Consul's Wife and *King's Evidence,* neither of which have survived,
but on both of which the heavy hand of Sabatini still lay. Rattigan now
joined the Classical Divisions in the Fifth form, where one of his class,
Victor Rothschild, went on to cricketing eminence. They opened the
batting together in their final years. Another member of the class was
Anthony Goldschmidt, a member of Druries house, just across the
High Street from the Park, who became a friend and was later acknowledged as one of the most brilliant classical scholars of his time.

The only cloud on Rattigan's horizon during his first full academic
year at Harrow was the school's insistence on army drill. Boys were
expected to parade in full uniform on two days of the week, Wednesday
afternoon (in place of part of games, which was highly unpopular) and
Friday mornings (in place of study, which was slightly more popular).
From time to time they were also expected to take part in military
exercises, once again dressed in full khaki, on Sunday mornings. The
strain of militarism was hardly surprising. Harrow had lost more than
a hundred old boys in the trenches of Flanders barely seven years before.
The walls of the school's chapel bore plaque after plaque commemorat-
ing boys who had lost their lives. Nevertheless, the whole business
irritated the young Rattigan.

Drill or no drill, he was still writing plays, often by candlelight after
the official 'lights out' at the Park, known as 'tollying up'. There were
fewer opportunities for theatre-going than there had been, since the
allowance he received from his father had perceptibly dropped, but
instead there were the printed plays stacked in their shelves along the
mahogany panelled walls of the school library, which lay barely 200
yards away from the Park in the High Street. He devoured them all,

disliking some – particularly Shaw – and admiring others – not least
Somerset Maugham.

As a member of the Classical Divisions, there were also the Greeks.
Aeschylus and Sophocles were often set for translation, especially *The
Agamemnon*. Though still a junior, Terence escaped the fate of being
taught by one of Harrow's less favoured classical masters of that time,
J.W.Coke-Norris, a desiccated clergyman with a distinctly prominent
Adam's apple which hypnotised his pupils. Coke-Norris took the more
backward classes and occasionally preached during the school service
on Sundays – always beginning his sermons with the words 'Thucyd-
ides tells us'. 'The budding playwright T.M.Rattigan', as he now styled
himself on the cover of each of his plays, mimicked Coke-Norris's
style and delivery remorselessly.

Rattigan was developing his talent, and Harrow was encouraging
him to do so. The long discussions, the reading into the night, and his
own writing drove him on. And the reason lay in his own emotions.
The young man who had had to maintain control at all times in the face
of his grandmother's affectionless nurture and his father's infidelities
allowed himself to experience – and express – those emotions in his
plays. They were, as they were always to be, his escape from his own
straitjacket.

> When, in early days, my heroines rushed into their second act
> paroxysms of hysterics and fell to the floor in dead, but graceful,
> faints; when my handsome heroes crushed some fatal document
> violently between the palms of their hands and stared with horror
> and amazement into space; when my villains turned quickly on
> their heels with curt, sardonic laughs and quietly left the room;
> and above all, when the curtain slowly fell – I never wrote of
> them as falling fast, for the reason, I suppose, that if they had the
> plays would have ended a second or so sooner, an unbearable
> thought – it was at such ecstatic moments that I was most
> conscious of being a member of my own audience, and of par-
> ticipating myself in the emotions that I, as author, had aroused
> in them.

How far he had come in expressing those emotions on paper was
demonstrated in his second full academic year at Harrow. In 1926, at
the age of fifteen, he completed a new play, *Integer Vitae* (a quotation
from Horace's *Odes*), the title of which he would later change to *The
Pure in Heart*. The only one of his plays from Harrow to survive intact,
it shows that he had begun to find his own distinctive voice. Gone are

the Sabatini Borgias and the fainting Contessas. In their place are a contemporary middle-class family about to encounter a formidable moral dilemma.

'A Play in Two Acts by T.M.Rattigan, author of *The Consul's Wife* and *King's Evidence*', *Integer Vitae* has a cast of nine, including the Father, the Mother and the Son, as well as the Maid, the Visitor, the Doctor, the Policeman and Two Men. The setting of Act One is 'The Drawing Room of a suburban house, an evening in winter,' and of Act Two, 'The same, two months later. Late afternoon.'

As he sets the scene, however, Rattigan displays something of the arrogance as well as the acuity that Harrow had burnished in him. This is his description of the play's Drawing Room:

It is scrupulously neat and has that air of shabby gentility that is usually to be found in middle-class houses. The wallpaper is of a dismal grey, a colour that was chosen probably because it does not fade. An attempt at brightness is made in the coverings of the armchair and sofa, an attempt that fails dismally.

The Mother is sitting, working at her sewing. She is a woman of about forty-five. She looks fifty-five. Care and trouble have brought premature wrinkles to her face. In an armchair by the fire, the Father is seated, reading a newspaper. He is a man of about fifty. The chief point in his appearance is his extraordinarily mild air. Every feature in his face tends to this, every feature that is to say except one. His eyes are not the eyes of a bank clerk, for that is his vocation, but rather those of an artist. In fact he is known by his colleagues to have 'queer' eyes. Except for this he is very ordinary – he possesses a pair of drooping moustaches . . .

Beneath the surface of this 'ordinary' life lies a pain that Rattigan was to return to time and time again in the years to come. The plot is hopelessly melodramatic, the dialogue stilted, the situation contrived, but the dilemmas faced by the characters are real and complex, and the play's proposition straightforward. Earlier that day the father has saved himself from being sacked by the bank by persuading his boss that he has a 'first-rate' reputation, and is therefore too good to lose. The boss has relented, providing he keeps his 'blameless reputation – for never doing anything I oughtn't'. The son has been given an expensive public school education (at Radley), and is always 'off with his high-class friends'. The father admits to his wife that he is convinced his son 'loathes the sight of me' and that he is getting to 'loathe him'.

The son – 'Aged about twenty-three, reasonably good-looking, his character is betrayed by his mouth, which is petulant, weak and sensual' – arrives home to confess that he has just killed a man. Why?

> SON: Because he deserved to die. And to save the honour of the girl I love . . . I don't regret it. (*With a slight air of martyrdom*) What I did was not for myself. But I'm quite prepared to take the consequences. I'm going out now to confess.
> FATHER: (*Vehemently*) You're not. You're going to stay here.
> SON: I know it means death on the gallows. But I'm ready to face that.
> FATHER: But I'm not. You're going to stay here.

The son reluctantly agrees, and the father suggests that he leave the country for Canada rather than confess. The son's integrity is now drawn into question, just as the father's has been. The son hesitates, but before he can make his decision the evening paper reveals that a burglar has been arrested for the murder that he intends to confess to. The curtain falls.

As Act Two begins, the son has decided to wait for the verdict at the burglar's trial before deciding whether to confess. If the burglar is found guilty, he will confess, if not, he won't. He finally arrives to tell his parents that the verdict is 'guilty', and he and his father go upstairs, on to the balcony at the front of the house, to discuss what to do next. The dilemma that is threatening the family is about to be increased by the fifteen-year-old playwright.

Offstage, the son falls from the balcony and is killed. His mother immediately accuses her husband of murdering not only her son, but also the burglar – whom it transpires a few moments later was actually found innocent rather than guilty (making the son's death even more futile).

> MOTHER: Do you realise what you've done? You've killed your son for nothing.

She decides she can no longer live with him, but he, after briefly considering suicide, decides that by far the best course of action is to go back to the office in the wake of his son's death, his reputation for 'blameless integrity' intact. The curtain falls on the line:

> FATHER: I never thought of that. It'll create a good impression.

Impressions, and appearances that had to be maintained, were to become a hallmark of Rattigan's work. The necessity of concealing the truth behind a façade of 'good behaviour' and 'blameless integrity' inhabits every play he wrote. His own father's conduct had shown him the way, and it was not by chance that, in *Integer Vitae*, it is a father and son who are forced to confront this issue. Nor is it an accident that the relationship between a father and son recurs throughout his work.

Integer Vitae was completed in candlelight after lights out, in the first months of 1927. But his appetite for games was undimmed. He played football for the house team, keeping goal – as he had at Sandroyd. His first love, however, remained cricket. The previous summer he had once been chosen to play for the Eleven – the youngest boy chosen – and was now spending as much time as he could in Harrow's newly completed covered cricket nets. Even here, though, he was not free from his father's reputation. That summer the *Daily Telegraph* reported: 'he is the son of the great player W.F.A. Rattigan, but he is quite young, and nowhere near the Harrow first pair, and it was hard if his father's reputation as a winner of matches made the son seem so formidable that he was made to play level with an experienced school representative.'

More than the writing of plays, or the uncomfortable relationship with his father, sex now pushed its way to the forefront of Terence Rattigan's life. Brief affairs with other boys were no longer quite enough. His 'worldly air' (and reputation) prompted something more adult. About this time his father had introduced him to the racing correspondent of the *Daily Express*, Geoffrey Gilbey. Gilbey took a shine to Rattigan, and Rattigan returned the feeling with enthusiasm and without, apparently, much sense of guilt. At the end of the summer term of 1927, and at the end of another successful cricket season, they began an affair.

But there was all the difference in the world between a flirtation, however physical, with another boy at Harrow, and a relationship with an adult from beyond the school walls. Homosexuality was a crime, and a serious one. Any man found guilty of a sexual relationship with a minor – and Rattigan was barely sixteen – faced a lengthy period of imprisonment, and ruin. To join the secret adult world of homosexuality and 'queers', which had its own rules and its own institutions, was a huge risk for a young man to take. Nevertheless Rattigan embarked on the adventure without a qualm. Far from being 'seduced', he was from the start a willing partner. 'He never for one moment questioned whether or not he was a homosexual,' a friend commented. 'He just knew he was, and it did not disturb him in the least.'

The affair lasted throughout his remaining years at Harrow. Gilbey would come down to the school to take him out to lunch – adding considerably to Rattigan's reputation as 'a man about town'. The lunches would have seemed harmless, no more than a friendship between a boy and one of his father's friends. That was the intended subterfuge. In reality, an element of secrecy had entered Rattigan's life which would from now on grow to become a major part of it.

CHAPTER 4

Lord's

◆

An old professor came down this afternoon and jawed about cricket, that Temptation was the bowler, and Honour, Purity and Truth the three wickets, and I was so flabbergasted at his hock- bottleness that I was nearly ill.

GERALD DU MAURIER, letter from Harrow

◆

Terence Rattigan's friendship with Geoffrey Gilbey got him into trouble, but not the trouble that he might have expected. During one of their lunches in the spring of 1928, Rattigan mentioned to him that the boys were so unhappy about the amount of drill that was still being forced on them as part of the Harrow Officer Training Corps (OTC) that they had written to the colonel in charge of the cadet force to complain. 'They have even threatened not to parade,' Rattigan told him. Gilbey, the journalist, was fascinated. The Prime Minister's old school refusing to parade: it was nothing short of mutiny.

And so ran the front page of the *Daily Express* the following morning. Gilbey had asked if it would be all right to 'mention it to my editor', and Rattigan had agreed. But he had not realised the significance of his decision. Though he disapproved of the OTC, he personally had not been involved in the letter demanding that the parades should be curtailed.

The school was in uproar. Newspapermen descended from the rest of Fleet Street and the headmaster was besieged with telephone calls not only from newspapers but also from irate parents, many of whom had lost sons in Flanders. Refusing to parade, and by implication to fight, was an insult to them.

The headmaster, Dr Cyril Norwood, who had replaced Lionel Ford at the beginning of 1927, was astonished that news of the 'rebellion' had got out. And he was furious that the *Daily Express* had come to hear of it. 'In the end Terry had to go and tell him,' Rattigan's contemporary in the Park Jimmy Stow recalls. 'It was not a particularly comfortable interview, but Norwood forgave him.' The mutiny at Harrow blew over, and the young Rattigan had learnt that the press had more power than he had imagined. It was a lesson he was to use to his advantage in the months to come. He was still determined to end the OTC parades. He wrote both to the school magazine, the *Harrovian*, and to *The Times*, a letter which attracted the attention of fellow Harrovian Stanley Baldwin, the Prime Minister, who raised the matter in the House of Commons. But the OTC parades continued.

The moment had arrived when Rattigan had to decide what subjects to specialise in for the rest of his time at school. Although his work in the first terms of the Classical Sixth had been inspired by the school's new young classics master, E.V.C.Plumtre – known as Plum – who had joined the staff in 1925 straight from Oxford, Rattigan decided to prepare for a scholarship in his other strong subject, history. Perhaps he knew that his friend and exact contemporary Anthony Goldschmidt, who was one of Plum's stars, would certainly win the major classics prizes, and he had never relished the prospect of being 'second best'.

Rattigan was equally determined not to be second best on the cricket field. In the summer of 1928 he was again selected for the Eleven, opening against Harrow Town, but was bowled by a 'yorker' before scoring. It made him even more determined, and in later matches he scored 20 against Charterhouse and 22 not out against the MCC schools. He was also a stalwart of the second eleven, and was awarded his 'flannels' in recognition of his performances, a considerable honour for a boy not quite seventeen. It meant that he could wear a white jacket instead of a blue one and sport the distinctive striped cap and silk scarf reserved for those who had been elevated to that exalted status. Firmly established in his own room on the Bottom Passage in the Park, just along the corridor from his friend Jimmy Stow, his life was the happiest it had ever been. Rattigan was to say later that his schooldays were the happiest of his life, and there is no reason not to believe him. He was a talented young man rising to the top of a great school, surrounded by contemporaries who respected and admired him. The vividness of the feeling was to remain with him for the rest of his life.

All the same, there were one or two flies in the ointment. His father had taken to appearing at the school unexpectedly, usually in the company of the latest blonde. Sporting a red carnation in his buttonhole, his waxed moustache perfectly in place and his smile as endearing as ever, the Major would introduce the young woman and Terry would welcome her warmly enough. But his father's behaviour embarrassed him in front of his peers, and after they had gone he would mimic him mercilessly. 'Terry was devoted to his mother, and very sarcastic about his father,' Jimmy Stow recalls. 'Major Rattigan was so clearly an Edwardian, that he seemed a relic of a bygone age to the boys of 1928. But that did not deter Frank from the conviction that Terry should follow him into the Diplomatic Service – and take the ambassadorship that he felt he had been denied.'

In the spring term of 1929 Terry won the second English literature prize, the St Helier, and that summer confirmed his place as opening batsman for the Eleven, often in partnership with Victor Rothschild. Always far more nervous than he appeared to be, he scored 27 against the Free Foresters, 67 against the Butterflies, 20 against Harlequins, 10 against Marlborough, 4 against Winchester, and 13 and 22 against the Harrow Wanderers. And playing against the touring Cambridge University team, the Quidnuncs, he managed his first century for the school, making 100 of Harrow's total of 272, including three sixes and ten fours. The innings provoked the *Harrovian* to comment shrewdly, 'A very creditable performance in spite of rather a shaky start.' Nervous or not, it was inevitable that he would be chosen for the match against Eton, the pinnacle of any Harrovian cricketer's career.

And so at eleven thirty on the morning of a blindingly hot day, 12 July 1929, Terry walked out to field for Harrow on the billiard-table turf at Lord's, the headquarters of English cricket. Played over two days, and with each side playing two innings, the great annual match between the country's two pre-eminent schools was still one of the highlights of the London social calendar, coming after the Fourth of June at Eton and after Ascot, but well before the Regatta at Henley. Another Harrovian, Aidan Crawley, who had played three years before, recalled that the match was 'one of the great fashion parades of the London season. That day there were said to be 25,000 spectators (only a few thousand fewer than a Test Match), all dressed in their best. Whole families came together, boys and girls all wearing dark or light blue buttonholes or ribbons.' Every man and boy in the crowd wore a top hat.

Proud families had traditionally parked their broughams, and now increasingly their cars at the nursery end of the ground to unpack their hampers for lunch. Open-topped carriages, which had become a feature of the Derby at Epsom, also made their appearance. During the lunch and tea intervals the crowd spread across the outfield, flooding the whole playing area except the pitch itself, which was roped off. Younger brothers watched, while their sisters gossiped. Frank Rattigan brought his wife, Vera, to watch their son play, rather than one of the young ladies whom he was given to calling his 'cousins'.

Harrow lost the toss, and fielded. Before lunch on the first day Terry caught a fine slip catch, but later in the day dropped an easier chance in the deep. Eton had amassed a formidable 347 all out before he and Victor Rothschild opened the batting for Harrow after tea. Perhaps because of his father's reputation – in his three years playing for the Eleven in the 1890s the school had never lost – Terry was even more nervous than usual, and it showed. In the first overs he got a thin outside edge, which only narrowly escaped the wicket-keeper's gloves to run away to third man for four. Gradually he relaxed, while Victor Rothschild went from strength to strength. At 67 for no wicket, however, Rothschild played on, leaving Terry to carry on with the new batsman. He did not last long, being brilliantly caught at slip off another thin edge.

In the second innings, the following afternoon, he managed to score only one run, but the school's performance was still acclaimed. They managed a draw against an Eton side which had outperformed them in almost every aspect of the game. It wasn't the triumph of Frank Rattigan's matches in the 1890s but it wasn't a disgrace, and Major Rattigan was visibly proud of his son. Terry's average for the summer's ten innings was almost 29 – while Victor Rothschild's was 39. They were firmly established as the opening partnership for the following summer of 1930, and there was every expectation that Terry would follow in his father's cricketing footsteps and appear against Eton again that year.

When he returned to Harrow after the summer holiday, Terence Rattigan was appointed a monitor, or prefect, responsible for discipline in the Park. Terry's friend Jimmy Stow was made head of house, responsible for any beating that was thought necessary. The housemaster traditionally left almost all matters of corporal punishment to his head of house, who had to ensure that the monitor was present when any beatings were administered. One new inhabitant of the Park at the time, Richard Walker, who was beaten by Jimmy Stow 'for whistling in the passage', remembered vividly afterwards that 'What wounded me far more was the behaviour of the monitor who witnessed the affair, Terence Rattigan eating an apple.'

Preparing for a history scholarship to Oxford, his father's ambitions for him in the Diplomatic Service in mind, Rattigan was recognized as 'one of the cleverest boys in his year'. But drama was still his passion. By now he had read almost every play in the Vaughan Library, including all the works of Shakespeare and the Greek tragedies of Aeschylus and Sophocles, and had even made an appearance in a school production of *Julius Caesar*. 'He would read by candlelight after lights out in the Park,' Jimmy Stow remembers. 'Night after night, when he was supposed to be sleeping.' The theatre had taken an unshakeable hold.

In the first term of 1930 Rattigan set down his views on drama for the *Harrovian*. 'There is, in fact, a ceaseless conflict being waged in the drama of today, Entertainment versus Instruction. Both camps have numerous allies,' wrote the would-be playwright. Rattigan firmly identified himself with the entertainers.

The Pinero–Jones school and the Shaw school have gone on developing side by side, and as yet show no signs of converging. They are founded upon two distinct principles. The Pinero–Jones school – ably being upheld by such excellent craftsmen as Somerset Maugham, Noël Coward, Benn Levy, Ashley Dukes – hold as their acknowledged criterion the box office. Not that any of them fit that famous description of the bestseller writer – 'he who has superior talents to the man in the street, but the same tastes'. It is only that they regard the financial success of their plays as their highest aim. Who indeed can blame them?

Rattigan concluded, 'Without an audience there cannot be a play.' He was to adhere to that same view throughout his life.

Drama apart, Terence Rattigan had lost none of his distaste for the OTC. On 3 April 1930 he again wrote to the *Harrovian* on the subject.

Dear Sirs, I gather it is the practice of at least one House to have extra parades on a Sunday. Though possessed of no strict Sabbatarian prejudices myself, I am a little bewildered by the inconsistency of the rule that forbids a boy to play a game of squash or fives on Sunday, yet allows him to be forced to dress in a khaki tunic, and exert himself in military exercises. That by doing so he is, as some assert, improving both his soul and his body, is immaterial. The inconsistency remains. I am, yours, T.M. Rattigan.

Nevertheless he was still prepared to turn out for the parades himself, on one occasion tartly reminding his fag, Michael Denison, who was later to appear in a number of his plays, that he had been putting too much Cherry Blossom boot polish on his Sam Browne belt. Rattigan summoned Denison. 'Look, old boy. I don't care about the OTC, but I do care about getting ticked off for something you are supposed to have done. So just learn how to do it, will you?' It was a tone of voice that he was to use throughout his final year at Harrow, a tone which would seep into his manner in the years to come. Cool, deprecating, but also a shade domineering, it reflected his view of the world around him. Nothing was a surprise, and no shibboleth should go unchallenged. He took great pleasure in passing round the works of Bertrand Russell, though they were banned by the school.

He was, however, capable of being shocked. Another contemporary in the Park recalls that on one occasion that spring Rattigan turned up in his room, unexpectedly, and alone, 'as if he had something to get off his chest'. Rattigan and he were not particularly close, 'but I think he trusted me in some way,' the boy, now a man of over eighty, recalls. 'In any case, he chose to tell me a secret that he clearly had not told anyone else at school: the reason for his father's sudden departure from the Diplomatic Service.'

'Terry told me that his father had somehow managed to get the Princess [Elisabeth of Romania] pregnant, and that she had been forced to have an abortion. When the King of Greece discovered that his new wife's former lover was Great Britain's Acting High Commissioner in Constantinople, he let his objections be known in London,' he explains. 'And in an effort to placate the King, Frank was asked to leave, although he was allowed to keep his small pension. The truth obviously affected Terry very deeply.'

It affected him so deeply that he did not tell his closer friends at school. Jimmy Stow was never told the story. Neither was anyone else. 'But Terry obviously wanted to tell someone – and someone who would not be likely to gossip about it,' he recalls. 'It was literally a confession, and it came as a great surprise. He even went into elaborate details about the special contraceptive that his father had told him he always used, which apparently consisted of two layers of rubber rather than one. Terry said his father still could not understand why it hadn't worked.' As Terence Rattigan left his room at the Park, he swore his contemporary to secrecy. It was a confidence that remained unbroken for sixty years, and was only breached 'because I thought it helped to explain a lot about Terry'.

In spite of Terence Rattigan's apparent worldliness, his fellow pupil remains convinced that his contemporary was deeply shocked by his father's behaviour and furious about the effect that it must have had upon his mother. 'Terry was devoted to her, and apparently she loved the diplomatic life, and found it terribly difficult to give up.' There is little doubt that the story had an impact on Terence Rattigan's own sexual development. His father's actions proved that anything was permissible, providing that you never, ever, got caught. Of course his father's heterosexuality did not appeal to him. Certainly, if it had, there would have been ample opportunity for Terence Rattigan to indulge it. The housemistress's daughter, Margaret Middleditch, had developed a passion for him in his final year, and took every opportunity to spend whatever time she could alone with him. 'Eventually I think he got rather scared of the whole business,' Jimmy Stow explains, 'but he was very funny about it when he escaped.'

Aged eighteen, a little under six feet tall, with fair hair, clear blue eyes and a round, almost oriental face, there was a feminine quality about Terence Rattigan at this time which he did nothing to conceal. He would openly discuss the attractiveness, or otherwise, of the new boys who arrived at the school, remarking on their prettiness, observing their reaction when flirted with. The taste he developed at Harrow for small, round-faced boys with wide-set eyes and oriental colouring was never to leave him. Like a grand actress he would swoop upon a younger boy, dazzle him with his wit and sophistication, and then – if the boy were willing – seduce him. But he also quickly came to accept that there was a price to be paid for the seduction. The younger boy would make his presence felt, if only for a time, and Rattigan recognised at once that there would be a good many tantrums before the relationship ended. The younger boy, the object of his seduction, had a power too. It was a recognition that he would bring to his work as a dramatist, and the taste for tantrums in his sexual life was never to desert him completely.

Gilbey was still there in the background, but there was also a new companion, the entertainer Douglas Byng, who sometimes performed in drag. Stow remembers going to the Café de Paris with Rattigan during one school holiday to see Byng. 'Terry rather liked all that, the groups of homosexual men. He always used to say that the Greeks had a good attitude towards sex, which the British people didn't apparently have. He was always after the Greek ideal.' It was clear to Stow, and to his other contemporaries in the Park, that Rattigan took pride in his homosexuality, even if he had to conceal it from the world at large.

Certainly the Greek plays were an inspiration. In his final year he persuaded the classics department to arrange a trip for all the senior boys to see a production of Aristophanes' The Clouds at Oxford. On Sunday afternoons he encouraged Jimmy Stow and others to attend play readings, and he and Stow would go to the London Palladium together during the holidays, to see Billy Bennett and Max Miller. 'Terry loved being in any theatre. He'd got a sort of longing to belong to it.'

At the end of the first term in 1930 Rattigan won the English Literature Prize, as well as the Modern History Prize, the Bourchier. Though he made light of the prospect, it looked very much as though he *could* win a scholarship to Oxford. 'The point was he *had* to win one, because of his father's departure from the diplomatic,' according to Stow. 'If he had not won a scholarship, he would not have been able to go up to Oxford and he could not bear the thought of not going up.'

Rattigan later described the experience, as ever contriving to conceal how hard he was trying by a well-honed deprecating tone of voice.

> On my paternally-planned course towards the British Embassy in Washington or Paris, which was then thought slightly superior, I was made in 1930 to sit for a history scholarship to Trinity College, Oxford, and to my parents' surprise and my own stupefaction, got one. To this day I don't know how. My idea had been, obviously, to fail, as the first move in the long battle of persuading my father that I would make a highly unsuitable diplomat, a moron fit only for the hazards of artistic creation.

He suggested that perhaps the examiners had confused his papers with those of a boy next to him called Rattray, who 'judging from what I could read, had scholarship material stamped all over him'.

The truth was that Terence Rattigan desperately wanted to win a scholarship to Oxford. The evidence of his contemporaries in the Park shows that he worked too hard, and too consistently, to sustain the myth that he was trying to fail. He had had a dazzling all-rounder's career, even adding, in company with Jimmy Stow, the squash and racquets cups to his earlier triumphs at cricket. He was a boy the younger ones admired, not always from afar. He was ambitious, but also vulnerable; and he craved success.

His father still wanted him to join the Diplomatic Service, however, and the friction between father and son increased as his final year at Harrow came to an end. Rattigan insisted that he would go to Oxford, but he still wanted to become a playwright. Frank Rattigan shook his head, and refused to discuss the matter. It seemed of little importance for the moment. Cricket was much more significant to Major Rattigan. As the summer began and Rattigan's scholarship to Trinity was duly won, he was also awarded the Simpson leaving scholarship, one of Harrow's principal prizes. The glittering school career had come to an appropriate end. All that remained was the Eton and Harrow match at Lords.

The pressures of the scholarship examination, however, had taken an unexpected toll on Rattigan's ability on the cricket field. Everything had seemed to begin well enough. He and Victor Rothschild had put on 170 for the first wicket against the Butterflies in just two and a quarter hours, with Rattigan scoring 67 to Rothschild's 106. In June *The Times* commented on his performance against Charterhouse in glowing terms: 'With Rattigan playing fine forcing cricket – some of his drives past extra cover were obviously hereditary.' His 42 was the team's highest score, but it was also his last success. As the Eton match loomed he struggled to make runs, losing confidence with each lapse. He made a duck in the trial against Harlequins and failed to reach double figures in either innings against the Old Harrovians after being dropped down the batting order.

'It was all that reading by candlelight,' Jimmy Stow maintained. 'He strained his eyes so much that he couldn't bat properly.' Whatever the reason, Rattigan was now in a quandary. Should he persevere, in the hope that his form would return, or should he offer to stand down from the Eleven before he was pushed out of it. 'In the end Terry decided to offer to stand down,' Jimmy Stow recalls, 'and rather to his surprise the team accepted it.' He was replaced as opening batsman by R.D.Stewart Brown, the head of school and a classicist. Disconsolate, Rattigan asked another friend, the future show-jumping commentator Dorian Williams, to send an overnight telegram to his father to tell him the news.

Frank Rattigan was horrified. How could the school possibly drop his son? It was an insult to him. In a rage he rushed down to Harrow and, to his son's embarrassment, visited the headmaster, his house-master, the games master and the cricket professional in an effort to persuade them to change their minds. His son was 'the finest batsman in the school', they could not possibly leave him out of the match at Lord's. It was to no avail; Major Rattigan left and his son was still not in the Eleven selected to face Eton.

In the *Daily Express*, Geoffrey Gilbey came to his young friend's defence. On the morning after the match, which Harrow lost, he wrote:

Only those who play games can understand how much it means to a boy to represent his school. Rattigan, who comes from a brilliant cricketing family, represented Harrow last year. There is no keener cricketer. This year he made top score in the first three school matches, but then he began to meet with misfortune after misfortune, and made few runs in the remaining matches. He did what not one in a thousand would have done in similar circumstances. He suggested to those responsible for choosing the side that he should be dropped. His resignation was accepted. The bitter disappointment to a cricketer who has longed for this Eton against Harrow match ever since last year can be understood . . . No one ever took a disappointment more philosophically.

The loyal Gilbey continued, 'It was very sporting of Rattigan and, I venture to suggest, a very great mistake to leave him out. Owners might just as well refuse to put up Richards after he had ridden ten consecutive losers, or Gloucestershire refuse to play Hammond.' But as the 1930 Eton and Harrow match unfolded at Lord's, 'the best class batsman in the side', as Gilbey had called him, was sitting with his father, mother and brother doing his best to conceal his pain. His life at Harrow had, momentarily, turned to dust, and though cricket remained one of his great passions, he never played it seriously again. Failure was the one thing that Terence Rattigan could never bear.

CHAPTER 5

Oxford

◆

I had not gone to Oxford to study. That was what grammar-school boys did. We products of the English public schools went to Oxford either for sport and beer-drinking . . . or for the aesthetic life and cocktails.

LOUIS MACNEICE, *The Strings are False*

◆

When Terence Rattigan walked into the Porter's Lodge at Trinity College, Oxford on 10 October 1930, he entered an even more cloistered world than the one he had just left behind. With barely 170 undergraduates, Trinity was a cosy, almost family, college. It welcomed sportsmen, particularly those who might add strength to the college boat, but it was more concerned with intellectual accomplishment. The University as a whole, however, did not see education as narrowly academic. The college set out not just to provide intellectual stimulation but to cultivate 'tolerance, articulateness, sociability and qualities of leadership and organization', as the official history puts it. Trinity provided its undergraduates with a tranquil haven for three years before they moved out into the world at large.

Rattigan was ushered by his scout along the gravel paths and past the cedar tree towards Room 18 on the second floor of Staircase 6 on the Front Quad. Opening his leaded light window to look out towards the even more beautiful Garden Quad, the college chapel, and Balliol beyond, he knew he wanted Oxford to be the launching pad for his career as a playwright. Across its stage had walked a string of

actors and writers whom he already admired. Its spires were the backdrop to the city of Harold Acton and Maurice Bowra, Evelyn Waugh
and Beverly Nichols, and he relished its reputation. For the first time,
he felt he could do precisely as he pleased. The constraints of school
had gone, and he intended to indulge himself, in the theatre, in writing,
and in the company of other like-minded young men.

Aidan Crawley, for whom Rattigan had been fag during his first
year at Harrow, had only just left Trinity, where he too had had a
'two-roomed set', in which 'male friends could sleep in the spare room
at any time'. For Crawley the most exciting thing about college life
was the experience of finally being grown up. 'Younger dons called
me by my Christian name and expected me to do the same to them.
One called nobody "sir" . . . I remember waking up one morning and
realising that from now on life was what one made it. If one liked
people, one cultivated them. One walked round to see them in the
morning, lunched together at a club or in college, played games in the
afternoon and dined with some other group.'

Undergraduates of the time were instantly recognisable, by their
gowns, their accent and – for many – their clothing: grey flannel
trousers, tweed jacket, collar and tie for ordinary occasions, white
flannels and blazer for sporting functions. Several colleges had long-
standing links with particular public schools, New College with Winchester and Christ Church with Westminster, for example. Only a
decade earlier, a fifth of Christ Church's intake and a sixth of Magdalen's had come from Eton alone. Friendships and 'fashions in clothing, culture and slang spread rapidly from public schools to Oxford'.

Rattigan quickly decided to put his 'hearty' cricket-playing days
behind him, and instead place himself firmly among the University's
'aesthetes'. As John Betjeman, who had arrived at Magdalen in 1925,
wrote, the division between the hearties and the aesthetes 'overrode all
social and college distinctions'. Inspired by Harold Acton's desire to
'escape into the universe of art', the aesthetes wanted to startle their
fellow undergraduates with extravagant language, cosmopolitan culture and fashion, and affected or genuine homosexuality.

Oxford University in the 1930s was also a quite overwhelmingly
male society. Of the 1,750 undergraduates, just 250 were women, and
what few women there were lived in all-female colleges or halls of
residence less centrally placed than the men's. Lord Hugh Cecil (the
MP for Oxford University from 1910 until 1937) was not alone in
welcoming the 'nervous intensity' of the University's predominantly
male community. For him close male friendships had made Oxford
and Cambridge 'the seed beds of movements of great importance to

the community'. In Beverly Nichols's novel *Patchwork*, published in 1921, male undergraduates walk about arm-in-arm, address one another as 'my dear fellow', and engage in intense heart-to-heart talks. This gave Terence Rattigan his lead. His first year had barely begun when he began to dress more and more flamboyantly.

Rattigan found Trinity delightful, but its traditional and sporting traditions were not what he had in mind. The college archivist, Clare Hopkins believes, that 'Rattigan clearly wasn't too concerned with life in college'. He saw himself as 'different' and looked down on many of his fellow undergraduates, particularly the sportsmen, as 'immature', with their addiction to hoaxes and horseplay. Even the bachelor dons living in college did not seem immune from a certain childishness. The President at the time was the Reverend H.E.D.Blakiston, a brusque, shy, short-sighted man of nearly seventy, familiarly known as 'Blinks'. Under his command, Trinity did not particularly welcome flamboyant new undergraduates, especially when they did not seem very interested in work. Rattigan was taught history by the man soon to succeed Blinks, J.R.H. (Reggie) Weaver, and in the first term he did little work. He did not borrow a single volume from the college library, and took out only seven books in his first year, most of them on the history of England before the Norman Conquest. Instead he directed his attention towards the OUDS – the Oxford University Dramatic Society. He joined at once. Many of his contemporaries were to become friends and colleagues for life.

The novelist Angus Wilson was to become a member, as was the fashion designer Bunny Roger. Rattigan's brilliant old Harrovian colleague Tony Goldschmidt, and another old Harrovian, John Bayliss, who, like Gilbey, regularly supplied him with racing tips, were already members. Another was Paul Dehn, the future dramatic critic and wit, who would write the lyrics for Rattigan's only stage musical, *Joie de Vivre*. Two directors he was to work with in the years to come – Frith Banbury, director of the first production of *The Deep Blue Sea*, and Peter Glenville, who directed *The Browning Version* and *The Winslow Boy* – were fellow undergraduate members. George Devine, who later directed the English Stage Company and who was to become Rattigan's nemesis, became its president during his second year.

Frith Banbury recalls how he first encountered Terry 'in a production of *Hassan* by James Elroy Flecker – with Peggy Ashcroft, who came down as a guest artist, Giles Playfair, George Devine, Hugh Hunt. I played the fighting ghost and Terry had a walk-on part.' The OUDS club rooms, where the members could read, eat and drink, were a regular meeting place, especially for breakfast on Sunday mornings.

But Rattigan was not an especially conspicuous attender in his first year. He was not yet dressing quite as flamboyantly as some of the other members, and was a little in awe of some, whose careers in the theatre already seemed all but launched. But he never disguised the fact that he was homosexual, which put him in the company of Angus Wilson, Frith Banbury, Peter Glenville and Bunny Roger. Roger remembers that the first time he encountered Terence Rattigan, 'he was in bed with rather a handsome young man. And did not seem in the least embarrassed.'

Even today there are some who find any suggestion of overt homosexuality at Oxford or in the OUDS thoroughly overdone. The official history concludes, 'Homosexual conduct may have been fashionable in some Oxford circles in the 1920s, but far more prevalent was an unselfconscious affection between male friends that is readily misinterpreted by more knowing generations.' In the case of Rattigan, and many of his friends in the OUDS at the time, such a view is absurd. Frith Banbury puts it politely but firmly: 'Terry was gay. I knew enough about him to know, after all I'm gay.' Bunny Roger is equally direct: 'Terry was homosexual at Oxford, that's all there is to it. I know one or two people he had affairs with who might want to deny it now, but that doesn't affect the truth of the matter.' 'Queer as a coot' was the current phrase used to describe homosexuals, and Rattigan 'was not in the least afraid of making fun of himself'. At the club's 'smokers', at which the members entertained each other, he developed the character of 'Lady Diana Coutigan' and presented waspish sketches about life in London and Oxford.

To flaunt his homosexuality among his friends in the OUDS was one thing, but when the Major and his mother came down to see their son, Rattigan's demeanour was much more restrained. 'Keeping up appearances' was already second nature to him. When the long vacation arrived in June 1931 he went so far as to take home four books, borrowed from the college library, to testify to his diligence. Nor did he object when his father decided that he should spend part of the summer at a 'crammer's' in France, to improve his French.

On 17 July 1931 Terence Rattigan duly found himself on a steamer from Dover to Boulogne, *en route* to a French language school for young English gentlemen near Wimereux run by a certain Monsieur Martin, an exponent of what he called the 'direct method'. Each of the ten young gentlemen in his charge at the Villa des Dunes had a room to himself 'for private study'. The only language permitted in the house was French. Every meal was taken with the belligerent Monsieur Martin, and every resident was also expected to have a daily tutorial with him. Rattigan did not enjoy his stay, and particularly objected to being persistently addressed as 'Monsieur Rottingham' by Monsieur Martin, whom he described as having a 'jutting grey beard, ferocious expression, dark serge suit, open necked shirt and sandals'. Rattigan also felt no particular empathy with his conformist fellow students, all of whom seemed perfectly content with the diplomatic careers their fathers had mapped out for them. It was a relief to get back to Oxford. There was nothing to restrain him there.

One of Rattigan's Oxford friends was Philip Heimann, a tall fair-haired South African who was reading law. They moved into digs together in Canterbury House, King Edward Street, where Peter Glenville joined them barely a week later. Trinity's room 18, which Rattigan could have kept for one more year, had been pleasant enough, but slightly restricting. He wanted to be free of Blinks and his scout, free of fellow undergraduates in the Junior Common Room with their noisy ribaldry and their lavatorial jokes. 'Canters' was one of the most fashionable places in which to have digs in Oxford. It also provided Rattigan with the inspiration for one of his first plots.

Heimann was having an affair with a voluptuous and distinctly dramatic female undergraduate nicknamed Va-Va. Her real name was Irina Basilewich. Aged twenty-six, already married and divorced, she seemed to the twenty-one-year-old Heimann and his twenty-year-old friend Rattigan an immensely sophisticated and exciting creature. Given that Rattigan's attraction to Heimann was unequivocally sexual, the situation had all the makings of a play; a piquant, homosexual variation on the conventional eternal triangle. Throughout the year Rattigan mulled over the idea, sometimes even discussing it with Heimann, who was only too well aware of his friend's attraction to him, but for the moment he put nothing on paper. That could come later. For the moment there were the OUDS smokers to concentrate on, he was having an affair with another undergraduate, a lawyer from New College two years his senior, and his friend Tony Goldschmidt had become co-editor of the university newspaper *Cherwell* and had asked Rattigan to become one of its film and theatre critics.

His first piece appeared on 31 October 1931 and was principally devoted to the delights of Mary Pickford, in a film he did not bother to name. But the following week he was dispatched to London to review Noël Coward's *Cavalcade*, which had just opened at Drury Lane. Another of the university's publications, *Isis*, had hailed Coward as a genius. Rattigan was less generous. After criticising Coward for failing to live up to his early promise as a striking new dramatist with plays like *The Vortex*, and further suggesting that he had succumbed to the lure of commercial success, he concluded tartly: 'He has the happy knack of feeling strongly what other people are feeling at the same time. If he has the ability to transform this knack into money and success we should not begrudge them to him. But such cannot be the qualities of genius.' It is unlikely that Coward, impregnably established, ever saw the *Cherwell* notice, or, if he did, that he would have remembered who wrote it. Had he done so, it would be possible to pinpoint this youthful squib as the seed of the antagonism which was to exist between the two men throughout their lives. As it was, he would one day find his criticism of Coward levelled, in almost identical terms, against himself.

In December Rattigan reviewed Lionel Hale's *Passing through Lorraine* in the same dismissive style. 'It would stand no chance if given the West End production that a reviewer had predicted for it,' he wrote. 'Yet there are certain indications that go to show that perhaps one day Mr Hale may write a successful comedy. But first he must learn the bitter lesson of his own limitations.' Again the critics would one day write the same of him.

While he brooded on the Heimann/Va-Va idea, Rattigan was working on other plays. Some of these efforts were thrown on to the flames of his coal fire in Canters, others were never to be completed. But some were shown to friends, and one even to George Devine, now President of the OUDS. The one-act play, which Rattigan later described as 'a highly experimental piece rather in the vein of Constantin's effort in *The Seagull*', was rejected by Devine, who pronounced: 'Some of it is absolutely smashing, but it goes too far.' Though he did his best to conceal his feelings by telling his friends that Devine was probably right, and had been 'very kind' to read the play, the snub rankled for years to come. Rattigan suspected that Devine, who surrounded himself with homosexuals, nonetheless disliked them, and he strongly suspected that Devine disliked him personally.

Still, Rattigan did not refuse to take part in Devine's production of *Romeo and Juliet* in February 1932. Determined to make his mark as President, Devine had invited the new star of the London Old Vic company, John Gielgud, to direct the play, and, to tempt him further, had persuaded Peggy Ashcroft to play Juliet. Gielgud agreed – it would be the first production he had directed – and in turn invited Edith Evans, who had just returned from Broadway, to play the Nurse. Women undergraduates were not at that time allowed to join the OUDS, and professional actresses were 'put up and loved', in Devine's words, in their place.

Gielgud was the first star Rattigan had witnessed in action at first
hand, and he was fascinated. Even though he had only a couple of
weeks to prepare the production, Gielgud insisted on auditions, finally
selecting Christopher Hassall to play Romeo, Devine himself to play
Mercutio, and William Devlin for Tybalt. Rattigan was chosen to play
one of the musicians who discover Juliet's body, which brought him
the single line: 'Faith, we may put up our pipes and be gone.' Gielgud's
acting commitments in London prevented him from staying in Oxford
during rehearsals, but Peggy Ashcroft and Edith Evans remained, regularly inviting groups of members to dinner, and arousing rivalries and
petty jealousies among the company, to Rattigan's amusement. Devine
was to use the production as his route to an acting career in London.

On the first night, at the New Theatre in Oxford, Gielgud was
shaking with nerves, but not as much as Rattigan, who had been
coached patiently by Gielgud to help him get his single line right. To
both men's amazement, Rattigan's line about 'putting up his pipes'
raised an enormous laugh. He liked to maintain in the years to come
that he was embarrassed by this reaction, and did everything he could
to try to avoid the laugh on subsequent nights, but in reality he relished
it, though he decided then and there that he preferred writing plays to
acting in them.

After the production Gielgud returned to London, to enjoy success
as both star and director of *Richard of Bordeaux*. Rattigan nevertheless
kept in touch with him through their mutual friendship with John
Perry, an Irish-born former actor turned writer, who had visited
Oxford during the production and who shared a house with Gielgud
near Henley-on-Thames. Rattigan became a regular visitor. There was
poker and ping-pong, a great many famous faces, and frequent Sunday
house parties. The same atmosphere of flamboyant high spirits prevailed as at Canters, where Rattigan and Peter Glenville had developed
a similar reputation for elegant and sometimes outrageous parties.

This was the magical star-studded world which Rattigan had longed
to be part of. It was also a world of homosexuals, which the theatre
accepted more readily, and more consistently, than any other profession. Gielgud's theatre company was certainly more welcoming to
homosexuals than some of the more conventional managements and
impresarios of that time; nevertheless, every homosexual knew only
too well the dangers that confronted them if they dared to advertise
their sexual appetites too brazenly. Any homosexual act between adults
over the age of twenty-one was punishable by months of imprisonment, while the punishment for an affair with a minor was even harsher
– and Rattigan was not even twenty-one. Queer-bashing was on the

increase, and not only among those who would shortly join Oswald Mosley's British Union of Fascists. Even the most civilised people strongly disapproved. Rattigan, like every homosexual of the time, was always on guard, preoccupied with preserving appearances at all costs, conscious of the need to protect his secret world.

Throughout 1932 Rattigan's visits to Perry and Gielgud increased. There he could relax in an atmosphere that delighted him, and he never wanted to leave. So when his father insisted that he again spend the summer at a French crammer, this time at La Baule in Brittany, he agreed with the greatest reluctance. It has been suggested that during the trip he contracted venereal disease from a prostitute, an experience which had already been bitterly embarrassing since he had been unable to reach a climax. 'He had felt driven to try a sexual experiment with a woman,' insists one acquaintance. But there is very little evidence to support the suggestion, especially in view of his own experiences at Oxford. If it is true, then it was to be Rattigan's only sexual experience with a woman. For, as one Oxford contemporary puts it, 'Terry was simply not interested in women in that way.'

At the beginning of his third and final year as an undergraduate, Rattigan began belatedly to do some work. An unexpectedly large number of books were borrowed from the college library, and his attendance at lectures increased, while his weekly tutorial hour was prepared for more diligently. The whole of Oxford teaching was based on the premise of 'ideas not facts, judgement not an index, life not death', in the words of the history don Cyril Oman. He insisted that his pupils 'get an idea' and 'work it out by illustration to the end', writing nothing 'without first considering construction, not mere verbiage'.

Rattigan warmed to the approach. He was studying the development of modern Europe, including the causes of the French revolution, the impact of Napoleon and the emergence of a German state, as well as the political thought of Aristotle and Plato, and the law of the British Constitution. He was still living in Canters, still infatuated with Philip Heimann, who was in the last stages of his law degree, and still conscious of the Oxford literary tradition of wearing knowledge, no matter how hard won, lightly. 'The greatest gift that Oxford gives her sons is, I truly believe, a genial irreverence toward learning, and from that learning love may spring,' is how the Canadian novelist Robertson Davies described it. 'Wearing your learning lightly' was to become the essence of Rattigan's approach to his work as a playwright. He was to conceal his seriousness every bit as determinedly as his homosexuality.

The pretence that the final goal was to be the Diplomatic Service was still being maintained, but only just. Rattigan's fearsome grandmother, Lady Rattigan, had recently died, leaving him a modest but comforting legacy of £1,000, which created in his mind the dangerous feeling that, so far as his personal life was concerned, everything would take care of itself.

In the larger world Hitler had just come to power. To any enlightened young Englishman, the thought of another war was repugnant, indeed intolerable. Rattigan was toying with the idea of becoming a communist, as his friend John Bayliss had done. 'There was always that in Terry,' Frith Banbury recalls. 'There was the good living and élitism on the one hand, and wanting to be a revolutionary on the other.' He was not alone. Speaking at the Oxford Union two years earlier, Philip Heimann had already proposed disarmament and pacifism as the only possible approach to a changing world order. The Union decided to debate the motion 'That this House will in no circumstances fight for its King and Country.'

Tony Goldschmidt spoke in favour, and he, Philip Heimann and Rattigan were among the 275 who voted in support. The motion was carried by 122 votes, provoking an outcry and causing Oxford undergraduates to be condemned by some sections of the British press as 'woolly-minded Communists, practical jokers and sexual indeterminates'. It was a description that Rattigan could laugh at, in private at least, and it had not the slightest effect on his equanimity. Instead he put a fraction of his legacy towards an advertisement in the *Morning Post* calling for play scripts. He and Heimann hoped to discover a new play which they could produce. Unfortunately they heartily disliked all but one of the scripts they received, and then when they met the author they dismissed him too as an 'uneducated second rater'.

Rattigan was confident he could better himself. His notebooks were full of playlets and ideas, scraps of dialogue and sketches for characters. As the Hilary Term of 1933 drew to a close, he drafted the outline of a play based on his own relationship with Heimann and Va-Va, the eternal triangle with a difference. He called it *Embryo*. He and Heimann discussed the text interminably, during seemingly endless walks round Christ Church meadow; but when he returned after Easter, he put the play on one side.

The time was approaching for him to take his final exams, and the archives of Trinity College library show that at last he was working hard. Over Easter he had taken out more books from the college than ever before, and in the weeks after the start of the summer term in 1933 the number increased again. In May alone he borrowed eleven books, more than he had ever done before in a single month.

But when the examination day arrived, Rattigan did not turn up. It was his first public act of defiance, the first time that he had openly confronted his father. Frank Rattigan was desperate that his son should graduate, particularly since he had failed to do so himself. Terence knew this, and he also knew that his father's plans for him to join the Diplomatic Service would probably be hindered if he declined to take his finals. There was also something else at the back of his mind. Rattigan had watched his mother's humiliation over the past few years, the string of blonde young 'cousins' Frank continued to parade round town. Even more disturbingly, his father had, on one occasion, invited his son to join him for the weekend at a country hotel. Major Rattigan had then registered his young female friend as his son's sister. The girl had hardly helped matters by displaying more interest in her 'brother' than in her 'father'. Rattigan's sarcastic comments to his friends about his father's pomposity and double standards had steadily increased in bitterness as a result. He had not even been able to bring himself to return to Stanhope Gardens during the summer vacations, preferring to take a house in the Thames Valley with Tony Goldschmidt and Philip Heimann.

The legend has grown up that Rattigan did not take his finals 'because he had written a play' which was about to be produced in the West End. This is untrue, though he had certainly done some work on *Embryo*. The truth was more private. His refusal to take his finals at the last moment was based on revenge. He saw no need to take his final examinations, even though one tutor later suggested that he would certainly have got a first; a degree was not essential for a playwright. Besides, if that annoyed his father, all the better. It was Rattigan's first public rebuff for his father.

In fact he was to remain a resident of Canters until the spring of 1934. But his tutor's book at Trinity for the summer term of 1933 notes simply: 'Went down without taking schools.'

CHAPTER 6

First Episode

◆

*He would live straight, not because it mattered to
anyone now, but for the sake of the game. He
would not deceive himself so much. He would not –
and this was the test – pretend to care about women
when the only sex that attracted him was his own.
He loved men and always had loved them.*

E.M.FORSTER, *Maurice*

◆

With Oxford temporarily behind him, Rattigan set off not for Stanhope
Gardens and his parents, but for Germany. He had already planned to
spend the summer there, and there seemed no reason why he should
change the arrangement. Then he would return temporarily to Oxford
for a time and plan the future carefully. For the moment he wanted
time to think, and to work with Heimann on *Embryo*. He had persuaded
Heimann to abandon the voluptuous and experienced Va-Va Basilewich for a few weeks, and to go with him to a crammer's in Marzell,
near Baden Baden. They could share a room together and work.

Rattigan's infatuation with Heimann had never been reciprocated,
though he had long hoped it would be. Only in the play they were
writing together could he express the emotions he felt. The conflict
between the affair between a young undergraduate and an older and
more experienced woman, and the effect this has on the young man's
relationship with his friend, a homosexual fellow undergraduate, was
to lay part of the foundations of his success as a playwright. Here

already were two themes that Terence Rattigan was to return to time and again in his work: the attraction of a man and a woman who can only harm each other, and the desperate illogicality of love and passion.

The play's setting is unmistakably Oxford, and the echoes of Rattigan's own experiences with Gielgud and Peggy Ashcroft at the OUDS the previous year are only too clear. A visiting actress, Margot, who is in her thirties and down to play Cleopatra in the University Drama Society's *Antony and Cleopatra*, falls for Tony, the young producer, who has been having an affair with the promiscuous but charming Joan. When he in turn falls for Margot, Tony passes Joan on to his close friend David, who then becomes convinced that Tony's affair with Margot will mean that Tony will fail his exams and threaten the friendship they have built together as undergraduates.

At first Margot fights her attraction to Tony. 'You're all so very young. It's almost stifling, the atmosphere of youth in this place.' After a week or two, however, she realises that she cannot fight the attraction. Tony wants her to go away with him. She refuses, and explains that she is 'so very much more in love with you than you are with me'. Tony objects: 'That's not true, Margot; I do love you passionately.' In a line that Rattigan would rework many times for characters in the years to come, she retorts: 'That's just it, and it may only be passion.' Nevertheless she agrees to go away with him.

After a few weeks Tony confides to David that he is tiring of Margot. She is just too difficult: 'If I don't say "Good Morning" in the right tone of voice, our whole day is spoilt. And she's absurdly jealous. She says you have a bad influence on me.'

Like Rattigan to Heimann, David is sympathetic, but he is also aware that Va-Va does not care for him. Indeed Rattigan then gives Va-Va the opportunity to present her side of the affair. He has Margot tell David exactly what she thinks of their friendship.

MARGOT: I'm part of him that even you can't separate.
DAVID: Why should I want to separate you?
MARGOT: Because you're just a filthy degenerate.
DAVID: God! How dare you? You come down here and seduce a boy half your age . . . you've done your best to ruin his life for him. He's up to his neck in debt and he'll go down without a degree, and all because of you – and you talk about degeneracy.

Margot snaps back a little later in the exchange, 'The friendship of young men can be very selfish.' 'But so impregnable,' David replies. Margot takes her revenge – by tipping off the Senior Proctor that David is in Joan's hotel room at a forbidden hour. This too concealed the truth. For Rattigan and Heimann were well aware that no producer or theatre owner would be prepared to present the real story that lay behind this part of the play, that David would, of course, have been in Tony's bed at the forbidden hour. To portray a real homosexual relationship on the British stage in 1933 was inconceivable. It was the love that dared not speak its name.

Margot's act of vengeance sees David sent down and Tony so angry that he drops her, while the hapless Joan is condemned to the arms of a brainless cricketer called Bertie. The intensity of the emotional triangle at the heart of the play, however, was weakened by a garnish of undergraduate pranks, larks, parties and general high jinks that conceal the serious heart of the play. With their sights firmly set on the West End of London Rattigan and Heimann were trying to present their story in a palatable form. There are funny lines, but they detract from the serious themes that Rattigan was pursuing. Nevertheless, the funniest line is one said to Joan, the 'tart with a heart of gold', by the ultra-naïve Bertie, who is trying to warn her about a potential seducer.

BERTIE: My poor child, do you know what he wants to do to you?
JOAN: (*mock alarm*) No, Bertie!
BERTIE: He wants to – he wants to – Joan, have you ever lived on a farm?

This frivolity colours the whole of the play, and fundamentally weakens it. The japes and hilarity, including a drunk scene for David and a great party to celebrate his picking the winner of the Derby (a feat which Rattigan had managed twice in his time at Oxford, with April the Fifth and Windsor Lad), make it seem no more than a frothy farce. Tony is just a boy, David and Margot simply unlucky people, caught up in his first romantic episode. The underlying seriousness of the plot is lost.

But a careful reading reveals the subtext, that sexual attraction can be dangerous, and that love can be illogical. Rattigan had set out to evoke the plight of those men who seem doomed to fail their women by the inadequacy of their passion; and the intensity and passion of men for each other. He was, in fact, using the play not only to examine his own emotions and sexual passions, but also to suggest the adjustment young homosexuals were forced to make in their friendships in a world which expected every man to be heterosexual. But he concealed this message beneath a froth of jokes, using his wit to conceal the pain.

Terence Rattigan loved Philip Heimann, and was sexually attracted to him. He suspected that Heimann loved him, but he knew Heimann was not a homosexual. The result was a painful sense of loss and longing, confused and compounded still further by the intensity of

their friendship. A friend of both men at the time remembers that
Heimann had once told him about a 'truth game' that Rattigan and he
liked to play as undergraduates at Oxford. 'The question they had
all asked each other was "Who in this room would you most like to
kiss?" Philip told me that Terry had not hesitated for a moment – "Oh,
Philip, definitely."' But Terence Rattigan's love could never be
reciprocated.

Heimann and Rattigan completed the final version of the play in
Germany in late July. They immediately sent it off to a London management with a reputation for putting on new work. On the frontispiece
to the play the author's name is given as Terence Rattigan, while Philip
Heimann's was added later. Just before it was dispatched, Rattigan also
changed the title to *Episode*.

Heimann left Germany for South Africa, but Rattigan was joined
shortly afterwards by John Perry. The two men had grown increasingly
close since the Gielgud production. They were regularly entertained
by the domestic quarrels of their hosts at the crammer's, where the
wife was an enthusiastic supporter of National Socialism while her
husband was not. To find out for themselves, Perry and Rattigan went
to a torchlight Nazi rally in Karlsruhe, which Rattigan thought 'very
pretty' and 'rather a joke'. In the end he told Perry, tongue slightly in
cheek, that the whole business was being taken 'far too seriously'. For
the moment, he was more concerned with his play.

To Rattigan's astonishment, he received not only an acknowledgement from the London management but also a suggestion that *Episode*
could be put on without delay. In a state of high excitement, he
borrowed the air fare from Perry and flew back from Germany at once.
It was not his only extravagance in support of his new play. He also
agreed to put up £200 of his grandmother's legacy towards the cost of
production.

But first the play required a licence from the Lord Chamberlain,
who was responsible for ensuring that no 'offensive or suggestive'
material was performed in public on the London stage. On 15 August
1933 Norman Gibson, the manager of the Q Theatre in Richmond,
where the play was to be produced, submitted *Episode* to the Lord
Chamberlain's office in St James's Palace.

The Lord Chamberlain's office followed the standard procedure for
every play that was proposed for production. It sent the script out to
one of its appointed 'readers', who was asked to submit a report, and
to comment on whether or not the play should be licensed for public
production. The reader was also asked to recommend changes where
these were thought appropriate – to protect the play's prospective audi-

ence from bad language, blasphemy, sexual explicitness, or anything else that the Lord Chamberlain felt might offend an audience.

The reader's report on *Episode* was submitted to the Lord Chamberlain the day after the play was received. H.C.Gane, the reader in question, had considered the work overnight, and after briefly summing up the plot, concluded by stating: 'I don't think anyone could take this play seriously, otherwise I should suggest a warning against dialogue or mounting the play . . . as I hardly think University life as depicted here would appeal to the authorities.' The play's frivolous tone, however, convinced Mr Gane that no one could be unduly offended, although he drew the Lord Chamberlain's attention to 'a certain amount of crudely sophisticated dialogue'. In particular he was uncomfortable with the use of the phrase 'filthy degenerate', saying 'there has been nothing to justify this', and that there were 'rather too many "Gods" in the early part of Act II and Act III'.

The Lord Chamberlain's office agreed with their reader, commenting on his typewritten draft, 'Terrible Trash, I quite agree', and taking exception to the use of the word 'pansies' in Act Two, during a discussion about homosexuality. 'Otherwise, unpleasant a play as it is, I think it can reluctantly pass.' The Lord Chamberlain explained in a letter on 21 August, 1933 that he would grant a licence for the production, providing there were a number of small cuts – mostly of discussions about Margot's sexual appetite – that the word 'pansies' be deleted from Act Two, and that some of the uses of the word 'God' be omitted. Norman Gibson accepted the suggestions, and the official licence was granted on 24 August 1933. Terence Rattigan's first play was about to be produced in public.

Still known as *Episode*, the play was produced by Muriel Pratt, who had been responsible for a series of productions at the Q Theatre on the north side of Kew Bridge over the Thames. She emphasised the humour of the piece, playing down the relationship between Tony and David, highlighting the pranks and parties, and it duly opened on 11 September 1933 for a 'brief season'. It was well received. In its review a week later the *Daily Telegraph* reported: 'An extremely able and amusing "first play", all unheralded and unchaperoned, popped up at the Q Theatre last week . . . It gives us an Oxford – or at least "a certain side of Oxford", as we can reassure ourselves – riddled with betting on horses, not averse to alcohol, and interested, to the point of mania, in young ladies. Nevertheless it has the ring of being an authentic side.'

Nor did the reviewer fail to detect the serious undertones. 'With a skill that is quite extraordinary in inexperienced hands, the authors have switched the play over in its last act from being merely a play of

juvenile high spirits into a play in which the characters are real enough
to feel pain.' He added, 'For the benefit of those who object that the
riotous side of University life is overdrawn, it may be mentioned that
the play is strictly moral in its values: it is the gamblers, drinkers and
those too interested in young women who feel the pain.'

The review gave the company, and its young author, an enormous
boost, especially as it concluded: 'It is claiming no prophetic gifts to
suggest that the play will probably be seen later in town'. This brought
a handful of London managements to see the play for themselves, and
one, Daniel Mayer, agreed to give it a try out in the West End. It
would have to wait until a theatre was available, probably after the
New Year. The success of *The Wind and the Rain*, another play about
student life, which was running at the time, encouraged Mayer to feel
that *Episode* might be worth the risk.

Rattigan was naturally overjoyed. Once the run in Kew had finished
in October, he set about revising the play in the light of the audience
reactions he'd noted during each and every performance. He would
prowl the back of the small stuffy theatre, carefully watching which
lines worked and which didn't, seeing where the action flagged, or
where the characters seemed stilted. Rattigan began by changing the
title of the play to *First Episode,* and then cabled Heimann in South
Africa to break the good news that they were about to get their first
play put on in the West End. Heimann cabled back that he intended
to be there for the first night.

Immediately after the New Year, *First Episode* went into rehearsal.
There were one or two cast changes from Kew. Max Adrian had been
brought in to strengthen the part of Bertie, which Rattigan had rewrit-
ten slightly to make it more interesting, while Barbara Hoffe was to
play Margot, William Fox Tony and Patrick Waddington David. The
plan was to open at the end of January at the Comedy Theatre in Panton
Street, one of London's smaller theatres just off Leicester Square. In
the meantime the new management had to have Rattigan's new version,
First Episode, licensed, and on 3 January 1934 duly submitted it to the
Lord Chamberlain's office.

Once again Mr Gane read the play, commenting this time: 'The first
version seemed to me utter trash, but the play has now been considerably cut about and generally pulled together so that it is now more
credible and effective.' He was still not tremendously impressed, however, concluding, 'It remains a trivial and unpleasant play.' He also
asked for a number of further cuts, in particular that the references to
'sexual intercourse', which Rattigan had added to the new version,
should all be removed, as indeed should any reference to 'physical

love'. Love was acceptable to the Lord Chamberlain, but 'physical' love was not. On 6 January, Daniel Mayer agreed to the cuts, and three days later the official licence was issued.

By the time Philip Heimann had arrived by boat from South Africa and set himself up in a small flat in Half Moon Street, just north of Piccadilly, the play was all but ready. It opened on Friday, 26 January 1934, with production by Muriel Pratt, dresses and hats by Lawler of South Molton Street, and champagne by George Goulet & Co. of Reims. The programme contained an advertisement for James Bridie's play *The Sleeping Clergyman* at the Piccadilly Theatre, near by.

The audience, which included Frank and Vera Rattigan, were enthusiastic if not ecstatic, and the two young authors took a brief curtain call after the cast. They had each received £100 in advance of their royalties for the transfer, but Rattigan had never recouped the £200 he had invested in the run at Kew. The money was of no consequence, however. The curtain had fallen for the first time on a Rattigan play in the West End of London, and the author was just twenty-two.

The next morning the critics were reasonably encouraging. *The Times* was a little stiff, but not ungenerous. 'The impression it gives of uncertainty is doubtless due to the determination of the two authors that there shall be something of everything for everybody; and it would be ungrateful not to acknowledge that the piece has liveliness to cover its rather more than occasional failure to make its development plausible', said its anonymous reviewer, adding: 'These adventures are set in a farce that is at times as uproarious as *Charley's Aunt*, or, shall we say, *While Parents Sleep*. And for all its somewhat self-conscious vulgarities the farce is alive.' The *Daily Telegraph* remarked: 'The dialogue is often neat, and the handling of the situations instinctively theatrical.' Even James Agate in the *Sunday Times* declared: 'This play should run.'

Terence Rattigan, delighted, threw a party for the cast in Heimann's Half Moon Street flat. And as the weeks passed, and the run continued, he held a series of parties for the young actors in the cast. There was no doubt in his mind: this was the life he wanted, and he intended to celebrate as often as he could. William Fox recalls, 'Terry was always inviting us to parties, and a good many of them were in Oxford.' Rattigan still had his rooms at Canters. That was the next thing to be sorted out.

Only two groups objected to the play, neither of them professionals. A pompous body of theatregoers, calling themselves 'The Public Morality Council', complained bitterly to the Lord Chamberlain just two weeks after the first night that *First Episode* was a 'thoroughly unpleasant and immoral play – full of irreverence, sex in its worst form and filthy language . . . University life is portrayed as evil and disgusting.' The ever dependable Mr Gane was this time dispatched to see the play. He reported that the complaints 'seem to me entirely unjustified . . . there's no undue amount of swearing, not many Gods and only two bloodies'. The Lord Chamberlain's office invited the Public Morality Council to a meeting on 14 February to mollify them. It worked. They did not pursue their objections.

But the Oxford University Proctors were rather less easily diverted. They took exception to *First Episode*'s depiction of university life, not merely because they too had received a letter from the Public Morality Council, but also because they were annoyed by newspaper headlines like 'Stage Shock for Oxford. Lurid Picture in New Play' in the *News Chronicle*. The Proctors summoned the new editor of *Cherwell*, Rattigan's friend Paul Dehn, and ordered him not to print any review of the play. Dehn reluctantly agreed. When Rattigan himself was called to see the Proctors he told them simply that he had already left the university.

Now came the task of telling his father that he had no intention whatever of sitting the Diplomatic Service examination. Since his son's childhood, Frank Rattigan had made no secret of his dislike for anything 'artistic'. His passions were sport and shooting, 'manly recreations' as he put it, 'proper pastimes' for a young man. Frank had made it equally clear that a young man's interests should also turn to young women.

Terence Rattigan and his father had for years argued about the future during his rare visits to Stanhope Gardens. His mother would look on in despair as the two men bitterly condemned each other's view of the world – the diplomat and the aesthete. Brian would chip in from time to time, always in support of his father. 'Brian was like Frank, not interested in culture' is how Rattigan's younger cousin, Roxanne Senior, remembers it. 'And Terry's decision not to go into the Diplomatic Service absolutely infuriated his father.'

But by now the posters outside the Comedy Theatre were announcing '50th Performance. Great success.' That fact that the play seemed set fair for a long run in London seemed sufficient excuse to its young author to 'come down from Oxford without a degree, issue a defiant manifesto to my father and rent a studio flat in London to pursue my now determinate career'. Rattigan was sharing the flat in question with Philip Heimann, at least for the time being. And in April 1934 *Theatre World* reported his decision: '*First Episode* has definitely decided him on a writing career instead of the Diplomatic Service. Much to the distress of his mother and father. Terry has finished another play with Heimann and has also written one by himself which Patrick Waddington says is brilliantly clever.'

But Rattigan did not have the courage to tell Frank of his decision face to face. Instead he sent him a letter, announcing that he was going to become a playwright, not a diplomat, and that he was going to live on his own in London, at an address he intended to keep to himself. In spite of the success of *First Episode*, it was the letter of a young man who had still not quite grown up, though it is easy to understand why he should not want to tell his father with whom he was sharing his flat.

His platonic idyll with Heimann was, in any case, to be short-lived. Va-Va arrived to re-stake her claim to the man she wanted to marry. Heimann hesitated for a moment, unwilling to leave Rattigan. Though it had never been physical, theirs was a far more intense relationship than any of their friends, and certainly his parents, had ever understood, or known about. But Heimann did not hesitate for long. Within a few days he announced that he and Irina were returning to South Africa to get married, and that he was going to join the family business. Rattigan could keep the play they had been working on since last summer, *Black Forest*, as a parting gift. But he was leaving.

Rattigan was shattered. They had been soulmates, destined, he thought, to remain together for ever. Now a woman had destroyed the dream. The shock was to remain with him for many years, and Irina too would become the second prototype for the man-hunting young woman who would, following the example set by his house-master's daughter, Margaret, loom large in many of his plays. Heimann later wrote a novel about his triangular relationship with Rattigan and the woman who did indeed become his wife, but he was never to work with his old friend again.

Heimann's defection was not the only shock to strike Rattigan in the last weeks of March 1934. Suddenly the box office for *First Episode* had collapsed. The play was no longer taking enough money to carry on. The Comedy told him it would have to close in early April. In common with most of the other actors, William Fox, who was playing Tony, 'could not understand why it all seemed to go wrong so suddenly'. Whatever the reason, Rattigan had not only lost the £200 he had invested in the play at Kew, but by now he had spent the £100 that he had been paid for the play's transfer to the West End. There was talk of a quick revival in London, even of the possibility of a trip to Broadway, but nothing was guaranteed. A little of his grandmother's legacy remained, but Rattigan was almost broke.

The 'defiant manifesto to my father' failed along with the play. 'It was an insufficient excuse,' he wrote. 'The play was a flop and within three weeks I was back under the parental roof, penniless though not entirely penitent.' By then Frank Rattigan had discovered where his younger son was living – though not the precise details of the ménage – and summoned him home to Stanhope Gardens. It was not too painful a mission. Under the influence of his wife, Frank had accepted at least part of the reality of his son's life and made him an allowance of £200 a year for two years 'to explore' his chosen career. If he failed to make a living and support himself by the end of that time he would have to accept his father's allotted fate, the Foreign Office. Meanwhile a writing desk was moved into his room under the eaves of the family's flat on the top floor of the five-storey building in South Kensington. 'In this I was lucky,' he wrote. 'Most writers, I know, have perforce to begin part time. I began whole time and as the end of the probationary period drew near, much more than whole time.'

Throughout the remainder of 1934 and the whole of 1935 Rattigan worked in a frenzy: plays, adaptations, screenplays, anything to keep him out of the clutches of the Diplomatic Service. Father and son stalked round each other, while Vera Rattigan did her best to keep the peace – not particularly aided by Brian. Rattigan removed himself to his room for long periods, and when he came out it was usually to leave the flat altogether. 'I just kept on writing until somehow I had finished a play,' he wrote. 'Then I started the next one.' As soon as one was finished he parcelled it up and posted it off to a succession of agents and managements.

As spring turned to summer in 1934, he spent whatever weekends he could with John Perry and John Gielgud, who had moved to a house near Finchingfield in Essex. It was Perry who introduced him to his next collaborator, Hector Bolitho, who lived not far away at Hempstead. A middle-aged writer of travel books and royal biographies, and distinctly old-womanish in manner, Bolitho had already written two novels and now wanted to adapt his third, *Grey Farm*, for the stage. If Rattigan would come and stay with him at Hempstead they could work on the adaptation together.

The outcome was disastrous. Rattigan rapidly came to despise both Bolitho and his novel, and took refuge in a local pub, or, when possible, in John Gielgud's house eight miles away. But he needed the money, so he struggled on, gritting his teeth, and being rude about Bolitho to John Perry whenever he saw him. No one could have saved *Grey Farm*, which was never to be produced in England. A homicidal version of the then popular play *The Green Bay Tree*, it revolved around the mania of a middle-aged man who feels driven to strangle his maid because his wife has died in childbirth and his nineteen-year-old son is getting married. When it was finally performed, briefly, on Broadway in May 1940, the *New York Post* remarked, 'The evening is more than a bore, it is a titan among bores', while the *New Yorker*'s Wolcott Gibbs called it 'a pathological melodrama about a man who feels he has to strangle people . . . It is a dull and unpleasant play, and Oscar Homolka's performance in the leading part is like nothing I've seen since an actor called Frank Vosper portrayed homicidal mania by eating a silk scarf.' Homolka, by contrast, relentlessly flexed his thumbs. *Variety* called the result 'a hopeless script' and 'a box office dodo'.

There were compensations. The rumour of a run on Broadway for *First Episode* had turned into reality. The powerful Shubert Organization wanted to bring over a group of new British plays about young people, and had decided that *First Episode* was to be the first. There was to be a brief out of town tour first, and then a Broadway opening in September. Max Adrian and Patrick Waddington had been allowed to retain their original parts in the American cast, and when the play opened in New Haven, Connecticut, one of the traditional venues for an out of town tour, *Variety* was encouraging. 'Play has all the ingredients of good theatre, mixing romance and humour with a touch of near tragedy. It's not the conventional type of happy-ending play, but it depicts a pretty accurate slice of English University life.' The New York papers were to prove less generous. When the play opened at the Ritz Theatre on 17 September 1934, the *New York American* called it 'a very poor and silly little play', while the formidable Brooks Atkinson in the *New York Times* wrote: 'An unpalatable mixture of tenderness and ear splitting farce'. But, he added presciently, 'If the authors were willing to pursue their theme earnestly *First Episode* might well be a disarmingly poignant drama.'

The reviews sealed the play's fate on Broadway. It stayed at the Ritz for just forty performances, and only lasted that long because the Shuberts wanted to set up their season and had made financial commitments to the English actors. Rattigan had not been able to afford the fare to New York, and the short run meant that once again he failed to see a penny from the production. But the experience had further confirmed his conviction that he was a playwright, nothing else. And Broadway brought him another, unexpected, benefit. *First Episode* was to be revived in London, at the Garrick Theatre in December. It too failed to bring its author a penny. Played for farce, it closed shortly after Christmas.

John Perry came to his rescue, this time encouraging Gielgud to consider Rattigan as a collaborator. Gielgud had just finished an immensely succesful tour of *Hamlet*, and was planning a stage adaptation of Charles Dickens's novel *A Tale of Two Cities*, which would allow him the licence to play both the heroic Sidney Carton and the wicked Marquis de St Evremonde.

Rattigan recalled that Gielgud had first mentioned the idea to him rather vaguely. 'I can't find anyone to do this *Tale of Two Cities*. You're not doing anything – I'm sure you're not doing anything. Would you like to do it?' and then wandering off before returning and saying, 'I wonder if it's all right to have anyone without any experience.' Gielgud was not above keeping the young playwright with only one West End production to his name firmly in his place. But it was still a remarkable opportunity. Gielgud was one of the theatre's young lions, his *Richard II* acclaimed around the world and his *Hamlet* one of the most popular productions of the play in modern times. He had directed both productions himself.

Gielgud simply wanted Rattigan to write the dialogue, leaving out most of the background – there was to be no storming of the Bastille, for example. He wished to restrict the play instead to the major characters. The two men started work in the spring of 1935 at Finchingfield, at the same time that Gielgud was rehearsing his leading role in André Obey's *Noah*, destined for the New Theatre in London.

Rattigan wrote a Prologue and the first two acts using straightforward English wherever he could rather than Anglicised French. There were even one or two jokes. 'You don't seem quite to realise what the Bastille is,' Jarvis Lorry remarks to Miss Pross. 'It's a prison, isn't it,' she replies, 'only French.' But it was the courtroom scene at the trial of Charles Darney at the Old Bailey which established Carton in the mind of the audience and showed Rattigan at his best.

When the Prologue and the first two acts were completed to his satisfaction Gielgud took them to Bronson Albery, for whom he was appearing in *Noah*. Gielgud had made the New Theatre virtually his permanent base since *Richard of Bordeaux*, and the two men were very close. Albery, who was responsible for running both the New and Wyndham's with his elder step-brother, Howard Wyndham, liked what he saw of *A Tale of Two Cities* and confirmed to Gielgud, whom he was anxious to please, that if the last act was as good as the first two he would certainly produce the play that autumn. When the third act was delivered a few weeks later he confirmed that he was happy with it. The frontispiece read 'Adapted for the stage from the novel by Charles Dickens by Terence Rattigan and John Gielgud'. Rattigan's career as a West End playwright looked set to continue.

However, it was not to be. Though Bronson Albery asked the Motleys, Elizabeth Montgomery and the two sisters Sophie and Peggy Harris (who had designed *Romeo and Juliet* for Gielgud at the OUDS – George Devine had later married Sophie), to create a spectacular set for the New, and began to assemble a fine supporting cast, including Fay Compton as Lucy Manette and Martita Hunt as Miss Pross, there was a snag. It came in the barely missable form of one of England's leading actor-managers, Sir John Martin-Harvey, who was then seventy-two and had been playing his own version of the same Dickens story, called *The Only Way,* since 1889. Gielgud had received an emotional letter from the old actor-manager, begging him not to put the new version on while he was still playing his. He took the letter to Albery, who – rather to Gielgud's surprise – got cold feet and insisted on consulting a number of the leading London critics, including James Agate, all of whom seemed to agree that Gielgud could not take 'bread out of an old man's mouth'.

Gielgud agreed without much hesitation. He had, in fact, already lined up an alternative for Albery, a new production of *Romeo and Juliet*, in which he and Laurence Olivier would alternate the roles of Romeo and Mercutio, and Peggy Ashcroft and Edith Evans would repeat the roles they had played for him at Oxford three years before. But when the time came to break the bad news to Rattigan, Gielgud could only bring himself to mutter: 'It's a pity about Martin-Harvey, isn't it? But it's lucky the design works for *Romeo and Juliet*, so that we can do that instead. Larry says he'll do Mercutio. Isn't it marvellous?' When he went back to his room in Gielgud's house at Finchingfield that night, Rattigan wept.

In an effort to lessen the blow, Bronson Albery sent him a cheque for fifty guineas and asked to see any other plays he might have written. He had already seen a number of Rattigan's plays, all of which he had returned, but there were still one or two which had been kept back. When Rattigan got back to Stanhope Gardens, he looked through the pile of a dozen manuscripts he had worked on in the past year. There were two possibles. One was *Black Forest*, a drama of 'tangled emotions' partly inspired by his time with Heimann in Germany; the other, a farce called *Gone Away*. The question was – which one to send?

'Better let him read a good farce than a bad drama,' said Vera Rattigan. Her son was less sure. Eight managements had already turned down *Gone Away*, which had started life as *Joie de Vivre* and had then briefly become *French Chalk*. He had even sent it to Albery once already under that title, and was far from confident that it would fare any more successfully this time. But Vera persisted. She put the manuscript into an envelope, sealed it and sent it off, thereby creating a theatrical bond with her son which would last for the rest of their lives. Ever afterwards he would take her opinion above almost anyone else's, and her support became a talisman for his success. If she liked something he did, that was enough. If she was amused, so would the audience be.

In fact Rattigan had been far more tempted to send *Black Forest* to Albery, knowing Albery's preference for drama. It was more serious, the work of a young man determined to become a professional play-wright, more representative of what he intended to write in the future. Set in a hotel, it tells the story of an ageing schoolmaster, William Bryant, on holiday there with his wife, of whom little is seen and less heard, their two sons, John, who is at Cambridge, and Peter, who is at the school at which Bryant is housemaster, and their twenty-six-year-old daughter, Mary, who is with her would-be fiancé, David Pleydell, another schoolmaster, who hopes to succeed to Bryant's house. Also at the hotel is Edward Watherstone, whom Bryant has had to sack from the school after he has been discovered making love to a kitchen maid in a churchyard.

Again the echoes from Rattigan's life are clear enough: Brian's adventures at Harrow, his own experiences with his housemaster, B.Mid, but as ever the events are transformed. The play opens on the first floor veranda of the Hotel Schönblick, and John is complaining bitterly about having to learn German. 'Good Lord, why? Frightful language, I should think. Sounds like one long retch.' He is equally unenthusiastic about his sister's choice of future husband. 'Can't stick his type really – you know, the friendly schoolmaster type, the sort that has boys to tea and talks to them as if they were human beings, but if they show any signs of being human beings gets them sacked.' Daringly, John even suggests to his sister: 'I think it's Peter he wants to marry and not you.'

William Bryant has apparently expelled Watherstone for having sex on a tombstone, but there is also the clear indication that he knows that his daughter is infatuated with the boy. When the play opens Watherstone has been wandering round Germany with a German girl, Toni. But within three days matters get out of hand. Bryant's son John proposes to Toni and Mary rediscovers her youthful passion for Watherstone. Mary and Watherstone decide to elope together. Once more Rattigan's theme hinges on the illogicalities of sexual attraction, and love.

At one stage Bryant describes love as 'a germ', and his daughter picks up the reference.

MARY: You heard what my father said about that virulent germ. He was right. If it attacks you you've got no hope. You forget about things like the standards of morality. What should I care what Teddy is?

DAVID: You'll care soon enough, when he leaves you for another woman.

MARY: Yes, I suppose so. It's against all reason that being the man he is won't cause me the most frightful unhappiness. But you know, David, reason is one of the things this germ makes you discard.

Black Forest ends after Toni goes missing. Mary and Watherstone are convinced she's killed herself, but she has, in fact, merely been sleeping in the woods. Alarmed at the passions they have stirred up, all the partners return to their original less than happy relationships, in what the critic B.A.Young called 'a characteristic Rattigan open ending'.

But for the time being at least, *Black Forest* remained in his drawer at Stanhope Gardens as *Gone Away* was sent off to Albery. Things were beginning to look bleak. Frank Rattigan took some pleasure in reminding his son that their two-year agreement ran out the following year. Rattigan knew he had to find a job, if only to keep the Diplomatic Service at bay. Before he found one, however, Albery rang about *Gone Away*. The impresario had read it on a train, and told him, in rather a surprised voice, 'It made me laugh out loud.' He had passed it on to Gielgud, who was also complimentary, suggesting that Albery mount it at the Embassy Theatre in Swiss Cottage with Jessie Matthews, but Albery kept that piece of information to himself. For the moment he simply offered a small fee for a 'nine-month option' to produce the play in the West End.

The small fee wasn't enough to sustain Rattigan, however. He needed a job, and in the first months of 1936 duly found one. On the strength of *First Episode*, he managed to persuade the head of Warner Brothers in England to hire him to work as a contract writer at their British headquarters on the Thames at Teddington Lock. The job provided a contract for seven years, and a salary of £15 a week, rising to £20 a week after two years. The post required of its writers that they work from ten until six for six days of the week, including Saturday (though they were usually allowed to go home early on Saturday afternoon). Their task was to write what were known as 'Quota Quickies', which had come into existence to 'assist' British film production – which insisted that for every foot of foreign film shown in a British cinema, there must also be a 'quota' of films made in Britain. In practice it simply meant that the American studios set up small bases in Britain, and hired British staff.

Rattigan started work for Warner Brothers in the spring of 1936, two years after *First Episode* had closed. His room in Stanhope Gardens was littered with rejection slips, and not one of the eight or so plays he had written during the period had ever been produced. Anthony Powell, who was also working as a writer at Warner Brothers at the time, recalled in his memoirs, *Faces in My Time*:

> Although he had sidestepped his father's efforts to put him into the Diplomatic Service, Rattigan was outwardly very much like the popular notion (as opposed to the usual reality) of a young diplomat, tall, good-looking, elegant in turnout, somewhat chilly in manner . . . His homosexuality, of which he made no particular secret, probably unswerving, was not at all obvious on the surface.

The two men worked together on one project for three weeks, but were never close.

> One was always aware in Rattigan of a deep inner bitterness, no doubt accentuated by the irksome position in which he found himself at that moment . . . He was a thrusting young man whose primary concern was to make himself financially independent, not interested in 'art' so much as immediate effect. Rattigan would talk entertainingly about the mechanics of how plays are written, always consciously from a 'non-artist' angle, though in a manner never to bring in doubt his own grasp and intelligence. One of his favourite formulas was: 'Take a hackneyed situation and reverse it.'

It was a judgement that Terence Rattigan would come to defend: 'In the thirties a playwright without means, and I was emphatically that, had to please an audience or starve. (Or, worse still, get a job in a bank if he could find one.) The choice was as marked as that.' For Rattigan there was no choice. 'It was a time of slump, jobs of all kinds were hard to come by and I had to make a career.'

CHAPTER 7

Without Tears

◆

*But men must know, that in this theatre of man's
life it is reserved only for God and angels to be
lookers on.*

FRANCIS BACON, *Advancement of Learning*

◆

To Rattigan's intense dismay, Bronson Albery did not renew his option
for *Gone Away*. He simply let it expire in the summer of 1936. Suddenly, all the promise of the previous year had disappeared. Albery
could not promise anything, and Gielgud was busy at the New Theatre
playing Trigorin in Komisarjevsky's new production of *The Seagull*.
Warners were paying him the not inconsiderable sum of £15 a week, but
the work was soul-destroying. More importantly, it was not leading
towards the only goal he really desired, Shaftesbury Avenue.

At Warners, 'There was no time for frills, the plot had to be told in
three lines,' Rattigan recalled. He did not find it easy. A script he
prepared from *Tzigane*, Lady Eleanor Smith's romance about gypsy
life, was torn up in front of his eyes by the head of production, Irving
Asher. A more experienced writer was then brought in to take over.
He was dismissed with the curt command to the older writer: 'Take
this young man away, and show him how to write scripts properly.'
It was a long way from the euphoria of *First Episode*.

In desperation Rattigan started sending *Gone Away* round to agents.
He had already received nine rejections from managements, but now
he had another idea. Perhaps an actress might like the idea of playing
Diana, the man-eating young woman at the heart of the comedy he
had written in an exercise book during a family holiday in Exmouth,

Devon, the previous year. 'We had to be back in London in four weeks' time for the Jubilee celebrations, so I simply got on with it,' he remarked. 'I wrote it in long hand.' And then, because he couldn't afford a typist, he typed it himself with two fingers.

Miraculously, one actress who received a copy of Gone Away by this rather naïve route did like it. Kay Hammond was a new young star, and loved the idea of playing Diana Lake, a decidedly more spirited leading part than many others she had been offered recently. She in turn sent it to a dashing young actor turned director, Harold French, who was then just thirty-six. The only question was, who would put it on? Everyone had turned the play down.

Knowing that Bronson Albery was desperate to find a replacement for his fast-fading production of The Lady of La Paz at the Criterion, starring Lilian Braithwaite, French suggested to Albery that he might try Gone Away – as a stopgap. To French's surprise, Albery agreed. But he was not prepared to take all the financial risk himself. There had to be one or two other producers alongside him for Wyndham's Theatres to put the play on at the Criterion. Encouraged by Kay Hammond's and Gielgud's enthusiasm, Albery talked the idea over with Rattigan's new literary agent, A.D.Peters. When he discovered that Peters would be prepared to put up £500 himself, about a third of the production costs, Albery agreed to mount Gone Away. Wyndham's Theatres would be its official producers, but they would spread the risk.

It was A.D.Peters, therefore, who actually bought the rights to Gone Away from Terence Rattigan. This was unusual, to say the least. A literary agent did not normally turn himself into a producer for the sake of a new play. Nevertheless, in exchange for £60 Peters took the rights to produce the play on 'condition that it played at a West End Theatre before December 30, 1936'. Rattigan was to get 5 per cent of the theatre's gross weekly receipts up to £900, 7½ per cent up to £1,100, and 10 per cent over £1,100. The Criterion's break-even for the production was expected to be a little over £800 a week, and the maximum it could take for a week a little over £1,625. Rattigan consulted his father about the terms of the contract, but signed it happily enough on 16 October 1936, the day after the first official read-through with the cast.

'Bronnie said I could do it if I could cast it – and then he gave me about five days to cast and ten days to rehearse,' Harold French remembers. Albery told him firmly that the entire production had to be mounted at a cost of less than £1,500, and that meant 'a young cast and a cheap set'. Albery 'thought it might have twelve weeks in it',

but that was all he needed until the play he had always intended for
the Criterion had finished its out of London tour and was ready to
open at the theatre. On 12 October 1936 he sent the play to the Lord
Chamberlain's office for approval, and for the licence he needed to
present the play. The reader was once again H.C.Gane, who had read
First Episode, and again he objected to the language of the play – in
particular the use of the term 'po-faced', which the Lord Chamberlain
insisted should be changed to 'pie-faced' before he granted a licence on
26 October.

There was certainly no time for elaborate casting discussions. Albery
had already pencilled in Jessica Tandy for the twelve weeks to cover
the gap as well as a young actor friend of John Gielgud's, Robert
Flemyng (who had met Rattigan at Gielgud's house), and a young actor
called Trevor Howard. Harold French then added Roland Culver, 'after
watching him play bridge at the Green Room Club', and the spectacularly robust Guy Middleton. Albery, in turn, suggested that the leading
man might be played by a young actor who was enjoying some success
in the West End in a play called *Heroes Don't Care* at the St Martin's.
Rex Harrison was then only twenty-eight, but had made his first
appearance in rep in Liverpool at the age of sixteen. French took Kay
Hammond to see him, but she wasn't impressed at first. It was only
after she'd watched him unpack a suitcase 'full of women's under-
clothes, which he did magnificently', as French recalls, 'that she
changed her mind'. There is not much doubt that she also found him
attractive.

Rex Harrison recognised his value to the play at once, and held out
for the best salary he could get. 'Of course, the script was always very
funny,' he wrote later, 'but it was regarded, at the beginning, as just
a nice cheerful little play.' He reckoned it needed him, and he asked
for £50 a week, plus a percentage of the takings after break-even. It
was a considerable salary for a young man still on the rise, but he had
heard it was what Kay Hammond was getting and he wanted parity.
He got it. After all, it was only going to be a short run.

The company, which Harrison later described as being 'almost
entirely young hopefuls', assembled for the first read-through in
Albery's office in the New Theatre at 7.30 pm on the evening of
15 October 1936. It was the earliest time that Rattigan could guarantee
to get there from his desk at Warners in Teddington. He need hardly
have bothered. No one took the slightest notice of him. He sat at the
back, beyond the semi-circle of ten cast members who were grouped
in front of French and Albery. 'Sometimes he chuckled, and once or
twice he seemed to be making a note,' French observed. 'I imagined

he must be an assistant stage manager making a list of the "props" that he would have to find.' It was Kay Hammond who told French during a break in the reading at the end of Act Two that the young man making notes at the back was the author.

The evening did not go particularly well. Roland Culver stammered a good deal, and there was only occasional laughter. At the end, to console him, French took Rattigan to the Green Room Club for a drink. Rattigan was overwhelmed. Here at last was the heart of the West End theatre, and he was being welcomed into it. French bought him a series of dry Martinis, and Rattigan watched the room fill up with actors – most of whom he recognised at once. 'Terry was star-struck,' French remembers. 'I think he always was.' The two men spent the rest of the evening together, finally getting round to discussing the subject that had been on French's mind from the moment they arrived – the play's title. '*Gone Away* suggested pink coats, horses, hounds and a lot of Tally Hos.' French wanted a change.

Shortly after midnight the two men parted and French went home. At 1.30 his telephone rang. 'This is Terry Rattigan here. I'm terribly sorry to disturb you, but I've been thinking, and you're quite right . . . er . . . this is only an idea, kick it out if you don't like it . . . but would *French Without Tears* be any good?' It was the name of a popular French primer of the period. There was only a slight pause before French agreed. *Gone Away* had gone.

The next problem to be tackled was the play itself, which was 'twenty minutes too short', according to Albery. He could 'lose' ten minutes by bringing the curtain up at 8.40 every evening instead of 8.30, but that was all. Rattigan had to find the extra ten minutes from somewhere. 'Where they were to come from nobody knew, certainly not the author,' Rattigan wrote. 'But come they did. God knows how, but not before the author had seriously toyed with the idea of bringing back to rehearsals a piece of paper on which he had written the words: "At the rise of the curtain the stage is left empty for ten minutes, at the end of which time Diana enters from the Right." He never made good the threat. His solution was to expand Alan's description of his novel and its pacifist content, as well as poking more fun at the elderly Naval Commander.

The next few days were frantic. Rehearsals stuttered somewhat, not least because there was a little tension between Guy Middleton and Rex Harrison – who were supposed to be friends at the French finishing school – over the attention being paid to Middleton's wife by Harrison. That crisis was overcome eventually, but the set was still terrible – 'All green and ghastly,' as Robert Flemyng recalls. In the end Harold French went off to Sandersons and bought wallpaper to put on to the canvas flats around the stage. It cost him £50. Albery did not give him his money back, instead he gave him a small stake in the production. That was the extent of his confidence in the venture.

The first dress rehearsal in the theatre took place on 4 November 1936, and it was not a success. Culver was still stammering, Rex seemed uncomfortable with the part, Middleton was blustering rather than acting, and only Kay Hammond seemed at home with life in the crammer's. On top of that, Harold French had a problem with the final curtain.

As Rattigan had written it, the man-eating Diana, finally foiled in her effort to ensnare Alan Howard (played by Harrison), rapidly settles on an alternative. Lord Heybrook is about to arrive at the crammer's, and he will be a better catch. As the play draws to its close, she disappears, to emerge again just before Heybrook's arrival wearing a bathing suit and a suitably seductive smile. Rattigan's final twist was that Lord Heybrook should be a 'blond, swishy queer', who sweeps on to the stage leading a languid borzoi dog and utters the curtain line: 'Come along, Alcibiades.'

In some respects this was Rattigan's revenge on Margaret Middleditch at Harrow, and on Va-Va Basilewich at Oxford, by condemning the man-eating woman to fall for a homosexual, as well as a way of introducing a homosexual element into the play, albeit flippantly. But there was more to it than that. With its homosexual overtones, the relationship between Alan Howard and Brian Curtis, in *French Without Tears*, was an echo of that between David and Tony in *First Episode*, even down to the name of the dog. (Alcibiades was one of the most brilliant but unscrupulous politicians and commanders in Athens, and his own sexuality was not exactly straightforward.) The English might want to keep up appearances, but in Rattigan's subtext there was always something else going on underneath.

In the event, it was the borzoi that fixed it, indirectly. The dog arrived at the first dress rehearsal languidly enough, but it also proceeded to raise a languid hind leg and ruin the curtain line. Harold French seized his opportunity. 'Why couldn't Lord Heybrook be a boy of thirteen or fourteen?' he asked. 'It would be just as big a smack in the eye for Kay, the twist to the play would be there, without the unpleasant taste.' Not being a homosexual himself, he was particularly anxious to remove the character of Lord Heybrook, whose presence he feared might offend the West End audience. The dog was a perfectly good excuse.

Faced with a choice between seeing his play do well in the West End and retaining an elaborate and, for him, important joke, Rattigan chose, for the first but not the last time, the easier option. He gave up his homosexual joke. Lord Heybrook did not have to be 'a queer'. By 2.30 the following afternoon the queer Lord Heybrook and his dog had been dispatched, to be replaced by a young man called William Dear (forever thereafter known as Billy Dear), who was rushed off to a boy's outfitter for a blazer and a straw boater.

At 6.15 that evening, Guy Fawkes' Night, 1936, the curtain went up on the second, and final, dress rehearsal of *French Without Tears* in the cramped setting of the Criterion Theatre on Piccadilly Circus. The rumble of the underground trains on the Piccadilly Line beneath rever-berated around the 600 or so red velvet seats. Terence Rattigan sat in the circle with his mother Vera, while Alban Limpus, another impre-sario, who had put money into Noël Coward's plays, sat beside Albery. Limpus had been brought in to reduce Albery's own financial risk. In the darkness Rattigan squeezed his mother's hand.

The mood on stage was nervous. No sooner had the curtain gone up than Trevor Howard forgot his second line. Harold French then recalls, 'Rex Harrison played as though he were constipated and didn't care who knew it. Roland Culver put in more "ers" than he had done at the reading, Jessica Tandy was so slow she might have been on a modern strike, and Percy Walsh forgot he was playing a Frenchman and every now and then lapsed into an Oxford accent.' Only Kay Hammond looked reasonably relaxed. When the new Lord Heybrook finally brought down the curtain the mood in the theatre had turned suicidal. Jessica Tandy looked across the footlights to her director and proclaimed, 'Mr French, you know we can't open tomorrow night. This isn't a play, it's a charade, and an under-rehearsed one at that.'

Albery stormed back to his office, muttering 'It won't last a week,' and set about finding a show to replace it. Limpus offered his share in the production to anyone in the cast for £100. 'None of us have got £100,' Rex Harrison told him. So the panicky impresario rushed to the telephone in the theatre manager's office and sold it instead to the theatrical agents and producers O'Bryen, Linnit & Dunfee. Only A.D. Peters and French kept their nerve.

Harold French was not to be put off. At the back of the stalls, from which he had been watching proceedings, he told his young playwright that he was going to hold the dress rehearsal all over again. 'I don't think I could stand it again,' Terence Rattigan said weakly. 'Balls,' French replied, and went off to tell the cast. Rattigan gloomily sent his mother home, and settled back into the stalls to watch the second dress rehearsal of the evening. It was an improvement, but not a substantial one.

To cheer himself up, Rattigan took himself off to the Savoy for supper – after all, he was about to see his second play open in the West End, even if it was going to close within a week. By coincidence, he came across his Oxford friend and contemporary, Peter Glenville, just back from playing Romeo and Mark Antony at Stratford. The two men gossiped, and Glenville finally offered him a lift home. As they turned into Piccadilly, Rattigan pointed to the Criterion and announced: 'They're doing a play of mine there tomorrow night. Don't congratulate me. They're only running it as a stopgap because another play has folded.' It was the first mention he had made to Glenville of *French Without Tears*.

The next day, Friday, 6 November 1936, was wet and miserable. Rattigan went to Teddington but left early for Stanhope Gardens, to change into white tie and tails, then the custom at West End first nights, and to collect his parents and take them to supper before the show. Gamely, he ordered champagne in an effort to dispel all their nerves. As she left Vera slipped the cork into her handbag for luck.

At the theatre, it was soon clear that the audience, even though they had struggled through the rain to see 'A Light Comedy in Three Acts', were in extremely good humour. When the curtain rose on Trevor Howard trying to finish his French composition, the actress Cicely Courtneidge giggled loudly in the stalls. By the time Guy Middleton had joined him in the living-room of Miramar, Monsieur Maingot's villa in a small seaside town in the south of France, to order his breakfast in the worst schoolboy French anyone had ever heard, the mood was set.

> KENNETH: If you're so hot, you'd better tell me how to say she has ideas above her station.
> BRIAN: Oh, yes, I forgot. It's fairly easy, old boy. Elle a des idées au-dessus de sa gare.

The audience roared, and for years to come, at cocktail parties and country house weekends, the exchange was repeated with affection and its eternal pay-off: 'You see, it wasn't that sort of station.'

Shortly after 10.30, Billy Dear made his entrance, the curtain fell, and calls of 'Author, Author' resounded around the Criterion. But the author was nowhere to be seen. He had left his parents in the circle and retired to a local pub for a drink to steady his nerves. When Harold French finally found him, Terence Rattigan was standing at the back of the stage 'green-faced and dithering, being supported by a convenient

back wall'. French told him, 'They're yelling for you. Go on and thank
them.'

'Come with me,' Rattigan begged. French shook his head, and Rattigan reluctantly made his way towards the centre of the stage, past the
jubilant members of the cast, to give what he was later to describe as
'an extempore speech I had been working on for five hours'. In actual
fact he never got the chance. The stage hands had given up hope and
as he reached centre stage they closed the curtains on him from both
sides. All the author could do was wave through them.

Kay Hammond took Rattigan and most of the rest of the cast back
to her flat to await the first editions of the morning papers and the
critics' verdict. As soon as they were delivered Rattigan lay on the
floor, scanning each one carefully, trying to gobble up every word. He
was not disappointed. 'The gift of real lightness is a rare one in the
theatre,' W.A.Darlington said in the *Daily Telegraph*, 'and Terence
Rattigan is a lucky young man to have it.' The conservative *Morning
Post* was just as complimentary. 'A brilliant little comedy, gay, witty,
thoroughly contemporary without being unpleasantly modern.' The
Daily Herald carped that 'It has no conceivable relation to British
Drama,' but *The Times* was in no doubt, complimenting its author on
his 'sly, cool, and delightfully opportune dialogue' and suggesting,
'What we are concerned with is a world in which nothing matters
except to be entertained. The entertainment, in its own frothy kind, is
beyond question.' At that point Rattigan rolled over on to his back
and whispered, 'I don't believe it. Even *The Times* liked it.'

The Sunday papers were a shade cooler. In the *Observer*, Ivor Brown
called it 'this happy-go-lucky charade' about a group of young men
'who appear to have stepped out of a short story by P.G.Wodehouse',
and concluded: 'Wit had not much chance among this nonsense, but
humour has, and the play rattles along, leading nowhere in particular,
but never flagging in jovial absurdity.'

There was one black spot. The formidable James Agate in the *Sunday
Times* hated it. 'This is not a play. It is not anything. It is nothing. Six
Marie Tempests and six Charles Hawtreys would not be able to redeem
it, because there is not a crumb of redemption in it. It is not witty. It
has no plot. It is almost without characterisation.' But he was forced
to add: 'There is one thing which the piece definitely and triumphantly
is – a success. Up to the time I left the laughter in the theatre was
deafening. I left, because I no more understand this sort of play and
acting than my cat understands Euclid. I am of the school which likes
the play to be about adults and acted by adults.' In the weeks to come
Agate was to return repeatedly to the attack.

No matter. It was youth and high spirits and escapist fun that the young people in the cast seemed to inspire – an enthusiasm that audiences wanted, young or old. Robert Flemyng remembers vividly listening to King Edward VIII's abdication speech in his dressing room only a few weeks after the play opened – and, perhaps in reaction to the general air of gloom in the country, 'from that day onwards there didn't seem to be an empty seat'. Winston Churchill had been the play's first famous visitor, coming to see it during the height of the crisis itself.

But the play also had 'quite a serious side to it', Robert Flemyng observed, 'about the boy being a pacifist. It was not long after the vote at Oxford, and I think that helped because Rex's speeches sending up the Naval Commander were very much in the air at that time. It was topical, but it still didn't offend people somehow'. Rattigan was speaking for a new generation of young people, in a language that they could understand, but in terms that did not offend the fathers and mothers who paid for their seats in the stalls. 'We became a vogue, a household word, and everybody, from royalty to aristocracy to café society, dropped in to see us – if they could get seats – before going on to some night club like Ciro's, or out to supper,' Rex Harrison recalled.

The new King, George VI, and his wife, Queen Elizabeth, went to see the play shortly after his accession to the throne. The following February Queen Mary also attended, making her first visit to the theatre since the death of her husband, in the company of the young Duchess of Gloucester. The audience stood and applauded as she took her seat, but a hush fell on the house at the point when Rex Harrison described Diana as a bitch. 'In those days that was rather shocking, you never said bitch in front of a lady,' Robert Flemyng remembered. There was a pause. 'Then suddenly the old girl laughed, and the theatre fell down.'

But there were layers of complexity and concealment beneath the play's froth. Alan Howard is an ambassador's son whose father is determined he should follow him into the Diplomatic Service, but who would rather write novels. He already has three manuscripts doing the rounds of the London publishers, with the rejection slips to prove it. Kit Neilan, the young juvenile, played by Flemyng, believes himself to be in love with the rapacious Diana, but is in turn worshipped by Jacqueline Maingot, the proprietor's daughter. For his part Kit is not in love with her. 'I'm frightfully fond of her, but somehow – I don't know – I mean you couldn't kiss her or make love to her.'

Kit and Alan discuss the impossibility of love, and their own uncertainties, much as Tony and David had done in *First Episode*, and the subtext is once again clear. They are attracted to each other, although neither would dream of saying it. Indeed, echoes of *First Episode* came through so strongly that after the first night Irina Basilewich's sister insisted that Rattigan had modelled Kay Hammond's character on Va-Va and accused him of getting 'a bit near the bone'. Rattigan did not deny the charge. 'The nearer the bone the sweeter the meat,' he said. The play's characters were all, to some extent, portraits from Rattigan's life.

There is certainly depth in his portrait of Diana. Though outwardly a bitch who is determined to get her man, any man, she is also the only character in the play prepared to give full vent to her emotions. All around her men are desperately trying to control themselves, because they are afraid that to fall in love, or to commit themselves, would be to lose that control. Rattigan was not only taking the conventional situation – the predatory male seeking a mate – and turning it on its head by making the predator a female. He was also underlining what he believed was the ordinary Englishman's one fatal flaw, his inability to accept emotion, and love. Rattigan's male characters dither, make speeches, but do not understand the realities of the sexual game they are playing. Only Brian, who saves his money to pay for a local prostitute, has sorted out the complexities of his sexual life satisfactorily. He prefers to pay for sex rather than to fall in love. It is safer that way.

Talking about the play shortly before his death, Rattigan said: 'I think it's a bit more serious than anyone has ever allowed. It's not a farce. I regard it as a comedy of mood and character. It's not simply a lot of young men romping about. Each of them has a point of view. The character first played by Rex Harrison is a writer who's just published a pacifist novel about two young men who make a pact that they'll desert the country if ever it declares war. And that's pretty much how I felt at the time. Remember, it was before Abyssinia and the absolute evil of Hitler . . . the play reflects how I and others of my generation felt.'

It certainly transformed his life. Within four weeks of the show's opening he was earning more than £1,000 a month in royalties alone, and within eighteen months it had brought him more than £23,000. At the age of twenty-five, Terence Rattigan had become one of the most talked-about young men in London.

CHAPTER 8

The Albatross

◆

*Youth is the time to go flashing from one end of
the world to the other both in mind and body; to
try the manners of different nations; to hear the
chimes at midnight.*

ROBERT LOUIS STEVENSON, *Crabbed Age and Youth*

◆

Everything happened very quickly. By the time King Edward VIII
slipped into exile on Friday, 11 December 1936, Terence Rattigan had
become London's latest theatrical star. It was his name, not Kay Hammond's or Rex Harrison's, that graced the front of the Criterion
Theatre. The 'tall, strikingly handsome boy who looked like an Oxford
undergraduate', and whom Emlyn Williams remembered encountering
two years before, was suddenly the toast of the town. Everyone wanted
to meet him, to shake his hand, to ask him if he was working on a
new play. He was never to forget the heady moments of that first
success, and never lose his desire to repeat them.

Yet this intoxicating youthful celebrity was to hang like an albatross
about his neck for the rest of his life. Rattigan could never quite escape
the feeling that his talent was evanescent, something that had bloomed
more by accident than design. This caused him to hide behind a mask
of languid flippancy, which few outside a usually small circle were able
to penetrate. What he was not to realise for a time was that it would
also blight his theatrical reputation because . . . once a lightweight
always a lightweight. Could the author of a stunning commercial success, a 'masterpiece of frivolity' to quote the London *Evening Standard*'s
verdict on *French Without Tears*, ever be a playwright of serious depth?

Not that Rattigan was aware of all this straight away. For the
moment he was too caught up in the maelstrom of his new celebrity.
The telephone hardly stopped ringing at Stanhope Gardens, and his
father, in particular, revelled in his son's triumph. Frank Rattigan took
to appearing in a box at the Criterion on most nights of the week with,
it need hardly be added, a succession of young ladies in tow. Rex
Harrison remarked that Frank was clearly there 'to show off his son's
play and, one presumed, himself too, for he was a very handsome
man'.

As for Vera, she sailed on like a ship in full sail, unruffled apparently
by her husband's infidelities or his gambling excesses on the horses,
for which his son was now expected to pay. Rex Harrison took to
calling Vera 'Old Blighty', although he could not remember quite why.
The Major's nickname, coined by another member of the cast, was,
more prosaically, 'the wicked old sod'.

Rattigan himself, in spite of his fame and new-found wealth, was in
the peculiar position of having to turn up at Teddington Studios six
days a week for a salary of £15, about a tenth of what he was now
receiving in weekly royalties. He had signed a contract, and Warners
were not about to let him break it. But A.D.Peters and Bronson Albery
had already been approached by the American producer Gilbert Miller
for an option on the American production of the play. There was
even talk of a film version – in spite of the fact that Irving Asher had
turned the project down for Warner Brothers a few months before
when Rattigan had first shown it to him. The rumour was that
Marlene Dietrich was interested in playing Kay Hammond's part
in the film, and was prepared to purchase the rights herself to ensure
she got it.

By the spring of 1937 *French Without Tears* was established in London
as one of the shows no one could afford to miss. Dietrich had taken
Douglas Fairbanks to it. The German Ambassador Ribbentrop took a
succession of Nazi dignitaries. Perhaps he viewed the play as conclusive
evidence of the decadence of young men in England, mocking as it
does the Navy and the Diplomatic Service, and confirming its hero's
reluctance to fight in the event of war. Whatever the reason, he saw
the play six times.

The only irritation was the continued sniping of James Agate. He
attacked the play week after week in the *Sunday Times*, belligerently
repeating his original criticisms when the play opened the previous
November. The young Terence Rattigan found it hard to understand
or swallow this bile. 'Why?' he would ask friends plaintively. 'Why
me?'

In March 1937 Rattigan turned down an invitation from O'Bryen, Linnit & Dunfee to write an English version of the American hit *The Women* for a London production. For the moment he was more intent on enjoying his new-found success, and he was still labouring for Warner Brothers during the day. In the evenings there were friends, parties, and other, less public pleasures, to occupy him.

There were one or two special friends who could not be taken every-where. His friendships were reserved for other homosexuals who knew the risks that they were running, and accepted them. But Rattigan was not a cottager. He did not frequent the public lavatories of Shepherd Market on the lookout for instant, unselfconscious sexual gratification with a stranger, though he might appreciate the attractions. Rattigan preferred more discreet relationships, an introduction at dinner, a flir-tation that might or might not lead to bed.

During the summer of 1937 the plans for a Broadway production of *French Without Tears* were finalised. Bronson Albery and Howard Wyndham were prepared to be its official backers this time, though A.D. Peters was allowed to invest and Gilbert Miller was to be the play's official American producer. There was to be a brief try-out at Princeton, New Jersey, before the New York opening in late Sep-tember. This time Rattigan was determined to attend. Never again would he allow one of his plays to be produced on Broadway without his being there, as *First Episode* had been. He wanted to be sure that *French Without Tears* was presented as he intended it.

As befitted a young man who was now earning more than £250 a week for his new play, and had just received £10,000 for the film rights, Rattigan set sail for New York on the SS *Champlain* and took a suite at the Waldorf-Astoria on Park Avenue. Warners had been persuaded to give him a holiday. Or rather, that's what they said. Shortly after he arrived, Irving Asher turned up in New York to tell him that War-ners had subcontracted his services to Hollywood, and that he would be expected to leave shortly for the coast. The studio were prepared to give him a rise – to £17.5s a week – but otherwise his terms and conditions would remain exactly as before. Rattigan refused point blank. Let Warners sue. He would return to England when his business in New York was over, not before. He would work at Teddington, but not in Hollywood.

Rattigan could afford to risk offending Warners. He had just read in *Variety* that the Barrymores were anxious to play Alan and Diana in the film. Besides, the play had also been produced in Paris, and an English tour was in preparation, as was another production in Amster-dam. With the Broadway opening only weeks away, Rattigan would have the distinction of seeing his play in production in the three major theatrical capitals of the world, London, Paris and New York.

In New York everything seemed set fair. The try-out at Princeton was a success, and Harold French had come over to direct the all-English cast, bringing Guy Middleton to play his original part of Brian. But now Frank Lawton was to play Alan, and Penelope Dudley-Ward was to play Diana. Another Englishman in the cast was the young Hubert Gregg, playing Kit.

Shortly before the New York opening, Rattigan agreed to write an autobiographical piece for the *New York Post*, to introduce the play and himself to American audiences. He took the opportunity to return to the subject that haunted him – his father.

> I think one of the first things I ought to do during my visit to America is to make it clear that my father and I are the fastest of friends. For I daresay the news has got about here, as it did in London, that I have put myself in the play, more or less (giving that alter ego some of the best lines, of course!), in the character of Alan Howard . . . and since [he] has some rather cutting things to say about *his* father, people might infer that there is a quarrel between *my* father and me. Well, it isn't so.

It was an odd line to take, since so few people in New York would have heard of his play, much less its young playwright, or his father. But Rattigan went on to describe how he had rejected his father's idea of joining the Diplomatic Service. 'What I wanted to do was write, especially for the theatre. My father didn't think much of that idea and said so with – shall we say – emphasis.' What the piece really showed was that he was still unable to confront his father, and that the best he could do was to pass off their disagreements as a joke. 'My father,' the readers of the *New York Post* were informed, 'enjoys saying those lines refer to him because he knows that they really don't, and that I've pointed them up a bit for the sake of the play.'

When *French Without Tears* opened at the Henry Miller Theatre in New York on Tuesday, 28 September 1937, Rattigan was, naturally, nervous. Everyone had told him the play was bound to work, although cautioning that it 'would, of course, still depend on the critics, and especially Atkinson' Unfortunately, the formidable Brooks Atkinson was not impressed. 'Although a great many people in the audience were amused by last night's capers,' he wrote in the *New York Times* the following morning, 'this column felt that it was looking into space. After the first act there seemed to be less on the stage than met the eye, old boy.'

The management did their best to combat the review, not least by extracting Atkinson's comment – 'So light it almost floats out of the theatre' – for their posters. But the damage was done. *Variety* summed it up when it commented a week later, '*French Without Tears*, another translated-from-London play, is captioned a "light comedy in three acts". It's light all right. Too much so, in fact, to stay anchored for long on Broadway. Not even . . . an expert cast can bolster it to any great degree because once having exhausted the class trade for which it is best primed, it will pass on quickly.' The entertainment industry's bible also wondered 'what Paramount has to make a film out of'. By the end of the year so did Marlene Dietrich. She withdrew from the project, leaving Paramount to find a replacement.

Unbowed, Rattigan volunteered to write a piece for the *New York Times* himself, to defend the English theatre from the charge that it was 'escapist – so it is dead'. Accepting that O'Neill and other American playwrights wrote 'plays that face the modern world and its problems fearlessly; they show life as it is in all its harassing aspects; they provide some message for its betterment', he insisted that the English theatre was by no means dead, even if its audiences preferred escapism.

From Shakespeare until Shaw Englishmen continued to go to the theatre to escape from the immediate problems of everyday life. English audiences listened to Shaw because he made them laugh. They went to Galsworthy's plays because he was a superb tech-nician and gave them characters that were real and situations which they found exciting. I don't honestly believe they cared much for the message which either of these dramatists contributed.

In a very thinly veiled defence of his own play, Rattigan concluded:

Whimsy is a word on every American critic's tongue in writing of English plays. (I can say this without prejudice. The word was not mentioned once in reviews of *French Without Tears* – to my grateful surprise.) It is used exclusively as a term of opprobrium and applies to almost any play that is not firmly rooted in mother earth. One might be permitted to wonder what kind of reviews *A Midsummer Night's Dream* would receive from the New York critics in their present mood if they were seeing the play for the first time.

It was evidence of his sensitivity to criticism. And his first experience in New York set the tone for years to come. No matter how much he tried to make light of criticism, it hurt him deeply.

By the end of the year the audience for *French Without Tears* in New

York had run out. The show closed on Saturday evening, 1 January 1938 after 111 performances, having taken an estimated $116,000 at the box office. It was a respectable run, but it had not been a hit. In contrast, the show was continuing to play to packed houses both in London and Paris, which made Rattigan's fury at the critics and their jibes about escapism, in particular Agate's repeated attacks, fiercer than ever. He persuaded Peters and Albery to make a copy of Agate's original review and put it outside the theatre, right beside the sign announcing 'The Biggest Success in the History of the Criterion Theatre'. When the display appeared Agate threatened to sue, much to Rattigan's amusement. The offending review was removed, but Agate went back to the attack in the *Sunday Times*.

It was John Gielgud who finally put an end to the acrimony between playwright and critic. In a letter to the *Sunday Times* he explained that he had read the play in manuscript and considered it 'particularly delightful and original both in conception and execution', and he condemned Agate for criticising a young playwright when the theatre was in need of new young writers. It was a brave act; Gielgud, like every other actor and director, depended on a good relationship with Agate and the other critics. 'I wonder,' Rattigan wrote soon afterwards, 'if anyone not actually in the theatre can understand the moral courage involved in the writing of that letter. Agate's good will must, I know, have meant just as much to Gielgud as it did to all of us, for Gielgud's season of classics in 1938 were more dependent on the major critics' support than were light comedies like *French Without Tears*. And that season was financed entirely out of his own pocket.'

The furore provoked the *Daily Telegraph* to send its own Sydney Carroll back to see the play, to discover what the fuss was about. On 14 April 1938 he told the paper's readers:

> Nothing provokes attack like success. The continuous and growing onslaughts upon the immensely popular Criterion comedy *French Without Tears* provide a striking example of this unfailing corollary . . . despite all the indisputable evidence of approval it has from its initiation been beset with critical ridicule, contempt, and even abuse. It has been treated by some who claim to be leaders of theatrical thought as a sign of the present degeneration in playgoing, and a piece of gross materialism.

Carroll liked the play, and concluded his article: 'The theatre that denies the right of a dramatist to score in trifles of this nature is puritanical and old-fashioned.'

Determined to show the critics, and Agate in particular, that comedy could have its serious element, and that he was capable of writing a play that was more than simply 'escapist', Rattigan started work on two new plays. The first, *After the Dance*, he had started drafting in New York the autumn before and had even discussed the outline with Hubert Gregg. The second, *Follow My Leader*, a comedy with distinctly serious overtones, was written in a rush in the early spring of 1938 in collaboration with his friend and contemporary at Harrow and Oxford, Tony Goldschmidt. The two of them disappeared to a house Rattigan was renting next door to the club house of Sonning Golf Club in Berkshire, to get it down on paper.

During the writing of *Follow My Leader*, Rattigan embarked on an affair with Peter Osborn, who was just making a name for himself in the West End as a juvenile leading man and was three years his junior. It was a relationship that was to last, off and on, for the next forty years. The playwright whisked the young actor into a new world: the Eton and Harrow match, the Ascot Gold Cup. 'Life seemed to be all smoked salmon or smoked trout or quail's eggs,' Osborn was to recall, 'and champagne, and strawberries and cream; first nights and star dressing-rooms; and then we would stay the night at the Mayfair Hotel, or the Savoy, or the Ritz – two separate rooms, but sometimes with connecting doors . . . I suppose I was really "being kept", except that I was still earning my living in the theatre.'

Both the plays Rattigan was working on illustrated his duality: the internal conflict between the hedonist in the Savile Row suit and the political idealist and pacifist. One moment he was marching down Whitehall with Peter Osborn and other members of Equity to Downing Street to demand 'Food and Arms for Spain', the next leaving the demonstration to dine at the Savoy Grill. 'Bring on the Revolution. But not quite yet,' was how one friend summed up his politics at the time. Rattigan agreed. His good fortune, he told one *Evening Standard* reporter, 'had had the unusual effect of turning his politics to the Left'.

Rattigan showed the two plays to Bronson Albery, expecting the impresario to be enthusiastic. Albery, however, liked neither of them. The comedy was too political, the drama too serious. He wanted another *French Without Tears*, a sequel, showing what happened to Diana after Alan left. Did she run after him? Did she finally get her man? Or was she doomed to failure? These two plays did not tell him any of those things. Worse, they sounded to him like polemic – not entertainment.

A.D.Peters was rather more enthusiastic. After all, he had made more than £50,000 from his original investment in *French Without Tears*, as had the theatrical agency O'Bryen, Linnit & Dunfee. Peters took the comedy *Follow My Leader* to them and to Gilbert Miller, who had presented *French Without Tears* in New York. Without hesitation Miller agreed to present it at the St James's Theatre in London that autumn. He acquired the rights from Peters and sent the play immediately to the Lord Chamberlain for a licence. Had he not been an American producer, and a distinctly abrasive one at that, Miller might have hesitated a moment before submitting the play, but he liked nothing better than to twist the tail of the British lion. Who could possibly object to a 'New Comedy' by the author of *French Without Tears*? If it was a 'bit of a bombshell', as he described it in his letter to the Lord Chamberlain, all the better.

But Miller had reckoned without the sensitivities of the British establishment. The play made no secret of the fact that it was a farce about Hitler's Germany, even if the mythical country it depicted was actually called Moronia. It was a young man's play, full of puns and practical jokes, a send-up of Nazism in the broadest comic terms, with an obvious political message, disguised as farce. The Moronians had chosen a plumber, Hans Zedesi, as their president, and greeted each other with raised arms and a cry of 'Up Zedesi'. Anthony Eden had just resigned as Britain's Foreign Secretary. Hitler had just annexed Austria. Few doubted, and certainly not the authors, that Czechoslovakia would be next on the Führer's list. But this was the last thing the British Foreign Office, now led by Halifax, wanted to have said in public.

It was against this background that Gilbert Miller submitted *Follow My Leader* to the Lord Chamberlain for a licence. Within a few days the Lord Chamberlain's office sent it out for a reader's report, and on 4 July 1938 H.C.Gane duly reported: 'This is a most difficult play to deal with. It is a farce, it satirizes the Nazi regime, it burlesques its leaders, but except in its more blatant moments the satirical effect is achieved more by innumerable minor touches of ridicule than by an obvious and direct method of attack.' Pointing out that the three central characters, Slivovitz, Baratsch and Zedesi, could clearly be seen as portraits of Goebbels, Goering and Hitler, he suggested the 'play should be sent to the Foreign Office for their opinion as it seems to me there are grounds for German objections to caricatures of their leading men'.

Unsure how to proceed, the Lord Chamberlain's office sent the play out for a second opinion. The second reader, Geoffrey Dearmer, was far less cautious, pointing out that the three main characters did not exactly resemble the three German leaders and that the dialogue was very 'English in character and humour' – the Town Hall clock was called Big Benito. Dearmer thought the play should be licensed, and urged that if it was to be sent to the Foreign Office their attention should be drawn to similar plays which had been given a licence. In particular he pointed out that George Bernard Shaw's *Geneva* 'deals, too, with the subject without making any attempt to disguise the personalities whereas this play carefully alters them. It is true that *Geneva* is high philosophy and does not ridicule, but it does criticise.'

Dearmer's conclusion was firm. 'If this play were banned the authors might complain with reason that preferential treatment is given to the GBSs and the Elmer Rices of the dramatic world.' Rice's play, *Judgement Day*, was on the same subject. 'The Censor has never been guilty of this,' Dearmer went on. 'I think the play is fair comment on national philosophies and politics, not an attack against particular nations exclusively.' The argument was to no avail. The Lord Chamberlain, Lord Clarendon, who had only just taken up the post, did not hesitate: he sent *Follow My Leader* straight to the Foreign Office.

Major Gwatkin, one of the Lord Chamberlain's senior officials, was on tenterhooks when he approached the Foreign Office. He apologised for disturbing them – 'but it is perhaps better that I should worry you now than that you should be worried later on by the German Embassy' – and suggested that 'It would help to talk things over rather than write a letter.' In a handwritten internal note he admitted, 'Although I don't like passing babies we had better have the Foreign Office view before we see the authors.' The Foreign Office took the rest of July to respond, and when they did so they were careful to accept Gwatkin's suggestion and not do so in writing. They hated the play.

The Lord Chamberlain's office had earlier sent a holding letter to O'Bryen, Linnit & Dunfee – 'in general' they were against the 'guying' of foreign heads of state 'when there is no doubt who is intended' – and on 28 July 1938 Gwatkin broke the news to Miller. 'The Lord Chamberlain has received the views of the Foreign Office who are of the definite opinion that the production of this play at this time would not be in the best interests of the country. Under these circumstances the Lord Chamberlain feels he cannot grant a licence.' He went on to explain that the ban was for 'this year anyhow – and I rather gathered that this time limit was a minimum', and then suggested that perhaps 'the play might be revised, ruritaniarised and chief characters altered so they could not be identified'.

The ban was a bad blow to Rattigan's morale, but he took it with his customary practised insouciance. Inwardly he was bitter, and angry. He and Tony Goldschmidt discussed the idea of putting the play on in a club theatre, which would get round the ban, and using newsreel extracts between the acts to counterpoint the comedy. In the end they gave up the idea, though not before Gilbert Miller had tried, in

November, to change the Lord Chamberlain's mind, putting the point which Dearmer had already made about George Bernard Shaw's *Geneva*. Major Gwatkin was unmoved. 'I am afraid objections to *FML* still exist. *FML* is a farce in which certain of the German leaders are definitely burlesqued, whereas *Geneva* is a politico-philosophic discussion in which the characters are abstractions rather than the personalities, so really the two plays are hardly comparable.' The reply served only to fuel Rattigan's sense of grievance, and his dislike of GBS.

To cheer himself up, Rattigan finally moved out of his parents' flat in Stanhope Gardens into a flat of his own at 20 Hertford Street in Mayfair, just round the corner from the one he had shared with Philip Heimann in Half Moon Street. He moved into the ground floor, and suggested to Peter Osborn that he should move into the top floor flat, which had become vacant at the same time.

'Terry said he would pay the rents for both flats,' Osborn remembers half a century later, 'and I should repay him when I was able . . . I can see that I ought to have turned this tempting offer down; but at the age of twenty-four, with a friend with whom I was very much in love, and who had contacts with everybody who was anybody in the West End theatre, I was only too keen to grab at this attractive offer.'

It was the first time Rattigan had actually considered living permanently in the same building as one of his lovers. In the past there had been shared houses during the summer, but the young men had stayed there behind the disguise of large numbers of other guests. Now Osborn was to become a fellow resident at Hertford Street. There were conditions, however. 'Terry had certain very strict reservations,' Osborn remembers. 'Firstly, his father . . . It was important that I should not be downstairs if the Major called . . . Not unnaturally I wanted to be wanted all the time, but this arrangement was quite impossible.' It was eventually to break Osborn's heart.

Rattigan was still indulging his father. He would purchase antiques and pictures from him at inflated prices, to subsidise without appearing to, and he would allow him to use the new flat to entertain his string of young actresses – each of whom was assured that she would be taking over from Kay Hammond in his son's play. 'The Bath Club was only just round the corner,' Osborn remembers, 'and the Major might frequently blow in from there without any warning.'

For his father's sake, the disguise that he was a heterosexual young man about town was to be maintained at all costs. But once Rattigan was out of his sphere of influence, he would take Osborn to parties, including a memorable one thrown by Ivor Novello in which the host took great pleasure in taking home movies of his guests bathing in the nude. 'Best of all, was that Terry and I were given our own bedroom, with a deep delicious double bed,' Osborn remembers. Rattigan had everything he wanted, except what he most desired: recognition as a serious playwright.

CHAPTER 9

After the Dance

◆

The young have aspirations that never come to pass, the old have reminiscences of what never happened.

SAKI, *Reginald at the Carlton*

◆

For the first time in his life Terence Rattigan realised that success had its drawbacks. He was the author of the most successful play in London, but somehow that was not enough. Peter Osborn noticed that, in spite of his public gaiety and charm, his friend and lover could also sink into depression, and the feeling surfaced in his new play.

In *After the Dance*, Rattigan's protagonist, David Scott-Fowler, is drinking heavily, neglecting his work, and living a life of pleasure that brings him no happiness. A rich man, with a flat in Mayfair, he has been married for twelve years, but he and his wife, Joan, have meticulously concealed their affection for each other beneath a contrived flippancy, with the result that Scott-Fowler is left craving the emotional warmth that his wife never shows him.

But in the Scott-Fowlers he also paints a portrait of what happened when the Bright Young Things of the early 1920s began to decline. More specifically, he was criticising the flippancy of Coward, and the apparently thoughtless generation that blossomed after the end of the war in Flanders. David Scott-Fowler knows the novels he writes are third-rate, but he goes on writing them because they help bring him a last remaining hold on decency. The endless round of parties which his wife throws are her attempt to make herself seem to be the kind of wife that her husband would not find boring. The gavotte of pretence each dances round the other is both ridiculous and sad.

Living with the Scott-Fowlers in their Mayfair apartment is the laconic, charming John Reid, an affable hanger-on and perennial commentator on the events around him. Reid and Scott-Fowler were both portraits of Rattigan's friends at the time, indeed the previous occupants of his Hertford Street flat. Though not presented as a homosexual in the play itself, Reid's attitudes are nevertheless those Rattigan recognised among his homosexual friends, cynical, world-weary, yet also capable of affection – and generosity of judgement. It is Reid who explains to Joan Scott-Fowler that all her husband really wants is 'someone to be in love with him'.

> JOAN: Not me. He doesn't want me to be in love with him. I'd have bored him to death if I'd ever let him see it. I know that.
> JOHN: It's awful how two people can misunderstand each other as much as you and David have over twelve years.

Reid cares deeply for both husband and wife, yet accepts that the pretence must go on.

Scott-Fowler has a younger brother, Peter, whom he hires as his new secretary, and whose fiancée, Helen Banner, takes it upon herself to reform David. Her plan is simple enough. She will separate him from his wife and marry him herself. When she hears about the scheme Joan remarks quietly, 'Let's have a quiet little divorce with only the family as guests.'

When, finally, Joan confesses to her husband that she does love him, but has been afraid of boring him, and he admits that he too has been trying to conceal his serious side, it is too late. In the midst of yet another party she walks on to the balcony of their third-floor flat in Mayfair and jumps to her death.

The third and final act sees disillusion everywhere. David has stopped drinking, but only temporarily, and he and Helen are bickering constantly. Peter has turned into a socialite who is only interested in having a good time. Once again it is Reid who provides the illumination.

> DAVID: Are you trying to tell me that Helen isn't in love with me?
> JOHN: No, I'm not. She's in love with you all right, and you're in love with her. The only difference between you is that in a year's time she'll be even more in love with you than she is now, and you'll undoubtedly hate her like hell.
> DAVID: What makes you think that?
> JOHN: The fact that you half hate her already.

The play ends with David returning to his old ways – too much drink and too many parties – thereby showing Helen his 'true side', as Reid calls it, which will inevitably lead to his own death. Only Reid sets out on a new course, by deciding to become a writer.

Though diametrically opposed to the mood of *French Without Tears*, there is no doubt that *After the Dance* was indicative of Rattigan's view of his life. No matter how it may have seemed to the friends who flocked to his Mayfair flat, Rattigan had a black side. Hidden behind the banter and the perpetual smile lay insecurity and a pervading sense of guilt. The desire to be taken seriously, the dream of becoming an 'important' playwright, gnawed at him, as did a feeling of unease that success had come too quickly, that it had not been earned. Peter Osborn saw it, and so did one or two of his closest friends. But for the most part Rattigan concealed it by putting on a brave face and throwing himself into his work. There was the screenplay of *French Without Tears* to be completed. He was to do so in partnership with two men who were to become a central part of his working life over the next two decades: Anatole de Grunwald and Anthony Asquith.

Born on Christmas Day 1910 in St Petersburg, the son of a Czarist diplomat, Anatole de Grunwald had escaped to England as a child during the Russian revolution, together with his younger brother, Dimitri. Histrionic and ambitious, he was making his début as a screenwriter with Rattigan's play. Asquith, by contrast, had already established himself as one of Britain's most gifted film directors. Son of the Liberal prime minister Herbert Henry Asquith, he had spent his formative years, between the ages of six and fourteen, living in Downing Street. In 1925, the year his father became Earl of Oxford, he had co-founded the British Film Society with Bernard Shaw, H.G.Wells and Julian Huxley. Known as 'Puffin' – a nickname given him by his formidable mother, Margot, as a result of his slightly hooked nose – Asquith had co-directed a successful film version of Shaw's *Pygmalion* in 1938 in partnership with the film's star Leslie Howard. *French Without Tears* was to be his next enterprise.

The trio, who began work on the screenplay early in 1939, made an unlikely team. Rattigan was to call the combination of talents 'combustible' on many occasions in the future. Nevertheless the mixture seemed to work. The eternally energetic Asquith set the pace, striding about the room and gesticulating wildly, while De Grunwald shouted his disagreement, and Rattigan sat quietly trying to make sense of it all, until finally offering to go away and try 'a little rewrite'.

Though Paramount had originally purchased the rights to *French Without Tears* from A.D.Peters for £10,000 in the firm belief that Marlene Dietrich would play Kay Hammond's part, the star of *The Blue Angel*, *Shanghai Express*, and *The Scarlet Empress* had backed away from the project in 1938. Nevertheless the studio also wanted the film version of Rattigan's play because it would help them to satisfy the 'quota' of British-made films that the American studios were forced to make under British legislation. By the beginning of 1939 Paramount wanted the film finished quickly. In desperation they shipped back to England one of their younger contract stars, Ray Milland, to play the Rex Harrison part. It was an unhappy choice: the Welsh-born Milland lacked Harrison's distinctive light touch, and it was compounded by the studio's decision to ask another of their contract stars, Ellen Drew, the daughter of a Kansas City barber, to play Diana.

Asquith had no choice but to accept Paramount's casting as far as the leads were concerned, but had more room for manoeuvre in the minor roles. He followed Rattigan's suggestion and asked Roland Culver and Guy Middleton to repeat their roles as the naval commander and as Brian. He also accepted Rattigan's recommendation of a handsome young actor called Kenneth Morgan to play Kenneth Lake. Round-faced, almost oriental-looking, with wide eyes and a schoolboy's smile, Morgan had also become Rattigan's lover, though Peter Osborn did not know it. The playwright's tastes, formed in the Park at Harrow, had not changed.

Filming took place during May and June 1939 at Shepperton Studios, to the west of London. The script was hardly familiar Asquith material, as it lacked a moral in the obvious sense, and had little or no social commentary, yet his enthusiasm for the play, as expressed to Rattigan when they had first met at dinner, was genuine, and helped to establish their friendship.

While Asquith and his editor, David Lean, were completing their final cut of the film, Rattigan was already working on the final production of *After the Dance*. A.D.Peters had agreed to put on the play himself, and had submitted the final version to the Lord Chamberlain's office on 15 May 1939. Neither Peters nor Rattigan wanted to miss the opportunity to exploit 'A New Play from the Author of *French Without Tears*'. If Albery was not keen, then so be it; they would go it alone. Peters recruited the help of another of his clients, J.B.Priestley, who was then a director of the Westminster Theatre, and Priestley in turn suggested Michael Macowan as the play's director. One reason for the haste, though Rattigan concealed it from everyone, was that he was running short of money. Another West End hit would help.

French Without Tears, which finally closed at the Criterion on 23 January 1939 after 1,030 performances, had earned its author more than £30,000 in less than two years, and he had spent almost all of it. The parties, the dinners at Ciro's or the Savoy Grill, the pictures, the new furniture, weekends in the country for his friends, an allowance for his father to support his gambling, living expenses for his mother, a Rolls-Royce, a rented house in the country, his own gambling, which included regular trips to casinos in France, and presents for his young lovers – now increasingly generous in the case of Kenneth Morgan – had seen the money disappear. Rattigan told one querulous accountant who dared to suggest that he might not be able to afford a Rolls-Royce, 'It's your job to make sure that I can afford one.'

Perhaps if Rattigan had written the sequel to *French Without Tears* that Bronson Albery wanted, he would have seen his financial problems disappear, and his success confirmed. But he was determined not to be seen as a one-dimensional playwright, and besides, the Lord Chamberlain had prevented his comedy, *Follow My Leader*, from reaching its audience. Rattigan wanted to give his audience something serious instead.

The Lord Chamberlain's office evidently took the point, commenting in its report that *After the Dance* was 'a surprisingly serious play . . . the idea being to compare a section of the post-war generation now in their middle thirties with the present-day twenty-year-olds, to the disadvantage of the former'. Accepting that there was 'no adultery or love-making business in this nicely balanced interplay of character', the reader concluded, 'Rattigan's work requires a certain amount of careless bad language for his careless characters . . . His portraits, however, are faithful and he is a dramatist of genuine good taste.' The play was licensed on 6 June, and its first performance took place at the New Theatre, Oxford, less than a week later, on 12 June 1939.

On 21 June *After the Dance* opened at the St James's Theatre in London, the same theatre that was to have staged *Follow My Leader* the previous year. Robert Harris and Catherine Lacey starred as the Scott-Fowlers, and Martin Walker as John Reid. The London papers had been asking 'Can He Do It Again?' Nervous as always, Rattigan ushered his father and mother into their box for the opening night. The Major was relaxed, rather more so than his son. His mother carried the champagne cork she had held during *French Without Tears*, and Rattigan too bowed to their joint superstition and had his hair cut, just as he had done on that earlier first night. This time, however, he did not watch from the back of the box, or the wings, but played chess with Peters in the manager's office, popping out from time to time to see how things were progressing.

The performance ended and it looked as though he need not have worried. There were cheers, and calls for the author – although this time Rattigan refused to appear. He said he did not want to risk being hit on the head by the curtain. Early the following morning – when he went out to collect the first editions – the message was clear enough. The *News Chronicle* headline ran 'Rattigan Does It Again', its critic concluding his review, 'It only remains to wish this play the long and prosperous run that it deserves, to congratulate its author on having justified so conclusively his departure from the realms of comedy and to look forward to a long series of his triumphs during the next forty or fifty years.'

The Times was every bit as flattering. 'Mr Rattigan's estimates of character are never fiercely prejudiced, and his method of allowing people gradually to reveal themselves gives to his play a genuine distinction.' W.A.Darlington in the *Daily Telegraph* agreed. 'Terence Rattigan has most successfully abandoned the light-hearted fooling of *French Without Tears* for something more serious,' he wrote. 'All these people are drawn with an extraordinary fidelity which both holds the audience's interest and inspires the actors. That is another way of saying that Mr Rattigan is a real dramatist; and it takes a real dramatist to contrive a dénouement to a play which is at once satisfactory and not obvious.'

At the weekend the chorus of praise continued, with only Ivor Brown in the *Observer* quietly carping that there was not one 'likeable' character in the play. But Agate, the scourge of *French Without Tears*, could hardly have been kinder.

> Mr Rattigan is the author of the most successful farce of modern times. Presumably it would have been easier for him to continue to provoke what Goldsmith so unkindly calls the loud laugh that speaks the vacant mind. But Mr Rattigan's mind is by no means vacant . . . I see nothing here that is not praiseworthy . . . I suggest that this play is worthy of respect.

This was a joy to Rattigan, who remained fixated on the opinions of the critics.

The English critic and playwright Charles Morgan wrote the most perceptive notice in the *New York Times*. Morgan noted that Rattigan had turned away from farce to write a serious play of discussion, contrasting two generations, and said:

> The nature of the contrast which he sees is, broadly stated, that the war generation wear over their seriousness a cloak of flippancy and over their deeper emotions a mask of indifference; while their successors, now in their early twenties, take themselves with open seriousness and even solemnity . . . Where he is drawing his major characters he reveals himself as a serious dramatist of real insight, who can write light dialogue that is never an interpolated comic

relief, but is always contributory to our knowledge of the mentality of the speakers.

'This', he concluded, 'holds out a real promise that in Mr Rattigan we have not only a successful writer of farce but a dramatist of serious consequence.'

This was praise indeed. As Rattigan accompanied Tony Goldschmidt to the Eton and Harrow match at Lord's, and witnessed his school's first victory since 1908, he had every right to feel that his ambitions had been fulfilled. He had done it again. But his optimism was not to last. As it became increasingly clear that war was inevitable, the mood of London's theatregoers subtly changed and the audiences for *After the Dance* began to trickle away. Though he could not have realised it at the time, Rattigan's fortunes were about to change.

During the first euphoric weeks after the play's opening, however, Rattigan had felt encouraged to see if he could breathe new life into *Follow My Leader*. On 24 July 1939 he wrote to Norman Gwatkin in the Lord Chamberlain's office, suggesting that 'Since last submitting this play to you, I think you will agree that circumstances, if not personalities, have considerably changed', and saying that he and Anthony Goldschmidt had 'revised the play and would, at all times, be agreeable to delete such passages as the Lord Chamberlain or the Foreign Office found objectionable . . . I really think that our Fuhrer would find it very hard to recognise himself in the person of Hans Zedesi, particularly played by Robertson Hare.'

The letter provoked a stir, and a flurry of internal memos swept across Lord Clarendon's desk, debating the play's merits and whether it would still be found offensive by the German Embassy. Clarendon was still at a loss. Geoffrey Dearmer, who had campaigned for the play a year earlier, returned to its defence in a new reader's report on the revised version, which he submitted on 29 July.

There was a reason for banning the play last year because of its central political situation and the policy of appeasement. Neurasthenia and Czecho-slovakia were very much alike. The 'protection' of the Neurasthenian minority and the impending invasion was much too imminent and likely to happen off the stage to be allowed on it. But this is now history. Surely a dramatist may echo by implication that Government's and the country's political views. To take the opposite view and ban a play because it makes fun of fascist ideology would be to hand over as a gift to the Censor's enemies the most weighty of ammunition.

The fastidious, fussy Clarendon was not convinced. He would rather not have had the problem in the first place. Gwatkin had sent a copy of the revised version to the German Embassy, and on 3 August received a stiff reply. 'It contains in its present camouflaged form without any doubt a lot of allusions to leading personalities in Germany, which can't but raise unfriendly feeling in the audience. Thus I don't think it would be helpful in improving Anglo-German relations'. Although the outbreak of war was now less than a month away, the Lord Chamberlain still dithered. He wrote to Gwatkin, 'I should like to ban all these anti-Nazi plays for they cannot help promote a better atmosphere, on the other hand a policy of appeasement cannot be said to have done much good so far.' Clarendon tried to play for time by referring the whole matter to the Foreign Office again, but Gwatkin disagreed and suggested instead that he talk to Rattigan.

When they met on 10 August, Gwatkin explained that there was no way in which they could license the play in its present form. 'Mr Rattigan was charming and professed he saw all the points,' Gwatkin noted afterwards. Rattigan admitted that it would be difficult to alter the play and wondered whether it might be possible to set it in England. In the end he told Gwatkin that he would think it over, as he and Tony Goldschmidt were considering trying it out that autumn at a Sunday evening club performance at the Gate Theatre, which would not need a licence from the Lord Chamberlain. Rattigan left the Chamberlain's office at St James's Palace and walked the few hundred yards to the St James's Theatre, where *After the Dance* had only three more nights to run. On 12 August, after just sixty performances, A.D.Peters reluctantly closed the play down.

Dejected by the collapse of both plays, Rattigan retired to a rented cottage near Farnham in Surrey, telling his friends that he was not sure how he was going to survive. 'I have not got a single idea: none.' There was talk of adapting a couple of comedies, one French, the other Italian, for Gilbert Miller, and Peters had mentioned the idea of reviving *A Tale of Two Cities* in the wake of Gielgud's phenomenally succesful *Hamlet*, which was about to be performed at Elsinore. But the talk came to nothing. His friends rallied round in an attempt to lighten his gloom. Finally Peters and Tony Goldschmidt suggested that they try to launch *Follow My Leader* just one last time. Rattigan was playing golf at Blackheath with Goldschmidt and Peter Osborn when war was declared on Sunday, 3 September. Surely now the Lord Chamberlain would grant a licence.

Rattigan hurried back to Mayfair. This time Peters himself wrote to Gwatkin to ask if a licence could be granted now that 'the war was on'.

Within three days Clarendon had relented. 'This play can now be passed for there is no longer any reason why we should be anxious not to hurt Nazi feelings.' Galvanised, Peters tried to launch a production at once, and take Rattigan back to the St James's Theatre, but that proved too ambitious, especially as the Lord Chamberlain had not withdrawn all his objections to the play. There was still the little matter of the use of the words 'piddling' and 'pansy' which the Lord Chamberlain's office would not accept. Rattigan suggested 'piffling' and 'cissie' as substitutes.

But the truth was that *Follow My Leader*'s time had passed. Had it been licensed in 1938, it might well have become a success. But by the time it finally appeared in front of an audience, in a try-out in Cardiff just before Christmas in 1939, the foolishness of dictators was no longer something the British audience felt like laughing about. Frith Banbury, who was to go on to become a director, appeared in the play and remembers, 'It was old hat by then. It fell on the floor because it wasn't the subject of humour any more. It was the time of the phoney war. But the Apollo was booked, and so we had to open'. The show's first director resigned, and Athole Stewart, an old comedy actor who was playing the King of Neurasthenia, took over. 'But even he wasn't able to do anything with it.'

In October, while *Follow My Leader* was still in preparation, the film version of *French Without Tears* opened in London, usually as part of a double bill with a propaganda film for the British Army bearing the ludicrous title *Arf a Mo, Hitler*. The distinctive charm of the play had been lost in its translation to the screen. Not even David Lean's efforts as editor could recapture its original theatrical verve. Also, by this time, its attempts at frothy lightheartedness were incongruous, not to say irrelevant. That alone was enough to sink it. Paramount's casting did the rest. The *New Statesman* noted tartly, 'Although this film is directed by Mr Anthony Asquith, it is less amusing than the play.' Ellen Drew was considered to have coarsened Diana almost beyond recognition, and Ray Milland to have turned Alan Howard into little more than a rather stiff young man with a mid-Atlantic accent.

Rattigan did not receive a screenwriter's credit, only credit as author of the original play. The screenplay was credited to Anatole de Grunwald and Ian Dalrymple. Rattigan could not complain. He needed the fee, and had been prepared to do anything the studio wanted, even down to allowing the film to end with Alan and Diana's wedding, contenting himself with devising a closing line for Guy Middleton and Roland Culver that suggested that the marriage would never last.

Almost the only critic who had a kind word to say for the film was Graham Greene, then coming to the end of his period as film critic of the *Spectator*. He called it a 'triumph for Mr Anthony Asquith', but added, to Rattigan's dismay, 'After the first ten minutes his witty direction and firm handling of the cast (Mr Ray Milland has never acted so well as this before) conquer the too British sexuality of Mr Rattigan's farce.' That 'national mixture of prudery and excitement' (which he appeared to attribute to Rattigan personally) would, he went on, 'be unbearable if it were not for Mr Asquith's civilised direction (unlike most adaptations from stage plays it is the padding that is memorable)'.

The fact that he concluded 'rather reluctantly' that the film was enjoyable was of little consolation to Rattigan. Nor was the opening of *Follow My Leader* at the Apollo on Shaftesbury Avenue on the snowy night of Tuesday, 16 January 1940. Even though his mother took her champagne cork again, there was nothing to be done. The attempts to improve the play since its disastrous try-out in Cardiff had not succeeded, and not even the combined talents of Reginald Beckwith as Hans Zedesi, Athole Stewart himself, who was still doubling as producer, and Marcus Barron as the British Ambassador could save it. The critics were respectful, but unenthusiastic. The London *Evening News* called the piece 'Dictatorship Without Tears . . . The humour is not very subtle, but it is hearty and unflagging', while W.A.Darlington in the *Daily Telegraph* described it as giving 'the impression of being a series of sketches strung together'. In the *Observer* Ivor Brown called it 'competent burlesque . . . unexacting comedy'. But it was left to Agate to make the central point in the *Sunday Times*. 'I just personally don't see that you can write a full-length burlesque about, say, the Plague when the Plague is an actual visitation.'

Follow My Leader lasted for just eleven days. It was Rattigan's first real flop, and the effect deepened further his sense of despair and bewilderment. He could not write, he was a one-hit wonder, his career was over. He also felt acutely that he had let down his lover, Kenneth Morgan, whom he had specifically requested be given the part of the young Trooper, Paul. It was Morgan's first West End part, and coming straight after his appearance in the film version of *French Without Tears* he and Rattigan hoped it might give his career a lift. 'Kenneth was ambitious, and Terry wanted him to succeed desperately,' one friend recalls.

As Peter Osborn knew, and Kenneth Morgan came to realise, Rattigan never allowed his male lovers to live with him. They might go out to dinner and a club together and then return to his flat, but he would always insist they left that night. He claimed that this was so that he could start work in the morning. But it also meant that he could, when the opportunity presented itself, fit in another brief affair.

Osborn would sit in the darkness at the top of the stairs in Hertford Street and wait to see if Rattigan was alone when he returned after dinner. If he was he might be invited downstairs, if not he would creep back into his own flat. But Rattigan was still fearful that his parents might find him out. Permanent residents or not, it was Morgan and Osborn who saw the dark side of his character, as others did not. They glimpsed what happened when despair really took hold.

When it did, as happened now, Rattigan's whole lifestyle changed. He took to going to bed at five o'clock in the afternoon, lying with the curtains drawn in darkness. He would stay there until the following morning, even though he might have invited someone to dinner. He would say that he had a migraine, and the guest would be sent away. It was his way of contracting out of the world, of putting aside the confusion and bewilderment he felt.

Asquith saw and understood this turmoil, perhaps because of his own ambivalent sexuality. 'There was an impenetrable side to Puff,' Rattigan wrote later, 'however close one was to him. He certainly liked being with young men, but it never went further than talking or going to a concert or playing cards.' Asquith's ceaseless, restless energy was an antidote to Rattigan's languid despair. Asquith took to arriving at his friend's London flat to demand that they went out together to dinner or a concert, conscious that Rattigan needed to be diverted out of his depression and the conviction that he had failed.

Close though they were, there was no question of a sexual relationship between them, and Rattigan doubted that Asquith had ever had a love affair with a man. Instead Asquith became Rattigan's confidant in a way that none of his lovers did. When they had first met, Rattigan admitted later, 'I more or less fell for him – fell for his personality, fell for his charm, fell for his enthusiasm and for his eagerness and for his way of life.' And when they worked together on the script of *French Without Tears* the affection grew. 'We discovered we had lots of private jokes,' Rattigan wrote. 'Those weeks of my introduction into films were weeks of giggling and laughing.'

Asquith also appealed to the snob in Terence Rattigan – the son of a Liberal prime minister, brought up in Downing Street, scholar at Winchester, Classics undergraduate at Balliol, one of the first British film directors to train in Hollywood, his mother continuing to influence Government even after his father had died. Shortly after the outbreak of war, when the Cabinet abruptly decided to shut the theatres and cinemas for fear of enemy bombing, Puffin was appalled, not least because the film of *French Without Tears* was due to open within a month. He persuaded his mother to invite several members of the

Cabinet to her house to discuss the matter. The intervention worked. The cinemas and theatres were allowed to reopen. This unlikely aristocrat in his crumpled clothes and oversized hat represented a world that Rattigan delighted in, even if he recognised in his heart that it could only truly be entered by the accident of birth.

Asquith and Rattigan were alike in ways they both recognised. Both were extravagant, and needed accountants to protect them from their own profligacy. Both drank determinedly and both smoked to excess. Both too were in awe of their mothers, Asquith of the redoubtable Margot, with whom he still lived in Bloomsbury's Bedford Square, Rattigan of the equally formidable but much less blunt Vera, whom he had established in a house near Luton, bought with the proceeds of the sale of his film rights. Only in their clothes did they markedly differ, the working men's boiler-suits affected by Asquith contrasting with the Savile Row equivalent for Rattigan.

Short, with tight curly blond hair tinged with red, and long delicate fingers gesticulating restlessly, Asquith became the single most important influence on Rattigan during the first months of 1940. The two men discussed the war and whether or not Rattigan should volunteer for the armed forces. Rattigan felt he could no longer sustain his once strongly held pacifism. They talked about music, which was Asquith's lifelong passion. Asquith enthused about opera, particularly Puccini, and Rattigan in turn tried to interest Asquith in cricket, with considerably less success.

In an attempt to shake off Rattigan's depression, Asquith told his friend that he had persuaded Paramount, who were sufficiently pleased with the performance of *French Without Tears* in England to want to maintain good relations with him, to allow Rattigan and de Grunwald to write the screenplay for the next film which they had in mind for him. It was a version of Esther McCracken's stage play, *Quiet Wedding*, a gentle English comedy about the preparations made for a large family wedding and the reaction of the prospective bride and groom to the event, and Asquith was well aware that it was exactly the sort of material that Rattigan could write brilliantly.

In the company of Asquith and de Grunwald, Rattigan's spirits began to lift. He was persuaded that his 'writer's block' was a figment of his imagination. They worked as a group, dictating their efforts to a male secretary, who was instructed to write down everything said. The result was one of the British cinema's gentlest but most enduring successes.

In the late spring of 1940, however, once the collaboration was over, the black mood once more descended on Rattigan, and as a last resort,

Asquith suggested he consult a psychiatrist whom he himself had just met, Dr Keith Newman of Oxford City and County Hospital. This strange man was to exercise an eerie, almost sinister, influence over both their lives for the next five years.

CHAPTER 10

Escape

◆

What revels are in hand? Is there no play,

To ease the anguish of a torturing hour?

SHAKESPEARE, *A Midsummer Night's Dream*

◆

Kurt Odo Neuman was one of the most bizarre figures ever to come out of the world of psychiatry. Born in Vienna, he trained as an analyst there before fleeing to England after the Anschluss in 1938, at which point he changed his name to Keith Newman. He was a short bald man, with a strong Austrian accent and a nose like Mr Punch, at first sight almost a caricature of a psychoanalyst. Every patient he treated, indeed everyone who came into contact with him, it seemed, described the uncanny influence he exercised over their lives. Newman seemed to come close to hypnotising his patients, even from a distance, so great was their dependence on him. Patients would consult him on all their decisions, would never do anything without his permission, and would take particular care never, on any account, to annoy him.

The actor Jack Watling remembers being taken to a wartime concert, to be conducted by Sir Adrian Boult. 'We weren't properly dressed. Newman just had an old sports jacket on, and I was in uniform, while everyone else was in white tie. But Newman wasn't in the least dismayed. He marched in at the beginning, and shouted "Boult" in a loud voice. Sir Adrian turned round, and meekly said, "Oh Newman, how nice to see you", and gave us two seats in the front row. That was the kind of man Newman was.'

In the first months of 1940, Puffin Asquith, Tony Goldschmidt and Rattigan all started to have hour-long sessions with Newman at Hertford Street, sometimes twice weekly. The first friend to be treated,

however, was Peter Osborn, who had briefly considered suicide over
Kenneth Morgan. Rattigan asked Newman to see him, and then started
treatment himself. Certainly Rattigan felt he had a great deal to talk
about. In the beginning he took the treatment to discuss his recent
'writer's block', but as the sessions went on he quickly discovered that
for the first time he could unburden himself of some of the feelings
and experiences that had weighed on him since childhood: the pain of
his father's unfaithfulness; his own sense of letting him down; the
recognition that his homosexuality was not simply a passing phase,
but something from which he could not escape and from which he
had no wish to escape; the scenes with Osborn and Morgan; and the
self-doubts engendered by his first success – had it all been, as he feared,
a fluke?

There was also the question of his politics, the confusion in his mind
over whether he should fight against Germany or not. 'I haven't really
campaigned against anything since the Spanish Civil War,' Rattigan
told him. 'I did march outside Downing Street carrying a banner
demanding food and arms for Spain.' Newman would listen impassively. 'That too is something we should discuss,' he would answer, in
his stern authoritative voice. He would explain that Rattigan clearly
needed more intensive treatment, and perhaps more sessions, in view
of the serious nature of his psychosis. This was what Rattigan had been
searching for – here was someone to provide him with a sense of
direction, and to absolve him from what he felt were some of his
unpardonable sins: his vanity, and his sexual appetite. Newman used
his influence ruthlessly. 'He seemed to want to control, completely
control, everybody he came into contact with,' Jack Watling suggests.
Watling himself was to come under Newman's spell in 1942, placed in
his hands by Asquith and Rattigan as a young man of nineteen. Five
years later Watling had the task of committing the analyst to a mental
hospital.

Newman's prescription for Terence Rattigan was unexpected. He
advised him to join the Royal Air Force at once. He emphasised to
Rattigan his need for discipline, the discipline that life in the armed
services could bring. 'Discipline is not only essential for practical life,
but for morality, art and science,' he wrote a year later. In particular
he argued that the younger, more flamboyant traditions of the RAF
would make it the most appropriate service for Rattigan, even though
he was the least technical, and least practical, of men. In turn, he advised
Peter Osborn to join the Navy.

There was no immediate need for Rattigan to enlist, however. By
the beginning of 1940 more than one and a half million Englishmen

were in the armed services, most of them in the Army, and every man aged between eighteen and forty-one was eligible to be called up. Twenty-seven-year-olds were not required to enlist until May, and twenty-nine-year-olds like Rattigan would not be conscripted until even later. Naturally, it was possible to volunteer early, and more than a million men did so, but there was no hysteria to join up, no strident recruiting posters, and no white feathers, as there had been in the Great War. Individuals could even argue for deferment of their military service on grounds of 'personal hardship'.

Nevertheless, shortly after the German invasion of Denmark and Norway in early April, which brought down Chamberlain as prime minister, Terence Rattigan volunteered to join the Royal Air Force. At the start of the interview his languid style did not impress the recruiting officer, but when Rattigan explained that he was the author of *French Without Tears* the conversation grew a good deal friendlier. He was accepted for training as an air-gunner.

Rattigan returned to his Hertford Street flat and packed up his belongings, taking most of them to his parents' house, Pepsal End, near Luton, and dividing the rest between Peter Osborn and Kenneth Morgan. In spite of his depression, his attachment to Morgan had intensified during the past few months, to the point where he grew jealous when he saw him with anyone else. Perhaps for the first time in his life he realised that he was falling in love. When he told Newman, the Austrian was noncommittal. He wanted his to be the sole influence.

Osborn, on the other hand, had taken Rattigan's affair with Morgan badly. 'There were evenings when he might send for me,' Osborn later wrote, 'and later I would creep upstairs again satisfied, and yet profoundly dissatisfied. I do not remember when, or on what occasion, I purloined his revolver . . . I know that there were fantasies of a double murder, to look like 'a suicide pact.' They came to nothing. When he discovered the revolver was missing, Rattigan summoned Osborn and told him that a doctor was on his way to see him. It was Newman.

While he was waiting for official notification of his call-up from the RAF, the play he had written six years before, *Grey Farm*, based on the Hector Bolitho novel, was produced on Broadway; and Asquith's film version of *French Without Tears* opened in America. Neither was a success. For the American release Paramount cut the British version from eighty-six to sixty-seven minutes, and left out the entire last act, in which Brian and the Commander rally round to save Alan from Diana. The result was to make the film pointless, as the *New Yorker* noted on its release in late April 1940. 'This screen version of one of the frothiest plays that ever bubbled through a season here was made in England . . . and perhaps should never have been made anywhere.'

Grey Farm fared even less well. For this melodrama about a father who feels he has to strangle people, in the wake of his wife's death in childbirth, the show's producer, Irving Cooper, had tried to persuade Charles Laughton to play the lead but Laughton had wisely turned it down. In his place, Cooper had turned to another European film actor, the whiskery and whisky-voiced Oscar Homolka, an Austrian, and persuaded him to make his Broadway début. It was a mistake.

Rattigan had never thought much of Bolitho's writing talents, and had even introduced a line into *Follow My Leader* dismissing them as a joke. The play's reception, when it opened on 3 May 1940, at the Hudson Theatre, New York, proved how right he was. The *New York Post* called it 'more than a bore, it is a titan among bores; in fact, it is several titans, all of whom just happen to be dumb'. The columnist Walter Winchell described it as 'a dreary show, barren of action and crowded with dialogue, none of it eventful'. It closed in a matter of days.

In spite of his declared pacifism at Oxford, Rattigan entered the RAF with something of the relief that he was to attribute to T.E.Lawrence twenty years later in his play *Ross*. He wanted to escape from the realities of his former life and to submerge himself in the humdrum details of military routine and the security of comradeship. Newman had prepared him for this change, and, once it came, he realised how much he had longed for it. Rattigan's sense of escape is all too clear in his letters to his parents at the time, as well as in his handwritten notes in his RAF notebooks. He took refuge in the minutiae of guns and gunnery, and then in wireless procedure, codes and morse, and, of course, the details of flying. Even the inevitable drill, which formed part of the horrors of basic training for every new serviceman, failed to dampen his sense of new-found freedom. He was not the only young man from a comfortable, even spoilt, background who was to feel that way at the beginning of the Second World War.

Inevitably, he hastened to describe all this to Newman.

Since I last wrote to you I have sprouted a few tiny feathers on my yet unformed wings . . . I have passed my tests 100 per cent, which is not unprecedented (or anything like it) . . . Such exercises aren't at all difficult, what is difficult is to do correctly all the hundred little things connected with the whole business – to forget none of them or, if one does (and one nearly always does) forget one, to be able to find the fault and not to panic. Which sounds like Kipling's *If*, I'm afraid, but to a person like myself, always prone to intense panic and by no means the cool-headed unimaginative type, it was a triumph to find that I had managed to stumble through all the tests while other worthier people were coming down from the skies in tears of desperation . . .

Rattigan's fragile confidence returned in this confined, protected world.

The concentration required is so enormous that from the moment one fell into the plane till the moment one jumped out and leant nonchalantly against the plane in the hope that someone on the road would think one was a fighter pilot, one was utterly and completely oblivious of one's surroundings, and conscious only of that infuriating medley of knobs and dials before one's face . . . However, I become a bore on the subject, and indeed think and talk of little else. Forgive me.

It was a glamorous time to be training for the RAF, even if only as a wireless operator/air gunner. In July, the Battle of Britain began. Indeed, the savage bombing of London interrupted Asquith's filming of *Quiet Wedding* at Denham no less than five times. Rattigan was brave enough, but he was not destined for Fighter Command. After passing out seventh of the forty-four in his class, with an average mark of 74 per cent, he was posted to flying training and eventually selected for officer training at RAF Cranwell in Lincolnshire. He was to join Coastal Command. Such was his enthusiasm that he decided to become a rear gunner, one of the most dangerous jobs in the RAF.

In his RAF notebook he recorded his first flight in the rear gun turret, making no mention whatever of fear, or even conscience.

The ground slipped away from me like a green carpet pulled by some invisible giant and presently the familiar hangars and buildings of Manby appeared momentarily below . . . as the Wellington turned and set course for the air firing range. This was the first time I had ever flown in a rear turret and I allowed myself the privilege of examining my sensations. They were not altogether disagreeable once I had overcome the feeling of being suspended in space in a small glass ball. This I effected by the simple expedient of turning the turret until it was possible to reassure myself visually that the small glass ball was, in fact, attached to a reasonably solid-looking aircraft and thus to convince myself that if I did not manipulate the turret too violently it would, in all likelihood, not drop off.

Like a new boy at Harrow, Aircraftsman Rattigan was concerned to ensure that he did nothing wrong.

> We approached the sea and I tried to remember the sequence of turret drills as I had been told it, not once but nearly twenty times over before taking off. Lower the doors. I had lowered the doors. Examine the reflector sight. I had examined the reflector sight. Test manipulation of turret . . . It only remained for me to report to the instructor and await his further instructions.

But neither had Rattigan lost his habitual sense of humour. On the front of the same notebook, he wondered in pencil: 'Do Barmaids Devour their Young?'

Unlikely though it may have seemed to some of his theatrical friends, Terence Rattigan was immensely proud of his new position in the RAF. It is clear in a letter he wrote to his father at the time, explaining that he was

> honestly delighted the Air Ministry chose to make me a Wireless Operator/Air Gunner instead of an AG pure and simple. The only snag is that the WO is by far the most responsible job in an air crew. He is the man who brings the plane home, and if his knob twiddling fails, the plane is apt to come down in the middle of the North Sea. Still the sense of triumph one gets from the signal 'R' (Received) is something far more acute than I've ever known before, and the equivalent shame at tuning off frequency is quite appalling.

Throughout the remaining months of 1940 Rattigan continued his training, returning to London and his friends only rarely, writing little except the notes and codes the Air Force demanded of him. He saw Newman and Asquith whenever he could, but his parents had to content themselves with letters. What time he had off was too precious to be able to fit in the longish journey to Luton and Pepsal End. There were plays to be seen, friends to be caught up with, not least Kenneth Morgan. Rattigan wrote to his father: 'I fully intended to come down to you for at least one day, but I found that there were so many things I had to see and do, and so many people asked me to so many parties that before I knew where I was my leave was up. Beyond that I make no excuses, and am really very sorry I missed you both.'

On one leave he did manage to catch up a little with his career. He saw Gielgud, and agreed to write a draft for an appeal he was conducting on behalf of the Institute of Social Psychiatry. His former mentor also asked him to consider writing a one-act comedy which he and Beatrice Lillie could perform for the troops. 'If I have time I will,' Rattigan wrote to his father, 'but judging from Cranwell I doubt if I will.' Asquith had also been angling for his friend's release from RAF service for two months to work on the script of a new film for him, and Rattigan was not about to reject the idea, no matter how keen he was to submerge himself in the world of the armed services. 'This would obviously be such an enormous financial help that I'm quite ready to incur the Air Ministry's displeasure by asking them to release me for the requisite period,' he wrote to Frank Rattigan, adding, 'Actually I'm quite sure they won't do it.'

But the Air Ministry did grant him a period of leave, allowing him time to work on two scripts, the first for producer Paul Soskin, for whom he had written *Quiet Wedding* – which was just about to open in London – and the second for Asquith's new employers, Gainsborough Pictures and Gaumont British. Soskin's film was to be directed by Harold French, four years after their partnership on *French Without Tears*. By now French had turned himself from an actor into a film director, and was preparing a story for Soskin about Norwegian freedom fighters who destroy a German U-boat base and are rescued by British commandos. The film was to be called *The Day Will Dawn*, and the screenplay would be written by Rattigan with his collaborator, once again, Tolly de Grunwald.

It suited Rattigan's mood to take refuge in films. There was none of the pressure on him of his name alone in lights on Shaftesbury Avenue. It was the stars and the director who attracted the limelight. No one noticed the name of the screenwriter. When *Quiet Wedding* opened in London in February 1941, the reviewers barely mentioned him, though Louis MacNeice did note in the *Spectator*, 'It has a lightness, a deftness and a celerity which most British peacetime films have notoriously lacked . . . It looks as if the now all but obsolete country household, when treated with this blend of nostalgia and burlesque, is just what people want for their escape-entertainment.'

Rattigan was still paying for the upkeep of his parents' house near Luton, and providing his father with a weekly allowance. He had plucked them out of the gloomy gentility of the top-floor flat in Stanhope Gardens, and he was determined that they should not return there. Screenplays, which paid well, could ensure they did not. He was all the more grateful, therefore, when the Air Ministry relented yet again, giving him the chance to write another screenplay for Asquith, this time in collaboration with the respected pre-war playwright Rodney Ackland.

Asquith's new film was *Uncensored*, the story of a group of Belgian patriots and their efforts to produce and distribute a free newspaper, *La Libre Belgique*, under the noses of the occupying German forces. It was very similar in theme to another of Asquith's films, *Freedom Radio*, which was just about to be released and dealt with an underground radio station in Vienna. Rattigan and Ackland worked on the script of *Uncensored* in Gainsborough's offices in London, as the bombing intensified in the first months of 1941. As soon as the script was finished Rattigan returned to the RAF.

By the end of March 1941 he had qualified as a wireless operator, and by the end of May as an air gunner, after a period at RAF Manby. From there he was posted to Invergordon in Scotland as a pilot officer (a title denoting rank rather than role) with Coastal Command. It was his first experience of long missions out over the Atlantic. He was transferred in September that year, and again in November, as his experience increased.

The missions carried a small risk of enemy fighter attack, but mostly they involved tedium rather than danger – the monotonous process of sweeping the sea for signs of German submarines or shipping, watching for British or Allied ships in distress, and reporting on conditions. With long periods on the ground when the weather was bad or the planes were being repaired, this regime gave Rattigan a great deal of time to recuperate, and to think. Keith Newman had been right. The RAF had given him a sense of pride and purpose, and renewed his confidence in himself.

Fourteen years later he wrote a narration for a thirty-eighth birthday concert for the RAF, which began: 'Youth may have its faults, we grant, but lack of pride is not one of them. In the family of Her Majesty's three services we may be the babe in arms, but it is a babe that, more than once in its short life, has changed the course of human history. To their Trafalgars and their Waterloos we have our answer.'

But there was another side to the service's appeal to him beyond the pride: the male camaraderie. At one stage in his RAF career Rattigan organized a drag show called *Boys in Blue, or Things in Wings*, during which, dressed in a tutu, he sang 'I'm just about the oldest fairy in the business. I'm quite the oldest fairy you've ever seen'. One of his fellow performers was the actor turned writer Anthony Creighton, who was later to collaborate with John Osborne on two plays.

It is hardly surprising, therefore, that the RAF provided him with the inspiration for the next play he would write alone – his first for more than three years. Nor was it surprising that the play should express the warmth of his feelings for the service he had come to love. On leave in early November, he had discussed the idea for a new play with Newman, who was magisterially encouraging. Asquith, who had just finished shooting *Uncensored*, was equally pleased to hear that Rattigan was ready to write again. 'Would you consider directing it?' Rattigan asked, knowing full well that Asquith had never directed for the theatre before in his life. His friend barely hesitated. 'Of course, dear boy, if you think I could.'

A few weeks later, after he had been posted to 95 Squadron, then based at RAF Calshot in the Solent, Rattigan began work on the play. He wrote it in the back of his RAF exercise books, in pencil at first and then in ink. The thin upright hand was as neat and precise, as straight along the lines on the page, as when he had written *Integer Vitae* at Harrow. But the man was different. He did not feel quite the same pressure to hide emotion behind repartee. He wanted to convey something of what being in the RAF meant to the members of the service themselves, and their families. He also wanted to write a play that would please Shaftesbury Avenue.

The sky over the English Channel grew greyer and greyer in the short November days of 1941, which meant that the Sunderlands were often grounded by bad weather, but this also left Rattigan more time than usual to sit and write. The plot for his new play had been gestating in his mind for six months, and now, within a fortnight, he had the draft of the first act written. Suddenly the situation changed. 95 Squadron were instructed to fly to Freeport in Sierra Leone, via Gibraltar, for further coastal reconnaisance duties, leaving immediately. The squadron took off in the third week of November. But before they reached Gibraltar, they ran into a series of attacks from German fighters, which forced some of them to wait for running repairs to be carried out. Rattigan's plane was one of those forced to wait.

When Rattigan's Sunderland took off again for the fifteen-hour flight to Freeport, everything went smoothly for the first hour or so. Suddenly a German Heinkel came into view. It made five passes at the slower and more cumbersome Sunderlands. The attack, as Rattigan put it in a letter to his parents afterwards, 'put four holes in our tailplane – rather near me incidentally', but ended indecisively. Not waiting for the Heinkel to attack again, Rattigan's Sunderland set off as quickly as it could. But the Sunderland's difficulties were not over. Still eight hours out of Freetown, one of the plane's four engines cut out 'and was in acute danger of blowing up'.

'We decided to come down in the sea,' Rattigan wrote,

although we were over 900 miles from the nearest help, Gambia. But the swell was too great to land, so there was nothing for it but to go on – on three engines, without enough petrol and apparently no chance of getting there. To maintain height we threw overboard everything that was detachable – less the first act of my play which I rescued from my suitcase just as it went over the side, and then, as we were still losing height, we used a fire axe on the aircraft and threw everything over the side that could be hacked off.

The first act of his new play was by now stuffed safely inside his flying jacket. 'Unexpectedly a beautiful God-sent thirty miles per hour tailwind sprang up, and blew us into Bathurst Gambia eight hours later with enough petrol for ten minutes more flying. Without that wind we had had it, in the Air Force phrase.'

In the two weeks they spent in Bathurst waiting for repairs, Rattigan wrote the second act of his play, including the scene in which a young aircraftsman breaks down. 'I was shitting myself like everybody else,' he told Jack Watling not long afterwards. He completed the play when the squadron finally reached Freetown in early December, had it typed and – on Christmas Eve – sent a copy each to his mother and father and a third copy to A.D. Peters. 'It is either my best or my worst,' he wrote to Frank and Vera,

> anyway quite different to anything I have written before, in spite of the echoes of *Black Forest* coming through occasionally. I hope you like it, and I have a suspicion that you will because, whatever else may be said about it, its theme and characters are, for once, quite pleasant. It may be too sentimental, but not for my taste and the happy ending, if phoney, should be commercial.

He was impatient for the next move.

> I have told Peters to get busy on it at once, but I would like you to stick pins in his behind at frequent intervals. The play's appeal, if any, is immediate and American dramatists are, I am sure, rushing out plays by the score about the gallant US airmen, and this play should reach New York, and the films – for which it should have an obvious appeal – first.

Rattigan did not like Freetown. He was no Somerset Maugham, happy amid the humidity and the servants. His natural habitat was the Savoy, not Sierra Leone. He enjoyed the flying, 'which is not quite as cissy as Sunderland trips are popularly supposed to be', but not the climate. The flying was a relief.

It does at least get me out of this spot, which is, to put it frankly, torture . . . infested not only by 95 Squadron but by lizards, giant spiders, giant centipedes, mosquitoes (not giant but not any the less pleasant), bats, bugs that nest under your skin and a particularly delightful monkey . . . The town itself is better not visited and certainly there is no reason to do so, although it boasts of one officers' club and one brothel.

It was unlikely that he would get back to Britain before March, as he was not due for leave until he had completed 300 hours of flying. In the meantime he would have to suffer at the hands of the native population. 'The expression "black devil" is one I am loath to employ only because it seems to me to understate,' he wrote.

After a few days of 'I say would you mind awfully' etc. I have now firmly descended to 'Fetchem master's shaving water plenty chop chop or master whip black boy's hide plenty bloody quick.' Even then the shaving water is not brought unless the threat is accompanied by the gift of a small coin – necessarily small because the recipient has stolen all the larger coins already.

'I hope you're both well, and not too starved,' he ended his letter home, 'and while I remember it. A Merry Christmas. Write soon, and let me know what you think of the play.'

Rattigan remained in Freetown for a further three months before leave brought him back to England for discussions about his new play: and not least about its title. Rattigan's original thought had been *Next of Kin*, but he was not certain. Asquith did not like it at all. Neither did Newman. 'Too bland,' he told Rattigan when asked to comment on *Next of Kin*. 'It should illuminate the world. That title does not. It must be called after those lights that show aeroplanes where to land – a flare path.' It was Newman, therefore, who came up with the play's title, *Flare Path*. In gratitude, Rattigan dedicated the play to him, not just because of this brainwave but most of all for sending him into the Air Force in the first place.

In Rattigan's absence in Sierra Leone, Peters had approached both Bronson Albery and O'Bryen, Linnit & Dunfee about the new play but neither had been enthusiastic. Albery in particular had been cautious about 'a war play', as he insisted on calling it. Undismayed, Peters took the play to Hugh Beaumont at H.M. Tennent, who had already established himself as the West End's most successful new young impresario. Over the next two decades the tall, elegant, slightly mysterious and most definitely homosexual 'Binkie' Beaumont was to become one of the most important influences on Rattigan's career. They were never lovers, merely two friends joined in mutual admiration and showing the same need to screen their true identities behind a mask.

Rattigan was to describe the man who helped him become Britain's leading commercial playwright as 'The bland, smiling, courteous, ingenuous seeming occupant of the managing director's office at H.M.Tennent Ltd, looking ten years younger than his age, chain-smoking, chain-tea-drinking, chain-telephoning, while suavely exchanging items of trivial gossip with the casual visitor . . . perhaps not altogether unhappy to be enabled – by some lucky chance – to hide his true personality behind the screen of an infantile nickname.' This nickname derived, so legend had it, from the remark of an old lady who looked into his pram one morning and pronounced: 'Oh, just another Binkie.'

Beaumont was born in Wales, some said the illegitimate son of a middle-class mother, and at the age of sixteen became the assistant theatre manager of the Playhouse in Cardiff. The following year he managed the touring version of *The Creaking Door* for Sir C. Aubrey Smith, and provoked the manager of the Barnes Theatre on the outskirts of London to say that he refused 'to be managed by a creature all puberty and spots'. The play went ahead in spite of this protest. While he was in London, Beaumont seized the opportunity to find another job and got one in the box office of the Prince of Wales Theatre, just off Leicester Square. H.M.Tennent, then managing director of the powerful Moss Empires chain of theatres, rang the theatre one day looking for tickets for that night's production of *The Blue Train*, which he was told was sold out. Tennent asked to speak to the manager and was put through to Beaumont, who quickly arranged for two house seats. Tennent, impressed, first invited him to lunch a few days later, then asked him to join Moss Empires. The ever-confident Beaumont accepted on condition that Tennent would eventually create a production arm 'limited to the production of straight plays'. He would have nothing to do with the music hall.

H.M.Tennent Productions finally came into existence in 1936, with both Tennent and Beaumont as its principals; and although the first productions were all flops – indeed the company was saved largely by a farce called *George and Margaret* – it soon afterwards became one of the most powerful production companies in London. *Flare Path* was one of the first plays that Beaumont took on alone, Tennent having died only a matter of weeks before. It was the first new Rattigan play to be presented for two years, and the first he had written for almost four. Binkie Beaumont agreed to present it in the West End, after a brief four-week tour, and submitted it to the Lord Chamberlain's office in April 1942. A month later Flying Officer Rattigan returned from Sierra Leone to his next posting in England, with the new rank of Flight Lieutenant. His career was back on the road.

CHAPTER 11

A One-Hit Wonder?

◆

Me – who am as a nerve o'er which do creep

The else unfelt oppressions of this earth.

SHELLEY, *A Lament*

◆

The Lord Chamberlain's reader's report on '*Flare Path*, also known as *Next of Kin*', observed that the play was 'Mr Rattigan in a more serious mood', and added, 'I do not suppose there is anything secret in this play, but it should be vetted by the Air Ministry before a licence is granted.' By the end of April both the Air Adviser to the Ministry of Information and the Lord Chamberlain had agreed that the play could be produced, and asked for only minor changes. The Air Ministry wanted Margate changed to 'say, Littlehampton' and did not want any character to say how many air raids they had taken part in. The Lord Chamberlain's office – as ever – decided to niggle about the language. In their formal letter to H. M. Tennent they insisted 'bloody' be changed to 'damned' in several places, that they would not accept 'a pissy type', 'pissed', 'caught with our knickers down' or 'stone the bloody crows'. Neither Beaumont nor Rattigan objected. The cuts were accepted and the licence was granted on 8 June 1942.

By then, Rattigan was a bundle of nerves. He telephoned Peters endlessly, demanding to know every detail of what was happening; he pestered Puffin Asquith, whom Beaumont had accepted as director, badgered Beaumont himself, and consulted Newman both in person and on the telephone. To outsiders Rattigan may have appeared his usual languid self, sipping champagne, cutting a dash in a London just recovering from the Blitz, but his friends – Asquith especially – knew the truth, his genuine fear that he might turn out to be a 'one-hit wonder' if his new

play failed to please. He resumed his sessions with Keith Newman, sometimes three in a week and always held in a darkened room.

Rattigan's anxiety increased even further when he learned that Beaumont was so unconfident about the play that he had declined to confirm
the booking of a London theatre. He had in mind the Apollo, in spite
of Rattigan's unhappy memories of *Follow My Leader* there, but was
not prepared to confirm it until the provincial tour had got under way.
'He doesn't believe it is going to work, and certainly isn't going to
waste his money on guaranteeing a London theatre,' whispered one
friend. Worse still, Peters told Rattigan that Beaumont was not prepared to risk his own money, but had offered shares both to Linnit &
Dunfee, who had invested in *French Without Tears*, and to the band-
leader and impresario Jack Hylton. It was even rumoured that he was
putting the play on as a tax loss. Rattigan's response was to drink
heavily. Asquith kept him company. Newman looked on impassively.

The urgent task of casting the play went ahead none the less. One
young actor whom Rattigan and Asquith auditioned was Jack Watling,
from Chingford in Essex, then just nineteen. Watling had just volunteered for the RAF himself, but had not yet been called up 'because
there was a bottleneck of people who wanted to join air crew'. Watling,
who had trained at stage school, was almost unknown in the theatre
when he was invited to meet Rattigan and Asquith in the cocktail bar
of the Savoy hotel, though he had appeared in two films. 'I'd never
been in anything like the cocktail bar of the Savoy,' Watling recalls,
'and I was totally overawed. But there was Rattigan, and Anthony
Asquith, and another bod, whom I didn't know.'

Asquith had worked with Watling once before, on his film *We Dive
at Dawn*. It was one of the stars of that film, Eric Portman, a friend of
Asquith's, who had suggested Watling as a candidate for the young
pilot in Rattigan's new play. Asquith gave Watling the script and asked
him to read 'the breakdown' scene in which the pilot, Teddy Graham,
admits to his wife Patricia how afraid he really is. It was the scene
Rattigan had written after his experience with the Heinkel 115 on his
way to Freetown, and the emotional centre of the play.

> You don't know what it's like to feel frightened. You get a beastly
> bitter taste in the mouth, and your tongue goes dry and you feel
> sick, and all the time you're saying – this isn't happening – it can't
> be happening – I'll wake up. But you know you won't wake up.
> You know it's happening and the sea's below you and you're
> responsible for the lives of six people. And you pretend you're
> not afraid, that's what's so awful . . .

'I read the scene,' Watling remembers, 'and they totally ignored me for a bit. Rattigan was at his most charming, and so was Puffin. The other fellow said nothing. Anyway, after a few minutes' discussion Rattigan said, "We'd like you to play the part – there's only one thing. Anthony Asquith's directing the play, and this gentleman will be directing you." The gentleman in question was Keith Newman. Watling was stunned.

'At that moment I'd never heard of such a thing, and I wish to God I hadn't to this day,' Watling says now. Newman was to all but wreck his life, and his career. During the run of *Flare Path* and for the next three years, Newman came to exercise as powerful an influence over Watling as he did over Asquith, Rattigan and Tony Goldschmidt. Newman insinuated himself into every aspect of the young actor's life, even insisting that Watling should live with him in his flat in Oxford. 'On the strength of *We Dive at Dawn* I'd been offered a contract by Gaumont British Pictures,' Watling recalls. 'I was a working-class lad, with no education to speak of, and all I wanted was to be a film star. But Newman told me, "Don't accept the contract. You are an actor."' The young Watling meekly agreed.

Phyllis Calvert had been signed to play Patricia, the young pilot's wife, and Martin Walker was to be Kyle, her American former lover. During rehearsals, which took place at the Apollo, Newman said nothing. 'He just sat there in the stalls, silent', according to Watling. 'But just before the play opened in Oxford, where I was to stay with him in his flat at Number 36 Holywell, he took me to the Lake District for three days of what he called intensive voice training.' The psychiatrist had devised a set of vocal exercises, which he insisted he practised for hours at a time. 'It was unbelieveable,' Watling recalls. 'He took over my life completely.'

Watling was not aware that the author of *Flare Path* was homosexual, or that his taste was for handsome, fresh, round-faced young men, as Watling was at the time. 'I didn't discover any of that until much later,' he explains now. 'But I did find out that Newman was telling Rattigan not "to bother with me". Certainly Rattigan never made a pass at me, as he did at some actors.' At this stage Newman had not made a homosexual pass at Watling. That came later. Newman simply frightened him beyond words. 'I couldn't do anything without asking his permission. I was heterosexual then, and I am now, but Newman pretty much gave me a nervous breakdown. I couldn't cope with him.' Why Newman had this power, or why people submitted to him, Watling is just as unable to explain now as he was then.

The pre-London tour of *Flare Path* opened on 13 July 1942 at the

New Theatre, Oxford, but with Rattigan called back to Coastal Command, only Newman and Asquith were on hand to witness its reception. Whatever Beaumont's reservations, the audience clearly liked it, and by the time it had finished its week, he had plucked up the courage to book the Apollo for the middle of August.

By coincidence, two of the films which Rattigan had co-scripted – *The Day Will Dawn* and *Uncensored* – were released about this time. *The Day Will Dawn*, which he had written with Tolly de Grunwald, had emerged in May to no more than lukewarm notices. 'It could have been, should have been, enormously exciting. But to my mind, it never gets beyond the inspired mediocre,' said the *Observer*'s C.A.Lejeune of this story by Frank Owen about the destruction of a U-boat base in Norway. 'Would have been a better film and no less popular if its climax had been subtly timed,' was the opinion of the *New Statesman*.

When *Uncensored*, which Rattigan had scripted with Rodney Ackland, was released in July, the critics were a little more enthusiastic, not least because Eric Portman was its star and Anthony Asquith its director. Dilys Powell in the *Sunday Times* complimented Puffin specifically, and called the screenplay 'a neat job'. William Whitebait in the *New Statesman* felt it 'a more finished piece of work than the same director's *Freedom Radio*'. Even so, none of the critics felt the film was as moving or as exciting as it could have been, though they thought Peter Glenville, Rattigan's friend and house-sharer from Oxford, deserved particular praise for his portrayal of the jealous partner who betrays the hero.

For once the reviews hardly interested Rattigan. His attention was focused on the fate of *Flare Path*. The Air Ministry not only approved of the play, but had also asked for seats for the opening night. Air Chief Marshal Sir Charles Portal, the Chief of the Air Staff, intended to be present. This cheered Binkie, who saw the publicity possibilities. So, on the warm evening of 13 August 1942, Rattigan established his parents in their box and went to stand with Asquith at the back of the circle as the first act unfolded. Inevitably Vera had brought the famous champagne cork in her handbag, and Rattigan had once again had his hair cut. As always, he observed the rituals and deferred to his superstitions. Now he was in the hands of Adrienne Allen and Phyllis Calvert, Martin Walker, Kathleen Harrison, Jack Watling, and a very young George Cole.

By the middle of the third act some women in the stalls were actually crying, and Rattigan risked whispering to Puffin, 'I think we've brought it off.' It certainly seemed so. Then a strange thing happened. The curtain slowly began to fall. It stopped half-way down, and stayed there for what seemed like an eternity, until, just as inexplicably, it began to rise again. There was hesitant applause from the audience, which grew to a storm a few minutes later, when the play actually ended and the curtain fell as it was intended. It was the warmest reception Rattigan had received since *French Without Tears*.

The Chief of the Air Staff sent a message to Flying Officer Rattigan, inviting him to his box to receive his congratulations. Newman summoned Jack Watling: but not to offer any praise. Sitting impassively in the stalls, he had been making notes on how his protégé could improve his performance. Rattigan and Asquith then retired to Puffin's house in Bloomsbury, to wait for the first editions. Applause was welcome, but what mattered to Rattigan were the reviews. He was worried, and rightly.

'Given technical competence,' *The Times* noted sniffily, 'a play on the subject of bomber pilots and of the women who wait for them to return from their raids can hardly fail to move a London audience today. But something more than mere competence is required if these semi-public figures are to reveal themselves and their problems.' Most of the rest of the dailies were equally cool, criticising particularly the 'unimaginative' characters, which the *Spectator* added at the weekend were never 'roundly drawn by the dramatist'.

By a strange irony only James Agate, scourge of *French Without Tears*, correctly assessed the play's strengths. 'Considered as entertainment Mr Rattigan's piece is extraordinarily lively. A laugh every minute, a roar every five minutes, and a tear every ten,' he wrote in the *Sunday Times*, adding, 'At times it is a little better than this.' Paying tribute to its author's 'craftsmanship', he concluded, 'Notable acting by everybody makes the piece safe for a year.' In fact it was to be safe for eighteen months.

Most of the critics had totally failed to appreciate the public mood, just as Beaumont and Bronson Albery had done when the play was first offered to them. London's theatregoers already had their 'entertainments'. Noël Coward's *Blithe Spirit* was playing almost next door at the Globe, also presented by Beaumont, while Gielgud, Edith Evans and Peggy Ashcroft were at the Phoenix in *The Importance of Being Earnest*. But there were no other plays in London which accepted the facts of the war, and none that brought those realities home in as palatable and moving a form as *Flare Path*.

Rattigan's experience of writing propaganda films for Asquith, coupled with his own sympathy for the everyday life of the airmen he had lived and served with, gave his play a quality with which the audience immediately identified. Finished on the veranda of a former school in Africa, with his fellow officers looking over his shoulder offering suggestions, the play's affection for its characters shone through. It touched a nerve, even if the critics thought it too sentimental. And, above all, it was optimistic. It carried the message that those fighting the war might just survive, no matter how long the odds. In the months after the fall of Singapore and Tobruk, while the British army was still being forced back by Rommel in the Western Desert, that message was welcome. Agate and the other critics may have called for a tragic ending, but Rattigan was, instinctively, a better judge of the country's mood. 'To be successful,' he wrote seven years later, 'a playwright must take so many factors into consideration; the changing background of everyday life; changing tastes; changing fashions; changing manners.' *Flare Path* showed he could do so.

Terence Rattigan had written his second hit, and it brought back his confidence. 'I don't know whether you have heard the figures,' he wrote to his father shortly after the play opened, 'but they are extremely good. First full week £1,287, second £1,305 and this week up a little, so far, on last. This is a better start than *French Without Tears*. I get a daily and eagerly awaited telegram telling me the returns.'

Flare Path also captured the public appetite for stories about the RAF. Air Chief Marshal Sir Arthur 'Bomber' Harris, head of Bomber Command, went to see the play shortly after it opened, and went backstage afterwards. 'Bloody disgraceful,' he bellowed at Jack Watling, 'showing cowardice in front of the enemy.' Harris knew that many of his own air crew would go to see the play and identify with the young pilot who was losing his nerve after so many missions. What he failed to understand was that the frank admission of fear could provide its own inspiration. Nevertheless he helped to speed up Watling's own admission to the RAF.

Even that, however, did not allow the young actor to escape Newman's clutches. By pulling strings the psychiatrist arranged for Watling to be posted to the Allied Squadron, where French and Polish officers were taught English at a base in London. This meant that Watling, even after his official call-up, could still perform. Newman meanwhile sat in the stalls for every single performance and watched his young charge in action. Though neither Rattigan nor Watling knew it, Newman was planning a book, which he would later publish himself, called *250 Times I Saw a Play*. When he sent a manuscript to George Bernard Shaw the playwright commented, 'I don't know what to say about this book. The experience on which it is founded is so extraordinary that an honest record of it should be preserved. But it would have driven me mad; and I am not sure that the author came out of it without a slight derangement.'

By the autumn of 1942, and in spite of Newman's brooding presence, *Flare Path* was established as the most popular new play in London. In late October Eleanor Roosevelt went to see it, writing afterwards in the *News Chronicle*, 'It was beautifully cast and acted, and I am glad it is going to the United States, because it is a true and moving picture of the RAF.' By then Gilbert Miller, together with the Theatre Guild, had bought an option on the play for Broadway, and were negotiating for Alec Guinness to make his Broadway début as the young airman. Meanwhile, with Rattigan's encouragement, A.D. Peters had turned down two offers for the film rights, £5,000 from Warner Brothers and £8,000 from Twentieth Century-Fox. Rattigan was determined they should get £15,000 at least, and he succeeded. Early in 1943 Fox bought the rights for £20,000 – almost as much money as Rattigan had made from the entire run of *French Without Tears* – and then failed to make the film.

Flare Path changed the course of Rattigan's life. Had it failed he might never have risked writing for the stage again, taking refuge instead in screenplays. Its success, and the remarkable impact it had on its audiences, had a cumulative effect on his confidence, which he was to draw on in the years to come. 'Each fresh success gives more confidence; more knowledge of the likes and dislikes of audiences; and, of course, more experience in stage technique,' he wrote later. Though his fear of failure was never quite to disappear, it was never again to be so intense.

When Winston Churchill went to see the play with his wife Clemmie and Margot Asquith in January 1943, shortly before leaving for the Casablanca conference with Roosevelt, he told the cast, 'I was very moved by this play. It is a masterpiece of understatement. But we are rather good at that, aren't we?' The Prime Minister's remark made up for the disappointment Rattigan had felt just a few days earlier, when the Broadway production closed after only fourteen performances at the Henry Miller Theatre. Though he had been in New York, arriving there on the *Queen Mary*, he missed the Broadway opening by one day. Under orders from the RAF, he had left to ferry Catalinas back from America to Prestwick in Scotland. He flew throughout Christmas Day 1942, his route via Bermuda, and took twenty hours to reach the Scottish coast, having got hopelessly lost. So it was some days before he discovered that the Broadway production had flopped. *Variety* prophesied:

It is doubtful if the American reception of *Flare Path* will approximate the click being enjoyed currently by the original London offering. Perhaps one reason for this lies in the fact that the play is somewhat ahead of its time over here. Being concerned with air raids and life under the immediate war conditions of embattled Britain, it is obvious that a London audience would look upon the drama as an actual piece of their existence lifted bodily on to a stage.

The other New York reviews confirmed this judgement. 'The drama seems sentimental, slow and confused,' wrote Lewis Nichols in the *New York Times*. Once again Rattigan felt, as he was to feel many times in the future, that he would never succeed in the United States. It was all the more galling because he firmly believed that he had put far more than mere propaganda into the events in the residents' lounge of the Falcon Hotel in Lincolnshire.

As Rattigan had explained to his parents in a letter, there were echoes of his unproduced *Black Forest* in *Flare Path*. It too focused on the fact that lovers, husbands and wives were often unable to express their emotions, even in the most extreme situation. Even more significantly, the central triangle in *Flare Path*, the young bomber pilot, his wife and her former lover, a Hollywood star who has returned to claim her, also mirrored a crisis in the playwright's own life. Kenneth Morgan had left him and gone to live with another actor.

Morgan's decision that he was not going to remain faithful had come as a tremendous shock to Rattigan, who saw himself as someone whom no lover should ever leave. The shock was so great that it was to colour his view of love in the years to come. It was to recur time and again in different guises throughout his later work. But, in this first instance, it meant that Rattigan put a substantial part of himself into *Flare Path*, and in particular into the character of the glamorous Peter Kyle, the movie star who is unable to recapture the woman he loves once she has discovered that her husband, a young bomber pilot called Teddy Graham, needs her more. And though Kenneth Morgan was eventually to return to him, the experience of being deserted by someone he loved deeply left a wound that was to remain with him throughout his life.

Flare Path's two subplots, one involving a Polish count (Gerard Heinz), whose wife (Kathleen Harrison) was a barmaid until they married and is convinced that her aristocrat husband will leave her once the war is over; the other concerning a cockney Sergeant, Dusty Miller (played by Leslie Dwyer), whose wife has taken enormous trouble to come down to the hotel for the night, only to see her husband disappear on a sudden bombing raid, are extensions and reflections of the triangle between Kyle, and Patricia and Teddy Graham at the heart of the play. Both subplots are designed to underline the fact that love can conquer, no matter how strange its twists and turns may appear. In fact the Polish countess discovers that her husband will never leave her, when Peter Kyle translates a letter from him after he has gone missing, and the cockney wife reveals how much she cares about her husband, no matter how gloomy she may appear. *Flare Path* passed this optimistic message to its audience.

Rattigan revelled in the play's success. He had struck a chord in the hearts of the London theatre audience. It was what he wanted. In the introduction to the first volume of his collected plays, published a decade later, he was even to overlook the critics' original unenthusiastic reaction. He wrote: 'At long last I found myself commended, if not exactly as a professional playwright, at least as a promising apprentice who had definitely begun to learn the rudiments of the job.'

Not that he was to practise his craft again for some time. In the Air Force his next posting was as Gunnery Officer to 422 Squadron, where his job was to devise training programmes for the air crew while still flying missions himself. He wrote to his parents, apologising that he could not tell them exactly where he was stationed, but explaining, 'The camp is large and damp and Nissen hutted. There is nothing to do and nowhere to go after working hours. To quote from a sergeant friend of mine, "We are fourteen miles from f- all."' The period of isolation was soon to come to an end. *Flare Path*'s success brought his transfer from active duty to the RAF Film Unit. He would still wear uniform, but his days as a serving air gunner and wireless operator were over. He was no longer expected to fly. His transfer took place in March 1943.

The RAF wanted Rattigan to collaborate with the American novelist and screenwriter Richard Sherman on a film about an airfield, meant to illustrate the collaboration between British and American air forces. The idea had come from William Wyler, the Hollywood director, now mobilised with the rank of Major and working on a documentary in Britain. In the end Wyler returned to America without working on the story that Rattigan and Sherman had come up with. It had grown out of *Flare Path*, but it was to be almost two years before the screenplay would finally reach the screen with Asquith's help.

Another project the RAF had in mind for Rattigan was based on the work of Flying Training Command. Produced entirely within the Film Unit, the film was to be directed by another serving Flight Lieutenant on secondment to the unit, John Boulting. He had worked as a producer with his twin brother, Roy, in the years before the war on films like *Thunder Rock* and *Pastor Hall*. The film was to centre on the life of two young men from the start of their initial training to their final posting to a Lancaster and their participation in a bombing raid. Rattigan wrote the script himself, without the customary collaboration from either Asquith or Tolly de Grunwald, and called it *Journey Together*. Again it was to take almost two years before the film was finished.

In the meantime Rattigan and De Grunwald worked on a script for a film that Harold French and Two Cities had suggested. It was to be called *English Without Tears*, and was planned as a sequel to his first great success. The project did not enthuse him. He could not see the point of bringing Diana back to life, but the fee was welcome, and he accepted de Grunwald's assurance that the job would not take long. This time he chose an English butler and manservant, Gilbey (another of his private jokes, this time on his friendship at Harrow), in the tradition of P. G. Wodehouse's Jeeves, to carry the comedy. Gilbey is the focus for the affections of the fickle but charming Joan Heseltine, who has launched an English class for Allied officers in her own contribution to the war effort. But, like Diana in *French Without Tears*, Joan proceeds to fall in love with a number of the officers she is teaching, including a Pole and a Frenchman, and forgets Gilbey, because he is only a manservant. Nevertheless, when she volunteers herself, she is posted to work for her former butler, now promoted to the rank of Major, and finds that she loves him. Even the neat ending could not conceal the flimsy nature of the piece. It was escapist entertainment, a way of earning money. Privately Rattigan despised it.

On Easter Day, 25 April 1943, the brutal reality of the war intervened when Anthony Goldschmidt was killed in battle. Handsome, brilliant, and a loyal friend since Harrow, though never a lover, Goldschmidt had married after giving up his career as a stockbroker to become a writer. His loss devastated Rattigan, and everyone else who knew him. Newman's strange book on *Flare Path* is dedicated to Goldschmidt's memory, though it never once mentions the name of Terence Rattigan. For a time Rattigan was so distraught that he could not bring himself to work. He and Goldschmidt had been friends for nearly twenty years, used to laughing at each other's jokes, Rattigan mimicking everyone they knew and Goldschmidt collapsing in tears as a result. Rattigan was thirty-one, Goldschmidt a year younger.

Theirs was a friendship that Terence Rattigan was to recreate within a few months in his screenplay for John Boulting's film *Journey*

Together. In his story, two young men share every experience, until finally they find themselves in a rubber dinghy lost in the North Sea after their Lancaster has ditched on its way back from a raid on Berlin. It was Rattigan's way of coping with his loss.

Flare Path continued to run successfully at the Apollo, surviving cast changes in January, February and June 1943. Leueen MacGrath replaced Phyllis Calvert and Griffith Jones Jack Watling. Inquiries for possible production rights were coming in from around the world, in spite of the play's failure on Broadway. The film rights money was safely lodged in Rattigan's bank, Coutts & Co. in the Strand. He was still paying for the upkeep of his parents' house at Pepsal End, including their grocery bills, and providing his father with an allowance for the usual undiscussed purposes, though he seldom went down to see them. Rattigan's affair with Kenneth Morgan had survived far less well. They had argued persistently until Morgan left. Rattigan had reproached him for his persistent unfaithfulness during his tours of duty with Coastal Command, but Morgan had responded by complaining that his famous partner would not let him live with him. Morgan would stump off in a huff, return, then stump off again.

Rattigan's brother Brian was another worry. Now drinking very heavily, he had finally managed to qualify as a solicitor but could not find a place in a London firm. The chip on his shoulder, which he had tried to conceal by his outrageous behaviour at Harrow, had never shifted. He relied on his parents for financial support. Though he did not realise it, indirectly it was Rattigan's generosity that sustained him while he completed his law exams. Like his younger brother, he also showed no inclination to marry, and Frank Rattigan had long since lost the little sympathy he had for his crippled elder son. The Major still had no time for him.

In spite of the financial burdens of his brother and his parents, which he bore without complaint, the success of *Flare Path* meant that Rattigan was considering taking an apartment again. The RAF had confirmed that he was to stay with the Film Unit rather than return to active service as aircrew. As always he favoured Mayfair, or somewhere as close to it as possible, and in June 1943 he took a small set of chambers in Albany, the elegant Georgian building just off Piccadilly that already housed his fellow playwright J.B.Priestley, another of A.D.Peters's clients. Byron had been one of its early inhabitants, as had Gladstone when he was prime minister, the historian Macaulay, and the novelist Compton Mackenzie. Built originally in 1771, and then called York House, it was one of London's most fashionable addresses. Applicants for sets were subject to discreet vetting. 'Mr Rattigan,' the trustees record, 'took a lease for two years in the set of apartments known as K5 from 24 June 1943 to 24 June 1945 at a rent of £250 per annum.'

CHAPTER 12

Shaftesbury Avenue

◆

Mirth resting on earnestness and sadness, as the
rainbow on black tempest: only a right valiant heart
is capable of that.

THOMAS CARLYLE, *On Heroes*

◆

It was at Albany in the second half of 1943 that Rattigan entertained
Puffin Asquith and Keith Newman as regular visitors. Asquith came for
endless discussions, while Newman arrived for the familiar one-hour
sessions, conducted in whispers in a darkened room. It was Albany
too that gave him the setting for his next play. Oscar Wilde had set
the first act of *The Importance of Being Earnest* in 'Algernon Moncreiff's
flat in Half Moon Street, W', just along the road; why shouldn't Rattigan go one better and use 'Albany W' for a whole play?

Rattigan had caught a bad cold during the late spring of 1943, and
acting on his mother's advice to 'go away and relax' and 'write a play
or something' he retired to the White Hart Hotel on the Thames at
Sonning in Berkshire. The experience of the officers' club in Freetown
had convinced him that words and inspiration came to him more easily
in places where he was no more than a visitor, a stranger. Now that
he had established that he was capable of writing more than farce, he
was happy enough to provide the audience with what Binkie Beaumont, echoing Bronson Albery, had taken to insisting that they
wanted, a light comedy: a sequel to *French Without Tears*. Rattigan
struggled with the first draft, tore it up, and wrote the entire play
again: this time back at Albany. Ironically, it was only after he had
moved back there that the play finally came to life.

He would write from shortly after ten in the morning until lunchtime, sitting on a sofa with a lined pad on his knee. At lunchtime he would take a break for two hours, then write again from four until eight, when he had dinner. If he was nearing the end of a play, he would write again after dinner for about an hour, before going to bed. When he was writing, he would try not to drink until six o'clock in the evening, at which time he would allow himself a whisky or two, but he would smoke incessantly throughout the day, the ash often falling on to the lined pad on his knee. The two drafts of the new play took him just ten days to complete. As he wrote later, 'I suppose it would be fair to say that I tried to recreate *French Without Tears*; I certainly set out to try to create some purely escapist laughter for those dark days of the war.'

Binkie Beaumont was delighted. It was just the play he had hoped for, and he wanted to produce it as speedily as possible. His contract demanded he approach Linnit & Dunfee to see if they were prepared to present it with him, and when they agreed – as they did with alacrity – he sent the text of *While the Sun Shines*, as the play was now entitled, to the Lord Chamberlain's office for a licence. Meanwhile Beaumont planned a short provincial tour and a London opening before the end of the year.

As ever, the Lord Chamberlain's office grumbled at some of the language, and also about the poor light the play seemed to throw upon the morals of English officers. The staff demanded a number of changes. But this time Rattigan was less anxious to compromise, and personally wrote back to ask the Lord Chamberlain to reconsider. 'The lines are . . . not inserted for the sake of raising salacious laughter from obvious innuendo . . . I would like to point out this is a light comedy not a farce. It is written and will be produced in exactly the same mood as *French Without Tears*. It is a comedy of character not of situation.' He invited the Lord Chamberlain to send one of his representatives to a final rehearsal of the play if he was in any doubt. After a series of letters a compromise was reached on 18 October 1943, a week before the first performance of its tour. The play opened at the Opera House in Manchester, then moved on to Oxford, Glasgow and Aberdeen before opening at Tennent's own principal theatre, where Beaumont had his famous office, the Globe on Shaftesbury Avenue.

Once again Asquith directed, and once again Newman made a significant contribution, this time suggesting the final curtain line 'Vive la France', when Rattigan was at a loss for one. But Asquith's touch with comedy was less sure on the stage than on celluloid, and at first the production creaked. Michael Wilding and Penelope Dudley Ward, the two principals in the film *English Without Tears*, which Harold French was just finishing, were to star in the new play at Rattigan's specific request (and with Newman's as well as Asquith's permission). Penelope later fell out with Asquith, and was replaced by Jane Baxter, the leading lady from Beaumont's first major success, *George and Margaret*. Meanwhile Beaumont was fretting – and so too was Rattigan – that Asquith might turn into a disaster what looked like a sure-fire hit.

Beaumont's solution, which he had privately agreed upon with Rattigan, was to see if they could persuade Harold French to lend a hand with the direction. Rattigan was designated to speak to French, who had fallen out with him dramatically over *Follow My Leader*. 'Naturally he gave it to me,' he recalls, 'and I said, "No, this is rubbish, not the moment for it, I beg you not to do it", and we had a terrible row about it, which is why I didn't see Rattigan for five or six years.' Now the two met again by chance at the Savoy Hotel, and at Rattigan's request, French went along to a rehearsal of *While the Sun Shines*, 'to see if I could help'. He suggested one or two changes. 'Puffin, I think, knew and didn't mind'; but French refused to take over entirely as the play's director.

Beaumont, still fretting, next asked Noël Coward, whose *Blithe Spirit* was still at the Duchess, to 'look in' on the production. The Master deigned to do so when the play reached Oxford early in November. He was not particularly complimentary, criticising in particular Brenda Bruce, who had come to the company from Birmingham Rep, as a 'dim little actress', and thereby threatening her nerve. Beaumont did nothing to help her, but Rattigan was at his best. He took her out to dinner several times during the four-week tour, and persuaded her to stay rather than disappear back to Birmingham. She responded by falling in love with this charming young man, who always appeared at the theatre in his Flight Lieutenant's uniform. She had no idea of his true sexual tastes, and he did nothing to enlighten her.

Unlikely as it may sound today, many of the young actors and actresses who appeared in a Binkie Beaumont production or a Terence Rattigan play at that time had no idea that either man was homosexual, or that homosexuality was part of the mortar that was holding together the edifice of the production. The designer Michael Weight, for example, also homosexual but not one of Rattigan's lovers, worked on the stage designs for *Flare Path* and *While the Sun Shines*, making the latter look exactly like Rattigan's rooms in Albany. One evening on the way home from the theatre in a taxi, he made a pass at Jack Watling. 'It shows you how innocent I was. He made a dive at me, and I said "You filthy disgusting swine" and hit him.' Watling was so incensed that the following morning he went to see Beaumont, in his office above the Globe. 'I marched in, and Binkie said: "What on earth do you want?" I said "Mr Beaumont, do you realise you've got a homosexual working for you?" It's unbelievable now, but it was absolutely true then. You simply did not realise how many homosexuals worked in the theatre at that time. It was something you didn't talk about.'

Theatrical customs were different then. *While the Sun Shines* opened at the Globe on Christmas Eve 1943, a night no producer would dream of using to launch a play today. But Binkie Beaumont was determined that his first night audience should be in the most festive mood possible, and he was not disappointed. They cheered the final curtain, demanding an appearance from the author, which Rattigan, following Beaumont's own example, refused. Rattigan contented himself with standing at the back of his parents' box and basking in the applause. 'Of all the productions I've been concerned with, this one has for me the happiest memories', Rattigan told a radio audience six years later. 'Even the first night was happy, and a first night is usually a rather miserable occasion for a nervous author.' There were no papers the following morning, but when the reviews appeared after Christmas they were almost uniformly good.

Ivor Brown told the *Observer*'s readers:

An obedient first night audience was entranced by the humours of a British duke astray in Albany and the French language. He is, incidentally, trying to marry his daughter to a two-million pound earl, now a naval rating . . . it will be an enormous success. The humours of an English earl, American airman and French sailor sharing a bed, while a brace of ladies wait in the offing, are war-time winners without a doubt.

Philip Page in the *Daily Mail* agreed, enthusing that Rattigan's new play 'caused so much laughter at the Globe Theatre on Christmas Eve that it is likely to run even longer than his play (now in its second year) at the theatre next door'. *Flare Path* was still running at the Apollo. And the two theatres – each with the name Terence Rattigan in lights above their entrances – were less than a hundred yards apart.

To Rattigan's enormous relief, most of the reviews were raves – 'not only the wittiest play in London, it is also the funniest', 'this gay farce', 'a dramatist of genius' – although one or two reviews hinted that he was to some extent retracing old steps. The *Manchester Guardian* was particularly impressed. 'Mr Rattigan's light-hearted text . . . has the inspired lucidity and economy of P.G.Wodehouse at his best.'

Rattigan was astonished, however, by the reaction of his old adversary James Agate, who began his review in the *Sunday Times* by comparing him to Oscar Wilde.

About 'An Ideal Husband' on its first production Mr Shaw wrote: 'It is useless to describe a play which has no thesis: which is, in the purest integrity, a play and nothing less.' And about its author: 'In a certain sense Mr Wilde is our only playwright. He plays with everything: with wit, with philosophy, with drama, with actors and audience, with the whole theatre.' The same might be said today of Mr Rattigan, a playwright with the brains not to take himself seriously.

Agate concluded: 'Mr Rattigan's one failure is the French lieutenant who, with an eye to the girl, argues the case for passion as the proper basis for marriage . . . What, however, is one failure against six major successes in a play whose test is delight not truth? And this piece is delightful, a little masterpiece of tingling impertinence.' Rattigan's stunned comment to Asquith was: 'One cannot grow from nothing into Oscar Wilde between one light comedy and the next – especially if the second has been modelled on the first.'

None of the critics made anything of the fact that when the play opens the Earl of Harpenden's bed is occupied by a young American officer, Joe Mulvaney, who is mistaken for a girl. Though the three young men at the centre of the plot, the Englishman, the American and the Frenchman, are all in pursuit of the same girl, just as they were in *French Without Tears*, so too do they make no secret of the fact that they share the same bed. Most homosexuals knew only too well that it was easy enough to pick up young servicemen during the blackout in London. Rattigan himself rarely indulged in the practice, but many of his acquaintances did. They would have got the joke: even if the critics didn't.

While the Sun Shines, just as all his other plays had done, drew on Rattigan's own experiences. The character of the Duke of Ayr and Stirling, played by Ronald Squire, for example, was a portrait of his father, Frank. The borrowing, the gambling, the taste for pretty young girls, the daft business ventures, the boundless enthusiasm for life, were all among Frank's traits. During the next ten years Frank Rattigan was to turn up in a number of different guises in his son's plays, but his appearance this time, which hugely amused Rattigan's friends, remained a private joke.

The *Daily Mirror* certainly did not catch on to Rattigan's jokes, private or otherwise. Hardly had the play opened than they complained

at the use of the word 'trollop' to describe the amateur tart Mabel
Crum, played by Brenda Bruce. Indeed they complained so forcefully
that the Lord Chamberlain's office felt compelled to send someone to
see the play, to see if there were grounds to the complaint. In the event
they found there weren't, and accused the *Mirror* of 'a cheap newspaper
stunt'. The publicity did the first weeks of business no harm whatever.

By the beginning of February 1944, *While the Sun Shines* had replaced
Flare Path as the most popular Rattigan play in London. The RAF
drama had begun to run out of steam and Beaumont decided to close
it at the end of that month. It had played for almost a year and a
half, and notched up 670 performances, including three matinées every
week. It had earned its author more than £15,000 during that time, in
addition to £20,000 from the film rights, and was to provide an income
for months to come during the provincial tour. The foreign productions
brought in even more royalties. The play's success convinced Rattigan
that he had, at last, turned the financial corner, and could celebrate by
buying a Rolls-Royce.

As *While the Sun Shines* settled into the Globe, for what seemed
certain to be a long run, Rattigan went back to the two film scripts he
had been working on the year before. *Journey Together*, which he was
writing for the RAF Film Unit and his fellow Flight Lieutenant, John
Boulting, was now needed urgently. Boulting had managed to persuade the American star Edward G. Robinson to play a small part in
the film, and he would be available only during that summer. The
other script, about Anglo-American collaboration, which had been
shelved when William Wyler had returned to the United States, had
been revived, and Rattigan, de Grunwald, and Asquith, who was now
to direct, were to work on it together.

Rattigan told his new publisher, Hamish (Jamie) Hamilton, with
whom he had begun to play squash from time to time, 'As you get to
know me better – your plain duty, as my publisher, but my pleasure
– you will learn to recognise and forgive a shocking reluctance on my
part ever to put pen to paper.' It was one reason why he had forced himself to leave Albany and retire to what he called 'the hideous uncomfortable country pub I have incarcerated myself in' – the White Hart Hotel
at Sonning – to work. 'I won't leave my prison,' he wrote to Jamie on 6
April, 'until I have finished two film scripts (official) and a play
(unofficial). It's for Gertie Lawrence, though she probably won't like it.'

Journey Together, the story of two young men joining the RAF and
training to become pilots, was to star Richard Attenborough and Jack
Watling as the young men, as well as David Tomlinson and Ronald
Squire. There was to be only one female star in the cast, Bessie Love,

from *Broadway Melody*, whom John Boulting had persuaded to play Edward G. Robinson's wife, and who – like Robinson – was appearing for nothing. The film was shot at Pinewood in July and August, in the wake of the Normandy landings. By that time London was suffering attack from the German V1 rockets, but even this seemed to have no effect on the size of the audiences for *While the Sun Shines*. General (later Field Marshal) Montgomery had been to see the play in April, going backstage afterwards to tell Michael Wilding how much he had enjoyed it. Soon afterwards one of the 'doodlebugs' landed on the Queen's Theatre, right next door. Even that did not deter the audience.

Unfortunately the same was not true of the theatre audiences in New York. There the show opened on 19 September 1944 at the Lyceum on 45th Street, presented by Max Gordon and directed by the legendary George Kaufman. Columbia Pictures, who had bought the screen rights for £30,000, also put up $15,000 towards the cost of staging the show. There had been a short tour before the opening, starting at Princeton. *Variety* had liked it there, calling it 'escapist fare of the first order. The laughs roll along with amazing rapidity, and no small credit for that must go to George S. Kaufman'. The entertainment industry's trade paper came to the conclusion that the play 'should keep on shining for many a moon'.

It did no such thing. Lewis Nathan killed the play with his review in the *New York Times*. '*While the Sun Shines* is not a good play basically, for it is contrived as though by a ruler, pencil and a pair of shears.' There were just thirty-nine performances. Terence Rattigan's fourth play on Broadway was his fourth Broadway flop.

Back in England, it was back to work with Asquith and de Grunwald. Reminiscing some years later, Rattigan described how Asquith was forever 'discoursing omnisciently and with zeal on subjects ranging from Chelsea's new centre forward to the obscurer seventeenth-century composers', while de Grunwald sat on one side, chain-smoking, but equally volatile, 'setting himself on fire twice', imitating Winston Churchill 'seven times' and using the telephone 'sixteen times' in the course of an average session. As for Rattigan himself, 'I had, apparently, been mainly occupied with practising golf shots with a walking stick, while occasionally varying this activity with an unimpressive display of new found ability to juggle with three apples.' Yet their peculiar collaboration continued to be extremely effective. 'I can only assume that in an association as close and harmonious as ours has been,' Rattigan wrote, 'it is possible that we have developed a form of mental shorthand which saves both time and tempers and allows us a chance of combining pleasure with even the most harassing business.'

During the V1 raids in 1944 the trio met for script conferences at Rattigan's chambers, K5 at Albany. De Grunwald and he had agreed to listen out for the rockets to cut off, the silence that was a sign that they were about to drop in the uncomfortably close vicinity. From time to time they would rush into the corridor if one seemed about to fall on them. On one evening Asquith was, as usual, pacing the floor and gesticulating wildly, when a V1 duly cut out above them. Rattigan and de Grunwald rushed into the hall, and fell on top of one another. The bomb landed near by. Returning to the room, they found Asquith still walking up and down, unaware that they hadn't been listening. 'This is no time for games,' he told them sternly. 'We're supposed to be getting on with the script.'

As 1944 drew to a close, it became increasingly apparent that by the time the script they were working on was made into a film the war in Europe might well have ended, and that as a result its theme of Anglo-American collaboration would lose some of its point. Rattigan suggested that they should turn the whole story into a flashback. 'We eventually decided to begin the picture with a shot of a bare derelict airfield and say on the sound track, "This was an airfield."' It was a simple solution, but it worked. *The Way to the Stars* has since been acknowledged as one of the finest British war films.

The cast was to be headed by Michael Redgrave and John Mills, with Trevor Howard, Jean Simmons (in her first film role) and David Tomlinson in support. Redgrave, who was to play Flight Lieutenant Archdale, an airman killed in action early in the film, was enormously impressed by Rattigan's script, calling it 'a marvel of its kind', and explaining, 'There are scripts, now and then, where every line seems so right that you do not have to learn them. It is enough to repeat the words a few times for every line to fall into place . . . The contrast of characters and situation were masterly. And his story contained a strong, clear idea . . . the conflict in temperament betwen the British and Americans in time of war.'

One crucial addition to the script, again suggested by Rattigan, was to include John Pudney's moving poem, 'For Johnny', which had first been published in the collection of poems *Dispersal Point* in 1942. In the finished film it is memorably recited by John Mills as he walks across the airfield, tracked the whole time by the camera. Out of shot he was tracked by Asquith too – who was so overcome by the perform-ance that he walked into a wall.

> *Do not despair*
> *For Johnny-head-in-air;*

He sleeps as sound
As Johnny underground.

Fetch out no shroud
For Johnny-in-the-cloud;
And keep your tears
For him in after years.

Better by far
For Johnny-the-bright-star,
To keep your head,
And see his children fed.

The extra emotional dimension the poem introduced into the film helped lift it beyond conventional propaganda, giving extra depth to its sense of mortality and Rattigan's evocation of the lives of the young pilots. Asquith was deeply affected during the filming, and often in tears, which he called 'suffering from the floods'. He was also drinking heavily, to the alarm of some of the crew, but solved this problem in his own particular style. He would take himself off to a transport café called Joe's, on the Great North Road near Catterick, when the pressures of the set, or life, grew too great. The wrap party for *The Way to the Stars* was duly held at Joe's, with passing lorry drivers and lads from the local racing stables welcomed as guests alongside the crew. Asquith, in boiler suit and black leather belt, was in his element, and Joe's Café became his bolt-hole for the next twenty-five years. Whenever he stayed there he would get up at five in the morning to help serve breakfast with the eponymous Joe, an ex-regimental sergeant-major, and his wife, Rita. Then Asquith would cycle round the district delivering newspapers. But the point was that when he was there he did not touch alcohol.

Rattigan now turned to revising the play he had told Jamie Hamilton in April was intended 'for Gertrude Lawrence'. Initially called *Less Than Kind*, its central characters had been conceived with that inimitable actress firmly in his mind. The leading man, he thought, could be 'someone like Cecil Parker'. But when Lawrence, the star of *Private Lives*, received the first draft, with a note from Beaumont that it 'was the play Terence Rattigan said he was going to write for you', she professed to know nothing whatever about it, and declined even to look at it.

The plot of the play centres on a young man returning from Canada to discover that his father has died and his mother is now living with a wealthy, but married, industrialist, Sir John Fletcher, who also happens to be a member of the War Cabinet. The boy, Michael Brown, who has grown up into an enthusiastic socialist, is horrified, not only that his mother, Olivia, is living in sin, but also that she is living with a man other than his father.

The parallels with *Hamlet* are clear enough. The boy broods, indulges his antic disposition, takes to wearing a black tie and an 'inky cloak', studies a book on poisoning, invites Sir John and his mother to a play called *Murder in the Family*, and confronts his mother – in Rattigan's equivalent of the 'closet scene' – with her betrayal of his father's memory. When his mother finally decides to leave Sir John's comfortable Westminster house in favour of a small flat near Baron's Court – 'Puffin's Corner' (another of Rattigan's little jokes) – the boy realises that he is being ridiculous, and there is no reason why he shouldn't get along with Sir John, whose wealth could help him influence a new girlfriend.

The prototype Michael was, of course, Rattigan himself. He too was a man who had struggled to retain his socialist principles in the face of the attractions of wealth and glamour, and, in the end, accepted the fact that money helped. He too was tempted to pose for effect, and he too felt that he had abandoned his high-flown principles. Rattigan too had accepted his father's less than committed attitude to marriage, and had seen his mother's desperate reaction. The relationship between the young man and his father provided the central force of the play, as it was for so many of his plays in the two decades to come.

Athough much dismayed by Gertrude Lawrence's rejection, Rattigan now had a stroke of luck. In the early summer of 1944, a 'doodlebug' fell on the Aldwych Theatre at the end of the Strand, near the flat of his friend and fellow homosexual, the composer Ivor Novello. As a result, Novello immediately realised that Lynn Fontanne and her husband Alfred Lunt, who were about to open in a new play there, would now be without a home for it. He also knew that the Lunts, who were based in the United States but were nevertheless an enormous attraction for London theatre audiences, had no intention of cutting short their time in Britain. What they needed was a new play – quickly. Novello suggested they might like to look at *Less Than Kind*.

Beaumont encouraged the idea, and arranged a meeting between Rattigan and the theatre's most famous acting couple. Rattigan was enthralled by the plump Lunt and his beautiful wife. They represented everything in the theatre he most admired. They were effortlessly glamorous, fêted in the United States – which Rattigan was still determined to conquer – and virtually guaranteed an audience for any play in which they appeared. After a couple of days, Lunt rang Rattigan at Albany. He and his wife 'would be proud to do your play', providing Rattigan would be agreeable to making one or two adjustments which he had in mind. And Lunt would direct it himself. Rattigan telephoned Beaumont at the Globe with the news. Both men were thrilled: the Lunts in a new play by Terence Rattigan, whose *Flare Path* had just started its post-West End tour in Brighton, and who still had *While the Sun Shines* playing on Shaftesbury Avenue. The new play was certain to be a hit. They were right, but not before it had been changed dramatically.

There was no question that the version of *Less Than Kind* Alfred Lunt had been given was written for a female star. The part of the dentist's widow, Olivia, was larger and far more significant than any other part – with the exception of her son, Michael. The role of Sir John, which Lunt would have to play himself, was essentially secondary. Lunt was determined to change that, even though he confided to the author, 'Sometimes Lynn has the play, and sometimes it's my play.' The truth was he wanted the balance changed.

'I didn't realise,' Rattigan was to admit subsequently, 'that he was asking me to write a new play. But he was right. In the end I wrote a far better play because of his suggestions. But at the time it was a rather trying experience.' 'Trying' was an understatement. Under Lunt's delicate nudging, an unlikeable Sir John became an amiable, indeed lovable, Sir John, and a central figure in the plot. And the play had been given a new title to mark its new manifestation. It was now to be called *Love in Idleness*. Alfred Lunt and Lynn Fontanne had wheedled and bullied Rattigan until he had created the play they wanted. It was a painful process.

In a letter to his mother Vera, Rattigan described the atmosphere during rehearsals and the process of rewriting as 'hysteria', which was 'apparently the only atmosphere in which they can work happily'. The experience did not dismay him unduly, he was used to it. It was, he told her, 'reminiscent of John with the *Tale of Two Cities*, only worse, because there are two of them'. For all that, Rattigan believed Lynn Fontanne was 'going to be at least three times as good as Gertrude Lawrence would have been and about twice as good as I thought anyone could ever be in the part. She brings out the comedy and at the same time very touching moments. She is playing exactly the part I wrote, and I could not get it played half as well by any other actress in the world.'

As for Lunt, 'Practically all the re-writing at the moment,' Rattigan wrote to his mother, 'is concerned with his part, and practically everything that has been done is a big improvement, though of course it is nearly all at the expense of the boy, of whose part they are both a little jealous.'

Rattigan described the experience of watching Lunt direct as 'exciting' and 'a refreshing change from Puffin Asquith', but admitted to Vera that

> The boy, poor little brat, is having a terrible time . . . Alfred's way of rehearsing him is to take him over three lines in three hours, finally reducing him to tears and hysteria. It is hard to see whether he will be good or not, but I am willing to bet that if he survives the next two months he is going to become the best juvenile actor on the English stage. If he doesn't survive we already have a long list of others to choose from.

The young man in question was Brian Nissen, who had just appeared alongside Anton Walbrook in the film *Watch on the Rhine*, and had also had a part in Olivier's *Henry V*.

The changes Alfred Lunt agreed with Rattigan were so extensive that Binkie Beaumont felt that *Love in Idleness* must be resubmitted to the Lord Chamberlain for a new licence, even though one had been granted to it as *Less Than Kind* in August. The Lord Chamberlain's office, which had been evacuated from St James's Palace to the safety of Windsor Castle, noted that the play 'does not differ in construction' but that now Sir John 'no longer resorts to the somewhat undignified expedient of persuading his wife Diana to vamp Michael'. In the revised version the job of seduction was passed to 'Miss Sylvia Hart', who does not appear, but who is equally revealed to be 'no angel'. 'The result is equally successful in humanising the "stern moralist."' A licence was duly granted on 22 November 1944, five days before the Lunts performed it for the first time, in Liverpool.

The critics failed to enthuse, but the audience were enthralled. Once again, the ever-cautious Binkie Beaumont, who had persuaded Noël Coward to come in with him as an investor, asked his friend to go and see the play on tour. And once again Coward did so, and was scathing about it. No sooner had the performance finished than he stormed backstage to tell the Lunts not to bother with it, and to abandon all thoughts of a London production. The advice was hardly unbiased. The only London première the Lunts had appeared in so far had been a play of Coward's own. He was certainly a little jealous that Rattigan had had two plays on Shaftesbury Avenue almost next door to each other for several months that same year, and that the achievement was about to be repeated. He was also jealous of Rattigan's growing reputation as a wit, and was not anxious to see his own reputation in that department challenged by the author of *French Without Tears*, who happened to be twelve years his junior. Coward's pre-eminence in the London theatre was under threat.

First in their dressing-rooms, and then later at the Adelphi Hotel, the Lunts listened as Coward systematically set about destroying the play. But his strategy did not work. First Lynn Fontanne and then Alfred Lunt took Rattigan aside to reassure him that 'no matter what Noël might say' they were going to do the play, and the following morning they assured him they were still very happy with it. The episode only intensified Rattigan's suspicion of Coward. Rattigan did not even see himself as belonging to the same generation – indeed that had been part of the inspiration for *After the Dance* – and he certainly did not consider that Coward had any right to make sweeping generalis-ations about the theatre or the state of England. He also thought Coward a pompous hypocrite, with his patriotic films and his private homosexuality. Rattigan had no wish to be bracketed with 'The Master' in any discussion of the state of the theatre. He saw himself as a serious playwright, not one who wanted to be remembered for no more than witty sayings and songs. Nor did he enjoy being criticised by the same man who had incorrectly predicted the year before that *While the Sun Shines* would not work.

But Rattigan also knew how deeply Beaumont was influenced by Coward's opinions, which might have stopped *Love in Idleness* even reaching London if the Lunts had not supported it. The fact that they did was all-important, and Rattigan would remain eternally grateful. 'There was far too much ballyhoo about the play before it opened,' he wrote to his mother. The Lunts 'laughed at me and told me that they had never felt so confident in a play in all their twenty-five years together'. But, he added, 'You had better touch wood when you read that, as I am doing now.'

Rattigan's confidence in himself and his work had, however, increased dramatically since the dark days before *Flare Path*; and Keith Newman's influence had consequently dimmed, making his visits to Albany far less frequent. The invitations to dinner and to country weekends, the stream of congratulatory letters and telegrams, the con-stant requests from actors and actresses to 'write a play for me', allowed Rattigan to bask in the acclaim. But adulation made it harder, not easier, for him to make friends he could trust. In private he was lonely. Peter Osborn had disappeared into the Navy. Kenneth Morgan, though he had taken to reappearing from time to time, could not be relied upon. And Rattigan did not like touring the homosexual clubs in London at

night in search of company. To any young man who even appeared
to like him, therefore, Rattigan was almost embarrassingly generous,
even though they were never to become his lover. He would give
presents of champagne or gold cigarette cases to people he knew only
slightly. Equally the first night presents he gave to every member of
the cast of his plays were extravagant – a perfectly chosen book, a
delicate watercolour, an engraved decanter. They were the gestures of
a man intent on being liked.

It is not difficult to understand why Rattigan was particularly generous to young fresh-faced actors. One who took his fancy at the time
was Bryan Forbes, whose name had been put forward for the role of
Teddy Graham in the tour of *Flare Path*. With the boyish looks that so
much appealed to him, the young Forbes was taken under Rattigan's
wing. Now a successful writer and director, Forbes later wrote, 'Terry
became my mentor and very close friend, though possibly, not as close
as he would have wished.' Certainly Rattigan wooed him with presents,
and persistent invitations to Albany. 'Terry not only encouraged me
as an actor, but was immensely helpful in guiding my attempts to
become a writer,' Forbes says. So much so, indeed, that he persuaded
A.D.Peters to take the young actor on to his books. He also sent a
novel that Forbes had written, entitled *Nourished in the Grass*, to his
own publisher, Jamie Hamilton.

In a covering letter to Hamilton, sent from Albany in October 1944,
Rattigan explained: 'I should very much like you to give an opinion
. . . I should imagine from reading it that it is unsaleable in its present
form, but he would principally like to have an expert opinion. It is, as
you will see, unfinished, but when I read it through – very hurriedly
I admit – I thought it showed in places remarkable promise.' Hamilton
duly received two rather unencouraging readers' reports, and politely
returned the novel, but this did not diminish Rattigan's enthusiasm.
He had even shown the young actor an early draft of *Less Than Kind*,
briefly entitled *A Little Less Than Kind*, and suggested that he might
be the right young man to play Michael – not least because of Forbes's
clearly heterosexual inclinations. An offer to play the part with the
Lunts on tour and in the West End never materialised. But their friendship was to last for some years.

Rattigan's Albany chambers must have bewitched many young men.
'Period furnishings, silver on the table, the rich food he managed to
serve even in wartime, wine, a butler – to my eyes it all seemed something out of a film,' Forbes wrote later. The mixture of theatrical gossip
and high camp was intoxicating for the young men who shared his
tastes. As one homosexual friend of Rattigan's put it: 'We really did

use to say ridiculous things like "We must get Mrs Car out of Mrs Garage and go and have dinner with Mrs Beaumont at Mrs Savoy."' Certainly Forbes, who was more sophisticated than the the young Jack Watling, was to conclude: 'Nobody who grew up in the theatrical scene during the war and post-war periods could be unaware of the homosexual dominance exercised by, amongst others, Coward, Novello, Rattigan and, of course, the ubiquitous Hugh "Binkie" Beaumont.'

Whatever intentions Rattigan may have had towards Forbes, not every young actor who appeared in his plays was the subject of such intense attentions. George Cole, who had played Percy in *Flare Path* since the start of its run, was never to receive either an invitation to Albany or a generous present. 'I never knew him socially at all,' Cole recalls. 'The only correspondence I had was a pencilled note, telling me that he couldn't hear me at the back of the dress circle.' Perhaps fortunately for him, Cole was not blessed with quite such a wide, round schoolboy's face.

On the evening of 29 September 1944, however, Rattigan was to meet a man to fill the void left by Morgan. He was invited to dinner by Juliet Duff in 'her little flat stuffed with French furniture and bibelots'. The words are those of another of her guests that evening, the American-born British Member of Parliament, Sir Henry 'Chips' Channon, destined to become Terence Rattigan's great friend and mentor in the years that followed. Channon recorded in his diary: 'Also there, Sibyl Colefax and Master Terence Rattigan, and we sparkled over the burgundy. I like Rattigan enormously, and feel a new friendship has begun. He has a flat in Albany.'

'Master Terence Rattigan' was no accidental phrase, for Channon, though married to Lady Honor Guinness, eldest daughter of the Earl of Iveagh, since 1933, was notably homosexual. Urbane in public and uninhibited in private, he had been befriended in his youth in Paris by both Jean Cocteau and Marcel Proust, and had emerged from the experience with a consuming interest not only in writers but also in the affairs of the world. Of lunch with Puffin's father in 1924, for example, he wrote:

Mr Asquith, benign, beautiful and patriarchal, presided at the end of the long table and talked, in his clear bell-like Jacobean English, with a wealth of metaphor. Mrs Asquith, distraite, smoked and read the papers during luncheon, and occasionally said something startling like, apropos of spiritualism, 'I always knew the living talked rot, but it is nothing to the nonsense the dead talk.'

Beneath all the gloss, 'the iron butterfly', as he was nicknamed, was prone to the same bouts of depression and self-doubt that plagued Rattigan. He too hid his uncertainty behind a glamorous, almost embarrassingly charming exterior and an extravagant lifestyle. As Lady Diana Cooper was to say of him, 'Never was there a surer or more enlivening friend . . . He installed the mighty in his gilded chairs and exalted the humble. He made the old and the tired, the young and the strong, shine beneath his thousand lighted candles. Without stint he gave of his riches and his compassion.' Some of those riches and some of that compassion he was to direct towards Terence Rattigan.

First he showered him with presents – a gold cigarette box from Cartier, an Aubusson carpet, an Augustus John drawing. And no clearer indication that the friendship was reciprocated could have been produced than the fact that on the first night of *Love in Idleness*, which took place at the Lyric Theatre in Shaftesbury Avenue on 20 December 1944, Sir Henry 'Chips' Channon sat in a box with Frank and Vera Rattigan and their son. In a matter of weeks Chips had become a central part of Rattigan's life, so much so that Rattigan dedicated the play to him.

Another homosexual, the notoriously bitchy Labour MP Tom Driberg, later reported in his autobiography:

Chips was one of the better known homosexuals in London, and he was rich enough to rent almost any young man he fancied – a handsome German princeling, a celebrated English playwright. His seduction of the playwright was almost like the wooing of Danaë by Zeus: every day the playwright found delivered to his door, a splendid present . . . In the end, of course, he gave in, saying apologetically to his friends 'How can one not?'

Driberg was distinctly jealous.

Noël Coward and Puffin's mother, Margot Asquith, were also in the theatre that evening, sitting in the stalls, as were the dancer and choreographer Robert Helpmann, the actress Vivien Leigh, and Duff Cooper, Lady Diana's husband and a member of the War Cabinet. It was another of Beaumont's glittering first nights, once again timed to catch its audience in good humour with the approach of Christmas. The travails of Liverpool and the penance of the rewrites were things of the past as the curtain rose on Lynn Fontanne describing a world that Rattigan had come to know even more intimately through his new friendship with Chips: the world of Westminster politics and the smart London dinner party.

It appeared at first, according to Beaumont's account, that the Lunts were prepared to play only for three months in London, as they were anxious to do a short tour for servicemen before taking their new plays back with them to Broadway. So this was the one play that every firstnighter wanted to see before any other. As a result the first night reception was the warmest that any play by Terence Rattigan had yet received. The reviews were almost as encouraging.

'An accepted wit has but to say "Pass the Mustard" to set the table in a roar,' reported the *Daily Mail* the next morning. 'Mr Alfred Lunt and Miss Lynn Fontanne are accepted players of comedy, and with their consummate art they made the performance of Mr Terence Rattigan's *Love in Idleness* a riot of laughter at the Lyric Theatre last night. Almost every remark was greeted with anything from a titter to a deafening guffaw.' The *Times* critic disliked the play, however, accusing the author of being 'insufficiently inventive'. But the London *Evening Standard* called it 'a most satisfying and dazzling piece of theatre, as last night's audience testified'. Even James Agate was impressed, calling the Lunts 'superb in the first act and good in the second; if their performance crumbled away at the end it was merely because the comedy had lost its sincerity'. Ivor Brown in the *Observer* thought it Rattigan's 'best piece'.

Now Terence Rattigan once more had two plays side by side on Shaftesbury Avenue, to vie with Coward's *Blithe Spirit* and *Private Lives*, which Binkie Beaumont was also presenting in the West End. Rattigan and Chips went to the first night party of *Love in Idleness* together. Noël contrived to miss it.

CHAPTER 13

A Secret Life

◆

It is the bright, the bold, the transparent who are
cleverest among those who are silent; their ground
is down so deep that even the brightest water does
not betray it.

NIETZSCHE, *Thus Spoke Zarathustra*

◆

To engage in any form of sexual relations with another man was, in 1945, to risk scandal, ruin and a period in prison. In the privacy of their own world, a world which understood and sympathised with the pressures that that fear brought, they could relax. But even there every practising homosexual had to exercise a caution that no heterosexual of the time had to. He risked his livelihood and reputation in every relationship that he entered into. No one understood that better than Terence Rattigan.

Homosexuals took refuge in their secret world, in private parties, and in private clubs. There they could relax, there too they might meet a companion who might be prepared to spend the night with them. It was a world unknown to millions, and certainly unknown to the vast majority of London's theatregoers. Yet the theatre was one section of British life which welcomed homosexuals, so much so that they had become a significant force.

'There were two different managements in London in those days, and you worked for one or the other. The heterosexual one was Linnit & Dunfee, and the homosexual one was H.M.Tennent. If you worked for one, you usually didn't work for the other. If you'd worked for Binkie, Linnit and Dunfee were convinced that you were of the other persuasion, and vice versa,' one actor suggested fifty years later. 'The old story was that the reason Binkie's lift was so small at the Globe – just room for two – was that he liked to find out if the new young men who came to visit him were interested or not.' Other actors fundamentally disagree. 'Binkie wouldn't cast anyone because of their sexuality,' one insists. 'He was only interested in getting the best possible people for the play.'

It is certainly true, however, that some young actors were simply too naïve to realise the significance of the suggestions that were sometimes subtly – and sometimes not so subtly – made to them. Certainly Jack Watling had not been aware of the significance of Rattigan's homosexuality, nor of Keith Newman's attraction to him, when he had first auditioned for *Flare Path*. Bryan Forbes also appears not to have been aware of the implications of Rattigan's interest in him, at least when they began. The experiences clearly affected some actors' lives, however. Watling admits today that when Newman started writing him love letters 'it gave me a nervous breakdown', and he was discharged from the RAF with 'nervous anxiety'.

On the other hand, some young actors took advantage of their looks, and the fear of a scandal that haunted their new-found 'friends', to exploit their position and obtain the best parts. 'You could say there was a gay casting couch on Shaftesbury Avenue in those days, and more than one young man on the rise took every chance to exploit it,' says one elderly actor now. Not all those young actors cared to recall their homosexual adventures in wartime London once their careers were firmly established. It was an unspoken bond, a shared confidence, that bound the theatre of the day together. But it was not to be discussed, or shared, with outsiders.

Had she known any of this Mrs Vera Rattigan would have been horrified. Her son, at least, thought so, and his efforts to ensure that she never found out even went so far as to tell one newspaper interviewer in 1945 that he intended to follow Arnold Bennett's example and not marry until he was at least forty – which gave him six years' grace. To his mother he remained the elegant, charming, generous son who had provided her with a house in Bedfordshire, plus an allowance for his father (and an unstinting appetite for the Major's 'bargain' antiques), and was now providing them both with a cook and a butler to look after them. Rattigan did not visit them all that often, but when they came to visit him in Albany he seemed exactly as he had always seemed, impeccably dressed and endlessly charming. The fact that there were rather more male than female guests at his parties was a mere coincidence.

Terence Rattigan was careful to avoid the squalid encounters that had marred the lives of some other writers of his day. But the price he paid for doing so was an oppressive self-consciousness, an awareness that no one who might be dangerous, or indiscreet, should ever be allowed into his private world. He could not afford to make the slightest mistake, for that would mean disagrace, not just for him, but also for his parents; and he was determined they should be protected. So when he introduced the young men who were his lovers to his mother, as he often did, it was simply as 'my dear friend'. 'Vera did not suspect anything,' one lover explained later. 'She never did.' She met Kenneth Morgan, for example, and Peter Osborn, but never realised that either was more to her son than simply a 'dear friend'.

But the world that Rattigan fought so ferociously to conceal from his family and from many of his professional colleagues had one singular advantage – it helped to fuel his inspiration. As the critic John Barber of the *Daily Telegraph*, himself a friend of Rattigan's, was to write many years later: 'Not to see how Rattigan mirrored and indulged the middle-class fear of sex is to ignore a fundamental part of his appeal.'

Terence Rattigan kept his own passions strictly, and relentlessly, under control, and as a result understood instinctively the desire to conceal emotion that existed in the English theatre audience of the day. He harnessed the pressures that concealment brought upon him, and by doing so identified himself with a generation and a class of English men and women who were only too used to doing exactly the same thing, albeit in heterosexual rather than homosexual life. The overwhelmingly middle-class audience for the West End theatre in the years before and during the Second World War was often uncomfortable with the loss of control that passionate sex implied. The desire not to reveal passion, not to give way to its worst excesses, certainly inhabited *After the Dance*, *While the Sun Shines* and *Love in Idleness*. It was to emerge in Rattigan's work even more vividly in the years to come, as he came to present all sexual passion as doomed. As John Barber reminded his readers in 1979, in one comedy, passion is 'sneered at' as 'white hot burning thingummy'.

One man who certainly helped Rattigan to view passion as something to be kept in its place was Chips Channon. Theirs may have been a sexual union, but it was one conducted at the most light-hearted level. There was no room in Chips's great house at 5 Belgrave Square, or indeed at K5 in Albany, for soulful declarations of undying love. This was an affair between two men anxious to preserve their public reputations, both equally certain that life had to be conducted in a civilised manner at all times. Rattigan liked to joke to his friends, 'Oh,

for God's sake get him drunk so that I don't have to go to bed with him.'
What he liked was the MP's style, and his friends. He was impressed by
the famous people Channon attracted to Belgrave Square, and he relished
being introduced as 'that celebrated English playwright'.

Rattigan's relationship with Channon was less the hurly-burly of the
chaise-longue than the calm of the marriage bed. Neither man wanted
his emotions stirred too greatly, his life disrupted too dramatically;
there were more important matters to concern them. They delighted
in each other's company, and laughed at each other's jokes, but they
were never star-crossed lovers. Neither were they entirely faithful to
one another. But it was Channon's encouragement, as the war came
to an end, that helped Rattigan's confidence flower. Channon finally
convinced him that he was no 'one hit wonder'.

The reviews for *The Way to the Stars* helped. The film opened shortly
after the end of the war in Europe in May 1945 to extensive publicity
– 'Sky-High Entertainment' the posters proclaimed – but it was the
critical reception that mattered. Dilys Powell complimented Rattigan
on his skilful script, adding, 'its true quality lies in its portrayal of
individual character'; while the *Daily Mail*'s critic commented that
Flight Lieutenant Rattigan's talent 'has carried him in wartime to the
ubiquity on stage and screen held during the last war by Somerset
Maugham'.

By this time Rattigan was working on a new play. Inspiration had
come from an article entitled 'Law in Action' by the formidable and
famously irascible American critic Alexander Woolcott, which had
been given to Rattigan by the Lunts. In it Woolcott described the case
of a thirteen-year-old naval cadet, George Archer-Shee, who had been
expelled from the Naval College at Osborne in 1908 over the alleged
theft of a postal order. Rattigan sensed that it would make a drama.
De Grunwald had been nagging him for some time to work on a
script about British justice for Puffin to direct, and a new book on the
Archer-Shee trial brought the case back into Rattigan's mind. He gave
de Grunwald and Asquith the book, but neither was all that impressed,
de Grunwald saying he thought it was dull.

Rattigan disagreed. 'The facts of the Archer-Shee case . . . had so
fascinated and moved me that unlike many ideas that will peacefully
wait in the storeroom of the mind until their time for emergence has
come, it demanded instant expression.' If de Grunwald did not want
to use the material as the basis for a film, he would write it as a play.
Asquith was sceptical, doubting that Rattigan would be able to make
the trial of the boy, which provided the climax to the story, work as

drama on the stage. Rattigan was certain that he could. If Puffin did not like the result then he would get a director who did.

The facts were fascinating. When the young Archer-Shee was expelled from the Royal Naval College at Osborne, he furiously denied that he had ever stolen a postal order from another boy. His father believed his son and protested, first to the Commander of the College, then to the Admiralty itself. His protests were in vain. Archer-Shee could not even bring a case against the college to court, because the college's decision was final. Osborne, as part of the Royal Navy, was the King's domain, and the King – at that time – could do no wrong. Archer-Shee's only possible redress was to appeal for what was known as a Petition of Right, which if it were accepted and endorsed by the Home Office and the Attorney-General could be put before the Crown. The King could then, as an act of grace, grant the Petition – and a legal case could come to court. The basis of the Petition of Right was the simple principle, 'Let Right Be Done.' Rattigan saw that as the basis for drama.

Once again, the tension between a father and his son provided Rattigan with a focus. Archer-Shee Senior had asked the celebrated King's Counsel Sir Edward Carson, who, as a younger man, had led for the prosecution at the Oscar Wilde trials, to handle the case. It was the father's fight to 'Let Right Be Done' that created the drama in Rattigan's mind. And, as ever, the characters rather than the precise details of the case fascinated him. 'I found that I could only write my play by allowing my characters to write their own story.' He began the task in Albany, just as the General Election campaign of July 1945 was getting started. Channon was away in his constituency in South-end, but was rushed back to London for a hernia operation, 'too ill and angry to reflect seriously on the disastrous Election results'. When he emerged from hospital, late in July, Rattigan explained his idea for the play over lunch on the day that Japan sued for peace. Within ten days Rattigan showed Channon the draft of the first act, and the forty-eight-year-old Conservative MP noted in his dairy, 'I suggested the title of "Ronny versus Rex", and he has temporarily adopted it.' Rattigan returned to his flat in Albany to work on it.

'The task, though not easy, proved on the whole a good deal less arduous than that of writing a light comedy,' he wrote later.

I wanted to create, not just to recreate. The plot was borrowed from life, but if the characters too had been borrowed from life then I felt the whole play might easily have been dead . . . Ronnie Winslow is not George Archer-Shee; Ronnie's father is not George's father, and Sir Robert Morton is not Sir Edward Carson.

As for Catherine and Dickie Winslow, and the other people in the play, they are entirely the figments of my playwright's imagination and, as far I know, had no counterparts whatever in the Archer-Shee story.

The play presented particular problems – not least how to avoid falling into the trap of having a great trial scene at the climax, which Asquith warned him he was certain to finish up doing. Instead Rattigan set himself the task of having all the major legal events take place off stage in order to restrict the production to one set and the cast to a manageable number. He wanted to write a domestic drama in the Edwardian style of Maugham and Galsworthy.

Though he began the first draft at Albany, Rattigan completed it in a house he had rented at Sonning. *Love in Idleness* had finally closed at the Lyric on 23 June, after a run of six months, having played to packed houses every night. It had brought Beaumont more than £60,000 at the box office, and Rattigan himself more than £10,000. This meant that he no longer had to suffer what he called 'the discomforts' of the White Hart Hotel. Besides, the Lunts were already planning the Broadway production for the beginning of 1946, so happy were they with the play, and Rattigan had received an advance from the American producers, the Theatre Guild.

Incarcerated in his rented house, he transformed the bare facts of the Archer-Shee case into his own drama. He retained the father's long struggle through the courts, and Sir Edward Carson's interrogation of the young Archer-Shee at the family home. But he made a number of radical changes to the family. Ronnie Winslow's father became less prosperous than Archer-Shee Senior, and his elder brother a frivolous Oxford undergraduate, rather than a retired Major and Conservative MP. Equally George's sister was not a suffragette, as Ronnie Winslow's was in the play, but a Tory like her father and elder brother. Rattigan has her engaged to an army officer whose father is uncomfortable with any kind of public display, and in turn adored by the family's faintly bumbling solicitor, Desmond Curry, who briefs Sir Robert Morton KC in the boy's defence. Rattigan also moved the year of the case from 1908 to 1912. But, more significantly, Rattigan neglected to make the Winslows a Catholic family, as the Archer-Shees were. The religious bigotry which underpinned the Archer-Shee case would have confused his central theme that right had to be done.

On 17 September Channon noted in his diary,

Terry returned to London, and we discussed his play, which he has now all but finished. It is being typed, and there are only a few touches still to do. I advised against the title 'The Hamilton Boy' and we decided on 'The Winslow Boy', which I suggested. Terry thinks only of his play, dreams and lives it, and it really is magnificent. What a genius he is. He has completed it in six and a half weeks.

Two days later Channon wrote again, 'Terry came to lunch, and afterwards we took off our coats and settled down comfortably while he read me the script of his play which took till six. I adored it, and made many comments, suggestions and criticisms.' In recognition of his efforts Rattigan dedicated the new play to Channon's son Paul, 'In the hope he will live to see a world in which this play will point no moral.'

Once he was satisfied, Rattigan sent the play to A.D.Peters, who in turn forwarded it to Binkie Beaumont. There was not a moment's hesitation. H.M.Tennent were only too keen to present a new Rattigan, especially as *While the Sun Shines* was still playing at the Globe, *Love in Idleness* had only just left the Lyric for a brief Forces tour on its way to Broadway, and *Flare Path*'s British tour had only just stopped raking in the profits. Beaumont had even used the Lunts' triumph – and their determination to go to Broadway – as a bargaining counter in his bid for permission to bring Thornton Wilder's highly successful *Our Town* to London from New York. There was no question about it. H.M.Tennent would be proud to present *The Winslow Boy*, once again in association with Linnit & Dunfee.

The question of casting was more delicate. Rattigan had written the role of Sir Robert Morton for John Gielgud. There had never been anyone else in his mind. He believed it was the first part he had written worthy of Gielgud's particular talent. But when Beaumont offered him the part, Gielgud turned it down. Whether he thought the part too small (Morton does not appear until Act Two), or whether he thought the play simply 'commercial', and therefore rather beneath him at that time, Gielgud has never made clear. Fifty years later, however, Sir John is willing to say that he 'rather underestimated the quality of Terry's work'.

Rattigan was deeply upset that his friend and one-time collaborator should reject what he believed was one of the finest, and certainly one of the showiest, parts he had ever written. He had felt a debt to Gielgud ever since Oxford, and offering him this part would, he hoped, be one way of repaying it. That his friend – and Binkie's even closer friend – should turn it down was not only hurtful, but baffling.

It was now up to Beaumont to make another suggestion. His

solution was to turn to the sometimes irascible and definitely pernickety actor Eric Portman. But Portman insisted that Morton was too small a part for him. He noted tartly that the barrister does not appear until almost the end of the second act, minutes before the interval. Finally Beaumont turned to another closer member of his group, the actor and playwright Emlyn Williams, who accepted. Rattigan had no alternative but to agree.

By the time the question of who was to play Sir Robert Morton had been settled, *Journey Together*, Rattigan's film for the RAF Film Unit, had been released to a rapturous reception. The *News Chronicle* called it 'One of the most realistic and brilliant films of the war in the air', and the *Spectator* added that it was 'one of the few really fine and exciting films to come out of the war'. The critics' only complaint was that it had taken more than a year to release, by which time the war had ended. Its author barely noticed. Together with Tolly de Grunwald, he had just finished a script of *While the Sun Shines* for Puffin to direct and was preparing to leave for New York to attend rehearsals for *Love in Idleness* with the Lunts.

The Lunts had not been seen in their native America for two and a half years, and they wanted to give themselves the best possible chance of a long New York run. So a pre-Broadway tour was organised to take in Toledo, Milwaukee, Madison in the Midwest and Washington. When Rattigan inquired why it was playing in Madison, he was told bluntly that it was close to the Lunts' farm in Wisconsin. As for the title, the discussions ranged back and forth until just before the tour began. *Variety*, reviewing the production on the first stop of the tour, alluded to the matter, concluding: 'Recently called *A Very Light Comedy* but now *O Mistress Mine*, after being known in England as *Love in Idleness*, the Lunts' latest play is light but should do well.' The Lunts' name alone helped ensure that there were $150,000 in advance ticket sales before it opened on Broadway.

When the play finally reached the Empire Theatre on 23 January 1946, the *Hollywood Reporter* spoke for all the New York critics when it reported,

> *O Mistress Mine* is simply a shell game being conducted by the most skilful of dealers, and you're a sucker if you don't let Lunt and Fontanne take you in . . . You may not think much of the play, but you must have the greatest respect for the players. Lunt and Fontanne have co-starred in twenty plays since they first appeared together under Theatre Guild sponsorship in 1924 in *The Guardsman*.

O Mistress Mine was to run for almost 450 performances, a record for the Lunts on Broadway, not closing until 31 May 1947. By then it had taken more than one and a quarter million dollars, making it Rattigan's most succesful play by far in the United States. Within a year the film rights had been sold to Howard Hughes's RKO Pictures for a further $140,000, and another tour of the play was being planned with the film actress Sylvia Sidney and John Loder. Rattigan was to estimate later that it earned 'about $200,000 for the British Treasury' in taxes.

As soon as he was back in England, Rattigan was plunged straight into preparations for *The Winslow Boy*. Kathleen Harrison, who had been in *Flare Path*, had been invited to play the Winslows' maid, Violet, Angela Baddeley Arthur Winslow's suffragette daughter, Catherine, and – very much against Binkie's wishes – Rattigan and the play's director, Glen Byam Shaw, had invited Jack Watling to play Ronnie Winslow's elder brother, Dickie. Byam Shaw took Watling to one side and said, 'You're not going to be difficult are you?' Watling was baffled. Only later did he realise that the question was a reference to his naivety over Michael Weight, which had obviously annoyed Binkie rather than amusing him.

After *Flare Path*, Watling had to face up to Keith Newman's continuing obsession with him. The Austrian had become increasingly unbalanced and unpredictable. 'I started getting the equivalent of love letters. "I can't live without you", that sort of thing,' Watling remembers. These homosexual advances were all the more unwelcome because he was, at that moment, on the brink of getting married. Finally Watling arranged for Newman to become a patient at a mental hospital near Oxford, and a few weeks later Newman was certified as being medically insane. Not long afterwards Watling 'got a call from Terry inviting me to stay with him at Sonning for a short time'. Watling suspects that Rattigan was feeling a little guilty, having taken no part in settling Newman's affairs. 'Anyway I stayed for about a week, but he was writing and I hardly spoke to him. I had nothing overt from Terry at all.' Perhaps the part of Dickie Winslow was Rattigan's way of thanking him. Actually to done said so would have been too painful.

The Lord Chamberlain's office voiced almost no objections when they issued their licence in early December, requesting only that the name of the public school attended by Dickie Winslow, which Rattigan had given as Repton, should be omitted, and that the female reporter who comes to interview Arthur Winslow about his son's case, and spends most of her time admiring the curtains, should not be identified as coming from the *Daily Mirror*. 'It seems unnecessary to single out a particular newspaper for derision.' The Lord Chamberlain could hardly be expected to recognise that this was another of Rattigan's jokes. He remembered the fuss the paper had caused him at the beginning of *While the Sun Shines* and was intent on returning the compliment.

The only other issue raised by the Lord Chamberlain was that the programme should include a note: 'This play is based on a famous case; but the characters are all fictitious.' When Beaumont's solicitors, McKenna & Co., saw the suggestion they immediately dismissed it as a 'non-sequitur'. 'If the play is based on the case in question then the characters could hardly be regarded as fictitious. They are merely hidden under a *nom de guerre*.' Instead McKenna recommended that the programme should include a sentence which read, 'This play was inspired by the facts of a well-known case, but the characters attributed to the individuals represented are based on the author's imagination and are not necessarily factual.' Their wording duly appeared.

The Winslow Boy was to begin its short tour at the Theatre Royal, Brighton, on 25 February 1946. That night Rattigan received a telegram from Keith Newman. It read, 'The Court of Artistic Law is going to lead the Winslow Flag of Triumph tonight.' Terence Rattigan was never to see Newman again. The man whose advice he had sought on every issue in his life, and to whom he had dedicated *Flare Path*, was to die in his mental hospital within a year, unvisited by either Rattigan or Puffin Asquith. His spell over both men had been broken, and his reason seems to have given way as a result.

On Thursday, 23 May 1946, when *The Winslow Boy* opened at the Lyric on Shaftesbury Avenue, which *Love in Idleness* had only vacated the previous June, there was to be no telegram from Keith Newman, but a veritable cascade from famous actors and actresses – Jack Buchanan and Alec Guinness, Basil Radford, Joyce Carey and Michael Redgrave. And, yet again, Beaumont made certain that the first night audience glittered. The film star Paulette Goddard arrived in a sweeping ermine coat, accompanied by Alexander Korda. Channon, Michael Redgrave and Puffin were there, as, naturally, were Major Frank Rattigan and his wife, whose handbag, as ever, contained the lucky champagne cork. Rattigan had taken care to have his hair cut.

He need hardly have bothered. Sir Robert Morton's first cross-examination of Ronnie Winslow, at the end of Act Two, immediately before the interval, brought sustained cheers from the audience.

SIR ROBERT: (*Bending forward malevolently*) I suggest your whole testimony is a lie –

RONNIE: No! It's the truth –

SIR ROBERT: I suggest there is barely one single word of truth in anything you have said either to me, or to the Judge Advocate, or to the Commander, I suggest that you broke into Elliot's locker, that you stole the postal order for five shillings belonging to Elliot, that you cashed it by means of forging his name –

RONNIE: (*Wailing*) I didn't. I didn't.

SIR ROBERT: I suggest that you did it for a joke, meaning to give Elliot the five shillings back, but that when you met him and he said he had reported the matter you got frightened and decided to keep quiet –

RONNIE: No, no, no. It isn't true –

SIR ROBERT: I suggest that by continuing to deny your guilt you are causing great hardship to your own family, and considerable annoyance to high and important persons in this country –

CATHERINE: (*On her feet*) That's a disgraceful thing to say!

ARTHUR: I agree.

SIR ROBERT: (*Leaning forward and glaring at Ronnie with the utmost venom*) I suggest, that the time has come for you to undo some of the misery you have caused by confessing to us all now that you are a forger, a liar, and a thief!

RONNIE: (*In tears*) I'm not! I'm not! I'm not! I didn't do it –

Grace has flown to his side and now envelops him.

ARTHUR: This is outrageous, sir –

John appears at the door, dressed in evening clothes.

JOHN: Kate, dear, I'm late. I'm most terribly sorry –

He stops short as he takes in the scene, with Ronnie sobbing hysterically on his mother's breast, and Arthur and Catherine glaring indignantly at Sir Robert, who is engaged in putting his papers together.

SIR ROBERT: (*To Desmond*) Can I drop you anywhere? My car is at the door.

DESMOND: Er – no – I thank you –

SIR ROBERT: (*Carelessly*) Well, send all this stuff round to my chambers tomorrow morning, will you?

DESMOND: But – but will you need it now?

SIR ROBERT: Oh, yes. The boy is plainly innocent. I accept the brief.

He bows to Arthur and Catherine and walks languidly to the door, past the bewildered John, to whom he gives a polite nod as he goes out. Ronnie continues to sob hysterically.

The curtain fell to tumultuous applause, and what the critic B. A. Young called 'one of the best *coups de théâtre* of modern theatre'. It remains just that, even today. But Rattigan, when writing it, had doubts. 'I thought you can't have so theatrical a curtain as that these days,' he said later, 'but then I thought, well, of course, in 1912 you could. So I left it in. Thank God I did!'

The scene certainly caught the attention of all the critics, who, once again, however, missed the play's essential message. Falling for the theatricality, *The Times* said 'a brilliant first act' was reason enough to see the play, but complained of a weak second half. Lionel Hale in the *Daily Mail* was prepared to admit that 'It is a tract most discreetly pointed and decked with all kinds of theatrical skill.' In the *Sunday Times*, James Agate pronounced, 'Mr Rattigan's play is intensely exciting for as long as his material holds out. He uses his magnificent sense of the theatre to extract the maximum of drama out of the subject,' but added, 'When the material runs thin Mr Rattigan is just the accomplished playwright turning poorish matter into goodish . . . All the same it is green corn pretending to be ripe corn.'

Most of the critics missed the large trial scene that Asquith had insisted the play could not do without. Rattigan had deliberately done without it, giving instead the critical line in the play to Catherine Winslow at the end of the third and penultimate act, when Sir Robert asks her for his instructions.

CATHERINE: (*In a flat voice*) Do you need my instructions, Sir Robert? Aren't they already on the Petition? Doesn't it say: Let Right be done?

It was that phrase, applied to a single British family, and in particular to the head of the family, Arthur Winslow, that lay at the heart of the play. Only Philip Hope-Wallace, writing in *Time and Tide*, picked up the point that Arthur Winslow, his search for truth and his defence of his son were a great deal more the play's central concern than the flamboyant antics of Sir Robert Morton. As Rattigan, on this occasion his own best critic, explained soon after the play opened, 'The drama of injustice and of a little man's dedication to setting things right seemed to have more pathos and validity just because it involved an inconsequential individual.'

Corn or not – and Agate was surely wrong – *The Winslow Boy* remained at the Lyric for more than a year, playing for 476 performances, before leaving first for a provincial tour and then for New York. There were to be French, German, Swiss, Swedish, Danish, Australian, South African, Greek, Norwegian, Czechoslovak, Israeli and Hungarian productions within the space of a year. By the early autumn of 1946, when Rattigan took a holiday at the Miramar in Cannes – and indulged his increasing passion for gambling – Peters had sold the film rights to Alexander Korda for £37,500 plus £625 a week throughout

the play's run on Broadway (after the first three weeks) up to a
maximum of £100,000. The payments were to be spread over a period
of five years. That was just as well. Rattigan lost a great deal of money
in the casino.

Once again Beaumont had two Rattigan and two Coward plays in
the West End. *Private Lives* and *Blithe Spirit* were still running, and
While the Sun Shines was rapidly approaching its 1,000th performance
at the Globe, just a few yards from *The Winslow Boy* at the Lyric.
Coward did not attend Rattigan's latest first night, but he did deign to
go to a performance a couple of weeks later. When he finally heard
that Noël had seen it, Rattigan immediately sent a telegram: 'I am
delighted to hear that you liked it when you saw it – at least that was
the report I got at the theatre last night. Do give me a ring and tell me
the truth, even if this report should prove unfounded.' The two men
were still stalking round each other like fighting cocks, Rattigan sus-
picious and sceptical, Coward patronising and a little too flattering to
be believed.

The Winslow Boy's success convinced Rattigan that he could now
afford to buy a house at Sonning, instead of simply renting one, and
that he could afford a bigger set of chambers in Albany. In September,
shortly after he came back from Cannes, he leased F2 at a rent of £650
a year, and surrendered K5. Ironically he had spent part of the summer
working on a film treatment of a novel by another resident of the
block. He, Tolly de Grunwald and Bill Linnit of Linnit & Dunfee had
bought the film rights to Graham Greene's 1938 novel *Brighton Rock*,
but after a lengthy negotiation had sold them on to John Boulting.
Boulting's company, Charter Film Productions, paid £12,000 for them.
Now Boulting wanted Rattigan to work with Greene on the screenplay.
Their joint fee was to be £6,000, to be apportioned 'to fairly represent
the services contributed by each of them respectively'.

Between the end of July and the end of August 1946, Rattigan
worked on the treatment. It was a rush, and on 15 August he wrote
to Boulting:

Dear John, You should never have asked me, and I should never
have agreed to do this treatment in so short a time. However, I
refuse to make excuses and provided the enclosed is not taken as
conclusive I feel it may well provide a useful basis for discussion.
I have altered Graham Greene's construction a fair amount – less
at the beginning than at the end – where I feel the tempo of the
physical action slows disastrously. I have also invented my own
murder. These and the other alterations I have made I trust you

and he will forgive. They are not, as I say, meant to be final, but merely to provide a basis for discussion.

The film was to be directed by Puffin Asquith.

In fact Rattigan's treatment of this story of Brighton's racecourse gangs laid as much emphasis on the character of the Cockney singer, Ida, as it did on Pinkie, the callous young crook. And in particular, it focused on Greene's hints about the Devil. In Rattigan's version, Kolley Kibber's tip for Ida was called 'Satan's Colt', and when a bookmaker asks her, 'Do you believe in the Devil, Ida?' she says no. 'And if there was a devil he wouldn't be a boy that age.' Throughout his version Rattigan used Ida as the direct counterpoint to Pinkie, the heterosexual against the homosexual, warm against cold, soft against hard, against the background of a discussion of good and evil.

In the end Boulting took over the direction of the film himself, relying rather more on Greene's approach than on Rattigan's, and therefore giving Greene's name first on the screenplay credit. Puffin had preferred Rattigan's approach, and had withdrawn from the production, but Rattigan had finished the dialogue and a final version for Boulting by the end of the year. The screenplay was not exactly to his liking, but he had been guaranteed £3,000 and a little over 11 per cent of the film's profits, which promised to be considerable. Associated British Pictures wanted to complete it quickly, and have it in the cinemas before the end of 1947. John Boulting had already decided that he wanted to use Richard Attenborough, whom he and Rattigan had worked with on *Journey Together*, as the villainous Pinkie.

Rattigan went straight on to write another film for de Grunwald, this time based on the story of a bride's trousseau – a wedding dress, a string of pearls, a veil and a bouquet. Each item was to be the focus of a separate story, and the four were to be presented together in a single film under the title of the place where each was to be purchased – *Bond Street*. It was a compendium approach which was to be copied by Gaumont Film Distributors with Somerset Maugham's short stories in *Quartet*, *Trio* and *Encore*. *Bond Street* was a confection which Rattigan did not take too seriously, but Tolly was prepared to pay him handsomely for the work, and it did not take long. Far more important was the film version of *The Winslow Boy* which Alexander Korda was planning.

Korda wanted a Broadway production of *The Winslow Boy* to whet the appetite of the American public for the film, and he pressed Beaumont to get a film star to take over the part of Sir Robert Morton for the New York opening. Beaumont agreed to the idea, and approached

Clive Brook, the London-born star of *Shanghai Express*. But Brook turned it down, telling Beaumont in a letter, 'I was so associated with these frozen faced parts in the movies for so many years, and indeed in this country as well, that it took the greatest possible effort to get away from them. Now, having done so, I do not want to risk going back.' Brook was not the only film star to turn the role down. Robert Donat also declined on the grounds that it wasn't 'the star' part, being 'obviously secondary to that of the father, if not to that of the daughter'.

In March the film version of *While the Sun Shines* had appeared in London to very mixed reviews. The *Daily Express* critic wrote: 'Oh dear, witty Mr Rattigan, why did you write it, the film I mean, not the play,' while Elspeth Grant in the *Daily Graphic* spoke for the majority of her British colleagues when she said, 'I do not think Mr Anthony Asquith, a director for whom I have the greatest admiration, has made a very good film of Mr Terence Rattigan's *While the Sun Shines* – but he has made a star of Mr Ronald Howard. Mr Howard is the son of the late Mr Leslie Howard, whom he startlingly resembles.' This was fine for Mr Howard but he, like the film, rather failed to quite fulfil the expectations.

Rattigan did his best to ignore the criticism and to concentrate on finishing the two parts of *Bond Street* that he was writing for Tolly de Grunwald. Meanwhile Korda was also pressing them both to get on with the script of *The Winslow Boy*, offering them £2,500 each to do so. Korda was also determined to succeed where Beaumont had failed and persuade Robert Donat to play the screen role of Sir Robert Morton, by tempting him with the offer of top billing and a substantial fee. Ultimately it was Rattigan's script, which he finished before he left for the New York opening of the play in October, which did the trick. Donat was given just a little more of a chance to 'star'. Korda's powers of persuasion did the rest.

When *The Winslow Boy* opened on 29 October 1947 at the Empire Theatre on Broadway, New York proved a disappointment once again. In spite of the success of *O Mistress Mine*, which had closed towards the end of March, Rattigan remained convinced that the show was the Lunts' success rather than his. That feeling in turn fuelled the insecurity that had always been a hidden ingredient of his own success. The fact that no one in the United States appeared to take his talent seriously served to heighten his private need for reassurance and make his desire to succeed in England all the greater. For no matter how it may have appeared, the playwright whose life and work depended on conceal-ment was nevertheless desperate for recognition and affection from theatre audiences, on whichever side of the Atlantic. If that did not come in New York, it made it all the more important in London.

Perhaps the lack of a Hollywood star for *The Winslow Boy* on Broadway made all the difference. In the end Binkie Beaumont, in association with the Theatre Guild and John C. Wilson, had merely imported most of the English cast for New York, giving Glen Byam Shaw another opportunity to direct, rather than adding a grandee of the movies to the cast. That downbeat approach had worked in England, where Rattigan had been given the first Ellen Terry Award on 30 June, after Ivor Novello had finally managed to launch what he saw as 'a British theatrical equivalent of the Oscars'; but it cut no ice across the Atlantic. As *Variety* commented during the play's brief pre-Broadway tour, it is 'so thoroughly impregnated with British humour and British approach that some of the force it must have had in England will be missing for the American audience, unless changes are made'.

None were. And the result was catastrophic. In the *New Yorker*, Alexander Woolcott, whose original article on the Archer-Shee case had fired Rattigan's enthusiasm for the project in the first place, offered distinctly faint praise.

> Since its author is a conscientious rather than an inspired playwright – *O Mistress Mine* was little more than a roomy Badminton court for the Lunts, and his preceding works that I can recall had also been driven by considerations other than art – *The Winslow Boy* can hardly be placed at the level of required theatre, but it should certainly go somewhere on your list of good, presentable entertainment, suitable for all the family and guaranteed not to antagonise important guests.

Brooks Atkinson in the *New York Times* was even less complimentary, 'Mr Rattigan's hackneyed technique very nearly conquers his convictions in his anti-climactic conclusion . . . [he is] only a practicing playwright when the occasion calls for an artist.' One review alone appealed to Rattigan. It read: 'Such a good play that one naturally wishes it could be perfect.'

In spite of the critical cold shoulder, however, *The Winslow Boy* was to last for more than 200 performances, staying on at the Empire Theatre for almost six months. It brought Rattigan £625 a week for twenty weeks or so, under the terms of his agreement with Korda, and did something to soften the sting of the reviews. It also meant that the play and the film version of *The Winslow Boy* had earned him more than £65,000 in eighteen months.

Alas, he was proving no more adept than before at hanging on to his financial gains. Rattigan's continued extravagance was driving his new accountant, Bill Forsyth of Chennall's in Chancery Lane, to distraction. No sooner had Rattigan Productions, the company set up to offset his tax liabilities, given him a cheque, than he – or his newly acquired secretary, Miss Mary Herring – would be on the telephone asking for another. Forsyth told his client angrily that he 'would have to sell the new house at Sonning – as you simply can't afford it, or afford to keep on putting all these people up'.

Rather shamefaced, Rattigan duly put the house on the market. But he did not fire Forsyth. Instead he took his strictures to heart. 'Just don't give me any money I can't afford to spend,' he told him. It was to be the system he would use throughout the rest of his life. Even when he went into the casino in Monte Carlo, Rattigan would divide the notes in his pocket into two halves. One was to gamble with, the other he would give to whoever was with him, with the strict instruction: 'Don't give that money back to me, even if I beg you for it.'

CHAPTER 14

The Crock

◆

The applause of a single human being is of great

consequence.

SAMUEL JOHNSON

◆

On the morning of 29 November, 1946, while *The Winslow Boy* was still running comfortably at the Lyric, Rattigan finished a one-act play of eighty manuscript pages. He had been working on it for just 'seven writing days', as he wrote proudly on the frontispiece. Barely three weeks later he was to finish a second one-acter, this time of ninety-nine manuscript pages, and within a further four weeks a third. It was one of the most productive periods of his career so far.

The first of these plays, *The Browning Version*, which he had first thought of calling *The Browning Story*, was typed up in the weeks before Christmas and sent directly to Binkie. The second, *Perdita*, and the third, *High Summer*, followed not long afterwards. They had all been written with just one actor in mind for the leading male part, the man who had turned down *The Winslow Boy* – John Gielgud. The reason for that was clear enough. When finally turning down Sir Robert Morton, Gielgud had promised Rattigan that he would do 'something else for you', and Rattigan had every intention of keeping him to his word.

Binkie lost no time in sending *The Browning Version* to Gielgud – and Gielgud, to Rattigan's delight, adored it. Sir John remembers now, 'I was immediately thrilled by *The Browning Version*, which I longed to play.' There was a snag, however. Binkie Beaumont hated *Perdita*, Rattigan's comedy about actors, which was to make up the second half of a double bill. 'Unfortunately the comedy which was to accompany it, a short burlesque piece, was thought so unsuitable by Binkie that he would not even show it to me for weeks,' Gielgud recalls.

There was more to Beaumont's disapproval of *Perdita* than met the eye. He was afraid the play might offend both Gielgud and the Lunts. 'Terry had remembered our Oxford meeting,' Gielgud remembers, 'and had conceived a sort of sketch on my behaviour at rehearsal as well as including a sort of imitation of Alfred Lunt, who might, he feared, be resentful of the implications.' So, instead of *Perdita*, Beaumont and Gielgud concentrated on the third of Rattigan's new one-act plays, *High Summer*, set in the grounds of White Manly, an English stately home, where the inevitable cricket match is in progress. The play revolved around the question of the house, and whether its owners, the Marquess and Marchioness of Huntercombe, would be able to afford to remain in residence.

By this time, Rattigan had taken on a new agent in New York, Harold Freedman of Brandt and Brandt. Short, eternally cheerful and unmistakably Jewish, he was to become his single most trusted adviser. Writing to Freedman in March 1947, Beaumont went so far as to confirm his agreement to stage *The Browning Version* and *High Summer* as a double bill, starring John Gielgud, who was also to direct *High Summer*. Beaumont anticipated opening the plays in the autumn of 1947, and told Freedman that Gielgud had committed to play for one year, including the provincial tour. He even told Rattigan that Gielgud and he were 'talking to designers' about *High Summer*, a play which they both felt was a 'period jewel'. *The Browning Version*, by comparison, did not need an elaborate design. Gielgud wanted Cecil Beaton, though Rattigan suggested his old friend Michael Weight, who had designed *Flare Path* and *The Winslow Boy*. The discussions over who should design the play rumbled on throughout the early part of 1947. Gielgud remained adamant that Beaton was the only possible designer, Chips Channon felt Rattigan did not need to remain loyal to Michael Weight. And Beaumont just looked on with his customary wry smile.

But Gielgud, in spite of his original enthusiasm, would not finally commit to an opening in London in the autumn of 1947. His mind was on other things. He was preparing a version of Dostoyevsky's *Crime and Punishment*, written by Rodney Ackland, which Komisarjevsky was to direct. Unable to stand the suspense, Rattigan eventually confronted Gielgud in New York. Walking through Central Park together, and after a great deal of elaborate courtesy by way of a warm-up, the best Gielgud could offer by way of an explanation was that he had 'to be rather careful of any new plays these days'. It meant that he was not prepared to commit to either of Rattigan's plays, at least for the moment. Rattigan's version of their conversation, which he took a pained delight in repeating to his friends, was rather different from Gielgud's, however, and rather more in line with the great actor's reputation for dropping the occasional brick. Rattigan remembered that Gielgud had told him, 'They've seen me in so much first rate stuff, do you really think they will like me in anything second rate?'

Rattigan was mortified. He cabled Beaumont, who was on holiday in Portugal, to say that reluctantly he had agreed to postpone the production of his two one-act plays until after Gielgud's *Crime and Punishment* had been produced. 'In future,' he added, 'am resolved act firmly on assumption plays will only be performed privately in Colney Hatch [a large North London mental hospital] whither the actor for whom they were written is plainly bound.' The ever diplomatic Beaumont cabled back, 'Let us pray madness will shortly lift as cannot feel Crime will prosper.' But the madness did not lift.

Gielgud's feet grew colder and colder. He decided he did not 'truly like' *High Summer* though he 'longed to play' *The Browning Version*. Throughout 1947, and the rigours of writing the screenplays for *Bond Street* and *The Winslow Boy*, Rattigan tried his hardest to persuade Gielgud to take on both roles, but the more he cajoled the more uncertain Gielgud became. On 11 January 1948, more than a year after he had first sent him *The Browning Version*, Rattigan accepted the inevitable.

'As I told you when I last saw you there could be nothing so stupid or dangerous as for either of us to continue in a venture of which we are not entirely confident, and that there is no earthly reason why either of us should feel obligated to the other because of a commitment given in haste over a year ago,' he wrote to Gielgud from Albany. 'So this letter is to release you entirely from any commitment you feel you have made – and to wish you well in whatever you decide to do next.'

A relieved John Gielgud cabled back, 'Greatly touched by your very sweet letter and understanding attitude,' and then wrote to Rattigan at length from New York, explaining the reasons for his uncertainty.

You know my childish and impetuous nature. If I don't start into something right away in the first flush of enthusiasm it is liable to go cold on me and then I am beset by doubts and fears . . . You are forgiving and sweet and believe me I do appreciate it and rejoice that our friendship has not been knocked for I should regret that more even than having a failure in the theatre. I still hope I may create a part for you one day not too far off.

Gielgud ended his letter by inviting Rattigan to go to Jamaica or Bermuda with him.

Grievous blow though it was, Rattigan decided that he was going to recast *High Summer* as a full-length play, and that he definitely wanted *The Browning Version* and *Perdita* put on as a double bill, no matter what Beaumont might say. The czar of Shaftesbury Avenue, as he was by now being called, then decided – without a moment's warning – that a 'double bill was always unlucky in the theatre'. Rattigan dismissed that idea completely. But with Gielgud gone, an atmosphere of bickering suddenly seemed to take over his entire life. Beaumont was still frightened of offending the Lunts. Chips Channon was offended that Rattigan had renewed his relationship with Peter Osborn. Kenneth Morgan had reappeared. Rattigan's secret circle seemed to be at each other's throats.

Rattigan turned to Laurence Olivier and Vivien Leigh for advice. Olivier had recently appeared in a double bill of two one-act plays, *Oedipus* and *The Critic*, and clearly did not suffer from Beaumont's prejudice against double bills. So early in January 1948 he sent Olivier a copy of *The Browning Version*. 'Dear Larry,' he wrote, 'This is the play I told you about. As far as Binkie and John G are concerned it is as free as the air – only I'd rather, for many reasons, you didn't mention the fact to them that you've read it.' Rattigan went on to explain that he wanted it performed with *Perdita*, but as the main piece of the evening. Olivier and Vivien Leigh had already read *Perdita*, and told Rattigan not only that they liked it, but also that they would consider appearing in it. But after reading *The Browning Version*, they did not feel it was right for them. Ironically, the Lunts had seen *The Browning Version* and liked it, but as Rattigan told Olivier, 'I haven't, of course, dared to show them *Perdita* – in which they would be superb.'

Within a couple of weeks of hearing from the Oliviers that they did not want to do *The Browning Version*, Rattigan had approached Alec Guinness, who liked the play and said he would do it. Rattigan then talked to Tyrone Guthrie, who had agreed to consider directing it, and to the film actor Clive Brook about the possibility of his appearing in *Perdita*. He was now effectively acting as his own impresario. 'Binkie knows nothing of this project,' he wrote to Harold Freedman in New York, 'but as he feels so venomously about *Perdita*, and as our original idea of John Gielgud has now fallen through, I feel I am completely free both morally and contractually to do as I like with these two plays.' He had been snubbed by Gielgud. He was not prepared to be snubbed by Beaumont.

Rattigan decided to jump before he was pushed and tell Beaumont that he had decided to offer his two plays to another producer, Stephen Mitchell. On St Valentine's Day, 1948, he sent Beaumont a long typed letter, explaining his decision.

> I know you will understand that this arrangement is absolutely without prejudice to our own association – past, present and future. I hope, too, that you will appreciate the reasons that have led me, temporarily, to desert your banner. Stephen, as I have told you, understands the situation perfectly, and is only anxious that you shouldn't feel he has intrigued against you in any way.

Rattigan, with a touch of mischief, then consulted Beaumont about how to avoid offending the Lunts with *Perdita*. He knew how important their goodwill was to Beaumont, and how much Beaumont wanted to remain close to them. The *Perdita* business could constitute a real threat, and so Rattigan blandly suggested in his letter to Beaumont that he should send them a copy before the two one-acters went into rehearsal – 'in order to avoid any affront to their dignity that might arise from their hearing of the play after it has come on', but concluding that he did not feel 'the likeness of my characters to the Lunts is any more marked than it is to – say – the Oliviers, the Liveseys or the Cassons'.

On the following Monday morning, Binkie sent a handwritten reply, in which he carefully avoided mentioning the Lunts, or his own view of *Perdita*. 'My dearest Terry,' he wrote.

> It was very sweet of you to write such a charming letter and I was deeply touched and happy that you had taken so much trouble. Of course, I understand your point of view about these plays and only feel a certain sadness that we are not doing them together. However I sincerely hope – as you say in your letter – this will make no change in our future plans together – as that would indeed make me very sad. No author could be a better partner than you . . . If, as you say, you are only leaving us for these plays my heart is fairly gay and I long to welcome you back.

The deed was done.

Rattigan had fought so hard, and worried so intensely about the fate of *The Browning Version*, because the play meant more to him at the time than any play he had attempted before. It represented his first major dramatic exploration of a theme to which he was to return persistently in the years ahead – the pain and loneliness that lie behind the restraint and reticence of English society, and especially the upper middle classes. Though Rattigan was now indisputably a figure in

London society, constantly photographed in Albany with his terrier, Tiffin, written about in the gossip columns, featured as 'one of the best dressed men in London', his apparently frivolous exterior concealed his own pain, uncertainty and loneliness. In his plays he was able to reveal some of the truths that hide behind the façades that people create for themselves. In *The Browning Version* he did so in one long fierce act that does not for one moment lose the attention of the audience.

As he was to explain to the *New York Times* some time afterwards, Rattigan had become convinced that the day was approaching when plays would last for between sixty and eighty minutes rather than having an interval (or two) during a performance. He wanted the opportunity to 'hook' an audience without an interval in which he would lose their concentration. He was convinced this would enable him to explore more fully, and more emotionally, the complex characters he was now determined to present. The one-acter, played without a break, would enable him to do this more effectively.

Some critics, in reviewing *The Winslow Boy*, had reproached him for 'suddenly turning rather serious'. They had failed to realise his truly serious ambitions. The battle to rid himself of the albatross, the epithet of Mr Terence 'French Without Tears' Rattigan, had never ceased. As he told a New Zealand reporter, his ambition remained 'not to be content with writing a play to please an audience today, but to write a play that will be remembered in fifty years time'.

The Browning Version, his one-act play about a forty-year-old man who has never managed to fulfil his own promise, or live up to the expectations of his wife, gave him the opportunity. He had been haunted by the idea of unfulfilled promise since his schooldays at Harrow, and his father's sudden retirement from the Foreign Office. Now, nearing forty himself, he was ever more acutely aware how painful the sense of lost promise could be. The figure he chose to convey this sense of loss was a classics teacher, Andrew Crocker-Harris, who has been forced to leave his post early through illness. Rattigan modelled the master on one of the classics masters at Harrow, J.W.Coke-Norris, who, though an Oxford first, had only ever been allowed to teach the lowest forms and had left the school long before the normal age of retirement, not long after Rattigan himself had done so. Coke-Norris had been responsible for drawing up the school's timetable for the two years before Rattigan arrived at Harrow, being what was known as the Organization Master, but had apparently been relieved of the task.

Another added dimension to the genesis of *The Browning Version* came from the bickering in his own emotional life. Rattigan had steadily fallen for Kenneth Morgan again, and Chips Channon, for all his professed taste for keeping passion at arm's length, was growing resentful. There lurked within Channon a sense of missed opportunity, which added poignancy to his barbed observations and his desperate desire to 'be at the heart of things'. Now aged fifty, Channon too had begun to feel old. Rattigan sensed it, just as he sensed his own need not to be dismissed merely as a 'farceur', and he tried to capture their emotions in the play.

So Andrew Crocker-Harris, the failed classics master in *The Browning Version*, was based on elements of both Chips Channon and himself. But Rattigan also put part of himself into the character of Taplow, the schoolboy being given private lessons by the Crock – as Crocker-Harris is known to the boys – in Aeschylus' play *The Agamemnon*. Certainly Rattigan himself loved Aeschylus, and dated his determination to become a professional dramatist from the time he first encountered *The Agamemnon* in the Vaughan Library at Harrow. Certainly too he liked the Browning translation, after which the play is named, although Rattigan was never taught by Coke-Norris himself, nor did he give the parson a present. Instead he used his experience with another master at the school, on whom he had developed a homosexual crush, as the inspiration for Taplow's gift to the Crock.

For Millie Crocker-Harris, the classics master's shrewish wife, Rattigan drew partly on his experience of Mrs Middleditch and her daughter, the demanding girl who had pursued him as a schoolboy, and so it follows that Frank Hunter, the science master with whom Millie is having an affair under the Crock's nose, was also partly a portrait of Rattigan. The Crock, Millie, Taplow and Hunter – bits of Rattigan existed in each of them, their debate and confrontation in effect a dialogue he was conducting with himself.

After Gielgud, almost the first person he consulted about the play was his father. Indeed the first expense he was to charge to the production almost eighteen months later was £90 for a gold cigarette lighter 'given to W.F.Rattigan for advice re *The Browning Version*'. The only other present of comparable generosity was the cheque for £37 and 10 shillings 'for criticism of the plays', made out in February 1947 to Kenneth Morgan.

Stephen Mitchell, the producer Rattigan designated to put on *The Browning Version* and *Perdita*, had only recently returned to London after his war service. During 1947 he had produced J.B.Priestley's *Ever Since Paradise*, and Ben Levy's *Clutterbuck*, which had been a considerable success, and before the war had put on Emlyn Williams's *The Corn is Green* in the West End. Rattigan and he had met casually at that time, but they had hardly seen each other since. Nevertheless when Mitchell received the two plays in the first weeks of 1948 he knew at once that he wanted to present them in London. And for the next nine months he and Rattigan struggled together to find the right cast. Their first thought was Alec Guinness, who seemed keen, but then thought he was not going to be available until later in the year. So in late February Rattigan contacted the film actor Frederic March, who had let it be known that he would like to appear on the London stage. Their conversation straggled on inconclusively through the early summer, during which time Rattigan also contacted Cedric Hardwicke before making a new approach to Guinness.

By July they had still not found an actor willing to play the Crock. They had, however, appointed a director. Peter Glenville, Rattigan's friend from Oxford, who as a young actor had been singled out for praise in Puffin's film *Uncensored*, had become a promising theatre director. Rattigan had decided to give him the play. Glenville suggested offering the part of the Crock to Eric Portman, the Yorkshire-born star of *Uncensored*, an actor legendary both for his fussiness and for his intense concentration. At first Portman turned the part down, but Glenville, undeterred, persuaded him to have a drink with Rattigan, Stephen Mitchell and himself at Rattigan's flat in Albany. In another flash of inspiration, Glenville also suggested that the trio of hosts should put on dinner jackets, in an effort 'to look very distinguished'. 'When Eric came through the door,' Stephen Mitchell recalls, 'he said "I can't resist this, I'll do it."' Rehearsals began a week later.

Perdita, the second one-act play, which Rattigan told Harold Freedman was 'to be presented as a work of no particular importance, but one which is required by the conventions of the theatre concerning the time an audience expects to sit in the theatre', he had decided to retitle *Harlequinade*. In a letter to Lynn Fontanne, enclosing a copy, he explained that it 'really is designed to serve the purpose implied by its title'. Rattigan, unlike Beaumont, felt confident that the Lunts would get the joke. *Harlequinade* was a farce about the dress rehearsal of a production of *Romeo and Juliet* by the celebrated acting couple, Arthur Gosport and Edna Selby, who were obviously a portrait of the Lunts. Equally clear were echoes of Gielgud's production of *Romeo and Juliet* for the OUDS, not least in the fact that a young actor (based on Rattigan himself) is given the line he had stumbled over so persistently in Oxford in 1932, 'Faith, we may put up our pipes and be gone.' Arthur Selby's direction of the play is clearly modelled on Gielgud. A further dig was the Selby/Lunt/Gielgud penchant for remembering the passing years only by events in the theatre.

Not surprisingly, the piece contained a series of barbed comments on the stage and its denizens, but it also demonstrated an affection for the absurdities of the theatrical life. Subsidised theatre, for example, gets a stiff jolt, as do plays with a social purpose. Here, for example, are Edna Selby and her aunt, who is playing the nurse:

EDNA: The theatre's gone through a revolution since 1900.
DAME MAUD: It was 1914 I played Juliet, dear. I remember the date well, because the declaration of war damaged our business so terribly.
EDNA: There's been another war since then, Auntie Maud, and I don't think you quite understand the immense change that has come over the theatre in the last few years. You see, dear – I know it's difficult for you to grasp, but the theatre of today has at last acquired a social conscience, and a social purpose. Why else do you think we're opening at this rat-hole of a theatre instead of the Opera House, Manchester?

It is a commentary reflected shortly afterwards in a conversation between the stage manager and the theatre's manager:

BURTON: Funny for them to choose to open up here, I must say.
JACK: Social purpose, Mr Burton.
BURTON: Social purpose? Now what the blazes is that when it's at home?
JACK: As far as I can see, it means playing Shakespeare to audiences who'd rather go to the films; while audiences who'd rather go to Shakespeare are driven to the films because they haven't got Shakespeare to go to. It's all got something to do with the new Britain and apparently it's an absolutely splendid idea.

Harlequinade also demonstrated Rattigan's dislike for the new verse dramas of Christopher Fry and Ronald Duncan, which were surfacing in London. He dismisses them with a reference to 'a modern play in verse called *Follow the Leviathan to My Father's Grave*', a title which he was to use repeatedly to decry all verse plays – which he found boring and pointless. But the play's comedy comes not only from its reflections of the state of contemporary theatre, but also from the characters of Arthur Gosport and his wife. It is Gosport who suddenly discovers that a young woman who has presented herself at the stage door believes herself to be his daughter, and that he is still officially married to her mother – making the famous theatrical couple's marriage bigamous. The theme of concealment, and the revelation which will – inevitably – result, is a lighthearted mirror image of *The Browning Version*, and one of the main reasons for Rattigan's determination that the two plays should be presented together.

In Rattigan's mind, *Harlequinade* was as important to *The Browning*

Version as *The Agamemnon*. Both illuminated his central theme. It is no accident that in Aeschylus' tragedy the hero is slain by his wife, Clytemnestra, while in *The Browning Version* the Crock is spiritually murdered by his wife, Millie. She is the only true villain Terence Rattigan ever allowed himself to create. He called her 'an unmitigated bitch'.

The Browning Version was so important to Rattigan, and so close to his heart, that – as Stephen Mitchell recalls now – 'there was not a line altered in the play from beginning to end. It was the only play I've ever known in which there was no alteration of any kind whatsoever. That has stuck in my mind ever since.' For a time Rattigan had considered giving the play a tragic ending, with the Crock's death from a heart attack, but he finally settled on allowing his future to remain unclear – condemned to a life without love, either alone or in the continuing thrall of his venomous wife.

Throughout the summer of 1948 rehearsals proceeded steadily, if not exactly calmly. Mary Ellis, who had been recruited to play Millie alongside Eric Portman's Crocker-Harris, did not like her co-star, and said so. During the brief tour on its way into London, she even took the trouble to write to Rattigan to tell him that Portman was demanding cuts in *Harlequinade*, 'because he didn't like listening and thought the audience would be bored'. Portman's confidence was famously fragile, and the closer the plays came to their London opening, the more fractious and nervous he became.

In an effort to calm his nerves, Rattigan introduced Portman to his real classics master from Harrow, E.V.C.Plumtre, who he hoped would help him with the Greek the Crock used during the play. It did not work. In fact Rattigan had also been consulting Plumtre himself throughout the year, but on another matter entirely. He had wanted Plumtre's advice on the life of Alexander the Great, which he was intent on dramatising for the stage. Their first talks had taken place during the early months of 1948, while the debates with Beaumont and Gielgud about the two one-acters were still going on. By the time rehearsals for the double bill were under way the new play, *Adventure Story*, had been completed and sent to Beaumont. Rattigan was unsure about it, telling Lynn Fontanne in a letter that it 'is an ambitious effort and perhaps I should never have written it at all, but I felt I had to try. Binkie, I am happy to say, seems to like it very much and I gather is going to produce it here in the autumn.' In fact Beaumont did not want two Rattigan openings at the same time, and had put *Adventure Story* away.

For Rattigan a great deal depended on the success of *The Browning Version*. His financial affairs were in a worse state than ever – in spite of his having sold the Sonning house to meet one of his tax bills. The successes of the war years were no longer there to live on, and he had refused to save any money. His overdraft at Coutts was increasing at a rapid rate, while he showed no sign of restraining his habit of entertaining his friends as lavishly as he had always liked to. 'I have taken a furnished house in the country for the months of June July and August – Sonning having been sold to pay off my debts – just for the purpose of entertaining you,' he wrote to the English-born Lynn Fontanne. 'Hideous little pink shuttered nook I'm afraid, but very comfortable. You really must give me at least one weekend.'

If the two one-act plays failed he was in grave danger of having very little money left. He did not own his chambers in Albany, having instead only purchased a twenty-one-year lease, entered into in 1947, and he had not worked on a film script since his version of *The Winslow Boy*, which he had delivered in September 1947. Film scripts as a method of shoring up his bank balance had been put to one side, to enable him to work on his play about Alexander the Great, and to wage the battle on behalf of *The Browning Version*. Rattigan vowed to himself that, if the play was a success, in future he would always save enough to pay his income tax bills at least.

Turning away from films – at least for a time – was no great loss, however, except financially. Rattigan was not particularly upset when *Bond Street* trickled out to miserable reviews in May 1948. 'The film is like one of those glossy, elaborate romantic magazines. The illustrations and the typography are much better than the stories. If you're looking for an unimaginative way of spending an evening, *Bond Street* is harmless enough,' said the London *Evening Standard*.

The film version of *The Winslow Boy*, which opened in London in September, was much more warmly received, not least because of Robert Donat's return to the screen after an absence of almost three years. 'It is Donat's tremendous authority (especially his easy brilliance in the law court and Parliamentary scenes) that gives the film its glittering centrepiece,' proclaimed the *Sunday Express*. Donat was 'brilliant, unselfish, and unimpeachably correct', wrote C.A.Lejeune in the *Observer*. This fastidious critic was less impressed by Rattigan's script. '*The Winslow Boy* had been adapted for the cinema by the author . . . and must be presumed to have carried out his intentions. In that case Mr Rattigan proves himself to be a better playwright than screenwriter,' she concluded. Nevertheless the film made money at the box office.

But it was *Playbill*, as the evening of his double bill of *The Browning Version* and *Harlequinade* was now to be called, that mattered. 'I am a playwright, not a screenwriter, that is all I have ever wanted to be,' he would tell his friends, and it was true. The Lord Chamberlain had put no difficulties in the way of either play, not a word needed to be amended to suit the censor, and the play had been licensed to Stephen Mitchell and London Theatrical Productions on 10 June 1948. Rehearsals had been fairly calm, with the exception of Eric Portman's fussing and Mary Ellis's obvious dislike of her co-star. But 'There was nothing we couldn't handle,' Stephen Mitchell recalls now.

Rattigan's only concern was that Portman was making the Crock seem like an old man. 'One thing I am determined on,' he wrote to Peter Glenville, 'is to put a line in which definitely states that Crocker-Harris's age is forty . . . Partly, I think the trouble is Eric's vanity, which stops him from playing the part of a physically unattractive man except by unconsciously adding twenty years to his age.' In the end Glenville persuaded him against the idea, and did what he could with Portman.

Finally, *Playbill* opened in Liverpool in the last week of July, at the beginning of a short pre-London tour. Rattigan gave Stephen Mitchell a set of golf-clubs and Peter Glenville two antique boxes as opening night presents, his habitual generosity undimmed by the wailing of his accountant. Beaumont wired his support, as did John Gielgud and Puffin Asquith. The next day Rattigan cabled Harold Freedman in New York, 'Reception notices really exceptional. All critics see point regarding contrast of plays and don't attempt comparison.' He repeated the same message in another wire to Beaumont, 'Eric gave a very exciting performance in both plays; pray God it will last.'

On the night of the final dress rehearsal at the Phoenix Theatre in London's Charing Cross Road, Portman threw his final tantrum, insisting that one vital prop had been removed from his desk, 'which is terribly destructive to one's confidence'. Rattigan and Stephen Mitchell agreed to walk the stage with him fifteen minutes before the curtain went up the following night, to make absolutely sure that there were no mistakes. Portman had not made an appearance on Shaftesbury Avenue for eight years, and was, not surprisingly, intensely nervous.

For the first night on 8 September 1948, Rattigan had invited everyone who mattered to him. His guests were spread throughout the intimate theatre. Chips Channon and Lady Juliet Duff were in the first row of the stalls, not far in front of Tolly de Grunwald and Puffin Asquith. His old lover Peter Osborn was in row N of the stalls, while Kenneth Morgan was in row D of the dress circle. They might know of each other's existence, but it was prudent to keep them as far apart as possible, especially in the light of his transferred affections. There

were more than a hundred telegrams wishing him luck, including one
from Beaumont – 'You clever clever boy. Enormous Success. Love
Binkie' – and an enigmatic one from the notorious Godfrey Winn,
'Dear Terry, I hope your success tonight will equal your success in
private.' Peter Osborn cabled, 'From the deep of my thought and in
love I say, 'Sweet is a grief well ended.''

A few minutes before the curtain went up, Rattigan and Stephen
Mitchell duly walked the stage with a nervous Portman. Everything
seemed to be in place. When the curtain rose on 'sitting-room of the
Crocker-Harrises' flat in a public school in the South of England
between 6 and 7 pm of a day in July', and Taplow made his entrance
in search of his private lesson, the chair he was to sit on had disappeared.
'He had the good sense to go and find another one,' Stephen Mitchell
recalls. It was the final straw for Rattigan. He walked out of the theatre
and across the road to a pub on the corner of Old Compton Street,
and had three large drinks very quickly. He did not say a word to
anyone. Seventy-five minutes later, as *The Browning Version* came to
an end, he walked back into the foyer of the Phoenix. Tumultuous
applause echoed around the theatre.

The audience had been transfixed by the two great climaxes at the
end of the play. The first comes when Taplow gives the Crock a copy
of Browning's translation of *The Agamemnon*, a gesture that makes the
schoolmaster break down in tears of gratitude; only to be destroyed
by the second climax minutes later when his wife Millie pours scorn
on the gift in the most venomous speech Rattigan had ever written, a
diatribe worthy of Clytemnestra herself:

> MILLIE: The artful little beast . . . I came into this room this afternoon
> to find him giving an imitation of you to Frank here. Obviously he was
> scared stiff I was going to tell you, and you'd ditch his remove or
> something. I don't blame him for trying a few bobs' worth of
> appeasement.

In the words of one critic present that night, 'the gasp of horror was
audible'. The defeat of Crocker-Harris is complete, the gift that might
have indicated that for once a boy had been touched by his own love
of Greek drama exposed, apparently, as a cheap schoolboy joke. Millie's
revenge on her husband for his failure to satisfy her – both as a schoolmaster and as a lover – has been achieved in the course of one brilliant,
brutal harangue. When Frank Hunter, horrified, tries to comfort the
Crock, the classicist once more retreats behind the mask he has so
carefully constructed for himself over the years – the façade of the
desiccated schoolmaster.

CROCKER-HARRIS: If you think, by this expression of kindness, Hunter, that you can make me repeat the shameful exhibition of emotion I made to Taplow a moment ago, I must tell you that you have no chance.

The Crock is trying to protect himself again, after letting his defences slip, and, as the play comes to its end, Rattigan sensed that the audience would want him to have some small triumph with which to console himself. He produced it at the very end of the play. Crocker-Harris telephones the headmaster to tell him that he will not be humiliated again at the prizegiving the following day by agreeing to speak before a more popular master. His right is to speak last, and he is determined to exercise it, even if he does so in phrases of utter restraint.

CROCKER-HARRIS: I am of the opinion that occasionally an anti-climax can be surprisingly effective.

As the curtain fell on this understated line, 'the heart responds as to the sound of a trumpet,' reported one critic. Harold Hobson, who had replaced James Agate as the dramatic critic of the *Sunday Times*, wrote to Rattigan shortly afterwards, 'I was particularly moved by *The Browning Version*, and if any of this came through in my notice I am extremely gratified.' He called the play 'nearly a masterpiece', and went on, 'Mr Portman's playing and Mr Rattigan's writing in *The Browning Version* are playgoing experiences one encounters only once in a thousand nights. If as often.'

The reception for *Harlequinade*, which was played second, was equally enthusiastic, though quite different. There was little or no emotion as it came to an end. The play was simply accepted as a 'refreshing romp, complete with Pantaloon and Policeman'. The critics avoided making any inept comparisons between the two plays. *The Times* called the second play 'good-natured and funny', without suggesting that it weakened the impact of *The Browning Version*. The *Daily Telegraph* called *Playbill* 'the best evening in the theatre for a very long time', while the *Daily Mail* added, 'For once a theatrical occasion in the grand manner; good writing, fine acting, and a glamorous first night audience justified of its rapture.'

The relief Rattigan felt was intense. He had been so tense that he could hardly bring himself to speak to anyone during the interval, certainly not to any of the critics, and instead put on his familiar, fixed smile. His public mask was still firmly in place for the evening. As he was to admit later, 'I am unconquerably shy of critics – as critics, no doubt, are of authors – and I never know whether an expression of gratitude for past "kind words" might not be misinterpreted as a base and smarmy attempt to ensure even kinder words in the future.'

With his friends he could let go. 'The plays,' he wrote to one the next morning,

> opened in London last night and I think I can say with that mastery of understatement which is supposed to be mine, that it went off quite nicely. Aunty Times, who I am pretty sure had taken that old brolly of hers with a parrot's head handle to whack me on the head with at the slightest provocation, had this morning put it away again in the armoury practically unused except for a few minatory flourishes. She has permitted herself the strangely typical Aunty Times observation about the evening 'being more satisfactory than satisfying' and has laboriously unearthed the theme in the Browning Version which is just as incomprehensible to me as it will be to most of her readers . . . The other notices are kind, some very kind indeed, and our first night was star-studded, overdressed, flashlight conscious, but with all vociferous.

A few days afterwards Rattigan left for a holiday. He went to Antibes to stay with Binkie Beaumont and talk about his play about Alexander the Great, *Adventure Story*. Ironically, by the time he returned to Albany, John Gielgud had contacted him about the possibility of playing Crocker-Harris on Broadway the following year. The play had been hailed as a masterpiece, and Gielgud was apparently only too aware that he might have missed an opportunity. An excited Rattigan cabled Harold Freedman in New York with the news. But, once again, there was a difficulty: Gielgud was committed to a season at Stratford-upon-Avon in 1949, and would, therefore, have to start in New York quite quickly. And meanwhile, of course, the whole matter had to be kept secret, 'for fear of upsetting Eric'. Predictably, after all the dithering that had gone before, the prospect of Gielgud as Crocker-Harris once again slipped away.

The Browning Version marked Rattigan's arrival as a British dramatist of serious consequence. Among the first to recognise this was the veteran critic Sydney Carroll, who had recently retired. After seeing *Playbill*, he wrote a long letter to Rattigan explaining just how considerable he believed his gifts to be.

'Having just seen your remarkable double bill at The Phoenix I cannot refrain from telling you how greatly I regret my inability to use my critical pen in tribute to your powers. Clearly you have a great career in front of you as an eminent British playwright. You must realise its full potential,' he wrote on 25 October, adding:

I have often been struck by the fact that dramatists of immense power and emotional effect have started their professional lives by fripperies and farcical lightweight manoevres – subsequently blossoming out and revealing themselves as keen observers of the depths and inner secrets of humanity and the fatalities of existence. Shaw, Barrie, Pinero, Jones, Ibsen, Galsworthy, Tchekov, Maugham, Barker, O'Casey, O'Neill and others whose name will strike you – I cannot but include you in my gallery of dramatic notables, whose early beginnings gave little indication of their finer flights of dramatic invention.

The letter affected Rattigan deeply. It was almost the first time a respected critic had written to him in such terms, and it satisfied a need that he had hardly dared to admit, even to himself, the need to be loved and admired. 'I can hardly begin to express to you what enormous pleasure your letter gave me,' Rattigan replied.

Naturally I take myself seriously as a writer – none of us, I suppose, would be able to write if we didn't – but to have moved a critic of your taste and discernment to express so high an evaluation of my work is an achievement of which I feel I have every right to boast. I hope you'll forgive me if I do – for I can assure you I have no intention whatever of modestly storing your letter in a dark and undisturbed drawer. It goes into my wallet to be shamelessly used as a weapon against scoffers and as a charm against my own doubts and depressions, which are sometimes acute

Carroll in turn wrote back, 'You do well to take yourself seriously. I am convinced that the world will do so before long and recognise you for the fine dramatist you undoubtedly are – Let us leave it at that.'

Rattigan had the grace not to lose his sense of fun, or proportion. When he took Jeremy Bullmore, then a Harrow schoolboy but later chairman of the advertising agency J. Walter Thompson, to see *The Browning Version* as part of a school English prize that he had endowed, Rattigan gave the young man a present at the end of the evening. It was the collected plays of Tchekov. The inscription to Bullmore read, 'I only wish I could say it was from the author.'

CHAPTER 15

Noble Failures

◆

I would prefer even to fail with honour than win

by cheating.

SOPHOCLES, *Philoctetes*

◆

The idea of a play based on the life of Alexander the Great had been in Terence Rattigan's mind since Harrow. He had been fascinated by the Greek commander's pursuit of his ambition to the end of the known world. Like many other schoolboys of his generation he had read Plutarch's *Lives* at school, and that in turn had fostered in him the idea that Alexander's life could be examined in rather the same way that Shakespeare had described the life of Henry V. It was a brave, not to say foolhardy, undertaking.

Rattigan started work on the play early in 1948, gathering around him an elaborate collection of books and other documents, including the *Cambridge Ancient History*, *Alexander of Macedon* by Harold Lamb, Sir Thomas North's translation of *Plutarch's Lives*, and *The History of Ancient Persia* by R.W.Rogers. On 16 February he started writing, leaving his chambers in Albany for a room he had taken at the Stag and Hounds pub near Binfield, not far from Reading. In the first week at Binfield he managed thirty-seven pages, the following week sixty, and the week after forty-six. The fourth week saw him complete the first draft with a final fifty-two pages. The manuscript was the longest he had written, and as usual he sent it first to Binkie Beaumont for his reaction. By then Beaumont knew that he was no longer to present *The Browning Version*, but he had no wish to antagonise the man who had written him four West End hits during the past six years. He immediately replied that he liked the new play.

But Beaumont's was not the only reaction that Rattigan sought. He had been asking E.V.C.Plumtre, 'Plum', for specific guidance throughout the four weeks he had been writing. In a letter, he explained how difficult he had found the task. 'I fully realise that I can hardly expect to carry all my audience with me in my view of Alexander. In any case I haven't really tried to create a fair and faithful portrait of the man. The play isn't meant to be a character study of Alexander – I think that would be impossible anyway.' In the course of writing, he had grown increasingly conscious that the experts on Alexander seemed to disagree about their subject. 'Plutarch also doesn't seem able to make up his mind and one or two of the more judicious biographers also seem to be perched rather uncomfortably on a fence.'

Rattigan came up with his own solution.

I decided to take a different approach and instead of writing a play about Alexander the Great to write a play about a man called Alexander who gained the whole world and lost his soul. I realise perfectly that it is highly debatable whether the real Alexander did indeed lose his soul, or even whether he had any soul to lose, but there is, as I know you will admit, at least some evidence on my side . . . And although the notion that absolute power corrupts absolutely is not exactly original it is something that can be said quite effectively in theatrical terms. I couldn't have said it about Napoleon, because my audience would have known far too much about him – even how he looked and how he stood – very frustrating to an actor. But who of my audience will know anything of Alexander, except that he conquered the world; sighed for more worlds to conquer; cut the Gordian knot and died young? Very, very few – because, thank heavens they won't all be Plumtres.

Once again Rattigan had set out to examine what motivated the man at the centre of his play. In particular he was guided by Plutarch's conclusion that 'you can sometimes learn more from an occasional remark than from the tremendous details of military success'. And, just as he had done in *The Winslow Boy*, Rattigan had constructed his play around a single phrase, this time the one uttered by Alexander in the first moments of the play when he lies on his death bed. 'Where did it first go wrong?'

As Rattigan admitted in a letter to Lynn Fontanne at the time, he knew he was attempting something ambitious, and perhaps he should not have done so, but 'I felt I had to try.' What he did not see was what might be called the language trap. Rattigan's natural ear for dialogue and his feeling for human emotion were honed in the drawing-rooms of middle-class twentieth-century England. His command of what many critics called 'middle-class vernacular' did not translate easily to Ancient Persia. As the critic Freddie Young puts it, 'In speech and thought, his Alexander is like a daring fighter pilot of World War Two.' Another friend puts it more gently, 'No matter how hard he tried, Terry could never write poetry.' Yet Alexander cried out for a poet.

Nevertheless, a new full-length play by Terence Rattigan was not about to be refused by H.M.Tennent. Since the first night of *Flare Path*, in August 1942, there had been a Tennent production of a Rattigan play running on Shaftesbury Avenue almost without a break. So in the spring of 1948, while Rattigan immersed himself in trying to find exactly the right man to play the Crock, Beaumont began searching for an actor to play Alexander the Great. His first thought was Alec Guinness, who said how much he liked the play. But Guinness was not prepared to commit himself to play the part for a year in the West End. That presented a difficulty for Rattigan because Binkie Beaumont was adamant he wanted a star who would play Alexander for at least a year. Negotiations with Guinness broke down.

Rattigan encouraged Beaumont to consider instead the group of young leading men beginning to emerge from the new Shakespeare seasons at Stratford-upon-Avon. One of them was the flamboyant and talented young Welshman Richard Burton who, Rattigan told Beaumont, 'would be a perfect choice' to play the combative Hephaestion, Alexander's friend and supporter. And there was another young star from the same distinguished training ground who would be absolutely right for Alexander. Paul Scofield's recent Hamlet had been called 'the finest performance since Gielgud'. Rattigan urged Beaumont to send him a copy of *Adventure Story*, and wrote to Lady Juliet Duff a few days afterwards. 'From the moment I re-read the play I was certain that Paul was the ideal actor to create "Alexander".'

Scofield leapt at the chance. In July he wrote to Beaumont to say, 'I told you I loved *Adventure Story*, but I am sure I didn't express adequately how much I love it – I really think it's a wonderful piece of writing and theatre. I am bursting with excitement about the whole thing.' Burton agreed to play alongside him, while for the regal, imposing Darius, Beaumont hoped he might manage to entice Jack Hawkins back from his career in films. At first Hawkins agreed, but then balked at the lengthy rehearsals and the six-week pre-London tour, because he was busy filming. There was another reason, as he told Beaumont firmly: 'I consider the play a starring vehicle for Alexander.' Finally, after a good deal of bickering, Hawkins backed out altogether and the part was played by Noel Willman. But Gwen Ffrangcon-

Davies, who had agreed to play the Queen Mother of Persia, was not put off in the least by the negotiations with Hawkins. It was to be her first appearance on the London stage after seven years away in South Africa. Robert Flemyng, who had played Kit in the original *French Without Tears*, was to play Philotas. William Devlin, who had been in Gielgud's *Romeo and Juliet* at Oxford in 1932, and three then little-known young actors, Stanley Baker, Terence Longden and Frederick Treves, were also in the cast.

Rehearsals began in late November 1948, while *Playbill* was still packing the Phoenix and *The Winslow Boy* was showing at a great many cinemas up and down the country. Peter Glenville had once more agreed to direct the play, and the full panoply of the Tennent organization's power in the West End theatre was to be thrown behind it. How could *Adventure Story* fail?

The Lord Chamberlain had granted the play a licence without demanding a single change, but privately, and without Binkie Beaumont ever being aware of it, the Lord Chamberlain's reader had raised a note of caution. In his internal memo he wrote: 'Alexander is a neurotic youth, spurred on by his attempts to justify himself to his dead father, Philip . . . The God-like youth becomes a dictator with all the implications of loneliness, suspicion, blood guilt and other neuroses.' Shrewdly, he concluded: 'This should be a sumptuous production, with its scenes in Babylon and Persia; but I cannot help feeling that this splendour is bound to overlay the author's attempts to get inside the mind of his hero.'

Privately, Rattigan was begining to share just this doubt. In a letter to a friend during the first weeks of rehearsals, he explained, 'As you can well imagine I am feeling more than a little apprehensive at my own temerity at having rushed madly in where so many angels have feared to tread – after all Shakespeare could read his Plutarch too.' As the rehearsals continued, so the author's apprehension grew.

By early December Rattigan and Peter Glenville were no longer certain that they wanted Richard Burton for the part of Alexander's friend and confidant Hephaestion, and later in the month they replaced him. Burton later explained that Rattigan had told him that he and Glenville were afraid the audience (and the Lord Chamberlain) might make a homosexual connection between the two men. But if that was the case, Paul Scofield, who was playing Alexander, was certainly not aware of it. 'There was a bond and an attraction between the two men,' but 'I don't remember any discussion of the attraction being a homosexual one,' he remembers now.

An alternative explanation was that Burton was not homosexual enough for Rattigan and Peter Glenville's taste, and was not capable of conveying the sort of intimacy that they were looking for in the two men's relationship. Certainly the unequivocally heterosexual Burton had not been altogether pleased when the play's author had made a rather drunken fumbling pass at him during rehearsals. Whatever the precise reason, Rattigan was gallant in his letter to Burton. 'The fault is entirely mine and Peter's,' he wrote, adding that they felt they needed 'a physique and personality different from yours. There was never any criticism of your performance, which was excellent.'

The uncertainties and apprehension over *Adventure Story* made the Christmas of 1948 far more gloomy for Terence Rattigan than it should have been. There were more than enough reasons for celebration, the enduring success of *The Browning Version*, and the first serious negotiations about a film version of the play, but neither seemed to cheer him. He was desperate for *Adventure Story* to succeed, and the fear that it might not led him to mope. Chips Channon did his best, by calling the Alexander play 'sublime' and giving him a blue velvet smoking suit as a present, but even that did not shift the playwright's anxiety. By now, in fact, Channon's attentions were rather less welcome than they had once been. Rattigan's infatuation with Kenneth Morgan had intensified again, and Channon's possessiveness was making it difficult for them to meet. Even more disturbingly, Morgan was once again demanding to become his permanent lover, and move in with him. Rattigan was still not prepared to agree to that, and said so. He did not say that he was still seeing Peter Osborn from time to time either. Nevertheless, Morgan's response was the same as it had been years before – to threaten to leave him for another actor.

When the provincial tour of *Adventure Story* began in Brighton, in January 1949, Chips drove down for the occasion. He found Rattigan in his room at the Grand Hotel, 'half-dressed, rather tight and maudlin, but lovable, as he always is before a First Night'. For good luck Channon gave him a 'coin minted in the reign of Alexander'. But the play itself disappointed him. 'Though it is magnificently produced, Paul Scofield as Alexander did not particularly impress any of us . . . We refused Terry's invitation to supper and drove back to London,' Chips wrote in his diary.

By now Rattigan was not the only person worried about *Adventure Story*. An extra source of concern was the fact that, because of its elaborate sets, the play was going to cost £7,500 to mount, about three times as much as a normal Rattigan. Even though Rattigan was putting up £3,000 himself, as well as paying for the music, Binkie Beaumont was growing increasingly anxious, and yet again he turned to Noël Coward for a second opinion. He invited Coward to take a look at the play in Brighton. Coward tore it apart after the Wednesday performance, just as he had torn apart *Love in Idleness*. But this time there was no Alfred Lunt to take Rattigan to one side and tell him not to worry.

Two days later Coward himself even wondered whether he might not have gone too far, and wrote to apologise. 'It was difficult for me to express on Wednesday night what I really thought of your play,' he explained, 'and I do hope I didn't sound too carping when I went on so much about the blue pencil.' Trying to pour oil on what were now very troubled waters, he continued:

> I was particularly impressed by the clarity and taste of your writing, and by the fact that you never once fell into the trap of vulgarization which so often happens when classical characters speak modern prose. As far as I can see everything you write is so much better than what you have written before. This is a very important achievement and I congratulate you with all my heart.

Rattigan was not appeased. If anyone was entitled to criticise his plays it was certainly not, in his view, Noël Coward. The Master had never done anything except try to unsettle him. Besides, he, Terence Rattigan, was his own sternest critic, he told Beaumont fiercely. Behind his ferocious reaction, however, may have lurked the nagging suspicion that perhaps Coward was right, though there were those who didn't think so. Harold Hobson, for one, had taken the trouble to seek out the play in Edinburgh in the first week of February, and had written a reasonably complimentary notice in the *Christian Science Monitor*.

The strain was beginning to tell, and Rattigan confessed his growing fears about the production to Freedman in New York. One thing which particularly distressed him were the slow scene changes. 'I was always a bit worried that if the scene changes did not move quickly and perfectly, and if the production were a little heavy, Scofield would have to have enough authority and power to dominate these difficulties.' Rattigan was beginning to have doubts on this score, in spite of Scofield's many strengths. The slow scene changes in Manchester had also given plenty of time for the critics there to blame the play 'rather than the performances'.

> Scofield is a very inexperienced actor, brilliant some nights and on other nights, having no technique to fall back on, quite hopelessly mechanical and artificial. It isn't that he doesn't try, or that he

doesn't understand the part, but this is the first time he's had to sustain a long part (*Hamlet* was only played once or twice a week at Stratford) and he needs continual guidance and coaching.

In Rattigan's view, Gwen Ffrangcon-Davies was also not to be relied upon.

> All the real emotion of the play should come from her, but although she gives a graceful and well-spoken performance, she seems incapable of showing even a shred of maternal feeling. That, I am afraid, is why so many critics seem to feel that the play hasn't the power to move them.

Rattigan's apprehension had translated itself into panic, and into attributing some of the blame for what may have been his own failures to those around him. He was convinced *Adventure Story* worked, and that it should be a success. He could not understand why other people did not share his view. After all, he had been right five times during the past seven years in the West End. Worse was to come.

Rattigan became convinced that Peter Glenville had turned against him. Glenville was now directing another play at the same time as *Adventure Story* was on tour, and that too was bound for London and a Tennent theatre. Was he quietly deserting the sinking ship of *Adventure Story* and putting his efforts elsewhere? Rattigan's neurotic mood led him to suspect as much, and even to believe that Beaumont might give Glenville's other play a better theatre. He became obsessed with the fear that *Adventure Story* would not open on Shaftesbury Avenue itself, as four of his previous five West End hits had, but instead be pushed off into a theatre less prominently positioned, like the St James's in King Street, well south of Piccadilly.

When he discovered that Binkie Beaumont had indeed given the Globe to Peter Glenville's other production, and that *Adventure Story* was now destined for the St James's, it was the final straw. The St James's was the theatre that had seen the collapse of another play which he had cared about deeply, and which had also suffered its difficulties, *After the Dance*. Rattigan tried to put as brave a face on it as he could muster, but a sense of doom overwhelmed him.

Suddenly everything Rattigan touched seemed to turn to dust. Noël Coward's waspish criticisms of *Adventure Story* had barely stopped ringing in his ears when Kenneth Morgan announced petulantly that he was leaving him. Morgan was going to live with a not particularly successful actor, whom some of his homosexual friends described as 'unreliable and bisexual'. Rattigan, being Rattigan, made every effort to conceal his real feelings, but he could not put Morgan out of his mind. He did not want to pursue him too ostentatiously, wounded though he was, but he wanted him back. He simply did not know what to do. How could anyone give up the life he was discreetly offering – the dinner parties at Albany, the weekend parties in Surrey, the butler, the cook, the Rolls-Royce, the expensive presents – in return for a small flat somewhere in Camden Town? It was beyond comprehension.

Perhaps if Rattigan had contacted Morgan and told him how much he needed him, and how badly he wanted him back, the actor might have returned. Perhaps it was a tiff, like so many of the tiffs between them in the past, to be made up with tears, apologies and homosexual love. In the years to come the thought would come back to haunt Rattigan in the darkest hours of the night. Certainly, had Morgan come back, the course of Rattigan's life, and his work as a playwright, would have been transformed. As it was, Rattigan's reticence, and the concealment of emotion that he had trained himself to abide by regardless of the consequences, changed his world for ever.

Six weeks later, on Monday, 28 February 1949, Kenneth Morgan killed himself. Rattigan was told the news that afternoon in his suite at the Adelphi Hotel in Liverpool, the last stop on *Adventure Story*'s tour before London. Bobby Flemyng saw him shortly afterwards. 'Terry was quite simply stunned. He could not believe it.' Morgan had taken an overdose of sleeping tablets, but when they had failed to kill him he had draped a tea towel over his head and held himself over a small gas ring, usually used to boil a kettle, until he had lost consciousness and died. It has been suggested that on the very same evening Rattigan told Peter Glenville, while they were going down in the Adelphi lift on their way to the theatre for the evening performance, that 'The new play will open with the body discovered dead in front of the gas fire.' Bobby Flemyng, who also saw Terry that evening, is less sure. 'I remember thinking, "I bet a play will come out of this."' It did.

No one, and certainly not Rattigan, ever discovered the reason for Kenneth Morgan's suicide. The pressures of being a homosexual had cost other young men their lives, especially if they were about to be revealed in public. The pain of losing a lover, whether male or female, overwhelmed many other young men and women. The fear of being left alone or abandoned threatened the sanity of stronger men than Kenneth Morgan. And the desire for private revenge, or for attention, from a previous lover could never be ignored completely as a motive.

But whatever the reason, Rattigan was never to rid himself entirely of the guilt that Morgan's suicide brought him. There had been other lovers, and there were still Peter Osborn and Chips Channon; but the worst of the blow was to his fragile inner confidence. Worse still, no homosexual at the time could admit publicly to an affair which might lead to suicide, for that would be to court publicity and danger. Terence Rattigan, a man who needed to be loved, realised only too clearly that he had failed a man whom he believed he had loved; and he could not display the emotion. Once again, he was to turn his life into art. That was his way of coping.

In public, as usual, he exercised his icy control. Whatever pain he felt was kept firmly inside. When *Adventure Story* opened at the St James's Theatre on Thursday, 17 March 1949, less than three weeks after Morgan's death, everything was as it had always been for a Terence Rattigan first night. There was a reserved box for Chips Channon and his parents, and another for Billy Chappell and Frederick Ashton. Alexander Korda was in the front row, as usual, alongside Lady Juliet Duff and not far from Cecil Beaton. Puffin was given his customary seat alone, while Peter Osborn was given two. As usual, Rattigan carefully bought presents for the cast. No matter what his private feelings were, he saw no reason to forgo the niceties that he believed belonged to the theatrical tradition. But he did allow himself the small joke of giving a gold coin to Peter Glenville, whose decision to bring another play to the West End at the same time might have been motivated by money. He gave the manuscript to Paul Scofield.

When the curtain rose, on George Wakhevitch's vast sets and to the music by Benjamin Frankel, for which Rattigan himself had paid £1,400, spontaneous applause broke out in the audience. But the author was not there to hear it. Just as he had done for the first night of *Playbill*, Rattigan had left the theatre the moment the house lights dimmed and retired to a nearby pub – where he proceeded to down several stiff drinks in rapid succession. He returned to watch the second half of the play, and Alexander's slow descent into madness, but refused once again to respond to the calls for 'Author' when the curtain fell to sustained applause. As they left the theatre the audience were congratulatory and respectful.

For once, some of the critics reflected the audience's enthusiasm. Leonard Mosley, in the *Daily Express*, wrote: 'That young playwright with the Midas touch, Terence Rattigan, failed to appear at the end of last night's show, but the excitement of the audience indicates that he has again produced theatrical gold.' *The Times* complimented both author and star.

While conquering the world held by Darius Mr Terence Rattigan and Mr Paul Scofield are alike at their best. It is extraordinary with what quiet ingenuity the author gives dramatic firmness and continuing interest to each stage of the young conqueror's progress from Babylon to Parthia; and Mr Paul Scofield matches the strong and pointful dialogue with acting equally strong and pointful.

But *The Times*, like the *Daily Telegraph* and the *Observer*, was distinctly critical of the exploration of Alexander's character. In the *Observer*, Ivor Brown accepted that

> It is natural, in this age of ours, for the psycho-analysts to set to work. Terence Rattigan who, with admirable courage, has tackled 'the great Emathian conqueror' . . . steps in where even Marlowe feared to treat. He follows the modern trend and discovers an Oedipus Complex in the ruthless destroyer of Oedipus's own city of Thebes. His Alexander, brilliant, shrill, so engaging that even a priestess of Apollo will unbend to his smile, is also sexually neuter, pours all his affection motherwards, and, when one mother is gone, must find a compensating dream mother in the enemy camp.

Rattigan's new supporter, Harold Hobson, in the *Sunday Times*, wondered why this Alexander made the transition from a young conqueror 'unmoved by women and indifferent to wine' into 'a Macbeth, luxurious in the Shakespearian sense, and a drunkard'.

But it was Beverley Baxter, MP and theatre critic of the London *Evening Standard*, who annoyed Rattigan the most. 'I commend Mr Rattigan's courage,' he wrote, 'and only wish I could acclaim another triumph, but the stern fact remains that Shakespeare did this kind of thing much better. I am very much afraid that *Adventure Story* will not turn out a success.' When it appeared on Friday, 18 March, Rattigan was deeply depressed by the tone of Baxter's review. But within a few days he had become infuriated by it. Here was a critic who seemed to imply that he should not even attempt to tackle so grand a subject. That rankled. Five weeks later he seized the opportunity to answer back.

In a foreword to the shortened, ninety-minute radio version of the play, which he had rapidly prepared for the BBC to keep interest in *Adventure Story* alive, he called such criticism arrant nonsense.

> When I read in the notice of an eminent critic that 'the stern fact remains that Shakespeare did this kind of thing much better', I

am heroically prepared to accept the fact, stern though it may be, but find difficulty in seeing its relevance . . . 'the stern fact remains' that neither Shakespeare nor Shaw has written a play about Alexander the Great – and I have, and as this is, they say, a free country it is hard to see why a subject should be banned to a playwright, however humble, because two great dramatists might have chosen that subject themselves, but did not.

It was an over-reaction, a sign of his own vulnerability. He hit out because he felt that his achievements were being overlooked, his seriousness of purpose called into question by critics. Only one, T.C. 'Cuthbert' Worsley, who had recently started reviewing for the *New Statesman* and was to become one of Rattigan's friends, offered a comment which, though unpalatable, he could accept. After complimenting Rattigan on his progress towards 'a real exploration of character' in *The Browning Version*, he wrote:

> Now he has taken a wild leap which has landed him between two stools. His new play is not mature enough to satisfy those who have already responded emotionally to the figure of Alexander; nor, unless I am greatly mistaken, is it sufficiently crude to appeal to that large public who enjoy seeing history reduced to a sort of contemporary slip-slop.

The fashionable London audiences were not going to miss out on the latest Rattigan, however, and for the first time his name alone was sufficient to carry the play. Within its first three weeks it had been visited by the Queen, accompanied by Princess Margaret and the King's Air-Equerry, Wing-Commander Peter Townsend, as well as by Queen Mary, the Duchess of Kent and the Princess Royal. Not everyone was enthusiastic, however. Shortly after the first night, Rattigan was in the foyer when two young women burst from the dress circle demanding their money back – even before the curtain had gone up on the evening's performance. 'I wouldn't see this play if you paid me,' one exclaimed to the other. The bemused author asked why. 'Because it's BC,' the woman replied, seizing her refund and marching out of the theatre. 'I'm afraid *Adventure Story* is indeed BC,' Rattigan told a radio audience not long afterwards. 'It really has to be.'

BC and the reviews took their toll. In July 1949, after 107 performances, the play closed. Beaumont wrote a note, 'I am very proud of *Adventure Story* and could not have enjoyed the adventure more – and long to get at the next Rattigan epic.' *Playbill* was still running. The closure was a bitter blow. 'Terry cared deeply about this play and his disappointment, in its lack of popular success, he felt very keenly,' Paul Scofield explains. Rattigan remained – in Scofield's words – 'very easily hurt by small unconsidered remarks that might imply criticism. He smiled with his eyes, the rest of his face expressing little, except a sort of indefinable pain.'

'The purpose of the play is to explain the deeds by the man, and not the man by the deeds,' Rattigan had told the BBC's radio audience, adding,

> Is it right to measure a man's greatness simply by his deeds? Isn't what you are more important that what you do? . . . Alexander's tragedy was that he set out to conquer the world before he first succeeded in conquering himself. 'For what shall it profit a man if he shall gain the whole world and lose his own soul?' That, I hope, is the story the play tells.

It was also, partly, his own story.

Of all his plays, *Adventure Story* became Rattigan's favourite, and was to remain so – 'no doubt for no more reason than that, like all parents, I nurture a special fondness for the child that died in infancy'. The child may have been dead, but he never gave up his battle to resuscitate it. Within two years he was trying to persuade Laurence Olivier to star in it in New York, and two years later still he was to revise it completely, first with Laurence Harvey in mind, and then for Tyrone Power. Neither production was destined to reach the stage. The next performance *Adventure Story* received was on BBC Television in 1959. The star was a young actor called Sean Connery.

Rattigan had described his Alexander to Paul Scofield as 'an artist as well as a man of action – his physical energy, strategic brilliance and determination being inspired by the love of his father . . . All Alexander's primary motivations came from the love of his elders.' The strength of his own feelings for his father and mother had not wavered. Frank Rattigan still exercised an extraordinary influence over him, and yet his son remained keenly aware of what he saw as his mother's suffering. The month that *Adventure Story* closed Frank Rattigan had a stroke. 'He was never the same again,' his son Terence told his friends afterwards. The Major was partially paralysed, and his memory had been badly impaired. Rattigan was so distressed that he refused to go to New York for discussions with the American producers about the Broadway opening of *Playbill*. His father's illness kept him in England for most of the rest of the year.

*   *   *

A major theme of Rattigan's work, Cuthbert Worsley was to write, was that 'the weak have a terrible clinging strength . . . they will always come back to haunt and weaken the strong with their misguided devotion'. It was true, and it applied to his relationship with his father. When Frank confessed to him at Harrow exactly why he had been asked to resign from the Diplomatic Service, one side of Terence Rattigan was deeply shocked, shocked by the apparently callous behaviour displayed towards his mother. But another side of him took account of two things: first that his mother, fond of her though he was, not only knew about, but also in a sense, condoned her husband's myriad liaisons; and, secondly, that his father's unceasing desire for conquest stemmed at least in part from an unsatisfied need to be loved, and by being loved to feel alive. Terence Rattigan recognised that trait in himself. His fixed determination to surround himself with a court of friends, whether homosexual or not, to fill with amusing remarks even the briefest lag in the conversation, to be gallant and charming come what may, and in the face of whatever slights – these were the signs of a lonely man unable to cope with his own lack of love. His father's weakness was also his weakness.

This gave the relationship between them a strange quality. Part of Rattigan's reaction to his father was amusement, as demonstrated by his relentless mimicry of him, but there was also real affection. And the tension between the two translated itself into drama. His father's weaknesses were the well-spring from which flowed his own sympathy for the oppressed, for lovers whose hopes were destroyed by the very intensity of their emotions, his ability to avoid making one-sided moral judgements – and his inability, except for Millie Crocker-Harris, to create a real deep-dyed villain. He had come to accept that just as his father's nature could never be completely transformed, neither could his. It was his understanding of his father's weaknesses that gave him the strength to be himself – to be, and remain, unashamedly homosexual, and to accept his sexuality as his father had accepted his.

To be prevented from going to New York to discuss *Playbill* was a blow, both professionally and financially. Rattigan was to have acted as co-director of the Broadway production with Peter Glenville, for a handsome fee already agreed, but he turned the opportunity down in order to remain with his parents and make sure that his father received the best medical advice. He kept in close touch with the family doctor, William Buky of Welbeck Street, making sure that his father told the doctor about the wounds he had received in Flanders during the Great War.

But he kept New York in his sights, determined that *The Browning Version* at least should receive the best possible Broadway production, and encouraging Harold Freedman, once Gielgud had slipped away again, to look for a replacement star. 'Prefer Brando to Garfield,' he cabled his New York agent, 'but know neither's work well and would appreciate your own opinion. Agree Kazan best proposition for director.' He was aware that for his double bill to do well he would need a specifically American production.

Sadly he was not to get one. His preoccupation with his father's illness, and the sheer Englishness of the two parts of *Playbill*, made their casting and direction by Americans intensely difficult. Each time Freedman seemed nearly to have managed it, so the prospective star or director disappeared. The English-born actor Brian Aherne, who had made a career in Hollywood, was interested, but nothing materialised. Frederic March considered the prospect, but finally decided it was 'too uncertain'. In the end it was Maurice Evans, the Dorset-born actor who had made his name in the West End production of R.C.Sheriff's *Journey's End* and had since been producing Shakespeare in the United States, who settled the matter. He wanted to play Eric Portman's role in both *The Browning Version* and *Harlequinade* and he was prepared to produce the double bill and risk his own money. In the absence of a better offer, Freedman recommended acceptance; that way the shows could open on Broadway that autumn. Rattigan agreed. Evans's 'Shakespearean reputation could help Harlequinade'.

As the negotiations in America wore on, *Playbill* smoothly continued its run in London, while productions were planned for Belgium, Switzerland, Germany and Holland. And hardly had *Adventure Story* closed in July 1949 than *The Browning Version* won Rattigan his second Ellen Terry award in three years, which he was to receive from the Duke of Edinburgh at the Savoy in early August. Shortly after the ceremony, and with Dr Buky confident of his father's at least partial recovery, he set off for Denmark – to discuss the Danish production. Rattigan was driven to Copenhagen by his chauffeur in his latest Rolls-Royce and with the ever-reliable Mary Herring as companion and secretary. On the journey they discussed the possibility of accepting a commission from the BBC to write a television play for the forthcoming Festival of Britain, due to open in 1951, and whether or not he should contribute an article to an anthology about the arts, to be called *Diversion*.

By the time he returned he had drafted a piece for the anthology. It concentrated on how little credit writers received for their work in the cinema. 'So let the screenwriter throw off the shackles of the director,' he proclaimed, '(and the camera) and remember that the screenplay is the child not only of its mother, the silent film, but also of its father,

the Drama; that it has affinities not only with Griffith, De Mille and
Ingram, but also with Sophocles, Shakespeare and Ibsen.' He concluded
firmly, 'I believe the camera to be the enemy of the screenwriter's art
. . . drama is inference and inference is drama.'

By the beginning of September, it was clear that the New York production of *Playbill* was going badly. Peter Glenville sent a telegram
complaining that Maurice Evans was not getting the Crock right, but
both men knew there was little or nothing they could do about it. If
Rattigan had been involved from the beginning, if he had been present
and able to act as co-director, if one of the other stars had actually
agreed to play the part, then things might have been different. As it
was the rehearsals were all but over and the play was to open in New
York at the end of October, with a short tour beforehand. There was
nothing to be done but prepare to accept the worst. Filled with fore-
boding, Rattigan set sail for New York in September 1949.

When he arrived, he discovered that Maurice Evans was insisting
on playing *Harlequinade* first and *The Browning Version* second. Evans
wanted other changes, many of which he had persuaded Glenville to
accept. Rattigan was horrified. No sooner had he settled into his suite
at the Waldorf-Astoria on Park Avenue than he found himself not only
desperately re-writing *Harlequinade* but also endeavouring to stave
off all kinds of 'tinkering' with *The Browning Version*, the one play of
his which had never had a word changed. There was one small consolation: Tolly de Grunwald had agreed to pay him £5,000 for a script of
Love in Idleness. Rattigan needed almost all the money to pay off his
overdraft.

When *Playbill* opened at the Coronet Theatre, New York, on 12
October 1949, the audience's reaction was sufficiently enthusiastic to
persuade its author to break the rule he had kept for almost a decade
and make a speech. Rattigan said little of significance, beyond explaining how much the plays meant to him, and how much he hoped they
would entertain an American audience. He still longed for success on
Broadway. This was his eighth play to be presented in New York, and
only *O Mistress Mine* could truly be called a hit. He wanted another
one.

Playbill was not to be it. The critics were respectful, but they did
not believe that New York audiences would appreciate the failings of
an English schoolmaster. There was an element of national pride in their
reaction, for some of the English critics had been less than generous in
their reception for Arthur Miller's *Death of a Salesman*, which had
recently opened in London. The American critics had not forgotten

the slight. Brooks Atkinson, the magisterial critic of the *New York Times*, encapsulated the American view:

> English writers are a good deal more preoccupied with the miseries and heartbreaks of schoolmasters than our writers are. In English playwriting the schoolmaster has become almost a convention; and conventions sooner or later come to be accepted without critical analysis. Some English critics have dismissed Willy Loman in *Death of a Salesman* as pure sentimentality, though most of us took him as a tragic figure. There is no accounting for this difference in attitudes, but it certainly exists; for me Mr Rattigan's schoolmaster is pure sentimentality and I cannot grieve over his misfortunes. He is a colorless, ineffectual little man – not strong enough to sustain a drama of emotion. The sorrow Mr Rattigan asks us to feel over his failure is maudlin, despite the expertness of the play's craftsmanship.

·In his own defence, and to answer Atkinson, Rattigan decided to write a piece for the *New York Times* himself. He wanted to discuss the 'hazards of play export'. He began by suggesting that 'the best plays are about people and not about things', and then wondering, if that were the case, why 'the play of character, when exported from its native country, seems to face far greater hazards than does the play of ideas'.

Rattigan then answered his own question. 'The fact is that plays of character, be they Russian, American, English or French, really demand a contribution from an audience, which, when that audience is foreign and unversed in the customs, idiom and idiosyncrasies of that dramatist's native country, cannot readily be given.' This was not the hysterical reaction of a playwright incensed at his ill-treatment at the hands of an American critic, but rather an attempt to solve the puzzle for himself, and to point out that other dramatists shared the same fate. He was convinced, for example, that his new friend Tennessee Williams had suffered it in England with his latest play *A Streetcar Named Desire*.

> Some of the English critics described the play as a 'picture of tenement life in New Orleans'. Well, I suppose if you care to look at it that way, that's what it is. But American audiences didn't look at it that way. They looked at it as the author intended they should, straight at Blanche du Bois and the surrounding characters and only vaguely took in the background, which Williams, like

any good painter, had designed simply to enhance his portrait. But in England the background has tended to obscure the whole picture.

Then Rattigan came to the point.

No comparisons are implied, but *The Browning Version* is also a play of character, with a background especially designed to show off that character . . . I have to admit that I was a little surprised to learn from several journalistic sources that I had written a play 'about life in an English public school'. Well, like my friend Tennessee Williams in a different context, I suppose I had, if you care to look at it that way. But it isn't the way English audiences did look at it – and I should really be very happy if I thought that American audiences wouldn't look at it that way either.

The debate highlighted the mutual incomprehension of Britain and the United States at that time. Rattigan was bitter about the Brooks Atkinson review, but in one way they are both saying the same thing. There is a divide, both cultural and emotional; and certain plays, and certain playwrights, may try all their lives to bridge it and still fail. That was Rattigan's fate. The very Englishness that glistened on the surface of his plays concealed for some the emotional reality he was addressing beneath that surface. But the American audience did not penetrate to it.

Less than two weeks after his article appeared, *Playbill* closed on Broadway. It had survived for just sixty-two performances, closing barely two months after its launch. In an effort to keep it alive, Maurice Evans had contemplated substituting another play for *Harlequinade*, but had finally decided against it, telling Rattigan in a telegram, 'It is the twin bill which frightens customers away. Whatever happens, and however much it will have cost, I wouldn't have missed the opportunity of playing Crocker-Harris for anything.' In private the play's author rather wished he had, but he did not say so, of course. That would have been too un-English.

By now Rattigan was on a new tack. He was writing a play in which a man in pursuit of pretty blonde girls is discovered to be leading 'a double life' by his long-suffering wife. In real life his father was by now almost unrecognisable: his face sallow and twisted, his speech impaired. Even his eyes had lost their particular sparkle. The stroke had affected his brain so badly that he was almost a husk, barely able to recognise anyone. Rattigan's new play would celebrate the man he once was. But a play about his father would also be a play about himself, with the blonde young women doubling for fresh-faced young men, and his 'double life' being discovered by one of his long-standing male lovers. Only nobody would need to know that. That would remain beneath the surface.

CHAPTER 16

My Father, Myself

◆

The greatest reverence is due to a child! If you are
contemplating a disgraceful act, despise not your
child's tender years.

JUVENAL, *Satires*

◆

In August 1949, Terence Rattigan gave up his chambers, F2, in Albany
and moved to 16 Chester Square in Belgravia. Here, in the first weeks
of December, he wrote the first fifty pages of a new play, an attempt
to explain his father's behaviour, and, by implication, his own, and to
make both a focus for comedy. It did not prove easy. The more he
toiled the less the result satisfied him. No matter how hard he tried,
he could not bridge the gap between explaining his father's and his
own selfishness and the art form of comedy. Shortly before Christmas
he tore up the first pages of the draft and started again.

But his sombre mood would not dissipate. Every time he tried to
draw the character of Mark, the philanderer at the heart of his story,
he seemed to freeze over the page – the character emerging only as
stilted and unlifelike. The longer he struggled, the less the play would
come to life. He simply could not make his serious points comical. In
despair, he resorted to the solution he had chosen for the confusion of
his own life. He resolutely concealed the serious purpose of the play
and broadened out the comedy.

This was the genesis of *Who Is Sylvia?*, as the new play was to be
called. 'It just wouldn't work in too realistic a vein,' Rattigan later
explained to Rex Harrison, to whom he sent two copies as soon as he
had finished. 'Too many awkward and uncomfortable questions were

raised which in light comedy can be gaily brushed aside, to wit, what happens to the discarded mistresses?'

Though he would never admit it, the process of writing the new play had made Rattigan uncomfortable. He had forced himself to examine himself and his father, and he had not relished the result. The shame he felt, and the shame he believed his father should have felt, was almost too painful to bear. Not that anyone would have guessed. He had written it as he had so many others, sitting on the sofa with his 'writing table' perched on his knee, scribbling in ballpoint on a foolscap pad. He had appeared to his secretary just as he had always done – self-effacing, polite, a man at ease with himself. Yet the reality was quite different. No matter how hard he had tried, Terence Rattigan could not make *Who Is Sylvia?* an excuse for his father's actions, or for his own. Neither he nor his father could laugh them off. The behaviour was not truly funny, even though he tried to treat the whole thing as 'a joke'. On the surface, when he finally plucked up the courage to read the play to them, Frank and Vera Rattigan shared it with him. The Major and his wife 'laughed until the tears ran down their faces, and gave me their blessing to use the material in this way,' he told a Scandanavian journalist shortly afterwards. Behind the smiles, however, lay a desolate truth. There was no excuse for sexual promiscuity.

Turning his and his father's behaviour into comedy had not solved the problems Rattigan had set himself to sort out by writing the play. The attempt to make the whole matter comic led to an unhappy, and unfunny, compromise. One man who sensed that at once was A. D. Peters, to whom Rattigan sent a copy shortly after Rex Harrison. Peters disliked the play intensely on first reading, and said so bluntly when they met in February 1950. Sarcastically, he added that if it were produced as it was the first night would be one that he 'would find extremely interesting'. Rattigan was mortified. He could not bear to accept the truth, and reacted bitterly, and brutally. He severed their professional relationship. Peters, who had put his own money into *French Without Tears* fourteen years before, and had helped create Rattigan's reputation, was abruptly dismissed. The two men would never work together formally again. Instead Rattigan turned to Harold Freedman in New York, and Dr Jan van Loewen in London.

Freedman too had his reservations, but was canny enough to express them diplomatically. 'I am just wondering,' he wrote carefully, 'whether or not in getting away from the heavy treatment you told me you had started the play out with, you have landed on too light a treatment for it. Not in the lighter scenes, which I think are wonderful, but in the fundamental emotional basis of the play.' He ended by suggesting that perhaps a serious resolution to the piece would be appropriate. Rattigan cabled back immediately: 'Many thanks first class analysis. Have been thinking along somewhat similar lines. But am very doubtful whether play should end with a serious scene though believe a serious note, i.e. three or four lines would help. Anyway will ponder deeply and do nothing until I see Rex.'

Rattigan also gave a copy of the new play to Glen Byam Shaw and Stephen Mitchell. But neither man, after reading it, wanted to be involved. Byam Shaw told him politely: 'I am not the right person to produce it. That is my limitation not yours. I should tend to give it a reality which you have so cleverly realised in the writing would be wrong.'

So *Who Is Sylvia?* went to Binkie Beaumont, who jumped at it. The idea of a new Rattigan comedy – no sweeping historical drama this time – was far too good an opportunity to pass up. And there was also the tempting possibility of bringing a star like Rex Harrison back to the West End. To Beaumont's delight, it really did look as though Harrison was serious. On 14 February 1950 he had written Rattigan a long letter from New York, explaining that he had been awaiting it 'with great excitement' and had found it 'a terribly funny play with a great great deal of simply glorious comedy'. He predicted that, even as it stood, it would be 'a huge success'.

But there was a sting in the tail. Harrison may have known a good deal about discarded mistresses himself, but he was not anxious to present the image of a rapacious philanderer to the London theatre audience. 'Mark is, after all,' Harrison wrote, 'a cultured, witty man of the world who has obviously mixed with varied and attractive feminine society, and even though the three girls do suggest "Sylvia" in appearance, it seems incredible to believe that he would become attracted to them.' The point was clear. There was no way Rex Harrison was going to be seen to fall for three such floozies in a production on the West End stage.

Rattigan replied from Chester Square offering his own analysis of Mark's situation and placing it in contrast with his counterpart in the play, a character called Oscar. Mark, Rattigan told Harrison,

suffers from arrested development and is in love throughout his life with the image of his own youth. Sylvia, in fact, is a fantasy and has no existence in reality. I suppose a deeper Freudian diagnosis would analyse Mark as a fairly straightforward Oedipus subject in love with the mother image which he neatly divides into two halves, the upper part being represented by his wife and the lower half by successive Sylvias. His conscious mind is acutely aware of the fact that the lower half of this image must never dominate the upper and he arranges his life accordingly.

The parallel with Frank Rattigan's succession of blondes, which, though obtrusive, were never allowed to wreck his relationship with Vera, and with Terence Rattigan's own succession of 'Sylvias', which he had hoped would not ruin his relationship with Kenneth Morgan, was precise.

Just in case Rex Harrison missed the point, Rattigan continued:

Certainly he [Mark] can persuade himself for a few brief moments that he is romantically interested in the girl, but it is a deliberate self-deception that does not go very deep. Oscar, by contrast – and he is really in the play only to provide that contrast – is a cold blooded amorist – the usual type – who pops in and out of bed whenever and wherever he can and for whom the pursuit of sexual gratification is the key to existence.

Rattigan did not want to make the three 'Sylvias' of his new play too intelligent or sympathetic because he did not want the audience to worry about them when they were discarded.

In fact it is to safeguard his marital life that he takes on extra-marital relationships and that is why he deliberately chooses his sex objects from among the silly and the commonplace. But the shortcoming of his life is not only sex . . . but is more importantly of that kind of romantic intoxication that the adolescent enjoys when he meets a pretty girl at a dance and which adults have reluctantly to give up after the first excitement of marriage settles down into the inevitable monotony of domestic life . . . Mark refuses all his life to come out of the emotional nursery.

Harrison cabled back, 'Would be happy appear London, New York or both.' Rattigan was overjoyed, cabling back to say how pleased he was that Harrison would be starring in 'another play of mine after fourteen years'. The joy was to be short-lived. Just two days later, Rex Harrison got cold feet again. This time he wanted to see some 'alterations' to help put his mind at rest. Rattigan refused, and told Harold Freedman to convey the message to Rex in New York. Freedman did so, and Harrison changed his mind back again. 'Trying to contact you telephone today,' he cabled Rattigan. 'Please bear with me until we meet beginning of April. Do very much want to play it.' Rattigan's reply was again to the point. 'Will bear with you till Kingdom come, or more specifically about the middle of April.' Less than a fortnight later, however, Rex cabled again, explaining that he had decided to stay in America with his wife, Lilli Palmer. Once again, the actor for whom Rattigan had specifically written a role had turned it down.

Binkie Beaumont acted quickly. Why not Michael Wilding, he suggested, who had done so well for them both in *While the Sun Shines*? Rattigan was not absolutely sure, but agreed, and Wilding was offered the part. He too accepted, only to discover that the film producer Herbert Wilcox, to whom he was now under contract, would not release him. 'Herewith your beautiful play,' Wilding finally cabled Rattigan, 'and some pieces of my broken heart. I would so love to have played it or tried to.' David Niven, who had loved *The Browning Version*, was now approached, and then John Mills. Both men politely said no. Michael Redgrave phoned Beaumont about the possibility of his playing the part, but he and Rattigan had by now begun to wonder whether Robert Flemyng, another of Rex's companions from *French Without Tears*, might not be the best choice. After all, Roland Culver, another veteran of the Criterion production, was scheduled to play Oscar. Perhaps Bobby Flemyng, whose career had been burgeoning in New York, might succeed as Mark. In the first week of May, he was offered the part. He accepted, but ironically not before raising exactly the same objections as Rex Harrison had done. He doubted that 'a man of Mark's obvious intelligence and character would build romance out of quite such silly girls'. He even argued, exactly as Harrison had done, 'that all that must be better explained, or somehow made more plausible. In other words we must feel that this pursuit is a more serious and romantic aspect of his life than it appears to be – at the moment it strikes me as a little too adolescent to be true.'

Unmoved, Rattigan declined to redraw Mark's character. He still could not confront completely the question at the heart of his idea for the play – was there an acceptable explanation for his father's philandering, or his own amorous adventures? The play was his attempt to explain his father to his mother, providing the woman he cared about so deeply with something approaching a reasoned explanation for her husband's behaviour, and incidentally for his own, though he doubted whether Vera would ever grasp that that was what he had in mind. Rattigan recognised his mother's preference for self-deception. Besides, he was not prepared to return to the painful process of rewriting that had seen him destroy his first fifty-page draft.

Instead he disappeared to Stratford-upon-Avon to talk to an open-faced young actor called Anthony Quayle, who had been director of the Memorial Theatre company there since 1948, and whom he hoped he could sign up as his director for *Who Is Sylvia?* Rattigan discussed the play in general with Quayle, and even sent him a telegram after their meeting: 'Agree Mark should have more definite point of view but must in no way approximate Oscar's.' But he did nothing fundamentally to alter his text. Beaumont was putting no pressure on him to do so, and he simply sidestepped every effort to make him confront the contradiction of the 'serious comedy' he had set out to write a year earlier. Instead he took refuge, as he had done as a schoolboy, in watching cricket. He had decided to use a cricket match as the basis for his television play for the Festival of Britain, and intended to spend the summer completing it, before rehearsals for *Who Is Sylvia?* began to take up too much of his time. He had been working on the idea since April, dividing his time between Chester Square and the Stag and Hounds at Binfield.

Financially things were looking up, in spite of the failure of *Adventure Story*. RKO had finally bought the rights to *Love in Idleness* for $125,000, and Cary Grant was to play the Alfred Lunt role, or so Harold Freedman had told him. Grant wanted Carol Reed to direct, but the negotiations had not been completed. Rattigan was also being summoned to Pinewood Studios for regular conferences on the film version of *The Browning Version*, which Gainsborough were to make, with Puffin directing. He had been paid £25,000 for the rights and a further £5,000 for his script.

There had been lengthy discussions about the casting of the Crock, until in the end Michael Redgrave had convinced Asquith that he should be given the film role. The quality of his performance in *The Way to the Stars* had tipped the scales. Rattigan had agreed to the casting, and was only too pleased to see Puffin directing the picture and working with him from his screenplay. The two men were still close, though not as close as they had been during the first years of the war, bound together, in part at least, by their shared tendency to underestimate their own achievements. Puffin sent Rattigan a present that summer – a small porcelain cockerel with the inscription, 'This small cock is to crow for you, as you are incapable of doing it yourself.'

There had been a smaller fee from BBC Television for his Festival Drama, while during the summer the BBC had exhumed for radio – again for a smallish, but nevertheless welcome, fee – the adaptation which he and John Gielgud had made of *A Tale of Two Cities*, with Eric Portman playing Sydney Carton. The broadcast had received respectful rather than overwhelmingly enthusiastic reviews and had revived in Rattigan the sense that he was still doomed never to be taken seriously, at least by those sections of English literary society who set themselves up in judgement on what was good or bad.

That spring, in the midst of his struggles with Rex Harrison, Rattigan also succeeded in stirring up a hornet's nest among British theatre
enthusiasts by expressing in public his long-held conviction that plays
were about people and not about things. In doing so, though he failed
to realise it at the time, he was making himself a sitting target, which
from then on he would remain, for all those who made it their business
or pleasure to attack the concept of the popular or well-made play.

The controversy began quietly. Rattigan had drafted a brief piece
for *Theatre News*, which he had called 'Concerning the Play of Ideas'.
A.D.Peters, then just still acting for him in such matters, wanted to
send it to the London *Evening Standard*, but Rattigan's new friend Cuthbert Worsley, now drama critic of the influential *New Statesman*,
grabbed it for his own paper. Rattigan was paid a fee of ten guineas
for his contribution.

On 4 March 1950 his article was published. The first two paragraphs
set out its author's intention.

> I am in fact a heretic from the now widely held faith that a play
> which concerns itself with, say, the artifical insemination of
> human beings or the National Health Service is of necessity
> worthier of critical esteem than a play about, say, a mother's
> relations with her son or about a husband's jealousy of his wife
> . . . I further believe that the intellectual avant-garde of the English
> theatre – or rather, let's be both brave and accurate, and say of
> the English speaking theatre, since in my view, the Americans
> are the worst offenders – are, in their insistence on the superiority
> of the play of ideas over the play of character and situation, not
> only misguided but old-fashioned.

In particular he pointed out that it was George Bernard Shaw, then
still alive at ninety-four, who in 1895 had campaigned for a 'new'
theatre, the 'theatre as a factory of thought, a prompter of conscience,
and an elucidator of social conduct'. He doubted that the 'present-day
proponents of "socially significant" drama' had taken one step beyond
the standpoint Shaw had taken up then. But that had not prevented
them from dismissing as valueless any play that did not fit into their
mould.

> So complete, in fact, has been the Shavian–Ibsenite victory that
> in 1950 any defence of the theatre they defeated is considered to
> be no more than a naughty heretical joke. Daily, we playwrights
> are exhorted to adopt themes of urgent topicality, and not a voice
> is raised in our defence if we refuse. That refusal is universally

and blandly taken to indicate that our minds are empty of ideas, and being so, are despicable.

He acknowledged that his view would land him in 'the intellectual and critical soup', but did not draw back from insisting that the avant-garde were mistaken.

The misconception on which your cult is founded is that ideology equals intellect. It doesn't. The mis-reading is of Ibsen, who was considerably less interested in his own ideas than were his followers, and considerably more interested in his own characters than were his critics.

His conclusion was no less sweeping.

From Aeschylus to Tennessee Williams the only theatre that has ever mattered is the theatre of character and narrative . . . I don't think that ideas, per se, social, political or moral have a very important place in the theatre. They definitely take third place to character and narrative, anyway . . . The trouble with the theatre today is not that so few writers refuse to look the facts of the present world in the face but that so many refuse to look at anything else.

Not for the first time, and certainly not for the last, Terence Rattigan allowed his pen to run away with him, without stopping to think what might be said on the other side. He presented himself as an outspoken critic of Shaw (still, at that time, a dangerous thing to do), and as someone unwilling to give the new generation of playwrights a fair hearing. At the same time he managed to antagonise many traditionalists.

The first riposte came from the Shavian camp, championed by the caustic pen of the Scottish playwright James Bridie. 'Shaw is a liberator', Bridie wrote the following week.

Rattigan has got him all wrong . . . He has made possible all our plays – Rattigan's, Priestley's, the whole boiling of them. He has broken the old moulds, with their insistence that there were only four kinds of play; that they must be about murder and/or adultery; and that there was only one way of doing each variety. This has allowed a number of intelligent craftsmen to make their own, individual contributions without being booed by the gallery or bullied by the critics. Rattigan, of all people, ought to be grateful. Does he imagine for a moment that *French Without Tears* or *While the Sun Shines* would have run for a fortnight under the old dispensation?

Bridie's argument was suported by Ben Levy. 'I should say the first essential of a great play is a heated intellectual or poetic imagination, and preferably both. Without either, characterisation and narrative breed no more than a novelette.' Then Peter Ustinov chipped in: 'I do not recognise a sharp dividing line between the plays of human relations and the plays of ideas. The best plays are, I believe, a felicitous blend of the two. Ideas are not confined to the dreary social message, and I would go so far as to say that there is no better purveyor of ideas than the play with a deep and subtle human interest'. And Sean O'Casey: 'No one can write about ideas without creating persons to express them; but it is one thing to have an idea in a head and quite another to place it in a play. It takes a mastermind to do that so that it will appeal to the imagination of an audience. Shaw and Ibsen are masters of this fancy.'

Finally Shaw himself entered the debate, summing up Rattigan as 'an irrational genius'.

He is, of course, vulnerable as a reasoner; but he is not a reasoner, nor does he profess to be one. The difference between his practice and mine is that I reason out every sentence I write to the utmost of my capacity before I commit it to print, whereas he slams down everything that comes into his head without reasoning about it at all. This of course leads him into all sorts of Jack o'Lantern contradictions, dead ends, and even delusions; but as his head is a bright one and the things that come into it, reasonable or not, are all entertaining, and often penetrating and true, his practice is pleasing.

After the compliments, Shaw proceeded to attempt to demolish Rattigan's argument:

Now there are ideas at the back of my plays; and Mr Rattigan does not like my plays because they are not exactly like his own, and no doubt bore him; so he instantly declares that plays that have any ideas in them are bad plays, and indeed not plays at all, but platform speeches, pamphlets and leading articles. This is an old story! It used to take the form of complaints that my plays are all talk . . . Mr Rattigan, not being a born fool, does not complain of this, but being an irrational genius, does let himself in for the more absurd complaint that, though plays must be all talk, the talk should have no ideas behind it, though he knows as well as I do when, if ever, he thinks for a moment, that without a stock of ideas, mind cannot operate and plays cannot exist. The quality of a play is the quality of its ideas.

Shaw's contribution closed the *New Statesman* debate, which had done Rattigan no good whatever, especially among the new generation of playwrights. The piece he had dashed off – just as he was to dash off the introduction to his first two volumes of collected plays three years later with every bit as disastrous results – seriously dented his standing as a playwright, so seriously that it would take almost half a century before he could again be considered as a serious playwright, rather than a mere entertainer. Already suspect for the flamboyance of his lifestyle, he could now be dismissed as facile and unthinking, a man who dismissed ideas and was interested only in commercial success.

In fact, the reality was far removed from this image. Terence Rattigan struggled to ensure that his plays dealt with complex emotions in an accessible form, and to see that his characters brought those emotions to life. In that he would not have disagreed with Shaw. But by leaping into battle with Shaw he had done his reputation untold damage, wounding it in a way that would take him another decade to understand. His reputation was fatally tarnished in the minds of the young playwrights and critics who were about to make their mark. His new play did nothing to alter their misconception.

In an effort to regain ground in the aftermath of the failure of *Adventure Story*, Beaumont had decided to try the new play at the Criterion, hoping to repeat the early success of *French Without Tears* there. Rattigan, too, hoped the theatre would bring him luck. It had 'a small gross but excellent atmosphere and tradition for light comedy', he cabled Freedman, 'thus obviating necessity excusing lightness of play'. He was getting on well with Anthony Quayle, who had agreed to direct, and he demonstrated his commitment by arranging with Bill Forsyth that Rattigan Productions should put up a third of the production's cost – an investment of £1,000. Beaumont, needless to say, was delighted. His risk had been cut.

The short try-out in Cambridge, which opened on 9 October 1950, seemed to go reasonably well, though after another week in Brighton, Rattigan became increasingly worried about Bobby Flemyng's performance as Mark. He was no Rex Harrison. No stretch of the audience's imagination could transform him into the adorable womaniser that Rattigan had had in mind. Binkie Beaumont and he even discussed replacing him with Nigel Patrick before the show opened in London, but finally decided it was safer to stay with Flemyng. Their leading man was under no illusion that what mattered above everything else to both men was that the play should be a success. Flemyng recalls now: 'The only thing that really mattered to Terry was success in the theatre. He was dedicated to it.'

The dress rehearsal did not help. As Mary Herring told a friend afterwards, 'It was dreadful, they were all as flat as pancakes.' Even the designs by Rattigan's friend and companion Billy Chappell, and the skill of Diane Hart, who was playing all three incarnations of Sylvia, could not save the production. Nevertheless Terence Rattigan put on his most urbane smile for the opening night in London on Tuesday, 24 October 1950. Once again his mother was in a box, and the champagne cork was in her handbag. Chips was in the front row, just in front of Tolly de Grunwald and Puffin Asquith. Rattigan had also reserved seats for his new friend Stephen Potter, now on the brink of fame as the inventor of the 'Lifemanship' joke, and for the film director David Lean, who wanted Rattigan to write a script for him. But once again Rattigan did not stay and watch the performance, and when he returned to witness the curtain call the applause was hardly rapturous.

The reviews were no more enthusiastic than the audience. W.A. Darlington, in the *Daily Telegraph*, wrote: 'Terence Rattigan had established well-deserved fame as about the best of our lighter dramatists at providing incidental amusement. In his new frolic . . . he relies almost exclusively on this particular skill. His other, more formidable, skill, that of telling a story, hardly comes into use at all.' *The Times* agreed. 'If his theme were treated seriously, and the first act is scattered with what seem to be the bits and pieces of a serious intention, the repetitiveness of the story would be its theatrical strength; but treated as a light comedy, entertainingly as it is told, divides itself into three short plays with too many points of resemblance.' The *Manchester Guardian* was blunter still: 'High comedy needs a philosophic touch, and the idea was too thin, too worn, and too obvious to stand it.'

The *Evening News* damned Rattigan for 'too airily and too casually' sketching the peccadilloes of a diplomat, while Beverley Baxter, in its rival the *Evening Standard*, concluded: 'Rattigan has established a level beneath which he must not fall. This play has neither the exuberance of inexperience nor the technique of a tired master. It was assembled, not written.'

Rattigan had been expecting harsh reviews, but remained convinced that at least his talent to amuse an ordinary West End audience had not deserted him. The morning after the opening he cabled Freedman in New York:

Above left: *Major Frank Rattigan* c *1900.* (*Theatre Museum, V & A*)
Above right: *Vera Rattigan as a girl.* (*Theatre Museum, V & A*)
Below left: *Brian Rattigan and three-year-old Terry (right).* (*Theatre Museum, V & A*)
Below right: *Terry Rattigan, c. 1918.* (*Theatre Museum, V & A*)

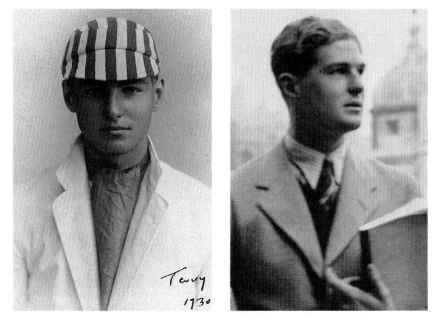

Terence at Harrow, 1930, in 1st XI cricket colours.
An Oxford undergraduate. (Theatre Museum, V & A)

The first cast of French Without Tears, *(including Rex Harrison, Kay Hammond and Trevor Howard). (Theatre Museum, V & A)*

Kenneth Morgan, Rattigan's close friend who appeared in Follow My
Leader *and the film version of* French Without Tears *and who knew
Rattigan well from 1939 until his death. (BFI/UIP)*

Anthony Asquith, film director. (R. Haupt/Camera Press)

Dr Keith Newman, Rattigan's Oxford psychiatrist in the early 1940s who helped him overcome writer's block, and earlier in the army uniform of his native Austria.

Right above: *A scene from* Journey Together, *with Richard Attenborough and Jack Watling, 1942. Rattigan wrote the screenplay.*

Right below: *Flight Lieutenant Rattigan, 1942.*

Rattigan is his Eaton Square flat in the early 1950s and in his Albany flat in 1976, near the end of his life. (T. Blau/Camera Press and F. Hermann/Camera Press)

Michael Franklin, who knew Rattigan well from 1949 until Rattigan's death. (Angus McBean)

Kenneth Moore and Peggy Ashcroft in the first production of The Deep
Blue Sea, *1952. (Theatre Museum, V & A)*

Rattigan, with Margaret Leighton at the première of Look Back in Anger,
8 May 1956. (Hulton Deutsch Collection)

Rattigan, who enjoyed the company of beautiful women, with Vivien Leigh at the first night of The Summer of the Seventeenth Doll, *April 1957.*

Above: *Rattigan and his mother,
1960. (Hulton Deutsch Collection)*

Below: *Kenneth Tynan, Rattigan's
principal critic, with his wife
Kathleen, 1970. (Hulton Deutsch
Collection)*

Opposite above: *Rattigan with his
mother, Vera, left and his secretary
Mary Herring at the investiture of
his CBE in 1958. (Hulton Deutsch
Collection)*

Opposite below: *Rattigan with
Harold and Pegs French at the
investiture of his knighthood in 1971.
(Hulton Deutsch Collection)*

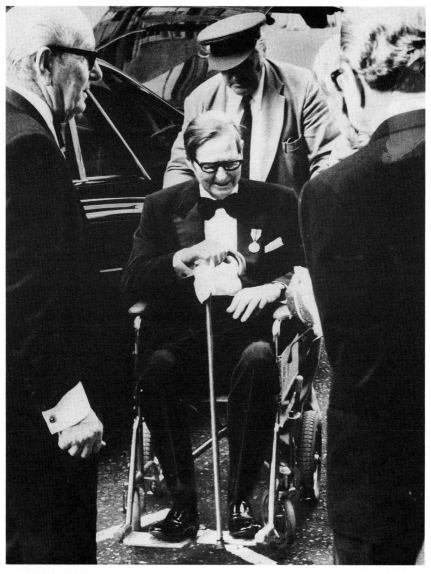

Rattigan arriving for his final first night: Cause Célèbre, *July 1977. (Hulton Deutsch Collection)*

Notices as expected guarded and patronising. Main criticism being that a serious subject has been treated too sketchily and frivolously. Stop. Consider myself main fault lies in Flemyng's inability to bring out the various relationships in the play notably with Oscar thus making their scenes together more like backchat between comedians than conversation between very close friends. Stop. Toughness of audience last night forced Flemyng into more thin-blooded performance than he gave last performances of Brighton week. Stop. Believe play will go much better with normal audiences and understand box office is quite active.

Barely a week after the opening, Rattigan set off for New York on the *Mauretania* to discuss a new script he had agreed to write for Korda, for which he was to be paid £10,000. He went on to take a short holiday in Jamaica before returning to New York to talk to Peter Brook, the man whom he was determined should direct the Broadway version of *Adventure Story*. This plan came to nothing, in spite of the support of the powerful American producer Irene Selznick. By the time he got back to England in January *Who Is Sylvia?* had been losing money for seven weeks. In a desperate attempt to keep the show going, Rattigan agreed to waive his royalties from each performance, and Beaumont accepted that Tennent would also relinquish their management fee. The show limped on.

'Rattigan could not bear to see it become a failure,' Flemyng recalled. 'That was his pride. He thought of himself as a successful playwright, and he wanted all his plays to be successful.' Harold French, who directed the film version of the play for Alexander Korda two years later, agrees. 'It should have been a flop but Terry kept it going because in those days you could, the get out was so small. That was the pride side of him. He couldn't bear a flop.'

This was all the more true because of all the play meant to him, and the extent to which it echoed his own emotions and life. In Act One, for example, Mark's friend Oscar warns him about the dangers of the double life he is planning. It was Rattigan talking about himself, as the critic Freddie Young was to point out later.

OSCAR: I'm always terrified of the disaster that looms ahead for a character like you who refuses to come out of the emotional nursery . . . You know what you are, Mark, don't you? You're an emotional Peter Pan.
MARK: Well, what's wrong with that? I prefer to keep my emotions adolescent. They're far more enjoyable than adult ones.

And here is Mark describing his son Denis, with whom Rattigan also identified.

MARK: He's a damn little slacker. He's been at this place in Tours for three months and he can't even write a line of a letter in reasonably correct French. Keeps complaining that the daughter of the house has fallen in love with him.

Who Is Sylvia? also contained one speech that Rattigan had always wished he had made to his own father. It occurs in Act Two, after Denis has announced that he does not intend to follow a career in the Diplomatic Service, but to become an actor instead.

DENIS: Father, may I say something? (*Mark looks at him in silence.*) I know it's none of my business – but really, you know I do think you're making rather a mistake chucking the Diplomatic. (*Very sincerely*) I know exactly how you feel and I do sympathise with you – really I do. But you've had such a brilliant career up to now – haven't you – I do think it'd be an awful waste to throw it all away now . . .

In the third and last act, Mark, speaking to Oscar, eloquently defends, by implication, Rattigan's own behaviour as a homosexual.

MARK: To divide the illicit from the domestic, the romantic and dangerous from the full and secure – to divide them into two worlds and then to have the best of both of them. Years ago in this very room you told me it couldn't be done – well, I've done it – not only here in London, but in Paris, in Rome, in Stockholm and in La Paz.

But in Act Three he also admits that duplicity can be found out. Mark's wife Caroline, played by Athene Seyler, makes a speech that Rattigan wished – perhaps – that his mother had made first to his father and then to him.

CAROLINE: You see from the beginning I thought to myself – well, this Mark Wright business must go rather deep. I'm his wife, and if he really wants to change his identity from time to time, then it must, in some way, be my fault. Something that I can't give him, that he wants and can find elsewhere. I would have liked to be Mrs Mark Wright, but I knew I couldn't be. I knew I couldn't ever be anything more than the wife of Mark Binfield – and as I wanted more than most things, to go on being that, I realised I had to give up all claims on Mark Wright. And I did. Except, of course, that I had to do my best to see that Mr Wright came to no harm. In Paris, for instance, we always have to have him followed by the Embassy detectives. He will go to such dreadful dives in Montparnasse . . .

When the play was published, Rattigan dedicated it 'To My Father. With love, with gratitude and in apology'. Frank Rattigan had not been well enough to attend the first night, and he was never to attend the opening of another of his son's plays. He could, however, read the reviews of the film version of *The Browning Version*, which was released in March 1951 while he was recuperating at a hotel in Exmouth, Devon. The critic Dilys Powell commented in the *Sunday Times*: 'Mr Rattigan, in adapting his own play, has allowed nothing to distract attention from the central figure; even when the man is not on the screen the audience is thinking about him.' Asquith's 'skilful' direction was praised by *Variety*, which called the film 'one of the best dramatic entertainments to have come from the J. Arthur Rank stables for a long time', while almost every critic praised Michael Redgrave as Crocker-Harris. The *Daily Mirror* called it 'one of the greatest performances ever seen in films'.

Frank Rattigan had every reason to be grateful to *The Browning Version*. He had benefited from its success in the theatre, just as his wife had benefited from the success of *The Winslow Boy*. Rattigan had arranged for half the profits from each play to go to each of his parents, and Frank had received a little over £5,000 from *The Browning Version*, most of which he had invested in stocks and shares. He was also entitled to 7½ per cent of the producer's profits – if there were any. They had also received income from the $125,000 Rattigan was to earn for the film rights to *Love in Idleness*. It was the first time Frank had had any money of his own – apart from his Foreign Office pension – since leaving the Diplomatic Service, for the money came to him directly, and not as an allowance from his son.

The influence a father could have on his son was also the theme of the television play Rattigan wrote for the BBC as part of the Festival of Britain celebrations. Inspired by Sir Donald Bradman's last appearance in a Test Match in England, *The Final Test*, which was broadcast on 30 July 1951, also focused on a son who both misunderstood and underestimated his father. Sam Palmer is a great English cricketer about to play in his final test match. His son Reggie is a budding poet, and not particularly keen on cricket, so instead of turning up as he has promised to watch the game, he goes to visit the poet/playwright whom he most admires, Alexander Whitehead, who lives near Henley. The playwright is not keen to see him, but when he finally agrees he suddenly realises whose son he is. A cricket lover, Whitehead immediately whisks the boy off to the Oval to see the match, thereby overturning Reggie's prejudice – that no poet or playwright could possibly admire cricket.

In his introduction to the play for the *Radio Times* Rattigan wrote:

I shall also be arrogant enough to beg those of you who do switch on, and who may be misguided enough not to share my enthusiasm for the game of cricket ('I have heard that such people exist,' as a character remarks in the play), not, on discerning to your horror that *The Final Test* does in fact mean the final test, to switch off too soon. Cricket is only the background. It is not, please believe me, the play.

Nowhere is that more clearly demonstrated than when Alex is finally introduced to Sam Palmer, the boy's father, after he has been bowled for a duck in his final innings:

ALEX: At the same time I have to confess I envied you a little.

SAM: Envied me?

ALEX: Your profession. Other professions aren't quite so rewarding – you see – my own for instance. If, later on, when the time comes for me to retire and I write my last play – well – if I'm bowled for a duck on the first night I don't think I can quite see my audience standing and cheering me for five minutes. There's more likely to be a very ugly sound from the gallery and a stampede for the exits.

SAM: But *your* profession – well I mean, it is a profession. After all, what you do lasts –

ALEX: Only as long as people read it. They may not, for very long.

SAM: I'm sure they will. But what I do – or what I've done rather – well there's nothing to show.

ALEX: (*Excited*) Nothing to show. You're out of your mind. (*Catching himself up*) I'm so sorry but I get excited about this. It's such an old argument, this complaint that the non-creative artist is forgotten when the creative artist lives on –

SAM: Am I – what was it – a non-creative artist?

ALEX: Of course. Now tell me, Mr Palmer, is Paganini forgotten? Is Nijinski? Is Garrick? Will Fonteyn be forgotten when she has ceased to dance? – may that day never come. Of course not. The non-creative artist – every time, because what they do, or have done, must get better and better as the years go on, until a legend of greatness is born that goes far beyond the actual truth. Look at W.G. for instance, I bet he wasn't really as good as we think he was today –

SAM: Well, I don't know.

ALEX: (*Interrupting firmly*) Of course he wasn't. Of course he couldn't have been. In 1881 what was he? No more than a pretty good cricketer, with a straggly beard and a very bad temper. Seventy years later, what is he? A God, an Olympus. But the creative artists – we wretched scribblers and composers and painters, why, damn it, we have to leave a record behind us, so that posterity will inevitably know for certain just how ordinary we really were. With such a handicap how can we poor creatures hope to join you on Olympus? That's why I envy you, Mr Palmer. I envy you most deeply.

The voice was authentically Rattigan's own.

To make a reputation as a playwright, in the face of his father's opposition and initial contempt, and to raise the Rattigan name and reputation among dramatists of the century had long been his greatest ambition. Now, during the first weeks of 1951, he started work at the Stag and Hounds on a play he hoped and believed would see that ambition fulfilled and his place as a serious dramatist in the world's and his father's eye confirmed.

Frank Rattigan lived only to read the manuscript of *The Deep Blue Sea*, not to see it in performance. As usual he and Vera had each received a typed copy shortly after it was finished. But within three days of its reaching the West End stage, the man its author had spent a lifetime trying to impress was dead.

CHAPTER 17

Hester or Hector

◆

*Death is the only pure, beautiful conclusion of a
great passion.*

D.H.LAWRENCE, *Fantasia of the Unconscious*

◆

The play Rattigan had been struggling with at Binfield in the first
weeks of 1951 represented a return to one of his abiding themes – the
illogicality of love. As he was to explain it to Laurence Olivier a few
months later, 'The phenomenon of love is inexplicable in terms of
logic. That was the theme of *The Deep Blue Sea*.' He had originally
planned the play as a long one-acter about a young woman trapped by
an imbalance of passion, 'beginning with the discovery of Hester in
front of the gas fire and ending with her preparations for a second
suicide attempt'. He explained later that his objective was not 'so much
to develop a character as to reveal it', and the character he set out to
reveal was Hester Collyer, the wife of a High Court judge, who –
when the play begins – has left her husband for a handsome young
former fighter pilot called Freddie Page. As the play took shape in the
first months of 1951, it extended to three acts.

In fact Rattigan was describing the life of Kenneth Morgan, who
left a wealthy and successful playwright, Terence Rattigan, for a
younger man. Hester's relationship with Freddie is doomed, and
the play opens with her being saved from suicide by the hand of
God – the money in her gas meter runs out, and the supply cuts
off before she can asphyxiate herself. Morgan had been more determined. His attempt to gas himself had succeeded on 28 February
1949, apparently after his relationship had come to a sudden, and
unexpected, end.

Rattigan's own experience coloured every line of the play. He saw Kenneth Morgan in Hester Collyer, and himself in her devoted husband, Sir William. But he also saw part of himself in Hester and part of his former lover Chips Channon in Sir William, anxious as he was – as Chips had been – to shower her with presents. Like *Who Is Sylvia?*, *The Deep Blue Sea* was, in many of its aspects, an intimate revelation of its creator's own life, and he made no attempt to hide the fact from his close friends.

The man he was determined should direct the play was Peter Brook, and he handed him a copy only a few days after he had sent his parents theirs. Within weeks a strong rumour began to spread that Rattigan had written a play about being a homosexual, and that Hester Collyer had started life as Hector Collyer. Certainly he was striving to come to terms with Morgan's death – 'and the best way Terry knew of doing that was to write a play about it', as one of his friends now puts it – but a decision to reveal himself publicly as a homosexual at that time, or even to hint at such a thing, would have contradicted the whole pattern of his previous behaviour. Stephen Mitchell, who had produced *The Browning Version*, is convinced that his friend would never have considered such a thing. 'Besides, he based the play, in part, on a married couple we used to play golf with together at Sunningdale, who were in the process of splitting up.'

Frith Banbury, the play's eventual director, himself a homosexual, also dismisses the idea. 'Nowadays it's always said that Terry wrote a homosexual play and then re-wrote it because it was banned, which was absolute rubbish. I knew . . . We talked a lot about Kenneth Morgan and he put bits of Kenneth into the play and himself too. But he would never have written a homosexual play *per se*, knowing that it would be very lucky to get two or three weeks at a club theatre. He was very commerciálly minded and he wanted his plays to make money. Never for one moment did he refer in any of his conversations with me at that time to a homosexual version.'

Nor is there any record of such a version in the Rattigan archive in the British Library, or in the H.M.Tennent archive. The Lord Chamberlain's files, which are now available for public scrutiny, show no trace of one, and neither do the files of the Rattigan Trust or of his solicitor. Although rumours of it persist, the director Alvin Rakoff, who worked with Rattigan in the 1960s, in particular on the first transmission of his original television play *Heart to Heart*, explains that Rattigan told him he could not conceive of the emotions in *The Deep Blue Sea* without thinking of Hester as a man. The critics Freddie Young and Anthony Curtis suspect that Rattigan might have had in mind

Hector Collyer, but that he would never have considered putting the idea down on paper.

Binkie Beaumont's friend and business associate John Perry certainly saw an early version of the play in September 1950, while Rattigan was still working on it, and sent him lengthy notes on its development, which he had clearly discussed with Beaumont. But the letter containing these notes – which is now in the Rattigan archive – gives no indication whatever that the original version had Hector Collyer at its heart, even though Bryan Forbes was later to suggest that he had seen an early draft in which Hester was Hector Collyer. Perry made no mention of it, urging only that the play needed more 'depth'. Had a homosexual relationship been at its heart, he would not have ignored it. No play with a homosexual theme would have received a licence from the Lord Chamberlain for a public performance.

Certainly Terence Rattigan was only too aware that the London theatre audience of the time would not be allowed to see a play with a homosexual affair at its centre. Many years later he wrote to his fellow playwright John Osborne:

> At last I can write about my particular sins without Lord Chamberlain-induced sex-change dishonesty . . . But my own sins bore me terribly, which may be the lethargy of old age creeping over me, or just the disinclination to join in the chorus of voices endlessly *shouting* the love that once dared not speak its name, from every housetop in the country. Perhaps I should rewrite *The Deep Blue Sea* as it really was meant to be, but after twenty years I just can't remember why I made all that fuss.

Rattigan wrote the play, as he wrote several others, with Puccini playing in the background, and it seems far more likely that the character he created at its heart was always a woman, like the tragic Cio-Cio-San in *Madame Butterfly*. The fact that those passions could also be shared by a homosexual did not make them any the less feminine. The genesis of the play may indeed have been in a homosexual's death, but Rattigan placed it firmly in a heterosexual context and it is hard to conceive reasons which would have impelled him to do otherwise, especially as he was determined his parents should never discover his secret.

It is possible, however, that after the change in the law on homosexuality following the Wolfenden report of 1958, Rattigan was tempted to recast his play using Hector instead of Hester. There is some evidence that he considered doing so, but that the friends whose advice he sought were not enthusiastic and as a result the project was abandoned. But even if such an attempted revision did take place, he would have kept it extremely private. Terence Rattigan was still anxious to present an acceptable face to the world, the face of a man who was not openly homosexual. 'Outing' was many years in the future.

Mordaunt Sharp's *The Green Bay Tree*, which focused on a previous homosexual attachment, had played in the 1930s, but the affair was treated in retrospect, after one of its participants had changed his way of life, and nothing sexually suggestive was apparent in the play's plot or dialogue. The whole construction of *The Deep Blue Sea* is entirely different. Hester's desire for Freddie is clearly in the here and now. Rattigan makes the sexual centre of the couple's ill-fated love abundantly clear at the beginning of the play's second act, when Freddie describes his relationship with Hester to his friend Jackie Jackson.

JACKIE: There must have been some rows.

FREDDIE: Very minor ones. Nothing like the real flamers we had when we first started.

JACKIE: What were they about?

FREDDIE: (*Uncomfortably*) Usual things.

    Jackie waits for him to continue.

(*Explosively*) Damn it, Jackie, you know me. I can't be a ruddy romeo all the time.

JACKIE: Who can?

FREDDIE: According to her the whole damn human race – male part of it, anyway.

JACKIE: What does she know about it?

FREDDIE: Damn all. A clergyman's daughter, living in Oxford, marries the first man who asks her and falls in love with the first man who gives her an eye. (*After a slight pause*) Hell, it's not that I'm not in love with her too, of course I am. Always have been and always will. But – well – moderation in all things – that's always been my motto.

Frith Banbury says of the Rattigan/Morgan relationship in its early days in January 1940: 'Kenneth was a wide-eyed kiddiwink really at that time, and very much Terry's type – he liked chaps that looked as though they were in their late teens, seventeen, eighteen and nineteen-year-olds – but were actually well into their twenties – which I think Kenneth Morgan then was – and could therefore make intelligent conversation after the event. I think they had an actual affair then, certainly Terry became rather obsessed with him.'

Rattigan and Morgan lost touch during the war, but not long after it ended, when they had come together again, Rattigan's obsession rekindled with a vengeance as his affair with Chips Channon began to wane. By 1949 he had become possessive. But just as Rattigan had become bored by Channon's relentless pursuit, so Morgan became weary of Rattigan's. In the last months of 1949 he had moved into another actor's small and rather seedy flat in Camden Town – the flat which provided *The Deep Blue Sea* with its setting. Whether Rattigan ever went there – in a desperate attempt to persuade Morgan to resume their relationship, as Sir William Collyer was to go to Hester's shabby apartment – is a matter of conjecture.

By the beginning of March 1951, with the celebrations for the Festival of Britain getting under way on the south bank of the Thames in London, Rattigan had sent a copy of his new play not only to Celia Johnson, whom he particularly hoped would play Hester, but also to Margaret Leighton. No hint was given to either actress concerning the genesis of the play – an approach Binkie Beaumont, who certainly knew about it, approved of. As Frith Banbury puts it: 'Binkie divorced his activities from his views and he didn't find anything strange about that.' No matter how outrageous he might be in private, in public he maintained an air of studious asexuality. Like Rattigan, details of his sexual life were shared only with those whom he knew well and trusted completely. He was, moreover, at this moment doubly anxious to keep out of trouble. Parliament was about to look into complaints about his activities, and his allegedly monopolistic grip on the West End theatre, and he would hardly have wished to add to his difficulties by announcing that he was to present a play with a homosexual scandal attached – even if it was a new play by Terence Rattigan.

Rattigan had wanted to send the play to Laurence Olivier, in the hope that he would both direct and appear in the role of Sir William Collyer, but Beaumont, afraid that Olivier's involvement might mean that it did not appear under the H. M. Tennent banner, dissuaded him. Instead Beaumont suggested Frith Banbury as director. He was anxious to push ahead with the new play as quickly as possible, not least because *Who Is Sylvia?* was finally limping to a close at the Criterion, and he had no wish to keep it going any longer even if Rattigan had contributed a third of the £4,000 necessary to mount the show. Banbury had worked as an actor, toured Europe in *While the Sun Shines* with Ronald Squire and Bobby Flemyng, briefly appeared in the West End production, and thereafter turned to directing. *Waters of the Moon*, with Edith Evans as its star, and Wynward Brown's hit *The Holly and the Ivy* had been two of his recent successes.

By July 1951 Banbury was casting. He wanted the best, and though he admired Margaret Leighton and Celia Johnson, was convinced that only Peggy Ashcroft could do Hester Collyer justice. But it was left to Beaumont to persuade her. 'Peggy was a very sexy person, but she didn't like to think of herself in that light,' Banbury says. As a result she refused the part point blank, calling Hester 'a silly woman'. But Beaumont persevered and in October finally convinced her. In jubilation Rattigan cabled Freedman in New York, 'Binkie considers it his greatest victory.' Her agreement, however, meant that the play would have to be delayed until the following spring, – the first moment she was available.

While the future of *The Deep Blue Sea* was gradually unfolding, Rattigan turned to another project, a film script that David Lean had asked him to do about flying faster than the speed of sound. Based on Lean's own idea, which he had sold to Alexander Korda, *The Sound Barrier*, as it came to be called, had no story. 'I'd always wanted to make an adventure film about man's exploration into the unknown,' Lean told the *New York Times*. 'Now here was this "sound barrier" – invisible, yet able to tear an airplane to pieces. Man's assault on this treacherous mass of air seemed to me the great modern adventure story.' Lean had taken a year to research the idea, and gave Rattigan a notebook containing 300 closely written pages. But it was not until Korda and he took Rattigan to watch a jet fly low at Farnborough, and he was introduced to the test pilots – 'quiet young men, absolutely unlike the types I had known during the war' – that he agreed to write the script.

Once again Rattigan drew on his father to help him create the film's central character, Sir John Ridgeway, the pioneering aircraft builder who achieves his ambition, but only at the cost of his son's life. Domineering, but frightened of being alone, craving human affection, yet unable to show his true feelings, he cannot even open up to his daughter after his son is killed on his first solo flight. The sound barrier is finally broken, but only at the cost of her fiancé's life. The film was shot during the late summer of 1951, with Ralph Richardson as the aircraft builder, Lean's then wife Ann Todd as his daughter, and Nigel Patrick, who had turned down *Who Is Sylvia?*, as her fiancé.

In New York Harold Freedman was still trying to interest a Broadway producer in *Adventure Story*, but without much success. Every producer he approached wanted a major star, and a complete revision of the script. Rattigan reluctantly agreed, but only when he had time. *The Deep Blue Sea* came first.

Peggy Ashcroft could begin rehearsals in January 1952, as could Roland Culver, veteran of so many Rattigan successes, who was signed up to play Sir William after Clive Brook had turned it down. Alec Guinness had declined the part of the enigmatic Mr Miller, who was finally played by Peter Illing, and Trevor Howard had turned down Freddie. What was to be done? Frith Banbury wanted the fair-haired former commando Jimmy Hanley, but Culver suggested a new young actor, Kenneth More, whom he had met playing golf. At his first audition, with Rattigan and Beaumont, More did not convince them. But Rattigan had a hunch that he might be right, and arranged a second audition at Chester Square. He gave the young More two stiff drinks before they started, to help him to relax, and this time he was excellent. Banbury was persuaded, and Kenneth More became the ex-fighter pilot Freddie Page, the role that was to make him a star.

Rehearsals were not without their dramas. Peggy Ashcroft was still nervous. 'I feel as if I'm walking about with no clothes on,' she told Banbury on one occasion. The remark was a revelation to him. He thought, 'Oh good, that's just what the character ought to be feeling, that's why you're going to be so marvellous in it.' At the start of rehearsals, with Rattigan on a brief trip to New York, Banbury and she had arranged for one or two changes, which the director then explained to Rattigan over dinner on his return. He did not appear concerned, but when Banbury left, he telephoned Beaumont and told him, 'They're trying to ruin my play.' It took Beaumont most of the night to calm his author down, but eventually he accepted the changes. 'In the end Terry was extremely cooperative,' Banbury recalls now.

In January 1952 the Lord Chamberlain granted the play a licence without demur. A brief try-out in Brighton was planned for February, then the West End opening at the Duchess would take place on Thursday, 6 March. In Brighton, Peggy Ashcroft first displayed the remarkable depth of her interpretation of Hester. Banbury recalls that when she first describes to her husband her first meeting with Freddie, she chose to 'sit down for the whole time and look out of the window'. 'Not my direction,' he explains. 'All I can claim credit for is not preventing her doing it.' The effect was utterly absorbing.

HESTER: That word you were talking about just now. Shall we call it love? It saves a lot of trouble.
COLLYER: You said just now that his feelings for you haven't changed.
HESTER: They haven't, Bill. They couldn't, you see. Zero minus zero is still zero.
COLLYER: How long have you known this?
HESTER: From the beginning –
COLLYER: But you told me –
HESTER: I don't know what I told you, Bill. If I lied I'm sorry. You must blame my conventional upbringing. You see I was brought up to think

that in a case of this kind it's more proper for it to be the man who does the loving.

>   *Pause.*

COLLYER: But how, in the name of reason, could you have gone on loving a man who by your own confession, can give you nothing in return?

HESTER: Oh, but he can give me something in return, and even does, from time to time.

COLLYER: What?

HESTER: Himself.

On 6 March 1952, when *The Deep Blue Sea* opened at the Duchess Theatre, with his mother in the audience, but not his father – who had gone to Exmouth to escape the worst of the winter weather – the final curtain was greeted with a burst of cheers. It was almost the first sound the audience had allowed itself all evening. As Philip Hope-Wallace wrote in the *Manchester Guardian*, the play 'was listened to with that unmistakable hush with which a first night audience, though calloused by current trash, still knows how to honour a finely written and superbly acted piece of emotional drama'. The *Daily Mail* reflected all the critics the following morning with its headline: Mr Rattigan Jumps Back to the Top.

Three days later, on 9 March, Frank Rattigan, the inspiration and provenance of so much of his younger son's work, died from a stroke at the Pencarwick Hotel in Exmouth. He was seventy-two. His body was cremated after a short private ceremony at the Golders Green crematorium in North London four days later. There was a brief announcement of his death in *The Times*, but no lengthy obituary. It was a gloomy counterpoint to the cheers.

'Terry was always more obsessed with his father than his mother,' Frith Banbury recalls now. 'He used to talk about him, make jokes about him, impersonate him all the time.' Certainly his father's influence extended into the play. But his father's was not the only influence at work in his new play. There was also the influence of Keith Newman. Terence Rattigan drew on both men in *The Deep Blue Sea*.

In Act Three, for example, when Mr Miller returns to stop Hester's second suicide attempt, Rattigan gives him a crucial speech. It is one which Keith Newman might have made and one which he rewrote no fewer than four times. For Mr Miller is, to a very considerable extent, Terence Rattigan's first stage portrait of Keith Newman. Miller's dialogue certainly bears astonishing similarities to some of Newman's utterances, and he is one of the play's crucial figures (which was one reason why Rattigan had originally wanted Alec Guinness to play him).

Miller had been disbarred from the medical profession for being homosexual, and not, as most theatregoers assumed, for being an abortionist;
and this is what Rattigan is talking about when Miller tells Hester:

> MILLER: Listen to me. To see yourself as the world sees you may be very
> brave, but it can also be very foolish. Why should you accept the world's
> view of you as a weak-willed neurotic – better dead than alive? What
> right have they to judge? To judge you they must have the capacity to
> feel as you feel. And who has? One in a thousand. You alone know how
> you have felt. And you alone know how unequal the battle has always
> been that your will has had to fight.

To some extent Terence Rattigan was describing his own will here,
and likening Hester's will to Kenneth Morgan's. But the conclusion of
the play, when Hester chooses to live instead of to die, aroused a
controversy that still goes on. Kenneth Tynan, the flamboyant critic
who was to become Rattigan's principal antagonist in the years to
come, wrote in the London *Evening Standard*: 'I shall never forgive
Rattigan for his last act. It is intolerable: his brilliance lays an ambush for
itself and walks straight into it . . . When finally she chooses survival, it
is for all the wrong reasons.'

Rattigan himself was aware that some people might take this view.
In fact, when the play was still what he called 'a long one-acter', he
had even considered ending it with Hester taking her own life. But, as
he was to tell a French correspondent, 'When I came to write it at full
length my artistic conscience revolted. In deciding that Hester should
live there was no thought in my mind, I assure you, of making any
moral point, I simply felt . . . that it was dramatically wrong for Hester
to kill herself at the end of the play.' The artist in him won out, as did
the determination not to be seen as simply the inheritor of Pinero's
mantle. 'Whereas in a short play,' he wrote a few months later, 'the
suicide ending might be logical and conclusive, in the dramatic sense
in a play of full length it seemed merely sentimental – like the suicide
of Paula Tanqueray.'

Sentiment was something he was determined to avoid. 'The strong-
est evidence that the present ending is right is that it is, of all Hester's
fates, by far the least popular. There is hardly a member of the audience
who would not prefer her to kill herself – a fact which, for me, would
make the so-called "tragic" ending not tragic at all and highly suspect.
Hester's real tragedy lies in life, not death.'

Rattigan's assessment of his audience reveals a great deal about him,
and his view of life. One of his most characteristic traits as a playwright

is to conjure an upbeat ending from the tragedy that surrounds his characters. Hester sends Freddie packing, but decides not to kill herself. In spite of everything, the Crock in *The Browning Version* gets his way about his speech. Even Alan is determined not to fall into the arms of the predatory Diana in *French Without Tears*. These acts of will were reflections of their author's belief that suffering, no matter how intense, did not exclude hope.

The shock of his father's death was to prevent Rattigan from working for some weeks, and just as he was about to start again the family was struck by another tragedy. Shortly after Frank Rattigan's death, Terence's elder brother, Brian, was diagnosed as suffering from lung cancer. Though they had never been particularly close, Brian's plight deepened the melancholy that Rattigan already felt at his father's death. As ever, he tried to conceal his feelings, by hiding in the midst of the noisiest party he could throw, and he bought a new house, Little Court, on the very edge of the Sunningdale golf course in Surrey, in which to throw the gayest parties. But the ruse did not work. For now when he invited his friends down for the weekend he was not well enough to entertain them. He took to disappearing to bed, leaving his cook and butler to look after them.

Even the excellent notices for the opening of *The Sound Barrier* in July, which C.A.Lejeune in the *Observer* called 'A triumph' and William Whitebait in the *New Statesman* insisted would 'enthral audiences everywhere as has no English film since *The Third Man*', did nothing to help (even though *The Sound Barrier* did become the most successful British film to play in London since *The Third Man*). The Queen expressed her enthusiasm for it. Noël Coward phoned Rattigan to congratulate him on breaking the box office record at the Plaza previously held by his own film *In Which We Serve*, and Churchill asked for a special screening. But for once Rattigan barely noticed. Apart from his own worries, his brother Brian's illness was on his mind, and he was able to keep the melancholy that enveloped him at bay only by burying himself in a film script for Puffin Asquith based on his television play *The Final Test*. He accepted a mere £1,000 for the script and £2,500 for the rights. He wanted something to keep him busy. Jack Warner had agreed to play the ageing cricketer Sam Palmer and Robert Morley the verse playwright, and Asquith was anxious to get on with it and shoot in the early autumn, before the sun and warm weather disappeared completely.

Rattigan had also agreed to finance the production of Rodney Ackland's play *The Pink Room*, first in Brighton and then in London. John Perry had turned it down flat for H.M.Tennent but Frith Banbury, an

old friend of Ackland's, had suggested it to Rattigan after Rattigan told
him that Rattigan Productions was looking for a tax loss that year.
Written in 1945, Ackland's play, which was retitled *Absolute Hell* in
the 1980s, concerned the lives and loves of a large group of men and
women at a London drinking club at the end of the war. In part, the
play reflected Ackland's own relationship with a male lover, but he
had deliberately transformed the relationship from a homosexual to a
heterosexual one although its true focus was on its characters' determination to 'run away from life'.

In spite of its large, sprawling cast and multiplicity of themes, Rattigan liked the play and believed it deserved a London production. In
June, just as *The Deep Blue Sea* reached its hundredth performance,
Ackland's play became his first official venture into the production of
another playwright's work. His faith in it touched Ackland deeply. On
the night before the Brighton opening, Ackland sent him a telegram:
'Whatever they may think of the play your courage and generosity in
putting it on deserves the success we hope for.' Now regarded by some
critics as one of the finest plays of the 1940s, *The Pink Room* was not
particularly well received. The *Manchester Guardian*, noting that the
gallery had been restless during its opening at the Lyric, Hammersmith
on 18 June 1952, called it 'an interesting failure'. Kenneth Tynan, well
aware of Rattigan's involvement, and displaying the disdain for Rattigan's seriousness that was to become only too familiar in the years
ahead, dismissed it: 'Mr Ackland examines his menagerie of escapists
sometimes with a commiserating grin, sometimes with an unlikeable
smirk, and sometimes with over-powering affection. But it takes, I am
afraid, a heart larger than his to write about the small sins of small
people without sentimentalism or shallow moralising.'

The Pink Room lasted just three weeks, and lost a little over £3,500.
Rattigan did not relish the smell of failure. 'When the play failed,'
Frith Banbury, its director, recalls, 'Terry never wanted to see Rodney
again.' The two men never met again. Ackland was so upset that he
eventually recovered the prompt copy of his play from the theatre and
virtually refused to show it to anyone for some years.

By the time *The Pink Room* closed, however, Terence Rattigan's
mind was elsewhere. His brother was dying. In late July, Brian had
been admitted to the London Clinic, off Harley Street, where he was
put on a strict diet of 'eating something or drinking a glass of Horlicks
every two hours', as he put it in a letter to his mother. The family
doctor, William Buky, tried everything he could, but by the beginning
of August there was little more that could be done. Brian was admitted
to University College Hospital and discovered – when a radiographer

left her notes on his bedside table – that he had a malignant tumour on his left lung. He wrote to his mother: 'Whatever happens I take the fatalist view, and swear to you that I am not worrying at all.'

His elder brother's illness provoked an intense reaction in Rattigan. The reserve he had always displayed towards him, the disdain he had felt towards his lack of determination, the superiority he had felt in the glow of his own success while Brian had struggled to qualify as a solicitor and then to find a job in the Ministry of Agriculture and then the Treasury Solicitor's office, left him feeling hollow. For once, and in private, he allowed himself to experience the emotion that he was always so careful to conceal and understate in public. On 19 August 1952 he wrote to his brother from his new house in Sunningdale, Little Court:

Dear Brian, It's rather late to write (2.15am) but I can't go to bed without getting this effusion (not a literary one, I assure you) off my chest.

It's been my profession all my life to use words dishonestly, and now when I need them to record, rather than induce, an emotion most genuinely and deeply felt, they seem to be taking their revenge on me. I can't really blame them I suppose. They've been wickedly exploited – for the vilest of motives – more cash.

So I think the best thing is just not to try and find the beastly things at all, but merely to tell you this simple truth – that if ever and whenever my own time comes to receive news as grave as the news you have received, I can only hope and pray I receive it as well as you have – but I deeply doubt it. I'm sure that embarrasses you for it carries the extremely fussing implication (fussing to a character whose previous life and conduct has not perhaps exactly provided a brochure on modern sainthood by the Archbishop of Canterbury and who, I'm sure, had no such ambition anyway) – the implication that, when the real test of character came, he has provided an inspiration (and a spiritual inspiration at that) to his weaker brother – an inspiration which may – I think which will – help me a lot when my own time comes.

But at this moment of trouble and anxiety I thought you should know how much your courage, resignation and unselfishness have helped those who care for you.

Sorry to be embarrassing, but I couldn't avoid it. Some things have to be said.

My love and every possible wish. Terry.

When his secretary, Mary Herring, arrived the following morning, he asked her to deliver the letter to his brother by hand. Brian Rattigan replied the following day, in a very shaky hand from his hospital bed.

Dear Terry, Your letter, which Mary handed to me this morning, has helped and encouraged me tremendously. You see when I first knew for certain what was wrong I felt rather like an actor who had been given an opportunity to redeem in the last act a pretty lousy performance in the preceding ones. I knew I was up against something real which I couldn't run away from, a problem which couldn't be solved by flying to the bottle.

In fact it gradually dawned on me that this was not so much an affliction as the opportunity to prove to myself (and possibly to others) that I am not wholly cowardly and selfish; and, of course, Old Boy, that is precisely why your letter encouraged me. It indicated that I haven't been entirely unsuccessful.

Please believe me Terry when I say that this is no Pagliacci act.

It is rather odd to think that if all this had never happened you and I would almost certainly never have revealed that we have a considerable affection for each other . . .

In the event of my retiring from the scene in the near future I would suggest that the final arrangements should be the same as in the case of Dad.

I certainly won't hold your letter against you in the event of my recovery, but I shall always value very highly its obvious sincerity. Love Brian.

The two men met just twice more. Brian died of carcinoma of the left bronchus on 22 September. He was forty-five. Mary Herring recorded his death at the local Registrar's Office the following day. Rattigan and Vera attended the cremation at Golders Green a few days later, their second visit to the crematorium within six months. The Rattigan family now consisted of just Terence and his mother. They were to become ever closer, even more devoted to one another than they had been in the years before.

A fan of *The Sound Barrier* happened to catch his mood when she wrote to him just before his brother's death: 'My feeling is, that when life gets us by the throat and we are shaken emotionally, as most thinking people are at times, we can either disintegrate, or take courage and go forward all of a piece to a life of more breadth and vision.' She was describing his two test pilots, but she could just as well have been describing his own emotions.

As he had done so often before in times of crisis, Terence Rattigan took refuge in his work. Harold Freedman in New York had told him repeatedly that the Americans were desperate to produce *The Deep Blue Sea* on Broadway, and that there was not a moment to lose. Freedman had also instilled the idea in his mind that Margaret Sullavan, the American actress who had deserted Broadway for Hollywood in 1944, might be tempted to play Hester in New York, and as a result Rattigan had taken her to see Peggy Ashcroft's performance in London in April. 'She's very frightened of the part,' he told his mother afterwards. Nevertheless Margaret Sullavan agreed to play Hester Collyer on Broadway, with Frith Banbury again directing the play.

Sullavan 'was this enchanting, tiny little thing,' Banbury remembers, 'but the moment of truth had come because she was forty-two or so and she told me "I'm of an age when I want to be a woman."' But when rehearsals started the American star could not capture the tragedy at the heart of Hester. Banbury tried to persuade her to stop acting like a little girl – 'which is what she instinctively reverted to' – but to no effect. She wanted another director. She did not want to be compared to Peggy Ashcroft. 'There were screams and shouts all the time,' Banbury recalls. Josh Logan was talked about as an alternative director, and so was Glen Byam Shaw. 'But Terry remained loyal to me,' Banbury recalls. As the short pre-New York tour wound on Sullavan grew more and more uncomfortable, angrier and angrier. But her dislike of Banbury and her fear of the role of Hester were not the only reasons for that.

Rattigan and Frith Banbury had tried to persuade Kennth More to leave the London production and recreate the part of Freddie Page on Broadway, but More had refused. He had just accepted his first starring film role, in *Genevieve*, and did not want to neglect his career in England. So Banbury turned to Jimmy Hanley, the man he had originally intended to cast as Freddie, who had taken umbrage and left England to play in a farce in 'Australia after being rejected for *The Deep Blue Sea*. Banbury immediately cabled Australia and offered the part of Freddie to Hanley, and the actor accepted instantly. When Hanley arrived in New York for rehearsals, however, the handsome young leading man that Banbury had wanted to cast looked considerably older and substantially fatter than he had done eighteen months earlier in London. Life in Australia had clearly agreed with him. But Hanley's transformation from a dashing juvenile lead, to a more mature, not to say a little weightier, performer horrified the woman who was supposed to give up everything for him on Broadway. Margaret Sullavan was apoplectic with rage. The already edgy leading lady all but refused to speak to the man she was supposed to have fallen hopelessly in love with – and her animosity came straight across the footlights.

Shortly before *The Deep Blue Sea* opened on Broadway in November
1952 Rattigan wrote to his mother from Washington, where it was
then playing, admitting that the play could not succeed because of
Sullavan.

> The simple truth is that she's not a good enough actress to play
> it. She has only two approaches to the part and both are inad-
> equate. Either she plays it all out for 'pathos', using her famous
> tearful voice (put on) in which case she is dull and self-pitying,
> and the play goes down the drain, or she plays it with her own
> voice and personality, in which case the play equally goes down
> the drain because the part becomes hard and matter of fact, and
> you lose patience with Hester, and can't see what all the fuss is
> about.

Rattigan was so distressed that he had even discussed not opening
in New York, but had reluctantly accepted that that would create too
great a fuss. 'Our single hope of success is to get good notices for her
– which she'll get at the expense of the play – and let people think she's
being wonderful in a banal little vehicle. This might just conceivably
happen.' There was a substantial advance at the box office on the
strength of Sullavan's name, but he suspected the play would not survive. 'In spite of all this,' he told Vera, 'I find I like her very much.
She genuinely loves the play, and wants to play it honestly. She just
can't that's all, and is hysterical because she knows she can't.'

The one thing that cheered Rattigan up was the increase in his
income. 'Money is wonderful,' he told his mother. 'This week alone
I shall make about £1,000 (not dollars) in royalties, and if the play gets
away with it in New York (sorry I mean if she gets away with it) I
should be quite rich.' Korda was still intent on buying the film rights,
and the opening of *The Sound Barrier* at the same time was helping to
keep his spirits up.

> I think about you a lot, and wonder how you're getting on . . .
> You mustn't think too much about recent happenings. You've
> had a terrible year, but from now on things are going to get much
> better for you. After all, you have a rich and loving son – and
> surely that's something. Keep fingers crossed and champagne
> corks grasped next Wednesday. Don't worry about it too much.
> After all we've had a great success in London.

Just as Rattigan feared, though the audiences seemed to like it, the
New York critics dismissed the play when it opened at the Morosco
on 5 November 1952. 'Played like this . . . it all seems like an ordinary

triangle story – what they call soap opera over here,' he had warned his mother. The *Daily News* dubbed it just that, while the *Post* called it 'slick magazine fiction'. In the *New York Times* Brooks Atkinson wrote, 'To London audiences Mr Rattigan's professional aloofness and his knack of understating may be evidence of skill and maturity. But Americans expect an artist to participate more actively in a theme – to have strong opinions about his characters, their experience, and the world in which they live. To our way of thinking Mr Rattigan is too easily satisfied with craftsmanship.'

Within a fortnight Rattigan had escaped from New York on the SS *Constitution* en route for the Mediterranean. On the way across the Atlantic he again wrote to his mother, finally posting the letter when the ship called at Gibraltar on its way to Cannes. He had 'slept solidly for at least three days, and adored waking up without caring whether Maggie Sullavan was in a bad mood, and needed talking to'. He was still concerned about money, however.

> Herring has probably told you of our wonderful first week's business at the Morosco. The film is also doing wonderfully. In fact I believe better than any other film on Broadway. Wasn't I silly to refuse a share of the profits, which I could have had instead of a sum down? They've already got their money back in England alone, and everything in America is sheer profit. They'll make a bloody fortune, damn them. Oh well.

Rattigan also took the opportunity to sustain the myth that he had carefully constructed for his mother – that he was living the life of a carefree bachelor. 'I'm being chased by a highly predatory female,' he told her, and as a result 'I've decided not to go on to Naples – her destination – but to get off at Cannes, and stay there for a few days.' He knew very well that this was what his mother would like to hear. 'The lady in question is extremely decorative, but – as I only learnt to my cost when it was too late – has just dumped a husband and very firmly on the look out for another. Added to which a child of six, and no visible means of support, as they say. So I'm making the excuse that you're joining me at Cannes – incidentally I wish you were – and am skipping off the boat the day after tomorrow. She doesn't know yet. There'll be hell to pay when she does.'

His plan was to stay at the Martinez in Cannes for about a week, no doubt with the intention of gambling a substantial proportion of his American royalties, before returning to England for Christmas. He invited Vera to Little Court for the holiday, and told her that while he was there he would 'try and think out the next play – a trifle about

Kings and Queens for the Coronation . . . I'll work on it when I get back.' His mischievous sense of humour had not deserted him. Terence Rattigan concluded his letter to his mother by describing his female pursuer as: 'A determined lady – but then so am I.'

The idea for a new play was the result of a conversation with Alexander Korda, who had offered Rattigan £10,000 to write a screenplay on monarchy, called *Le Roi*. He had turned Korda down, but had been struck by the idea of a play on the subject – 'Though you mustn't say so,' he told Vera Rattigan, 'or I shall be sued.'

Back on Broadway, the strong first week takings for *The Deep Blue Sea* had continued. In spite of the notices the play made money steadily, closing at the Morosco after 132 performances, and then continuing to do so on a ten-week nationwide tour. Nevertheless Rattigan had hoped that, at last, the Americans would accept him as a serious playwright. They refused. The choice of Margaret Sullavan to play Hester had put paid to that. Even a nomination for an Oscar for his screenplay for *The Sound Barrier* could not make up for the disappointment. Terence Rattigan retired behind the defence he had adopted so often in the past – his work.

CHAPTER 18

Aunt Edna's Entrance

◆

Conceit is the finest armour a man can wear.

JEROME K. JEROME

◆

A frenzy seemed to overtake Rattigan. He was still only forty-one, but the deaths of his father and elder brother within the space of a few months instilled a fear that he too was probably doomed to die young. From the moment he and his mother were left alone during the Christmas holiday of 1952, he seemed ever more determined to live each day as though it were his last. The weekend parties at Little Court grew bigger and bigger, the trips to the casinos of the south of France more and more frequent. A sense that his life might be snatched away from him at any moment came to infuse his entire being. He drank more, gambled more, and explored his sexual appetites more fully than ever before.

He moved from 16 Chester Square to a new and grand flat at 29 Eaton Square. Here he played the part of the man he sometimes called, only half in jest, 'the prettiest playwright in London'. He paid even more attention to his mother. Vera Rattigan had told him at Christmas that she did not want to spend her entire time alone in Pepsal End, but wanted to spend at least the winters in London, near her son. After some debate, it was agreed between them that she should take a set of rooms at a small private hotel almost opposite the family's old flat in Stanhope Gardens, South Kensington. It was called the Stanhope Court Hotel. Vera would spend the winters there, and the summers in Bedfordshire.

Because of this arrangement, it became even more important than formerly that his lovers should never actually live with him, and that they should maintain a discreet distance whenever Vera was likely to call. She had been introduced to Kenneth Morgan, but merely as a friend. She had met Chips and Peter Osborn, without questioning her son's relationship with them. If Vera Rattigan, who had been confirmed into the Anglican Church in the wake of her husband's death, ever came to suspect her son's sexual leanings, she kept this secret to herself. To those who escorted her to functions at Rattigan's request, she would simply say, 'I do think he's rather keen on Margaret Leighton, don't you?'

The only woman who knew rather more of the details of Rattigan's private life was his secretary, Mary Herring, now established during the daytime in the small study in Eaton Square as guardian of his affairs, in every sense. Unmarried, with a little house in Clapham, and 'utterly devoted' to Rattigan, Mary Herring was a director of Rattigan Productions and keeper of her employer's reputation. When Vera Rattigan was once told by one of her fellow guests at the Stanhope Court Hotel that her son was homosexual, she immediately rushed round to ask Mary Herring if it was true. The ever loyal Miss Herring categorically denied it: much to Vera Rattigan's evident relief. Miss Herring was also the person on whom devolved the responsibility of ensuring that Rattigan had enough money to sustain his extravagant lifestyle. Hers was the task of asking his accountant, Bill Forsyth, to supply more money whenever it seemed to be running low.

To Forsyth's frustration, money was required more and more often. Rattigan had borrowed £18,000 back from the money he had given his parents to buy Little Court in Sunningdale – and was repaying it at 5 per cent interest. He had recently received £22,000 from the sale of the film rights in *Love in Idleness* and £5,000 from those in *The Browning Version*. The exasperated accountant eventually wrote to his client, 'From Miss Herring's constant demands for more money I gather you are living above your income to the extent of many thousands a year. I could understand that last year, when you were furnishing Little Court, but surely that must have been over some time ago, so that I can only imagine that your weekend parties and normal running expenses are costing much more than even you can earn net.' His demand that Rattigan should bring down his 'living standards' had no effect. Spending kept the demons at bay, and the spiral was now established.

There was another reason for Rattigan's extravagance – a new lover had entered his life. Short, with the boyish round face he invariably went for and with considerable energy, Michael Franklin was nineteen, half English by birth but brought up largely in America, from where he had recently returned to live in West London. The critic Freddie Young, who first encountered him in 1948, says that he then seemed 'determined to make his mark in one way or another'. Openly homo-sexual, Franklin made no secret of his ambition to find a well-known lover. Messages would be left for him at Young's flat, as he could not afford his own telephone. One was from the composer Benjamin Britten. Young describes him as 'anxious to be looked after', and by the spring of 1953 Rattigan was sending telegrams to Young, one of which read: 'Please see to Michael's requirements which do not include a Jaguar. Love Terry.'

Franklin, who was rapidly given the nickname the Midget by Ratti-gan and his friends, was to remain the playwright's companion and friend throughout the rest of his life. Tempestuous, temperamental, possessive, insecure, argumentative, and yet capable of enormous affec-tion towards his friend and mentor, the Midget was to become a fixture in the Rattigan household, even though he was never to take up per-manent residence there. Indeed when Vera Rattigan was invited to Little Court for the weekend, he was studiously not invited. No matter how intense the rows, how mighty the scenes that took place in private (on one occasion the Midget threatened to throw himself off the bal-cony of the Martinez Hotel in Cannes), the necessity of maintaining the outward proprieties – especially in front of his mother – remained, for Rattigan, paramount.

'If there was a row between Terry and Michael,' Freddie Young recalls, 'it was generally solved by my putting Michael's case to Terry over drinks, with lunch for Michael the next day when I could put the other case.' Bunny Roger, another of Rattigan's friends, explains: 'There was something about Terry that loved all that hysteria that the Midget liked to bring – the threats of cutting his wrists, or throwing himself off the balcony. Though Terry didn't appear to be like that himself – quite the opposite – he adored it in the Midget. It was an aspect of his life that other people did not see.' The bickering and the flouncing off into the night, the stormy scenes and the private reconciliations, were part of a deepening sexual relationship.

Now in his forties, Rattigan needed a steady companion. 'I think he wanted to settle down and not be sleeping around quite so much,' says Frith Banbury. 'But he wanted sex, and Michael was there. He was a service as it were. It sounds sad put like that, but it was true.' Rattigan had little appetite for chance homosexual encounters – at least while the English law took such a stern view of them – and the Midget represented safety. Rattigan was to embark on many other homosexual affairs throughout his life, but they would all be conducted among men who knew that he wished to preserve his public reputation, and no one ever completely replaced the Midget in his affections.

Rattigan's mania for concealment impregnated his professional life. It even affected the explanations he gave for his plays. In late November 1952, in his letter from Gibraltar, he had told his mother how a chance conversation with Alexander Korda had sparked the idea of 'a trifle about Kings and Queens'. But when, twenty years later, he came to describe the genesis of the play that he worked on that winter, he remembered events in a rather different light. 'On January 1, 1953 I woke up with the customary blinding hangover and, later in the day, to the equally blinding thought that this was Coronation Year and I ought to do something about it.' He then added: 'Other creative talents, I knew, were busy churning out odes, stirring chorales, ballet homages and patriotic extravaganzas for the occasion, I just thought I'd like to join the party.' But he also felt that if he was to do anything, 'it had to be something light and happy and even a little ironic. I was in no mood for portentousness.'

His father's role in the Coronation of 1911 provided the idea for a play about a foreign prince – could it be the Prince of Romania? – attending the festivities and falling in love with a most unlikely partner, a chorus girl named Mary Morgan (another little joke) who was playing the character of Elaine Dagenham on the stage. The story of his own birth helped too. 'It was probably my remembrance of the fact that my arrival into this world prevented my mother from attending the Coronation of 1911 – I was born ten days before it – that decided me on my choice of period. What she had lost by my importunity I would try to restore for her in make believe.' He also brought Vera to life in the shape of the Grand Duchess, whose acceptance of her husband's succession of 'girlfriends' 'has not the slightest tinge of jealousy or regret or any other of the emotions that will arise from such a triangle on a lower level'. The play, he soon decided, was to be 'an occasional fairy tale' – 'a rather shrewd device, I thought, for telling the critics that they mustn't take it too seriously and that it was, in fact, a *pièce d'occasion* and nothing more'.

Rattigan wanted Laurence Olivier and Vivien Leigh to head the cast, but Beaumont was firmly against the idea – so much so that Rattigan angrily considered asking Stephen Mitchell, with whom he had done *Playbill*, whether he would be prepared to produce the new play. In the end Beaumont relented and on 20 February Rattigan cabled Freedman, 'Have finished play . . . lightness has been quite a strain though trust will not give this impression. Gather there is still a fairly good chance of the Oliviers here. Advise possibility of Audrey Hepburn New York for Autumn if you think right.'

The new play was based on his familiar device of standing a dramatic cliché on its head. In *French Without Tears,* as Rattigan wrote later, 'a femme fatale, far from destroying a friendship between two men who are rivals for her love, actually makes a friendship between two deadly enemies'. He intended to spring an equal surprise on the audience in *The Sleeping Prince,* as the new play was to be called. Its hero, the Regent of Carpathia ('a name,' Rattigan wrote, 'carefully chosen for its echoes of Anthony Hope and Strauss operettas'), is far from being the irresistibly attractive Prince Charming who 'longs to escape the bondage of Royal duty for the bliss of anonymity and the joys of ordinary love'. He is, on the contrary, 'a quite unattractive, very conscientious, extremely mundane little man who is dedicated to the routine of his job, which happens to be that of Acting Head of State, but, apart from the accident of birth, could equally well have been that of Stationmaster at King's Cross'. As for the joys of 'ordinary love', the Regent 'finds them agreeable enough provided that in no circumstances whatever may they interrupt his rigorous routine, nor endure longer than an hour . . . He is the kind of Prince who will expect to be called Royal Highness even in bed. Prince Uncharming in fact.'

But when a chorus girl is hastily acquired to minister to the appetites of this uncharming prince, she proves, 'to the Prince's intense dismay, to prefer the romantic cliché to the unromantic reality'. If she is to be seduced it has to be with the accompaniment of 'Tzigane music, quotations from *Antony and Cleopatra* and dialogue about her eyes being like "twin pools" . . . about the burdens of Royalty and the Prince's need for the "ennobling love of a pure young woman".' Rattigan's Prince Uncharming duly says all the expected words, 'but then, to his horror and anguish, finds that she had taken them all seriously, and had decided to stay with him not for an hour, but for life. His frenzied attempts to disentangle himself makes thereafter the whole play; together with his genuine transformation from Prince Uncharming, if not into Prince Charming at least into Prince Half-Way-Human.'

Within four days of receiving the first draft of *The Sleeping Prince,* Freedman had cabled back 'Utterly delightful', and Rattigan had confirmed in turn that Olivier was reading the play. Meanwhile Vivien Leigh was filming in Ceylon, where her co-star was the handsome Australian actor Peter Finch, who had first come to England as Olivier's protégé four years previously. She was to go on to Hollywood from Colombo to complete the picture, and a script was sent out to her there. Meanwhile Beaumont's idea for a director came as something of a surprise to Rattigan. He wanted Alfred Lunt, who – to Rattigan's surprise in the wake of *Harlequinade* – agreed at once. And now Vivien Leigh was equally enthusiastic. On 2 March, she cabled Rattigan in a style that would now be questioned as a rather too effusive, but which then remained a commonplace, 'Darling. You are Wonderful. Can't wait to start.' He replied, 'It's you who are wonderful. Very happy and thrilled.'

At that moment it looked as though Rattigan's 'occasional fairy tale' would get off to a fairy tale start in June 1953 as his contribution to the Coronation celebrations. But the mood of the actress who had become a star as Scarlett O'Hara in *Gone with the Wind* was not to last. Within three weeks, she was to sink – as she had done before during her career – into the bleakest depression, a depression which was to culminate in a nervous breakdown. The reason had nothing to do with *The Sleeping Prince*. She was, in Laurence Olivier's words, 'hopelessly lost in the floodtide of the all-consuming passion' for Finch.

Neither Beaumont nor Rattigan knew any of this. They were still pressing ahead rapidly with their plan to launch the play in London a week after the Coronation, after a brief provincial tour. Beaumont had submitted the play to the Lord Chamberlain, whose reader had reported enthusiastically, 'Mr Rattigan has written a charming pseudo-Ruritanian comedy, as a change from anything he has previously done.' Vivien Leigh's illness put paid to all their plans. Olivier flew out to Hollywood to arrange for her to be brought back to London for a course of psychiatric treatment, which included electric shock therapy. It was clear that *The Sleeping Prince* would not be able to open in London on time.

Reluctantly Rattigan accepted that the production would have to be postponed until the autumn. Olivier told him that he genuinely believed his comedy might help his wife recover her health, which gave him real pleasure. But there were few other consolations. The delay meant that Alfred Lunt would no longer be able to direct. Worse still, it also meant that the '*soufflé*' Rattigan had cooked up for the celebrations would now become exactly what he had not wanted in the first place – a major new play by Terence Rattigan for the London theatrical season. As the year went on, as he was to write later: 'The press of the world were now announcing its advent almost daily, the already over-expectant public had now got themselves into such a frenzy of excitement that they had bought out the entire Manchester Opera House at double prices for the entire pre-London week within hours of seats going on sale, and the queues for the Phoenix stretched out of sight.'

Meanwhile *The Deep Blue Sea* had folded on Broadway, and was now touring profitably in the United States. Interest in the film version, however, was undiminished. The Rank Organization in Britain had opened the bidding the previous autumn with an offer of £10,000 down and a further £5,000 for the script, but Freedman was not keen. When Puffin Asquith and Teddy Baird, the team who had made *The Final Test*, entered the scene, Freedman was able to tell them that he was negotiating with Twentieth Century-Fox. And that Bette Davis wanted to play Hester.

Even Marlene Dietrich started to express enthusiasm, cabling to say that she would very much like to play Hester, and keeping up the pressure for almost two months. There was little real progress, however. Fox were gradually going cold and Rank had withdrawn. Then Alexander Korda entered the negotiations, offering Rattigan £10,000 for a screenplay and £40,000 for the rights to the play itself, if Anatole Litvak could direct Olivia de Havilland as Hester. But then Fox refused to release Litvak and negotiations came to a halt again. It served only to increase Rattigan's unease. Even the London run of the play was drawing to its close, although Googie Withers, who had taken over from Peggy Ashcroft to great acclaim, took the production on tour to Australia.

Only the London opening in April of his film version of *The Final Test* gave Rattigan any real pleasure. The normally taciturn C.A.Lejeune in the *Observer* positively glowed, calling it 'a perfect entertainment of its kind. It does with skill, wit and affection just what it sets out to do: make us laugh, touch our hearts a little, supply words for some of our unformulated thoughts, keep us for ninety minutes in the most delightful company, and send us home refreshed and happy. It also manages, through gentle gibing, to convey an uncommon lot of common sense and truth.' In February of the following year, when it opened in the United States, *Time* magazine was to describe it as 'the funniest picture to come out of England since *The Captain's Paradise*' – which was to feature alongside it in many critics' lists as one of the ten best films of 1953.

To console himself for the postponement of *The Sleeping Prince* and relieve his overwrought nerves, Rattigan threw a party at Little Court for Royal Ascot, two weeks after the Coronation. The guests of honour were, naturally, the Oliviers. But also invited were John Mills and his wife, who recall the event now as 'great fun – but with a tremendous amount to drink. There always was when you went to Little Court.' There was also a slightly frenzied air about the host which betrayed the strains of bereavement and professional setbacks, and which seemed to his friends to manifest itself in a lack of perspective and balance.

This had been evident earlier in the year during his row with

Beaumont about *The Sleeping Prince*. Even their disagreement over *Perdita* and *Playbill* had not equalled the bitterness of Rattigan's note to him on 29 January: 'Just about the only thing I want to know is what you are going to do with it. Who is going to direct it? Who design? What sort of cast can we get? What theatre? When rehearse?' He refused to accept any criticism of his play. His father, for all the ridicule that Rattigan had poured on him, had been a steadying influence, surprising though it might seem. Now that influence was gone.

One of the results was the unwelcome appearance of 'Aunt Edna', the woman who was to attract the opprobrium of Rattigan's professional and theatregoing opponents for the rest of his lifetime and beyond. She made her first appearance in the impetuous introduction to the two-volume edition of his selected plays which the publisher Hamish Hamilton was preparing for the autumn of 1953. Rattigan regarded its publication as a great honour, and wanted to use the opportunity to explain himself to his critics, and to the audience. But he also wanted to be sure that only the plays he approved of were to be included. After discussing the matter with Roger Machell, a director of Hamish Hamilton and a fellow resident of Albany when he had lived there, Rattigan had decided that the first volume should include *French Without Tears*, *Flare Path*, *While the Sun Shines*, *Love in Idleness* and *The Winslow Boy*, and the second volume *The Browning Version*, *Harlequinade*, *Adventure Story*, *Who Is Sylvia?* and *The Deep Blue Sea*.

The fact that he decided to omit his two pre-war flops – *After the Dance* and *Follow My Leader* – from the first volume, but to include two post-war flops, *Adventure Story* and *Who Is Sylvia?* – in the second, was evidence of the lack of perspective that was afflicting him at the time. There was certainly a strong case for including *After the Dance* in Volume One if *Who Is Sylvia?* was to be included in Volume Two. But Rattigan was determined to present the first volume as an example of his successes, and to present the second as evidence of his increasing maturity as a playwright. He felt that *Adventure Story* had been misjudged, while *Who Is Sylvia?* was too personally significant to him to be omitted, flop or not.

In late May Rattigan set about writing introductions to both volumes. The tone he chose was defensive, evidence of just how vulnerable he still felt, in spite of all his success. His resentment at the critics and their dismissal of him as a 'lucky fluke' permeated the introduction to Volume One, which was completed on 5 June. He fiercely pointed out that his plays had been dismissed time after time for being popular and well constructed, designed only to ensure his success as a 'popular dramatist'. Yet Rattigan was also prepared to acknowledge, in a note to himself, that 'I could not possibly expect others to know of the high theatrical ambitions that burned in me nor of my intense longing to be taken seriously as a professional playwright.' Undeniably, the introduction to the first volume of his collected plays was not the work of a playwright confident of himself and his talent. It was a sustained exercise in self-justification, a battle with the ghosts that haunted him fought out between hard covers.

Nowhere is his sensitivity more obvious than in a paragraph which he finally cut from the published version of the first introduction, but which survives in his collected manuscripts. Rattigan was determined to dismiss the charge that anyone could write a popular play. 'No open flattery of an audience will ever work,' he wrote. 'They will see through it at once and despise the author. Only to the subtle flattery of apparent participation are they responsive. And responsive they must be, or they will not come, and then there is no play. For a play without an audience, though it may provide study for the scholars and pleasure for the reader, is dead.'

This craving to be recognised as a serious and ambitious dramatist is the theme of the entire first introduction. He could not understand why popularity with the public should ensure condemnation by the critics and some members of the new literary smart set. What he failed completely to realise was that his whole lifestyle, his blatant pleasure in popular and commercial success, his expensive suits and cars, his famously extravagant parties, did not appeal to the British appetite for understatement. Rattigan's class, his accent and his bearing were beginning to tell against him. This blind spot was all the more ironic in a man whose plays, as he admitted in the first of his introductions, depended on 'the implicit rather than the explicit' to give effective life to their scenes.

But if the first introduction was defensive, the second was disastrous. He returned to his theme that a play did not exist in a vacuum, by reasserting that a play can 'neither be great, nor a masterpiece, nor a work of genius, nor talented, nor untalented, nor indeed anything at all, unless it has an audience to see it . . . Plays, though they may give incidental pleasure in the library, are first intended for the stage.' But then he went on to define its audience, to draw what he called 'a simple truth' – which was that the theatre could not afford to offend a 'nice, respectable, middle-class, middle-aged, maiden lady with time on her hands and the money to help her to pass it . . . Let us call her Aunt Edna.' In his first draft of the introduction he had called her Gladys, but changed it to Edna, the name he had used for Lynn Fontanne's character in *Harlequinade*, and – shades of his mother – during the winter months he had her reside at 'a small hotel in West Kensington'. Aunt Edna could be ignored by some artists. 'Not so, unhappily, the playwright, for should he displease Aunt Edna he is utterly lost . . . The playwright who has been unfortunate or unwise enough to incur her displeasure, will soon pay a dreadul price. His play, the child of his brain, will wither and die before his eyes.'

The introduction backfired on him, resoundingly and from the start. 'Aunt Edna' did indeed become a catch-phrase in theatrical arguments, and on the principle that bad publicity is better than no publicity, this was not without its value. But the overall effect was to make Rattigan seem what most devoutly he did not wish to seem – nothing more than a craftsman determined to win commercial success, and prepared to compromise his own vision and creativity to do so.

But Aunt Edna's creator did not realise any of this. So taken was he with his creation that he proceeded to claim all manner of strengths for her. 'She is universal and immortal, and she has lived for over two thousand years . . . I believe she was shocked and intrigued by Euripides, impressed, if a little bewildered, by Aeschylus, and dissolved into gales of laughter by her favourite, Aristophanes. At the Elizabethan Globe Theatre, too, her sway was absolute.' It was essential for every dramatist to know her 'likes and dislikes, her tastes and foibles . . . however much they may despise her intellect or deplore her influence'. Rattigan compounded his mistake by explaining that he could not have written his own plays without her. 'Aunt Edna, or at least her juvenile counterpart, was inside my creative brain and in pleasing her I was only pleasing myself.' In the eyes of his opponents, particularly the new young critics and playwrights, he had condemned himself out of his own mouth. What they could not see was that Rattigan was grappling with his own self-esteem.

Towards the end of the introduction, he modified his position – slightly. Aunt Edna had stood him in good stead for *French Without Tears* 'and the plays that immediately followed'. They were joined in 'a friendship that I trust will never be broken'. Nevertheless, as time passed 'and I made efforts to develop as a serious writer for the theatre, I began to realise more clearly that the friendship, rewarding though it be, must never become too close . . . I was learning, in fact, that although Aunt Edna must never be made mock of, or bored, or befuddled, she must equally not be wooed, or pandered to, or cossetted.'

Rattigan admitted that he had been regarded only as a 'fairly skilful exponent of good theatre' rather than a 'dramatist' until *The Browning*

Version, and that *Who Is Sylvia?* was a product of his earlier 'over-Aunt-Edna-conscious self'. *Adventure Story*, by contrast, he described as 'consistent with the artistic development of an author who was trying to subdue the Aunt Edna in his soul. Aunt Edna, in fact, proved this conclusively herself. She refused to come.' But he had no regrets, she 'has never rejected the best. It is only with the second best, the third best, and the bad that she is so unpredictable in her imperious choice, spurning the one and favouring the other, often for no discernible reason. I have no complaint, therefore, about her judgement on *Adventure Story*. It was not, I agree, the best. It was merely the best that I could have written: and that was apparently not good enough.'

That was more rational, but the damage had been done. When the two volumes appeared in November, even Rattigan's friend John Barber could not conceal his irritation. Writing in the *Daily Express*, he condemned the Introduction: 'You keep coming back to "the critics' assessments of my comedies as romps and charades". You are hurt by "the jeers of the serious minded". You even mention "beastly bullies". Do you expect every word I write to be undiluted praise?' Then he added bluntly: 'I know why you are cross. We are disappointed in you now. Your later comedies make us cross. We did praise you, and we have stopped. That is what hurts.' In desperation, Barber went on, 'You say you don't want to pander to Aunt Edna in the stalls. Then don't. I shall go on nagging you to forget her and write as well as I know you can. Isn't that my duty? That is what you cannot bear. You know I am right.' 'Sad isn't it?' Barber concluded. 'To be so prosperous, so gifted . . . and spoiled. For that is what it comes to – to be so avid for more success and more success that it gets harder every morning to sit down in humble obedience to your own finest instincts.'

Barber wrote from the heart, Kenneth Tynan used his feline instincts. Not that Tynan had started out as Rattigan's implacable enemy: rather the reverse. In an article for the American edition of *Harper's Bazaar* to mark the opening of *The Deep Blue Sea* on Broadway, the twenty-four-year-old-critic, freshly down from Oxford, accepted that he had been wrong to conclude, after *Adventure Story* and *Who Is Sylvia?*, that 'We had . . . a competent but minor playwright.' Tynan admitted that he had missed a clue in Crocker-Harris's speech near the end of *The Browning Version* when the Crock tells Hunter, the young master who has been having an affair with his wife, that there are:

Two kinds of love. Hers and mine. Worlds apart, as I know now, though when I married her I didn't think they were incompatible.

In those days I hadn't thought that her kind of love – the love she requires and which I was unable to give her – was so important that its absence would drive out the other kind of love – the kind of love that I require and which I thought, in my folly, was by far the greater part of love.

Tynan recognised that this conflict of two incompatible passions lay at the heart of the play, just as it lay at the heart of *The Deep Blue Sea*, which he thought 'by far the best thing' Rattigan had written.

When Tynan came to rework the piece for his British employer, the London *Evening Standard*, however, in July 1953, he was less fulsome in his praise, omitting his statement in *Harper's Bazaar* that *The Deep Blue Sea* was 'the most striking new English play I have seen for a decade'. Tynan suggested instead that 'the third act lacks resolution'. Rattigan, in the new version, was a 'master builder', but cursed by the description and by his reputation for 'good theatre'. He hoped that 'it may be Rattigan's mission to take the curse off that snide, dismissive phrase', but the tone of his piece implied that he felt it fitted him, and when the *Collected Plays* were published in November, this became even clearer. Rattigan had now become 'the bathtub baritone of the drama', who was blind to the simple fact that Aunt Edna only went to *Hamlet* because highbrows had told her to. As for his own plays, they set out to please her by using that 'quality known to cynics as ingratiation . . . tact, understatement, avoidance of cliché – the hall-marks, in fact, of the "gentleman code" which holds so much of West End playwriting in curious thrall'. Tynan's final condemnation was sweeping. 'The greatest plays are those which convince us that men can occasionally speak like angels. The rest, which conspire to imply that angels speak exactly like men, deserve and achieve respectable acclaim, but they must not repine if, finally, their passports to immortality are found wanting.'

The damage that Aunt Edna might cause had not struck Rattigan's publishers. The views of Hamish ('Jamie') Hamilton are not on record, but Roger Machell, Hamilton's partner and Rattigan's editor and close friend, found Aunt Edna 'awfully amusing, written slightly tongue in cheek, I couldn't imagine anyone taking it completely seriously. I never thought it would be used as a stick to beat him with.' In Rattigan's carefully sealed, mainly homosexual world, inhabited by people who had often benefited from his generosity, there were few who would have been prepared to suggest to their friend and host that he might have made a mistake.

In fact a whole new theatrical world was about to be born, but in the Coronation summer of 1953 that was still a little difficult to predict. At Little Court the pink champagne continued to be served, the charades went on till dawn, and the rounds of golf were as keenly fought as ever. Rattigan's own handicap had recently been cut from twelve to nine, and he liked to play in the afternoon when he was writing. He was finishing the film script for *Who Is Sylvia?* for Alexander Korda, who had contracted the ballet dancer turned actress Moira Shearer, star of *The Red Shoes*, and wanted Rattigan to change the script to allow her to play a ballet scene. The male lead was to be John Justin, and because Shearer was red-haired, the title was to be changed to *The Man Who Loved Redheads*. Harold French was to direct. Looking back he now admits: 'I shouldn't have done it, I knew it was a bad script, but it was partly love of Rattigan that made me do it.' French and Korda rowed relentlessly throughout the shooting, and the film was eventually dismissed as 'a terrible mistake'. But Rattigan was paid almost £10,000 for only a few weeks' work. He could also console himself with the fact that the final script bore almost no resemblance to the original play, which was still close to his heart.

At the end of August, with the screenplay of *Who Is Sylvia?* completed, and the summer weekend parties at Little Court now at an end, rehearsals finally began for *The Sleeping Prince*. In spite of his desire for the Oliviers to be the play's stars, Rattigan now privately wondered whether he had been right that they were the best choice for the Regent of Carpathia and his chorus girl Mary Morgan. 'How on earth could Larry persuade an audience that he was "Prince Uncharming" when he had made even Richard the Third into one of the most sexually attractive characters ever to disgrace a stage? And how on earth could darling Vivien, one of nature's grand Duchesses if ever there was one, walk on to a stage as a chorus girl thrilled to her Brooklynese death at the prospect of meeting a real grand Duke in the flesh?' He was also aware that his 'trifle' would never bear comparison with the *Antony and Cleopatra* which had been the occasion of their last West End triumph. But it was too late to worry now. The die was cast. It had even been agreed that Laurence Olivier Productions would present the play with H.M.Tennent, although with a £1,000 contribution from Rattigan towards the £4,000 production cost, and that Olivier himself would direct, not least in an effort to minimise the pressure on his wife. Olivier wanted the play to be presented in three acts, rather than the two acts Rattigan had drafted, and after a prolonged debate got his way. Alterations and amendments to the script went on throughout

September, and were still in progress when the play opened its brief provincial tour at the Opera House in Manchester on 28 September, on its way to a London opening in November 1953 at the Phoenix.

Vivien Leigh's return to the stage after her *tour de force* as Blanche du Bois, and her first public performance since her breakdown in March, ensured a massive turn-out in Manchester for the play's first night. The crowd were not disappointed. The actress was rewarded with fifteen curtain calls, and the *Manchester Guardian* commented stiffly, 'The Oliviers in the new Rattigan comedy carried Manchester on so high a sea of enthusiasm last night that, voyaging by these stars, there seemed some danger of losing the play altogether.' Their stately progress by Bentley continued via Glasgow, Edinburgh, Newcastle and Brighton to London, where the first night, coinciding with Vivien Leigh's fortieth birthday, became one of the most glamorous of the year. It was Guy Fawkes' Night.

Somerset Maugham made a rare appearance, alongside David Niven, Noël Coward and John Mills, all of whom were invited to a party at Eaton Square afterwards. Michael Franklin was there, as were Puffin Asquith and Roger Machell, Tolly de Grunwald and the Rattigans' family doctor, William Buky. As usual, Rattigan was unable to bear the strain of watching the first night performance, although he had already watched what he called the magic of Olivier's performance on tour. 'Where I had expected my flimsy little fairy tale to be burst asunder by the vastness of his talent, it was in fact held firmly in shape by his quietly magisterial performance.' Rattigan's fears of Olivier becoming Prince Utterly Irresistible 'were forever laid to rest when, at the dress rehearsal, I went into his dressing room just before the curtain to be confronted by a rather dull looking little man, with an anaemic complexion, a thin, prissy, humourless mouth . . . and a sad looking monocle glued over his right eye'.

But even Olivier's performance could not satisfy the critics. The 'occasional fairy tale' – which Rattigan was later to dedicate to 'Hugh Beaumont with affection, admiration and gratitude' – was tepidly received, John Barber in the *Daily Express* speaking for many of the critics as he described the play as beneath Olivier's talents, Milton Shulman in the London *Evening Standard* calling it 'almost aggressively unimportant', and *The Times* comparing its comedy to a 'leaden soled boot'. After reading the first reviews at Rattigan's party at Eaton Square, Olivier stood up and addressed the crowd of almost a hundred people. 'On behalf of my wife and myself as actors, and personally as your director, I would like to apologise, dear Terry, for mucking up your play.' Rattigan did not hesitate. Jumping to his feet, he replied:

'Darlings, both, on my behalf, as an author, please forgive me having written such a mucky trivial little play' – which in turn provoked Noël Coward to top them both by announcing: 'Children, may I say – on all your behalves – that as an author, producer and actor I have frequently managed to muck up my own acting, plays and productions and still survive.'

And so indeed it turned out. Even the equally unenthusiastic reviews in the Sunday newspapers failed to deter the audience. The box office receipts showed every sign of breaking Rattigan's own record for *The Browning Version* and *Harlequinade*. He managed to persuade Olivier to reinstate the two-act form of the play after the first week, and the run looked set to continue at least until the end of June, when the Oliviers' contract ran out. When it did, however, neither Olivier nor Vivien Leigh were anxious to repeat the experience, which meant that an alternative cast would have to be found for Broadway.

This was not a great worry. As Rattigan wired Freedman: 'Whole critical reaction obviously influenced by general feeling held for some time past Larry is subordinating his career to hers.' Broadway would allow him a different Regent and a different chorus girl, as he again told Freedman when he reached New York at the end of November. But another important subject beside the Broadway version of *The Sleeping Prince* lay behind his talks with the agent he now wholly trusted. Rattigan wanted to revise, and relaunch, *Adventure Story* in New York.

In the end this was to prove an abortive enterprise, but only just. In February 1953, unknown to Binkie Beaumont, Rattigan had dinner at the Caprice in London with Laurence Harvey, the Lithuanian-born star of the film *The Black Rose* who had made a meteoric impact on the London stage straight from the Royal Academy of Dramatic Art. He and Margaret Leighton, whom he was about to marry, were regular guests at Little Court and great friends. On the inside of a Dunhill cigarette packet at the Caprice Harvey wrote: 'I hereby agree to play the role of Alexander the Great in the play *Adventure Story* by Terence Rattigan in New York at a date and terms to be subsequently agreed.' The contract was witnessed by the two other guests at the dinner that evening, Yvonne de Carlo and Rattigan's old friend, the designer Billy Chappell.

In fact Harvey was not the only candidate Rattigan had in mind for the part. Harold Freedman had told him that the film star Tyrone Power was 'very interested', and Cathleen Nesbitt had sent a script to Marlon Brando, who, she cabled Rattigan, was 'fascinated' by it. After discussing the possiblities at length with Freedman, Rattigan returned

to England to redraft the play completely, with the idea of sending it
to both Harvey and Tyrone Power.

The work kept him occupied for the first three months of 1954, and
he made no compromises with the critics. He retained the 'middle-class
vernacular' that so many of them had condemned, but which he still
felt appealed to Aunt Edna. He did, however, accept that the rhetorical
question with which he had opened his first version, 'Where did it first
go wrong?', should be abandoned. In its place, he created a new first
scene in which Alexander is being sculpted and his father Philip appears
on stage.

> ALEXANDER: And when you disown me father, in favour of your new
> bastard? What lies will you tell the Council about me?
> PHILIP: There'll be no need for lies. I shall tell them that I have no
> intention of bequeathing the leadership of all Greece and the command
> of the best army in Europe to an effeminate weakling, a mother's darling
> of doubtful paternity, so little fitted to be king that at twenty he hasn't
> even shown that he possesses the instinct of a man.

Once again, the theme of father and son echoed throughout the new
version, as Rattigan refocused his play on Alexander's battle with himself to overcome his father's influence. In Act Two, he crystallised this
in new dialogue:

> QUEEN MOTHER: Isn't the true reason for your despair and misery at this
> moment that only now, at last, are you beginning to know yourself.
> *Pause.*
> ALEXANDER: Am I as vile as that?
> QUEEN MOTHER: (*With a smile*) It's not you who are vile. It's what is in
> you.
> ALEXANDER: My devil?
> QUEEN MOTHER: Yes.
> ALEXANDER: And my devil is hatred?
> QUEEN MOTHER: Of a man who is now dead.
>   *Pause.*
> ALEXANDER: And all I have done adds up to no more than the antics of
> a little boy when he tries to show his father that he too can be a man?
> QUEEN MOTHER: And succeeding so well that now he has ceased to be a
> little boy and become – his father.
>   *Alexander leaps up. He throws his head back and laughs sharply.*
> ALEXANDER: Gods in heaven! What a revenge! Do you hear that, father
> Philip! All my life I hated you so much that now, at the last, I have
> become you. There's a joke for you to relish, if you're not too drunk
> up there to hear it.

(With shaking hands he is pouring himself some wine.)
Philip drinks to Philip, drunkard to drunkard, despot to despot, murderer to murderer.

In a new final scene the voice of the dead Hephaestion replaces Alexander's original soliloquy, and the Queen Mother returns to offer the dying man peace. The final dialogue is between them.

ALEXANDER: *(Speaking with great difficulty)* The adventure is over now, isn't it?
QUEEN MOTHER: Yes, it's over.
ALEXANDER: What a pity! *(Almost inaudibly)* I've shown him, though, haven't I, mother? I've shown him.
QUEEN MOTHER: *(Gently)* Yes, my son. You've shown him.
(Alexander dies and the people gather round the throne.)

Rattigan's final stage direction in his revision of *Adventure Story* reads: 'The circle of people around the chair are beginning to cast wary glances at each other. The lights begin gradually to dim. Finally only the chair is visible, cold, impersonal and menacing, until that too fades into darkness.'

He handed the completed manuscript to Mary Herring on 26 March 1954. The new version went to Tyrone Power as soon as it was finished, and Rattigan cabled him on 7 April:

Dear Ty, Forgive my long silence but I have found task more extensive than had imagined owing necessity research and determination not to do patch up job. Have finished and sincerely believe play is now as good as I can make it. Can safely say anyway that it is more mature than before which is hardly surprising in view of the fact that its author is more mature dammit. Will send you copy soonest and will anxiously await your judgement.

Power cabled back three weeks later: 'Adored Same.' But the revised *Adventure Story* was never to reach Broadway. The effort of revision was in vain. Like the chair and the people at the end of its last act, it faded into darkness. It was to be six years before another major production brought it back to life.

CHAPTER 19

Table by the Door

◆

The body is a house of many windows, there we
all sit, showing ourselves and crying on the
passers-by to come and love us.
ROBERT LOUIS STEVENSON, *Virginibus Puerisque*

◆

As always, Rattigan's notes for a new play were handwritten on sheets of lined foolscap. 'Table By The Door – Reverse of DBS. Better for evil affinity to torture each other than to be tortured alone,' he wrote about the new play that was begining to form in his mind as 1953 came to an end. 'DBS' was, of course, *The Deep Blue Sea*, and his aide-memoire continued: 'Great beauty in decline. No love in her life. Cold. Friendless too. Therefore alone. He alone because of scandal – drink, prison? Not liked by fellow guests as it is known her is famous. Her need for him and his for her incompatible.'

For the moment these were merely doodles, the outline of something that had been growing in his mind throughout the winter as he visited his mother week after week at the Stanhope Court Hotel in South Kensington. Rattigan had watched fascinated as the hotel's inhabitants gathered and gossiped about the lives of their fellow guests. The loneliness in their lives was tangible. He had even begun to sketch the inhabitants of his own imaginary private hotel. There was 'Lady R and companion: most money. Eccentric: dreams, sex and betting. Lady D: cheerful, down in the world. Boy, girl: undergraduates. Retired schoolmaster: anxiously awaiting son who neglects. Manageress: bright, cheerful, ruthless and lonely. "None of your sow-faced land-ladies."'

These notes formed the outline of a play that he would complete at Little Court in the spring of 1954. It would be one of a pair, both one-acters. There was even a little dialogue:

> He doesn't like women very much.
> Why did he marry you?
> He wanted a wife.
> Why did you marry him?
> I wanted a husband.
> You surely could have done better for yourself than that.
> I suppose so. But he was gentle and kind and rather funny and I went into it with my eyes open. I thought I could make it work. I was wrong. (*Laughs*)
> What's the joke?
> A nice question for a woman's page. Now girls, which would you rather have, a husband who loved you too little or a husband that loved you too much?

On another foolscap page Rattigan went on:

> So I don't know if I could ever satisfy your need. I know you can't satisfy mine for you.
> I could try.
> So could I, and we'd both fail. Our two needs are like two chemicals . . . that when brought together can blow up the universe. Our universe.

Rattigan identified with the world of the Stanhope Court Hotel. Though there were the weekend parties at Little Court, he was – as he had always been – a lonely man. He knew instinctively how much the inhabitants of a private hotel craved companionship. The need for company, and for a sexual partner, was never far from his mind. That was why he remained devoted to Michael Franklin, and why he could sympathise with other homosexuals who found it difficult to discover new sexual partners without finding themselves threatened with the full might of the law. A homosexual in Britain in 1954, no matter how successful he might be, was still in fear of this fate.

One man who had recently suffered the public humiliation of arrest for what the law still called 'indecent behaviour' was John Gielgud, Rattigan's collaborator on *The Tale of Two Cities* almost twenty years before, and the man he had more than once tried to inveigle into acting in his plays, who had been charged in the autumn of 1953. In the event, Gielgud was only fined £10 and told by the magistrate to see a doctor, but his reputation was undoubtedly, if briefly, threatened. The arrest came as a tremendous shock to the homosexual community in Britain. Many of Gielgud's friends in the theatre feared that he would be booed off the stage when he next appeared, which he was due to do a few days later in Liverpool. But quite the opposite happened. Gielgud was not booed, he was given a standing ovation. As Rattigan was to explain to the *New York Times* some years later: 'He had enough courage to go on and the audience had enough grace and sympathy to accept him purely as an actor . . . The acceptance by these very ordinary people of something about which they had little understanding was very moving.'

Rattigan made use of this experience in the new play he was working on about life in a hotel like his mother's, the Stanhope Court, but 'situated near Bournemouth'. It was the perfect setting for an exploration of two of the themes that had always preoccupied him: the suppression of emotion and the difficulty the English found in accepting sexual deviance. As he privately insisted, in a phrase that he would later use in a play: 'You know what the real Vice Anglais is? It's not flagellation or pederasty, or whatever the French think it is, it's the inability to express emotion.' Rattigan wanted to bring those ideas to life in his new play, and he needed a character to help him to do so. He went back to his original notes, and the 'Eccentric: dreams, sex and betting'. The eccentric was to become the 'Major', his own father's nickname.

Two years later Rattigan described his intentions to the man who would eventually produce the two one-acters in America. In a letter of August 1956, he told Bob Whitehead:

The play as I had originally conceived it concerned the effect on a collection of highly conventional people of the discovery that one of their number was a sexual deviant, and that deviation I had naturally imagined as the one most likely to cause a dramatic shock, the one most likely to be outside the sphere of their sympathetic understanding; the one which the Major would be most ashamed of their finding out and the one for which the whole of the part of the character of the Major was originally conceived: obviously homosexuality.

By the spring of 1954, however, he had realised that he was, in fact, writing two plays about the residents of Stanhope Court. One, as he had put it in his early notes, was 'the reverse of *The Deep Blue Sea*', where the doomed affinity of two heterosexual lovers for each other would this time see them condemned to stay together rather than part as Hester and Freddie had done. The other play was about 'the Major'.

By the end of May, just as *The Man Who Loved Redheads* was released – to distinctly unflattering reviews – he was deeply engrossed in his new double bill of plays: so engrossed that it had failed to strike him that the Lord Chamberlain was highly unlikely to license a play for production on Shaftesbury Avenue which featured an acknowledged homosexual in a leading role and, what is more, asked the audience to view the character sympathetically. As Rattigan explained to Whitehead, 'It is literally true that when I began the play . . . I had already reached the point where the Major's offence was to be revealed before I realised that, if I were to get the play done in the West End at all, I would have to find a way round the Lord Chamberlain's present objection to any mention of this particular subject.' So he made the Major's 'sexual deviance' an urge to molest young women in the cinema.

In the other play, embodying the 'reverse of DBS', a similar subterfuge had to be employed, for in Rattigan's mind, the doomed relationship between his two lovers was every bit as applicable to homosexuals as Freddie and Hester's. If he had put part of himself and part of Kenneth Morgan in Hester, and part of himself in her husband, Sir William Collyer, so was he was to put another part of himself into the character of John Malcolm, the former junior minister once imprisoned for assaulting his wife and now writing anonymous articles for a left-wing weekly while living in the equal anonymity of a residential hotel.

But just as there was a good deal of Rattigan in John Malcolm, so there was a considerable amount of his lover, Michael Franklin, in the character of Malcolm's ex-wife, Anne Shankland. Franklin's appetite for tantrums and deceit, his narcissism and his compulsive lying all surface in Anne Shankland's character. Nevertheless, just as Malcolm and his ex-wife end their time in his new play together, reconciled to their fate as partners, so Rattigan felt, would he and the Midget. Though some of his friends may have longed for him to choose a more appropriate lover – to choose the hotel manageress Miss Cooper in the play – he knew in his heart that he was certain to remain with Franklin.

If there was a part of Rattigan that longed to be open about his sexuality, so perhaps there was also a part that longed to leave the 'impossible' Michael Franklin for one of the more adoring homosexual 'Miss Coopers' who regularly presented themselves. But that dream would never be realised, and Franklin understood it. The Midget's reaction to the play, as retailed to one friend, was 'Our audience (lumped together in his mind as Beaumont, Noel, you – indeed all my friends) *longed* for your ending up with Miss Cooper and they all *hated* your ending up with me again.'

But Anne Shankland was not only Michael Franklin. She was also based on Rattigan's friend the model Jean Dawnay, who regularly acted as his hostess at the weekend parties at Little Court. Dawnay had once told him about a fight she had had with a boyfriend which had grown so violent the police had to be called, and that too found its way into the play, in the brutal action Malcolm takes against his wife. When she read one of the first drafts of the play, Dawnay was so disturbed that she begged Rattigan to change some of the details to conceal any possibility that she might be recognised.

'Nothing is ever a portrait,' Rattigan concluded, but John Malcolm's passionate speech in the first of the two plays nevertheless reveals the passions raging within Rattigan himself:

ANNE: If all I wanted to do was to make my husband a slave, why should I specially have chosen you and not the others?
JOHN: Because where would your fun have been in enslaving the sort of man who was already the slave of his own head gardener? You wanted bigger game. Wilder game. None of your tame baronets and Australian millionaires, too well mannered to protest when you denied them their conjugal rights, and too well brought up not to take your headaches at bedtime as just headaches at bedtime. 'Poor old girl! Bad Show! So sorry. Better in the morning, I hope. Feeling a bit tired myself, anyway.' No, Anne dear. What enjoyment would there have been for you in using your weapons on that sort of husband? But to turn them on a genuine, live roaring savage from the slums of Hull, to make him grovel at the vague and distant promise of delights that were his anyway by right, or goad him to such a frenzy of drink and rage by a locked door that he'd kick it in and hit you with his fist so hard that you'd knock yourself unconsconscious against a wall – that must really have been fun.

Rattigan too had felt the desire for 'delights that were his anyway by right', and in the privacy of his own relationship with Franklin had demanded them. Rattigan understood how Jean Dawnay could still find herself in love with a man who abused her. 'Part of Terry loved the Midget because of the tantrums and the dramas that he caused,' one of his homosexual friends recalls. 'Terry would laugh when he threatened to throw himself out of the window or cut his wrists. That was their way. There was a part of Terry that liked it, and longed for it.'

Before Royal Ascot in the middle of June, when he held another house party at Little Court with Jean Dawnay as hostess, Rattigan had completed a draft of the two plays, which he had decided should together be called *Separate Tables*, and were dedicated to his mother. The first play, about John Malcolm, was to be called *Table by the Window*. The second, about 'the Major', he called *Table by the Door*. Rattigan also intended that the leading parts in each of the two plays – Malcolm and his ex-wife Anne Shankland, and the Major and the young girl who sympathises with him, Miss Sibyl Railton-Bell – should be played by the same actor and actress.

This time, however, he did not send his new plays to Binkie Beaumont. The harsh treatment he felt he had received when he had submitted *The Sleeping Prince* to Tennent a year earlier had not been forgotten. On top of that Beaumont had only just decided it was going to be impossible to replace Olivier and Vivien Leigh in *The Sleeping Prince* at the Phoenix and had therefore decided to announce the end of its run. 'I therefore feel that by making this announcement at once we may very easily add to the box office,' Beaumont explained in a letter. Rattigan did not agree – he had even asked Freedman to see if the movie actor Charles Boyer might consider taking over Olivier's role. Officially it was a Tennent/Olivier production, even though he had put up a quarter of the cost, and he had no real say. In the circumstances, it was hardly surprising that he saw no reason to give Binkie Beaumont the impression that he had the 'first choice' of any new play he might write. Besides, these were two one-acters, and he had always told Stephen Mitchell that if ever he were to write a successor to *Playbill* he would give him first sight of it. Rattigan kept his word. For good measure, and perhaps a little in spite towards Beaumont, he also gave the plays to Laurence Olivier.

Both Mitchell and Olivier adored the plays. Olivier was so keen to keep them for Vivien and himself that he tried to persuade Rattigan to postpone production for eighteen months, by which time he would have completed the film version of *Richard the Third*, which he was committed to make for Alexander Korda. Rattigan was grateful, but nonetheless declined, suggesting instead that perhaps he and Vivien might consider doing the plays in New York – if they worked in London. On his side Mitchell wanted to press ahead without delay. By the middle of July he had submitted both plays to the Lord Chamberlain for a licence. The Lord Chamberlain's office made no objection. The reader's report specifically praises both plays, the first for its 'impeccable' taste in dialogue, the second for 'being in no way far-fetched in plot'. Far from suspecting any homosexual undertones, the report called the one-acter about the Major 'a little masterpiece'.

Shortly after *The Sleeping Prince* came to the end of its run in June 1954, Rattigan and Peter Glenville – with whom he was on speaking terms again after *Adventure Story* and who had agreed to direct the two plays – started rehearsals. A short pre-London tour was planned for the end of August, before coming in to the St James's Theatre in late September. Both men wanted to reunite the team that had made such a success of *The Browning Version* and *Harlequinade*, and both wanted Eric Portman to play both John Malcolm and 'Major' Pollock. Portman agreed at once. They had even considered asking Mary Ellis to join him but, remembering the dreadful arguments during rehearsals for *The Browning Version*, opted instead for David Lean's new wife, Kay Walsh, to play both Anne Shankland and Sibyl Railton-Bell.

After two weeks of rehearsals, however, it was abundantly clear to both Rattigan and Peter Glenville that Walsh was not the ideal choice for Anne Shankland. This time Rattigan decided not to suffer the same débâcle that he had with Margaret Sullavan on Broadway. Walsh had to be replaced as quickly as possible. The only question was, by whom? Rattigan was in no doubt. Margaret Leighton, now Laurence Harvey's wife, Birmingham-born and just thirty-two, would be absolutely right. She accepted with a little over two weeks to go before the first performances of the provincial tour. It was the first time she had actually appeared in one of Rattigan's plays, but she was already established as one of the actresses he most admired.

As the opening grew nearer, one point agitated Rattigan. He was deeply concerned that what he was later to call 'the bowdlerisation of the original' might suggest to some members of the audience that the Major and Sibyl would finally 'get together'. The thought horrified him. If that was the implication, he wrote later, he would be 'hammered (rightly) for tacking on to a serious play an improbable ending'.

Fortunately no such *malentendu* occurred. The first audiences for *Separate Tables* sympathised with both John Malcolm and the Major – and with Anne Shankland and Sibyl Railton-Bell – for the obvious pain of their plight, just as they had sympathised with Hester Collyer two years before. As in *The Deep Blue Sea*, Rattigan had created plays which could be understood and enjoyed by audiences of any kind. Hester Collyer had appealed to thousands of women who did not know that her inspiration was her creator's affair with Kenneth Morgan. Just as powerfully, the Major's predicament as a man shamed into confronting his weaknesses captured the imagination and the emotions of the audience. It was the humanity in both portraits that gave them their strengths, not the specific sexual details of their genesis.

When the plays opened at the St James's Theatre on 22 September

1954, the critics concentrated on the fact that the Major recaptured his dignity at the end of the second play, which Rattigan had decided at the last moment to retitle *Table Number Seven*. Harold Hobson in the *Sunday Times* was in no doubt that the second play was

> one of Mr Rattigan's masterpieces, in which he shows in a superlative degree his pathos, his humour, and his astounding mastery over that English language . . . And it is all the better because, in these days of minor statements and too easily accepted despair, it affirms ringingly that there is no sorrow which need prove fatal, no disaster that cannot be retrieved.

Not every critic was as enthusiastic. John Barber thought both plays 'flawed' while admitting they put 'middle-class loneliness under a miscroscope's eye'. *The Times* suggested – after a passing reference to Aunt Edna – 'Mr Rattigan's determination to consult her wishes on this matter doubtless accounts for a faint streak of falsity which runs through these extremely entertaining stage stories.'

·Kenneth Tynan, in the *Observer* the following Sunday, was the only critic to sense Rattigan's true intentions. He transformed his review into a duologue between a 'young perfectionist' and Aunt Edna herself in 'the dining room of a Kensington hotel not unlike the Bournemouth hotel' in which the plays were set. His piece concluded:

> A.E. Yet you sound a trifle peaky. Is something biting you?
> Y.P. Since you ask, I regretted that the major's crime was not something more cathartic than mere cinema flirtation. Yet I suppose the play is as good a handling of sexual abnormality as English playgoers will tolerate.
> A.E. For my part, I am glad it is no better.
> Y.P. I guessed you would be; and so did Mr Rattigan. Will you accompany me on a second visit tomorrow?
> A.E. With great pleasure. Clearly, there is something here for both of us.
> Y.P. Yes. But not quite enough for either of us.

The day after Tynan's review appeared Rattigan cabled Harold Freedman in New York: 'Sunday Press excellent excepting Tynan's *Observer* being funny about Aunt Edna in otherwise very appreciative notice. Anyway judging from box office and agency reports think I can now safely say we are a great big vulgar satisfying smash.'

Whatever Tynan may have implied, to the vast majority of playgoers the success of either play in *Separate Tables* did not depend on an understanding of the hidden reality behind the Major's offence. But Terence Rattigan did not believe that. He was to remain convinced that the play's audience had actually grasped the true reason for the Major's arrest. As he was to insist two years later, 'They fully realised that the Major's peccadilloes (in the cinema) were in fact only symbolical of another problem of which, at that time (just after several prominent cases), they were most sensitively conscious. An English audience knew my problem and accepted the fact that I had to skirt around it. They got the full impact of the play, as I subsequently learnt from many conversations'. He did not say who those conversations were with, but there is little doubt they were mostly with friends well aware of his own sexual preferences.

The ambiguity in Major Pollock's speech to Sibyl after he has been revealed as a liar and a coward remains one of the most effective Terence Rattigan ever wrote:

> POLLOCK: You couldn't guess, I know, but ever since school I've always been scared to death of women. Of everyone, in a way, I suppose, but mostly of women. I had a bad time at school . . . Boys hate other boys to be timid and shy, and they gave it to me good and proper. My father despised me too . . . (Getting a commission was my one success) . . . It meant everything to me . . . Being saluted, being called sir – I thought I'm someone now, a real person. Perhaps some woman might even . . . But it didn't work. It never has worked. I'm made in a certain way, and I can't change it.

The Major's admission in turn provoked Rattigan to a defence of his lifestyle and that of his friends, in an apologia which he gives in the same play to the newly married Charles Stratton:

> STRATTON: He presumably understands my form of lovemaking. I *should* therefore understand his. But I don't. So I am plainly in a state of prejudice against him, and must be very wary of any moral judgements I may pass in this matter. It's only fair to approach it from the purely logical standpoint of practical Christian ethics, and ask myself the question: 'What harm has the man done?' Well, apart from possibly slightly bruising the arm of a certain lady, whose motives in complaining – I agree with Lady Matheson – are extremely questionable – apart from that, and apart from telling us a few rather pathetic lies abut his past life, which most of us do anyway from time to time, I really can't see he's done anything to justify us chucking him out into the street.

It was a plea for tolerance which captured the imagination of London's West End audiences, just as it was later to capture the imagination of audiences in France, Germany, Holland, South Africa, Australia and the United States. But it did nothing to still the fear that Rattigan himself felt at the possibility of his being identified publicly as a homosexual. He could not bring himself to revolt against the public disgust at homosexuality. The habits of his own upbringing, the desire for concealment, the tradition among homosexuals in the theatre – as well as the moral temperature of the times – militated against it. This was not a time in Britain when a homosexual could 'come out' with pride.

During the provincial tour of *Separate Tables* Alexander Korda again turned up with proposals for a film version of *The Deep Blue Sea*. This time he knew who he wanted to play Hester – Vivien Leigh, and she had agreed. Before *Separate Tables* opened in London Harold Freedman had struck a deal with Korda which not only paid Rattigan £7,500 for the rights to his play but also gave him a further £4,000 for the first draft of the screenplay. Korda wanted Kenneth More as Freddie and Charles Boyer as Mr Miller, but he also told Rattigan that Vivien Leigh would not accept Puffin Asquith as the director. 'She feels he is too sentimental and inhibited for the project.' In Puffin's place Korda suggested Alfred Hitchcock, George Cukor or Max Ophuls. Though disappointed for Puffin, Rattigan was delighted at the prospect of any of the alternatives.

He began work on the screenplay immediately after the première of *Separate Tables*, retiring as usual to write at Little Court, with Mary Herring, a cook and a butler to look after him. He wanted to ensure that the script would work for an American audience. Vivien Leigh's last starring role in Hollywood, as Blanche du Bois in *Streetcar*, had won her a second Oscar, and he longed for her Hester to repeat the success.

So in his first notes for the screenplay Rattigan was at pains to bring Hester Collyer to life for this new public. In particular he was anxious that Hester and Freddie's first attraction for each other should be captured, 'the awakening of her protective instinct towards him and of his own need for her', as he noted on a lined pad, and 'their furtive life together before the decision to tell her husband. Her decision, not his, incidentally. (The first of their flamers).' He wanted the film version to make absolutely clear that it was 'Hester's recovery of her self-respect that makes her live'.

To convey that message he painstakingly rewrote the final section of the play for the screen. 'Miller's scene has now a different approach,' he wrote to Korda.

The 'emotional catharsis' by which would-be suicides are psychiatrically restrained from self-violence can be played down. In its place will be a cold, logical and more pointed exposition that

Hester's death wish is rooted in her sense of shame and that shame has become an intolerable burden through her need for a man who she believes doesn't need her. In fact, he does and if she could ever find out how strongly he does her respect might return. And with self-respect a will to live.

The screenplay did not, however, prove easy. Vivien Leigh was intensely nervous at the prospect of attempting Peggy Ashcroft's role, not least because she would be laying bare some of the unhappiness she too had suffered during the previous two years. Rattigan wanted to be sure to give her the clearest guidance to Hester's state of mind. On the final scene, for example, he wrote:

> Miller leaves. The Freddy–Hester scene that follows makes even plainer than the play Freddy's virtual certainty that she is going to beg him to stay and that after a few faint protests he has decided to do so. In fact, he will reveal not only to us but to Hester his need for her. Her last firm goodbye to him, which he can scarcely believe, will thus be more clearly seen to be the symbol of the final victory over herself, her self-hatred and over her will to die.

Vivien Leigh's fragile hold on the role of Hester was shaken still further when Alexander Korda made a deal with Twentieth Century-Fox to allow them the right to distribute the film, in return for which they would provide the £400,000 budget and have the right to choose the director. The deal made Korda a profit, but it left Fox in complete control. The studio did not hesitate; they nominated the Russian-born Anatole Litvak, director of the Oscar-nominated film *The Snake Pit* in 1949, as both director and producer. It did not turn out to be a happy choice, especially as Fox also insisted that the film be made in their new wide-screen Cinemascope process, and in colour. The delicate subtlety of Rattigan's original dingy, slightly squalid first-floor flat was to be lost even before shooting began in December 1954. Under Litvak's guidance, Vivien Leigh became the star rather than Hester Collyer.

As Christmas approached, and Rattigan worked on the screenplay with Litvak in Paris – for which Korda was to receive rather more than he had paid Rattigan – casting for the film version was completed. Charles Boyer had not been prepared to accept the part of Mr Miller, and Litvak had offered it to Eric Portman, at Rattigan's instigation, just as he had offered the part of Sir William Collyer to another friend, Emlyn Williams. Kenneth More had agreed to play Freddie Page, and even Jimmy Hanley was offered a small part. Rattigan had forgiven him for his part in the Broadway fiasco. Litvak, however, was to present more of a problem than the whole cast put together.

Kenneth More hated the script, claiming, 'There's too much Litvak in it and not enough Rattigan. I'd almost go so far as to say all the Rattigan has come out and all the Litvak has gone in.' It was a mild exaggeration. In his determination to co-operate as fully as possible in making the film a success, Rattigan had converted most of the director's wishes into reality, but, as he had done before, he had compromised too far, which became abundantly clear as filming got under way. By the time the shooting was over in March 1955, Terence Rattigan was telling his friends that he would never again work with that 'humourless and heavy-handed' man Litvak.

Between them, but at Litvak's relentless insistence, they had attempted to 'open out' the film, by including the scenes in which Freddie and Hester first meet and in which his crash and the end of his career as a test pilot are established. But the harder Rattigan tried to appeal to a cinema audience the more surely the claustrophobic atmosphere of the original piece was sacrificed and the particular compelling quality of Hester's cramped first-floor room began to disappear. Each embellishment succeeded only in diluting the drama, turning it finally into what *Time* magazine would describe as 'if not a soap opera' then 'no better than a detergent drama'. Terence Rattigan's 'fascination' with stars, and his desire for international success, had diminished his work.

But that had not just been happening with *The Deep Blue Sea*. The fate of the film version of *The Sleeping Prince* was also plaguing Rattigan. The screenwriter Garson Kanin had suggested to Darryl F. Zanuck, the vice-president in charge of production at Twentieth Century-Fox, that the play would make an ideal film; and, in particular, would provide a marvellous starring role for Marilyn Monroe, the actress then under contract to Zanuck and Fox. In his reply, Zanuck did not mince his words. 'We had considered it several times for Marilyn Monroe. The Mythical Kingdom idea frightened that away, particularly after such a splendid film as *Roman Holiday* was a disappointment at the box office. Our own *Call Me Madam* suffered the same fate. I guess this just isn't the year for Mythical Kingdoms.'

Beaumont wondered if Rattigan might not 'write a brilliant letter to Mr Zanuck', even if he did add the proviso that 'Maybe it is not really worthwhile.' Fascinated, however, by the possibility that the star of *Gentlemen Prefer Blondes* and *Niagara* might play Elaine Dagenham, Rattigan did not hesitate. In March he wrote to Zanuck:

As an admirer of Miss Monroe, I believe her to be . . . an actress of high potentialities which have hardly yet been, and then only most grudgingly, acknowledged by the critics . . . I would love to see her in the part . . . because I think it would be a brilliant piece of personality casting . . . The chief quality which the part requires in an actress . . . is 'style'. That, it seems to me, is a quality that Miss Monroe shares almost equally with Vivien – certainly as regards this kind of comedy.

Zanuck's reply was cautious. Miss Monroe, he told Rattigan, had two pictures waiting for her which would keep her busy for the rest of 1954, but he did not dismiss the idea completely.

I have been most interested in your play in spite of the fact that I have certain enormous fears about anything that happens to be 'light and frivolous'. I am not talking about my own taste, or the taste of certain discriminating metropolitan audiences. Like all producers I am constantly faced with problem of selecting stories that have what is known as 'mass audience appeal'.

For the moment Rattigan put the idea of Marilyn Monroe as Elaine Dagenham to one side, but she was not forgotten.

Beaumont and he then tried to persuade Jose Ferrer to take on the film, but once again were met by the excuse of 'the financial failure of Roman Holiday'. 'Deplorable and regrettable as this point of view is,' Ferrer told Beaumont, 'I need not tell you how it typifies a certain kind of thinking that one finds out here.' Nevertheless he attempted to interest Arthur Freed, the legendary producer of On the Town, An American in Paris and Singing in the Rain, but without success.

Rattigan, however, was so certain that a film version of The Sleeping Prince would eventually come about that he asked Bill Forsyth, his accountant, to create a new trust for his mother. He intended to place all the proceeds of the sale, when it finally took place, into the trust 'for the benefit of Vera Rattigan . . . during her life'. Only after his mother's death would the capital or the income return to him. It was to be one of the most generous acts of his life, for when the film rights were finally sold – in March 1956 – they fetched $175,000, more than £75,000.

But as the first signs of spring began to creep across Eaton Square towards the balcony of his flat at number 29, so the possibility of a film version seemed to be slipping gently away. In the meantime, Harold Freedman was still intent on pulling a Broadway production together. He wanted Monroe for the stage version, and Grace Kelly for the film, but it rapidly became clear he would be unable to get either. Freedman had also approached Robert Donat, whose asthma was now so debilitating that he turned the possibility down, as did Judy Holliday and Audrey Hepburn, who told Freedman that she did not 'want to play another Cinderella'. Rattigan himself had approached Alec Guinness about the possibility of his playing the Regent on Broadway, but he was committed to something else. 'My dear Terry, I seem fated not to appear in any of your plays and there's nothing I want to do more.' The Broadway production of *The Sleeping Prince* was proving almost as difficult to launch as the film.

Exhausted by the negotiations, and by the battles over the filming of *The Deep Blue Sea*, Rattigan took off for a tour of Australia, where a season of his plays was about to be presented. When he left he was a playwright at the peak of his powers. *Separate Tables* was firmly established in London. One of his champions, the critic Harold Hobson, had just paid him the compliment of suggesting in the *Sunday Times* in January 1955 that he was one person whom early success had not spoiled. 'Mr Rattigan began with a huge popular success. This success made my predecessor deeply uneasy. It need not have done. Mr Rattigan could hardly have developed finer qualities if, in his early days, he had been as viciously attacked as Ibsen.'

By the time Terence Rattigan returned from Australia the theatre that he and Aunt Edna had come to know and love over the past two decades had undergone a radical – and permanent – change.

CHAPTER 20

Never Look Back

◆

If you've no world of your own, it's rather pleasant

to regret the passing of someone else's.

JOHN OSBORNE, *Look Back in Anger*

◆

While Rattigan was away in Australia, Kenneth Tynan was writing his epitaph. 'Mr Rattigan is the Formosa of the contemporary theatre, occupied by the old guard, but geographically inclined towards the progressives.' It was the harbinger of his decline in critical and public esteem.

As his friend Harold Hobson recalled in his autobiography two decades later, 'There was discontent, often unjust, with the conventional drama of the day, which began to be attacked with a bitterness that surprised and distressed me. Terence Rattigan, in particular, was made the target for abuse and vilification, the violence of which broke his gentle and chivalrous spirit.' Without knowing it, or knowing why, Rattigan became the English theatre's sacrificial lamb – ripe for the slaughter. The old order of 'french window drama' – and there were a great many french windows in his plays – was out. The kitchen sink was in.

Cocooned within a select circle of friends, who would hear no criticism of their host and benefactor, Rattigan was taken completely by surprise. He was engrossed in the commercial success of his plays and films. That was what mattered. That was what proved his value as a playwright. That also brought him Savile Row suits, Rolls-Royce cars and dinner after the show at the Savoy Grill. Rattigan did not pretend that he did not relish the company of stars or princesses, from Vivien Leigh to Princess Margaret. Why should he? He had earned it. Rattigan saw no virtue in hiding his light under the nearest available bushel: quite the reverse. From his upper-middle-class seat in the stalls, life was good, and the old order apparently unchanged.

There was no signpost that the theatrical world had changed. Considering the period a few years afterwards, Kenneth Tynan himself admitted: 'The climate as a whole was listless. We quarrelled among ourselves over Brecht and the future of poetic drama; in debate with foreign visitors we crossed our fingers, swallowed hard and talked of Terence Rattigan; but if we were critics, we must quite often have felt that we were practising our art in a vacuum.'

By the time Rattigan returned to England, by way of the south of France, where he gambled and worked on an idea for a screenplay based on the life of T.E.Lawrence, the first signs that the vacuum was about to be filled were arriving in the West End. *Waiting for Godot*, a new play by Samuel Beckett, another cricketer, who had played for his university, Trinity College in Dublin, was just transferring into the Criterion from the Arts Theatre in London. Directed by the new star of Cambridge university theatre, Peter Hall, Godot was to transform the way in which London audiences saw the theatre. Allegorical, uncompromising, it was the antithesis of Rattigan's carefully observed naturalism. Audiences who instinctively empathised with Hester or the Crock found Vladimir and Estragon considerably harder to adjust to. But a younger audience was waiting in the wings.

Typically, Rattigan's own circle of friends were dismissive of Beckett's effort. Gielgud said he didn't understand it, and that he doubted it would ever be seen as an important play, while Somerset Maugham described it as 'two dirty old men picking their toenails'. Rattigan, to his credit, went to see it almost at once. Unfortunately, he then committed his own unfavourable opinion to print. In October 1955 he published a piece in the *New Statesman* under the heading, 'Aunt Edna Waits for Godot'. Although, in an imaginary conversation between Aunt Edna and her 'nephew', he was at pains to point out that she had actually enjoyed her evening, she still complained:

How could I like the play, seeing that Mr Samuel Beckett plainly hates me so much that he's refused point blank to give me a play at all? . . . Even a middlebrow like myself could have told told him that a really good play had to be on two levels, an upper one, which I suppose you'd call symbolical, and a lower one, which is based on story and character. By writing on the upper level alone, all Mr Beckett has done is to produce one of those things that thirty years ago we used to call Experimental Theatre – you wouldn't remember that, of course, and that's a movement which led absolutely nowhere.

Rattigan utterly disregarded the effect this flippant approach might have on a younger and more serious generation. He was more concerned with the film and Broadway versions of *The Sleeping Prince* and who would replace the Oliviers in each case. This had still not been settled. Barbara Bel Geddes, who had been starring in Tennessee Williams's *Cat on a Hot Tin Roof*, had told him that it was 'the best comedy ever written' and that she would love to play it on Broadway, if he was prepared to wait for her run to finish. Rattigan liked the idea, and told Freedman so, but who should be her leading man? Donat had turned the part down, and although Michael Redgrave was expressing some interest, there were not many other candidates.

At this point Freedman came up with an idea for the film version. He suggested contacting William Wyler, with whom Rattigan had worked during the war, as a possible director. Rattigan agreed without hesitation. He still thought that his film version would work, providing it was placed in the right hands, and Wyler was certainly the right hands. The director was vital. The critical reception of *The Deep Blue Sea*, which had just been released, proved it. The English critics were respectful, but not over-enthusiastic, while in the United States the *New Yorker* decided that Hester's predicament was 'boring'. And who was to blame for that except the director, Anatole Litvak?

Wyler too was aware of what had happened to *The Deep Blue Sea*, and suggested that Rattigan come to Hollywood early in November to discuss *The Sleeping Prince*. He cabled him in London, 'Preliminary to our meeting I want to affirm my feeling that the play as written must act principally as a basis for the development of a screenplay. I hope that we could broaden the scope of the subject and the situations involved so as to create a great amount of new material.' 'Dear Willie,' came the reply. 'Thanks cable, which neither alarms nor desponds but only makes me more eager hear your ideas in detail.'

Rattigan was anxious to keep the idea of Wyler secret until he was sure that it would lead to something. The reason was simple. He had informally offered the film rights to both Beaumont and Tolly de Grunwald, and did not want to run the risk of offending either. But he was nevertheless fascinated by the idea of Wyler. So instead of telling the truth to his regular collaborators, Terence Rattigan pretended he was off to watch the Ryder Cup golf tournament between Britain and the United States at Palm Springs. This, he told Wyler, 'pleasure apart gives reasonable alibi interested parties here my sudden semi-global dash'. But one person knew what he was doing, and why. No sooner had his plane touched down in New York, on route to Los Angeles, than Rattigan received a message from Miss Marilyn Monroe. Would he be prepared to have a drink with her that afternoon in Manhattan, before flying on? He was later to claim nonchalantly that he was not 'electrified' by the invitation, but the fact was that he was intoxicated by it. Intensely nervous, he arrived at 4.30 for the scheduled appointment, only to find the cocktail bar deserted.

Rattigan sat there for an hour, and consumed three Martinis, before the star finally appeared. She was wearing dark glasses, and – as he was to put it later – 'greeted me with that deliciously shy self-confidence that had overwhelmed so many thousands of tough and potentially hostile press men'. He could not understand more than about one word in three that she spoke to him, and was equally sure 'she didn't understand a word I said'. Nevertheless she managed to convince him that she wanted to buy the rights to *The Sleeping Prince* if Wyler declined. Then she asked Rattigan, bashfully, if 'Sir Larry' would do it with her.

> Gazing into those beautiful and childishly knowing eyes – she had removed her dark glasses – what could I reply but yes? I was sure 'Sir Larry' would leap at the chance, I said, and I would leave no stone unturned to see that he did.

The meeting with Wyler in L.A. appeared to go well enough, but after Rattigan's return to England the director pulled out. Relieved rather than dismayed, he then told Freedman to let Monroe know that the rights were available if she wanted them. Strictly and legally speaking that was true, but Rattigan had neglected to explain to Monroe his commitment to de Grunwald, who, acting in good faith, had approached John Huston and asked him if he would like to direct. For a moment Rattigan, an admirer of Huston's work, thought the two approaches could be combined, but Huston wanted Jean Simmons in the part – an obviously less alluring alternative than Monroe backed by 'Sir Larry'. On Boxing Day 1955 he cabled Freedman, 'Imbroglio getting beyond me. Do hope positive results soon.' Within a week John Huston had bowed out, muttering darkly about 'a doublecross' and holding Rattigan responsible.

Unperturbed by the accusations, Rattigan cabled Freedman on 5 January 1956. 'Delighted at news. Please tell little lady most pleased and happy and am hopeful get Larry to come with me Queen Mary January 12.' He ended with the news that he had also finished the first draft of his script on Lawrence of Arabia for Puffin. 'Slightly longer

than Seven Pillars,' he wrote. 'But much more moving.' It was the
Regent of Carpathia, however, rather than the complex figure of
Colonel T.E.Lawrence, who was to demand his time and energy in
the months to come.

'Sir Larry' was indeed persuaded to come to New York, where a
meeting was arranged with Miss Monroe and her business manager,
thirty-five-year-old Milton Greene, who had at one stage been her stills
photograper. By the time the meeting was over it had been agreed not
only that Miss Monroe would buy the project, but also that 'Sir Larry'
would be its director as well as its leading man. 'By the end of the
day,' wrote Olivier a quarter of a century later, 'one thing was clear
to me: I was going to fall most shatteringly in love with Marilyn, and
what was going to happen?' What happened was that 'Sir Larry' would
pay a great deal more attention to Miss Monroe's view of Rattigan's
screenplay than to its author's.

The film was officially announced in New York on 9 February, and
Rattigan agreed to have a first draft finished by the middle of April.
Within a month of his return to Little Court in the middle of February
he was cabling Freedman miserably to explain that he and Olivier 'have
had serious disagreements', adding, 'He insists complete collaboration.
I insist writing new scenes alone after preliminary discussions then
working together on basis my script . . . must confess would rather
relinquish script unless can work my own way.' Rattigan left it to his
agent to pass on his thoughts, and to work out with 'Sir Larry' the
terms of a compromise that would enable the script to be delievered.
Freedman managed it, and sent the two men away to Gleneagles in
Scotland to finish by the agreed date. After its completion, Rattigan
cabled Freedman, 'Have feeling Larry really prefers his authors dead.'

To offset the heartache, there was a considerable financial sop. Marilyn Monroe's production company paid Rattigan Productions $125,000
for the rights to The Sleeping Prince; and a further $50,000 for Rattigan's
screenplay. Most of the money was put into the trust Rattigan had
specifically created for the purpose, to benefit his mother during her
lifetime. On 5 May he cabled Monroe, enclosing the script. 'I am very
conscious, of course, that it is overlong but Larry preferred, in my
view quite rightly, that I should make it too full rather than too bare.
We are now engaged in cutting it . . .' Miss Monroe was happy enough
to set a date for her arrival in England to start filming. She would
arrive in July with her new husband, Arthur Miller.

In the meantime, Rattigan also heard that the Broadway stage production was to get under way. His suggestion that Michael Redgrave
might star alongside Barbara Bel Geddes seemed to be working out,

even though Redgrave was nervous of treading in Olivier's footsteps and was insisting that the show be launched on Broadway before the film opened so that there could be no comparison between them. To make sure Broadway came first, Redgrave offered to take over part of the management himself. Suddenly everything seemed to be happening at once. Stephen Mitchell was even trying to launch another American production of *The Sleeping Prince*, in Los Angeles, starring Shirley Maclaine. The productions in Copenhagen and Stockholm were already established, while the Paris production was about to start.

In April, just as Rattigan was putting the final touches to the script for Olivier, Redgrave wrote asking if he could direct, and asking for Rattigan to 'reassure' him that the Regent was 'meant to be a trifle younger' than Olivier had made him in London. The 'reassurance' took the form of a long explanation from Rattigan of the characters of both the Regent and his wife, which had been honed over the long months of working with Olivier, first on the play itself, and then on the film script. First, Rattigan told Redgrave, he had always meant the Regent to· be 'about forty . . . a confirmed, experienced and rather bored lady killer'. It was essential that the audience should never be allowed to get the impression that he and the Grand Duchess 'could ever have had any normal marital relations'. For, 'if they do it is fatal, because the Grand Duchess instantly takes all the sympathy', which 'not only killed the comedy but made us dislike the Regent'. Not a precise 'portrait' of the author's mother and father, perhaps, but a clear reference to their relationship. 'She is lady trained by heredity and strict upbringing to put duty before love, without even feeling the slightest qualm . . . She would never have expected her husband to behave in any other way sexually or emotionally than he does . . .'

Redgrave dithered, backed out, then quickly changed his mind again and finally committed to rehearsals in August for a New York opening three months later. By a strange coincidence, partly created by Peter Glenville's sudden decision that he was now available to direct the New York opening of *Separate Tables*, Rattigan now had not one but two Broadway openings within days of each other, with *Separate Tables* just beating *The Sleeping Prince* to the post. All this just as he had sent off the first script of Lawrence to Tolly de Grunwald, who was talking about Laurence Harvey or Richard Burton for the role of Lawrence, and just as Marilyn Monroe was arriving in Britain to start shooting with 'Sir Larry'.

Rattigan hardly had a moment to breathe, and certainly less time to go to the theatre himself than he usually did. Nevertheless Binkie Beaumont persuaded him to take an evening off on 8 May 1956 to join

him and Margaret Leighton at the first night of a new play being
presented by the English Stage Company at the Royal Court in
London. It was one of the first productions by the company, which
was now run by Rattigan's contemporary at the OUDS, George
Devine, and dedicated to putting on the work of new dramatists. The
new dramatist on this particular occasion was a young actor, John
Osborne, who had written a new play, called *Look Back in Anger*.

Rattigan and Beaumont sat in the stalls of the cramped theatre in
Sloane Square on that mild spring evening, and watched one of the
seminal moments in the history of modern English drama unfolding
on the stage in front of them. Osborne's hero, Jimmy Porter, launched
into a brilliant, eloquent attack on almost everything that a man educated at Harrow and Oxford, who lived in Eaton Square, played golf
and enjoyed weekend house parties stood for. It was a full frontal attack
on the class privileges that Rattigan had taken for granted throughout
his life, and a punch on the nose for the comfortable worlds of South
Kensington, Albany, Little Court and Cannes. The one significant
figure of authority in the play is an elderly colonel, whom Porter calls
'one of those sturdy old plants left over from the Edwardian wilderness
that can't understand why the sun isn't shining any more'. To Rattigan
it seemed as if the attack was at least partly aimed at him.

At the interval, Beaumont announced that he did not like the play
and intended to leave. Rattigan was about to follow him when he met
his friend, the critic Cuthbert Worsley, who was enthusiastic about the
play and saw its significance. Rattigan did not share his view. He was
prepared to accept only that it was 'quite well written', though 'badly
constructed', and he could not see what on earth Jimmy Porter had to
be angry about. Nevertheless Worsley persuaded Rattigan to see the
play through to the end.

Cornered by a reporter from the *Daily Express* after the curtain had
come down, and asked for his opinon, Rattigan replied that John
Osborne was saying, 'Look, Ma, I'm not Terence Rattigan.' It was a
foolish and conceited remark, and would count against him for almost
four decades. But once more Rattigan was oblivious to the effect his
words would have on other people. Back at home, secure in his well-
cushioned world, he set about preparing plans for Marilyn Monroe's
visit to London. He had already found a house for her to live near his
in Sunningdale, so that she could travel easily to and from the studios
at Pinewood, and both he and Olivier intended to welcome her and
her husband to Britain with two spectacular parties. Olivier's was to
be in London, Rattigan's at Little Court, and they would go fifty-fifty
on the total cost of both.

Rattigan's note to himself about the people to be invited to his party at Little Court on 24 July 1956 was couched in customary flippant vein. 'Preliminary list of Cosies, Cups of Tea and Close Chums to be invited for no other purpose but to give me entertainment, and, I hope, Mr & Mrs Miller (but that is a secondary consideration).' The list included Chips and John Gielgud, Puffin and Peggy Ashcroft, Beaumont, Cuthbert Worsley, the Guinnesses, the Mores, the Scofields, Edith Evans, Peter Glenville, Jean Dawnay, Eric Portman and Tyrone Power; but it was later extended a little to include the American Ambassador, the Duke and Duchess of Buccleuch, the Mills, Sybil Thorndike, Lewis Casson and the legendary Hollywood columnist Louella Parsons, who had come to England specially to cover the star and her husband's arrival. Rattigan did not neglect to invite Michael Franklin, even though Vera, his mother, would be there too. The Midget could be expected to hide in the crowd.

Chinese lanterns filled the garden of Little Court and threw a gentle glow on the white cloth of the tables as the first guests began to arrive shortly after nine. Margaret Leighton did not get there until after 10.30, but Marilyn Monroe did not make her appearance until close on eleven, although she stayed until nearly three. She and Rattigan danced the Charleston – 'even though Terry was a terrible dancer'. The last guests filtered away, past the special police cordon which Rattigan had arranged, just as dawn broke over the golf course. It was a million miles away from the world of Look Back in Anger.

The filming of The Sleeping Prince went a good deal less smoothly than the party. Olivier's passion for Monroe was quickly doused by her legendary ability never to appear on time. 'A very short way into the filming, my humiliation had reached depths I would not have dreamed possible,' he confessed later. But the more he fumed, the later she arrived. When she did turn up, Monroe managed to enrage Olivier still further by bringing with her Lee Strasberg's wife, Paula, as her 'personal adviser'. In desperation Olivier tried to bully her, but that too failed abysmally. When he lost his temper and swore at her, she simply replied, 'Oh, do you know that word in English too?' By the time she and Miller flew home, Olivier could barely bring himself to speak to her.

In New York, where Rattigan decamped in late August, the stage version of The Sleeping Prince was not faring much better. Redgrave's fussing was driving him to distraction. First he was going to appear, then he had to direct, then he did not think he could do both, then he was not certain about Barbara Bel Geddes, then she was all right, then Ina Claire, whom he had wanted as the Grand Duchess, began to worry him. The complications seemed to grow and grow. In May Rattigan had cabled Freedman, 'Am still doubtful his humour, however, perhaps for States more serious approach might be preferable'. During the first rehearsals in New York, Redgrave proposed alterations to the script, for the sole purpose, he claimed, of underlining the fact that the Regent was not a monster, and did like the Grand Duchess. Reluctantly Rattigan agreed, though he put his foot down at the proposed line: 'She says she always has had a protective feeling for me, like an elder sister.' 'This is, perhaps, flogging the point a bit too far,' he suggested through clenched teeth.

Surprisingly, the Grand Duchess was also causing problems with the American film censor. While he and Olivier had been working on the screenplay, the Breen Office (then responsible for censorship in the American cinema) had told Rattigan that his story violated two of the basic clauses of the American film production code. First, 'Seduction can never be a subject for comedy'; second, 'Pictures shall not infer that low forms of sex relationship are the accepted or the common thing.' Rattigan could hardly believe it. In deference to these feared bureaucrats – almost worse than the Lord Chamberlain – he had already transformed the Grand Duchess from the Regent's wife into his mother-in-law. Now he was being asked to make further amendments for even more ludicrous reasons. 'If the Breen Office really feels that the reform of a libertine by a romantically minded little chorus girl does not make a fit subject for comedy,' he wrote to Olivier, 'perhaps we could change the whole thing into a tragedy about an idealistic prince seduced from a high view of love to a "low form of sexual relationship" by an unromantic leading lady.'

In the end the Breen Office relented, but censorship troubles were not the only ones to dog the film. Warner Brothers, who were to distribute it, also wanted a change of title. Their first choice was *The Prince and the Showgirl*, but – as Olivier told Rattigan – 'other suggestions include "A Night in Love" and "The Purple Pillow". Horrified, Rattigan countered by proposing 'The Royal Pleasure, or Kings Pleasure', adding fiercely, 'believe anyway madness give up so much free publicity on present title'. But the studio had prevailed. *The Prince and the Showgirl* it was.

Hollywood's instincts may well have been right. Only weeks before the play's scheduled opening on Broadway on 1 November, the world watched in horror as Russian tanks crushed an anti-communist revolution in Hungary, and now fears were growing at the Egyptian threat to nationalise the Suez Canal. In the circumstances, Rattigan's lines for the Regent, 'I will not have my country made the pawn of British imperialism and French greed'; and his dismissive reference to 'probably some Hungarian violinist' were unlikely to be hailed as timely.

Redgrave realised the danger and asked to cut them. 'But Terry, convinced that art outlives contemporary events was insistent they be spoken,' Redgrave wrote later. 'Not for the first time, contemporary events proved themselves the stronger.' Had there not been the struggles with Olivier and the Breen Office, and had Redgrave himself not been quite so pernickety about so many other things, Rattigan might have seen the point, and accepted that the lines were ill-judged at that particular moment, but he did not – just as he did not see that the British theatre's own revolution had begun on 8 May 1956 at the Royal Court.

Rattigan was far more concerned with the details of the Broadway opening of *Separate Tables*, which was now scheduled for 25 October at the Music Box theatre. After a series of heated disagreements, he had finally agreed with Stephen Mitchell that the West End run should end in late July, because the London cast had been accepted for Broadway. More importantly, after long discussions with Peter Glenville, Rattigan was determined to introduce one crucial change. He wanted to make it abundantly clear that the reason that Mrs Railton-Bell and the other residents of the Beauregard Hotel in Bournemouth did not view Major Pollock with a 'good regard' was that he had been arrested as a homosexual, and he was convinced that American audiences would accept and sympathise with him.

On 29 August he wrote to Bob Whitehead, his American producer, to explain what had originally been in his mind when he had written the part, saying that he believed that 'an English audience knew my problem and accepted the fact that I had to skirt around it. They got the full impact of the play . . . An American audience, on the other hand, not conditioned to censorship and to the evasiveness to which British dramatists are now forced, may well take the Major's stated offence not as a symbol at all, but as a literal fact.' Rattigan, in his desire to be accepted as a dramatist prepared to tackle sensitive issues, intended to see to it that they were not allowed to remain under any illusions.

If the Major's peccadilloes are not more than what the Lord Chamberlain had forced me to pretend they are then everybody's reactions in the play are exaggerated . . . I had in fact appealed over the head of the Lord Chamberlain to the sensibilities and particular awareness of an English audience. I was in fact saying to them, 'Look, Ladies and Gentlemen, the Lord Chamberlain has forced

me into an evasion, but you and I will foil him. Everybody in
the play is going to behave as if there were no evasion at all
and as if the more important and serious theme were still the
issue.'

Rattigan told Whitehead that if he cared to examine the text of *Table
Number Seven* he would see that the characters behaved as if homosexuality were indeed the issue.

Mrs Railton-Bell's firm determination that he must leave the hotel
. . . 'The dreadful, the really ghastly revelation has still to come
. . . The Major has pleaded guilty to a criminal offence of a disgusting nature.' Lady Matheson's horror . . .' Oh dear, I don't
know how I shall ever look at him in the face again.' Sibyl's
hysterics . . . 'It makes me sick. It makes me sick . . . He's done
a horrible beastly thing.' Mr Fowler's comment . . . 'I once had
to recommend a boy for expulsion.' Charles's defence . . . 'The
Major presumably understands my form of lovemaking. I should
therefore understand his . . . To me what he has done, if he has
done it, seems ugly and repulsive. I have always had an intense
dislike of the more furtive forms of sexual expression.' Jean's
hostility . . . 'I think that people who behave like that are a public
menace and deserve anything they get'; and finally Miss Cooper's
remark . . . 'The word normal applied to any human being is
utterly meaningless.'

Rattigan's letter catalogued the lines. He saw them all as comments
'that such characters would normally make about a man pleading guilty
to a homosexual offence'.

This was frankness indeed and left far behind Rattigan's cautious
concealment of Hester/Hector and the debate about *The Deep Blue Sea*.
Of course the Major's sexual nature was only one issue among a
number of others laid out in the course of the short piece. None the
less this letter must rank as one of the most revealing statements Rattigan ever made about his work, and it is hard to know exactly what
prompted it, except that it lay at the heart of his hopes for the play.
He wanted nothing more than to be respected as a playwright capable
of dealing with complex human emotions, and not simply condemned
as being no more than a polished theatrical 'craftsman'.

'What is much more important,' he told Whitehead,

is that the essential feeling of each scene that follows the revelation
is enhanced and made much more by the Major being self-
confessedly an altogether different being from the others, and his

behaviour quite outside their normal experience. It is in fact their final acceptance that, though a *different* being from the others and in fact an 'outsider', he is still a *human* being that makes the last scene moving without being sentimental.

Rattigan told Whitehead that he did not want to alter a single word of the Major's part, though he did want to change some of the jokes about 'nudging' women that he had included in the original. In particular he believed the change of his offence to a homosexual one made the Major's long revelatory speech about being scared of women much more poignant, and that it also helped to explain his reluctance to stay with a friend in London, '. . . you see, it's rather a question of birds of a feather'. The only substantial change would be in the details of the Major's offence, which Lady Matheson reads out from the *West Hampshire Weekly News*: that the Major had 'pleaded guilty to a charge of persistently importuning male persons' by asking four different men for a light on the Esplanade between eleven o'clock and one o'clock at night.

Rattigan did not want to offend – or unduly shock – his American audience, and to guard against this he had asked the advice of several of his friends before actually proposing the change to Whitehead. Alec Guinness had said he thought the change was right, as had Olivier, Vivien Leigh and Billy Chappell, and, of course, Peter Glenville. Rattigan and Glenville had already raised the idea with Margaret Leighton, who was 'wildly enthusiastic', but had not yet had the courage to put it to Eric Portman.

'I think it is shocking enough to put any audience on its mettle and to force them to realise that the play is a serious challenge to their own prejudices,' Rattigan's letter to Whitehead continued. 'It makes it plain that we are dealing with a serious (and not uncommon) issue and that the play is not just a rather mild little comedy about an eccentric bogus Major and the hysterical behaviour of the people with whom he shares the hotel.' He also made it clear that he had been pondering the change for many weeks. 'I did not want you to think this was one of those sudden ideas that one gets excited about one vinous night and then forgets with the morning hangover . . . I am firmly and definitely convinced.' Terence Rattigan was so convinced that he proposed that a press release should be quietly issued in New York, explaining that 'Certain details in the play in its English performance . . . had to be re-written.'

Whitehead's reaction was the reverse of what Rattigan had hoped for. Whitehead was horrified. 'I think it is a mistake, and I urge you to reconsider very very carefully,' he wrote back on 5 September. 'In being so specific about his "offence" I feel the play becomes smaller, it becomes "a play about homosexuality", which it isn't.' He believed it would dilute the play's message fundamentally.

> The play has seemed to me to say that in spite of certain spreaders of hate and violence (i.e. Mrs Railton-Bell) there is some impulse in most of us that can and must contribute to the cause of man's humanity to man rather than man's inhumanity to man. I am afraid that with the change the thesis will seem to be on accepting the homosexual and helping him find his place in society etc. This should only be embodied in the larger meaning of the play.

Whitehead also argued that New York had seen so many plays about homosexuality that it had 'almost become a cliché on the Broadway stage'. More significantly, he warned that the change would undoubtedly lead to a great deal of 'distasteful' publicity, about homosexuality in the English theatre and John Gielgud's case in particular. 'It will serve to further "label" the play and detract from its essential size and meaning.' This, he argued, was doubly unnecessary because he knew that a number of 'New York's important critics' had already accepted 'the play's symbolism'.

Crossing the Atlantic on board the *Queen Mary* with his mother for company, Rattigan debated what to do. But by the time he had reached New York, he had still not made up his mind. Anxious that the 'true' version of *Table Number Seven* be played, he had Mary Herring type out his revised dialogue for Phyllis Neilson-Terry and Jane Eccles, who were again playing Mrs Railton-Bell and Lady Matheson, to use during rehearsals in New York. Peter Glenville was in favour of their doing so, but Bob Whitehead was certainly not. Whitehead was determined the Major's offence should be the same as it had been in London – and that *Table Number Seven* should not become a 'homosexual play'. And Whitehead had a powerful ally. Eric Portman did not wish to portray Major Pollock as a homosexual.

Portman had not been anxious to appear on Broadway in the first place – he had not acted there since 1938 – and he certainly did not wish to portray himself in this particular guise. Like Rattigan, he believed that homosexuality was a private matter between consenting friends, not a subject for public debate, and like Rattigan, he had always conducted that side of his life with great discretion. Portman had no desire to suffer the fate of Gielgud – which was still, of course, a risk. Against this, the benefits which might or might not accrue to the play from intensifying the outraged feelings of Mrs Railton-Bell were of little consequence.

In the face of Whitehead's arguments, and his star's intense personal feelings, Rattigan retreated. *Table Number Seven* was played in the United States in its original form, and his new dialogue for Mrs Railton-Bell and Lady Matheson has never been performed in public. It is a great loss, for it was no circumlocution, no 'appeal over the head of the Lord Chamberlain', 'no masterpiece of understatement' from a 'craftsman with a fine touch for light comedy'. In its new form, *Table Number Seven* was blunt, entirely to the point, and clearly heartfelt.

MRS RAILTON-BELL: No, no. Ex-officer bound over.

LADY MATHESON: (*Brightly*) Oh yes. (*Reading*) Ex-officer bound over. One a.m. arrest on Esplanade . . . (*Looking up*) On Esplanade? Oh dear, do we really want to hear this?

MRS RAILTON-BELL: (*Grimly*) Yes, we do. Go on.

LADY MATHESON: (*Reading resignedly*) On Thursday last, before the Bournemouth magistrates, David Angus Pollock, 55, giving his address – (*She starts violently*) – as the Beauregard Hotel, Morgan Crescent. (*In a feverish whisper*) Major Pollock? Oh!

MRS RAILTON-BELL: Go on.

LADY MATHESON: (*Reading*) Morgan Crescent – pleaded guilty to a charge of persistently importuning – (*Her voice sinks to a horrified murmur*) – male persons – (*She stops, unable to go on. At length*) Oh no. Oh no. He must have been drinking.

MRS RAILTON-BELL: He's a teetotaller.

LADY MATHESON: Perhaps just that one night.

MRS RAILTON-BELL: No. Read on.

LADY MATHESON: A Mr William Osborne, 38, of 4, Studland Row, giving evidence, said that at about eleven fifteen p.m. on July the eighteenth Pollock had approached him on the Esplanade, and had asked him for a light. He had obliged and Pollock thereupon offered him a cigarette, which he accepted. A few words were exchanged, following which Pollock made a certain suggestion. He (Mr Osborne) walked away and issued a complaint to the first policeman he saw. Under cross-examination by L.P.Crowther, the defendant's counsel, Mr Osborne admitted that he had twice previously given evidence in Bournemouth in similar cases, but refused to admit that he had acted as 'a stooge' for the police. Counsel then observed that it was indeed a remarkable coincidence. Inspector Franklin, giving evidence, said that following Mr Osborne's complaint a watch was kept on Pollock for roughly an hour. During this time he was seen to approach no less than four persons, on each occasion with an unlighted cigarette in his mouth. There was quite a heavy drizzle that night and the Inspector noted that on at least two

occasions the cigarette would not light, and Pollock had had to throw
it away. None of them, he admitted, had seemed particularly disturbed
or shocked by what was said to them by the defendant, but of course
this was not unusual in cases of this kind. At one a.m. Pollock was
arrested and, after being charged and cautioned, stated, 'You have made
a terrible mistake. You have the wrong man. I was only walking home
and wanted a light for my cigarette, I am a Colonel in the Scots Guards.'
Later he made a statement. A petrol lighter, in perfect working order,
was found in his pocket. Mr Crowther, in his plea for the defendant,
stated that his client had had a momentary aberration. He was extremely
sorry and ashamed of himself and would undertake never to behave in
so stupid and improper a manner in future. He asked that his client's
blameless record should be taken into account. He had enlisted in the
army in 1925 and in 1939 was granted a commission as a second lieutenant in the Royal Army Service Corps. During the war he had held a
responsible position in charge of an . . .

Rattigan's instructions then simply read: 'Continue as existing.' This
was the only change he proposed to make. Had he made it there, there
is a strong case for saying that it could have transformed his reputation
as a dramatist overnight. The fact that he did not reveals Rattigan's
eternal uncertainty about himself, his intense desire to be loved, and
his fear of giving offence. Had his mother also not decided to take her
first trip to New York for twenty years to see his two premières on
Broadway, he might well have been more persistent. As it was, he
refused to take the risk. Rattigan turned his back on a unique opportunity.

Whatever might have been had his changes been pushed through,
the New York critics were still impressed by the version they saw.
Brooks Atkinson in the *New York Times* called *Separate Tables* the finest
thing Rattigan had written. He went on:

> Although Mr Rattigan has written some popular fictions in the
> past that seemed almost too cleverly contrived, *Table Number
> Seven* is a masterpiece in miniature. The writing is reticent, but
> the pity and insight are admirably expressed. Certainly this is the
> most penetrating enquiry into the human spirit that Mr Rattigan
> has yet written, and it considerably alters his reputation as a theatre
> writer.

At the end of the week *Variety* welcomed it as 'the smash that traditionally marks the real start to the new Broadway season' and added that
'the author is writing about pitiful people shorn of their pretence and

without psychological defences. Implicitly but inescapably, the plays are a plea for tolerance and compassion.'

Separate Tables was to remain on Broadway for almost a year before spending a further six months on an American tour, becoming his biggest American hit since the Lunts and *O Mistress Mine*. A film version was inevitable. Harold Freedman had already sold the film rights to the producer Ben Hecht and his new partner, the film actor Burt Lancaster, for a minimum of $175,000, rising to a maximum of $350,000 on certain conditions, and Rattigan was about to be paid a further $50,000 for the script, which had to be delivered by 1 June 1957, plus another $15,000 in 'expenses'. After his experiences with the Breen Office over the script for *The Sleeping Prince*, he knew only too well that a forthright description of Major Pollock's 'true' offence would certainly not have been accepted. Given the money at stake he was not even inclined to suggest it.

The reception of Michael Redgrave's version of *The Sleeping Prince* at the Coronet a few days later was a sorry – and crushing – contrast. Brooks Atkinson called it 'the indulgence he [Rattigan] is entitled to ask for having done a good deed' in bringing *Separate Tables* to Broadway. 'This little prance back through the years is quite a long ride. Neither the views nor the conversation along the route is enlightening.' *Variety* simply said, 'It's a bit early for Christmas decorations. Too early, at any rate, for such a frail wisp of tinsel.' Redgrave later called the first night 'a disaster', adding, 'I am inclined to shoulder at least half the blame. When one is half the management, the director and the leading man, one can but say "Le débâcle, c'est moi."'

Rattigan generously disagreed. His own explanation for the play's failure was a belated recognition of the changed political climate. 'The fairy tale on the stage now ricochets connotations,' he wrote in a note to himself. 'World events have taken a grim and menacing turn.' Four days after the play opened the American President, General Dwight D. Eisenhower, ordered the British and French forces attempting to occupy the Suez Canal to withdraw. Carpathia was hardly in keeping with these changed times. The world had no appetite for occasional fairy tales. *The Sleeping Prince* closed before Christmas.

Rattigan had been to Princeton for the opening of *Separate Tables*, then to Boston to work on *The Sleeping Prince*, back to Princeton for the opening of *The Sleeping Prince*, back to Boston for *Separate Tables*, and on to Philadelphia for *The Sleeping Prince*. Exhausted by the shuttling about, he sailed back to Europe with his mother. He confessed, 'I'm haunted by a terrible fear of re-writing a scene for *Tables* and sending it to the director of *Prince* with instructions that it must

be inserted in the second act.' It was not entirely a joke; the scene he
had in mind – Lady Matheson's statement of the Major's true offence
– was in his luggage.

Just as he was leaving, the *New York Post* published a lengthy appreciation of his work which came closer to getting to the heart of his talent
than many British critics were to do in the years to come. 'Because the
best of his works have such surface brilliance,' wrote its author, Richard
Watts,

> and such shining virtuosity, we are tempted to hail them a bit
> patronisingly as expert stage equivalents of deft slick paper maga-
> zine fiction and neglect their solid core of dramatic worth . . . The
> fact is, I think, that beneath the sparkling surface of showmanship,
> theatrical facility and deft technical skill, there lies dramatic writ-
> ing of notable insight, sympathy, emotional truth and keenly
> observing intelligence.

For some considerable time afterwards Rattigan kept the clipping in
his wallet: a talisman against the sense of disquiet that was beginning
to creep through him. As a young man Somerset Maugham had warned
him that a playwright could only expect to remain popular for twenty
years. His twenty years had just run out. And even though he had
spent more than three months in the United States, he could no longer
blind himself to the success of *Look Back in Anger*, which had now
transferred to the West End. He even conceded to one American writer
that the play was 'odd and powerful' – a very different comment from
his first flip dismissal.

Perhaps he was not angry enough? The idea was tempting, but Rattigan dismissed it. On the way back across the Atlantic, he wrote an
introduction to the work of Noël Coward, in which he defended himself and his apparent lack of passion:

> The more turbulent emotions are not always conducive to the
> best work. Despite the recent prevalence of 'angry' plays by
> 'angry' young men, I have always held the, perhaps, prejudiced
> view that it is really the gentler emotions – pity, nostalgia, com-
> passion, love, regret – that are likely to inspire the most worth-
> while and durable drama. Anger rarely breeds understanding, and
> without understanding a play becomes too subjective to make
> good drama.

What Rattigan could not accept was that both forms of drama could
exist together. Anger, he concluded, was 'exciting, perhaps, at its
immediate impact; but forgotten soon afterwards'. Those were his feel-

ings as he finished the piece and the ship passed Gibraltar on its way to Cannes, where he and his mother were to stay at the Martinez for Christmas. It was to prove an impetuous and rather muddle-headed misjudgement.

CHAPTER 21

Theme and Variations

◆

Why are you so suddenly interested in me, any-
way? You've never cared much before about what
I was doing or what I was trying to do or the
difference between them.

Shelagh Delaney, *A Taste of Honey*

◆

On the surface, 1956 looked as if it was the peak of Terence Rattigan's career. *Separate Tables* had run successfully in both London and New York. *The Prince and the Showgirl*, the film version of *The Sleeping Prince*, had been completed, with one of the most dazzling female stars in the world playing the lead, while the play itself ran throughout Europe and enjoyed a conspicuous success in Australia. Rattigan had received by far the best notices of his career on Broadway, and was much in demand to write screenplays in Hollywood. He had earned more than £100,000 from the sale of the film rights to his plays, as well as a further £50,000 from film scripts and the plays themselves: all within the year.

In the decade since the end of the war Rattigan had established himself as unquestionably the pre-eminent English dramatist, setting the tone for serious theatre in London with *The Winslow Boy*, followed by *The Browning Version*, *The Deep Blue Sea* and *Separate Tables*. There had been the failures of *Adventure Story* and *Who Is Sylvia?* of course, but the commercial success of *The Sleeping Prince* had made up for them. His plays were the touchstone by which millions of theatregoers around the world judged English drama. The verse dramas of Christopher Fry, which had threatened to revolutionise the English theatre, had failed to do so. Among living English dramatists in those first months of 1956, the name of Terence Rattigan was pre-eminent.

Nor was his reputation restricted to the theatre. In the cinema he had been acclaimed for his scripts for *The Way to the Stars* and *Brighton Rock*; he had been nominated for an Oscar for his screenplay for *The Sound Barrier*, and he had seen his first television play, *The Final Test*, turned into a successful feature film. His own screenplays for *The Winslow Boy* and *The Browning Version* had attracted huge audiences around the world, while Hollywood's Cinemascope and East-mancolour version of *The Deep Blue Sea*, much as he disliked it, had been a notable commercial and critical success, once more compensating for the odd failure such as *The Man Who Loved Redheads*.

And now, at forty-five, Rattigan was financially better off than ever before. By bullying him relentlessly, and never allowing him to write a cheque for more than £10, Bill Forsyth had prevented him from spending everything he earned. Forsyth had carefully protected the large payments from the film sales into trust for his mother. The flat at 29 Eaton Square was on a long and advantageous lease, and Little Court at Sunningdale was bought and paid for. Forsyth had even encouraged Rattigan to pay off the remaining mortgage to his bankers, Coutts & Co. It seemed, at last, as though even the financial fears of the past were behind him.

Yet this was the very moment at which everything was to change. As he was to remark ruefully near the end of his life, 'There I was in 1956, a reasonably successful playwright . . . and suddenly the whole Royal Court thing exploded, and Coward and Priestley and I were all dismissed, sacked by the critics.' As the drama historian Christopher Innes eloquently explains in *Modern British Drama*, his review of the century of British drama between 1890 and 1990, Rattigan was 'relegated to critical oblivion at the height of his career'.

The shock of his sudden fall from grace was to transform the rest of his life. Terence Rattigan did not change, the theatre around him changed. He was swept aside in a tidal wave of 'new drama', more modern-seeming than his subtle, discreet examinations of human emotion. The softer cadences of his plays were lost amid the clamour of a new generation of playwrights. The noise of their anger drowned him.

The speed of Rattigan's consignment to oblivion was to destroy his spirit and hasten his death. His fragile self-confidence, protected as it always had been by his generosity and wit, was too frail to withstand the sudden withdrawal of public approval. Like an orchid deprived of tropical rain, he withered and crumpled without applause, wilting in front of his admiring public's eyes. It was a brutal fate, made all the more tragic by the fact that neither he nor his friends could fathom the reason for it.

And yet there was at least one explanation. The young writers living in bed-sitting-rooms and small flats, working on their first plays, naturally resented the gilded upper-middle-class figure Rattigan presented to the world. They condemned him as much for his lifestyle as for his plays, for he epitomised all that they most disapproved of about the old-fashioned, elaborate dignity of Shaftesbury Avenue and the smooth, plush image of H.M. Tennent in particular. To them Rattigan came to represent all that had gone wrong with the British theatre, and their view was echoed by the new wave of English critics, led by Kenneth Tynan. It was Tynan, more than anyone, who had first trumpeted the power of *Look Back in Anger*, and Tynan who put Rattigan to the sword. What neither the new critics nor the new young playwrights noticed, however, was just how close was Terence Rattigan's work to that of the man who had apparently rendered him extinct.

A careful study of *Table by the Window*, the first of the two *Separate Tables*, shows exactly how close it is in structure and approach to *Look Back in Anger*. As Christopher Innes says, 'It is worth noting here how ironic it was that *Look Back in Anger* should have relegated Rattigan to critical darkness, since its dramatic situation is almost identical to the first half of *Separate Tables*.' His double bill had been running for twenty months when John Osborne's play opened at the Royal Court.

Both the Rattigan and the Osborne play deal with a 'triangular relationship in which a cool and self-possessed woman fails to replace the upper-class wife of a socialist from a proletarian background'. Miss Cooper, the manageress of the Beauregard Hotel, does not succeed in keeping John Malcolm after his wife, Mrs Shankland, reappears. Equally Helena does not manage to hang on to Jimmy Porter after his wife, Alison, finally returns in the third act. 'Each marriage has erupted in violence, which leads to separation, but the battered wives' emotional need drives them both back into their husbands' arms.'

Jimmy Porter was a graduate without a job, rather than a former cabinet minister reduced to journalism, the victim of society in general rather than his own violent temper in particular and guilty of mental rather than physical cruelty, but his similarity to John Malcolm is striking. As Innes observes,

> The wives in each play are not only beautiful, accused of sexual frigidity and characterised as 'predictable' (Rattigan) or 'pusillanimous' (Osborne). It is also the revelation of weakness beneath their apparent dominance, their abasement that finally wins back

the husbands . . . The description of 'a genuine, live, roaring savage from the slums of Hull' is equally appropriate to both males, who share much the same passionate verbal monologues and political commitment. What is different is primarily Rattigan's objectivity.

Objectivity was not what the new dramatists, or the new critics, craved. They were seeking new heroes to replace the old, and were prepared to sacrifice anyone in their determination to get them. At the English Stage Company at the Royal Court, for example, George Devine, Rattigan's Oxford contemporary, was determined to leave his own distinctive mark on the postwar English theatre, and he brought to the task the same single-minded ambition he had shown as President of the OUDS more than twenty years before. It was a determination that failed to treat people who came into contact with it gently, a determination that would brook no opposition, nor any suggestion that it might be overstating or oversimplifying its case. Devine was perfectly prepared to make his reputation at anyone's expense, and particularly Rattigan's. Perhaps it was envy, perhaps opportunism, perhaps both, but there is no doubt that Devine had not cared for Rattigan's ways twenty years before, and he did not care for them now.

'Like many a lifetime radical of his generation,' John Osborne wrote thirty-five years later, 'George was unaware of his own bigotry and sentimentality, which he saw as a harsh endorsement of plain honesty.' But there was another reason for Devine's dislike of Rattigan, which Osborne also identified. Devine believed 'that the blight of buggery, which then dominated the theatre in all its frivolity, could be kept down decently by a direct appeal to seriousness and good intentions from his own crack corps of heterosexual writers, directors and actors'. It was a distrust and dislike of homosexuality that Devine shared with Tynan.

'It is no very serious criticism of the English Stage Company,' Harold Hobson wrote in 1978, 'to say that it missed some of the most promising talent of its time. A greater objection is that it often appeared to be completely lacking in a spirit of generosity, and to be animated by motives of personal hatred and jealousy. Whilst it ostensibly demanded higher standards of social justice, it made no attempt to respect these standards in its attitude to those who opposed it.' One person whose standards it specifically did not respect was Terence Rattigan.

His themes of loneliness and sexual repression, of the need for disguise and the deceptiveness of appearances, had been evident in his work for the past decade; but because he had always wanted to avoid a confrontation with Aunt Edna sitting in the stalls he had deliberately and subtly underplayed these themes. If Aunt Edna noticed them, well and good, if she did not, at once, then no matter, for she could still enjoy the play. The depth of meaning could emerge with time, because, as Innes puts it, 'Beneath the apparent lack of intellectual challenge there is a subtle probing of the spectators' responses.'

Rattigan had never believed in shouting to get his audience's, or anyone else's, attention. He had always preferred to invite his audience's interest obliquely by the creation of character, rather than by polemic or ideology. The roots of that lay in his own sexuality. Rattigan, like his characters, relied on disguise. Without disguise life posed too great a threat. But the new breed of playwrights believed that the purpose of drama was to 'give lessons in feeling', as John Osborne himself put it, to proclaim their beliefs. Terence Rattigan could not, and would not, see drama in that way.

This altered climate was to have an additional damaging effect on Rattigan's work. For it was not only the strictures of the Lord Chamberlain's office, or the demands of Binkie Beaumont and Aunt Edna, that had led Rattigan to keep his twin themes of sexual obsession and repression implicit rather than explicit in his plays. It was also the precise reflection of his own character. To be free of the necessity of disguise – by the creation of a theatre in which everything could and must be spoken openly – was to threaten the sublimation at the very heart of his imagination. To take off the mask that he had so carefully constructed for himself – as the insouciant, affluent author of successful light comedies 'and one or two other plays', as he sometimes liked to joke – would be to risk too much. Without the mask, the whole edifice of his life and career would come tumbling down. The tragedy was that by not revealing it he found himself dismissed as irrelevant.

As Innes puts it: 'Removing the necessity for disguise made Rattigan's drama less – not more – effective when he turned to explicit treatments of homosexual characters or relationships' – as he was to do in the seven years after 1956. If Rattigan had had the courage to *insist* that the Major's crime be presented in its homosexual form in New York in 1956, it is entirely possible that he would have been welcomed as a member of the vanguard of the new dramatists emerging in England – the elder statesman who had at last found the courage to break out, and expose the truth. He would not have found himself in that position by design or inclination, but nevertheless it could well have transformed the way in which he and his work were judged.

In the first months of 1957, however, Rattigan was less concerned with being judged than with delivering the screenplay of *Separate Tables* to his new producers, the dancer turned producer Harold Hecht and his partner, Burt Lancaster. In January he flew to Hollywood for a series of story conferences. It was to be his first extended experience of California and he did not enjoy it. He was used to retiring to Little Court to work, not emerging until he was satisfied with his draft. Now he was engaged in endless discussions and conferences with an endless stream of executives, all of whom seemed to have different notions of 'what he was trying to say' – bearing little or no relation to the reality.

While working on the script he stayed with Rex Harrison in his house in Beverly Hills, and this presented a crisis of its own. The actress Kay Kendall, whom Harrison was about to marry, had just been diagnosed as suffering from terminal leukaemia, and Harrison had decided that the awful reality of her illness must be kept from her. To see the once vivacious star of *Genevieve* in this condition and his old friend under such strain – for their disagreements over *Who Is Sylvia?* were a thing of the past for both of them – was a harrowing trial for Rattigan, and hardly a conducive atmosphere for work.

During the six weeks he stayed with Harrison, Rattigan managed to write barely a third of the *Separate Tables* screenplay. Finally the 'general hysteria', as he described it, got him down. And he did not wish to intrude on Harrison any longer. In spite of the sun and the swimming-pools, in spite of the fact that Harold Freedman had assured him that there were 'four more projects just waiting for him', with fees atttached to them of more than £200,000, he could stand it no more. He slipped quietly out of Hollywood, took the train for New York, and boarded the *Queen Mary* for England. He would complete the script at Little Court.

The screenplay was scheduled for delivery at the end of May, and he had been asked to merge the two stories. Rattigan accordingly produced screen treatments of the two plays and then a draft screenplay of each, before merging them into one. The reason for the merged screenplay was that Hecht and Lancaster had decided that the same actor and actress would no longer play both John Malcolm and the Major, Anne Shankland and Sibyl Railton-Bell. The roles would be separate.

By the summer, Rattigan was ill. The family and professional strains of the past five years had finally caught up with him. He delivered the screenplay on time, but in June he wrote to Harold Hecht in California to apologise for not staying on in Hollywood. 'The truth is that my health in the last three months has gone a bit to pieces and I don't know why. I'm not blaming Hollywood for that, but I just don't feel strong enough at this moment to go through the hurly burly of story conferences etc.' To recuperate he took off for the Martinez in Cannes, with Michael Franklin for company. They were both lovers and friends. For once, the Midget did not throw too many tantrums – threatening to throw himself off the balcony of their adjoining suites only once – and in the intervals between gambling and sitting in the sun they even managed to finish a novel together. It was a comic concoction, thought up by Franklin, called *Vice Versa and Versa Vice*, with the authors' names given as 'Michael Rattigan and Terence Franklin'. Rattigan had it bound in leather. Many years later Franklin was to confess, 'It still makes me chuckle – in the way Terry could get smiles, and tears, from re-reading his own writings.'

Back home, and refreshed, Rattigan returned to his screenplay about T.E.Lawrence. It seemed that the Rank Organization might be prepared to finance the film, once another draft of the script had been completed. Rattigan worked on this until the autumn, when Hecht again demanded his services. He was to be paid $1,000 a day for ten days to do a 'polish' on his *Separate Tables* screenplay, which was now being cast. What Rattigan did not know at that moment was that another screenwriter, John Gay, was also working on the screenplay in California.

United Artists had decided to start shooting the picture before the end of the year, and they wanted to be certain the script worked. They had managed to land the acclaimed television director Delbert Mann, who, two years before, had won an Oscar as director for his first feature, *Marty*. The studio believed *Separate Tables* might have a chance of its own Oscars, and wanted to leave nothing to chance. By the time Rattigan had finished his polish and Gay had reworked his earlier version of the screenplay in California, the studio were ready to go. Burt Lancaster, who had bought the rights originally, was to play John Malcolm opposite Rita Hayworth as Anne Shankland, while Deborah Kerr was to play Sibyl Railton-Bell and David Niven Major Pollock.

Although Rattigan had slightly amended the nature of the Major's admission of his crime, he had made no attempt to transform him into a homosexual. He had even been persuaded to accept the fact that the audience might want to believe exactly what he had always been determined that they should never believe – that the Major and Sibyl might 'somehow end up together'. To endear himself to Hollywood, and to ensure the film's commercial success, he was once more prepared to compromise his convictions about his own characters.

At the point where Major Pollock first tries to explain his actions in the cinema to Sibyl Railton-Bell, Rattigan's new dialogue read: 'I'm made in a certain way, and I can't deny it. It has to be the dark, you see, and strangers – because . . .' And again, a little later, he has Pollock say to Sibyl, 'Just that we're both frightened of other people, and yet we've both somehow managed to forget our fear when we've been in each other's company. Speaking for myself I'm grateful, and always will be. Of course, I can't expect you to feel the same way now . . .' Nor were these the only changes. In reply to Sibyl's question: 'Why have you told so many awful lies?' Pollock now answers: 'I don't like myself as I am, I suppose. So I've had to invent another person. It's not so harmful really. We've all got daydreams. Mine have just gone a step further than most people's. That's all. Quite often I've even managed to believe in the Major myself.' The effect was to soften and blur the Major's character still further.

By the time shooting started, shortly before Christmas, neither the producers nor the studio bothered much to keep Rattigan in touch. He had returned to England, and did not even know that anyone else had worked on the screenplay until he discovered the truth by accident. Then Rattigan learned that there was a plan to deny him credit for the screenplay. This provoked an angry and defensive reaction from the ever-devoted Mary Herring to Harold Freedman on his behalf: 'Whatever John Gay did on the script he was working from Rattigan's script, the whole of which was Terry's work . . . It was Terry's work that integrated the two plays into one script – no one else's.' Freedman stepped in and Rattigan's credit was restored, albeit alongside John Gay's. In fact, neither he nor Mary Herring need have worried. The script clearly worked. Rattigan relaxed shortly after Christmas, when he received a cheery thirteen-page letter from David Niven.

My dear Terry, I don't know if anyone has taken the trouble to give you news of the progress on 'Separate Tables'. If they have – just tear this up, if not – then you may be relieved to hear that, in my humble opinion at any rate, your beautiful plays have been placed side by side with the minimum of distortion and the maximum of loving care. I don't suppose more than two dozen actual lines have been written for this piece so all your wonderful dialogue is virtually intact . . .

Just one new scene, Niven added, 'accounts for 90% of all the new dialogue'. Placed at the opening, Niven told Rattigan, it introduces both Major Pollock and Sibyl to the audience, and 'gives both characters a chance to present themselves and their relationship to each other; also it sets up Mrs RB as the heavy!'

'As to the Major!' Niven went on.

Obviously I have never had a better part in my life and I shall do
everything humanly possible to live up to it . . . I am approaching
him from pretty much the same angle as Eric does . . . The only
difference perhaps (and because of the added scene I have a chance
to), I am letting him revel in his majorhood a bit more so that the
pricked balloon effect at the end will be a bit easier for me to attain.
The reason for this is that on the stage the actor has the audience with
him from the start in the second play because there he is transformed
before their eyes from the first one – in the movie I have in effect
got to come on cold and get that character established in the first
minute or two when for the last twenty-five years they have seen
me giving one performance in a variety of hats!

Six thousand miles away in London, Niven's enthusiam came as a
great relief. 'It all sounds very exciting,' Rattigan cabled back cautiously
on 7 January 1958, 'and I wish I could be with you. One thing I am
sure of is that you are going to be wonderful and I hope the film is
too.' His hope was to be fulfilled. At the Academy Awards ceremony
fifteen months later, *Separate Tables* won Niven his first and only Oscar
as Best Actor, and Wendy Hiller another as Best Supporting Actress
for her portrayal of Miss Cooper. In addition it collected five other
nominations, including a second one for its author for the screenplay
he had nearly not been credited with. By coincidence, while the filming
was taking place, Eric Portman arrived in Los Angeles in the touring
version of the American stage production, in which Geraldine Page
had replaced Margaret Leighton. Niven went to watch Portman's performance after shooting.

The experience of Hollywood and the hassles of *Separate Tables* had
confirmed Rattigan's belief that, though films might provide the lux-
uries of life, his true interest remained – as it had always been – the
theatre. He had been working on an idea based on the recent trial of
the English mass murderer John Christie, whose crimes had been
blamed on a mentally deficient young man, Timothy Evans, who had
shared Christie's house in Notting Hill, London. Evans had been
hanged for the crimes before Christie himself was charged with them.
Rattigan had spent some time at the trial, and had become so fascinated
by the character of Christie that he had worked on a sketch for a play,
tentatively entitled *Man and Boy*, which he had then put aside.

In its place, he had decided to write about something closer to home.
Rex Harrison's tragic relationship with Kay Kendall was not the only
one he had watched closely during 1957. He had also seen Margaret
Leighton, whom he had come to adore since *Separate Tables*, fall help-

lessly in love with Laurence Harvey, the young man with whom he had once signed a contract on a cigarette packet. They had married on a ship moored off Gibraltar in August. Both relationships supplied Rattigan with material, although for the moment it was the tempestuous affair between Leighton and Harvey that was to provide his main inspiration. As he was to explain to the London *Evening Standard* the following year:

> In *The Deep Blue Sea* I showed two people who were quite unsuited to each other. But I didn't really go too deeply into that part of it. I just said they had fallen in love and the audience had to accept it as a fact. In this play I am trying to show why people fall in love. I try to analyse love in terms of emotional needs, not sexual needs. My heroine is a woman whom nobody has ever needed, except in bed, and that is her problem, and tragedy.

But there was another, unspoken inspiration – Michael Franklin. For although Rattigan's projected play was ostensibly the portrait of the affair between an older woman and a younger man, it was also a portrait of the relationship between an older, more successful man and his younger male lover. As he worked on the new play, alone in Little Court during the first weeks of 1958, Rattigan found it harder and harder to complete. Somehow the play was almost too intimate, too intense a self-portrait, this time in the shape of his new heroine, Rose Fish. The whole process was so painful that for a time he even considered calling the play *Heart and Soul*.

Rattigan's notes made his intentions clear. His careful, handwritten memorandum to himself read, 'The bitterness of having achieved an ambition and having nowhere to go', and continued: 'First theme: *Expel nature* with a pitchfork – yet she will always return. *Waste of Ambition*. The life she has achieved was never worth achieving, and can never be again.' Here Rattigan was describing not only his feelings about Margaret Leighton, but also his disillusion with himself. His last note read, 'Second theme: Certain women get bored with being loved, and want to do the loving. It's not him that she needs – it's his need for her.' Rattigan's own need for the Midget was little different. He was prepared to admit that to himself. But, on the surface, the main concern of his new play was one of which Aunt Edna would approve – the love affair of Margaret Leighton and Laurence Harvey, transformed into Rose Fish and Ron Vale in an updated version of *La Dame aux Camélias*. In an early draft he even called his heroine Camilla Brown. Rattigan temporarily called the play *Rose by Another Name*.

'Two self-sufficient people meet and find they need each other,'

Rattigan noted. 'He needs her materially, at first, later maternally – possibly sexually. She needs him first cold-bloodedly for fun. Then more warmly for a pet, finally because of his need for her.' To Rattigan's watchful eye, Laurence Harvey's need for Margaret Leighton – and her considerable wealth – was comparable to Michael Franklin's need for him. 'She started it as a game,' he wrote to himself, 'letting herself be used – because she found it such a funny revenge to be treated the way she'd treated so many others. Then found herself getting stuck – and now suddenly jealous. Give him up. No. Why not? I don't know. I just can't. Maybe it's time she did the loving.' The parallel with Franklin was clear.

Much later Rattigan sought to explain his particular variations on Dumas's two themes in *La Dame aux Camélias*, which had first been dramatised in 1852. Of the first theme, in which the courtesan falls victim to a passion, he explained, 'the variation on it is to bring the story into the present day and to treat it not romantically but realistically, as modern theatre taste would – rightly in my view – seem to require'. At the same time, he had also decided to change Armand Duvall, who

> though full of high sounding phrases about the depth and purity of his love . . . seems to have had no compunction whatever in wittingly living off his beloved's immoral earnings, and is only outraged when he discovers that the earnings are not only for past but also for contemporary favours . . . In short, whatever his words, his actions are those of a gigolo and in my play I have made the transcription from Armand Duvall to Ron Vale – a self-confessed adventurer – with due and careful intent.

The second theme, even more important to Rattigan – was the theme of need – 'the need of one human being for another, or, more particularly, in the case of Rose Fish, my heroine, the need of one human being for another's need of her'. The first act curtain line, when Rose tells her companion, Hettie, 'I'm needed by Ron,' drives home the point, if any emphasis is still needed.

In the dancer Ron Vale Rattigan created a montage of the men with whom he had shared his own life. There were elements of Kenneth Morgan, of Chips Channon, and of Adrian Brown, a young dancer he had met in Paris while working with Litvak and whom he had helped to launch on a director's career. Above all, however, there was Michael Franklin. No matter how much Ron embarrassed Rose, or Michael Franklin embarrassed Rattigan, the love and need of one for the other could not be ignored. Rattigan put his feelings into the mouth of the play's homosexual ballet master, Sam Duveen:

SAM: (*Slowly*) . . . I see you're rather new to this business of being needed by Ron. You don't seem to understand that the Rons of this world always end by hating the people they need. They can't help it. It's compulsive. Of course it probably isn't plain hate. It's love-hate, or hate-love, or some other Freudian jargon – but it's still a pretty good imitation of the real thing . . .

Rattigan portrayed Michael Franklin's own resentment at being excluded from Little Court, and from Eaton Square, when anyone important was there. Franklin had even been banned by Rattigan himself from setting foot on Sunningdale golf course. On the one occasion Franklin did so, the man who had been his lover for seven years tried to pass him off to the club secretary as his golfing partner's 'nephew'.

RON: I wonder. Have you ever thought what it's been like for me, asked over here a couple of odd evenings a week whenever there're no important people around – because common Ron mustn't meet important people – oh dear no – that'd never do – and then when I'm shoved around, needled, sent up – everyone talking about people I don't know, and things I don't understand . . .

He even included the rows he and Franklin had had at the Martinez in Cannes.

RON: . . . I don't understand it. I hardly ever see you, when you call me in the mornings we don't say much to each other, just gossip, your friends treat me like dirt and so do you, only more polite, and yet I can't damn well do without you. I need you in my life. For some bloody silly reason which I can't explain, I need you in my life.

Franklin himself was well aware of his part in the finished work. His first-night telegram to its author read, 'From Michael, without whom this play would never have been written.'

Another unseen influence was, as so often before, Major Frank Rattigan, who appeared in the play's first draft in the guise of Ron's father, Alf Vale. Rattigan later removed the father from his draft, putting his emotions instead into the mouth of Sam Duveen. This allowed him to stick more closely to Dumas's orginal story and to enlarge on the relationship between Duveen and the young dancer – who has not succumbed to his homosexual advances. Rattigan's handwritten notes to himself include a quotation from Horace, in Latin, which he translated: 'If you drive out nature with a pitchfork, she will soon find a way back.' It was his own view of the behaviour of both his father and himself.

'As I get older it gets harder and harder for me to write,' Rattigan told a reporter from the London *Evening Standard* shortly after he had finished the play. 'It is an absolutely shattering experience. I get very annoyed that people should think I can toss off a play with a laugh between rounds of golf.' To recuperate from the effort, Rattigan left London for St Moritz shortly after Christmas to join Rex Harrison and Kay Kendall. As he left he dispatched the new play to Beaumont, and to John Gielgud, who he hoped might be prepared to direct it. He had finally decided to call it *Variation on a Theme*.

By the time he returned in February both men had agreed. Beaumont had accepted the play and Gielgud had said he wanted to direct it as a major Tennent production at the Globe, with a major provincial tour before a London opening in early May. It was the first time in a friendship stretching back more than thirty years that Gielgud's name was to appear alongside Rattigan's on a playbill, and more than a decade since John's famous snub: 'I've got to be so careful about new plays.' Rattigan was thrilled. He could hardly contain his excitement. Not only was this a Gielgud production, it was also the first new Terence Rattigan play for more than three and a half years.

In early March 1958 the manuscript was sent to the Lord Chamberlain, whose reader brought forward few objections, despite the character of Duveen. He called it, on the contrary, 'Rattigan's best play, which is high praise indeed.' The Wolfenden report on homosexuality had recently been published, and times were changing as even the Lord Chamberlain was becoming aware. Rattigan agreed to omit the line 'F.U.Jack' and to change the name of one of the characters from Lady Huntley to Lady Hunterscombe, and the casting process began.

On the surface, that should not have presented a difficulty. The part of Rose had been written specifically for Margaret Leighton, who had already agreed to play it: even Rose's background in Birmingham reflected her own upbringing there; and Rattigan had dedicated the play to her. But there was still the question of who should play her young lover, the ballet dancer Valov, the pseudonym of Ron Vale, also from Birmingham. When, in January, Rattigan had sent the first draft to Margaret Leighton in New York, he had made the tentative suggestion that Laurence Harvey might play the part himself, but, after reading it, Harvey refused point blank. Finally, after a great deal of scrambling about, a young actor called Tim Seeley was chosen, and rehearsals started. The opening was to take place at the Opera House in Manchester on 31 March.

The tour began well enough. The audiences in Manchester were enthusiastic, as they were also to be in Glasgow, Brighton, Streatham and Golders Green. But gradually Gielgud and then Rattigan himself began to doubt that Tim Seeley could produce the Ron Vale they both felt the play demanded. Seeley looked so young and handsome that the audiences seemed convinced that it was a play simply about an older woman's passion for a younger man, and did not grasp the mutual passion that came to engulf them both. One provincial critic even described it as merely a play about Margaret Leighton's 'cradle snatching'. The review sent a shudder of horror through the author and the director. Something had to be done. With only two weeks to go before the play was due to replace Graham Greene's *The Potting Shed* at the Globe, Rattigan agreed with John Gielgud that Ron Vale must be recast. In place of Seeley they chose a young actor called Jeremy Brett, whom Rattigan thought looked 'much more like Laurence Harvey'.

On the evening of Thursday, 8 May 1958, Rattigan ushered his mother into the same box she had sat in fifteen years before, for the first night of *While the Sun Shines*. Vera Rattigan sat in the same chair, clutching the same champagne cork that had accompanied her to her son's last thirteen first nights, and, once again, Rattigan could not bring himself to watch the performance, and retired to the circle bar. Everything seemed set fair. Beaumont had persuaded Norman Hartnell to design Margaret Leighton's dresses, in an effort to upstage Cecil Beaton's designs for the musical *My Fair Lady*, which had just opened at Drury Lane. Leighton herself had not been seen in the West End since *Separate Tables*, and Gielgud was expressing the greatest confidence in the play.

But as Rattigan returned to the back of his mother's box on that May evening, he finally realised the changes that had been taking place in the London theatre. The audiences which had cheered every curtain of *The Winslow Boy*, applauded at each interval in *The Deep Blue Sea* and roared with delight at *The Sleeping Prince* had disappeared – to be replaced by a more sceptical set of spectators whose tastes were for *Waiting for Godot* and *Look Back in Anger* and would soon be applauding Arnold Wesker's *Roots* and Harold Pinter's *The Birthday Party*. This tale of a rich woman who had succeeded in nothing more than separating her four previous husbands from their money, and had now gone off with a young ballet dancer distinguished only by his self-pity, failed to capture their imagination.

Ron Vale might have been romantic, but to the audience of 1958, with the sounds of the angry young men – and Elvis Presley – in their ears, the theme was too old and tired to seem worthy of any variation.

The new audience did not want another Camille, they did not hanker
after the glamour of Garbo, nor did they cast themselves as tragic
heroines or temperamental young lovers. The age had become too
brutally realistic for that. While even Aunt Edna may not have wanted
her heroine to be quite so unsympathetic. Rattigan had satisfied neither
his new nor his old audience. After the first night he threw a party at
Eaton Square for Rex Harrison and Kay Kendall, Margaret Leighton
and Laurence Harvey. But as his friend Freddie Young left the party
Rattigan told him, 'I know they hated the play.'

The critics certainly did. The following day almost every morning
and evening newspaper bitterly condemned *Variation on a Theme*. 'I'm
afraid I couldn't swallow it' . . . 'Not for a moment was I put on the
rack of tragedy' . . . 'This shoddy, novelettish romance' were typical
of the comments. Even Rattigan's staunchest defender, W.A.Darling-
ton in the *Daily Telegraph*, could not find a good word for the play,
concluding: 'Mr Rattigan is out of form.' It was, inevitably, left to
Kenneth Tynan to deliver the *coup de grâce* in the *Observer* the following
Sunday. He did not disappoint. 'As far as I could see the star of the show
was Norman Hartnell,' he declared. 'Even the Birmingham accents are
phony . . . I didn't spot much real acting going on, but then there
wasn't much reality there to begin with.'

Only John Mortimer, the young barrister about to turn playwright,
found a kind word to say. He called Ron Vale 'Terence Rattigan's
angry young man', and could not help liking Margaret Leighton once
'she got out of her dresses and into shirt and trousers'. Alan Brien in
the *Spectator* was equally sharp and came closer to the point. Alone
among the critics, Brien sensed Rattigan's true objective. 'The subject,'
he said, 'should be a homosexual relationship between a bored and
ageing rentier and a sharp, oily male tart.' 'It would have been so easy
for me to make it an Aunt Edna play,' wailed Rattigan a few days
later, 'to have given the woman a heart of gold. But I purposely took
the most Aunt Edna play of all time, *La Dame aux Camélias*, and showed
up the characters for what they really are.' The attempt did Rattigan
no good whatever. By the early summer of 1958 his theme and variations were as remote as a Pinero problem play, a dinosaur from
another era.

Only a few weeks later, this was underlined conclusively at the
Theatre Royal Stratford, in East London, where the mercurial director
Joan Littlewood had created a company to perform the works of new
playwrights. Littlewood often created the plays she worked on from
an idea during improvisation with her group of actors. And, not long
after *Variation on a Theme* opened at the Globe, she received a brief

manuscript written by a young Lancashire woman who had taken a fortnight's holiday from her job as a photographer's assistant in Manchester to write her first play.

The young Shelagh Delaney had seen Rattigan's play during its provincial tour, and had been so incensed by what she'd seen – and so angered by what she saw as its 'ridiculous attitude to homosexuality' – that she had decided she could do better herself. In a fury, she had typed out her own play on the kitchen table of her Salford council house. She called it *A Taste of Honey* and sent it to Joan Littlewood. Within four weeks of receiving it, Littlewood had mounted the play as part of her Theatre Workshop. And she made no attempt to soft-pedal the fact that it had been inspired by the failings of *Variation on a Theme*.

A Taste of Honey opened just three weeks after Rattigan's play and attracted enormous publicity. Two styles of theatre were at war across London. And there was little doubt which would win. *Variation on a Theme* closed at the Globe within four months of its opening, while *A Taste of Honey* was to transfer into the West End the following February, presented at Wyndham's by none other than Bronson Albery's son Donald.

Cuthbert Worsley tried to draw the sting from the attacks on Rattigan by a defence of him in the *New Statesman*. *Variation on a Theme*, he said, was

> Rattigan's best play so far . . . passionate, raw and truthful . . .
> No play of his has been written with such economy and weight; a single line of deceptive simplicity will carry three meanings . . .
> In no play has he compromised less. It is this, I suggest, which has dismayed his critics. Recently in these columns my colleague David Sylvester bracketed him with John Piper as an artist fatally contaminated with too great a wish to please. The charge can no longer stick. How easy it would have been for a writer of his temperament to produce a modern version of *La Dame* which did please and how his detractors would then have enjoyed their sentimental evening with the additional luxury of being able to sneer! Deprived of their enjoyment in the obvious sense, they have merely sneered.

The defence fell on deaf ears. The age of Rattigan had come to its end, even if the playwright himself did not want to accept it.

CHAPTER 22

The Bubble Bursts

◆

*In two years and twenty-eight productions the
Royal Court has changed all that. To an extent
unknown since the Ibsen riots, it has made drama
a matter of public controversy. It has buttonholed
us with new voices, some of them bawdy, many of
them irreverent, and all of them calculated to bring
gooseflesh to the evening of Aunt Edna's life.*

Kenneth Tynan, *Curtains, 1958*

◆

The pain of the bad reviews was almost physical. Rattigan seemed to
shrivel under the onslaught; shrinking back into his private world,
insulating himself against the possibility of any repeat. To escape, he
took off for the south of France, and the Martinez in Cannes, once
again in the company of Michael Franklin. The news that he had been
awarded the CBE in the Queen's Birthday Honours in early June
reached him there, but it did little to make up for the disappointment.

'I take my notices seriously,' he had admitted in the preface to the
first volume of his *Collected Plays*. 'I don't admit for a moment that I
have ever been guided by them in my subsequent work, or influenced
by them in my own judgement of it. I just take them seriously.' So
seriously, in fact, that this latest batch were to depress him for the
entire summer. But the reception for *Variation on a Theme* was not the
only source of his disappointment.

Just as the play was opening in Manchester, Puffin Asquith and Tolly de Grunwald were beginning the final preparations for the filming of his script about Lawrence of Arabia. The Rank Organization had agreed to provide the £700,000 budget, on condition that an hour was cut from the three-hour script which Rattigan had submitted, and had also accepted Asquith's suggestion that the part of Lawrence should be offered to Dirk Bogarde, unquestionably one of Britain's few international film stars, and much in demand – he had recently turned down the part of Jimmy Porter in the film version of Osborne's *Look Back in Anger*. Rattigan cut the script, while Bogarde and Asquith had begun to dissect the character of Lawrence for his performance. Asquith and de Grunwald then set out for Arabia to scout for locations, and discuss with King Feisal the possible use of his army.

'So lost was I in preparation and absorption that I took little, if any, notice of what was going on around me,' Bogarde wrote twenty years later. 'All I could think of was the strange blonde wig which was slowly, and carefully, taking shape in Make Up, and the probable starting date in the desert of April 7th.' That starting date was destined never to be met. On 14 March 1958 Rank pulled out, giving neither Bogarde nor Asquith any clear reason for their decision, although all or part of it lay in the fact that another film about Lawrence was in the pipeline, produced by the powerful American Sam Spiegel, to be directed by David Lean from a script by Robert Bolt. Rank did not want to offend Spiegel, whose film *Bridge on the River Kwai* had won six Oscars the previous year. Bogarde called the decision 'my bitterest disappointment'. But he and Asquith took refuge in making Shaw's *Doctor's Dilemma* for MGM in the United States. No such consolation was on hand to cheer the screenwriter.

Enraged by the prospect of what he called 'three years' work, albeit intermittent' being completely thrown away, Rattigan sat down, on his return to England in September, to adapt his screenplay for the stage. The original frontispiece of his screenplay had borne a quotation from Winston Churchill on Lawrence: 'I deem him one of the greatest human beings alive in our time. I do not see his likeness elsewhere.' Rattigan's interest lay in Lawrence's character, in the mixture of guilt and vanity occasioned in part by his sexuality which he understood only too well – just as he understood his need for solitude. For Rattigan's gregariousness was always partly façade. The man who had to retire from 'all social life', as he put it, once he began to work on a play clearly glimpsed more than a little of himself in the figure of Colonel T.E.Lawrence.

As he had done when writing about Alexander the Great, Rattigan took considerable pains to discover everything he could about his hero's

character, and even his manner of speech and phrasing, basing his notes
on Lawrence's letters. He decided early on to call his play *Ross*, after
Lawrence's first pseudonym in the RAF, to draw attention to the concealment, and, as with Alexander, he intended to illuminate the difference between the greatness of a man's deeds and the man's greatness
as a person. Ever since Harrow he had been fascinated by the nature
of 'heroic' acts. Now was the chance to study them. As in *Adventure
Story*, he was to begin his quest for the character of his hero with a
single question, 'Oh Ross – how did I become you?'

Rattigan was in no doubt that Lawrence's masochism, revealed to
him once and for all when he was sexually humiliated by his Turkish
captors in Deraa, was the key to his character. He wrote in his notes:

> Lawrence – whose original motive in going to the desert and
> escaping from 'muddy intellect' was to *find* himself, is *shown* him-
> self by the General, and the shock is enough to make him a mental
> suicide and destroy his will and purpose . . . *Therefore*, he goes
> to Allenby and gives up . . . He must refer, however obliquely,
> to the traumatic experiences he has just been through as the main
> reason for his giving up. The others – shooting prisoners etc –
> are subsidiary – but have to be mentioned . . . When he goes back
> he is a changed man – soulless, unfeeling, without anything but
> disgust in the whole undertaking . . . 'I should have left myself
> undiscovered – and grown into middle age a dull, frustrated, over-
> thinking archaeologist who never, in all his life, would have done
> anyone any harm. Not even himself.'

This perception of its subject dictated the structure of the play, which
opened at the same point that his screenplay had done, with Aircraftsman Ross attending a dinner party at Cliveden and then returning
to barracks. In his notes he reminded himself that the play's first act
should deal with the history, leaving the second to 'concentrate
on Lawrence himself, and the predicament of his masochism, dor-
mant homosexuality, his self-discovery (brought on by his own
ambition . . .) and consequent degradation and despair'. Rattigan concluded, 'The "human will", as a false idol with feet of clay, should
possibly be emphasised a bit more.' It was this portrait that he struggled
to bring to life in the last months of 1958. He completed the first version
of the play on the morning of 13 February 1959 and immediately sent
the typed manuscript to Binkie Beaumont.

By coincidence the British première of the film version of *Separate
Tables* took place that evening, and Rattigan had to endure the sour
verdicts of the London critics, who were markedly less enthusiastic

than the Americans. While *Variety*, the *Hollywood Reporter* and *Time* magazine had heaped praise on the film, Nancy Spain in the *Daily Express* called it 'an agonising bore', C.A.Lejeune in the *Observer* said that it reminded her of 'a jigsaw puzzle, one of the more expensive sort'; and the *Manchester Guardian* insisted that 'two Mr Portmans were worth more than one Mr Niven and one Mr Lancaster'. Only Paul Dehn in the *News Chronicle*, Rattigan's friend and future collaborator, gave the film an unqualified rave. But the reviews cut little ice. The film quickly became the biggest box-office hit in Britain, growing even more popular once David Niven's Oscar was announced six weeks later. Rattigan, deopressed by the British critics, though still firmly in their thrall, set off on a trip round the world, first to Australia and then back by way of Hollywood to New York.

In California he was once again asked to write a string of scripts – including the film version of Vladimir Nabokov's novel *Lolita*, which Stanley Kubrick was to direct. But he turned them all down, intent on returning to England and the theatre. There was, in addition, one delight in store. In New York, before sailing home on the *Queen Mary* with Margaret Leighton, he watched John Gielgud finally play the part he had written for him more than a decade earlier – Andrew Crocker-Harris in a television version of *The Browning Version* directed by John Frankenheimer.

When Rattigan reached home in May, he immediately set to work on the revisions to the script of *Ross*. Beaumont had decided to stage it that autumn. Alec Guinness had agreed, after giving the matter much thought, to appear in the title role. Glen Byam Shaw, who had not worked with Rattigan since *The Winslow Boy*, was to direct. There remained, however, one or two obstacles to overcome. Rattigan's 'portrait' of Lawrence was broadly based on *The Seven Pillars of Wisdom* and on Basil Liddell Hart's biography, *T.E.Lawrence: In Arabia and After*, but his theory that Lawrence's will had been broken by a homosexual assault was not confirmed by either book. To place such emphasis on it was his own theory entirely.

Knowing that his portrait of Lawrence might cause offence to some, Rattigan had been at pains to consult the Lord Chamberlain's office, and in particular Brigadier Sir Norman Gwatkin, whom he had been dealing with in the Lord Chamberlain's department for almost twenty years, before the play was formally submitted. Gwatkin was encouraging, but reminded Rattigan that Lord Scarborough, the current Lord Chamberlain, was sensitive about plays 'depicting actual people'. When Gwatkin handed out the play for a reader's report in late May, the reader in question rightly noted that the Rattigan thesis was 'that Lawrence suffered sexual assault by Turkish soldiers when he was captured and that that indignity broke his spirit and caused his subsequent odd behaviour'. In the past, he concluded, 'we have had plays about celebrities passed by the Lord Chamberlain and remote relations have popped up and made trouble. I suggest, therefore, that if the Lord Chamberlain does issue a licence for this play, it is on the understanding that the management makes every effort to find any near relatives of Lawrence who are still alive, and get their consent.'

That presented Beaumont and Rattigan with a major difficulty. The Rank Organization had been offered a share of the profits from the theatrical production to waive their interest in the screenplay, but it was now a confirmed fact that the film producer Sam Spiegel had purchased the rights to *The Seven Pillars of Wisdom* from Lawrence's closest surviving relative, his brother, the archaeologist Professor A.W.Lawrence. And obviously Spiegel would be determined to ensure that his film would be the only dramatic portrait on offer until after it had been launched. He could do this by persuading Professor Lawrence to withhold his consent to a stage version.

Reluctantly, towards the end of June 1959, and under pressure from the Lord Chamberlain, Rattigan sent the manuscript of his play to Professor Lawrence, via his publishers Jonathan Cape. In a letter to Cape on 24 June, he explained the history of the project, and how he had started by writing a screenplay. 'First because of my fervent sympathy with the subject, and second because I felt – perhaps arrogantly, but none the less honestly – that of all present writers in the dialogue form I was the one best fitted to do justice to the memory of T.E.L.' The screenplay had taken eighteen months, he explained. 'I never felt those months had been wasted. It had given me the opportunity of exploring again the mind and character of a man I admired above most others, and of attempting to communicate my feelings about him to a very wide audience.'

But he made clear that the play was 'a dramatic portrait' and 'by no means simply the screenplay reshaped to another medium'.

I began work on the play for the simple and straightforward reason that after three or four years I still found my writer's mind obsessed with the character of T.E.L. and, in looking for a subject for a new play, found myself unable to conceive of anything I wanted to write about more. I realised the subject would have to be – for a much smaller and better informed audience – entirely re-studied and entirely revisualised. The screenplay, in fact, was little help to me. In some ways it was a hindrance. But my motive remained exactly the same in both screenplay and play . . . to do full justice to the character and memory of a very great man . . . I thought you might need reassurance that, whatever my shortcoming as a 'dramatic biographer', my heart, at least, is in the right place.

His 'favourite character in all dramatic literature – Antony – lives and breathes for us far more movingly and truly by grace of his dramatist than his biographer', Rattigan went on. 'I am sure you understand my general point. It is the portrait I believe to be true, and in Alec Guinness I think we have the actor who can best give it life.

Professor Lawrence did not accept that Rattigan's heart was in the right place. He was appalled by the play. 'The "portrait" of T.E.Lawrence conveyed by the play to my mind is that of a weakling with a compensatory blood-thirst and other uncontrolled neurotic impulses,' he wrote. 'If that impression had been due to his reading of the source material I might think he had a right to form the opinion, mistaken though I should consider it. In fact, however, he builds up his "portrait" by a series of passages which contradict source material.' Not only did Professor Lawrence not approve of the play, but neither – he insisted – would his mother and elder brother, 'who know of the play from me'. Without their consent, the Lord Chamberlain would not grant a licence. The West End production looked doomed.

Uncertain what to do, Rattigan consulted Glen Byam Shaw, who suggested that they should mount a campaign to support the play's 'portrait' of Lawrence. In the first instance, he suggested getting the opinions of other people who knew Lawrence well, and whose views on his life might be accepted as just as authoritative as those of his brother. Shaw wanted to send a copy to Siegfried Sassoon, and suggested that Rattigan or Beaumont should send a copy to Robert Graves; both had known Lawrence well.

Sassoon replied promptly. 'My impression,' he wrote in September, 'is that the play – with Alec G. – would be very effective . . . The portrait of T.E. is, as you say, fully sympathetic and understanding. For me, it is always painful to read about what T.E. suffered in his interior life, but I welcome anything which defends him against the attacks which have been directed at his integrity. (He was a modern Hamlet.)'

Graves was less supportive. He had already heard about the play from Alec Guinness, who had gone to visit him in St Thomas's Hospital in London, where he was being given blood transfusions as a result of

'an unexplained tendency to haemorrhage'. In response to a letter from
Beaumont's office at Tennents, he replied, 'Broadly I think the play's
all right, but there are certain changes which I'd advise him [Professor
Lawrence] to ask Rattigan to make as out of character. One can't libel
the dead but on the other hand one can be prevented from misrep-
resenting the dead by the copyright laws . . .' In particular Graves felt
Rattigan had made Lawrence 'behave at times like the comic knut from
The Ghost Train' and that, though Lawrence was 'a humorist about
popular fame' he was not 'vain and never admitted it'. He did not tell
him that he was also being consulted by Sam Spiegel about the film
version David Lean was planning.

When he saw the letter to Beaumont, Rattigan wrote to Graves
himself. 'I am genuinely anxious to make such changes and emen-
dations as I can which, without destroying the play's theatrical life,
will bring it nearer to the historical truth.' Graves wrote back, telling
him that Professor Lawrence had come to visit him in St Thomas's
and Graves had 'put him wise'. But he had his reservations
about Rattigan's play. 'Now about dramatic portraits,' he wrote
on 16 October:

> This seems a form of literary expressionism in which the author
> presents himself in terms of the sitter, and is particularly common
> in dramatic representations of Jesus the Galilean. But Jesus is any-
> one's guess, and Lawrence isn't. And though the play is damned
> good theatre, there seems no reason to flout history and cause
> distress to a great many people who knew T.E. and could not
> even begin to understand that you were burnishing the name of
> a man you admired – for the sake of good theatre.

Now it seemed both Graves and Professor Lawrence were ranged
against the play.

Nevertheless, Beaumont was still keen to go ahead. He and Rattigan
first decided to purchase the rights to the Liddell Hart biography as
their 'official source', and recruited the help of Peter Carter-Ruck, a
London solicitor recommended to them by Bill Forsyth. Liddell Hart
was offered 1 per cent of the gross weekly receipts. Then, in late
October, Beaumont produced a long memorandum of events for the
Lord Chamberlain, which argued forcefully that Professor Lawrence's
consent was 'now being unreasonably withheld'. Beaumont pointed
out that the play could be produced abroad or on television without
the benefit of the Professor's consent; that in spite of repeated offers
from Rattigan to amend the play the Professor was not prepared even
to discuss the possibility; that the Professor had already agreed to Sam

Spiegel's film; and finally that no member of the Lawrence family was mentioned in the play at all, 'and there is no hint of the illegitimacy question raised by Aldington and others. In fact T.E.'s domestic background is left completely obscure. This was done entirely to avoid giving offence, even at the risk of appearing to critics and the public as a shortcoming in a play labelled "a portrait."

Beaumont suggested that they had done all they reasonably could to satisfy Professor Lawrence, and that they would now like to go ahead with the production; although the programme would include a note stating, 'This play is based on the life of a famous historical figure, but no claims are made that either the events depicted or the characters portrayed are necessarily factual.' It was another version of the note Tennents had used for *The Winslow Boy* fifteen years before. Sir Norman Gwatkin, in the Lord Chamberlain's office, agreed with Beaumont, and prepared an internal note for Lord Scarborough saying so. 'Far more publicity and public discussion will be invited if the play carries the notoriety of being banned and clearly the ban cannot be upheld for many more years.' A few days later the Lord Chamberlain agreed, and Gwatkin confirmed the decision to Beaumont: 'The Lord Chamberlain has come to the conclusion that it would not be in the best interests of the relatives for him to refuse a licence. At the same time, he is sure that Mr Rattigan would endeavour to meet objections to any particular passage which Professor Lawrence put forward.' A delighted Beaumont wrote back confirming that Tennents would be happy to agree to the other small changes the Lord Chamberlain had requested – principally that 'Arab' habits should instead be called 'Eastern', and that the word 'sod' should be omitted. The production could now go ahead. Rattigan put up £2,250 of the £10,000 it required himself.

In the weeks over Christmas 1959, he made what were meant to be the final changes to his script. And on 22 February 1960 rehearsals began in London for *Ross: A Dramatic Portrait* by Terence Rattigan. The frontispiece read, 'The action of the play begins and ends at a Royal Air Force Depot near London, in the afternoon, the same night and following morning of a day in Winter, 1922. The central passages cover the two years 1916–18 and are set in the Middle East.' The play was dedicated to Anatole de Grunwald, 'who brought Lawrence to me and me to Lawrence'.

But Rattigan was still not satisfied with the play. Throughout the rehearsals he amended it further in an effort to focus more closely on the two principal themes that had interested him from the start: the difference between the 'greatness' of deeds and the 'greatness' of a person; and the question of what constitutes 'heroic'. As ever, he took the greatest pains over his curtain lines. For the ending of Act One, for example, Rattigan continued to refine his original draft until – in much the same way as in *Adventure Story* more than a decade earlier – he had its protagonist addressing the audience:

> LAWRENCE: . . . War is war, after all. The enemy has to be killed and our own men have to die. And surely, at least I've been more sparing of them than any red-tabbed superman?
>
> *Pause.*
>
> (*Angrily*) What is wrong in trying to write my name in history? Lawrence of Akaba – perhaps – who knows?
>
> *Pause.*
>
> Oh Ross – how did I become you?

Then, in the key scenes in Act Two, in which Lawrence's fate is forged by his treatment at the hands of his captors, he made a series of further small amendments to the Turkish General's speeches at the end of Scene 2 and Scene 4, to make their message completely clear. In the climax of Scene 2, the prelude to Lawrence's downfall, for example, Rattigan's final version read:

> GENERAL: . . . The Arab's readiness for statehood is a lie and he knows it. That should give his interrogator a considerable advantage. To get him to admit that it's a lie? Difficult. With a man of faith, a real fanatic – like Feisal – impossible. But with an intellectual Englishman who believes only in his own will – and his own destiny – well, such faiths might be shaken. And another faith too – even more vulnerable – what I hear he calls his bodily integrity. One would probably have to start by teaching him a few of the facts of life.
>
> CAPTAIN: Surely if he's an intellectual he must know the facts of life.
>
> *The General laughs.*
>
> Have I said something stupid?
>
> GENERAL: Don't let it concern you. (*He finishes his glass.*) Yes, it's a strange relationship I have with Lawrence. He doesn't even know of my existence, while I probably already know more about him than he knows about himself. I wish all relationships were so pleasant and uncomplicated.
>
> *He looks at the Captain and turns away.*
>
> There's one thing I don't know about him. I wonder if he really believes that all the sacrifice is worth it.
>
> *The General has poured himself another glass of wine.*
>
> CAPTAIN: Sacrifice? Sacrifice of what?

GENERAL: (*Taking a sip of his wine and ruffling the Captain's hair*) Oh, of everything that makes life worth living.

At the end of Scene 4, Rattigan uses the homosexual attack on Lawrence by the Turkish guards as the fulcrum of the play, and again gives the Turkish General the vital curtain lines.

GENERAL: . . . I do pity you, you know. You won't believe it, but it's true. I realise what must have been revealed to you tonight, and I know what that will have done to you. You can think I mean just a broken will, if you like. That might have destroyed you by itself. But I mean more than that. Far more. (*Angrily*) But why did you leave yourself so vulnerable? What's the use of learning if it doesn't teach you to know yourself as you really are?
    Pause.
It's a pity your desert adventure couldn't have ended cleanly, in front of a firing squad. But that's for lesser enemies – not for you.
    He kneels down.
For you killing wasn't enough.
    He lifts Lawrence's head again.
You had to be – destroyed.
    He lowers Lawrence's head, and stands up.
The door at the bottom of the stairs through there is unlocked. It leads to the street.

As he had done in so many of his plays, Rattigan was examining his own weaknesses, and in particular the pain that being a homosexual had brought him. The shame that part of him felt, and which had expressed itself from time to time in his earlier plays, surfaced again in *Ross*. While accepting his own vanity, and his wilfulness, he nevertheless saw what those weaknesses had cost him. Rattigan expressed his regret, and the pain that recognition entailed in a scene with Aircraftsman Dickinson, who reveals the true identity of Aircraftsman Ross to the newspapers. Their final dialogue was amended slightly, but this earlier version clearly reveals his intention.

DICKINSON: How did you lose your soul?
LAWRENCE: The way most people lose it, I suppose. By worshipping a false god.
DICKINSON: What god?
LAWRENCE: The will . . .
DICKINSON: (*Hotly*) Self-pity – that's all it is. There's nothing in the world worse than self-pity.
LAWRENCE: Oh yes there is. Self-knowledge. Why shouldn't a man pity

himself if to him he is pitiable? But to know yourself – to see yourself, betrayed by your own god. (*Laughing gently*) Those silly Greeks! How wrong they were. Yes. To know yourself . . . that's the worst thing that can happen to any man . . . to any man . . . alive.

'You're lucky you're not a homosexual,' Rattigan once said to his golfing partner Stephen Mitchell. He repeated the remark often, regularly telling Harold French, another golfing friend as well as his director, 'Be grateful you're not a homosexual.' Rattigan's Lawrence was not a self-portrait, how could it be, but it did present part of its author's and its subject's shared fears; the disguised quality of both their lives, the disgust at their own needs, the suspicion of their own will. It was one reason why Rattigan could not get Lawrence out of his mind.

Rattigan's notes to himself also reveal how much trouble he took to discover all he could about Lawrence's 'coldness', a quality which he recognised in himself, and which some of his friends acknowledge as his 'chilly side'. Frith Banbury calls it 'his ruthlessness – when you didn't deliver what he thought you should'. Above all else, his notes on *The Seven Pillars of Wisdom* show his fascination with Lawrence's self-disgust. 'I long for people to look down upon me and despise me,' Rattigan notes Lawrence saying. 'I'm too shy to take the filthy steps which would publicly shame me and put me into their contempt. I want to dirty myself outwardly, so that my person may properly reflect the dirt which it conceals.'

By the beginning of April rehearsals at the YMCA off Tottenham Court Road were all but completed. There was to be a one-week try-out in Liverpool, beginning on 29 April, and the London opening was scheduled for 12 May 1960 at the Haymarket Theatre. Beaumont would normally have put the play into the Globe, the headquarters of the Tennent empire, but Ralph Richardson and Paul Scofield were happily ensconced there in Graham Greene's *The Complaisant Lover*. There was also another Rattigan enterprise for which he would have to find a theatre – a musical version of *French Without Tears*, which Rattigan had been persuaded to write the previous autumn by Beaumont himself, Billy Chappell and Paul Dehn. Yet again, there would be two Rattigan openings in London within a few weeks of each other.

Had Professor Lawrence not objected to *Ross*, the two Rattigan projects might never have become confused. But by the time the arguments were over, and the Lawrence arguments resolved, Alec Guinness had become temporarily unavailable for *Ross*, so the production had to be delayed. It was during this interval in the winter of 1959 that Rattigan got down to adapting *French Without Tears* as a musical. It had originally been Billy Chappell's idea, and he was to direct. Paul Dehn was to write the lyrics and Robert Stoltz, who had done the music for the pre-war hit *White Horse Inn*, was to write the score. The projected spectacular was to be called *Joie de Vivre* and Beaumont was convinced it would 'make a marvellous musical' – and provide competition for the hugely successful *My Fair Lady* at Drury Lane, of which he was distinctly jealous.

For the show's star, Beaumont and Rattigan had decided on Donald Sinden, who had been under contract to the Rank Organization for the previous eight years, making a string of successful British films including *The Cruel Sea*, and had just returned to the stage. Rattigan had rung Sinden and asked him if he could sing. 'No,' Sinden told him, which was absolutely true. But, as Sinden recalled twenty-five years later, 'Terry assumed I was being flippant rather than honest,' and offered him any of the leading male parts. 'Choose whichever part you like and it will be built into the lead,' Rattigan told him. 'You know what they can do with musicals.' Sinden opted for Guy Middleton's old part of Brian, rather than that of Alan Howard, and was immediately plunged into singing lessons for his two solos. His co-star was to be Joan Heal, who had begun her career as a soubrette in revue but had also recently starred in the comedy *Grab Me a Gondola* in the West End. The cast of eighteen was to be supplemented by thirteen dancers and four further singers.

Now, as a result of the objections of Professor Lawrence, *Joie de Vivre* was to begin its short pre-London tour at the New Theatre in Oxford a few days before *Ross* opened in the West End. Billy Chappell began rehearsals for the musical in rooms in Drury Lane, in the shadow of *My Fair Lady*, while Glen Byam Shaw was still rehearsing *Ross* in Tottenham Court Road. Rattigan shuttled unhappily between the two, the painful memory of the double opening of *The Sleeping Prince* and *Separate Tables* on Broadway four years earlier still fresh in his mind. Before the rehearsals of either play were complete, however, he had been taken to the London Clinic with viral pneumonia, possibly brought on by strain. It was his first serious illness. He was allowed home only two days before the opening of *Ross* on Thursday, 12 May, but nothing would persuade him to miss it.

There was no first night party at Eaton Square, however. Rattigan was simply not well enough, and went home to bed early, hopeful that the critics would like his sixteenth West End play. They did. Indeed the better reviews for *Ross* were to provide his only consolation in the desolate years to come. As ever, though, the few bad reviews were the ones that stuck in his mind. Milton Shulman in the London *Evening Standard*, for example, positively hated the play, suggesting it did 'no more than punctuate the dot at the bottom of the question mark' which was the enigma of T.E.Lawrence, and he roundly criticised Rattigan for failing to point out his protagonist's flaws, as well as his illegitimacy. Mercifully from Rattigan's point of view, Kenneth Tynan was absent from his post on the *Observer*, so he could take some comfort from the rest of the critics, who were rather more complimentary. 'Ross could have been a greater play . . . but only by being a different play,' wrote Alan Brien in the *Spectator*. 'Unless the real Lawrence was abandoned altogether I do not see how his life could be staged with less fiction and more integrity.' Sitting in bed the following morning, surrounded by the newspapers, Rattigan blandly told a reporter, 'I love reading my reviews.'

He did not enjoy reading them eight weeks later when *Joie de Vivre* finally reached the Queen's Theatre on Shaftesbury Avenue after its lengthy provincial tour. But they did not come as a shock. As they had done so many times in the past, he and Beaumont had taken enormous trouble to invite a glittering audience to the show's first night, and Rattigan had also recovered sufficiently to throw a party afterwards at Eaton Square. He had invested in the production himself – the total cost was approaching £20,000 – and had even managed to persuade the Lord Chamberlain to allow him to reinstate the word 'Merde', which he had had to omit from the play. 'It is a word which, though vulgar, is in fairly common usage in France and is inscribed freely by highly respectable ladies sending first night telegrams to French actors,' he had told the Lord Chamberlain. He seemed to have done everything possible to ensure success. Nevertheless, by the time the second act got under way on Bastille Day 1960, the audience were baying for its author's blood.

'I was standing at the back of the stalls,' Rattigan reported the following morning, 'when they began to get ugly. I'd already been warned by my secretary, who was in the upper circle, that someone had told her in the interval, "It's going to get the bird." But I couldn't believe it. It seemed to be going so well.' When Barrie Ingham, who was playing Alan Howard, announced, 'This is Hell,' there was an audible roar of approval from the gallery. Rattigan took one look at Billy Chappell and went backstage to warn the stage manager that if the barracking continued, he was to bring the curtain down at the end and leave it down. There were to be no curtain calls.

By the time Alan uttered one of his final lines, 'Stop laughing, you idiots. It isn't funny, it's a bloody tragedy,' only to be greeted by a shout of 'Too bloody right,' there was no hope. 'The final curtain fell to a tempest of booing and did not rise again . . . I can only guess that the fabric of Rattigan's original play was too flimsy to support the weight of decoration now piled upon it,' W.A.Darlington noted next morning in the *Daily Telegraph*.

What *The Times* called a 'fatuous attack on the Royal Court drama-tists' in the song 'I'm sorry but I'm happy' had made matters worse. Rex Harrison, coming to the first-night party from his own nightly triumph in *My Fair Lady*, gallantly tried to commiserate. But Rattigan accepted later that 'It wasn't the hatchet men among the critics. It was the audience. They just didn't like the play. They thought it was a trivial, meretricious little piece, hopelessly dated.' Just three days after the opening, Binkie Beaumont closed the show, losing Rattigan all but £1,000 of the £8,000 he had put into it.

As Donald Sinden walked in the Queen's stage door for the Saturday matinée on 17 July, three girls waiting to collect his autograph told him how sorry they were the show was closing that night. It was the first he had heard of it. Rattigan did not intend to let the occasion pass without comment, however. After the final curtain that evening, he gave a small party on the stage for the cast, and made a speech. 'Natur-ally he was rather distressed,' Joan Heal recalled. None of the cast realised how much. It was to be three years before he would risk another Shaftesbury Avenue first night.

The immediate aftermath was a bout of verbal fisticuffs between Rattigan and Kenneth Tynan, who revealed in the *Observer* that he had left 'when the first act ended' and whose review was not merely predictably adverse but insulting to boot. The director, Billy Chappell, was 'Michael Benthall *en cocotte*' (a reference to another director, the homosexual overtones of which Chappell considered to be actionable); while Rattigan was 'Pinero *en gelée*'; and Stoltz's music appeared to have 'come from some other show'.

'Dear Ken, I hoped to reach you in time to stop you wasting your space on *Joie de Vivre* which, as you will now know, closed on Satur-day,' Rattigan wrote.

I wish I had succeeded because I am a well-wisher of yours – although I recognise that the feeling is hardly reciprocated. I am afraid Billy Chappell is going to sue . . . I shall try and stop him, but why – oh why – are you so boorishly abusive? And – since the *New Yorker* – so dull and ill-tempered and ideological. So you didn't like the musical. Neither did 95 per cent of your colleagues.

But none of them expressed their dislike one tenth as boorishly as you. They didn't lose face by their (comparative) restraint . . .

Rattigan's anger was clear in his conclusion to Tynan.

If you persist in thinking and stating that Brecht is the only near-contemporary writer worth serious consideration you will lose those thousands of readers who obstinately continue to think him a cracking, pedantic, didactic, ill-translated old Marxist bore . . . I'm angry because it's all so unnecessary. Why couldn't you just have said 'I hated the whole thing and left half way through', and left it at that?

Rattigan's temper was not improved by the tone of Tynan's reply. 'Dear Terry,' the letter began:

I really don't know why you put up with me. There must be moments when you wonder whether it's all worthwhile. I'm sorry you find me 'dull and ill-tempered and ideological'; but I've tried being sparkling and good-tempered and mindless, and it doesn't seem to work out. And isn't there, by the way, a trace of kettle-calling in your charges . . .

At the end of his letter, Tynan added a tart PS. 'Have you noticed this season's recipe for success? Write a play with a monosyllabic title beginning with "R".'

Rattigan was furious. Tynan was rude, impolite, and had offended Billy Chappell. He replied at once. 'Yes, there was a trace of kettle-calling in my letter,' Rattigan told Tynan.

I was in a flaming temper. A few hours after digesting a notice which appeared to begin by stating that I hadn't had a fresh or original idea in six years and had definitely ended by describing my serious work as jellified Pinero (I took that to include the piece now wobbling gelatinously over the boards of the Haymarket) I was called upon to defend the very man who wrote it from a determined – if hysterical – onslaught by my best friend. And that, the morning after suffering one of the whoppingest flops in theatre history. Wouldn't you have been in a flaming temper? Wouldn't even Brecht? Or would alienation have rescued him? I mean that, isn't the logical end to the alienation theory that you succeed so fully in alienating the audience that the gallery boos and the critics tear you apart for having made the gallery boo?

Pressing on, Rattigan added:

When I called you 'ill-tempered, dull and ideological' the first two epithets can be dismissed entirely, as products of my own distemper on that Sunday morning. I only find you ill-tempered and dull (and then not invariably) when you write about me, and as you happily spend very little of your time doing that, I don't find you ill-tempered and dull. But ideological is another matter. It is, I hope you'll agree, a daunting thought for the uncommitted writers, and we are legion . . . that each new play of ours will inevitably receive a stern frown of disapproval from the Observer for not being the kind of play that the Observer thinks it should have been. Anouilh, Ionescu, Wesker, Pinter and Bolt have all (it seems at least to this reader) been frowned on at different times for precisely this reason, and sometimes for no other. (When I am frowned on it is usually for a lot of other reasons beside the main one, so I count myself out of it. But even for me, the main one is daunting.) Now isn't it a criterion of good criticism that a work should never be blamed for failing to be what it was never intended to be? I think I'm quoting David Cecil in that, but I can quote Trigorin more accurately. 'Everybody must write as he feels and as best he may.' You believe (I think) that you have the right to criticise him if he doesn't feel as you feel. Or perhaps you don't believe that quite yet, but you give the impression of coming to believe it . . . I believe that you only have the right to criticise Trigorin's writer when 'his best' is not good enough. And that, I suppose, is exactly where we differ. But only in the friendliest – I hope – possible way.

Rattigan could not quite bring himself to endanger completely his relationship with the man who had become Britain's single most influential theatre critic. His diplomatic inheritance, and what he described to Tynan as his 'reactionary, public school upbringing', both made him stop short of that. But the effect of Tynan's review, and the catastrophic collapse of *Joie de Vivre* following the failure of *Variation on a Theme*, was to confirm the decline that was to last for the rest of his life.

Not even the £75,000 that the producer Herbert Wilcox was paying for the film rights to *Ross* – including an immediate down payment of £10,000 – was sufficient to counteract the sense of unfairness, coupled with failure, that seized Rattigan. Viral pneumonia had weakened him, failure made him sink still lower. He became convinced that England had turned against him: the only solution was to retire abroad.

Rattigan had also begun to fear for his health. Kay Kendall's death

from leukaemia the year before had frightened him. He had watched
her shrink and waste before his eyes with horror. He had comforted
Rex Harrison after her death, inviting him to stay at Little Court, and
promising to write not one but two new plays for him. Now the damp
air of England seemed to hang on his chest, delaying his recovery and
adding to his despair. Michael Franklin sensed his fear, and suggested
that the sea air of Brighton might help. Rattigan agreed, and allowed
the Midget to buy a flat in Embassy Court. When he saw it, however,
Rattigan hated it, though he wondered nevertheless whether perhaps
he should buy a house there as well. His pneumonia gradually passed.
His spirit, on the other hand, did not recover.

As his physical health improved, Rattigan started work on a double
bill for Harrison tentatively entitled *Like Father, Like Son*. The first,
Like Father, focused on the life of Bert Leavenworth, a famous Bloomsbury painter whose son, Augustus, is forced to reveal that he is a
conformist, not a Bohemian, when he gets engaged to a field marshal's
daughter and brings her home to meet his father. There were sundry
jokes and sub-plots: Suzie, the painter's girlfriend, wants to legalise
their relationship. Leavenworth and the field marshal turn out to have
been Eton contemporaries; and all are amazed when Augustus and his
girlfriend reveal that they have never even slept together.

By the end of November he had finished a full three-act version of
Like Father, but was not sure what to do with it. He was not prepared
to send it to Beaumont – whom he blamed for not protecting Billy
Chappell and *Joie de Vivre* – and besides, the failure of *Variation on a
Theme* was too recent. So he simply stored the draft, marking it 'Discuss with TR before presenting'. In the end the play was never shown
to a management, or performed. It was the first of almost a dozen of
Rattigan's plays and screenplays written during the 1960s that would
never be seen anywhere.

In late October he left England for the United States, to discuss two
projects. One was the possibility of a Broadway production for *Ross*,
which was still playing to packed houses at the Haymarket, the other,
another new musical, this time a version of *The Sleeping Prince* with
lyrics by Noël Coward and the provisional title of *The Girl Who Came
to Supper*. The start of the trip brought an unexpected inspiration, for
while Rattigan was waiting in the VIP lounge at Heathrow airport a
fog came down – 'like the curtain at the Queen's Theatre' – and he was
stuck there all day. By the time the fog lifted, he had an idea for a film
set in the VIP lounge at a large airport. It was to be called *The VIPs*.

In New York, he had discussions with David Merrick, who was to
present *Ross* with Tennent. He agreed to put up $30,000 towards the

production. Then he flew on to Hollywood to see Tolly de Grunwald, who had just been given a producer's contract by Metro-Goldwyn-Mayer. By the time he flew home again he had sold Tolly the airport idea. Back in England, he rapidly drafted a seventy-two-page outline, which he dispatched to de Grunwald before the end of November. In short order he received a commission from MGM to write a screenplay for a fee of $100,000 – not far short of £40,000.

Soon after the New Year Michael Bryant replaced Alec Guinness in *Ross* at the Haymarket and Kenneth Tynan reviewed the change of cast. He used the opportunity to mount a stinging attack on the talents of the play's author. 'My main objection to *Ross*,' Tynan wrote, 'is not that its view of history is petty and blinkered; so, it might be urged, is Shakespeare's in *Henry V*. What clinches my distaste is its verbal aridity, its flatness of phrase, and – above all – its pat reliance on the same antithetical device in moments of crisis.' He proceeded to list eight examples, beginning:

1. I've an idea you don't care for authority, Ross.
   I care for discipline, sir.
2. There's nothing in the world worse than self-pity.
   Oh yes there is. Self-knowledge.
3. And so he will win his battles by not fighting them?
   Yes. And his war too – by not waging it.

Tynan's list ended:

7. You're going to make it hard for me, are you?
   I see no reason to make it easy.
8. You sicken me.
   I sicken myself.

Taken out of context Tynan's snippets made Rattigan's work look banal and clichéd. But antithesis had always been one of Rattigan's favourite and most effective techniques. Now it was being used to show that he could not write dialogue. It was the final straw. Disillusion and paranoia began to creep into his system – even someone he knew and trusted, like Olivier, seemed to have 'turned against' him by agreeing to appear in Osborne's play *The Entertainer*. Worse still, Olivier made no secret of his admiration for Tynan. There was nowhere to turn. Perhaps he should leave the country. Bill Forsyth and Peter Carter-Ruck presented him with an excuse – he could avoid paying so much tax if he took a complete year away. Though he would miss England, Rattigan agreed.

★   ★   ★

During the next three years Terence Rattigan travelled endlessly. Little Court was sold and a house in Marine Parade, Brighton, bought in its place, complete with a 'permanent bedroom for Margaret Leighton', both as a gesture to his friend and as a signal to his mother, but he hardly visited it. Eternally restless, Rattigan instead filled his time with pointless parties, and increased his drinking, which had always been heavy, 'almost as if he wanted to destroy himself'. Nothing pleased him: not even Rudolph Cartier announcing that he was to direct a television version of *Adventure Story* starring the young Sean Connery for the BBC, an accolade if ever there was one. When it was transmitted, in June 1961, Rattigan was not even in the country and did not see the respectful reviews. 'As in the theatre,' the *Daily Mail* remarked, 'it lacked only elegance of language to turn it into a piece of real stature.'

Rattigan took refuge on the Italian island of Ischia, where he rented a villa from Sir William and Lady Walton, who had settled there permanently. The faithful Michael Weight, who had been his major-domo for a decade, was dispatched to oversee the move and prepare for his arrival. He would spend the spring and summer there, writing, seeing his friends, and drinking. The critics could find someone else to attack.

Rattigan sympathised with the American Vice-President Richard Nixon, who had recently said much the same thing about his political career – in what became known as the 'Checkers' speech. Nixon's suggestion that the critics could get 'someone else to kick around' had given Rattigan the idea for another play, which he intended to work on in Ischia. But first there was his screenplay for *The VIPs* to discuss with MGM in Hollywood. He had delivered the draft in April 1961, but the studio wanted some amendments before they started shooting later in the year. Rattigan had added an extra ingredient to his original draft outline. He had drawn the torments of Olivier and Vivien Leigh into his story.

Five years earlier, in December 1955, not long after Rattigan had helped her to get Hester's role in the film of *The Deep Blue Sea*, Vivien had twice tried to leave Olivier for Peter Finch. The first time she had been coaxed back from France. But on the second she and Finch had been trapped in the VIP lounge at fog-bound Heathrow. Rattigan took the experience and turned it into the basis of his screenplay. By the end of the year, the woman who had been Rattigan's next-door neighbour in Eaton Square would see herself portrayed on the screen by Elizabeth Taylor, and her husband by Richard Burton. 'Vivien saw through the ruse,' Rattigan admitted to the critic and author Alexander Walker some years later, 'but if Larry did too he didn't say anything.'

Rattigan's trip to Hollywood from Ischia was a success. The studio 'loved' *The VIPS*, his first original idea for an American studio. Sol Siegel was to produce, and Vincente Minelli, whose sure touch for mainstream entertainment was clearly evident on *Meet Me in St Louis*, *Bandwagon* and *Gigi*, was to direct. Rattigan returned to Ischia convinced the film would be a success. By the time he had settled in Ischia, however, his thoughts were already returning to the stage again: but Broadway, not Shaftesbury Avenue.

But *Like Son*, the second play Rattigan had been working on for Rex Harrison, was not to be the second half of a double bill – *Like Father* had already turned out to be a full-length piece anyway. He had decided that *Like Son* was to be another full-scale play, and he wondered whether the two might use the same cast, as *Separate Tables* had done. This time the plays could be performed on alternate nights rather than on the same evening. While he was planning it in his mind, Rattigan decided to give *Like Son* a new title. It became *Man and Boy*.

Rattigan had made no secret of his ambition in a remarkable interview in the *Daily Mail* during the interminable negotiations over *Ross*. 'I have always wanted to be something better than just a Shaftesbury Avenue boy. My credo is that the audience is the judge, but my aim has always been to write a masterpiece.' Not long afterwards, he had given a second interview, and added bitterly, 'What I resent is that everyone thinks it's so terribly simple to write a play that will run for fifteen months. In New York it took a hell of a time before they took me seriously. They've always considered me polished but insincere, a journeyman hack. But when you've been shedding tears over a script it annoys you when they tell you that're just smooth and insincere.'

The two greatest dangers to the middle-aged playwright 'are sentimentality and disenchantment', he concluded. Rattigan did not seem to realise that he had fallen victim to both.

So what, he asked reflectively, was there left? 'Play golf. Travel. One day to write the masterpiece.' On Ischia, in the summer of 1961, Terence Rattigan prayed that he had, at last, written that masterpiece.

CHAPTER 23

The Heart's Voices

◆

Extreme hopes are born of extreme misery.

BERTRAND RUSSELL, *Unpopular Essays*

◆

There was only one reason to go on working – 'the hope of increasing my reputation' – as Rattigan told Binkie Beaumont in a letter from Ischia in June 1961. Nothing else mattered. If he could not convince the critics that he deserved to be taken seriously as a dramatist then he might as well retire. The play that he hoped and prayed would win back his reputation, and become the masterpiece he had always dreamed of writing, was the one he was on the brink of finishing, *Man and Boy*.

Rattigan wanted to complete it quickly, not least to re-establish his reputation, but he wanted Binkie Beaumont to launch it on Broadway, in partnership with 'dear Irene' Selznick rather than in London. The Shaftesbury Avenue critics were not going to have another opportunity to lambast him for the time being. Rex, of course, would play the part that had been written specially for him. Rattigan summoned Mary Herring to Ischia from London to decipher his handwriting, as she had done so many times before, and produce a clean typed manuscript. The first copy would go to Tennents in London, the second to Rex Harrison in New York, the third to Glen Byam Shaw, who had agreed to direct. Of course Rex was pretending to be a little reluctant, but he always did that. Rattigan felt sure that he would come round.

'I understand Rex's predicament,' he told Beaumont in a letter in June, 'because it is also my own. Rex – in the fifties, with a high reputation as a skilful performer, but not so high as he would like (or deserve) wants to "better" himself. I think, in this he is quite right. So do I. He no longer needs money. *My Fair Lady* has taken care of that, for life – or at least for the foreseeable future. I am in roughly the same boat . . . Rex doesn't need to work for ten years, moneywise. Moneywise I don't need to work for five.' It was not the money, or the glamour of a Tennent production, that drove him on – though 'God knows,' he told Beaumont, 'I don't scorn them.' But 'they don't, any of them, come near the point – which is terribly simple – namely will the new play be good or bad? Nothing else matters, nothing at all. To write a play that would be remembered in fifty years time, that would be sufficient reward for my labours.'

In the first week of July Mary Herring was dispatched back to London with the completed version of the play in her suitcase, while Rattigan, in a state of some excitement, wrote to Rex to explain why he was so keen on opening on Broadway first.

> The play is set in Greenwich Village – at least three of the seven parts must be played by Americans anyway – the play, in feeling and temper (and having to do with high finance) is more likely in some ways to appeal to the Broadway 'expense account' audiences than to our own browbeaten Shaftesbury Avenue creatures, scared to death (by Muller, Levin, Tynan et al) to admit to having enjoyed a play with a beginning, a middle and an end.

A week later Beaumont rang from London with his first reaction. It was enthusiastic enough, but wary. He wanted to hear what Rex and Glen thought first before deciding how to proceed. Rattigan countered by suggesting he come out to Ischia with his partner, John Perry, to talk it over. They could stay in another villa, which he had rented from Robin Maugham for the benefit of his guests. Beaumont politely refused, and in the weeks that followed Rattigan's hopes steadily began to sink. First Glen Byam Shaw cabled with one or two reservations. Rattigan sensed that he wanted to 'soften' his play, 'to make what I meant to be chilling and horrifying into something just fashionably shocking', as Rattigan put it to Harold Freedman. 'To transform a character I mean to be as evil and fascinating as Iago into a character as cosily naughty and charming as Raffles . . . Raffles, I know, with Rex, would be sure-fire, but I want something more shocking than that.'

Then Harrison himself telephoned from New York. He was uncertain, worried about the character of the man he was being asked to play, the financier Gregor Antonescu, who was obviously pretending to be a homosexual in the second act. He was even worried about the title, with its homosexual connotations. After the call, Rattigan's fears grew ever deeper. The arrival of Glen Byam Shaw for a week's discussions did nothing to allay them. Like Harrison's, Byam Shaw's reservations centred on the element of homosexuality in the play. Rattigan suggested that Herries, Gregor Antonescu's rival, was probably married, with two or three children, even though he was a homosexual. This provoked Byam Shaw to 'launch himself into a violent diatribe about the emotional "viciousness" of such a man', according to the account that Rattigan later set down for Binkie Beaumont. 'A homosexual who uses the camouflage of marriage is an unspeakable monster, a vicious bastard, a frustrated brute whose jaded sexual appetites require "sudden jets of lust" . . . to keep him functioning at all,' was Byam Shaw's view.

Rattigan took it with more than a pinch of salt. Two of Kenneth Morgan's lovers had later married and put their homosexual past behind them, but other married men he knew had remained homosexual. Neither unduly concerned him. That was for them to choose. But the fury of Byam Shaw's reaction surprised him. As far as he was concerned Herries was simply a great industrialist 'who has a sexual predilection which he believes is known to no one at all save to a few of his closest and most intimate friends'. This, of course, was exactly what he believed about himself.

Both Harrison and Byam Shaw wanted Antonescu's son, who was to be used as bait to trap his father's business rival, the homosexual Herries, cast as an intensely virile and masculine young man. But Rattigan wanted him to be portrayed as slightly effeminate. If the son were to be persuaded by his father into a brief homosexual affair – in an attempt to save his business – that would not necessarily make him an 'unspeakable' monster.

'Effeminacy = weakness = softness = contrast to virile father and minus abnormality happens to be the play, and that's that,' he wrote after his meeting with Byam Shaw. 'Rex doesn't want (Glen says) to pretend to be a member of "The brotherhood of buggers" – exact quotation. This utterly bewildered me as the whole of the second act is built on exactly this premise.' The conversation not only bewildered Rattigan, it also affronted him. 'I would far rather not have the play done at all, than done in a watered down, emasculated version,' he told Beaumont.

In the villa in Ischia, the atmosphere of cheerful abandon that Terence Rattigan had practised to maintain among his friends for more than two decades, began to give way to paranoia. The friends who came for the summer watched in horror as their host became ever more convinced that there was a conspiracy against him. The play which he had set such store by seemed to be in danger of disappearing before it had even been performed. 'Any doubts, any fears from any of us,' Rattigan told Binkie Beaumont in late August, 'myself included (my confidence is not after all indestructible) and it would really be far better to drop the whole project – at least with the present set up. I don't mean this idly. It comes from the heart.'

In particular Rattigan was devastated that Rex Harrison could not see the difference between 'acting' the part of a homosexual and 'acting pretending to be one': and he felt strongly that Harrison was a fool not to understand that playing a monster would not imply that he himself was monstrous. In Gregor, Rattigan was 'showing the audience the devil . . . Any watering down of this and we're into Raffles, and not *Man and Boy*,' he wrote. But Harrison steadfastly refused to compromise, and by September Rattigan had decided that his old friend was probably the wrong choice for the play's central character anyway. Rattigan did not want its impact halved or even wiped out by Harrison's wilfully cosy reading. Nor did he want Harrison aided and abetted by Glen Byam Shaw. Gregor Antonescu was the devil, and that was that. Intent on preserving his own vision of his new play, Rattigan decided that both Harrison and Shaw would have to go.

The summer produced another disappointment. Vincente Minelli and Sol Siegel had both withdrawn from their commitment to direct and produce *The VIPs*. The film now looked as if it were going to be just another de Grunwald production. 'Oh well!' Rattigan confided to Harold French, 'I suppose, I shall say "never again with Tolly" afterwards.' It was a little harsh. He had been paid $100,000, and de Grunwald had persuaded MGM to hire him in the first place. De Grunwald was also about to spend almost the entire summer flying across Europe in pursuit of his two stars, Elizabeth Taylor and Richard Burton, who were already scheduled to appear together in Twentieth Century-Fox's spectacular production of *Cleopatra*. De Grunwald wanted to get in first.

Rattigan's mind was elsewhere. He was consumed by *Man and Boy*. He had arranged to see Peter Glenville in Venice, which he and Michael Franklin would be visiting in September. He and Glenville duly met there in the middle of the month, and again a week later in Paris. For a moment, Rattigan's despair at the faltering progress of his play lifted. It became clear at once that Glenville had grasped the play's point. Was Gregor's inhumanity 'God-given or man-given?' he had asked. 'Peter's first question is the most important question the play should try to answer. The rest is subordinate,' Rattigan wrote to Beaumont in delight.

That same day he wrote to Glen Byam Shaw, explaining that the play that Shaw wanted to direct was not the one that he had written. 'Perhaps your play is better. But it doesn't seem to be mine.' Rattigan went on to describe Rex Harrison's views as 'absurd, damaging and utterly unacceptable'. Within a month he had travelled to Rome to tell Harrison himself exactly what he felt. It was unexpected behaviour from a man who usually avoided confrontation at all costs. 'Terry never spoke to you directly. If he didn't like something, he would always call your agent, and get them to do it,' one friend recalls. 'He was too polite to do anything else.' The face-to-face meeting with Rex Harrison proved how deeply he cared about the fate of *Man and Boy*. But while there was Peter Glenville there was hope.

By the middle of October 1961, however, even that hope had disappeared. Glenville too had withdrawn, because, he said, his 'non-resident tax status' would be jeopardised if the play was to be presented in England. The play Rattigan had hoped would be his masterpiece had lost its star and its director, and might even be in danger of losing its producer. What could its author do to save it? As in the past when everything seemed lost, Rattigan turned to Laurence Olivier, hoping he would be willing to direct it, star in it, produce it, or even make a film of it. 'The play's future in London, New York, and indeed in the world depends on your answer . . . Darling Larry, you know you can say "No" to all the questions listed above without the faintest risk to our friendship. But I do hope one (or more) will be Yes. I do, do hope.'

Darling Larry said No. He could not guarantee a London production, nor was he certain what the audiences at the Chichester Festival – which he had just taken over as its first director – would expect. Also the play itself frightened him. He was not sure how much he wanted to shock them in a modern play, Olivier explained. 'I mean passing off your own son as a queer and all that; I mean it's no good if they are simply not going to understand what the hell is going on – it's not that I'm frightened of shocking them.' It was the final straw. Rattigan put the play away, and did not look at it again for six months.

Instead, he started work on a television play. The BBC had invited him to write an original play which would also be broadcast by the thirteen other members of the European Broadcasting Union of that time, including Italy, Sweden, France, Germany and Belgium, thereby bringing a potential audience of 80 million people. The project was to be called *The Largest Theatre in the World*, and the fee on offer was £35,000, a substantial increase on the £300 he had been paid for his only other original television play, *The Final Test*, almost a decade earlier. The money was attractive. By the late autumn of 1961 he had finished his first draft. He sent it off before leaving for New York to discuss the Broadway production of *Ross* with David Merrick.

The role of Lawrence on Broadway was one subject for discussion. Alec Guinness had explained that he did not want to leave England at this precise moment, and Michael Bryant was still playing the role at the Haymarket, although there were signs that the play might be about to come to the end of its run. (In fact it was to last until March 1962 and amass a total of 762 performances – almost three times as many as *The Browning Version* and the longest run of any of Rattigan's serious plays in the West End.) For the part of Lawrence on Broadway, Rattigan had settled on John Mills, a friend from Little Court days, and Geoffrey Keen was to shift from London to New York to play the central figure of the Turkish Military Governor, who is referred to in the text of the play as the Turkish General. Rattigan's relations with Glen Byam Shaw were a little strained in the wake of their disagreement over *Man and Boy*. Nonetheless, he was to direct, just as he had done in London.

Ross was due to open at the O'Neill Theatre on Boxing Day 1961, Rattigan's twelfth Broadway production in the twenty-seven years since *First Episode* had struggled into the Ritz Theatre under its American title of *College Sinners* and the critic George Nathan had commented: 'The title was changed. They could have changed it to Hamlet: it would make no difference. It remains a first episode.' For the New York production of *Ross*, Rattigan made Lawrence's sexual violation at Deraa a little more explicit. He wanted the American audience to be in no doubt of his thesis. He also took pains to tell the *New York Times* before the opening, 'Lawrence went into the RAF just as a man goes into a monastery. He undoubtedly was a masochist – the evidence is there . . . But then at Deraa, a revelation of sexual masochism – suddenly realising that the whole thing had a dirty sexual basis – would have been enough to disturb any man.'

Neither the amendments to the text nor Rattigan's explanation succeeded. New Yorkers simply preferred Tennessee Williams's new play *The Night of the Iguana*, which opened just two nights later starring Margaret Leighton and Bette Davis, to the Rattigan analysis of a man they had only dimly heard of. The *New Yorker* dismissed *Ross* as a 'Portrait without Depth', adding that Rattigan's thesis was 'dramatic all right, but it is just a little too superficial as an explanation of Lawrence's strange behaviour after he left the Desert'. The influential critic John Simon said fiercely: 'This series of loosely connected, unpenetrating vignettes is pasted on to the stage like so many decals in which a third dimensionless Lawrence becomes neither divine nor human.' In the

New York Times Howard Taubman agreed: 'It does not vitiate the brilliance of Mr Rattigan's writing or the power and excitement of his play.' To Rattigan's astonishment, some of the tabloid newspaper critics even thought he was suggesting that Lawrence had been castrated in Deraa. 'Just tell me how I could make it clearer – without being offensive,' he asked the *New York Post* plaintively.

Ross did not work on Broadway. Rattigan's suspicion of the 'sea change' between London and New York had proved correct once more. The play ran for only three months at the O'Neill. In April 1962 it transferred to the Hudson, but not even a determined effort by Merrick – and Rattigan's agreement to waive his royalties – could keep it alive. It closed the following month, with losses rumoured to exceed $70,000. Rattigan had even confessed to the American critic John Simon that his interest in Lawrence had become so passionate that he had started to 'commune with him at night' – 'I got myself into such a state of semi-mania that I really came to believe that noise on the hot water pipes was a form of Morse code with which Lawrence was talking to me.' But his own passionate fascination with Lawrence had failed to cross the Broadway footlights. Once again in New York Rattigan was doomed to be seen as 'polished but insincere'.

Nevertheless, while in New York Rattigan had found time to amend his screenplay for *The VIPs* once more, this time in an effort to persuade Margaret Rutherford to play the eccentric Duchess of Brighton. She had turned down the part at first reading, feeling that 'the part had no background . . . there was nothing to get my teeth into'. In response, Rattigan gave the character a background and a job to go to – as the social director of a Miami Beach hotel. His efforts were to win Margaret Rutherford an Oscar.

On his way back to Europe, Rattigan stopped at Noël Coward's home in Jamaica to recuperate from the rigours of New York. Since the disappointments of *Man and Boy* he had been drinking ever more heavily, and as a result his health had deteriorated. He was not at all well. The viral pneumonia a year earlier had also left him susceptible to lengthy colds and regular bouts of flu. Nevertheless, he was working. He had dispatched the first version of his BBC television play, which he had decided to call *Heart to Heart*, in tribute to the BBC's own interview programme, *Face to Face*, chaired by the journalist John Freeman. In Jamaica he worked on revisions. The subject he had chosen was, on the surface, television itself.

But his script began with a dialogue that would not have been out of place in a number of his other plays, a further attempt at self-analysis in his work. Even before the titles appear, the interviewer David Mann is cross-examining his latest victim, the successful barrister Sir John Dawson-Brown QC.

> DAVID: (*In an incisive voice*) Sir John, how does a man fulfil himself in life?
> SIR JOHN: I would say that a man fulfils himself by the knowledge that he has always tried to do what is right rather than what is expedient.
> DAVID: Can a man always distinguish between the two?
> SIR JOHN: I think so.
> DAVID: How?
> SIR JOHN: There's a thing called conscience –
> DAVID: Consciences vary, don't they? To one man a certain action will seem right, to another wrong.
> SIR JOHN: Oh, I agree. I'm not claiming there are absolute standards. But the only certain rule in life is that happiness lies in doing one's duty. And one's duty is to do what seems right to one at the time – even though it may, perhaps, ultimately prove wrong.
> DAVID: Or even if it may harm not only yourself but other persons?
> SIR JOHN: Oh, yes. There can be no doubt at all about it – in my mind, anyway. A man must always try to do his duty as he sees that duty at the time. I don't think there can be any escape from that, Mr Mann.

Rattigan put the final touches to the script at the Hotel Martinez in Cannes in March, and waited there to meet the softly spoken Canadian Alvin Rakoff, whom the BBC had chosen to produce the play. 'Terry was a great one for questions,' Rakoff remembers. 'The first one he asked me was, "Wouldn't you be rather working on the new Wesker or Pinter or Arden?" He was feeling the new generation breathing hotly down his neck.' The two men spent a short time in Cannes, and then went on to Rome and Ischia to polish the draft still further. One reason for going to Rome was to persuade Richard Burton to play the part of the television interviewer David Mann. Burton was there preparing for the filming of *Cleopatra*. 'Burton said he wanted to do it,' Rakoff recalls, 'which was wonderful as we already had Sir Ralph Richardson on board to play the other lead, the Cabinet Minister, Sir Stanley Johnson.'

The more time Rakoff spent with Rattigan on Ischia, the more he came to respect him. 'He was very self-analytical. It was the way he would talk about his father and mother, and his relationship with the Midget, who was the love of his life. He thought his homosexuality was not the fault of his mother, but the result of a bad father relationship . . . He said he never gained his father's love, and that I think hurt

Terry enormously. A lot of Sir Ralph's character in *Heart to Heart* was his father, I believe.'

Rattigan would read his dialogue out loud to Rakoff, as if to convince himself that it had quality. The subject of David Mann's crucial interview was to be a politician who had accepted that his hotel bill should be paid by a Brazilian businessman involved in a bribery scandal, and had endeavoured to conceal the fact. The politician, Sir Stanley Johnson, has recently been made Minister of Labour, his first Cabinet appointment, when he is interviewed by David Mann. During the live interview Johnson breaks down and confesses to the audience that he did accept the Brazilian's hospitality, and that he will be resigning the following morning.

More than thirty years later the plot remains extraordinarily apposite. On the surface, Rattigan's inspiration may have been Richard Nixon's television farewell and John Freeman's British programme *Face to Face*. At a deeper level, however, the character he had created was closer to Major Frank Rattigan, the man who had claimed publicly that his resignation from the Diplomatic Service had not been as a result of a love affair with too eminent a lady but a disagreement with Lord Curzon. Now, a decade after his death, Rattigan's father is allowed to apologise and explain himself under the guise of Sir Stanley Johnson.

> SIR STANLEY: . . . Still, that doesn't excuse me for what I did, and I don't
> mean it to. I broke the law, and must take the consequences. From
> tomorrow on I'm just plain Stan Johnson – not Minister of Labour –
> perhaps not even an MP if my constituency chucks me out – which they
> have every right to do, mind – just common old Stan, who once made
> a bloomer and four years later had to pay the price.

The play ends with a direct appeal from the Minister to the television audience for justice – and forgiveness. Rattigan had originally intended it to end with the Minister's destruction at the hands of his interviewer, but had decided at the last minute that that might be condemned as too facile, too neat. His alternative was less expected, more in keeping with the play's inspiration.

> SIR STANLEY: . . . I'd like to say that old Stan here feels pretty damn badly
> about having let you down, and only begs for a chance, if one day you'll
> forgive him, to serve you again, in whatever capacity might seem good
> to you. But if you don't forgive him – and, mind you, he doesn't think
> you should – well, then, he'll take his medicine, and you'll hear nothing
> more from him. He'll blame no one at all – except himself – otherwise
> no one – and least of all his Grand Inquisitor, Mr David Mann, and

this great fine truthful show, 'Heart to Heart'. Good night, ladies and gentlemen.

Rakoff believes that there was a great deal of the author's personal convictions in the play. 'We're all contradictions, but Terry was a moralist, even though he was blatantly a homosexual when it was almost dangerous to be a homosexual.' The more time the two men spent together the more Rakoff came to sympathise with his collaborator's torment. 'Things preyed on his mind, like was he being replaced by Wesker, or did people hate him because he was gay, and they preyed on his mind more than they did on others.'

After completing the new draft, the two men set off for Cannes, where they were to meet another BBC executive to discuss the production. No sooner had they arrived at the Hotel Martinez than Rattigan set off for the casino. He took out a large sum of money and then gave Rakoff his wallet, telling him forcefully, 'I'll come back for this when I've lost the other – don't give it to me.' Rakoff went back to the hotel, where Rattigan did indeed arrive and ask for his wallet. 'But then he decided not to go back,' Rakoff remembers. 'That was his form of self-analysis, knowing that he was a gambler, but knowing that he was with someone who wasn't, and using that to keep his self-control.'

Every form of human weakness and sexuality fascinated Rattigan. 'He was also always intrigued about heterosexual relationships,' Rakoff recalls. 'He questioned me endlessly, and he questioned my wife, about our relationship and all sexual relationships.' He also adored gossip about sex, not least gossip about his neighbour on Ischia, William Walton. 'He loved the idea that this famous composer might be as naughty as he was, but in a heterosexual way.'

By the time he flew back to London to prepare the production, Rakoff had realised that Terence Rattigan always tended 'to belittle his own work. He didn't seem to believe then that people had enormous respect for him, especially within the profession.' But 'he loved being in the business, being in the arts, being in showbusiness. He would go to the theatre at the drop of a hat. He wasn't blasé at all. He loved talking about the business'. It was during one of their long evenings together on Ischia that Rattigan showed Rakoff his first draft of *Man and Boy*. 'It struck me forcibly that here was the father manipulating the son when I read it.'

Binkie Beaumont had recently been in touch with Rattigan to tell him that he had talked to the film star Charles Boyer about the possibility of his starring in the play in London and New York. The

French-born romantic star, who had played opposite so many of the
cinema's leading ladies as a 'great lover', had first expressed interest
after coming across the manuscript at a party in New York given for
William Walton and Rattigan, but at that time there was still hope of
Olivier. Boyer, however, had not given up the idea, and shortly after
Rakoff returned to London to prepare for the shooting of *Heart to Heart*
in May 1962, he replaced him as Rattigan's guest.

Rattigan himself had never considered Boyer for the part of Gregor
Antonescu. After both Rex Harrison and Olivier had turned him down,
he had been too downhearted for a time to think of anyone else for
the role, although he had cabled Beaumont in April to suggest Charles
Laughton. 'Surely he will be quite impossible,' came the reply. But
the idea of Boyer did not particularly appeal. And when the two men
met Rattigan was far from confident that one of the screen's great
lovers could actually transform himself into what he saw as the personi-
fication of evil. If *Ross* was a play about a man who tries to be God,
'then this is a play about a man who tries to be the Devil,' Rattigan
maintained. Boyer did not seem in the least dismayed. Indeed the longer
the two men talked the more enthusiastic he became – the reverse of
Rattigan's reaction.

Beaumont was still anxious to capture a star, preferably a movie
star, to help to ensure a box office hit, and pressed Rattigan to accept
that Boyer would be 'ideal for the part', even though he might not be
available for another year. Besides, Boyer, he cajoled, had another
advantage, 'He would be happy to open the play on Broadway.' If
there was to be a run in London it would have to be very short. Boyer
had no wish to spend long away from his adopted home in Hollywood,
especially if his absence would jeopardise the chance of a major film
role. In the past few years Hollywood had not called on Boyer quite
as often as it had once done. Perhaps *Man and Boy* might reverse the
trend. Rattigan told Beaumont he would consider Boyer, but he refused
to commit himself.

Even if he agreed to Boyer, however, there was still the question of
who would direct. He had fired Glen Byam Shaw, and Peter Glenville
had pulled out. Peter Wood had been mentioned, and so had Garson
Kanin, whom Irene Selznick in New York had said was 'very enthusiastic'. Binkie Beaumont would not have Kanin and suggested Elia
Kazan instead, but Kazan had other commitments. The discussions
dragged on.

Still uncertain exactly how he should proceed, but aware that his
year of enforced tax exile was reaching its end, Rattigan returned to
England in July to take up occupation of the new house in Brighton

he had bought at Michael Franklin's urging, which had been decorated for him by Michael Weight. When he arrived, he hated it. 'It's uninhabitable,' he told Freddie Young. 'There isn't a single room I can bear to sit in.' He went back briefly to the flat in Embassy Court, which he also disliked, and then decided to play golf in Scotland. He was restless and depressed.

Back in London, he at least found time to go to the theatre. The fascination he had felt as a boy in the gallery had not deserted him, and he was anxious to see what the new young playwrights were doing. He went to Arnold Wesker's new play, *Chips With Everything*, and to Harold Pinter's hugely successful *The Caretaker*, which he admired greatly. Rattigan liked Pinter; indeed, as he was to tell one American interviewer a few months later, 'he generates excitement in the theatre, an extraordinary achievement when sometimes one isn't at all sure what it's all about'. Not long afterwards, he and Pinter were introduced. 'Feeling rather pleased with myself,' Rattigan later remembered, 'I said, "It's about the Old Testament God and the New Testament God, with the Caretaker as humanity – that's what it's about isn't it?" Pinter said, "It's about two brothers and a caretaker."' But the reply did nothing to damage his enthusiasm for the playwright.

Wesker was another matter. 'I don't believe in commitment,' Rattigan told the *New York Times*. 'I am concerned with people as they are rather than what they stand for. Shakespeare wasn't committed. It's impossible to tell where he stood in the political context of his time.' Rattigan knew that he could not change. 'I am what I am. I cannot deny it, and I certainly won't apologise for it. I write about people I know – just as, for instance, Wesker does. It would be very silly of me to try to write about life in the East End.' What depressed him most was that entertainment seemed to have become a dirty word in the theatre. It was that he cared about most. 'Entertainment is what moves you, whether to laughter or tears. *King Lear* is entertainment. The essential thing is that you care about what's going on every moment.' Rattigan was not sure that he cared about what went on in *Chips With Everything*, but he sensed that Wesker represented the classless future of the English theatre, whereas he and Binkie Beaumont were the class-ridden past. The knowledge only deepened his depression.

While the discussions over *Man and Boy* dragged on through the autumn, it became abundantly clear that Richard Burton was not going to play David Mann in *Heart to Heart* on television. *Cleopatra* was still filming in Rome, and Burton was not certain that he would be free of it in time. It was another blow, and Rattigan took it personally. He had thought that he and Burton were on friendly terms – even though he had fired the now famous star from the London production of *Adventure Story* thirteen years earlier. 'Surely Richard could arrange to get away if he really wanted to?' he complained to Rakoff. But it made no difference. Another actor had to be found, and it was only when Kenneth More agreed to take over the role that Rattigan relaxed. In the meantime, he had also to fight off the BBC's suggestion that the television play should be re-titled *Footnote*. 'Damn ridiculous,' he told Rakoff. 'It sounds like the bottom of the page. The play is meant to be uplifting.' The BBC wilted. *Heart to Heart* the title remained.

By the time of the filming in November 1962, Rattigan's health had deteriorated still further. He caught a string of colds, and then, shortly after *Heart to Heart* was made at BBC Television Centre in West London, he was struck down by jaundice. He managed to attend the first screening of the play, at which Burton and Taylor failed to appear but which Noël Coward graced with his presence, before he was readmitted to the London Clinic on Thursday, 5 December 1962. He watched the final transmission on the television set in his room.

The television critics had none of the reservations of their colleagues in the theatre. In the *Daily Herald* Dennis Potter, then on the brink of his own career as a television playwright, called the two-hour play 'well produced and compellingly acted' and with 'just that sense of occasion, that weight of impact, which the little screen so rarely provides'; while in the *Daily Express* Herbert Kretzmer insisted 'it might have sprung white-hot, from John Osborne's typewriter or Mr Wesker's tormented belly, so deadly is its questioning of the moral values of our time . . . Triumphant play. A triumphant evening.' It was some consolation at the end of a terrible year.

Not that there were too many financial worries. Shortly before this he agreed to do another screenplay for Tolly and MGM. It was partly their idea, and Rattigan had no particular emotional commitment to it, but it represented a convenient way of making a large sum of money quickly. The studio were offering a total of $125,000. And just as *The VIPs* had been a variation on the theme of *Grand Hotel*, so now the new idea was a variant on *Bond Street*, which he and Rodney Ackland had worked on with Tolly just after the war. This time, instead of a bride's trousseau, the story would focus on the adventures of a Rolls-Royce. The idea had partly come from a discovery de Grunwald and Puffin had made on their ill-fated trip to discover locations for Lawrence. They had come across General Allenby's car in a garage, dusty, smeared with grime, but unmistakably a Rolls-Royce. The idea was to trace the life of a car like that – and to relate what happened to its owners. In the draft outline to his screenplay, Rattigan described the old, neglected yellow Rolls-Royce as 'like a dowager after one too many martinis at a garden party . . . to her mockers she may just be an expendable piece of junk. To herself she is still a Rolls-Royce.'

By the time he was finally allowed to leave the London Clinic, shortly before Christmas, he was unfortunately not up to working. Instead, to recuperate and 'to escape the damp of the English winter', he asked Michael Weight to book them both on a cruise to Hong Kong. From there they would cross the Pacific to Hollywood, call on MGM, and then travel across the United States, first to New York to talk to Harold Freedman about *Man and Boy*, and then back to Noël Coward in Jamaica. On the way he intended to work on *The Yellow Rolls-Royce*.

The trip seemed to succeed. By the time he returned to Europe in March 1963, he was ready to deliver the first draft of the new screenplay to MGM, and over the next six weeks he worked on two further drafts. Like *Bond Street*, the new film was to have four separate stories – although, like its predecessor, it would eventually be cut down to three. It was, he explained in a foreword to the screenplay, 'a story about a thing . . . and I must make it plain, at the outset, that the thing should be made to seem as important as any of the people who own it, or are carried in it . . . In fact, more important . . . The car must have life, and its life is the film. Also its death. When it plunges to destruction in the last shot of the film it should affect us as much as if a much loved character had died. If not, it will be the film that will die.' The explanation was partly to convince himself that he had not changed his view that 'a play should be about people and not about things'. This time the car was a person.

Rattigan's reputation as a screenwriter was increasing rapidly. *The VIPs* was due to be released in the autumn to coincide with Twentieth Century-Fox's release of *Cleopatra*, MGM having calculated that while there was an audience who – after all their publicity – actually wanted to see Elizabeth Taylor and Richard Burton in a film together, some might find the four hours of *Cleopatra* too long. They were to be proved triumphantly right, and Rattigan's stock rose higher still. Harold Freedman began to get even more calls from Hollywood asking what his client might like to write next. He had sold the film rights in *Heart to Heart* for $40,000, and both an American producer and Binkie Beaumont had approached Rattigan to turn it into a stage play. Freedman had even received a suggestion that Rattigan should write another musical, though this time not one based on his own work. Ray Stark, a former agent recently turned film producer, was anxious to follow the success of his Broadway show *Funny Girl* with another hit.

What Stark had in mind was a musical about the ballet. And he had already approached Michel Legrand to write the music and Herbert Ross to choreograph and direct. All Rattigan had to do was to come up with a suitable story. The success of *Funny Girl* and of Stark's first film, *The World of Suzie Wong*, had already helped to make him one of the most powerful American producers, able to pay the highest fees. Rattigan accepted the challenge. He was confident he knew enough about the ballet – after all, Frederick Ashton had been a friend for years and could always advise him – and it was a marvellous opportunity.

But before he could start work on the new project Rattigan was felled by further ill-health, starting with headaches in the first weeks of the summer. Friends such as Robin Maugham, who was staying on Ischia at the time, at first dismissed this simply as 'Terry's hypochondria', but the pain grew steadily worse, his temperature shot up and down and he felt perpetually exhausted. Hypochondriac or not, he had already had three bad years. Now, at the beginning of June 1963, Rattigan had lost a stone in weight, found difficulty eating, and was gasping for breath. He struggled home to England to see his own doctor, William Buky, who knew exactly what his patient was thinking.

Rattigan told his friends that he seemed to have some sort of 'blood condition', which the doctors 'are trying desperately to diagnose', but Margaret Leighton for one had her own ideas about what was the matter with him. She had watched Kay Kendall die of leukaemia and jumped to the conclusion that Rattigan had contracted the same disease. In fact only one of the ten different specialists Rattigan consulted was prepared to say definitely that he was suffering from leukaemia. As Rattigan told Irene Selznick in a letter in July: 'Only Bodley Scott of ten doctors is prepared to say definitely it is. I know his reputation, but some of the others have reputations too – notably Lord Evans – and the majority verdict, with a negative sternum test is still only "suspect", "not to be excluded", "too early for any positive diagnosis" etc., etc.' Emergency cortisone treatment had improved his blood count, and 'I feel much better,' he told her. Above all he was determined not to say too much to his mother. Vera must think it was just another viral infection. He returned to Ischia, where she was to join him for her summer holiday.

Once he had recovered from what he later called 'the alarming discovery that I am mortal', Rattigan decided to give a series of interviews. If he was to die, and to die more quickly than he had expected, he did not intend to be forgotten. Nor did he intend to allow Osborne and

Wesker to have things all their own way. He began his campaign by returning to Aunt Edna. He had, he explained in a piece for the *Daily Telegraph*, all but decided to kill her off in the preface to the third volume of his collected plays, which Hamish Hamilton had been delaying to coincide with the production of *Man and Boy*.

'It has more to do with my concern over the unhappy thought that of all the characters I have created during the last twenty years the only one who seems certain to outlive me is Aunt Edna,' he wrote. 'But I fear that even her creator won't be able to destroy her. Ten years ago I said she was immortal, and that is just what I am afraid the old girl is. And that is sad for my hopes of being accepted by the post Osborne generation as a dramatist of serious intentions.'

Two weeks later he returned to the theme in the *Daily Express*. 'I am an unfashionable word,' he declared.

> Most unfashionable. Oh, I've learned to live with that. That doesn't matter so much. Except, you see, I'd love to be taken a little more seriously by the critics. It is still assumed by some critics that I am still writing to lift the hearts of those Aunt Ednas of mine. I have tried to keep pace. Yet continually I am reading articles about the need to demolish the old theatre – and blow up Coward and Rattigan. I tell you, I don't dig that at all. I can't write a bit like Osborne and Wesker. I can't because you see I've grown up . . . The truth is anger isn't so becoming in a middle-aged playwright.

The following week rehearsals finally began in London for *Man and Boy*. Before its two week try-out in Brighton in August 1963, Rattigan emphasised to Michael Benthall, who had finally been chosen as its director, and to Charles Boyer, that he had always meant the play 'to be about the rejection of proffered and needed love'. He wanted Gregor Antonescu, Devil though he might be, to demonstrate to the audience how much he still craved the love of his son. 'It never occurred to Gregor that his son could possibly grow up and become his conscience.' As the opening approached he became more and more preoccupied, more and more desperate, more and more fearful.

Rattigan was desperate not to lose the emotional shape of *Man and Boy*. As his notes to himself reveal, his intentions were clear:

> Act One: revelation to the audience that boy, despite protestations to the contrary, loves man. Act Two: revelation to the audience that man, despite his brutal treatment of his son, loves boy . . .
> Act Three: Final and irrevocable rejection by Man of Boy, without

letting the boy know of his own need and his own love. Gregor's last victory in fact. A barren one, but at least he remains true to his own inhumanity, and succeeds in dying as he lived.

The Lord Chamberlain's office presented few difficulties. Even though the story of the financier was plainly based in part on the life and career of the Swedish match tycoon Ivar Kreuger, whose fall marked the climax of the 'Great Depression', this time there was no suggestion that the relatives should be appeased. Rattigan's plays as a whole were 'emotional, but with a faint chill', noted the Lord Chamberlain's reader, but his only objection was to the use of 'Jesus'. The author suggested 'Geepers', which was agreed.

But Rattigan was still fretting – haunting the rehearsals, supervising the sets, tinkering with the dialogue, fussing about the curtain lines. The more he fussed, the more he unnerved Michael Benthall and the more Charles Boyer seemed to distance himself from the fray. He was trying too hard. To Beaumont's astonishment, he was even planning to write to every critic in the national press to explain the play's intentions and his argument.

By the time the play opened at the Theatre Royal, Brighton, Rattigan could hardly contain himself. Instead of retiring from the theatre for a drink once the performance had begun, and returning to see the curtain fall, he took to pacing the back of the stalls, watching every movement, every exit, to see whether it worked for the audience. Each morning he would give a whole series of fresh notes and instructions to Michael Benthall, and then retire to brood over whether or not they would work. It was abundantly clear to everyone around him that to Terence Rattigan, 'dramatist', the night of 4 September 1963, when the play would transfer to the Queen's Theatre in Shaftesbury Avenue, had assumed an importance greater than any other in his career. It might even be the last first night he would ever attend.

CHAPTER 24

The Twilight of Aunt Edna

◆

*Each blade of grass has its spot on earth whence it
draws its life, its strength; and so is man rooted to
the land from which he draws his faith together
with his life.*

JOSEPH CONRAD, *Lord Jim*

◆

The Queen's Theatre in Shaftesbury Avenue did not hold the happiest
memories for Rattigan. It was the scene of his last first night, three
years before, when the gallery had booed *Joie de Vivre* off the stage.
Though he did his best to hide it, the theatre itself made him edgy.
Even his familiar routine of a haircut, meeting his mother for supper
before the show, and making sure she had the famous champagne cork
safely in her handbag did not entirely settle his nerves. As they walked
into the theatre, past the assembled photographers, Vera Rattigan could
sense the tension in her son. His laughter was just a little forced, his
mannered gaiety a shade too self-conscious.

The Queen's Theatre was not the only cause of Rattigan's nervousness. He had also neglected to tell his mother that the specialists could
not agree whether he was suffering from leukaemia or from a 'series
of viral disorders which demonstrate similar symptoms to leukaemia';
nor was she aware that he had taken the unprecedented step of actually
writing to one or two of the critics to explain the intentions of his new
play. All Vera Rattigan knew for certain, as she settled into her box at
the Queen's on 4 September 1963, was that the programme on her
knee announced *Man and Boy* as 'A New Play by Terence Rattigan',
and that the author was 'indebted to Robert Shaplen for suggestions

contained in Mr Shaplen's book 'Kreuger, Genius and Swindler', parts of which originally appeared in the *New Yorker* magazine'. Her son had told her that Gregor was 'loosely' based on the Swedish tycoon, but – as the programme in front of her also noted – 'the characters attributed to the individuals represented are based on the author's imagination and are not necessarily factual'. It was almost exactly the same disclaimer that had appeared in the programme of *The Winslow Boy*.

After the curtain went up to reveal a two-room basement apartment in Greenwich Village, New York, on a July evening in 1934, Rattigan slipped out of the box and went upstairs to the bar. He had three large whiskies, one after another. There was nothing he could do to change the play now. Boyer had written to him the day before to say, 'Whatever happens tomorrow night I want you to know how thrilled and proud I am to portray your Gregor in your magnificent play,' and Beaumont had been equally encouraging; but Rattigan was not sure. He was still not certain that Boyer would make Gregor Antonescu as evil as he had always intended him to be. Part of him still longed to be watching Rex Harrison in the part he had written for him. Besides, there had been so many obstacles along the way, so many directors, so many actors, so many disappointments and disagreements, that *Man and Boy* seemed somehow jinxed.

The direction was another cause for concern, another reason for another whisky. Rattigan missed Peter Glenville desperately. Michael Benthall was good, but he did not have Glenville's touch, and they had never worked together before. He was also worried that Austin Willis would not be able to bring Mark Herries, Gregor's homosexual business rival and the man who could ensure his ruin, properly to life. He realised that the play was only being tried out in London before the more serious business of the Broadway opening, which Alexander Cohen had planned for November, but it was here on Shaftesbury Avenue that his reputation had been born, and it was here that Rattigan wanted it restored.

Man and Boy was to have been his masterpiece, the final proof that he had earned his place as a serious English playwright, more than a mere 'polished craftsman'. And he had returned to the theme that inspired so much of his work, the relationship between father and son, this time extending it still further. When the fugitive financier Gregor Antonescu turns up at his son Basil Anthony's apartment in Greenwich Village, the two have been estranged for five years. But for all that, Gregor is able to persuade the boy to allow him to use his rooms for what he thinks will be a crucial meeting, to encourage him to dress up to appeal to the homosexual Herries, and, even more – though at first Basil Anthony fails to realise this – to ensnare his rival by leading him to believe that the boy is his lover rather than his son.

GREGOR: Well, dear boy – now a rather decisive meeting, perhaps the most decisive of my life. (*He smiles*) As a good socialist I know you must hope it fails. As my son, it would help me to have your blessing.
BASIL: You have my blessing, Father.
GREGOR: Thank you, chéri. Come in only when I open the door. Oh – and better not call me Father. Our friend is a little – straitlaced about such things.
BASIL: Yes, Father.
GREGOR: So you remain Basil Anthony. Right.
BASIL: Right.

In Act Two Antonescu springs the trap, by insinuating to Herries that Basil might be available to him. At this point the boy grasps the truth of what is happening, but, not willing to see his father ruined, agrees to give his telephone number to Herries. He barely utters another word to his father for the remainder of the act, beyond saying:

BASIL: (*At length, and with quiet intensity*) You are nothing. You live and breathe and have being and you are my father – but you are nothing.

With that he storms out of the apartment, thereby giving Gregor's business assistant, Sven Johnson, his cue to ask him why he tries to make his son hate him.

GREGOR: . . . It shouldn't have been a son, of course. That's obvious. I think I could have endured a daughter loving me – Yes. A girl might have been different. But I doubt it. (*After a pause of intense concentration*) It was all right when Vassily was a child. Even more than all right, remember?
SVEN: Very clearly.
GREGOR: I suppose I felt I could have let him love me then without danger.
SVEN: What danger?
GREGOR: Danger to me, to my way of life, to my universe. The whole world can hero-worship me, and some of it does, and there is no danger. But to be loved and worshipped by one's own boy – and by this boy above all . . . Oh, no. No, I will take almost any risk – you know that, Sven – but not the risk of being so close to the pure in heart. 'And virtue entered into him' – isn't that from the Bible?
SVEN: The New Testament.

GREGOR: I prefer the Old. Yes. Then here's your answer. It's perfectly clear. It shouldn't have taken me so long to see it. If I wanted to make my son hate me instead of loving me it's because I can, at least, understand hatred. I don't feel it, for anyone or anything, but I can understand it, and even relish it. And surely a good father should always try to understand his own son.

When the curtain fell, a few moments later, on this tense second act, it did so to a ripple of subdued applause. Rattigan heard it from the back of his mother's box, where he was standing almost hidden by the curtains.

Act Three introduced a theme even more insistent in his work – the inability of men and women to accept love, with the introduction of Gregor's second wife, and Basil Anthony's stepmother, Countess Antonescu. Rattigan's note to himself, written while he was drafting the play, read: 'Was a typist. Made pass at her. She gave way, then refused. Nothing short of money, title etc. He fell for it. (His only moment of human weakness, regretted at once.) In a sense Florence is still being punished for having once nearly made him love her.'

While the Countess is trying to explain that she loves her husband, she is interrupted by the return of Basil carrying newspapers with the headlines announcing Antonescu's imminent arrest by the FBI, and that the Bank of the City of London has brought an action against him which has nothing to do with his plots against Mark Herries. When Antonescu hears the news he suffers a slight stroke. His son offers to smuggle him to his girlfriend's apartment, but Gregor refuses and instead asks Sven to find him a revolver. Once more, he rejects his son's offer to help him, and his son's love.

GREGOR: Dear God, what a boy! Isn't there anything I can do to kill it?
BASIL: No. Not anything. But why do you have to try?
GREGOR: I don't know. (*Shrugging*) Perhaps, because – having had to live all my life without a conscience – it would be rather – unmanly – to acquire one now, don't you think? Go and return that two-seater to its owner.
    Pause.
BASIL: (*Desperately*) Isn't there any way – isn't there any way at all, Father, I can be of use to you at this moment?
GREGOR: No. (*Gravely looking at him*) I wish there were.

The play ends with the financier, revolver in pocket and suicide note written, listening to the radio news. 'Wherever he may be tonight . . . it is certain that this suave, cool, elegant and utterly charming personality is showing the same unruffled front that he has always shown to the world, through every crisis that has beset him,' the announcer intones. 'Is it not truer to say . . . that to be absolutely powerful a man must first corrupt *himself* absolutely.'

But Gregor Antonescu does not kill himself, just as Hester Collyer does not kill herself at the end of *The Deep Blue Sea*. As the curtain falls, he 'goes to the front door, switching off the lights there'. The cheering that had greeted so many Rattigan first nights was replaced by a gentler murmur of appreciation. Next morning, the verdicts were mixed.

Herbert Kretzmer, in the *Daily Express*, disliked it. 'Mr Boyer apart, the play is a great disappointment. Without its star, it would be revealed as a superior and extremely glib melodrama that has been given such a high gloss and polish that audiences here and on Broadway, where it opens in November, may well be tricked into believing that it actually has something profound to say.' David Nathan in the *Daily Herald* agreed: 'The next time 'disgusted' writes to complain that our young playwrights are obsessed with squalor and homosexuality and cites Terence Rattigan as the preserver of all the traditional values, I will recount the plot of *Man and Boy*.' And Nathan concluded: 'The whole play in fact seems false and hollow with much more profundity intended and none achieved . . . The play is here for only eight and a half weeks before going to New York. New York is very welcome to it.'

Bernard Levin, however, totally disagreed, calling *Man and Boy* 'Mr Rattigan's best play, and one of the most fascinating pieces of theatre to have come our way for many years'. The sometimes brutal Levin waxed lyrical about its author's strengths.

His dialogue, apart from a few touches of glibness; his unfailing dramatic cunning; his narrative power, faultless in its patient unwinding; above all his restless imaginative curiosity about the springs of human activity; these fuse, hot and glowing, into his finest work, and a play that outdistances all but a handful of authors writing in English today.

Cuthbert Worsley in the *Financial Times* supported Levin whole-heartedly.

The art of Terence Rattigan's theatre consists in crystallising in a bare one or two hours the character patterns that shape a personality; and his deceptively simple (because so engrossing) narrative epitomises the attitudes of a lifetime and the relationships that spring from them. Thus the subject of his new play . . . is not the last hours of a financial swindler of the thirties, trying to bring off a final coup, failing, and walking bravely out to his death. Its subject is humiliation, which has indeed been the subject of all Mr Rattigan's serious plays.

But in spite of Levin and Worsley, Rattigan's conclusion was that *Man and Boy* had failed. Neither the new audience relishing Bill Naughton's play *Alfie* at the Duchess, nor the one packing the stage version of C.P.Snow's novel *The Masters* at the Savoy would – according to most of the other critics – like the play. He was deeply disappointed – 'as much disappointed by the reviews for *Man and Boy*,' Freddie Young remembers, 'as he had been about *Variation on a Theme*.' Rattigan was convinced the English critics would never give him a fair chance. The only hope was Broadway.

Man and Boy closed after its scheduled run of eight and a half weeks and sixty-nine performances, but none of the company left the theatre with a spring in their step. Everyone felt deflated. And, inevitably, the recriminations started. Michael Benthall wrote from France that 'the accent of the play is in the wrong place', and Alexander Cohen sent four pages of notes and suggestions for changes that might be made before the opening in New York. Rattigan himself wrote to Beaumont to complain:

> The play I wrote two years ago has not been directed – it has been staged. I am grateful enough . . . but now we must just see it is directed – a term which includes re-writing, re-fashioning and re-casting. It doesn't necessarily mean a new director. I have never said that, and I never will unless you say it to me. The only person who has said it is Michael himself, on the telephone before he left, suggesting Peter Glenville.

After a pause, Rattigan had found himself laughing – he had always wanted Glenville.

Throughout the next four weeks the company fought to save what its author still just hoped would be his 'one great play'. There were amendments to the script, and to the staging, changes in the direction of the performances, and encouragements to each and every member of the cast, all but one of whom – Alice Kennedy Turney, who played Basil Anthony's girlfriend Carol – was to travel to Broadway. Glen Byam Shaw was even asked privately if he would be prepared to help with the transfer. In spite of being fired as the play's director two years earlier by Rattigan himself, he agreed. A delighted playwright told his star, 'So please keep your spirits high. Blucher is on the way to the battlefield – though perhaps Waterloo isn't the most tactful example to give to a Frenchman, come to think of it. Forgive my Englishness.'

Shouldering all the responsibility for the changes, Rattigan kept up the pressure. Boyer was co-operative, and looking forward to New York, but some members of the cast were more apprehensive. Austin Willis's performance as Herries was still giving Rattigan concern, and he even asked Boyer if he could give the British actor 'guidance'. 'Heaven knows he's getting little enough now,' he told his star.

When *Man and Boy* opened at the Brooks Atkinson Theatre on 12 November 1963, Rattigan's hopes were finally dashed. In the *New York Times* Howard Taubman wrote its epitaph. The play qualified 'as entertainment', but 'do not expect a great deal more than modest entertainment' even though 'given its premise you are entitled to expect something more'. The best he could say was that 'Mr Rattigan apparently has chosen to settle for what he can do so well. He has told a story built around believable people.'

The new weekly paper *Village Voice* chose to contrast him with Brecht – as Brecht's play, *The Resistible Rise of Arturo Ui*, had just closed. The comparison did not favour Rattigan. 'Mr Rattigan is writing not for the ages but for the middle class. His aim is not to change the world but to provide some brief diversion from it – and perchance a little insight.' *Newsday* was even less flattering, calling it 'a battering bore'.

By coincidence, while *Man and Boy* was limping along at the Brooks Atkinson, *The Girl Who Came to Supper*, the musical based on his play *The Sleeping Prince*, with lyrics by Noël Coward and a script by Harry Kurnitz, opened at the nearby Broadway Theatre. The show was to survive well into 1964, for a total of 113 performances. To Rattigan's irritation, a number of critics specifically remarked on how much Kurnitz had improved on his original. The only consolation was that he was on 2 per cent of the gross weekly takings at the box office.

Man and Boy closed before Christmas, after just fifty-four performances. The only British theatrical entertainment the New York audience seemed to want was a revue being performed only a few hundred yards away called *Beyond the Fringe*. It was to be eleven years before another new Rattigan play would be presented on Broadway, while *Man and Boy* became the only one of his plays never to be revived either in London or in New York in the years to come. His ambition to write one 'great play' had failed. As Rattigan set off back across the Atlantic, he doubted whether he would ever write a play again.

★   ★   ★

In the weeks after the closure of *Man and Boy* in New York, Rattigan busied himself with the final amendments to the preface for his third volume of collected plays. He had delayed the volume specifically so that *Man and Boy* could be included, to demonstrate to the sceptics that he was prepared to offend Aunt Edna. He had even told Roger Machell that his 'nice respectable, middle-class, middle-aged maiden lady with time on her hands' was about to meet her 'lethal end'. But when it came to the point he could not bring himself to murder the 'hopeless, lowbrow' lady in the stalls.

Instead he chose to defend her against his own charge that she was both hopeless and lowbrow. 'The image I gave to Aunt Edna in 1953,' he wrote in a preface that he structured as a libel case – with himself as the defendant – 'applied – I want to be quite honest – far more truthfully to the nineteen-thirties than to the nineteen-sixties. In fact, in writing the passage in question, I was guilty of looking back rather than of looking forward.' The drama of the thirties had lasted well into the nineteen-fifties, he explained, and that was how the confusion had come about.

It was now 1964, and Aunt Edna had become a classless, no longer middle-aged, 'most-likely Liberal' voter, who was also 'a lady of some sexual experience, either practised or imagined'. She went to Osborne and Wesker, and enjoyed Pinter, Ionescu and Beckett, even though she sometimes found them mystifying. 'Aunt Edna enjoys being mystified, but she loathes being baffled', and she was certainly not a lowbrow. 'Browless' was what she should properly now be called, 'a part of the majority audience for which true theatre exists, and has always existed'.

While updating Aunt Edna, Rattigan also attempted to defend himself against the charges that had piled up against him over the past seven years. Specifically, he sought to dismiss the two that hurt most, the first that he was simply a 'playwright of the thirties'; the second that he was linked in some way to Noël Coward. Only two of his plays had been produced in the thirties, he wrote defensively, and Coward was not only twelve years his senior but had also had his first play produced sixteen years before the first of Rattigan's own.

He ended his preface by reverting to Aunt Edna, the woman he called his most famous character – and the cause of so much trouble to him since he had first let her loose.

Aunt Edna remains Aunt Edna, with only two basic demands of the theatre – first, that it excite her to laugh or to cry or to wonder what is going to happen next; and second, that she can suspend her disbelief willingly and without effort. It's only Aunt Edna's emotions that a playwright can hope to excite, because we know for sure that she does bring those to the theatre . . . She is unchanging and unchangeable, immortal and everlasting, and all, she ever brings to the theatre is her undying love for it. Long live Aunt Edna! Long live the theatre! For the two are one and the same.

While Rattigan was telling the theatre critics what he thought of them, the cinema provided some consolation. *The VIPs* had opened to remarkable notices, and excellent business, in both London and New York. Unlike his colleague Howard Taubman – who had returned to the attack on *Man and Boy* for a second time shortly before it closed, calling it 'slick, superficial entertainment' – the *New York Times*'s film critic, Bosley Crowther, applauded *The VIPs* as 'a lively, engrossing, romantic film cut in the always serviceable pattern of the old multi-character *Grand Hotel*'. *Variety* called his script 'literate, witty and sometimes touching'.

As Rattigan suspected they might, the film critics in England took a very different line. And the fact that *The VIPs* was to become Metro-Goldwyn-Mayer's most commercially successful film of 1963, and helped to establish him as one of the highest paid screenwriters in the world, only made them more irate. The *Sunday Telegraph* dismissed it as 'well-written tosh', while the novelist Brigid Brophy, writing in the *New Statesman*, called it 'a super packaged box of chocolates' which was 'licking the boots of money and rank'.

Rattigan's riposte was to invite one of his most outspoken attackers, Alexander Walker of the London *Evening Standard*, to come and see him. He proceeded to spell out in the course of an interview how upset he felt at the perpetual insistence in Britain that he was 'glib' or 'insincere', and that his work was 'unfelt'. He told Walker exactly how painful it was to be accused of having 'a cliché-ridden mind' and how he had come to dread the word 'craftsmanship', whenever it was applied to his work, because of the insinuation that he was merely being 'slick'.

The outburst made him feel better, but only temporarily. His confidence was failing. Long bouts of solitude, punctuated with morbid telephone calls to his few friends, now replaced the jolly weekends at Little Court. His old friends saw less of him. He left London, stopping in Paris for what he called 'the odd adventure' and then going on to Cannes to gamble. His physical health seemed to improve, but his mental health did not. 'It was as if someone had switched the light off,' one friend recalled. 'Terry only seemed to flower when he was a success as a playwright. Once that had gone, nothing seemed to matter so much any more.'

Mary Herring, who had been his secretary since the week before *The Winslow Boy* had opened at the Lyric in May 1946, watched Rattigan's slow decline. He no longer seemed the man she once knew. Finally, not long after his return from New York, she telephoned him in Paris and told him that she was leaving. 'You'd better write me a letter about it,' was his reply. When she did so, the man she had served unstintingly for seventeen years never once asked her to change her mind. It was as if he were intent on cutting himself off from everyone around him, determined to prove that he did not need the support or friendship of anyone.

Nor was his work much consolation. Only the fees he could command for his screenplays cheered him up. He hired a new secretary, Sheila Dyatt, who had once worked for Stephen Mitchell and more recently for Binkie Beaumont at Tennents. She found him aloof, the chill that had always been part of his nature accentuated now as the sense of disillusion increased. He took to working more and more at night rather than during the day, retiring to bed with a notebook, sleeping late in the morning, and appearing just before lunch with a few pages for her to type.

At the weekends, when in England, he would entertain in Brighton, but the relaxed atmosphere of golf at Sunningdale was a thing of the past. Rattigan had almost given up the game because 'he could no longer go on improving', according to one golfing partner. 'He could not bear just being average.' And now the jollity was more forced. As Sheila Dyatt remembered later, he seemed surrounded by 'lots of people who liked him, but no one who really cared for him'. Vera would telephone from time to time, but Brighton was too far for her to travel – she was nearly eighty – and, in any case, he preferred to keep it for his homosexual friends. Cuthbert Worsley was, as always, a regular visitor, as were Billy Chappell and Frederick Ashton, and the Midget was usually in evidence. The flat in Embassy Court, Hove, had been rented for his use, so that Rattigan could continue to maintain the illusion that he was a bachelor living alone. No matter who was there, however, the spirit was backward-looking, full of memories of past glories rather than a celebration of the present.

The one bright spot was his physical health. In spite of some of the gloomy prognoses of the specialists he had consulted the previous spring, he did not appear to have leukaemia after all. He was a little more lethargic than formerly and unable to work long days – even if he had the inclination to do so – but the death sentence had been lifted, temporarily at least. Nevertheless his strain of hypochondria, the conviction that he was living on borrowed time, seemed to increase.

By the spring of 1964 he had recovered sufficiently to tell his mother how worried he had been; and to give an interview to the *Daily Mirror* admitting that he had been given 'only six months' to live. 'I'd use my illness ruthlessly as an excuse for not going out and not doing what I didn't want to do.' Illness, he added, was 'an excellent excuse, especially when you can back it up, as I did, with looking ghastly and losing a stone in weight'. What he did not reveal was his depression.

Shortly afterwards, he was taken to see the first work of a new young playwright called Joe Orton. *Entertaining Mr Sloane* had just opened at the Arts Theatre Club, and Rattigan was invited to meet the playwright with a view to his investing in the play. He had invested before, usually with financially disastrous results – in 1958, for example, he had lost more than £2,500 on a play called *Tabitha* by the actor Arnold Ridley – but the experience had not totally put him off. Besides, Rattigan admired Orton's play. He liked its author even more.

Orton was flattered by the attention he received from one of England's most renowned playwrights, as he confided in his friend and lover Kenneth Halliwell and their mutual friend, the comic actor Kenneth Williams. The two men's attraction for one another was to last for more than a year, until Rattigan offered to take Orton on holiday – on condition that he left Halliwell behind, a suggestion that Orton refused. As a result their friendship began to fade, although Rattigan remained an investor in Orton's plays, even persuading Vivien Leigh to join him in backing the young playwright's second success, *Loot*.

Shooting of *The Yellow Rolls-Royce* was due to begin at the MGM studios in May. Rattigan had wanted Ralph Richardson for the part of the Marquess of Frinton, but now, ironically, Rex Harrison volunteered to do it. The man who had not been prepared to risk being thought of as a 'member of the brotherhood of buggers' was quite happy to become a cuckolded husband in a Rattigan comedy for MGM, where money and prestige were involved. De Grunwald and Asquith intended to repeat the formula they had employed for *The VIPs* and collect a major group of stars to appear in the supporting roles. The French actress Jeanne Moreau was to play an English marchioness, the French actor Alain Delon and the American star George C. Scott were to play Italians; the Swedish-born Ingrid Bergman was to play an American and the Egyptian Omar Sharif a Yugoslav. Rattigan stayed away from the set.

Nevertheless, he did attend Tolly de Grunwald's elaborately glamorous charity première on 31 December, together with Rex Harrison, and enjoyed his brief return to celebrity as the flashbulbs went off in Leicester Square. Three mornings later, the pleasure turned to ashes.

Rattigan woke up to find himself once again the target for a bitter attack from Kenneth Tynan, who, having become literary manager of the new National Theatre under Laurence Olivier's direction, had switched roles on the *Observer* from drama critic to film reviewer. His piece was unusually vicious. 'There is a smiling, gracious staleness about *The Yellow Rolls-Royce* that gives it the air of some long forgotten ceremonial occasion . . . The stately blandness of its manner is quite at odds with the fusty triviality of what it has to offer: it condescends from a great depth,' his review began. Its three stories 'have two common factors: sentimentality and an expensive motor car, gaudily painted . . . This kind of Rattiganesque Runyonesque dialogue would shrivel the tongue of any self-respecting American actor who tried to speak it.'

Rattigan was incensed. On Sunday morning, 3 January 1965, he fired off a telegram to Tynan: 'Larry and others who have read your notice tell me I should not answer critics however bilious their criticism, how obvious there [*sic*] envy . . . but I do intend to answer yours.' Tynan sent no reply. Rattigan followed with two more letters, this time suggesting that he was considering legal action for defamation.

Rattigan was convinced that personal animosity lay behind Tynan's attacks, which he suspected was based on the critic's intense dislike of homosexuals. Cuthbert Worsley shared this view and had implied as much in his defence of Rattigan in the *London Magazine* two months earlier. Finally, at the end of January, Tynan replied. 'I've never in my critical career written a line that was consciously motivated by personal animus. I agree that my review was both charmless and graceless. Alas, as I get more silvery round the temples, I find myself setting less and less store by charm and grace "when honour's at stake" . . . I can't imagine why you should think me envious of you.'

On 13 February Rattigan wrote back from Brighton:

Of course I don't blame you for disliking the film. If you had ever asked me what I felt about the finished product, I might have had to ponder a bit . . . Which brings me to the only remaining point – but much the most important one, because it involves all the charges I made against you of spleen and personal bias, because it covers the whole question of fair and unfair criticism, because, in short, it is my whole case against you. It's this. Why pick on me?

He could only conclude, he added, 'that Cuthbert Worsley's accusations against you (and others) of personal bias against me . . . were fully justified. It seemed so, too, to most of my friends, and to neutrals that your notice – the first to appear about me since Cuthbert's attack was launched – seemed at best a very unconvincing denial of personal malice.' His bitterness could not be disguised.

> On the basis of my last three efforts at serious play-writing, you appear to have written me off in that field altogether (*The Deep Blue Sea* was thirteen years ago). To you (and some others) I have become, as a dramatist, a dirty, ex-Shaftesbury Avenue word. Not even as succcessful as I once was. Well, I haven't complained – at least not to you. I accept your right to that opinion. I don't agree with it, of course, and shall try again. Meanwhile I keep a roof over my head and a 'Phantom Five' under my bottom by writing for Hollywood, helping them – so far with success – to churn out their money-spinning glossies. (The question of conscience doesn't arise. I haven't got one, according to you.) But to be taken as a dirty word in that context seemed to me – and still seems – unfair and abusive. Also defamatory.

The two men bickered by letter and telegram in the months to come, Rattigan calling one Tynan review bad, sad and rather mad, and Tynan demanding he withdraw the word mad. On the point of leaving Britain for Hollywood in early April, Rattigan wrote his last words, denying that 'I think that you personally are a madman. Or that you, personally, are a bad man. Or even a particularly sad man. Just, in this particular instance (and one or two others) a misguided man.'

Whatever his hurt, Rattigan had lost his head and his sense of proportion, writing overwrought letters to an opponent who would probably only snigger at them. Subsequently he probably thought – as many others of his class and position were accustomed to think at the time – that success and wealth should command a certain 'respect'. To attack so impudently was simply not the done thing. 'Isn't it slightly a question of manners?' he challenged Tyan in another letter, written on board a Pan American jet-liner flying over the North Pole. 'Or do you deny their existence?' He even boasted that the success of *The Yellow Rolls-Royce* had made him 'the highest paid screenwriter in the world'. It was hardly the way to impress an egalitarian. Indignation was the worst way to deal with this particular adversary, and if ever proof was needed of the soundness of the old adage, 'Never reply to a bad review', Rattigan's intemperate attempts at self-justification supplied it to the hilt. His defensiveness meant that he remained sublimely unconscious of the fact.

Like a dog with a stick, Rattigan had taken to shaking Tynan obsessively whenever the opportunity presented itself, without questioning whether there was the slightest point in the exercise. The reality was that Tynan's position at the National Theatre, and his influence over a generation of theatregoers and critics, ensured that it was his voice, not Rattigan's, that would be listened to. But that hardly mattered.

Before the row started, indeed while the filming of *The Yellow Rolls-Royce* was only just getting under way, plenty of offers were coming in for Rattigan's consideration. Projects were milling about in his mind. Suggestions had been made that he might consider writing a script about the life of Lord Baden-Powell, the founder of the Boy Scout movement, as well as a film about the Duke of Windsor, whose abdication from the British throne still fascinated millions. But somehow they were hard to concentrate on. The money was attractive, but the subtlety and delicacy that he had always brought to his work had deserted him. His friends noticed this. There was a bluntness in his style that had not been there in the past, a desire to get the job of writing over with quickly. The facility remained, but the heart had gone out of him.

Rattigan had latched on to his money-spinning role. Part of him believed that it was all that was left for him, as he wallowed in his private despair. Besides, how otherwise could he afford his own Rolls-Royce, with its personalised numberplate, TR100, and his extravagant lifestyle? If he was called a 'slick craftsman', why should he care? It was a pretence, the same pretence that he had used to conceal his own shyness and uncertainty, the same pretence that he had used to hide his fragile confidence for so many years. He hid behind his carefully practised façade, the wealthy English gentleman.

Yet another part of him recognised that that too was not the whole truth, that he lacked the natural confidence of an English aristocrat. No matter how assured Rattigan may have appeared, he privately longed for real respect, for acceptance in the heart of the British establishment. Perhaps this, more than anything else, persuaded him to write a television play which was to be introduced by the Duke of Edinburgh. Lew Grade, the agent turned television tycoon, and chief executive of Associated Television, had offered him a deal to broadcast two of his stage plays, *Variation on a Theme* and *The Browning Version*, if he would also write a new play for television. Part of the proceeds from worldwide sales would go to the Duke of Edinburgh's Award Scheme for young people and part to another charity of the Duke's choice, a fund to save the sailing ship *Cutty Sark*. At a meeting at Buckingham Palace, Rattigan tentatively mentioned his idea of writing a play about Nelson, but 'I can't write about anybody for whom I can't feel compassion,' he explained. 'I prefer failures.' It was the Duke who pointed out that Nelson too had had a striking failure. He had failed to persuade the British public, and his friends, to accept his mistress Emma Hamilton.

'I thought isn't it just possible that no one liked her,' Rattigan said later. 'That she was an absolute cow.' He came to the conclusion that Nelson's wife was a cold woman, and 'though he'd probably spent a lot of time in brothels, this was the first time he'd done it with an expert'. The fusion of two of his favourite themes, the distinction between spiritual and sexual love (personified by Lady Nelson and Emma Hamilton in his mind), and the question of what motivates a famous man to act in a particular way, provided the inspiration for the play he was first to call *Tom Tit in Tears*, in a reference to Lady Nelson's nickname, and finally *A Bequest to the Nation*.

A second project, also from the heart of the British establishment, materialised almost simultaneously. The brainchild of the BBC's Head of Light Entertainment, Tom Sloan, it was an offer to write the script for a birthday tribute to Sir Winston Churchill, to be broadcast that November. It was a straightforward job – a ninety-five-minute programme, which Churchill had approved in principle, consisting simply of a selection of songs from the previous ninety years linked by a commentary on Churchill's life and achievements and with Noël Coward acting as compère. The approach was not altogether original. Rattigan had done something not dissimilar for the thirty-eighth anniversary of the foundation of the RAF several years earlier.

When it was broadcast on 29 November 1964 the programme was broadly welcomed, although Peter Black in the *Daily Mail* wrote next morning that 'The script was addressed to Sir Winston, who was presumed to be watching the programme; a device of doubtful worth. In the first place he almost certainly wasn't, and, in the second, it led the writer and narrator into some deplorable excesses of sentiment.' Churchill himself was pleased enough with it, however, and sent a telegram to the BBC the following morning thanking everyone involved.

In spite of these boosts, Rattigan's mood worsened until, as one old friend confided to Freddie Young, he went 'completely round the bend'. The bouts of solitude, locked up in Eaton Square, refusing to speak to anyone, drinking alone, were matched by manic, compensatory weekends in Brighton. Two of the themes identified by Cuthbert Worsley in a fierce defence of Rattigan's work in the *London Magazine* seemed epitomised in his behaviour – humiliation and obsession. A grateful Rattigan suggested to Worsley that the two of them should sail round the world together for a year, but the plan was shelved when he fell ill again. In the first months of 1965 he caught three more virus infections, and decided he could stand the cold English winters no longer.

When the tax year ended in April 1965 Rattigan retired into exile: exile both from the cold and from the future clutches of the Inland Revenue. MGM had come up with a plan for a musical version of *Goodbye Mr Chips*, with Rex Harrison and Julie Andrews as the stars, music by André and Dory Previn, and Vincente Minelli as director. The financial incentive added fuel to his desire to escape, for he had no savings and was increasingly afraid that he would not be able to afford to sustain his lifestyle in his old age unless he moved abroad and avoided paying the Labour Government's punitive income taxes at the same time. The $150,000 on offer to write the screenplay, if he could hang on to most of it rather than lose it in tax, would be a start towards a nest-egg.

Rattigan announced that he was surrendering the lease on the top flat at 29 Eaton Square, which was now threatened, in any case, with a substantial rent increase. And he considered putting 79 Marine Parade on the market, though he agreed that Cuthbert Worsley could continue to stay there until it was finally sold. At Michael Franklin's suggestion, he decided that Brighton was the best place to store his furniture and pictures, the leather-bound copies of his plays, the Broadway handbills and cuttings books that documented his life. He was still renting the Christobello, the villa on Ischia, and now he was out of Eaton Square his lawyer, Peter Carter-Ruck, suggested that he might consider renting a flat in Paris, where he could stay if he wanted to be not too far from his mother, who would celebrate her eightieth birthday in 1965. The plan was to take two flats, one above the other. Rattigan would live in the upstairs one, when he was there, and Pegs French, wife of Harold, the original director of *French Without Tears*, who had helped him run Little Court in the past, would live downstairs and ensure that he was cared for. He had steadily come to rely on her.

From now on, he would be free to spend his time as and where he wished. His business affairs would be left in the hands of Bill Forsyth and Peter Carter-Ruck. Pegs would look after Paris and Michael Weight Ischia, as he had done for the past three years. Sheila Dyatt's brief reign as his secretary would come to an end. When the news of his plans leaked out, it was said that he was leaving Britain to escape a £60,000 tax bill. This was not true. Rattigan did not owe any income tax at the time. He was leaving to escape humiliation.

His depression, which now amounted almost to a form of persecution, deepened still further in the spring of 1965 as he began a period of restless shuttling from Hollywood to Paris to Ischia to Paris again, to America again, and then to Ischia. Sometimes an old friend such as Billy Chappell would travel with him; sometimes Michael Weight would arrange for a party to arrive in Ischia, sometimes Michael Franklin would meet him in Paris. Sometimes he would simply spend days on his own in Paris, occasionally picking up a young man on the street, in spite of the danger of blackmail. Shortly after midnight on one occasion he telephoned down from his apartment to Pegs French below, demanding that she come upstairs 'at once', to save him from being compromised.

Rattigan delivered his television play, now retitled *Nelson: A Study in Miniature*, in August 1965. The play was to be broadcast by Independent Television the following spring, with Michael Bryant – whose achievement in taking over from Alec Guinness in *Ross* Rattigan had much admired – as Nelson. Celia Johnson (who had similarly taken over from Peggy Ashcroft for a time in *The Deep Blue Sea*) was to be Lady Nelson, and Rachel Roberts, by then Mrs Rex Harrison, Emma Hamilton. The play was set in the twenty-four days Nelson spent in London and at his country house prior to his final voyage to the battle off Cape Trafalgar.

His inspiration, he explained to Lord (Lew) Grade of Associated Television, came from a letter from Lady Nelson to her husband, dated 18 December 1801, which was returned to her marked 'opened by mistake by Lord Nelson but not read'. 'How could the man I know from all his writings to possess a gentle warm-hearted and very simple personality have done anything so wildly uncharacteristic?' he asked. The answer, he felt, lay in Lady Nelson's determination always to turn the other cheek; a proof that she loved her husband too much rather than too little. Nelson's only weapon against her, once he had fallen in love with Emma Hamilton, was hatred. As Rattigan put it in a note to himself, three souls joined in one – *tria junta in uno*, the motto of the British Order of the Bath – lay at the heart of his play. The canker that he recognized beneath the glittering façade of the British establishment fascinated him.

When the play was transmitted in March 1966, the ever loyal Cuthbert Worsley, obliged to retire from nightly theatre reviewing because of ill-health and, in consequence, now the television critic of the *Financial Times*, did not take that point. Instead, he warmly welcomed the piece as 'a most touching and moving drama of a hero seen in the round', and described its author as 'our leading professional playwright'. In the *Sunday Times*, however, the poet Adrian Mitchell

denounced the 'epigrams' in the dialogue and condemned its author
for not writing about the fact that 'four-fifths of Nelson's sailors had
been press-ganged to fight so gloriously'.

Little had changed. Some critics were still criticising him for not
writing something he had never intended to write. If that was what
they thought criticism was about, so be it. They could think what they
liked, they would not have him to abuse. Rattigan gratefully returned
to his self-imposed exile.

CHAPTER 25

The Movies, Hollywood, Everything

◆

The first hint that I should stop producing plays
came when I misjudged Look Back in Anger *and*
A Taste of Honey. *The theatre was changing,*
but I wasn't changing with it.

IRENE MAYER SELZNICK, *A Private View*

◆

If Terence Rattigan had been a different man, had he been as carefree and cavalier as he liked to pretend, depression might never have entered his soul. Certainly there was no reason why it should. Every film producer in America and Europe, or so it seemed, suddenly had a proposal to put to him. The Baden-Powell story had not disappeared. There was also a substantial offer from Switzerland for a screenplay for a film about the Battle of Britain, an idea about two turn-of-the-century explorers in Australia that might possibly make a movie, and a suggestion that he might write a drama about airmen in the First World War. Harold Freedman even believed that his script on Nelson might work for Hollywood.

But none of the offers truly inspired Rattigan. Though he did everything in his power to convince himself and his friends that he was content to give up the theatre and make a comfortable living from films, it was a pretence. 'If the theatre has given up Terence Rattigan, he would give up the theatre,' he would insist, but it was a lie. To be separated from the theatre was to threaten his entire existence. As the critic Anthony Curtis was to recall a decade later, 'Terry admitted to me just before his death that the Hollywood years were a betrayal of his talent, and were largely motivated by his need to make money.' It was a tragic waste.

But Rattigan could not afford to stop. The money the movies offered meant that he could sustain his lifestyle, and continue to pretend to himself that he did not care. The screenplays helped him do just that, and now the most pressing task was *Goodbye Mr Chips*. MGM wanted him to start work at once, to allow them to capitalise as quickly as they could on the success of *The VIPs* and *The Yellow Rolls-Royce*. And they wanted him right there in Hollywood. Rattigan accepted his fate. He took up residence in the autumn of 1966 and before long was writing a long memorandum to the producer Arthur Jacobs expounding his view of James Hilton's famous 1934 novel and the film adaptation that had won Robert Donat an Oscar in 1940.

> I think, in general, that the original version is far too obviously sentimental for today . . . I believe, therefore, that we need an entirely different approach to the character. I don't want to write another Crocker-Harris . . . although, in strict confidence, I'll plagiarise myself quite happily if I think it is good for the film and Lord Rank won't sue.

What Rattigan wanted was to retain the sentiment but discard the sentimentality, and at the same time to bring the novel 'a little more up to date, while keeping its period flavour'. He thought that by doing so, 'we are only doing what he [Hilton] would most probably have done himself, if he had written it today'. With this in mind he proposed to move the story from the turn of the century to the era of his own childhood, the early twenties, the days of flappers, long cigarette-holders, Oxford bags, and Irene Brown wowing London in *No, No Nanette*. To sustain the musical that MGM wanted, he turned the future Mrs Chippings into a soubrette in a musical comedy called *Hi There Hettie*. But his underlying aim remained serious. It was the elderly schoolmaster Chips himself who fascinated him, with his doubts about his marriage and what he had done with his life.

'In the story as now planned,' he told Jacobs,

> these doubts . . . are not resolved until almost the last scene between them, just before her death (not in childbirth, but in a 1944 flying bomb blitz) when, having lost his expected head-mastership and on the point of retirement, he confesses to her both his failure and his fear of having blighted her life. She tells him, very quietly and very convincingly, that marrying him has,

in fact, saved her life . . . And this, of course, we will know to be true, because we will have seen it. But Chips, although he too has seen it, had never been – how could he be? – quite sure. Now he knows.

Rattigan's intentions, however, were never translated to the screen. Rex Harrison, for whom he was to write the part, was to prove as difficult as ever to keep attached to a project, and eventually bowed out. Richard Burton was approached, but did not feel confident enough about the singing. Then MGM suggested Albert Finney and Peter O'Toole. Meanwhile Julie Andrews too slipped away, and the studio approached, at various times, Audrey Hepburn, Lee Remick and the singer Petula Clark to play Katherine, the future Mrs Chippings. Rattigan, having completed the first draft of the screenplay, left the script in Jacobs's hands and embarked on another project, *The Nine Tiger Man*, based on Lesley Blanch's book about the Indian Mutiny. He was guaranteed at least $100,000 for the first draft. But now he decided to follow the old Hollywood advice to screenwriters – he took the money and ran. Los Angeles was too much for him. He ran back to Europe – to Ischia and Paris.

There now began an even stranger, and more unsettling, period in Rattigan's life: as stateless performer for whoever would pay the largest cheque. He was prostituting his talent to finance a lifestyle for himself and for those he cared about – and one that did not depend on the whims of the London theatre critics. But it had its price. Even when his mother was taken to hospital, he could not risk breaking his tax exile, although he telephoned her every day at the London Clinic from Paris. His generosity remained. When Michael Franklin needed money, he arranged for Pegs French to provide it; when Cuthbert Worsley wanted to stay on in his Brighton flat he agreed. But Rattigan also knew in his heart that he had taken a wrong turning. He knew he was a playwright or nothing. He was drowning his private disgust in champagne, caviar and cash.

But there were, sometimes, small compensations. One of the scripts he worked on in this period was another screenplay for his Chips employer, Arthur Jacobs in Hollywood, this time based on a Frederick E. Smith novel about fighter pilots in Flanders during the First World War and called *A Killing for the Hawks*. Major Julian Seymour is a British pilot with more than seventy 'kills' to his credit, and an Oxford contemporary and great friend of another pilot, John Mandeville. Seymour admits to Lady Helen Morgan, the girl he has plans to marry, that he 'loves' Mandeville, but that their 'Platonic love' is 'entirely free of such muddy, grotesque and vicious thoughts as her over-sex-conscious brain' is capable of playing with. Seymour marries Lady Helen, but when, three years later, Mandeville is revealed as having had an affair with a junior officer since killed in action, Seymour turns against him.

Mandeville kills himself by flying into a barrage balloon, but a young American who has tried to protect him from Seymour's anger then falls in love with Seymour's wife. The two men set out to fight their version of a duel above the trenches of France, but, at the last moment, Seymour restrains himself. He refuses to kill the young American. Instead he sends him to see his wife and to talk to her about a divorce. At the last moment, the American realises that Lady Helen stands for a way of life he can never accept. He breaks off their relationship and he and Seymour meet one final time in a bunker on the night of General Haig's 'big push' in 1918.

This overheated plot at least allowed Rattigan to reiterate one of the central themes of his work: the need to be true to 'one's own nature'. The young American attacks Seymour for not 'fulfilling' his nature by accepting that he has always been – implicitly – a homosexual, like his dead friend, John Mandeville. Seymour admits that, had he allowed himself to, he might have loved Mandeville as much as he could 'love' any man, but that did not mean anything explicit. The explicit, for ordinarily constituted men, he maintains, is kept for women. But the implicit can be as strong as the explicit – even stronger. The American condemns him outright. In denying his own nature, Seymour has made himself a fraud. The following morning Seymour saves the American's life in an air battle and is killed. Rattigan's screenplay ended with Seymour's dying question to himself: 'To be cured, at last, of ignorance? Is that it? Or is it to find out, at last, the truth?'

This proved too much for Hollywood. Though the laws against homosexuality had just been relaxed in England, Hollywood was a very different place from Joe Orton's Shaftesbury Avenue. Rattigan's screenplay of A Killing for the Hawks was shelved, never to be produced.

Another project was for Richard Zanuck at Twentieth Century-Fox, who had commissioned a screenplay based on Gerold Frank's book about the Boston Strangler, the notorious American serial killer. In a foreword to his first treatment, Rattigan suggested: 'This could and should be one of the most exciting films ever made. I hope it will be. This author will certainly do all he can to make it so.'

To this end, and to compete with the film of Truman Capote's novel In Cold Blood, which he knew was on the brink of shooting for

Columbia, Rattigan upped the ante by introducing into his outline, among those involved in tracking down the strangler, a hypnotist and a psychiatrist. 'All male children wish to copulate with their mothers . . . and of course the converse is equally true. All grown men wish to murder their mothers,' announces the psychiatrist in his address to the detectives. In this character Rattigan was resuscitating none other than the man who had had such an impact on his own early life, Dr Keith Newman, and the actor he hoped would portray him was Peter Sellers, who had recently become an international star in Stanley Kubrick's *Dr Strangelove*. His wish was never fulfilled, for Rattigan's version was discarded, in spite of a number of rewrites, in favour of a version by Edward Anhalt.

With Hollywood now occupying almost all of his working life, Rattigan needed a more accessible base. The long flights tired him, but when he travelled by sea he seemed to be constantly plagued by fellow passengers asking interminable questions about his work, which was even worse. Rattigan knew he could afford something luxurious. Each screenplay was bringing in at least $100,000. The place he chose was Bermuda. He had called there in 1942, when flying Catalinas back to Britain from the USA. But why he really decided on it was because Noël Coward – who now lived on nearby Jamaica – had dismissed it as being 'Surbiton in mid-Atlantic'. In February 1967 Rattigan rented a house near the third green of the Mid Ocean golf club in Tucker's Town, and turned it into a Caribbean version of Little Court. Pegs French was even translated from England to look after it for him. The house was called Sitting Pretty.

In the next ten years Bermuda was to become as much Rattigan's home as anywhere in the world. By the spring of 1967 he had established himself as a 'non-resident' for tax purposes, and though allowed to make brief visits back to Britain, he did not always relish them. The only contacts he maintained were his memberships of the MCC and the Garrick, for which he had allowed himself to be renominated after resigning in despair after *Variation on a Theme* in 1958. He had seen to it that his mother was well looked after, and more of the Hollywood money was destined for a trust to provide an income for her during the rest of her life. But there was nothing to keep him in Britain. Michael Franklin could meet him in Italy, or come to Bermuda, and so could those few friends he remained keen to see. Binkie Beaumont had extracted a vague promise from him to write a stage version of his television play about Nelson, but he was in no particular hurry. London, even in the late spring, was damp and 'not particularly welcoming', so he skipped it, preferring to wait for the summer and Ischia. Then it was Hollywood, Bermuda and more movie projects.

Rattigan wanted to work on the old ballet project for the producer Ray Stark, which he had shelved for several years. The former agent wanted Rattigan to write what he described as a 'modern love story' set in a ballet background. A girl dancer falls in love with a homosexual and plans to marry him, but has the problem of making the arrangement work, and of not knowing how to compete with a man for her lover's affection. The project was to be called *Pas de Deux*. There was also an idea about young fighter pilots in the Arabian desert during the Second World War, called *Signed with Their Honour*, and he still had more work to do on *Mr Chips*, which was now to star Peter O'Toole and Audrey Hepburn and be filmed in England in 1968.

But Rattigan could not quite bring himself to give up the theatre altogether. In between times he amused himself by writing a fifteen-minute monologue for Margaret Leighton, which he first called *Duologue*, because the actress was addressing her dead husband. In it, he returned to his theme of the two loves, spiritual and sexual, and the despair that the failure to achieve either can bring. His protagonist only realised she loved her husband after his death, and was blaming herself for denying him the sexual pleasures that she knew he wanted. She was also trying, vainly, to convince herself that her hard-drinking husband had died by accident, and not by committing suicide. In the event it was to surface not in the theatre at all, but on the new BBC2 in September 1968, under the title of *All on Her Own*. Rattigan, however, was not in the country to see it.

The filming of *Goodbye Mr Chips* had begun, with O'Toole still starring but Petula Clark back on the set in place of Audrey Hepburn. During the shooting, Rattigan was to have his own brush with death. Visiting Pompeii from his villa on Ischia to watch the shooting of the scenes in which Chips first meets his young wife, he was suddenly seized by terrible stomach pains. He was suffering from acute appendicitis and was rushed to hospital in Naples, where he was operated on immediately; however, due apparently to a lack of hygienic precautions in the hospital at the time, gangrene set in within the week. He was to spend the next two weeks in a state of delirium, watched over by Michael Weight and Dr Buky, the Rattigan family doctor who happened to be on holiday in Italy. On more than one occasion Rattigan seemed almost on the point of death and Buky left the hospital convinced that he would not last the night. He recovered, but his hold on life seemed to grow frailer.

Rattigan's ordeal in the Neapolitan hospital persuaded him that he never wanted to see the inside of an Italian hospital again. There must be a safer place for a fifty-seven-year-old to escape the damp English winters. He started to investigate the possibilities of buying a house in the south of France, 'where the hospitals are a little more trustworthy'. In the meantime, there was still Bermuda, where he felt confident that Pegs French would make sure that he never found himself abandoned in an unsympathetic hospital again. When he returned there, after recuperating in Switzerland and Baden Baden, he moved into a new home, Shaw Wood House in Shaw Park. It was there that he started work on another screenplay, this time about the nineteenth-century Australian explorers Burke and Wills. He called it *Return to the Cooper* and told John Boulting, who was anxious to see it, that he wanted it to be an 'epic' in the style of David Lean's *Lawrence of Arabia*.

A number of factors militated against it. For one thing, he was stronger on portraiture than on epic scenes. For another, his dialogue was inclined to impede the action, while his insistence on strict historical accuracy in conveying the 'true nature' of the Australian outback in 1860 also entailed an unhappy ending. Both explorers died on their journey, and the only survivor was saved by the 'native Australians', the Aborigines – a conclusion more acceptable now than in the American studios in 1969. A speech attacking 'the powerful ones on the earth', who were accused of 'using their power to take the land away from the less powerful ones, even if the less powerful ones go about naked, have some customs we don't like, are a different colour from us, and haven't heard of Jesus Christ' also failed to find favour. John Boulting was not entirely happy, and the Americans were even less so. The project staggered to a halt. A two-and-a-half-hour version of the story, called *Burke and Wills* (which had become Rattigan's title), written by Michael Thomas, would finally be produced, although not for another sixteen years.

For all that, Rattigan had reason to feel grateful to Hollywood. In London the reception of a revival of *The Sleeping Prince* in the autumn of 1968 showed that he was still out of favour, whereas Fox were taking another look at *O Mistress Mine* – although struggling to see how they could make the willing mistress conform to the demands of their production code. In the meantime, he continued to work on *Pas de Deux*, his ballet story for Ray Stark.

Set backstage in a ballet company, his screenplay told the story of a new young male dancer, David Taylor, who has been prepared to accept the homosexual love of an Ambassador to promote his career, but then falls in love with the young woman, Amy Reid, with whom he is to dance the *pas de deux* in the company's new ballet. In the course

of the first act, the young woman asks the Ambassador: 'Tell me, what
is it that makes a man prefer boys to girls?' The Ambassador replies,
'Well, in one word infantilism,' to which explanation he then adds
three other words, 'Retarded emotional development.' So, 'In loving
David you're just loving yourself when you were young. Right?' asks
the young woman. He declines to reply, but instead seduces her himself. The Rattigan twist comes at the end of Act One, when the
Ambassador is 'forbidden' by his wife to see Amy again. Young male
lovers she can tolerate, young female ones, never. It is a characteristic
Rattigan contradiction – part of his restless search for the 'true' emotions that lie behind the pretence that colours so many lives.

The second act was never completed to Rattigan's satisfaction. Like
Burke and Wills and *The Boston Strangler*, it was destined to remain
in his filing cabinet in Bermuda for the rest of his life, unseen and
unperformed, a symbol of his fascination for the interplay between the
sexes, the contradictions implicit in both homosexual and heterosexual
love, particularly when they become intertwined.

Throughout 1969, he remained mainly in Bermuda, playing a little
occasional golf – usually by himself – and working in the late afternoons
and evenings. He was not well. The illness in Naples had weakened
him to such an extent that he simply did not feel strong enough to
travel or to entertain. He was unable to travel to England for Noël
Coward's birthday party in December 1969, and the following July he
was telling his publisher, Jamie Hamilton, 'I'd better write you my
autobiography fairly soon, because this damp and lazy place is death
to the memory. I can only remember that "shot over the bunker that
rolled up dead" if it happened yesterday. The day before I'm lost.'

He was certainly not tempted to attend the launch of *Goodbye Mr
Chips*, which was released in the United States in November 1969, and
in England, with a royal première, two weeks later. The reviews were
scathing. *Newsweek* warned that it was 'a good example of how the
old guard of the movie industry has lost track of itself, misplaced its
magic wand . . . muddled old and new as woefully as poor Chips',
and called it 'an unmusical musical'. In England only Peter O'Toole's
performance as Chips himself, and Rattigan's screenplay, were singled
out for praise. But even then, 'The sentiment of the nineteen-thirties,
even with the love story taking precedence over the school story, won't
work in the late nineteen-sixties,' according to Dilys Powell in the
Sunday Times.

Rattigan had agreed to rewrite the screenplay of *Chips* because he
felt he could bring something to the characters. It was the only way
he could work. When he did not feel this he would usually turn a job

down, no matter how attractive the offer. He had done so in the case of *The Bridge on the River Kwai*, which Sam Spiegel had asked him to undertake in the 1950s, and again a few years later when the same producer had invited him to adapt William Golding's *Lord of the Flies*. 'My forte as a film writer,' he once wrote to a producer,

> is dramatic rather than filmic. I have always had to rely on a Puffin Asquith or David Lean to remind me that films are made with cameras, and that character can sometimes be projected as easily by a single close up as by three pages of subtle dialogue. Reminded thus I have usually worked very happily in a medium which I know not to be my own, but which can, I feel, be benefited sometimes by the dramatist's eye for character, for 'theatre' in the non-theatrical sense, and for dramatic narrative.

It was this potential for adding something new to character that kept him tinkering with his story of Nelson and Emma, which Binkie Beaumont was so keen for him to convert from its original television version into a full-scale piece for the stage. He was at his most comfortable with dialogue, at his most relaxed within the confines of a proscenium arch. By the spring of 1970 the play was ready. Retitled *A Mutual Pair*, it delighted Beaumont, who accepted it at once. Rattigan wanted Peter Glenville to direct it, even though he had not directed in London for sixteen years, and offered him the film rights to the piece as an encouragement to do so. Bob Whitehead agreed to produce the play in America, and his wife, Zoë Caldwell, would star as Lady Hamilton in a production that Beaumont wanted to launch in the autumn. With good reason, Rattigan dedicated the new play to Michael Franklin, the man who had proved as unacceptable to his own friends as Emma Hamilton had to Nelson's.

In the second scene of Act Two Nelson spells out the consequences of the sexual obsession which lies at its heart, as it lay at the heart of *The Deep Blue Sea* and *Variation on a Theme*:

NELSON: . . . Six years ago, in Naples, I wittingly and of my own free will, deserted a loving and loyal wife for the embraces of a notorious charmer. How much did you all laugh in the wardroom of the Vanguard when you saw that happening? 'Not leaving his wife for that woman', did you say? 'Not for the one who displayed herself naked for show at fourteen in Vauxhall Gardens, who was sold by Greville to Hamilton as payment for a bad debt, and has been bedded by half the nobility and gentry of England before becoming Sir William's wife? Not leaving his wife for *her*! Not for *Emma* Hamilton!' Do you think I never imagined how loud that laughter must have been?

    Pause.

HARDY: My Lord, the wardroom could not have guessed that you were so aware. I did not guess it myself, until this minute. You pretend very well, you see.

NELSON: Oh God, Hardy – how do you think I can keep my sanity and not be aware?

    Pause. He turns his face from Hardy.

My Divine Lady? God in Heaven, Hardy, when Emma throws a glass of champagne after an insult to my King don't you think I see exactly what you see, a drunken, middle-aged woman making a fool of herself and of me. Do you think I relish the gutter-talk, don't wince at the vulgarity, and have lost the capacity to smell liquor on the breath? Do you think I don't feel blasted with shame nearly every day that I spend at Emma's side?

The explanation Nelson offers for his obsession is the same as Hester's: only stated more starkly. It is the realisation of, and pleasure in, physical love.

NELSON: . . . To the forty-year-old Admiral who had never known or enjoyed what most other man have enjoyed and long since forgotten – that in the release of bed there lies an ecstasy so strong and a satisfaction so profound that it seems that it is everything that life can offer a man, the very purpose of existence on earth . . . You must remember, you see, that, even at that age, I was still the rector's son who, from the cradle, had been preached the abomination of carnal love, and the ineffable joys of holy wedlock. But when at last I surrendered to Emma, I found – why should I be ashamed to say it? – that carnal love concerns the soul quite as much as it concerns the body. For the body *is* still the soul and the soul *is* still the body. At least they are for me. You must understand that there is nothing in Emma I would change, Hardy. I love her and I want her exactly as she is – because I am obsessed and I want her *absolutely*.

When *A Bequest to the Nation* opened on 23 September 1970 at the Theatre Royal Haymarket, with Ian Holm as Nelson and Leueen Mac-Grath as Lady Nelson, his long-suffering and always forgiving 'Tom Tit', it had been seven years since Rattigan had last had a new play produced in London, and more than a decade since his last hit, *Ross*, had opened at the same theatre. In the intervening years his self-imposed exile, and the transformation in the theatre itself, had seen him ignored and reviled. Rattigan prepared himself for the worst.

But some of the critics were kinder to *A Bequest to the Nation* than the author had feared they might be. The *Daily Mail* called it 'a genuine theatrical shock . . . a play of weight, entertainment and shapeliness', and *The Times* added that 'What Mr Rattigan offers is a boardroom portrait of a great patriot who maintains his dignity even amid the ugliest struggles of an irregular private life.'

Six weeks later, and to Rattigan's surprise and pleasure, there was another Rattigan opening, only this time a revival. Kenneth More had decided that he would like to play the part of Sir Robert Morton in *The Winslow Boy*, which Donald Albery had agreed to mount at the New. Frith Banbury was to direct, and Rattigan stayed on in London to be present at the first night. When Banbury asked him, 'Tell me, how much do you want to be referred to,' he simply replied, 'As little as possible, but I would like the American version to be done, the one with the cuts in it.' The effort of the new play, and the travel to England, had taken their toll; he was suffering from chest pains, and severe headaches, so severe that he was sometimes unable to get up to dine with his friends, even if he had invited them.

Two plays in the West End of London presented the English critics with an opportunity to reflect on the Rattigan career, and their conclusions confirmed his worst fears. In *New Society* he was again dismissed as nothing more than a smug craftsman. 'It's . . . facile knowingness that's at the heart of Rattigan's theatre. For if he sacrifices everything to plausibility it's not because of some dramatic theme, it's because that's the way he responds to his material. Every complexity can be explained away, every facet of human experience reduced to a simple matter of manipulation.' Obtuse and insulting as it was, Rattigan found it impossible to dismiss the gibe entirely. It served to confirm his melancholy. He felt irrelevant, a shibboleth in the English theatre, a creature, like Aunt Edna herself, to be mugged or abused at will.

The audience did not exactly share the critics' view. *A Bequest to the Nation* survived at the Haymarket for three months and 124 performances, while *The Winslow Boy* stayed at the New for almost six months. And at least one critic sprang to his defence. Ronald Bryden, Kenneth Tynan's successor as drama critic at the *Observer*, insisted in his review of *The Winslow Boy* in November 1970 that although: 'The new dramatists and critics pride themselves on their tolerance . . . There hasn't been much tolerance in, for instance, the treatment of Rattigan and his recent works.' Bryden pointed out that any playwright in England in ·the 1940s and early 1950s had been forced to hide 'the play he wanted to write behind the one his audience would accept', and Rattigan was no exception. 'Against the gains our new theatrical freedoms have brought us should be set one major loss: Terence Rattigan . . . The play stands up, a monument to the playwright we lost to permissiveness.'

Rattigan was not there to read the review. He had retired to Bermuda to finish another screenplay, this time an adaptation of Barry England's West End hit, *Conduct Unbecoming*, about events in the officer's mess of a British regiment in India in the 1890s. A cadet is accused of assault on a lady, but the real culprit is one of his seniors whose increasing madness has been overlooked by his brother officers in their desire to preserve the reputation of the regiment. On the surface this should have been a natural Rattigan subject, but he never seemed entirely comfortable writing it; feeling perhaps that it lacked subtlety. Whatever the reason, his screenplay was destined not to be used in the film British Lion were to release three years later. Robert Enders was given the final screenplay credit.

In the early spring of 1971, Rattigan was forced to return to England hurriedly and unexpectedly. His mother had contracted pneumonia and it was feared she might not survive. She had insisted on returning to her house near Luton from the small hotel she had moved on to from the Stanhope Court after celebrating her eighty-sixth birthday on 9 April – another of the whims that Rattigan, though outwardly dutiful, was finding a little irritating. On 23 April she died at Pepperstock, in the house in which both she and her husband had been supported by Rattigan's generosity over so many years.

Pegs French registered the death, and Vera's body was cremated three days later at Golders Green in North London, as her husband's and Brian's had been in their turn. Now only one member of Frank Rattigan's family remained. And he was not sure what to do. Rattigan asked Bill Forsyth to organize the sale of Pepsal End, and for the contents to be stored, while he thought about the future. He would be sixty in June, and part of him wanted to return to England for what he already believed would be the last few years of his life. His health was little improved, in spite of the Bermuda climate, and for the first time he began to wonder whether he would not rather die in his native country. In the end his mind was made up for him.

To his intense delight, a few weeks after his return to Bermuda in the early summer of 1971, Rattigan learnt that he was to receive a knighthood in the Queen's Birthday Honours list in June for 'services to the theatre', only the third playwright of the century to be honoured in this way – Noël Coward, the first, having received his knighthood eighteen months before, in January 1970, and Pinero his in 1909. It was a mark of his acceptance, and one which meant far more to him than any of the new generation of young playwrights would under- stand. It was the honour he felt his father had been denied, and a clear acknowledgement of his own theatrical worth. But it was also a shield against the critical abuse that he felt so keenly, and he hid behind it determinedly throughout the rest of his life. It also gave him the cour- age to plan his return to England. Stewart Trotter, the young director of a revival of *The Browning Version* the following year, noted that never once during their collaboration did Rattigan suggest that he might call him Rattigan. He remained 'Sir Terence' throughout.

Before the official announcement of his knighthood, Rattigan was back in a suite in Claridges, in time to attend the Test Match at Lord's and to announce determinedly to the world that he was returning from exile because he missed his friends, cricket and 'home'. When the news of his knighthood broke, one newspaper wondered whether he ought not to 'have waited for the official announcement before giving us all that guff', which infuriated him so much that he demanded, and received, an apology, even if there had been an element of truth in the claim.

Leaving Michael Franklin to look for a house 'near a golf course', Rattigan returned to Bermuda to work on two screenplays, and decide whether to sell his house there or not. He had already instructed Bill Forsyth to make sure that he was officially registered as a British resi- dent for tax purposes once the present financial year ended in April 1972. Meanwhile Roger Machell was investigating the possibility of finding him new chambers in Albany to provide him with a London base.

Rattigan was working on the film version of *A Bequest to the Nation*, and a project about William Joyce, the American-born but British- educated broadcaster from wartime Germany whose sneering voice had brought him the nickname of Lord Haw-Haw, and who had been tried, convicted and hanged for treason in London in January 1946, though he was not a British citizen. Rattigan considered him to be one of the most remarkable characters thrown up by war. In a memor- andum to accompany his outline treatment for the film, which he sent to Quadrant Investments, who were to pay him a total of £75,000 if he completed a final screenplay, he wrote, 'Let us agree that William Joyce as Lord Haw-Haw was a deadly threat to our war-time morale, and a phenomenon unparalleled in the history of warfare (for the other Axis broadcasters were mere walk-on parts compared to him). He was a great star, and hated the more by us because we recognised all his unique stellar qualities.'

Once again Rattigan's fascination with the outsider, the man condemned by his temperament and his actions to a life beyond 'respectability', was the spark for his imagination, as Ivar Kreuger had once sparked it. But, in this case, the project was stillborn. The ambiguities and paradox of Joyce's life would bring him the opportunity to explore the contradictions inherent in British society, but the screenplay was never commissioned and the idea was abandoned.

He returned to work on the screenplay of *A Bequest to the Nation*, which he was now writing for the legendary Hal B. Wallis, producer of *Casablanca*, who was anxious to make it for Universal Studios. Wallis had recently had hits with two other costume dramas based on British history, *Anne of the Thousand Days* and *Mary, Queen of Scots*, and he wanted to continue the tradition. Wallis hoped to get Richard Burton, who had appeared in *Anne*, and Glenda Jackson, who had appeared in *Mary, Queen of Scots*, to play Nelson and Emma Hamilton.

Rattigan worked on the screenplay throughout the autumn. He was due to deliver by 15 January 1972, and was being paid £70,000. He had all but finished when he went to England for his investiture at Buckingham Palace as a Knight Commander of the British Empire. The Queen was suffering from chickenpox, and the ceremony was conducted by the Queen Mother, but he was in no way disappointed. The whole occasion delighted him. After the investiture he travelled to Paris to stay in his apartment in the Rue des Vignes, to rest, to see Michael Franklin and other friends, and finish the screenplay. Back in Bermuda during the autumn, he had suffered another searing bout of flu, but he brushed it aside as 'nothing whatever to worry about'. In fact, he worried about it a great deal, and not without reason.

The screenplay was finished by the middle of January as scheduled, and copies dispatched to both Hal Wallis and Glenda Jackson, the Lancashire-born actress who had won her first Oscar for *Women in Love* three years earlier. Rattigan told his prospective leading lady that he was sure she would be superb with not a dry eye at the fade-out, certainly not his own. She replied that she liked the script, but wished her clashes with Nelson could be more strongly and clearly defined, a suggestion to which he agreed without demur. Hal Wallis's criticisms were much more serious, however. He wanted Emma Hamilton to make her appearance much earlier than in the screenplay. It was wrong that the audience should have to wait for almost half an hour before seeing the actress whose name was above the title.

Rattigan could not accept this. He was a craftsman and anxious to preserve the element of surprise that he felt the delayed meeting between Nelson and Emma would produce. Back in Bermuda, he wrote to Wallis to explain his problem.

I have given three whole days to thinking out a score of ideas, whereby such a scene might give you what you want, two hungry lovers meeting after a lapse of two years, while retaining the film's one essential element of suspense, which lies in the all important question . . . 'What does Nelson see in her?' And why has he left a loyal and loving wife for a 'vulgar drunken slut'? (Emma's own accurate description of herself).

But the harder he tried the harder he found the request. 'It's no exaggeration,' he told Wallis sadly,

to say that this question, and its various answers . . . represents virtually the whole story . . . the essence of the film must lie in Nelson's sexual infatuation with an 'ageing charmer' whose manners and behaviour make him 'wince' and 'shudder' and 'retch', whom he nevertheless loves 'absolutely'. This, of course, means that an early appearance of Emma must risk unbalancing our fragile story line by giving away too much, too soon.

So passionate a defence of his own screenplay was decidedly out of character for a screenwriter whom bitter experience had convinced that protest was usually pointless. But *A Bequest to the Nation* had been part of his life for six years. He had no wish to see it ruined.

An impasse was just avoided. Hal Wallis insisted on the rightness of his view and seeing his female star on the screen earlier. Rattigan compromised slightly. But by that time Richard Burton had bowed out of the project, to be replaced by Peter Finch, and Hal Wallis had chosen as director of the film, which was scheduled to start shooting at Shepperton in late July, a young Welshman by the name of James Cellan Jones who had directed for television but never for the cinema. Had he lived, Puffin Asquith might well have been called on by Wallis, but Rattigan's longest-standing collaborator in films had died of cancer four years earlier, working on the film version of Morris West's novel, *The Shoes of the Fisherman*, only a few months after the death of another of Rattigan's oldest friends, Vivien Leigh.

Before the filming started, Rattigan returned to England to see his doctor, and to inspect the chambers in Albany which Roger Machell had found for him. They were the 'double set' of H5 & 6, and he was to take over the lease from Mrs Alexander Stuart Frere in June 1972, settling himself in the meantime into a suite at Claridges. He decided there was a 'considerable amount of work to be done, which the Midget can oversee'. Michael Franklin meanwhile had found a 'house near a golf course'; but it was a Scottish golf course rather than a Surrey one.

The house was in Fife, thirty-five miles from Edinburgh and twenty miles from the home of the Royal and Ancient Golf Club at St Andrews, where Rattigan was a member. Called Newton Hall, it had three reception rooms and six bedrooms, and was set in grounds of a little over five acres with views south to the Firth of Forth. Without seeing it, Rattigan told Michael to go ahead with the purchase and to make himself responsible for its renovation and decorations. But when Rattigan did see it himself, he hated it at once.

Rattigan was never to live in Newton Hall, just as he was hardly to play any more rounds of golf. His fatigue and anaemia had not abated. When he consulted Dr Buky in Bentinck Mansions in the early spring of 1972 the doctor asked to take another series of tests. By the beginning of April Buky had confirmed what Rattigan had secretly feared, that the leukaemia that had been diagnosed in 1963 had actually existed after all, and that the disease had not been cured but rather had gone into a long and extended remission. This time Buky was blunt. There could be no doubt. The condition was incurable, the only question being how long it would take to kill him.

At Kay Kendall's memorial service in London in September 1959, Rattigan had written a brief speech about her for Vivien Leigh to pronouce. 'It was as if she had a premonition that the gift of life which she relished so greatly would not be hers for very long – with such intensity and fervour did she pack every minute of her stay on earth.' The same would now be true of its author. The disease provoked him to return to work on the play he had tried but failed to write a decade earlier. He knew he had to write it.

CHAPTER 26

The Memory of Love

◆

It is the image in the mind that binds us to our lost

treasures, but it is the loss that shapes the image.

COLETTE, *Literary Apprenticeship*

◆

When he moved back into Albany in the summer of 1972, Terence Rattigan dug out the red-covered writing block that he had balanced on his knees so often in the past, and went quietly back to work. He could not write as quickly as he had been able to in the years just after the war, but he still worked in the same way. The play took shape in handwriting on his familiar lined foolscap paper. The writing might be a little more shaky now, but the emotions it was trying to capture were every bit as strong. He was writing about Kay Kendall's illness, and about his own. He was trying to describe Rex Harrison's attempts to conceal her illness from her, and about his own attempts to conceal his from his friends. Above all, he was writing his own obituary; his apologia for his own life.

But there were interminable interruptions. Although he had spent the months since April thinking about the new play, he had not been well enough to start work on it. The weeks at Claridges had been followed by a fortnight in a private hospital near by in Bryanston Square, where Dr Buky had tried to build up his strength. And Hal Wallis had demanded still more amendments to his screenplay for *Bequest to the Nation*. Shooting itself began at Shepperton studios in late August, and the first feet of film had hardly been exposed before the arguments broke out.

Glenda Jackson did not see eye to eye with James Cellan Jones, her director, and as she was not only the star but also the holder of an

Academy Award she believed her view should prevail. Rattigan, in turn, felt he should support Cellan Jones against some of her more dramatic outbursts, and gave him encouragement whenever he came to Albany to discuss the script, urging him not to lose heart. 'Terry was obviously very ill,' Cellan Jones remembers now, 'but immensely fastidious, almost over-polite, and terribly sensitive.' Whenever he telephoned, Rattigan 'would always ask to speak to "Mr Cellan Jones", and never use my Christian name. He was from a different generation; but he was also a little vulnerable.'

As the filming drew to a close, however, the two men grew increasingly close, Rattigan finally commiserating with Cellan Jones over his leading lady's performance, and telling him, 'Don't fret, love. I've been through this so often before. In a lot of scenes she's very very good . . . All you have to do now is to make it appear not merely possible, but actually probable, that Nelson loved her.'

Bequest to the Nation was not the only interruption. The British ITV company Thames Television had approached the agents of a number of well-known playwrights to see whether they had any little-known plays that might be adapted, and his agent had sent along an old manuscript of his, *High Summer*, one of the three plays he had written for John Gielgud back in 1947. It was far from his best work, but the television company expressed their eagerness to put it on, if he would just 'make one or two alterations'. When Rattigan looked back at the play his heart sank. 'It's awful, isn't it?' he told Peter Duguid, the director Thames had appointed, when he came to see him. But he let the project go ahead nevertheless, suggesting only that Margaret Leighton should play the lead. She did, and the play went out in September 1972. The *Daily Express* described it politely as a 'total anticlimax'.

High Summer was a relic of a bygone age, an evocation of a world of stately homes and village cricket matches. Conceived before *The Sleeping Prince* or *The Deep Blue Sea*, and set in 1906, it concerns the eldest son of the Marquess and Marchioness of Huntercombe, who has run away to Paris to become a painter after having disgraced himself in the Diplomatic Service. Having inherited the title, he returns to his parents' country estate, White Manly, determined to sell it – until he realises that his actions are motivated by a possessive love for his mother and he decides to return to Paris to resume his career as an artist.

The familiar echo of his father's life, and his own perennial fascination with hidden emotions and the concealment of 'true feelings', albeit expressed in the studiedly flippant style of *French Without Tears*, are umistakable, even in this minor work. There is also a key passage,

truer of Rattigan and the generation to which he belonged than of
the decade in which the play was finally produced, in which George
Franklyn-Pearce, an old family friend, tells Jack, the new young Marquess, 'The trouble with you always has been that, as a boy, you played
too many amateur theatricals.'

> JACK: You mean – I dramatise myself?
> GEORGE: Of course – as the Artist, as the Bohemian, as the Enemy of
> Society, as the great Philanderer – as all sorts of grotesque and splendid
> things. And all the time, my dear Jack, you are nothing but a little boy
> – a little Marquess – dressing up as Robin Hood, and contriving, for all
> his careful disguise, to look the dead spit and image of his grandfather
> – and – if it comes to that – of his great, great grandfather too – the
> Regency one – the one that built the west wing and designed furniture,
> and was the friend of Edmund Kean.
> JACK: So I'm a slave to my class, am I?
> GEORGE: We all are, my dear boy, we all are. There is nothing to be done
> about it.
> JACK: Yes, there is. One can try to break the fetters.
> GEORGE: Oh yes. One can try that, if one's so disposed. But one will
> merely succeed in causing oneself and everyone else a good deal of
> unnecessary trouble and distress – without any result whatever. You will
> die with the fetters still in your hands.

As autumn turned to winter, Rattigan gradually began to get down
seriously to his new play. The hullabaloo over *Bequest to the Nation* had
died down. Cellan Jones was reconciled, for the moment, with his star,
and only sorry that Hal Wallis was refusing to stump up the money
for any seaborne battle scenes. But Rattigan let that wash over him.
In the afternoons he found the strength to write again. The new play,
though based on his stay with Rex Harrison and the dying Kay Kendall
in Hollywood in 1958, placed the couple in Islington, north London,
in 1972 and called them Sebastian and Lydia Cruttwell.

The Harrison figure is no longer an actor but a literary critic, and
Rattigan borrowed some of the characteristics of his old friend Cuthbert
Worsley to flesh out the portrait, while his wife is not a Hull-born
comedian but an Estonian refugee. They married at the end of the war
to get her out of the Russian zone in Berlin and thereby gain her a
British passport, but Sebastian over the years has grown to love her
so deeply that he doubts whether he can live without her. But before
he can admit that staggering fact to himself, or to his wife, he discovers
that she is suffering from a terminal illness. She does not know, and
he cannot tell her, or demonstrate to her how much he cares for her,

because if he does she will guess at once exactly how ill she really is. He wants his wife to spend the last months of her life without being conscious of the death sentence hanging over her.

As the play took shape a subsidiary plot began to emerge, focusing on the love of Sebastian Cruttwell for his son Joey, who has written a half-hour television play. But this love too Sebastian feels he dare not reveal, for fear that this second piece of uncharacteristically affectionate behaviour would further alert his wife to the fact that something is wrong.

In the play's final version, Rattigan decided that Lydia should suffer from poly-arteritis rather than leukaemia: partly in an effort to persuade Rex Harrison to play the part by disguising the parallels with his marriage to Kay Kendall. The disease itself was less important to Rattigan than his character's reactions. Lydia Cruttwell conspires with her doctor, a direct descendant of Mr Miller in *The Deep Blue Sea*, to persuade him to send encouraging reports of her progress to Sebastian. What she does not know is that he is also acting for Sebastian, and sending him honest reports. In fact Sebastian has been arranging for specialists to attend her sessions with her own doctor in the hope of finding a cure. One bad biopsy report makes him forget to come home to see his son's television play, and provides the link between the two plots.

Rattigan wanted the new play to convey emotions every bit as strong and sweeping as he had done in *The Browning Version* and *The Deep Blue Sea*, and in doing so to return to one of his abiding themes, the inability of the English to express their emotions, and particularly the emotion of love. The difference this time, in Rattigan's approach to the theme, was that the love in question was genuinely heterosexual. This was not the love that dared not speak its name, but the romantic love of a man for a woman to whom he has been married for almost thirty years.

He worked on the play throughout the winter, taking it back with him on a trip to Bermuda after Christmas, and returning with it all but completed towards the end of February. He wanted to spend the spring in England, to attend the première of *Bequest to the Nation*, which was scheduled for late April, but also to discuss the new play with Binkie Beaumont. Entitled *After Lydia*, it was only seventy minutes in length, and he had envisaged it being performed as the first play of a double bill. The second would be a brief farce, called *Before Dawn*, which he had written to conclude the evening. It was based on his favourite opera, Puccini's version of Sardou's story *La Tosca*, in which the heroine is faced with the dreadful choice of either making love to her captor, Scarpia, or allowing her lover, Mario Cavaradossi, to be executed.

Rattigan's farce turned this situation on its head. Tosca stabs Scarpia in the back, as in the Sardou/Puccini version, only to discover that he is wearing a knife-proof jacket. Then, at the moment when she thinks her fate is sealed, Scarpia turns out to be impotent. To conceal this terrible secret from the world he arranges for the lovers to be shot together – but by rifles loaded with blanks. Thus they will both escape. Only at the end is it revealed to the audience that Tosca's love for Cavaradossi is spiritual rather than physical. He prefers his boyfriend, Angelotti.

How H.M.Tennent – or, for that matter, opera lovers – would respond to this spoof Rattigan was far from sure. Even more important was whether they would rescind their rule, imposed in 1948, and be prepared to put on a double bill of his one-act plays. Beaumont had, in fact, been trying for a decade to encourage his friend to write 'a comedy about death' based on Kay Kendall's fate, and when he heard that Rattigan had finally done so he immediately suggested casting Rex Harrison and Celia Johnson as the principals. He was not at all happy about the play's short duration, nor that the heroine was Estonian, not English. Nevertheless, on the evening of 21 March, Binkie Beaumont settled down to read *After Lydia*. As soon as he had finished it, and still lying in bed, he rang Rattigan at Albany from his house in Lord North Street to tell him how much he liked it, and to suggest that John Gielgud might play Sebastian if Rex Harrison refused.

The next morning, Rattigan received another telephone call. It was to tell him that Binkie Beaumont had died from a heart attack during the night. Rattigan could hardly believe it. A thirty-year friendship and collaboration was at an end.

It was at this moment, perhaps, that Rattigan finally realised that the glamorous world of Shaftesbury Avenue, into which he had been launched in 1936, in all its glory of white ties and tails, had finally disappeared. No matter how bitchy he may have been, how capricious and how difficult on occasion, Beaumont had stood for civilised entertainment, for the well-made play, for Aunt Edna's world at its best. His genius for casting, and his impeccable taste and style, had left an indelible impression. Like Rattigan he had kept his private life well screened from the public gaze, but within his own circle, he had, like Rattigan, made no secret of his homosexuality, or its importance to him. The two men shared an outlook, and a discretion, that was precisely reflected in their view of the theatre. Emotions were to be implied, even concealed, rather than trumpeted: subtlety rather than

brash outspokenness was to be praised, and prized. But this philosophy
had been forced out of fashion in the course of the past decade. As a
tribute to his friend, Rattigan dedicated his double bill, now fittingly
called *In Praise of Love*, to Beaumont and his companion John Perry.

Inevitably, Beaumont's death delayed discussion of the double bill
and it was not until after the royal première of *Bequest to the Nation*,
on 25 April, that the matter of his two plays was raised again by John
Perry on Tennent's behalf. In the meantime Rattigan devoted what
energy he could muster to publicising the new film. He was badly
needed, not least because shortly before the opening Glenda Jackson
had given a television interview suggesting that she had been miscast,
and had, therefore, given a poor performance. This was the sort of
behaviour that Beaumont would never have tolerated from one of
his leading ladies. Rattigan felt it was 'inappropriate'. Pressed by one
journalist, he allowed himself to say: 'Perhaps it is the new fashion to
knock the film you're in. But she has not, so far as I know, returned
her cheque.' It was a pity, he continued, that they had not secured
Elizabeth Taylor, who 'would have done it for practically nothing'.
Of course, Miss Jackson 'did leave rather a lot out – Emma Hamilton's
love for Nelson, for one thing, which is quite important. She played
her as a mean-spirited bitch, instead of a great-hearted whore, but I
suppose that is her range.'

Fortunately both *Variety* and the *Hollywood Reporter* paid tribute to
Rattigan's screenplay when the film opened in the United States in
April under the new title, *The Nelson Affair*. *Variety* called it 'a deliberate, though stylish and genteel, deglamorization of the affair between
Lord Nelson and Lady Hamilton', while the *Hollywood Reporter*
believed his screenplay 'replaces stuffy costume drama with vibrant wit
and engaging melodrama'. Judith Crist in *New York* magazine added,
'Rattigan's gift – as he showed in *The Winslow Boy* – is in seeing a
period and people through the eyes of the young.' Only Andrew Sarris
in the *Village Voice* discounted the film, calling it 'not only a very
tedious movie' but also 'a very tedious idea for a movie'.

But the Nelson film script mattered to Rattigan far less than *In Praise
of Love*, his first new venture for the theatre for a decade. So it was
an enormous relief when he heard that John Perry, who remained at
H.M. Tennent in the wake of Beaumont's death, had agreed that they
would mount his double bill and had suggested John Dexter to direct it.
The eloquent, extrovert, and mischievous Dexter had been the original
director of Arnold Wesker's trilogy for the English Stage Company at
the Royal Court, as well as an associate director of the National Theatre
during Kenneth Tynan's period there, and was, therefore, hardly an

obvious choice for a Rattigan double bill. Nevertheless he had told Perry that he liked the plays, and even wrote to his friend, the composer Stephen Sondheim, calling them 'very good'. Dexter and Rattigan set off to spend a week in Cannes to work on the script. The double bill was to open in September.

The casting of Sebastian Cruttwell had long been one of Rattigan's chief concerns. The part was based on Rex Harrison, and he had always envisaged Harrison playing it. But he was well aware how sensitive Harrison was to any mention of his former wife, and how difficult he could be about playing parts which were not sympathetic. Rattigan knew that in extending his portrait of Cruttwell he had made him appear both bad-tempered and boorish. In the end, after lengthy discussions with John Dexter, Rattigan decided not to approach Harrison and take the risk of being rejected again. Instead he and Dexter settled on the English actor Donald Sinden, who had starred, albeit for only four performances, in one of his last West End openings, the ill-fated musical *Joie de Vivre*. Rattigan had promised him another leading role, and this was his chance. And to play Lydia Cruttwell, Rattigan suggested the London-born Joan Greenwood, whom he much admired, and who had twice successfully played Ibsen's Hedda Gabler in the West End in the past ten years.

The two plays were to open at the Duchess, site of Rattigan's triumph with *The Deep Blue Sea*, on 27 September 1973. But during the public previews he and Dexter became increasingly concerned that the order of the two plays was wrong. The sombre *After Lydia* seemed to drown the light-hearted *Before Dawn* if it came before it, and worse still, lessen its own impact. As a result, and after a good deal of heart-searching with Dexter, Rattigan agreed to reverse the order. 'We both of us like to think,' he wrote in the programme afterwards, 'that the impact of the substantial on the audience is even stronger than that of *The Browning Version*. It is certain that they seemed in no mood for any subsequent frivolity.' *Before Dawn* was now to be performed solely as a 'curtain raiser', and the main piece, instead of being called *After Lydia*, was to be given the title he had previously attached to both plays, *In Praise of Love*.

Before the decision was made, Rattigan had explained the point of the juxtaposition of the two plays to a reporter from the *Guardian*. 'The aim and object is to raise a tear in the first play and raise a laugh in the second. The first play is really about le vice Anglais. And this is not pederasty or flagellation. It is about the inability of the English to express emotion. The second play is about Italians who talk about love too freely but do not love enough.' In the event, the decision to reverse the order of the play of laughter and the play of tears was not destined to help either. The critics so disliked the 'curtain raiser' that it clouded their judgement when it came to the main piece. *Before Dawn* led many of the critics to underestimate both the intentions and the significance of *In Praise of Love*.

Milton Shulman in the London *Evening Standard*, for example, ended his review by suggesting, 'It is nice to have Sir Terence writing plays again but *In Praise of Love*, in spite of its adroit ability to handle death in such a chirpy manner, is not likely to be counted amongst his most important works.' *The Times* was even less generous: 'I cannot recommend anyone to go to what I can only see as a prologue.' While in the *Guardian*, Michael Billington, an admirer of Rattigan's, was equally disappointed: 'The famous Rattigan craftsmanship seems to be in abeyance,' he wrote. Billington concluded that by comparison with *The Browning Version* 'the work seems a rather crude and obvious piece of audience manipulation'. The worst review, which prompted Rattigan to write a bitter letter to its author, came from Michael Coveney in the *Financial Times*, who called it 'The product of a spirit languishing in the glow of a former heyday, a being in some way intravenously supplied with news from the outside world.' It was 'witless junk paraded under the banner of a reputation'.

The Sunday reviewers, Harold Hobson in the *Sunday Times*, and Frank Marcus in the *Sunday Telegraph*, were a great deal more complimentary. Hobson called *In Praise of Love* a 'play of unostentatious courage'; and Marcus insisted it was 'one of the finest plays Sir Terence has written'. But some damage had been done. *In Praise of Love*, together with its 'curtain raiser', survived for just 131 performances, and as John Dexter later admitted, it would have been taken off sooner without the two Sunday newspaper reviews.

The daily critics were wrong. The play, as Freddie Young wrote later, 'is the best-written play in the whole of Terry's work', and he listed the strengths of this 'masterpiece of deceit'.

> Casual as the language is in which the dialogue is couched, it gives the impression of care that is missing from the earlier plays . . . But the ability to reproduce everyday conversational English is the least of the merits the play exhibits. It is a technical masterpiece. A good deal of the dialogue is comic; Rattigan considered calling the play a comedy. *After Lydia* is not a comedy, however, so much as a thriller. There are as many hidden clues in the story as in an Agatha Christie detective play, but the clues are psychological rather than practical.

The interplay between the Cruttwells, their son Joey and the family's friend Mark Walters, a successful novelist, is brilliantly woven. As Young puts it:

> What is so interesting is that the problem is a different one for each character. Sebastian knows Lydia will die and must not say anything about it. Lydia knows she will die and may tell Mark but not Sebastian or Joey. Mark knows that Lydia will die but does not know at first that Sebastian knows it. Joey never knows it. So often praised for his stagecraft, Rattigan never wrote so clever a play as this.

But the Rattigan era had passed, and for the majority of his audience – and the daily critics – that meant that he was no longer capable of writing a serious or a significant play, especially one preceded by a farce. It was a sad misjudgement, but something he had grown all too accustomed to. He kept the play running with his own money during its last weeks at the Duchess, and hoped that New York would redress the balance. But for Broadway he knew he needed a star, and the only person he wanted to play the part of Sebastian was the man who had inspired it. He had taken Rex to see the London production himself.

In the autumn of 1973, and the first months of 1974, Rattigan resumed his wandering. In the early part of the year he had been to New York and to play golf at Turnberry in Scotland, as well as making a trip to stay at the Martinez in Cannes. In September he was in Brighton, staying at the Metropole, in October at the North British Hotel in Edinburgh, in November at the Carlton in Bournemouth. More often than not Michael Franklin would travel with him, otherwise Pegs French would go. At Christmas he went back to Bermuda, and stayed until the weather in Europe improved, working on a television play for the BBC on the life of the dancer Nijinsky. In April he returned to Albany, and in May 1974 he went to Glenrothes in Fife to see the house that Michael Franklin had bought and decorated for him. But he never once slept there. He was convinced the place was haunted.

By July 1974 the plans for an American production of *In Praise of Love* were well advanced. After the experience of London, Rattigan had decided it should be performed alone, and its length extended to something like eighty-five minutes. He had written the extra scenes, particularly a lengthy description of Lydia's escape from execution, during the winter in Bermuda. The only matter still to be decided was the casting of Sebastian Cruttwell. After careful thought, Rattigan decided to take the plunge and write to Rex Harrison – only to find that a London newspaper had disastrously jumped the gun with an article claiming that plans were afoot for Harrison to 'play himself on Broadway'.

Harrison, then staying at Portofino in Italy, was horrified and enraged, and once more, as so often in the past, Rattigan had to mollify his temperamental friend and star. He did so in the course of a long and passionate letter explaining exactly why he was convinced that Harrison should consider playing Sebastian Cruttwell, and suggesting, in spite of what the newspapers were claiming, that he would not simply be playing himself.

'Sebastian Cruttwell is not Rex Harrison,' he wrote.

Rex Harrison, to play Sebastian Cruttwell on stage, must play a character part, i.e. he must do everything to avoid any identification by the audience of two totally dissimilar characters . . . I'm not saying it's going to be easy for you – or for me when I rewrite – to stop an audience making that sentimental, wrong-headed and, I believe, utterly disastrous identification; but somehow we both have to do it.

Rattigan went on to outline precisely how he saw Cruttwell, telling Harrison that they had to

persuade an audience that Sebastian is a self-centred, Winchester-Balliol-Intelligence Service, ex-novelist, literary (high-brow) critic. (Cyril Connolly I kept thinking of when writing it) . . . who married an Estonian refugee girl he slept with in Berlin twenty-eight years ago . . . who finds out, one day, six months before the play opens, and twenty-eight and a half years after they've got married – that in fact he loves her, and doubts if he can live without her. But he can't let her know that, or she'll know she's dying. And he doesn't, by continuing to act the shit that in fact he's always been since the beginning of time. You do see, as our late lamented friend would have said, how very, very different a character that is from my dear friend, who once met a lady, loved her at first sight (as she loved him), contemplated marriage, was told by her doctors that she had a mortal disease and had no more than, perhaps, two years to live: who nevertheless went ahead and married her – not to give her a passport, but for the highest kind of love . . . and who behaved, throughout his long appalling ordeal, as well as any husband could. That was no uncaring shit (or 'cad' or 'bastard' or 'rotter' or whatever that word turns out to be), it was no 'uncaring' anything . . . It was you, and it was a million miles from Sebastian.

'The play is called *In Praise of Love*,' he continued, 'and it is: because it's only Sebastian's ability to feel it rather than just write about it that makes him a man and not just Ken Tynan . . . but that "caringness" must – repeat must – come as a surprise – or, at the least, creep up on us very belatedly – because if he is shown early on as "caring" then we have no play.'

Rattigan finished by insisting, 'The play I did write – inspired, I admit, by certain events that deeply moved me, but not at any time by the characters – relies entirely on the element of surprise.'

His appeal worked. Harrison agreed to play the part on Broadway. His co-star was to be Julie Harris, who had recently won her second Antoinette Perry award in New York, this time for her portrayal of Mrs Lincoln. And the play, to be directed by Fred Coe, rather than John Dexter, was to open in December.

No sooner had the plans for New York been finalised than Rattigan was struck down by pneumonia. He had been campaigning for the Liberal Party candidate in the forthcoming general election in Rich- mond-on-Thames, and had caught a cold which had steadily worsened. It was his severest attack for two years, and Dr Buky was so concerned that he arranged for him to be admitted to the Wellington Hospital, next door to Lord's Cricket Ground in Marylebone. Buky was worried that his patient's immune system might have been weakened so severely by the effect of his leukaemia that he might not be able to fight off the disease. In the event it took Rattigan more than two months to recover any strength at all, and almost three months before he felt well enough to travel to New York to see his play.

When he finally caught up with it, in Washington during its pre- Broadway tour, he was horrified. Rex Harrison was ruining it. Instead of playing the critic as bad-tempered, boorish, and indifferent to his wife, Harrison was playing him as a sympathetic, affectionate husband from the very beginning. He was even found looking at Lydia's medical reports at the opening of the play, thereby conveying to the audience his concern for her condition. It made Sebastian's transformation from indifference to passionate and undying love – an event Harold Hobson had called 'one of the great moments in the British theatre' – into a nonsense. It removed the surprise that Rattigan himself had explained to Harrison lay at the heart of his play.

But Harrison refused to change his performance. 'People will think I'm a shit,' he argued, unless he made it plain he was concerned about his wife. When Rattigan reminded him that that was the whole point of the play, and exactly what the audience were supposed to think, Harrison ignored him, and asked instead whether some of Lydia's lines could not be cut, as Harrison felt she was receiving more attention than he was. Rattigan refused point blank. The proposed cuts would make a mockery of the speech he had so carefully prepared for Sebastian in Act Two, in which the boorish critic finally admits his passion for his wife to Mark Walters.

> SEBASTIAN: No I could – but I've got to get used to – try to get used to – oh damn! Did I feel about her like this from the beginning? It's possible. It's possible. And wouldn't allow myself to? Yes, possible. (*Angrily*). Do you know what 'le vice Anglais?' – the English vice – really is? Not flagellation, not pederasty – whatever the French believe it to be. It's our refusal to admit to our emotions. We think they demean us, I suppose.
>   *He covers his face.*
> Well, I'm being punished now, all right – for a lifetime of vice. Very moral endings to a Victorian novel. I'm becoming maudlin. But, oh Mark, life without Lydia will be such unending misery.

Harold French, who had travelled to Washington with his wife Pegs to help to look after him, tried to explain Rattigan's view to Harrison but without success. He also tried to persuade Rattigan to remove some of the longer expositions about refugees that he had added to the play. In the end, neither Harrison nor he would compromise, and the play opened at the Morosco Theatre on 10 December 1974, with an obviously sympathetic and affectionate Sebastian Cruttwell, and somewhat lengthy speeches about the fate of Estonian refugees. Even so, the New York critics were a shade more impressed than their colleagues in London had been. *Variety* called it 'a touching but not depressing comedy drama', the *Daily Post* 'moving and beautiful', and Rex Reed, in the *Daily News*, described it as 'an extraordinary evening of rare perfection'. The play was to run for 199 performances, although more on the strength of its star names than its intended message. It was to be Rattigan's last new play for Broadway.

Rattigan retreated to Bermuda. He was 'heart-broken' at the notices, Harold French remembers. 'They still mattered to him a very great deal.' He was also very weak, the result of travelling too much in the wake of pneumonia. Pegs French had taken over looking after him completely and he decided to buy another house there, once again on the edge of a golf course. If he could not play himself, at least the prospect of watching other people's toe-shots might provide some amusement. He could not face returning to live permanently in London again; the danger of catching another cold which could develop into pneumonia was simply too great. In December 1974 he resigned his lease on the double set H5-6 in Albany. Only the house in Scotland remained, and he had no intention whatever of living there. Michael Franklin, and those few friends who cared to, could come and visit him in Bermuda. It was as if he was preparing himself for death. That summer he even signed a contract with Jamie Hamilton to write his autobiography before the end of 1975. It was to be called *Without Tears*.

He hardly had the strength to work. Only during short periods in the course of the afternoons did he feel able to write. His script about Nijinsky, which Cedric Messina had commissioned as a 'Play of the Month' for the BBC, had run into difficulties. Nijinksy's widow, Romola, had objected to her husband being depicted as a homosexual, by a writer who she believed was also a homosexual. The BBC insisted that she had no case, but Rattigan himself was sensitive to her view, and anxious not to offend her. He decided he did not want the work produced during his lifetime, even though he was proud of it.

The 105-page manuscript focused on the 'two most famous lovers since Romeo and Juliet', as Rattigan called them: Nijinsky and his choreographer Diaghilev. Their relationship ends when Nijinsky fathers a child by Romola de Pulszky, and Diaghilev withdraws his love. Rattigan brings this ending to life with a brutal argument between the two men in a lawyer's office. In a stage direction, he added: 'You must imagine a scene between two estranged and passionate homo-sexuals whose love and estrangement is known to the whole civilised world, having matters out – the essence of these matters anyway – against a background of stiff collared, puritanical lawyers, putting documents away, red faced with embarrassment.' Sensitive and beauti-ful though it was, the play was destined never to be performed. Romola Nijinsky's objections died with her four years later, but the play remained only a manuscript.

Without Tears did not even become a manuscript. The expense of buying his new house, Spanish Grange in Tuckers Town, the cost of removal from Albany, and his living expenses, had substantially eroded the capital Rattigan had built up from his years of screenwriting. And the failure of *In Praise of Love*, which he had supported financially in London towards the end of its run, had further drained his resources. This meant that he could not afford to turn down any profitable offer. One such was an invitation to work on an idea for a love story that could form the basis for a musical by the composer and book and lyric writers of *My Fair Lady*, Alan Jay Lerner and Frank Loewe. He was also considering updating an old project about First World War pilots. But finally he accepted another commission from the BBC. He agreed to write a play for radio for £6,000.

And all this when he could only find the energy to work for a few hours at a time. Pegs French ran the new house for him, and made sure the servants did what was required. Meanwhile Rattigan would sit and watch the golfers struggle on the third green at the end of his garden. He had not given up smoking. The cigarette-holder was still in evidence, although not flourished with quite such panache if no visitors were present. And he was still drinking. Harold French, who came out on a visit from England, watched as Rattigan left glasses of all kinds around the house. 'There might be a gin and tonic beside the sofa, a glass of red wine in the loo, a scotch in the garden. Rattigan would forget he had one drink and pour himself another.' But his faculties in other respects were unimpaired. He was still capable of writing, and writing dialogue.

Memories of his parents' flat in Stanhope Gardens, Kensington, were all around him. Spanish Grange was filled with photographs of his mother and father. That was where he had written his first plays alone, after his abortive collaboration with Philip Heimann on *First Episode* all those years ago. That was where he had learnt his craft, and he remembered his feelings with astonishing clarity. The genteel flat, his mother worried that he would not be able to support himself, the manuscripts posted off (and usually returned), the bus rides into the West End to see a show. He could almost smell the petrol-driven buses, hear the newspaper sellers shouting the evening headlines, see in his mind's eye the red velvet curtain with its gold tassels in the Globe.

It had been during one of his trips to the theatre that Rattigan had first seen a newspaper placard announcing details of what was called 'The Rattenbury Case'. The case and the trial that followed had stayed in his mind ever since. 'I remember I was on top of a bus in Park Lane in 1935,' Rattigan remembered forty years later. 'I saw the headline, "Mrs Rattenbury Kills Herself", and I thought then . . . as a budding playwright . . . My God, what a revenge on her detractors, of whom God knows I was one. I was with everybody else in thinking she was the bitch of all time . . . I couldn't use it then, but I thought one day I could have a shot at it.' The Rattenbury case contained every suppressed human emotion that he had made his own as a playwright, and it was set in a world that he knew well, the genteel, apparently respectable, but sometimes empty and solitary world of the English upper middle class.

Alma Rattenbury, a mildly successful composer of popular songs, and an attractive woman of thirty-eight, had married an elderly, retired and comfortably off businessman who was unable to satisfy her sexually. The couple lived in Bournemouth, and, unlikely to meet many other men, she had advertised for, and appointed, a handyman and chauffeur, George Stoner, aged eighteen, whom she had rapidly made her lover and taken on holiday to London. When they had returned to Bournemouth, the young man had become extremely jealous of her husband, particularly when he found out that she was still having sexual relations with him. The elderly Mr Rattenbury was then beaten to death with a wooden mallet, and both Stoner and Mrs Rattenbury were charged with the murder.

In 1935 the case became a *cause célèbre*. Alma Rattenbury was a 'scarlet woman' who had led a young man astray. The question was – had she encouraged him to kill her husband? When the two came to trial at the Central Criminal Court at the Old Bailey in London, the jury found Mrs Rattenbury innocent of the charge of murder and she was released. But George Stoner was found guilty and sentenced to be hanged. A few weeks after the sentence, and convinced that her young lover was to die on the gallows, Alma Rattenbury stabbed herself to death with a knife. A few weeks later, her young lover was reprieved, and his sentence commuted to life imprisonment. By the 1950s he had been released and – as far as Rattigan knew – was still alive. But he had never once given an explanation of what really happened on the night of Mr Rattenbury's death. It had always been pure raw material for a Rattigan drama, and he knew it. But he did not simply want to recreate the events of the trial. He would use the case as another opportunity to explore the English attitude to sex, to emotions, and the reactions of reticence and fear both regularly prompted. The fact that his own sexual drive had all but subsided since his illness had worsened did not mean that its legacy no longer haunted him. It remained a subject of the deepest interest to him.

To exploit it as drama, Rattigan created another plot, one of the most painfully honest – and autobiographical – that he had ever introduced. As a counterpoint to Mrs Rattenbury and George Stoner, he introduced a juror, Mrs Davenport, a lady of almost identical age to Mrs Rattenbury and portrayed as living in a Kensington flat almost identical to the one he had been brought up in himself. This juror also had a sexually incompatible husband. But it is she, not he, who is the sexual puritan, and he – not she – who responds by taking a string of young female lovers. The audience discovers all this as a result of a lengthy conversation between Mrs Davenport and her teenage son, Tony, who is a boarder at an English public school.

Mrs Davenport is, to all intents and purposes, a portrait of Rattigan's dead mother, Vera Rattigan. She is even described as the child of a distinguished family of lawyers, as Vera herself had been. And Tony is an attempt by Rattigan to explain to himself part of his own development. Mrs Davenport loves her son excessively, in compensation for her failed marriage. But she will not accept his own developing sexuality. Indeed she refuses even to discuss the subject. With money from his father, who is not living with the family (and is an obvious echo of Frank Rattigan), Tony decides to experiment with his own sexuality by going to a prostitute, but with disastrous results. (Rattigan was to imply after finishing the play that he had based the event on an experience of his own, though many of his friends doubted it.)

Humiliated, Tony rejects the possibility of heterosexuality and returns instead to an affair with a younger boy at his school. During the course of the play, Tony also discovers that the dark picture painted of his father by his mother is an exaggeration, and that his father's affairs were often no more than brief encounters, prompted by his wife's inability to respond to him sexually. Mrs Davenport has used them as an excuse to sustain her own position as 'the wronged party' in their marriage. In an ironic double reference to Alma Rattenbury and Mrs Davenport, alias Vera Rattigan, Rattigan called the play *A Woman of Principle*.

For almost three years he had been attempting to conceal the full extent of his illness from his friends. Now, as 1975 progressed, he knew he could not keep his secret much longer. And he knew that he wanted to spend at least a part of his time with Michael Franklin. In April 1975 they travelled together to Scotland, to stay near the Fife house that Franklin had bought for him, but that he had never lived in. Two months later they were at Turnberry in Ayrshire. But the effort exhausted Rattigan. By the middle of July he was back in the London Clinic in the hands of Dr Buky. In August he made a brief sortie to the Martinez in Cannes, and the following month he returned to the Grand in Brighton. But the pain had become intense. Throughout the autumn there were a series of exploratory operations. The results confirmed what he had known for a long time, that the cancer in the bone marrow of his back was malignant, and spreading more quickly than it had been in the preceding years. When he returned to Bermuda for Christmas, to escape the worst of the English winter, he was dying.

Rattigan had prepared himself carefully for this moment. He wanted to play it as lightly and gracefully as he had tried to play every other major crisis in his life. His friend and publisher Roger Machell said later, 'He took the whole thing outwardly very much more lightly than the characters in *In Praise of Love*,' while Freddie Young recalled that 'He treated it as light-heartedly as if it were a cutting from a gossip column.' For Rattigan it would have been a betrayal of his life's principles to do anything else.

Yet he could not always control his tears. And when the floodgates opened now, there was little of his old reserve. Not long after Christmas, and back in London for more treatments and more tests, Alvin Rakoff, who had worked with him on *Heart to Heart* more than a decade before, took him to a showing of a version of *In Praise of Love* which he had made for Anglia Television, starring Kenneth More and Claire Bloom. It was the first time Rattigan had seen the play performed as he had envisaged it, with More precisely capturing the transformation of Sebastian from a boor to a man who can hardly bear the thought of losing his wife. In the small private viewing theatre the tears poured down his face as he watched this acknowledgement of his own brilliance – and of his own mortality.

It was not the only time he was to burst into tears. A new production of *The Browning Version* was about to be launched at the King's Head pub, a fringe theatre in Islington, north London, and Terence Rattigan very much wanted to attend the first night. He was anxious to collaborate in any way he could. He had considered rewriting parts of it, because he was afraid the language would sound old-fashioned; and he suggested that there might even be an interval. To provide a first-act curtain, he felt that the Crock might ask where his own translation of the *Agamemnon* had gone to, only to be told by Millie that she had burnt it. But in the end, at the request of its young director, Stewart Trotter, he left the play as it was.

At the first night in January 1976, he again broke down in tears. Stewart Trotter told Freddie Young afterwards, 'The play really took off that night, and at the end it was difficult to say who was crying most – a group of trainee teachers at a table to our left or Rattigan himself.' After the final curtain, Trotter took Rattigan back stage to meet the cast, which included Nigel Stock as Crocker-Harris. 'But the treatment he was having made him pee a lot. So first I took him upstairs to the grotty King's Head loo. Standing outside, I heard a gurgling sound that made me happier than I can say. It was Rattigan singing.' The revival was such a success that there was talk of a transfer to the West End, and he was asked if he would adapt his television monologue for Margaret Leighton, *All on Her Own*, for use as a curtain raiser. He did so within a few days, and retitled the piece *Duologue*, but the transfer never happened.

Disappointed at the failure of *The Browning Version* to transfer to the West End, Terence Rattigan returned to Bermuda, to work as much as his pain allowed. He pretended he could still manage four hours writing a day, but this was not usually true. When the pain subsided he could, but more often than not it it did not. He had turned down an approach to write a film script for Lisa Minelli, who just three years before had won an Academy Award for her performance as Sally Bowles in the film of the musical *Cabaret*. The task was too demanding, and he did not know whether he would manage to complete it. He did not want to let anyone down. When he could, he was working on a stage version of his radio play on the Rattenbury case, which the BBC had broadcast in October 1975 and called *Cause Célèbre* but which he still preferred to call *A Woman of Principle*. The play had been commissioned by the British impresario John Gale, who wanted it for production in the autumn of 1976 and had approached Dorothy Tutin to play the doomed Alma Rattenbury. Rattigan could not have been happier – perhaps in the wake of *The Browning Version* at the King's Head, it was another small sign that the tide had turned in his favour again.

In the meantime, he was planning yet another play, which had also been in his mind for years. It was to focus on the Asquith family, and the Battle of the Somme in 1916, which Rattigan believed had brought the 'end of a form of Western Civilisation'. His uncle Cyril, his father's brother, had been killed in the battle, and so had Puffin Asquith's brother Raymond, while their father was still Prime Minister. 'It was in Asquith's power to stop the war,' Rattigan told the American critic and academic Holly Hill later. If he had done so, and there had been a negotiated peace rather than the unconditional surrender demanded two years later, the fate of Europe, Rattigan believed, would have been transformed.

The spark that had convinced him there was material for a new play had come from Puffin, who had once told him that his father had gone to visit the British commander, Field Marshal Sir Douglas Haig, six weeks after the Battle of the Somme began, and that Haig had arranged for Raymond to come to see him. During this visit, Asquith could have asked for his son to be reassigned, but he did not do so, and Raymond was killed a week later. His father was pushed from office barely two months after that. Rattigan saw tremendous significance in this episode. The father had been unable to convey to his son how passionately he loved him, and the son had been unable to overcome his own rigid self-discipline. 'They never touched each other at all,' Rattigan later told Holly Hill. The emotional repression and the desolation revealed in the lives of even the brightest Englishmen fascinated, moved and appalled him. But he was too ill ever to complete even a first draft.

In the spring of 1976, Buky told his patient that he would be lucky to survive for much more than a year if the disease continued at its present pace. The news came as no shock. Rattigan had been receiving regular monthly reports on his condition for some time. But it did spur him on to complete *A Woman of Principle*, which he was now describing as his 'last play'. That was not turning out to be easy. A director, appointed by Gale, came to visit him in Bermuda, but the two men did not get on and Rattigan asked for a replacement. Gale picked on Peter Coe, partly because of his long line of successes with episodic material like the Rattenbury case, but Coe wanted to drop the Davenport sub-plot, and Rattigan would not hear of it. Plucking up his courage, he asked Gale to try again. But at this point Tutin suddenly became unavailable and the production came to a halt.

Still, a new production of *Separate Tables*, starring John Mills and Jill Bennett, was in preparation, and there was also talk of a new version of *The Deep Blue Sea* with Sheila Hancock. A touring version of *In Praise of Love* was in prospect, as was a touring version of *Flare Path*. Another British impresario had taken out an option on *The Sleeping Prince* for the Queen's Jubilee celebrations in 1977, and there was talk too of the French actress Jeanne Moreau playing Hester in New York. Rattigan himself wondered whether he should adapt Anthony Trollope's novel *The Warden*, which had last been produced in London half a century earlier, and offer it to John Gielgud, but in the end he simply felt too ill.

Finally, John Gale persuaded Robin Midgley, the artistic director of the Haymarket Theatre in Leicester, to work on the stage version of the Rattenbury play, and Midgley flew to Bermuda to see Rattigan in January 1977, having carefully reconstructed the play from the original radio version and Rattigan's own first draft for the stage. The two men got on, and spent the next two weeks refining still further the play that Rattigan was insisting should be called *A Woman of Principle*. In early February Midgley flew back to England to plan for the production. It was to open in Leicester, run there for three weeks, and then transfer to the Her Majesty's in London. Rattigan was determined to be present.

By now in perpetual, agonising pain, he flew back to London from Bermuda on 28 April 1977, but instead of installing himself in a suite at Claridges, as he had been able to do only fifteen months before, he now had no alternative but to allow himself to be admitted to the King Edward VII's Hospital for Officers in Beaumont Street in central

London. He did his best to put on his customary brave face but there could be no disguising the fact that he was deteriorating rapidly. There was a suggestion that he should have a quick operation, in an effort to reduce some of the pain, but he did not want to risk this before seeing his play in Leicester, even though there was no possibility that he would be able to attend the first night. Instead he suggested to Midgley that perhaps he should come and see a Saturday matinée. The first chance for this would be on 21 May.

But before the play even opened a number of crises struck. Dorothy Tutin had pulled out and Glynis Johns had taken her place as Alma Rattenbury. Then she too had withdrawn and Heather Sears had taken over. Charles Gray, as the defence lawyer O'Connor, at one point dropped out too, but in due course returned to the role. In great pain, Rattigan finally made the long car journey from London to watch his last play, and at the end discussed the production and the performances with Midgley. Then he climbed painfully back into his car and set off back to London to await his operation. With some trepidation, he had set it for 1 June.

CHAPTER 27

Death's Feather

◆

I, born of flesh and ghost, was neither

A ghost nor man, but mortal ghost.

DYLAN THOMAS, 'Before I Knocked'

◆

On the warm summer evening of Monday, 4 July 1977, Sir Terence Rattigan CBE was gently ushered into the foyer of Her Majesty's Theatre in the Haymarket to attend the first night of the twenty-first of his new plays to be presented in London's West End. Half an hour before the curtain went up, the wheelchair that was bearing him was pushed into the Royal Box. He was wearing a dinner jacket, as he had done on each of these special occasions over the past forty-three years, and he had had his hair trimmed that afternoon. However ill, he was not about to neglect the superstitions that had more often brought him good luck than bad since they had begun two hundred yards away in Piccadilly Circus. As he settled himself painfully into his red plush seat with its gilt surround, the pain in his hips making every movement excruciating, he looked down at the stalls. It was to be an evening filled with ghosts.

So many had gone. His mother and father were not beside him as they had been for the first night of *French Without Tears*, and so often afterwards. Nor were A.D.Peters, Bronson Albery, Chips Channon, Puffin Asquith, or Binkie Beaumont, all of whom had shared so many other first nights with him over the years. Vivien Leigh was not there, nor Kay Hammond, nor his beloved Margaret Leighton. Philip Heimann was not there, nor Eric Portman nor Michael Wilding. Kenneth Morgan was not there, nor Peter Osborn.

In their place, the man sitting at his side was Michael Franklin. He

too was wearing a dinner jacket, and smiling as though to assure Rattigan that everything would go smoothly. He had even leant across
to squeeze his arm. The young man who had slipped into his life
before the first night of *The Deep Blue Sea* twenty-five years earlier
was now approaching fifty. Rattigan, slightly bloated by the drugs
he was obliged to take, shifted in his seat as the pain in his hips
returned.

Beneath him, the critics gradually took their seats. There too the
ghosts lingered. Many of his old friends and adversaries had also disappeared. Even Kenneth Tynan had left England for the United States,
as saddened and dispirited by the artistic atmosphere of his own country
as once Rattigan himself had been. And tonight, for the first time in
more than twenty years, Cuthbert Worsley too was absent. News of
his death had been cabled to Rattigan by John Gielgud in February. It
had been a terrible blow. Cuthie had championed his work when it
seemed as though almost every other critic in London was determined
to destroy it. Rattigan would never forget him.

As the house lights went down, his old nervousness returned. He
liked the young director, Robin Midgley, and Glynis Johns had rejoined
the cast, although Charles Gray had been replaced by Kenneth Griffith.
The sweat built up, as it always did, on the palms of Rattigan's hands,
but he was no longer mobile enough to slip quietly out to the circle
bar for a drink as the first act got under way. Instead he was obliged
to sit and watch the first night in its entirety. He was not relishing the
prospect.

Just as it had done for *The Winslow Boy*, the programme for *Cause
Célèbre* contained a note pointing out that 'The play was inspired by
the facts of a well-known case, but the characters attributed to the
individuals represented are based on the author's imagination, and are
not necessarily factual.' And the stage, as it had been for *A Bequest to
the Nation*, *Ross*, and *Adventure Story*, was to represent a variety of
different places, including, 'at various times, Court Number One at the
Old Bailey and other parts of the Central Criminal Court in London, a
villa in Bournemouth, the drawing-room of a flat in Kensington, and
other places'. Rattigan had wanted it made absolutely clear that the
curtain was to fall 'only at the end of each of the two acts'.

The red velvet curtain swung up to reveal Alma Rattenbury pleading
not guilty to the charge of murder. But soon it became abundantly
clear that it was his secondary characters, Mrs Davenport and her son
Tony, rather than the principals, Mrs Rattenbury and George Stoner
(renamed George Wood), who were to dominate the opening scenes.
It was Tony and his 'best pal at Westmnster, Randolph Browne', two

adolescents fascinated by sex, who were to recreate the ghosts of his Kensington youth.

TONY: I wonder what our parents think we do between thirteen and twenty-one.

BROWNE: Solo, I should think, or else have cold tubs and brisk trots.

TONY: It's such damn humbug. Of course they know we're safe – apart from Shuttleworths, which they don't like to think about. You should have heard my mother on this Mrs Rattenbury. The murder apart, my mother seems to think she's the monster of Glamis, just because she's twenty years older than Wood . . . And why not? Look at her. (*He slaps the paper*) She's damned attractive.

Still a virgin at seventeen, Tony decides to experiment sexually, and go to a prostitute in Paddington. From her he contracts a venereal disease which necessitates a painful course of treatment and fundamentally affects his whole attitude to women and sex. As he finally tells his mother:

TONY: Mum – twice a day for maybe six weeks, maybe longer, I'll have to lock myself in there – (*He points off*) – and you'll hear a tap running. Do you honestly think I can hope to come out of there without knowing what you're saying to yourself: 'My son has committed a filthy, disgusting act, and he's been punished for it with a filthy disgusting disease and a filthy, disgusting treatment –'

Exactly how close the parallel between Tony's life and his own, Rattigan left his friends to speculate. Few of them believed that he had ever experimented sexually with a woman; but several suspected that he had, at some stage, contracted a venereal disease as a result of a homosexual encounter. Certainly Rattigan was extremely sensitive about the subject, and had, over the years, been at pains to disguise the fact that some of the illnesses to which he had become increasingly prone might have owed part of their origin to his sexual activities. But, unlike Tony, however, Rattigan would never have discussed his sexual experiences with his mother.

His memories of repressed sexual desire and their consequences permeated the play's first act, as they had suffused the first act of *The Deep Blue Sea* and the first part of *Separate Tables*. Yet again, sex was to set the emotional tone of the play. As Tony was suffering from its pressures, so too were Alma Rattenbury and her new young lover, George Wood. George's passion for Alma is not so very different from Hester's passion for Freddie in *The Deep Blue Sea*, or John Malcolm's for Mrs Shankland in *Separate Tables*. The handyman even explains it to his defence counsel as the first act draws to its close.

CASSWELL: You are of age to be hanged, Mr Wood.

WOOD: I know.

CASSWELL: You are disposed then to die?

WOOD: No. I'm not. I want to live – Christ, don't I want to live. But I'm not going to say *she* made me do it. They can tear me apart before they'll get me to say that.

CASSWELL: I don't think you quite understand.

WOOD: (*Violently*) It's you who don't bloody understand. Alma Rattenbury, sex-mad drunken bloody cow that she is, lying deceitful bitch too come to that – she's the only woman I've ever had, and the only one I've ever loved, and I'm not going to shop her now . . . No, it's you who don't bloody understand, Mr Casswell, nor the others either.

During the interval, Rattigan chatted to Pegs French and Michael Franklin. Part of him was not entirely happy with the play. The structure was not perfect, but he had not felt well enough to go on making amendments, though he had written it four times, starting with the radio play. And there had been the difficulties with the casting – and with the director. Still, it seemed to be going well enough.

In the second act, more ghosts. Tony's father explains his unfaithfulness to Mrs Davenport, in words that his own father might have used to his mother. Davenport has written his wife a letter, which he reads aloud after she has refused to read it herself.

DAVENPORT: . . . I must tell you with complete truth that there is no other woman in my life. No single other woman, that is. The one you know about left me some months ago, with no regrets on either side. She wasn't important to me. No woman has ever been important to me except yourself. I admit that I've had occasional affairs, but they were necessary to me – you know why – always brief, and usually with a mercenary tinge. Without you, Edie, and without Tony, I have been a very lonely man. So, I believe, are you lonely without me. Please let me come back into your life. If you do I promise to behave as well as I can. That doesn't, I'm afraid, mean as well as you'd want me to. It can never mean that, Edie darling, as you know. But if you can only bring yourself to overlook an occasional late night at the office, or the odd dinner at the Club with the Permanent Secretary, I swear a solemn oath to you that you will never otherwise be humiliated. I renounce my conjugal rights entirely, but I earnestly entreat you to let me once again be your loving husband. John.

In contrast Alma Rattenbury's explanation of her sexuality, when she finally agrees to give evidence in her own defence, shows her partner in a different light.

> O'CONNOR: And what attitude did your husband take to all this?
> ALMA: None whatsoever.
> JUDGE: You mean he didn't know of it?
> ALMA: Oh, I think he must have known of it, My Lord.
> JUDGE: Then he must have taken some attitude – even if it was one of tactful silence?
> ALMA: I just don't think he gave it a thought.

Sexual passion – and the inequality of desire between two partners – lay at the heart of this last play, as it had in so many others in the past. Rattigan even let the repressed Mrs Davenport throw the spotlight on himself – unknown to most of the audience – when she repeats one of Alma Rattenbury's remarks: 'When an older person loves a younger, it's the younger who dominates, because the younger has so much more to give.' This was part of his own passion for Kenneth Morgan and Michael Franklin. And was he expressing in part his own desire when Alma, acquitted of murder, stabs herself in the last moments of the play, crying out: 'Thank God for peace at last'?

As the curtain fell the applause was loud and sustained, and Rattigan acknowledged it for the benefit of those who recognised him. But there was not the frenzy that had marked some of his past first nights. The days of gushing ovations had disappeared, to be replaced by a more measured enthusiasm, and the following morning the daily critics reflected this. In the *Guardian* Michael Billington welcomed the play's return to Rattigan's theme: 'the hypocrisy of the English about sex and the unequal distribution of passion in any two-sided relationship', adding that it underlined 'Rattigan's own passionate hatred of English puritanism and noble, unwavering affirmation of life'. At the weekend Bernard Levin in the *Sunday Times* described the play as 'by a man who knows that in every human being there is the capacity to reflect the living, and that it is love in all its forms, from the noblest to the most tawdry, that is most likely to show the gleam of that reflection. His play is theatrical in the best sense of the word, and I hope he will be spared to write many more such.' He was not to be.

'Well, that'll be my last first night,' Rattigan told Pegs French as she helped him back into his car to return to hospital. Nevertheless, the good notices cheered him. Two mornings later he was so elated that he decided to take a walk around the outside of the building. His first biographers, Darlow and Hodson, who saw him later the same day, recalled that 'He scared himself by finding out how weak he really was.' Even so, he was in sufficiently good spirits to tell Sheridan Morley how pleased he was to find himself acclaimed again by the London critics. 'I didn't think it would happen to me. I had hoped, though, that it might . . . I always thought that justice would one day be done to me.'

Somerset Maugham had warned him as a young man that he would enjoy only twenty years in fashion before being replaced by someone else, but he had never been able to accept the idea. He could not believe that the theatre was subject to the cruel swings of taste that Pinero had described in *Trelawney of the Wells*. The years had taught him otherwise. After a time, he told Morley, 'I discovered that any play I wrote would get smashed. I just didn't have a chance with anything.' Then he paused, and added, 'But perhaps I should have stayed and fought it out.' His fragile vanity was still, just as it had always been, his Achilles' heel.

All Rattigan wanted now was peace, to escape the pain of his illness. He disliked hospitals, which was one reason he insisted on sitting on his bed wearing outdoor clothes – 'It gave him a sense that he wasn't really there,' in the words of a friend – and he had no intention of staying in hospital a moment longer than was necessary. As soon as his treatments were over, he wanted to return to Bermuda: to die there in peace, and privacy.

He was still a man of the theatre, however, with all his theatrical instincts intact. He intended to bid farewell to London, and to England, with as much drama as one of his own curtain lines. With Roger Machell's help, Rattigan arranged for copies of each of his plays to be specially bound in leather – and delivered to Buckingham Palace. He then asked to be driven round London's theatreland, where there were now not one but two Rattigan plays running – *Separate Tables* with John Mills and Jill Bennett at the Apollo, and *Cause Célèbre* at the Her Majesty's.

In the first week of August, with tears in his eyes, Rattigan was swept by car down Drury Lane to the Duchess Theatre where Peggy Ashcroft had launched *The Deep Blue Sea*, then up across Cambridge Circus to the Phoenix, home to Eric Portman's Crocker-Harris and Olivier's Sleeping Prince, back down Shaftesbury Avenue past the Globe, the Lyric and the Apollo – where once *Flare Path*, *While the Sun Shines* and *Love in Idleness* had all but run side by side. Then it was on down the Haymarket, round what had once been the St James's Theatre, site of the failure of *Adventure Story* and the triumph of *Separate Tables*, along the Mall to Buckingham Palace, then back again and up

Lower Regent Street to the side of the Criterion, where *French Without Tears* had launched his career more than forty years earlier. As the car carried him west towards Heathrow airport and his house in Bermuda, he felt that everything had been taken care of with his customary panache.

Pegs French travelled with him, as she had grown accustomed to doing over the past handful of years. This cheerful, unfussy blonde woman settled Rattigan back into Spanish Grange in the middle of August. Her husband, Harold, was to remain in London, and would visit in September. But Rattigan was weakening fast, and though a nurse was hired to come to the house every day there was little that could be done. The operation on 1 June had only relieved the pain slightly. It could not halt the leukaemia.

On their way back to Bermuda Rattigan had begged Pegs French never to allow him to be sent to another hospital. But when he started complaining of terrible headaches she had no choice. In the local hospital, meningitis was diagnosed. Rattigan's friends in England feared the worst and Michael Franklin flew out at once, only to see his lover make a miraculous recovery, and be persuaded by him to return to London. In the meantime Harold French had arrived in Bermuda, to see Rattigan and Pegs, play golf and, incidentally, direct an amateur performance of *The Winslow Boy* for the Bermuda Musical and Dramatic Society.

'I had a room near his,' French recalls. 'Because I read a lot at night Pegs and I from very early on in married life had separate rooms, and I remember him coming in with his nurse. I was in bed reading the paper, and I said to him, "Look, if you're going to go on coming to see me in my bedroom I'll have to get some frilly pyjamas." He roared with laughter, and said, "I don't think that will be necessary." Then he toddled off with his nurse and I went to play golf.' It was the morning of Wednesday, 30 November 1977.

That afternoon, while the nurse was taking a lunch break and Harold French was playing golf, Pegs French was sitting beside Rattigan on his bed when he gave what she later called 'a slight smile' and let his head drop on to her shoulder. At that instant she knew he was dead. There were no dramatic last words. On that sunny Caribbean afternoon, Terence Rattigan had simply slipped discreetly out of life. He was sixty-six years old.

News of his death reached London later that evening, in time for most of the daily newspapers to print their obituaries the following morning. *The Times* was the most respectful, describing Rattigan as 'an enduring influence on the English theatre' and 'one of the leaders of the twentieth-century stage in what has come to be known as the

Theatre of Entertainment . . . he wrote some of the most enduring narrative plays of his period, designed for a "commercial" theatre and using traditional techniques Pinero and Henry Arthur Jones would have recognised.' It was not to be the only reference to his nineteenth-century predecessors. John Barber, in the *Daily Telegraph*, called him 'a prolific writer in the sleek tradition of Pinero, Maugham and Coward'.

This seemed a rather grudging farewell from an old friend. Michael Billington's tribute in the following day's *Guardian* was infinitely more sensitive. Billington described him as 'a much misunderstood drama-tist', and added: 'Because he was commercially successful, because of his urbane Harrovian manner and because of his cryptic style, it was often assumed that he was simply a purveyor of good middlebrow entertainment. And he himself fostered the illusion through his creation of the archetypal English playgoer whom he dubbed Aunt Edna.' Bil-lington was convinced that there had been far more to his talent than this, and said so eloquently. 'His whole work is a sustained assault on English middle-class values: fear of emotional commitment, terror in the face of passion, apprehension about sex. In fact few dramatists this century have written with more understanding about the human heart than Terence Rattigan.'

The following Sunday, by which time Pegs French had discovered that it was going to be almost impossible to accede to his wish to be cremated in Bermuda (in the end she arranged for the ceremony to take place in Canada), came a panegyric in the *Sunday Telegraph* from his fellow playwright, William Douglas-Home. 'Not for him,' Douglas-Home proclaimed,

> the passing fashions or the lure of topicality. He wrote what, in his heart, he wished to write, regardless of the current trend, and wrote it from his heart . . . Inevitably this, at times, incurred the wrath of the progressives and the innovators – they described him as old-fashioned and they said he wrote plays for his 'Aunt Edna', a fictitious lady, prim and straitlaced, and determined not to give offence for fear of losing popularity. They failed to realise, how-ever, that to be old-fashioned need not be a failing – that, for instance, Notre Dame, too, is old-fashioned but, at the same time, a thing of beauty not to be disparaged, save by philistines. They also failed to realise that his 'Aunt Edna' was a woman of integrity and dignity and quite outstanding worth.

Douglas-Home, whose own plays had also served Shaftesbury Avenue well, praised Rattigan's humour, integrity and compassion.

No member of the audience, unless his heart be made of stone, will go into the street at curtain-fall without a lift in spirit and a fuller understanding of mankind as his companion. That is Rattigan's achievement and his triumph. That, so long as theatres exist and players strut their hour upon the stage and speak the dialogue he wrote for them, is his eternal monument. And that is what ensures his place in history, for as long as it continues to be written, as a dramatist of genius.

Harold Hobson in the *Sunday Times* described him as 'the greatest natural talent for the stage of any man this century', but then wondered whether he had quite lived up to what the critics believed he promised? 'If Rattigan had had the spirit of Coward and Home he would have gone on writing the plays of his choice, whatever people said. But he had not that kind of resilience. His nature was delicate.'

It fell to Arthur Marshall, ex-schoolmaster, humorous monologist and newspaper columnist, to speak as a friend (and a close friend also of Rattigan's editor, Roger Machell). Writing in the *New Statesman*, he said:

Most of the other obituary notices that have appeared about him seem to me to have been less than generous . . . They certainly covered the ground but with little hint that here was a quite exceptional talent and a warm humanity, no suggestion that the plays were masterpieces of dramatic construction. No writers sought to mention the enormous pleasure they have brought, and still bring . . . His aims were simple and remained the same – to please.

Pegs and Harold French settled Rattigan's affairs in Bermuda. Eventually, Pegs brought his ashes back from Canada to England, where she lodged them quietly with those of his father, mother and brother in the family vault at Kensal Green Cemetery in west London. There was no ceremony. That was to come later. At noon on Thursday, 9 February 1978, a memorial service was held in his honour at the church of St Martin-in-the-Fields in Trafalgar Square.

The congregation included his old friend Laurence Olivier, his fag at Harrow Michael Denison, Denison's wife Dulcie Gray, Dame Wendy Hiller, who had won an Oscar for her performance in the film version of *Separate Tables*, and John Gale, whose production of *Cause Célèbre* was still running at the Her Majesty's. The service began with the overture to *The Prince and the Showgirl*, and the hymn 'And did those feet in ancient time?' Sir Alec Guinness read from the Book of Ecclesiastes, Elizabeth Vaughan sang 'Vissi d'Arte', one of his favourite arias, and Donald Sinden read an address written by William Douglas-Home.

As he read out the tribute, Sinden's sonorous voice filled the beautiful church.

> And, it is by those works – let us remember – and not by the memory of having known and loved him, that posterity will judge him. And that judgement, I submit without much fear of contradiction, will be that that gentleness, inherent in his character, enabled him to write his plays, without flamboyance and vulgarity, but with, instead, compassion and integrity and humour and a wealth of understanding, which ensured that, in no single one of them, was any line penned that, in any way, diminishes the dignity of man – rather, enhances it. And this is why whatever anyone may write about him, now or in the future, is and will be, in a sense superfluous. The fact is – let us thank God for it – he, himself, with his own works, inscribed his own unique and indestructible memorial.

The congregation filed out on to the church's worn stone steps a few yards from Trafalgar Square and the memorial column to his hero, Nelson. They formed a series of groups of friends, each representing part of his life: Pegs and Harold French, whose friendship had started with *French Without Tears* and ended in Bermuda; Peter Carter-Ruck and Bill Forsyth, his executors and the organizers of the trust that would administer and dispose of his royalties over the years to come; his producers, John Gale, Stephen Mitchell and John Perry; old friends from weekends at Sunningdale and Brighton such as Billy Chappell and Roger Machell. But one man stood apart, feeling the loneliness more than anyone. Gone were the tantrums, the rows at Cannes a hazy memory. When Rattigan's life stopped, 'my life stopped too – or nine-tenths of it,' said Terry's Midget, Michael Franklin. He was to survive his friend and lover by thirteen years, before succumbing to AIDS in 1990.

After Rattigan's debts were settled, there was less money left than many of his friends had supposed. Neither Michael Franklin nor Billy Chappell, a steadfast friend through so many years, received a vast amount under the will. For both there was nearer £10,000 than £30,000, as there was for Cuthbert Worsley's friend and companion, John Luscombe. Mary Herring benefited a little, but Pegs French rather more. The bequests would have been more generous had Rattigan spent less and earned more in the last years of his life. But the demands of Bermuda, and his private hospital treatment, had forced him to sell many of his most prized belongings, not least his collection of Chinese porcelain, his Cartier and Fabergé cigarette cases, and his mother's pearl, diamond and emerald brooch. One or two of the finest pictures, including a Vuillard, had also gone to auction that summer.

As for the revival of his professional reputation, for which he had prayed so fervently for so many years, this made slow progress to start with. The revival of *Separate Tables* had closed by the time of his memorial service in London, and *Cause Célèbre* was to struggle on for only a few more weeks. The plans for a revival of *The Sleeping Prince* in London came to nothing, as did similar plans for *The Deep Blue Sea* on Broadway. *Cause Célèbre* was not taken up by Hollywood, in spite of John Boulting's efforts; and the BBC never pursued *Nijinsky*.

For a time it seemed that the small white marble tablet erected to his memory on the west wall of St Paul's in Covent Garden, 'the actors' church', just above two similar memorials to Noël Coward and Charlie Chaplin, would be his only lasting monument. No theatre was named after him, no auditorium launched in his honour at the National Theatre. With his death, Terence Rattigan slid into temporary critical oblivion, a neglected, unfashionable figure, and although there were to be occasional notable revivals, it was to be fifteen years before the critic Michael Billington had fresh occasion to reflect in the *Guardian* that their author had been 'an infinitely more complex figure than he, or we, ever dared to admit'.

CHAPTER 28

Pretend Like Hell

◆

Do you know what 'le vice Anglais?' – the English

vice – really is? Not flagellation, not pederasty –

whatever the French believe it to be. It's our refusal

to admit our emotions.

TERENCE RATTIGAN

◆

Nothing is ever as it seems in a Rattigan play. Major Pollock is not a major, any more than Freddie Page is truly 'a ruddy romeo'. The Himmler of the Lower Fifth is nevertheless capable of tears, just as that 'uncaring shit' Sebastian Cruttwell is deeply in love with his wife. The raffish Alan Howard is actually afraid of the man-eating Diana, while the 'scarlet woman', Alma Rattenbury, kills herself for love, not rejection. Not even Aircraftsman Ross is the hero we expect. The calm, ordered surface of every Rattigan play conceals a more turbulent world beneath.

Exactly the same is true of their creator. Terence Rattigan lived a life of disguise and concealment. The painstakingly constructed mask he presented to the world, of a suave, charming figure, holding court in Eaton Square or Sunningdale, brandishing a cigarette and a glass of champagne, was every bit as much of a lie as Major Pollock. Like the Major, he wanted to be held in 'beau regard', but he feared that the grim reality was that he never would be. That insecurity infected his entire life.

To the outside world he exuded an effortless confidence, bred, like his accent, in the closeted world of the English public school and the Oxford college. His were the manners of an English diplomat, elegant,

sinuous, but unfailingly controlled. Yet in private he was obsessed with
the possibility of failure, and, therefore, of the reaction of the critics.
A more confident man might have laughed them off, but that was
beyond him. So fragile was his confidence that when they and the
theatrical world turned against him in 1956, his health gave way,
though he was only forty-five. Within a few years the disease that was
eventually to kill him had taken hold. Indeed, if there is a villain in his
story it is those critics who failed to give him credit for his subtlety,
his seriousness and his talent.

The critics clearly felt they had no need to treat him carefully. To
them, and to his audience, it seemed that nothing could possibly shake
him. He was, after all, one of the most successful playwrights in the
history of the English theatre. In the twenty years between the West
End opening of *French Without Tears* in 1936 and the closure of *Separate
Tables* in 1956, he was Britain's single most successful playwright. In
those two decades, two of his plays received more than 1,000 performances in a West End theatre, a record that no playwright has equalled
since, and three more were performed more than 500 times. At one
point in the 1940s, Rattigan plays occupied three adjoining theatres on
Shaftesbury Avenue for almost five years. Only Somerset Maugham
enjoyed such consistent success in the West End.

His success did not protect him, however. Quite the reverse. It made
him vulnerable to the jealousy and envy of lesser talents. In spite of
his spectacular triumphs, Rattigan was suddenly cast aside by the
British theatre with almost unimaginable brutality. First prized for his
humanity and his craftsmanship, treasured for his characterisation and
recognised as someone with a caring, affectionate eye for the weaknesses of every human being, he was then abruptly and summarily
dismissed as dated and irrelevant, period and precious, the creator of
plays that only middle-aged maiden aunts could possibly like or admire.
It was a monstrous judgement on his delicate, gentle talent, but the
stigma lasted for thirty years. Only now are audiences and the theatre
itself coming to accept that the critics were wrong. Only now is the
distinctive humanity that he brought to so many of his plays being
accepted again as a rare and vital contribution to the English theatre of
the twentieth century.

That is not to say that every Rattigan play is a masterpiece. *Who Is
Sylvia?*, *Follow My Leader*, *Harlequinade* and *Before Dawn* could hardly
be described as anything but lightweight trifles. *Love In Idleness*, *The
Sleeping Prince*, *While the Sun Shines* and *French Without Tears* are lightweight too, but still demonstrate an affection and charm that it is all
too easy to sneer at. There is a generosity of spirit in Rattigan that is

not always present in Coward or Priestley. His two major historical plays, *Adventure Story* and *A Bequest to the Nation*, fail at the highest level, not least because he was – in the words of the actor and director Kenneth Griffith – 'a beautiful miniaturist with a heart'. The poetry that both subjects demanded was not part of his creative equipment. Like the painter L.S.Lowry, his was an eye for the commonplace rather than the heroic, the flawed rather than the sublime.

But revivals of *The Deep Blue Sea*, *Separate Tables*, *The Browning Version* and *The Winslow Boy* in recent years have demonstrated conclusively just how much his finest work retains its capacity to fascinate an audience. His characters have lost none of their humanity through the passing of the years; their emotions remain the emotions of millions of us. Hester Collyer and John Shankland are as relevant today as they were when they first stepped on to the West End stage, as are Andrew Crocker-Harris and Arthur Winslow. Each one of them still speaks for the hopes and fears of a modern audience, as I believe they will continue to do for generations to come. For they address emotions we as spectators share. The characters invite our sympathy and respect, despite their failings, and they remain in the mind long after the curtain has fallen on them. Those four plays, together with *In Praise of Love*, *Cause Célèbre* and *Ross*, constitute a magnificent legacy to the theatre.

Terence Rattigan's sympathy and affection for his characters sets him apart from some of his contemporaries. He empathised and understood their plight because he suffered it himself. He was a man who craved our understanding every bit as much as the characters he portrayed. And it made the rejection he suffered all the more painful. When the theatrical tide turned against him, he did not know how to respond because he felt it was so unjust and capricious. He would never have treated one of his own characters as harshly. But he could not fight back. He more than anyone suffered from what Sebastian Cruttwell so memorably describes as the English vice – 'our refusal to admit to our emotions. We think they demean us, I suppose.' He felt they demeaned him, and as a result he refused to admit to them in public. Instead of tears, he attempted to swallow his pride, and his grief, by hiding in Hollywood and Bermuda. The only result was to hasten his death.

To have reacted any differently would have been to betray everything he believed in and felt he stood for. This member of the Royal and Ancient Golf Club, the MCC and the Garrick, could only protest in the mildest, least declamatory, tones. As the critic John Lahr said of him recently, 'He honoured feelings not ferment.' Terence Rattigan was as incapable of demonstrating public passion as was his character

Sir William Collyer. His whole being had to be restrained and monitored lest something were to get out of control. That made him a man who 'was always intensely aware of himself', as friends put it, 'someone who was always watching how he behaved'. It also meant that he took any slight or failure immediately to heart.

The only place Rattigan truly allowed his emotions to surface was in his plays. And even there they were conveyed by implication and subterfuge rather than in sweeping histrionic speeches and dramatic action. As he put it himself, 'It is the implicit rather than the explicit that gives life to a scene.' He went on to suggest that the most 'vital problems' in the craft of playwriting were 'what *not* to have your actors say, and how best *not* to have them say it'. So it was with his own life. It was the implicit world beneath the surface of the explicit that revealed the man.

As Lydia Cruttwell tells her son Joey in *In Praise of Love*:

LYDIA: . . . Honesty between people who love each other, or let's say should love each other, is the thing that matters least in life.
JOEY: (*Outraged*) We should *pretend*, you mean?
LYDIA: Pretend like hell.

That is exactly what Rattigan did throughout his life. To protect himself, he created the mask that was eventually to become his prison. He pretended not to care that his father was thrown out of the Diplomatic Service, and that he, therefore, had to win a scholarship to Harrow and then to Oxford. He pretended not to care that he was dropped from the Harrow Eleven in 1930, and pretended not to care that he did not, in fact, finish his degree. He pretended not to care that the six plays he wrote after *First Episode* were not a success, just as he pretended not to care that *After the Dance* and then *Follow My Leader* failed to repeat the triumph of *French Without Tears*.

He affected not to care that both *Adventure Story* and *Who is Sylvia?* were flops – yet he cared so much that he kept the latter going with his own money. He affected not to care that the young man who had come to obsess him, Kenneth Morgan, chose to leave him for another man. Later, he affected not to care about the Midget, the young man who came to replace Morgan, but he nevertheless remained loyal to him throughout the rest of his life.

Rattigan did his best to pretend that he did not care when his plays became unfashionable after 1956, just as he pretended not to care that American audiences and critics never took him to their hearts. He pretended not to care that when he decided to desert the English theatre in the 1960s and seek his fortune in Hollywood as a screenwriter no one in the country he loved seemed to miss him. He pretended not to care that the new English National Theatre in London, run by his old friend and colleague Laurence Olivier, never saw fit to revive one of his plays while he was still alive.

He affected not to care that when he was dying he had been forgotten by a theatrical world that had once described him as one of the three most significant playwrights of the century, alongside Shaw and Coward. He affected not to care that their reputations remained intact, while his sank until he had become a pariah. The rejection brought a disillusion and bitterness that he found almost impossible to bear. The chalice of success he had earned was snatched away – for reasons that he could not understand. His response was to hide his disappointment behind a studied indifference, which made it appear once more that he did not care. The reality was that it hurt him deeply, but he could not respond in any other way. The habits of a lifetime could not be unlearned.

It was this contradiction that lay at the centre of his life. Behind the apparently carefree mask lived a man crying out to be loved and appreciated, but a man who was also incapable of demonstrating that need. But this contradiction also provided one of the well-springs of his dramatic imagination. As the critic Anthony Curtis put it shrewdly, shortly after Rattigan's death, 'He appeared to be a complete model of the conforming upper-class Englishman just as his works appear to be perfect specimens of the well-made play, in reality he was not in the least conforming . . . there was a deeply Proustian ambivalence at the heart of him.'

It was a view supported by the playwright David Rudkin, who wrote to Curtis:

I detect in his plays a deep personal, surely sexual, pain, which he manages at the same time to express and disguise. The crafts- manship of which we hear so much loose talk seems to me to arise from deep psychological necessity, a drive to organise the energy that arises out of his own pain . . . I think Rattigan is not at all the commercial middlebrow dramatist his image suggests but someone peculiarly haunting and oblique who certainly speaks to me with resonance of existential bleakness and irresoluble carnal solitude.

When Rattigan himself heard that judgement, less than a year before he died, he admitted, 'He's quite right of course . . . but I never thought my slip showed as much as that.' He certainly did not mean it to.

Rattigan's upbringing and his own character insisted that he maintain a façade created in another era, England in the thirties. Tragically, that was to act against him, making him by 1958 England's least fashionable playwright. Part of that unfashionability came from the transformation in the habits of theatre-going during his life. When Terence Rattigan's career began the English theatre was still dominated by Shaftesbury Avenue. A first night was an occasion for white tie and tails, furs and the occasional tiara. Even at an ordinary evening performance the stalls would be filled by dinner-jacketed men whose wives and companions were in evening dress. They would have had a brief dinner before the performance, and would almost certainly go on to supper somewhere afterwards. It was a closeted, comfortable, upper middle-class world.

Terence Rattigan's attitudes and convictions were born at that time. His ambitions were to entertain and inform that audience, but – in spite of their dress and their manners – their interests and concerns were no different from today's infinitely less formal theatregoers. The human condition, and the complexities of human emotion, remain every bit as real today as they were then, and it is those that Rattigan's plays address. To ignore his plays, simply because they appear to come in an old-fashioned wrapper, is to ignore the importance of those emotions to every member of their audience. His humanity, like Hester Collyer's, is gently stated – not shouted from the rooftops. But it is none the less real for that. As he admitted to the critic and broadcaster Sheridan Morley shortly before his death, 'It's all very well to dislike one's plays, but they ought to be disliked for a better reason than that they're out of fashion.'

One member of the new generation who was not misled by Rattigan's delicacy of touch was Harold Pinter, who, while still an actor, played the Major and John Malcolm in *Separate Tables* in rep in Torquay in 1957. The two men became friends during the sixties. Pinter and his first wife, Vivien Merchant, were then living in Worthing, and Pinter was introduced to Rattigan by their mutual friend Enid Bagnold, who lived in Brighton. The two men got on so well that Pinter invited Rattigan to Boxing Day lunch in 1965. The lunch took place in Pinter's house in Worthing, and apart from Pinter's family the only other guest was Michael Franklin, Rattigan's lover. After lunch Rattigan took them all out for a drive in his Rolls-Royce. 'Terry had a charm which was regarded as suspect, I suppose, in some quarters,' Pinter recalls now. 'But in actual fact it was true charm. He wasn't at all pretentious. He was an extremely nice man, but he was suffering from the way he was being treated, and was somewhat rueful and bitter.'

Pinter has no doubt about the reasons for Rattigan's anguish. 'It was fashion and spite that saw him booted about. There's always been plenty of that about in the theatre. There was also a great deal of envy. One thing people don't like in this country is success.' Pinter was brought up on Rattigan, and remembers distinctly seeing Eric Portman in *The Browning Version* and Peggy Ashcroft in *The Deep Blue Sea*. 'I was able to be quite true and sincere in my admiration for him when we met.'

The sympathy and respect the two men felt for each other remained throughout Rattigan's life, and Pinter still holds Rattigan's work in the highest esteem. 'Terry had a tremendous respect for the craft of playwriting,' Pinter insists. 'No one could have taken it more seriously, and he was immensely skilful, very very entertaining, and very very shrewd about human nature. I never found him to be a safe playwright at all. I always found him to be very adventurous.' Pinter feels strongly that Rattigan was dismissed unfairly by the critics. 'We used to joke about it, because I had also had my critical ups and downs, but I think the problem for Terry was that he'd had such a wonderful career when suddenly it was cut off.'

Terence Rattigan had the misfortune to straddle the transformation that swept through the English theatre, the change from the conformist theatre of the thirties to the declamatory, permissive theatre of the fifties and sixties, and he suffered miserably and unfairly as a result. But his themes – the illogicality of love; the conflict between heavenly and earthly love; the pain of loss of promise; the defeat of greatness by human foible – are not weakened for one moment by the fact they are not expressed in the brashest tones.

Rattigan's style and themes came from his own life, and from the world he saw around him. 'Nothing is ever a portrait, of course,' he wrote to a friend, but, to some extent, everything was. In particular, the feminine side of his nature enabled him to create three of the best female roles in English drama this century – Hester Collyer, Lydia Cruttwell and Alma Rattenbury. 'He was a very very shy man,' says the former model Jean Dawnay, now Princess Galitizine, 'and that made him much more sensitive to women. He knew instinctively how a woman's psyche worked, you didn't have to dot the i's or cross the t's.'

Certainly his own sexuality influenced his work. It is no accident that his plays often revolve around a triangular relationship in which the leading character is torn between two others – and two differing definitions of love. In *Flare Path*, *The Browning Version*, *The Deep Blue Sea*, *Variation on a Theme* and *Cause Célèbre*, an older woman exhibits a passion for a younger man. It is the passion that Rattigan himself felt for a number of younger men. It both fascinated and repelled him. In

Who Is Sylvia?, *While the Sun Shines*, *Love in Idleness* and *A Bequest to the Nation* a man is torn between two women, and again their creator was also torn. Time and again he confronted his own reaction to occasional passionate, mainly sexual, affairs, with his longer-lasting, more permanent relationship with the Midget. And time and again, he failed to reconcile himself to the choice. This schizophrenic sexuality echoed throughout his plays. His characters were condemned to live with the contradictions of their own sexuality. The fact that the sexuality he was condemned to live with was, for most of the time, against the law only served to heighten the tension.

To him there was always a pursuer and a pursued in a sexual relationship: though the balance between one and the other could shift. His conclusion was that, more often than not, it was the partner who appears the weaker who ended up dominant. Millie Crocker-Harris seems dominant, but in the end loses out to the Crock. Freddie appears the stronger partner, but in the end it is Hester's strength that ends their relationship. Anne Shankland appears the stronger in *Table by the Window* but still her former husband makes the decision that they should try again, after she has broken down in front of him. Alma Rattenbury appears the stronger, but she realises that she cannot live without Wood.

> ALMA: . . . . Ever since this case began the only thing I've heard is how I must have dominated this boy. Well, I can only say that if anyone dominated anyone else, it was George who dominated me.

The appearance of self-assurance in each case concealed an inner weakness, and the parallel with his own life is clear. Behind every character, every action, lies another deeper purpose. In his comedies, Rattigan's intentions were almost always serious. In each of his comedies there is the ever-present theme of a conflict between emotion and reason. The characters struggle to reconcile the two. The same holds true for his histories. The three heroes he attempted, Alexander, Lawrence and Nelson, are revealed as men struggling to reconcile their reason with their emotions, and by doing so to control their own nature. They are each portrayed as men humbled by their weaknesses in the face of their own ambition. And each of them comes to realise his flaws during the course of the play. They too are a reflection of their creator.

In the first act of *Ross*, for example, Rattigan has Lawrence explain to his fellow airman Dickinson, who is intent on selling his story to the press, that he lost his soul by worshipping 'a false god' – 'the will'.

DICKINSON: (*Hotly*) Self-pity – that's all it is. There's nothing in the world worse than self-pity –

LAWRENCE: Oh yes there is. Self-knowledge. Why shouldn't a man pity himself, if he is pitiable? But to know yourself – or rather to be shown yourself – as you really are – (*He breaks off*) . . .

Rattigan struggled with his own will, and his homosexuality, throughout his life. It may be going too far to suggest that he suffered the degree of self-loathing that he portrayed in *Ross*, but there is little doubt that he struggled subconsciously to come to terms with his homosexuality against the background of the then overwhelmingly heterosexual society that existed beyond the theatre. Part of him took pleasure in his differentness, while another part was swathed in guilt. 'Self-sufficiency . . . being alone, that's the blessed state – if you've the character for it,' he once wrote. He knew he did not quite have the character for it. And the tension became one of the founts of his dramatic work.

But he did not believe in beating his breast in public, in revealing his failings openly in the theatre. Instead, he believed that the playwright owed the public a story. It was the aim of generations of playwrights before him, but it became the stick that was used to beat him nearly to death. 'So steadily does he aim to please,' Kenneth Tynan sneered, 'that in his whole oeuvre there is but one "unpleasant" character . . . Elsewhere the negative virtues predominate: tact, understatement, avoidance of cliché – the hallmarks, in fact, of the "gentleman's code" which holds so much of West End playwrighting in curious thrall.' It was a code that Rattigan held dear. 'He did not see anything wrong at all with being a craftsman,' one old friend remembers. 'But when the word was used as a criticism of him, it made him very angry indeed.'

When Tynan himself left England in 1976, four years before his own death, he wrote, 'Distaste, disdain, revulsion – the nouns of withdrawal, of contact rejected or scorned – these evoke the characteristic behaviour of only one country. They are the nouns of England.' Ironically they were also the nouns used to destroy Terence Rattigan's reputation as a playwright. Why?

One reason, of course, was Rattigan's image. His languid, affluent, upper-class lifestyle made him an easy target. He was a dinosaur to be slain by the angry young men emerging from post-war austerity. To them, he could not possibly understand the concerns, or the emotions, of ordinary people – and besides, he never put any 'ordinary' people in his plays. He was too controlled, too upper-middle-class for that. This was a grotesque oversimplification, but it stuck.

Precisely because Rattigan did not wear his heart, or his sexuality, on his sleeve, so he suffered for it. As Christopher Innes puts it:

> To the extent that his plays reflected the psychological repressions and hypocrisy of post-war Britain, they came to epitomise the evasion of emotion that seemed to characterise the society Osborne castigates . . . this sense of his work as period pieces, and his identification with the Establishment (signalled by a knighthood), was what made him the primary target for a younger generation of playwrights.

Rattigan became, in the words of the critic Irving Wardle, 'the main scapegoat of the age', because of his class and upbringing.

But there was also a distaste for his homosexuality among the new breed in the English theatre. The strength of the antagonism towards him among some members of the English Stage Company, and particularly George Devine, was certainly a reaction to his sexuality. In spite of Devine's own 'drag history: the line of breast-plated Wagnerian sopranos and rampaging Amazon queens', which Irving Wardle describes in his book on Devine's theatre, the director was utterly determined, as John Osborne later made abundantly clear, to replace the homosexual theatre of Binkie Beaumont and Terence Rattigan with his own heterosexual version. And he found a willing propagandist for that cause in the flamboyantly heterosexual Tynan.

Rattigan's homosexuality, though it was known to his colleagues in the theatre, remained a secret to his audience; and he had no wish to alter that perception during his lifetime. Terence Rattigan never considered 'outing' himself. The possibility would have appalled him. Indeed, even one of his lovers alive today will not consider it. To almost any member of the generation born before 1914, it is all but inconceivable. Not for Terence Rattigan the openness of his contemporary Tennessee Williams. Indeed, as Innes points out: 'Removing the necessity for disguise made Rattigan's drama less – not more – effective when he turned to explicit treatments of homosexual characters or relationships.'

The opaqueness that he brought to his own life was an essential part of his plays. This, together with his delicate subterfuge, was his singular contribution to English drama, and it bears comparison with Pinter. For both men it is what is left unsaid that speaks volumes. And, like Pinter, his themes are more subversive than many have been prepared to accept. The critic Michael Billington put his finger on this when he wrote:

It was often assumed that he [Rattigan] was simply a purveyor of good middlebrow entertainment . . . Yet his whole world is a sustained assault on English middle-class values: fear of emotional commitment, terror in the face of passion, apprehension about sex. In fact few dramatists this century have written with more understanding about the human heart than Terence Rattigan.

Time and again the theatre critics failed to look beneath the surface. The understatement that informed his work, and life, was mistaken for superficiality. The fact that his plays were 'well-made' and often included in the set a pair of 'french windows', was interpreted as a lack of seriousness of purpose, even though Rattigan himself retorted: 'Ibsen had french windows.' His commercial success was judged to mean that he was not intellectually respectable, even though, as he also pointed out: 'I am not in the least tempted to believe that the failure of a play with an audience means that it must therefore possess some special artistic merit.'

Had Terence Rattigan not so transparently relished his own commercial success; had he spoken in the classless accent of Philip Larkin and lived in obscurity in Hull rather than in Eaton Square; had his work not been so readily accessible to such a wide range of audiences; had he not rejoiced in Savile Row suits and Rolls-Royces in the midst of post-war austerity; had he not – as a result – become bracketed in the public mind with the playwright who was twelve years his senior, Noël Coward; had he not been a romantic when the world around him was so patently becoming infinitely less so; had he not been quite so fastidiously, understatedly English – then, perhaps, just perhaps, his reputation might not have suffered its rapid, tragic, and undeserved, decline.

As it was, Rattigan's joyous, uninhibited, ostentatious affluence sowed the seeds of the envy and the jealousy that were eventually to lead to his public humiliation. His accessibility was decried as a lack of intellectual seriousness, his affluence confused with a lack of integrity, his social conscience overlooked. In the process his subtlety, intelligence and compassion were dismissed with barely a moment's hesitation. This gentle, generous, shy, civilised, clubbable man, who loved golf and cricket and whose ruthlessness was usually a disguise for the fragility of his own confidence, found himself exiled from the one world that he had always loved, the theatre. The critics 'despised him with a scorn almost incredible in its ferocity', as Harold Hobson was to recall after his death. 'This broke his spirit and deprived the British theatre of much gaiety and happiness.'

Rattigan's natural obliqueness was swamped by the noisy clamour of the 'angry young men'. His characters never bellowed their misfortunes, screaming at the unfairness of the world. They suffered instead with a quiet, pained dignity. And their creator did the same. But he treated them with a forgiveness, humanity and affection that confirms his place as one of the finest dramatists this century, a playwright whose work deserves to be prized, and praised, for the intensity of its emotions. The fact that he sought to conceal himself and the true intentions of his work behind a carefully prepared façade does not mean that they were any the less keenly felt. His scream was no less powerful, or less poignant, for being almost strangled.

Select Bibliography

ARCHIVAL SOURCES

The principal textual sources for this book are the papers of Terence Rattigan himself, now held in the Manuscript Collections of the British Library.

The Rattigan papers are not, at this moment, fully catalogued, and it is not possible therefore to detail the exact location of each reference. The boxes of original manuscripts, letters, notebooks and diaries are mixed by subject and date in almost every case.

Beyond this principal textual source, however, lie two other important ones, also held in the Manuscript Collections at the British Library: the Lord Chamberlain's correspondence 1900–1968 and the Kenneth Tynan correspondence.

Other principal sources are the files of the Rattigan Trust, held at the offices of Peter Carter-Ruck and Partners, 75 Shoe Lane, London EC4A 3BQ, and the Hamish Hamilton archive in the special collections at the library of the University of Bristol.

The Public Record Office in Holborn provided copies of Terence Rattigan's birth certificate and that of his brother Brian, as well as copies of his parents' marriage certificate and the death certificates for his brother, father and mother.

Other important sources were: the archives of Sandroyd School, Dorset, Harrow School, and Trinity College, Oxford; the Times Room at the London Library; the theatre collection at the Garrick Club; the Trustees of Albany (for details of Rattigan's periods of residence there), and the Bermudan authorities for the same purpose.

Also consulted were the Theatre Museum in Covent Garden, and its H.M.Tennent Collection, housed near Brook Green in West London; the British Film Institute library in London; the Academy of Motion Picture Arts and Sciences library in Los Angeles; and the Billy Rose Collection at the New York Public Library at Lincoln Center.

PERSONAL TESTIMONIES

The references to interviews given by Terence Rattigan or to articles which he himself wrote are included in the following bibliography, as are the details of reviews and articles written about him.

Where individuals have spoken to me, or written to me, I also include the details in this bibliography, unless they have specifically asked that their recollections or comments be kept confidential.

I conducted lengthy and extensive interviews, details of which I have included in the text, with Frith Banbury, Peter Carter-Ruck, James Cellan Jones, Anthony Curtis, Jean Dawnay (Princess Galitzine), Robert Flemyng, Harold French, William Fox, Kenneth Griffith, Mary Herring, Holly Hill, J.V.L.Ivimy, Bernard Levin, Terence Longden, Sir John Mills, Stephen Mitchell, Peter Osborn, Harold Pinter, Alvin Rakoff, Mrs Roxanne Senior, Donald Sinden, Sir John Stow, Bunny Rogers, Frederick Treves, Jack Watling and B.A. (Freddie) Young. In contrast, Peter Barkworth, Paul Channon MP, George Cole, Bryan Forbes, Sir John Gielgud, Paul Scofield and Michael Sissons preferred to write.

BIOGRAPHICAL AND CRITICAL STUDIES

There are three published works on Rattigan: They are:

Michael Darlow and Gillian Hodson, *Terence Rattigan: The Man and his Work*, Quartet Books, London, 1979.

Susan Rusinko, *Terence Rattigan*, Tawyne, Boston, 1983.

B.A.Young, *The Rattigan Version*, Hamish Hamilton, London, 1986.

Only two lengthy pieces of academic research have so far, and to my knowledge, been written about the plays of Rattigan. The most complete piece of academic research is the earliest, *A Critical Analysis of the Plays of Terence Rattigan*, by Holly Hill, which was the author's thesis for a doctorate of the City University of New York in 1977, and which can be obtained through University Microfilms International. A further doctoral thesis, by Mohamed Bahaa El-Hassan A. Wasfy, for the Royal Holloway College at the University of London, was produced in 1994. Wendy Pollard wrote a shorter examination of Rattigan for her Open University BA in 1989.

THE PLAYS

Terence Rattigan's published plays are as follows:

The Collected Plays of Terence Rattigan, Volume One (French Without Tears, Flare Path, While the Sun Shines, Love in Idleness (O Mistress

Mine), The Winslow Boy), with an introduction by the author, Hamish Hamilton, London, 1953.

The Collected Plays of Terence Rattigan, Volume Two (The Browning Version, Harlequinade, Adventure Story, Who Is Sylvia?, The Deep Blue Sea), with an introduction by the author, Hamish Hamilton, London, 1953.

The Collected Plays of Terence Rattigan, Volume Three (The Sleeping Prince, Separate Tables, Variation on a Theme, Ross, Heart to Heart), with an introduction by the author, Hamish Hamilton, London, 1964.

The Collected Plays of Terence Rattigan, Volume Four (Man and Boy, A Bequest to the Nation, In Praise of Love (with *Before Dawn), Cause Célèbre)*, with an introduction by B.A.Young, Hamish Hamilton, London, 1978.

These, together with Terence Rattigan's *After the .Dance*, Hamish Hamilton, London, 1939, are the major published works, although acting editions of some of the works are available from Samuel French Limited, 52 Fitzroy Street, London W1.

Methuen, London, also published two paperback collections of Rattigan plays in 1985, each with an introduction by Anthony Curtis.

Where reference is made in the text to Rattigan's other plays, specifically to *Follow My Leader, Black Forest* and *High Summer*, or to his screenplays, copies of each work are to be found in the Rattigan papers at the British Library. Copies of his radio play, *A Tale of Two Cities*, written with Sir John Gielgud, and the original radio version of *Cause Célèbre*, are also to be found in the British Library.

ESSAYS AND JOURNALISM
Terence Rattigan's own contributions to books, magazines, newspapers and theatre or film programmes, which I have referred to in the text, are as follows:

'French Without Tears', *New York Post*, 25 September 1937.
'Drama Without Tears', *New York Times*, 10 October 1937.
'Sea Change Problem', *New York Times*, 4 December 1949.
'A Magnificent Pity for Camels', in *Diversions*, ed. John Sutro, Max Parrish, London, 1950.
'Concerning the Play of Ideas', *New Statesman*, London, 4 March 1950.
'Aunt Edna Waits for Godot', *New Statesman*, London, 15 October 1955.
'Marilyn, Sir Laurence & I', *Daily Express*, London, 25 June 1957.

'Noël Coward, an appreciation of his work in the theatre', in *Theatrical Companion to Noël Coward*, by Raymond Mander and Joe Mitchenson, Rockcliff, London, 1957.
'Why is entertainment a dirty word?', *Daily Mail*, London, 2 September 1963.
An introduction to Harold French, *I Swore I Never Would*, Secker & Warburg, London, 1970.
'Bequest: a Royal Inspiration', in the programme for the World Première of *Bequest to the Nation*, London, 23 April 1973.
Olivier, ed. Logan Gourlay, with a contribution from Terence Rattigan, Weidenfeld & Nicolson, London, 1973.

RADIO TALKS AND INTERVIEWS
Terence Rattigan gave a series of radio talks and interviews during his life, some of which are referred to in the text. They include the following:

Rattigan's radio talk, *Theatre Sense*, referred to in the text, broadcast on the BBC Home Service on 22 March 1949.
Details of his brief introductions for radio to *While the Sun Shines*, *The Winslow Boy*, *Adventure Story* and *The Deep Blue Sea* for the BBC Home Service were recorded on 17 September 1957 and are to be found in the files of the Rattigan Trust.
Terence Rattigan, interviewed by Derek Hart, BBC Radio Four, 26 November 1969.
Rattigan's Theatre, including an interview by Anthony Curtis, BBC Radio Three, 30 March 1976.
Terence Rattigan, interviewed by Sheridan Morley, BBC Radio Four, July 1977.

Michael Darlow's television obituary of Terence Rattigan was broadcast on BBC1 in 1978.

CRITICISM
The principal contributions on Rattigan's life and work by both critics and academics, referred to in the text, are as follows:

Anthony Curtis, 'Professional Man and Boy', *Plays and Players*, Vol. 25(5), February 1978.
Richard Foulkes, 'Sir Terence Rattigan,' in *British Dramatists*, St James's Press, London, 1994.
Richard Foulkes, 'Terence Rattigan's Variation on a Theme', *Modern Drama*, Vol. 22(4), December 1979.

Robert F. Gross, 'Coming Down in the World: Motifs of Benign Descent in Three Plays by Terence Rattigan', *Modern Drama*, Vol. 33(3), September 1990.

Holly Hill, 'Rattigan's Renaissance', *Contemporary Review*, Vol. 240, No. 1392, January 1982.

Barry Hyams, 'Terence Rattigan', *Theatre Arts*, New York, November 1956.

Christopher Innes, 'Terence Rattigan: updating the well-made play', in *Modern British Drama 1890–1990*, Cambridge University Press, 1992.

John Simon, 'Rattigan', *Theatre Arts*, April 1962.

John Russell Taylor, *The Rise and Fall of the Well-Made Play*, Hill & Wang, New York, 1967.

T. C. Worsley, 'Rattigan and His Critics', *London Magazine*, September 1964.

The debate on the play of ideas, which Rattigan launched in the *New Statesman*, London, in March 1950, was continued by James Bridie on 11 March 1950, Ben Levy on 25 March 1950, Peter Ustinov on 1 April 1950, Sean O'Casey on 8 April 1950, Ted Willis on 15 April 1950, and was concluded by George Bernard Shaw on 6 May 1950.

ARTICLES ABOUT RATTIGAN

The principal contributions by journalists and critics to magazines and newspapers about Rattigan, referred to in the text, are as follows:

John Barber, 'Rattigan's Return', *Daily Telegraph*, London, 30 July 1973.

Keith Baxter, 'Between the middle classes and the deep blue sea', *Sunday Telegraph*, London, 10 January 1993.

Michael Billington, 'Terence Rattigan, an Obituary', *Guardian*, London, 2 December 1977.

Hector Bolitho, 'Terence Rattigan Conquers New York', *Queen*, London, 3 March 1948.

Fergus Cashin, 'To Kill Aunt Edna', *Daily Sketch*, London, 10 March 1963.

Terry Coleman, 'The Claridges Version', *Guardian*, London, 2 August 1970.

William Cook, 'Look Back in Languor,' *Guardian*, London, 4 January 1993.

Sheila Duncan, 'How Terence Rattigan faced life when told he had only six months left', *Daily Mirror*, London, 12 May 1964.

Peter Evans, '52 Without Tears', *Daily Express*, London, 8 July 1963.

Olga Franklin, 'Golden Boy Rattigan', *Daily Mail*, London, 23 November 1956.

Arthur Gelb, 'Terence Rattigan', *New York Times*, 21 October 1956.

Harold Hobson, 'Terence Rattigan', *Houses and Gardens*, London, 1949.

Ruth Jordan, 'Another Adventure Story', *Woman's Journal*, London, August 1949.

Irma Kurtz, 'Terence Rattigan', *Nova*, London, March 1967.

John Lahr, 'Untutored Hearts', *New Yorker*, New York, May 1994.

Sheridan Morley, 'Terence Rattigan at 65', *The Times*, London, 9 May 1977.

Robert Muller, 'Soul-searching with Terence Rattigan', *Daily Mail*, London, 30 April 1960.

Robert Muller, 'The Rattigan Version', *Daily Mail*, London, 23 September 1959.

Philip Oakes, 'Comédie Anglaise', *Radio Times*, London, 15 May 1976.

Philip Oakes, 'Living for the Present', *Sunday Times* London, August 1976.

Jonathan Raban, 'Cause Célèbre', *Radio Times*, September 1976.

C. Patrick Thompson, 'Terence Rattigan', *Good Housekeeping*, London, June 1945.

Kenneth Tynan, 'An Inner View of Terence Rattigan', *Harper's Bazaar*, New York, November 1952.

Kenneth Tynan, 'Jackpot Rattigan', *Evening Standard*, London, 1 July 1953.

Irving Wardle, 'The Top Drawer', *Independent on Sunday*, London, 3 January 1993.

The individual newspaper and periodical criticism of Rattigan's plays, films or television plays, referred to in the text, can be located in the archives and the newspaper libraries listed above.

The obituary notices, also referred to in the text, are available from the same sources. Copies of William Douglas-Home's address at Rattigan's memorial are in the Theatre Museum collection in Covent Garden.

PUBLISHED REFERENCES TO RATTIGAN

The principal published reference to Terence Rattigan's early life is:

Frank Rattigan, *Diversions of a Diplomat*, Chapman & Hall, London 1924.

There are numerous published recollections of Rattigan, including:

Michael Billington, *Peggy Ashcroft*, John Murray, London, 1988.

Sheila Birkenhead, *Peace in Piccadilly, The Story of Albany*, Hamish Hamilton, London, 1958.

Dirk Bogarde, *Snakes and Ladders*, Chatto & Windus, London, 1978.

Chips – The Diaries of Sir Henry Channon, ed. Robert Rhodes James, Weidenfeld & Nicolson, London, 1967.

Stephen Citron, *Noël and Cole*, Sinclair-Stevenson, London, 1992.

The Concise Oxford Companion to the Theatre, ed. Phyllis Hartnoll, Oxford University Press, Oxford, 1972.

Aidan Crawley, *Leap Before You Look*, Collins, London, 1988.

Roland Culver, *Not Quite a Gentleman*, William Kimber, 1979.

The Diaries of Kenneth Williams, ed. Russell Davies, HarperCollins, London, 1992.

Nicholas de Jongh, *Not in Front of the Audience*, Routledge, London, 1992.

Michael Denison, *Double Act*, Michael Joseph, London, 1985.

Michael Denison, *Overture and Beginners*, Gollancz, London, 1973.

Alan Dent, *Vivien Leigh – A Bouquet*, Hamish Hamilton, London, 1969.

John Dexter, *The Honourable Beast*, Nick Hern Books, London, 1993.

Tom Driberg, *Ruling Passions*, Jonathan Cape, London, 1977.

Anne Edwards, *Vivien Leigh*, W.H.Allen, London, 1977.

Virginia Fairweather, *Cry God for Larry*, Calder & Boyars, London, 1969.

Bryan Forbes, *A Divided Life*, Heinemann, London, 1992.

Bryan Forbes, *That Despicable Race*, Elm Tree Books, London, 1980.

Harold French, *I Swore I Never Would*, Secker & Warburg, London, 1970.

Harold French, *I Thought I Never Could*, Secker & Warburg, London, 1973.

John Gielgud, *Early Stages*, Macmillan, London, 1939.

Halliwell's Film Guide, ed. John Walker, HarperCollins, London, 1991.

Halliwell's Filmgoer's Companion, ed. John Walker, HarperCollins, London, 1992.

Rex Harrison, *A Damned Serious Business*, Bantam Press, London, 1990.

Rex Harrison, *Rex – An Autobiography*, Macmillan, London, 1974.

Ronald Hayman, *John Gielgud*, Heinemann, London, 1971.

Harold Hobson, *Indirect Journey – An Autobiography*, Weidenfeld & Nicolson, London, 1978.

Harold Hobson, *The Theatre in Britain*, Phaidon, Oxford, 1984.

Michael Holroyd, *Bernard Shaw, Volume Three 1918–1950*, Chatto & Windus, London, 1991.

Richard Huggett, *Binkie Beaumont*, Hodder & Stoughton, London, 1989.

Ephraim Katz, *The Film Encyclopedia*, Putnam, New York, 1979.
Cole Lesley, *The Life of Noël Coward*, Jonathan Cape, London, 1976.
The Letters of Kenneth Tynan, ed. Kathleen Tynan, Weidenfeld & Nicolson, London, 1994.
The Letters of Kenneth Williams, ed. Russell Davies, HarperCollins, London, 1994.
Basil Liddell Hart, *T.E.Lawrence – In Arabia and After*, Jonathan Cape, London, 1948.
Arthur Miller, *Timebends: a life*, Methuen, London, 1987.
R.K.Minney, *Puffin Asquith*, Leslie Frewin, London, 1973.
Edwin Montagu, *The Archer-Shee Case*, David and Charles, London, 1974.
Kenneth More, *Happy Go Lucky – My Life*, Robert Hale, London, 1957.
Kenneth More, *More or Less*, Hodder & Stoughton, London, 1979.
K.O.Newman, *Mind, Sex and War*, Pelago Press, Oxford, 1941.
K.O.Newman, *250 Times I Saw a Play*, Pelago Press, Oxford, 1944.
Gary O'Connor, *Darlings of the Gods*, Hodder & Stoughton, London, 1984.
Laurence Olivier, *Confessions of an Actor*, Weidenfeld & Nicolson, London, 1982.
Laurence Olivier, *On Acting*, Weidenfeld & Nicolson, London, 1976.
The Orton Diaries, ed. John Lahr, Methuen, London, 1986.
John Osborne, *A Better Class of Person*, Faber and Faber, London, 1981.
John Osborne, *Almost a Gentleman*, Faber and Faber, London, 1991.
The Oxford Companion to English Literature, ed. Margaret Drabble, Oxford University Press, Oxford, 1985.
Michael Redgrave, *In My Mind's Eye: an autobiography*, Weidenfeld & Nicolson, London, 1983.
Margaret Rutherford, *Margaret Rutherford*, W.H.Allen, London, 1972.
A.J.P.Taylor, *English History, 1914–1945*, Oxford University Press, Oxford, 1965.
J.C.Trewin, *The Edwardian Theatre*, Basil Blackwell, Oxford, 1976.
Wendy Trewin, *All on a Stage*, Harrap, London, 1986.
Kathleen Tynan, *The Life of Kenneth Tynan*, Weidenfeld & Nicolson, London, 1987.
Kenneth Tynan, *A View of the English Stage*, Davis-Poynter, London, 1975.
Kenneth Tynan, *Curtains*, Longmans Green, London, 1960.
Hugo Vickers, *Cecil Beaton*, Weidenfeld & Nicolson, London, 1985.
Hugo Vickers, *Vivien Leigh*, Hamish Hamilton, London, 1988.
Alexander Walker, *Vivien*, Weidenfeld & Nicolson, London, 1987.

Irving Wardle, *The Theatres of George Devine*, Jonathan Cape, London, 1978.

Who Was Who, 1897–1915, Adam and Charles Black.

Who Was Who, 1951–60, Adam and Charles Black.

Who's Who, Adam and Charles Black.

Who's Who in the Theatre, concise 16th edition, ed. Ian Herbert, Pitman, London, 1976.

Michael Wilding, as told to Pamela Wilcox, *Apple Sauce*, George Allen & Unwin, London, 1982.

T.C.Worsley, *The Fugitive Art*, John Lehmann, London, 1952.

Maurice Zolotow, *Stagestruck – Alfred Lunt and Lynn Fontanne*, Heinemann, London, 1965.

Stage Plays, Feature Films, and Television Scripts

STAGE PLAYS
London and New York openings

First Episode (in collaboration with Philip Heimann),
(US title *College Sinners*)

London: Q Theatre, Kew, 11 September 1933, then transferred to Comedy Theatre, Panton Street, London, 26 January 1934. Directed by Muriel Pratt; starring Max Adrian, Meriel Forbes-Robertson, Patrick Waddington and William Fox. Approximately 80 performances.

New York: Ritz Theatre, 17 September 1934. Directed by Haddon Mason; starring Max Adrian, Gerrie Worthing, Patrick Waddington and John Halloran. Approximately 40 performances.

French Without Tears

London: Criterion Theatre, 6 November 1936. Directed by Harold French; starring Rex Harrison, Kay Hammond, Roland Culver, Guy Middleton, Jessica Tandy and Robert Flemyng, 1,030 performances.

New York: Henry Miller Theatre, 28 September 1937. Directed by Harold French; starring Frank Lawton, Penelope Dudley Ward, Cyril Raymond, Guy Middleton, Jacqueline Porel and Hubert Gregg. 111 performances.

After the Dance

London: St James's Theatre, 21 June 1939. Directed by Michael Macowan; starring Martin Walker, Catherine Lacey, Hubert Gregg and Viola Lyel. 60 performances.

Follow My Leader (in collaboration with Antony Maurice (Goldschmidt)

London: Apollo Theatre, 16 January 1940. Directed by Athole Stewart; starring Reginald Beckwith, Francis L. Sullivan, Walter Hudd and Athole Stewart. Approximately 15 performances.

Grey Farm (in collaboration with Hector Bolitho)

New York: Hudson Theatre, 3 May 1940. Directed by Berthold Viertel; starring Oscar Homolka, John Cromwell, Jane Sterling and Adrienna Morrison. Approximately 35 performances.

Flare Path

London: Apollo Theatre, 13 August 1942. Directed by Anthony Asquith; starring Martin Walker, Jack Watling, Phyllis Calvert, Leslie Dwyer and Kathleen Harrison. 679 performances.

New York: Henry Miller Theatre, 23 December 1942. Directed by Margaret Webster; starring Arthur Margetson, Alec Guinness, Nancy Kelly, Gerald Savory and Helena Pickard. 14 performances.

While the Sun Shines

London: Globe Theatre, 24 December 1943. Directed by Anthony Asquith; starring Michael Wilding, Hugh McDermott, Jane Baxter, Ronald Squire and Brenda Bruce. 1,154 performances.

New York: Lyceum Theatre, 19 September 1944. Directed by George S. Kaufman; starring Stanley Bell, Lewis Howard, Anne Burr, Melville Cooper and Cathleen Cordell. 39 performances.

Love in Idleness (US title *O Mistress Mine*)

London: Lyric Theatre, 20 December 1944. Directed by Alfred Lunt; starring Lynn Fontanne, Alfred Lunt, Brian Nissen and Peggy Dear. 213 performances.

New York: Empire Theatre, 23 January 1946. Directed by Alfred Lunt; starring Lynn Fontanne, Alfred Lunt, Dick van Patten and Esther Mitchell. 451 performances.

The Winslow Boy

London: Lyric Theatre, 23 May 1946. Directed by Glen Byam Shaw; starring Emlyn Williams, Frank Cellier, Angela Baddeley, Clive Morton and Jack Watling. 476 performances.

New York: Empire Theatre, 29 October 1947. Directed by Glen Byam Shaw;

starring Frank Allenby, Alan Webb, Madge Compton, George Denson and Owen Holder. 218 performances.

Playbill: *The Browning Version* and *Harlequinade*

London: Phoenix Theatre, 8 September 1948. Directed by Peter Glenville; starring Eric Portman, Mary Ellis, Hector Ross and Peter Scott. 245 performances.

New York: Coronet Theatre, 12 October 1949. Directed by Peter Glenville; starring Maurice Evans, Edna Best, Ron Randell and Peter Scott-Smith. 62 performances.

Adventure Story

London: St James's Theatre, 17 March 1949. Directed by Peter Glenville; starring Paul Scofield, Gwen Ffangcon-Davies, Noel Williams, Julian Dallas and Robert Flemyng. 108 performances.

Who Is Sylvia?

London: Criterion Theatre, 24 October 1950. Directed by Anthony Quayle; starring Robert Flemyng, Roland Culver, Diane Hart and Athene Seyler. 381 performances.

The Deep Blue Sea

London: Duchess Theatre, 6 March 1952. Directed by Frith Banbury; starring Peggy Ashcroft, Kenneth More, Roland Culver, Peter Illing and Raymond Francis. 513 performances.

New York: Morosco Theatre, 5 November 1952. Directed by Frith Banbury; starring Margaret Sullavan, James Hanley, Alan Webb, Herbert Berghof and Felix Deebank. 132 performances.

The Sleeping Prince

London: Phoenix Theatre, 5 November 1953. Directed by Laurence Olivier; starring Vivien Leigh, Laurence Olivier, Martita Hunt and Richard Wattis. 274 performances.

New York: Coronet Theatre, 2 November 1956. Directed by Michael Redgrave; starring Barbara Bel Geddes, Michael Redgrave, Cathleen Nesbitt and Rex O'Malley. 60 performances.

Separate Tables

London: St James's Theatre, 22 September 1954. Directed by Peter Glenville; starring Eric Portman, Margaret Leighton, Phyllis Neilson-Terry, Beryl Meason and May Hallat. 726 performances.

New York: Music Box Theatre, 25 October 1956. Directed by Peter Glenville; starring Eric Portman, Margaret Leighton, Phyllis Neilson-Terry, Beryl Meason and May Hallat. 322 performances.

Variation on a Theme

London: Globe Theatre, 8 May 1958. Directed by John Gielgud; starring Margaret Leighton, Jeremy Brett, Michael Goodliffe and George Pravda. 132 performances.

Ross

London: Theatre Royal, Haymarket, 12 May 1960. Directed by Glen Byam Shaw; starring Alec Guinness, Harry Andrews, Geoffrey Keen and Mark Dignam. 762 performances.

New York: Eugene O'Neill Theatre, 26 December 1961. Directed by Glen Byam Shaw; starring John Mills, John Williams, Geoffrey Keen and Paul Sparer. 159 performances.

Joie de Vivre

London: Queen's Theatre, 14 July 1960. Directed by William Chappell, music by Robert Stoltz, lyrics by Paul Dehn; starring Donald Sinden, Joan Heal, Joana Rigby and Robin Hunter. 4 performances.

Man and Boy

London: Queen's Theatre, 4 September 1963. Directed by Micahel Benthall; starring Charles Boyer, Barry Justice, Geoffrey Keen and Austin Willis. 69 performances.

New York: Brooks Atkinson Theatre, 12 November 1963. Directed by Michael Benthall; starring Charles Boyer, Barry Justice, Geoffrey Keen and Austin Willis. 54 performances.

A Bequest to the Nation

London: Theatre Royal, Haymarket, 23 September 1970. Directed by Peter Glenville; starring Zoë Caldwell, Ian Holm, Leueen MacGrath and Michael Aldridge. 124 performances.

In Praise of Love

London: Duchess Theatre, 27 September 1973. Directed by John Dexter; starring Donald Sinden, Joan Greenwood, Don Fellows and Richard Warwick. 131 performances.

New York: Morosco Theatre, 10 December 1974. Directed by Fred Coe; starring Rex Harrison, Julie Harris, Martin Gabel and Peter Burnell. 199 performances.

Cause Célèbre

London: Her Majesty's Theatre, 4 July 1977. Directed by Robin Midgley; starring Glynis Johns, Kenneth Griffith, Helen Lindsay, Bernard Archard and Patrick Barr. 282 performances.

FEATURE FILMS

French Without Tears: Paramount/Two Cities Production, Great Britain, 1939. Directed by Anthony Asquith; screenplay by Terence Rattigan (uncredited), Anatole de Grunwald and Ian Dalrymple based upon the stage play by Terence Rattigan; starring Ray Milland, Ellen Drew, Roland Culver, Guy Middleton. Running time 85 mins: black and white.

Quiet Wedding: Paramount/Paul Soskin Production, Great Britain, 1940. Directed by Anthony Asquith; screenplay by Terence Rattigan and Anatole de Grunwald based upon the stage play by Esther McCracken; starring Margaret Lockwood, Derek Farr, Marjorie Fielding and A.E.Matthews. Running time 80 minutes: black and white.

The Day Will Dawn (US title *The Avengers*): Paramount/Paul Soskin Production, Great Britain, 1942. Directed by Harold French; screenplay by Terence Rattigan and Anatole de Grunwald from a treatment by Patrick Kirwan; starring Ralph Richardson, Deborah Kerr, Hugh Williams and Griffith Jones. Running time 98 minutes: black and white.

Uncensored: Gaumont British/Gainsborough Production, Great Britain, 1942. (US release Twentieth Century-Fox, 1943.) Directed by Anthony Asquith; screenplay by Ronald Ackland and Terence Rattigan based upon the book by Oscar Millard adapted by Wolfgang Wilhelm; starring Eric Portman, Phyllis Calvert and Griffith Jones. Running time 108 minutes (US 85 minutes): black and white.

English Without Tears (US title *Her Man Gilbey*): Rank/Two Cities Production, Great Britain, 1944. Directed by Harold French; original screenplay by Terence Rattigan and Anatole de Grunwald; starring Michael Wilding, Penelope Ward, Lilli Palmer and Margaret Rutherford. Running time 89 minutes: black and white.

Journey Together: English Films/RAF Film Unit, Great Britain, 1945. Directed by John Boulting: original screenplay by Terence Rattigan; starring Richard Attenborough, Jack Watling, Edward G. Robinson and Bessie Love. Running time 95 minutes: black and white.

The Way to the Stars (US title *Johnny in the Clouds*): Rank/Two Cities Production, Great Britain, 1945. Directed by Anthony Asquith; screenplay by Terence Rattigan from a story by Terence Rattigan, Anatole de Grunwald and Robert Sherman; starring Michael Redgrave, John Mills, Rosamund John and Douglas Montgomery. Running time 109 minutes: black and white.

While the Sun Shines: Pathé/Stratford Pictures Productions, Great Britain, 1947. Directed by Anthony Asquith; screenplay by Terence Rattigan and Anatole de Grunwald based upon the stage play by Terence Rattigan; starring Ronald Howard, Bonar Colleano, Ronald Squire and Brenda Bruce. Running time 81 minutes: black and white.

Brighton Rock (US title *Young Scarface*): Associated British/Boulting Brothers Production; Great Britain, 1947. Directed by John Boulting; screenplay by Graham Greene and Terence Rattigan based upon the novel by Graham Greene; starring Richard Attenborough, Hermione Baddeley, Harcourt Williams and William Hartnell. Running time 92 minutes: black and white.

Bond Street: Associated British/World Screenplays (Anatole de Grunwald) Production, Great Britain, 1948. Directed by Gordon Parry; screenplay by Anatole de Grunwald (Terence Rattigan and Rodney Ackland, uncredited); starring Roland Young, Jean Kent, Derek Farr and Kathleen Harrison. Running time 107 minutes: black and white.

The Winslow Boy: British Lion/London Films Production, Great Britain, 1948. Directed by Anthony Asquith; screenplay by Terence Rattigan and Anatole de Grunwald based upon the play by Terence Rattigan; starring Robert Donat, Margaret Leighton, Cedric Hardwicke and Jack Watling. Running time 117 minutes (US 97 minutes): black and white.

The Browning Version: Gaumont Film/Javelin Films Production, Great Britain, 1951. Directed by Anthony Asquith; screenplay by Terence Rattigan based upon his play; starring Michael Redgrave, Jean Kent, Nigel Patrick and Wilfrid Hyde White. Running time 90 minutes: black and white.

The Sound Barrier (US title *Breaking the Sound Barrier*): United Artists/London Film Productions, Great Britain, 1952. Directed by David Lean; original screenplay by Terence Rattigan (Academy Award Nomination); starring Ralph Richardson, Ann Todd, Nigel Patrick and John Justin. Running time 118 minutes (US 109 minutes): black and white.

The Final Test: Rank/ATC Film Production, Great Britain, 1953. Directed by Anthony Asquith; screenplay by Terence Rattigan based upon his television play; starring Jack Warner, Robert Morley, George Relph. Running time 90 minutes (US 84 minutes): black and white.

The Man Who Loved Redheads: British Lion/London Films, Great Britain, 1954.

Directed by Harold French; screenplay by Terence Rattigan based upon his stage play *Who Is Sylvia?*; starring John Justin, Moira Shearer, Roland Culver and Gladys Cooper. Running time 90 minutes: colour.

The Deep Blue Sea: Twentieth Century-Fox/London Films, Great Britain, 1955. Directed by Anatole Litvak; screenplay by Terence Rattigan based upon his stage play; starring Vivien Leigh, Kenneth More, Eric Portman and Emlyn Williams. Running time 99 minutes: colour.

The Prince and the Showgirl: Warner Brothers, Great Britain, 1957. Directed by Laurence Olivier; screenplay by Terence Rattigan based upon his stage play *The Sleeping Prince*; starring Marilyn Monroe, Laurence Olivier, Sybil Thorndike and Richard Wattis. Running time 117 minutes: colour.

Separate Tables: United Artists/Hecht, Hill and Lancaster Production, United States, 1958 (Academy Award Nomination). Directed by Delbert Mann; screenplay by Terence Rattigan and John Gay (Academy Award Nomination) from the stage play by Terence Rattigan; starring Deborah Kerr (Academy Award Nomination), Rita Hayworth, David Niven (Academy Award), Wendy Hiller (Academy Award) and Burt Lancaster. Running time 98 minutes: black and white.

The VIPs: MGM/Anatole de Grunwald Production, Great Britain, 1963. Directed by Anthony Asquith; original screenplay by Terence Rattigan; starring Elizabeth Taylor, Richard Burton, Maggie Smith, Rod Taylor and Margaret Rutherford (Academy Award). Running time 119 minutes: colour.

The Yellow Rolls-Royce: MGM, Great Britain, 1964. Directed by Anthony Asquith; original screenplay by Terence Rattigan; starring Rex Harrison, Jeanne Moreau, Edmond Purdom, Shirley Maclaine, Ingrid Bergman, George C. Scott and Omar Sharif. Running time 122 minutes: colour.

Goodbye Mr Chips: MGM/APJAC Production, Great Britain, 1969. Directed by Herbert Ross; screenplay by Terence Rattigan based upon the novel by James Hilton; music and lyrics by Leslie Bricusse (Academy Award Nomination); music supervised by John Williams (Academy Award Nomination); starring Peter O'Toole (Academy Award Nomination), Petula Clark, Michael Bryant and Michael Redgrave. Running time 147 minutes: colour.

Bequest to the Nation (US title *The Nelson Affair*): Universal/Hal B. Wallis Production, Great Britain, 1973. Directed by James Cellan Jones; screenplay by Terence Rattigan based upon his stage play; starring Peter Finch, Glenda Jackson, Michael Jayston and Margaret Leighton. Running time 116 minutes: colour.

TELEVISION SCRIPTS

The Final Test: BBC, 29 July 1951. Directed by Royston Morley; original script by Terence Rattigan; starring Jack Warner and Patrick Barr.

Heart to Heart: BBC, 6 December 1962. Directed by Alvin Rakoff; original script by Terence Rattigan; starring Ralph Richardson, Kenneth More and Angela Baddeley.

Ninety Years On: BBC, 29 November 1964. Produced by Michael Mills. Tribute to Sir Winston Churchill, script by Terence Rattigan.

Nelson, A Study in Miniature: ATV, 21 March 1966. Directed by Stuart Burge; original screenplay by Terence Rattigan; starring Michael Bryant, Rachel Roberts and Celia Johnson.

All On Her Own: BBC, 26 September 1968. Directed by Hal Burton; original script by Terence Rattigan; starring Margaret Leighton.

High Summer: Thames Television, 12 September 1972. Directed by Peter Duguid; script by Terence Rattigan based upon his own unproduced stage play; starring Margaret Leighton, Christopher Gable and Roland Culver.

Index